INTERPRETATIVE REPORTING

INTERPRETATIVE
REPORTING

Curtis D. MacDougall, **Ph.D., Litt.D.**
PROFESSOR OF JOURNALISM, NORTHWESTERN UNIVERSITY

FIFTH EDITION

The Macmillan Company, New York
Collier-Macmillan Limited, London

© Copyright, CURTIS D. MACDOUGALL, 1968

All rights reserved. No part of this book may be reproduced or transmitted in any form or by any means, electronic or mechanical, including photocopying, recording or by any information storage and retrieval system, without permission in writing from the Publisher.

FIRST PRINTING

Earlier edition entitled *Reporting for Beginners* copyright 1932 by The Macmillan Company. Earlier editions entitled *Interpretative Reporting* copyright 1938, 1948, 1957 and © 1963 by The Macmillan Company. Copyright renewed 1960 and 1966 by Curtis D. MacDougall.

Library of Congress catalog card number: 68-10070

The Macmillan Company, New York
Collier-Macmillan Canada, Ltd., Toronto, Ontario

Printed in the United States of America

PN
4781
.M153
1968

Acknowledgements

Many of the improvements made in the fourth and fifth editions of this book were made upon the advice and with the assistance of a number of professional journalists. The author is grateful to those listed below. They, of course, bear no responsibility for any shortcomings which remain.

Baden, Leon, Harrisburg (Pa.) *Evening News*
Beinhorn, Sherman, Middletown (Conn.) *Press*
Black, Creed C., managing editor, Chicago *Daily News*
Blade, Joseph, Minneapolis *Star*
Blanchard, Robert O., Salt Lake City *Tribune* (now American University)
Block, Mervin, Chicago's *American* (now Columbia Broadcasting System)
Botts, Jack C., Lincoln *Journal* (now assistant professor of journalism, University of Nebraska)
Cade, Dr. Dozier C., head, Department of Journalism, Georgia State University
Carty, James Jr., Nashville *Tennessean* (now Bethany, W.Va. College)
Cockrell, James, financial editor, St. Louis *Globe-Democrat*
Croft, Duane, Toledo *Blade*
Dansker, Emil, Cincinnati *Enquirer*
Dedmon, Emmett, editor, Chicago *Sun-Times*
Driscoll, Thomas, city editor, Peoria *Journal-Star*
Eskey, Kenneth, Pittsburgh *Press*
Fisher, Prof. William, Kent State University
Francois, William, Dayton *Journal-Herald* (now Marshall University)
Full, Jerome, Salt Lake City *Tribune* (now Eastern Airlines)
Garrison, Jerol, Little Rock *Gazette*
Geiselman, Arthur Jr., York (Pa.) *Gazette & Daily* (now Baltimore *Post*)
Gibson, Martin, Houston *Chronicle*
Hart, Ronald, Pittsburgh *Press*
Hayes, Charles, Paddock Publications, Arlington Heights, Ill.

Hinson, Daniel, city editor, Orlando (Fla.) *Sentinel*
Hodell, Melvin, editor and publisher, Upland (Calif.) *News*
Kole, John, Washington bureau, Milwaukee *Journal*
Lambeth, Edward, Washington bureau, Gannett Newspapers
Little, William, Peoria *Journal-Star*
Littlewood, Thomas, Washington bureau, Chicago *Sun-Times*
Lunger, Phillip, Buffalo *Courier-Express*
MacDougall, A. Kent, *Wall Street Journal*
Mazzatenta, Ernest, city editor, Peru (Ind.) *Tribune* (now Omaha *World-Herald*)
Nofziger, Fred, Toledo *Blade*
Peeks, Edward, Charleston (W.Va.) *Gazette*
Perry, John L., development director, Center for the Study of Democratic Institutions, Santa Barbara, Calif.
Price, Jo-Ann, New York *Herald Tribune*
Pride, William, Denver *Post*
Reynolds, Edward, San Francisco *Examiner*
Smart, Kenneth, assistant city editor, Dallas *Times-Herald*
Spaid, Ora, Louisville *Courier-Journal* (now Economic Opportunity Council, North Carolina)
Spiegler, William, *Newsday*, Long Island, N.Y.
Stanley, Robert, Dallas *Times-Herald*
Walz, Margaret, York *Gazette & Daily*
Watson, Harry, Milwaukee *Journal* (deceased)
Werthimer, Prof. Jerrold, San Francisco State University
Williams, Edward, Milwaukee *Journal*

History and Purpose

The preceding four editions of this book and its predecessor, *Reporting for Beginners* (1932), have reflected changes in newsgathering practices and in journalism school methods of teaching reporting. This edition continues the effort to keep up-to-date.

Many of the features dropped as this book has developed over 36 years were made obsolete because of the tremendous growth of the journalistic media. For example, students once pored over facsimiles of the front pages of newspapers which appeared in the appendices of early editions. Today the papers themselves are available in school reading rooms or at news stands. They are bought when they are red hot off the press by students on vacation in all parts of the land. Pictures of attractive newspaper buildings and of newsrooms and other departments also have been eliminated because they are superfluous in this day of travel and electronics.

Elaborate descriptions of the newspaper organization as both a newsgathering and business institution now are contained in other textbooks which are used in introductory courses before the college student is introduced to reporting techniques. Long bibliographies of books in all fields of journalism are made unnecessary by the growth of school libraries and reference rooms. The development of the teletypesetter has led to the adoption by most papers of the Associated Press Style Book, so no author or teacher needs to prepare his own any more. Descriptions of the symbols used by copyreaders and proofreaders are available in many places.

No journalism curriculum today is complete without separate courses in History of Journalism, Law of the Press, and The Press and Society, however different their title designations may be. Hence, mention of the material included in such courses need be only minimal in a basic reporting text.

Whatever other courses a student takes should contribute to the background and understanding of his role as a newsgatherer—that is, reporter. All journalism, including editing and editorial direction, involves reporting or the reportorial point of view. This book is essentially a how-to-do-it book. As the title suggests, however, it goes beyond preparing a young person for his first newsgathering job. Rather, it attempts to impart a point of view related to his professional future. In training himself to be a good cub reporter, the student of this book should also be laying the groundwork for future positions which will require more than mere ability to observe and report the routine.

It is presumed that the first experience of the journalism graduate will be to cover local news. Unlike some of the preceding editions, this one stresses such coverage. The examples are types of stories which the young reporter may conceivably be asked to handle early in his career. By learning well at that level, he is building a sound foundation on which he later can become a Washington or foreign correspondent. He cannot, however, wait for the arrival of such an opportunity to be aware of the responsibilities which are necessary for a journalist in a democracy and in a confused, endangered world.

The author remains convinced that the first step upward in journalism is through mastery of the fundamentals of thorough, objective reporting. Thus, the contents and slant of Part I, Principles of News Writing, remain virtually unchanged. The fourth (1963) edition represented a thorough revision, retaining or restoring what was proved best from all of the preceding editions. All of the chapters in this edition have been updated and enriched, and about one-fourth of the material is new. The author had the valuable counsel of several outstanding professional veterans in making these and other revisions. As in the past, most of the new material was contributed by professional journalists.

Although a great deal of attention has been given to communications theory and research methodology, it has not diminished the great need of the practicing journalist to perfect his skills and to remain dedicated to the task of making the American free press contribute to the maximum in our democracy. As the Founding Fathers knew, only a fully informed people can succeed in governing themselves wisely. The responsibility of the mid-20th century journalist is to know as much about as many things as possible, especially in the social sciences; and to become a specialist on top of it all. The beginning reporter who envisions the goal ahead can prepare himself to reach it on every routine assignment. This book is intended to show him how to do it.

C. D. M.

Contents

PART ONE
Principles of News Writing

1	The Modern Newsgatherer	3
2	Problems of Newsgathering	31
3	Organizing the Facts	49
4	Playing Up the Feature	63
5	Making It Attractive	82
6	Making It Readable	92
7	Saying It Right	117
8	Winning Reader Confidence	128
9	Keeping Up-to-Date	156
10	Giving It Substance	185

PART TWO
Handling Important Assignments

11	Persons and Personalities	213
12	Meetings, Conventions, Speeches	237
13	Illness and Death	256
14	Police, Crime, Criminal Law	286
15	Courts, Civil Law, Appeals	322
16	Politics, Elections	349
17	Government	372
18	Business, Finance, Labor, Agriculture	409
19	Religion, Science	452
20	Sports, Reviewing and Criticism; Features	473
	Index	507

PART ONE
Principles of News Writing

A Newspaperman's Credo
BY MAX LERNER

1. I believe in the integrity of the newspaperman to the facts and events with which he is dealing. He must give the event as it actually happened, the facts as they actually are, to the best of his descriptive power. His obligation to what actually happened is as exacting as the obligation of a historian, and his regard for evidence must be as scrupulous.

2. He has also the obligation, whenever the facts or events do not speak for themselves, to give the frame within which their meaning becomes clear. This may be a frame of history, or a broader interpretative frame of fact. In doing this he must make clear the distinction between fact and event on the one hand and his own opinion on the other.

3. In deciding what to include or omit he must use to the best of his ability the test of what is newsworthy in the minds of his readers, and what is of importance in the flow of events. He must resist the temptation of including or excluding on the basis of what will help or harm whatever team he is on and whatever crowd he runs with.

4. This means that he must give a hearing even to unpopular causes, including those which he may himself detest. He has the obligation to keep the channels of the press open for a competition of ideas, since only through such a competition will the people be able to arrive at their own decisions of what is right and good.

5. In any contest of opinion he has the obligation to state, as fairly as he knows how, the opposing viewpoints. At the same time, if he is presenting opinion in an editorial or a column, he has the obligation to set forth his own position honestly and forthrightly as his own, regardless of the consequences.

6. Beset as he inevitably will be by favor-seekers, special interests, press agents, public relations men, and operators of all kinds, he must keep himself scrupulously independent of their favors and pressures. This means that he must be strong enough to make himself unpopular with those who can smooth his path or make life pleasant for him.

7. He must resist all pressures from outside, whether they be from advertisers, government officials, businessmen, labor organizations, churches, ethnic groups, or any other source which has an effect on the circulation or revenue of his paper. This applies whether the newspaperman is a publisher, editor, reporter, reviewer, or columnist. Since the danger in many cases is that he will anticipate the pressures before they are exerted, and censor a news story, review, or opinion which may hurt circulation or revenue, he has the obligation to resist the voice from within himself which tells him to play it safe.

8. His responsibility is to his craft and to the integrity of his mind.

Editor & Publisher

1

The Modern Newsgatherer

I JOURNALISM, TODAY AND TOMORROW

II THE NATURE OF NEWSPAPER WORK

III REPORTORIAL QUALIFICATIONS
1. Valuable Traits
2. Nose for News
3. What Is News?
4. The Need for Interpretation
5. The Growth of Interpretation

IV HOW TO PREPARE
1. Informational Background
2. Academic Preparation
3. Cub Reporting
4. Occupational Aids

V THE ETHICS OF JOURNALISM
1. The Reporter's Prerogatives
2. Newspaper Policy
3. Invasion of Privacy
4. Reportorial Decision Making
5. Freedom of the Press

NO MATTER WHAT CHANGES—SOCIAL, ECONOMIC, POLITICAL OR OTHER—occur in the future, it is inconceivable that there ever will come a time when there will not be those whose full-time function it is to find out what is going on and to transmit that information to others, together with a proper explanation of its significance.

Journalism, Today and Tomorrow

As the world's population zooms and it becomes possible to visit all parts of the globe in a few hours, possibly even minutes, the problems and areas of interest with which the editor of the future must be concerned will multiply many times. The complexity and interdependence of all aspects of human living, furthermore, continue to enlarge both the opportunities and responsibilities of the newsgatherers and disseminators. And it will make no difference what the future medium of distribution is: slave runners, town criers, newsletters, carrier pigeons, telegraphs, telephones, printing presses, motion pictures, radio, television—or thought waves.

This also seems certain: It is going to take better men and women to report and edit the news of the world in the future than it has in the past. The qualifications required of those who enter journalism will continue to broaden as they have been doing steadily during the past quarter century. More and better education will be required and there will be an augmented need for those capable, after adequate preparation as general practitioners, to become specialists in a multitude of fields.

The improvement in the quality of the personnel engaged in journalism will continue to be both a business necessity and an essential to the future existence of democratic society. Only a competent and responsible journalism can provide the knowledge and understanding the masses of mankind need in order to maintain government of the people, by the people and for the people. From the standpoint of the young person choosing a career, this means that there is no other field of endeavor more likely to provide challenges and opportunities for personal development and service to mankind.

This book is for the benefit of beginners in this field who aspire some day to be newspaper publishers, magazine editors, radio or television commentators, foreign correspondents, editorial writers, syndicated columnists or authoritative journalistic experts on specialized subjects for any or all of the media. Just as the youngster who dreams of growing up to be a concert pianist begins with scales, finger exercises and Bach two-part inventions, so must the journalistic neophyte acquire the basic skills which he later can use regardless of the specific activity in which he is engaged.

No matter what electronic devices are developed for the use of the communicator, the need for a permanent record will persist. This means that there always is going to be something akin to the newspaper. This is so despite the fact that the huge expenditures involved in contemporary publishing have reduced the number of daily newspapers in the United States from approximately 2,600 to about 1,750 in a half century during which the population has more than doubled. Despite the decline in the number of newspapers, their total circulation reached an all-time high of close to 60 million at the end of the same period. About 150 million Americans read some newspaper every day.

Anyway, whatever the future may bring, as of today the daily newspaper still provides the best basic training for beginners in journalism, no matter what their lifetime ambitions may be. No other medium comes anywhere close to duplicating its efforts at speedy, accurate and thorough coverage of the news of the world. Acquiring the skills necessary for success as a newspaper reporter, therefore, is the smartest "first step" that anyone can take in the field of journalism. News magazines, television stations and other media prefer employees who have such experience.

Understandably, the young person considering a newspaper reportorial career asks himself:

1. How do I know I would like it?
2. How do I know I am qualified?
3. How should I prepare myself?
4. What about the ethics or morality of journalism?

The Nature of Newspaper Work

Old-time movies notwithstanding, newspaper reporters do not often emulate detectives in exposing murderers, kidnapers and subversives, nor do they shout "stop the presses" and compose headlines over the telephone after profanely "telling off" unreasonable superiors. Rather, they work regular eight-hour days in and out of remarkably quiet and orderly newsrooms, where they remove their hats.

In large cities, some reporters spend their entire working days on "beats" in the press rooms at police headquarters, city hall, the county building, the federal building and other places where it is certain important news will originate. They telephone their information to rewrite men in note form or they dictate it, composing as they go along. On smaller newspapers, beat men visit their news sources once or twice daily, returning to their offices to compose their own accounts. They also may double as "general assignment" reporters, covering news which occurs at places other than the familiar spots. In all instances they are under the careful direction and scrutiny of the city editor who in turn is responsible to the managing editor who has general charge of the entire news-editorial operation. How departmentalized a newspaper operation is and how split up the managerial and operational functions, depend upon its size. On even small papers the sports and society (or women's) departments usually are separate. Someone is in charge of handling news that reaches the office via the teletypesetters or leased wires of the press associations (Associated Press and United Press International), so there may be a telegraph or wire desk or, on larger papers, a foreign news department with a cable desk as a part of it. Large newspapers also have a central copy desk where most stories from whatever source are checked for style, accuracy, etc. and given headlines. Makeup (deciding where stories and other, mostly illustrative, material are to appear) may be handled by a separate makeup editor, by a news editor or by someone else performing multiple duties. Perhaps no two newspapers are organized exactly alike, but the process of putting out a paper is the same no matter how the labor is divided. It is only by operating routinely on a predetermined schedule that it is possible to produce papers which appear daily at the same hour.

As for the reporter, despite the fact that he may consider himself haunted constantly by deadlines (the last minutes at which copy can be submitted to make editions), there is generally less monotony and consequently danger of "getting into a rut" in newspaper work than there is in almost anything else he could do today. This is the age of the Organization Man in which white-collar as well as blue-collar workers increasingly are becoming comparatively smaller and smaller cogs in huge industrial machines, the total operations (or even purposes) of which it is difficult for them to understand. Many recent authors have deplored the extent to which the contemporary economy puts a premium on conformity, stifles imagination and originality and, consequently, destroys initiative and even self-respect.

There is, of course, considerable sameness in the news from the same source day after day. Nevertheless, no two stories ever are exactly alike. The principals at least are different and so are their reactions to whatever befalls them: arrest, accident, honor, etc. And, even though the swashbuckling days of Richard Harding Davis are long since past, there is still a thrill, or at least a satisfied feeling, with every assignment successfully concluded. There is a greater pride of workmanship and sense of accomplishment than is possible for workers in most industries and offices in late-twentieth century.

Even though he may consider himself low man on the press' totem pole, the cub reporter carries more prestige with the public than is true of apprentices in most other fields. At the scene of a fire or riot he flashes his press pass and is allowed across police lines. On the routine beat he is courted by those who want to get something in or to keep something out of the paper. From the very start of his journalistic career, by the very nature of his work, he "is somebody," and this fact cannot help but be gratifying to the human ego.

His is not a dream world or fool's paradise. The reporter actually *is* a responsible person. Several other persons will have a part in determining how whatever news he handles appears in the paper. Nevertheless, he has "first crack" at it. The original judgment which he exercises in determining whether and/or how something is to be reported is of the utmost importance. He, in other words, is the backbone of the newsgathering and disseminating operation. Truly, every reporter is also an editor and, conversely, the best editors continue throughout their future careers to maintain the attitudes of reporters.

The occupational disease that newspapermen must guard against is cynicism. Whereas skepticism is a journalistic asset, a hard-boiled or flippant attitude toward the so-called "realities" of life can lead not only to a flagrant disregard of the public interest but also to personal deterioration. Many of the public figures with whom he comes into diurnal contact, the reporter knows, do not deserve public adulation but are, to use the vernacular, stuffed shirts or phonies. Disillusionment comes also with discovery that the "rules of the game"—as the game actually is "played" in politics, business and many other aspects of life—are often crass, mercenary and hypocritical. Overcoming gullibility and learning the "facts of life" can be valuable, provided they lead to intelligent sophistication.

Much superfluous effort has gone into the attempt to determine whether journalism is a profession, business or trade. What really counts is the attitude of the individual toward his work. Professionalism can be present or absent among carpenters, hotel clerks, nurses, doctors, lawyers, taxi drivers, newspapermen and anybody or everybody else. As for journalism, there is no field which offers greater opportunities for the development of a professional point of view, idealism, public service and the like. It is the place for the starry-eyed youngster who wants to help "save the world." There is no better way for one who wants to help make democracy work more effectively to devote his talents. As in every other worthwhile endeavor, the road to the top is long and strewn with obstacles. At the summit, however, are the prestige and power which make the struggle worthwhile.

Reportorial Qualifications

As regards the myth that newspapermen are born and not made, Joseph Pulitzer, patriarch of the old New York *World*, and founder of the Pulitzer School of Journalism at Columbia University, said years ago:

> The only position that occurs to me that a man in our Republic can successfully fill by the simple fact of birth is that of an idiot. Is there any

position for which a man does not demand and receive training—training at home, training in schools and colleges, training by master craftsmen, or training through bitter experience—through the burns that make the child dread the fire, through blunders costly to the aspirant?

The "born editor" who has succeeded greatly without special preparation is simply a man with unusual ability and aptitude for his chosen profession, with great power of concentration and sustained effort.... Even in his case might it not be an advantage to have a system of instruction that would give him the same results at a saving of much time and labor?

Early in the century, Dr. John H. Finley, the scholarly editor of the New York *Times*, issued a challenge to those who own and operate newspapers, those who expect to work for them and those who prepare the latter for their life work when he said:

> If I were to make a plea to the colleges and universities on behalf of the press, it would be to prepare a few all-around men and women who should be competent to perform a planetary service, not only geographically but intelligently, to be in this democratic age what Democritus was in his day to his little world. Such men as one whom I knew who was prepared when the tomb of Tut-Ankh-Amen was opened to enter intelligently with the archaeologist; who when Einstein propounded his theory had some notion of what he was talking about; whom I found one day trying to find geometrically the area of a triangle in the terms of its sides; who in the midst of the last campaign wrote a two-column editorial on the new planet and yet who could tell you the baseball champions for the last ten years or the presidential returns for the last century.

A few years later a committee on schools of journalism of the American Society of Newspaper Editors reported:

> We want the departments of journalism to turn out men ... capable of appraising the changed and new world which will be theirs tomorrow. We want these boys—of course, they will start at the bottom—capable of rising to the posts of great newspaper power, equipped to wield that power intelligently. In other words, we wish them, while they are collecting police news and reporting banquets, to carry the mental equipment which, rightly directed, will one day invest them with editorial control. Each graduate ought to have in the knapsack of his mind the baton of the editor and publisher.... This society knows it is far more vital to the welfare of mankind that the men who make its journals of public opinion be culturally superior than it is that the surgeon or corporation lawyer be a man of manifold intellectual attainments.

Altogether too many college freshmen think training for journalism consists primarily in learning how to write. They are mostly students who did well in high school English and were inspired with literary ambitions by teachers who were surprised and grateful to find fewer than the average number of grammatical errors in their themes. Unfortunately, there is no such thing as "just writing," in journalism or any other field. William Shakespeare is immortal, not because of vocabulary or style but because of greatness of thought. He had an incomparable knowledge of history, psychology, geography, philosophy and many other fields. He and other masters of past centuries are read today because they had something extraordinarily worthwhile to say.

Because great ideas rather than beautiful words and phrases make for superior writing, everything that a journalism student studies is of potential value to him. The subject matter of journalism includes all that is taught in courses in political science, history, economics, sociology, chemistry, physics and other subjects too numerous to mention. The student who recognizes this fact in his freshman year has a big advantage. By the time he takes his first journalism course in his sophomore, junior or senior year, he will have more than the average liberal arts student's superficial interest in and knowledge of the contents of the innumerable textbooks he will have studied. He should have his head and files full of information on which to rely when he starts wandering on and off the campus in quest of news. It is the purpose of his journalism courses to make his textbook knowledge come alive, to show him how to utilize it in understanding and interpreting the contemporary scene. Through experience in hiring both liberal arts and journalism school graduates, editors have learned that a so-called "broad background" of general courses is not in itself adequate preparation for newspaper reporting. Liberal arts courses are mostly theoretical and purposeless; journalism courses are practical and purposeful. Since, however, the journalist deals mostly with news related to the subject matter of courses in the different social sciences, the student who discovers he has little or no interest in political science, economics and sociology should take stock to determine whether he really is wise to aspire to a career in journalism.

VALUABLE TRAITS

The young person who should be encouraged to go into journalism, therefore, is the one who wants very badly to spend his adulthood saying or writing worthwhile things. His chances of success may be judged by the extent to which at any early age he becomes interested in the world of affairs. There is no sense aspiring to a newspaper career unless one finds newspaper reading pleasurable as a youth. The more cosmopolitan the interests the better, as long as the news which will be mentioned in the political science, sociology and economics textbooks of the next few decades is included, for that is the kind of news with which the beginning reporter is most likely to come into contact.

Most of the personality traits usually listed as valuable for the journalist are ones which would be equally essential for success in most other professional fields: intelligence, friendliness, reliability, imagination, ingenuity, nerve, speed, accuracy, courage, endurance, ability to organize one's activities, perseverance, mental alertness, honesty, punctuality, cheerfulness, the power of observation, shrewdness, enterprise, optimism, humor, adaptability, initiative and the like.

If there is any clue to be discovered in childhood by which to estimate journalistic capacity, it probably would be in the extent to which the boy or girl demonstrates curiosity and skepticism. A newsgatherer's stock in trade is his ability to keep on asking questions until he has exhausted all angles of an assignment. The youngster who wears out his parents by his querulousness may be worth encouraging as a potential journalistic great.

NOSE FOR NEWS

Usually listed first among the special qualifications which a newsgatherer needs is a "nose for news," which means the ability to recognize the news possibilities of an item of information and involves:

1. The ability to recognize that the information can be made of interest to readers.
2. The ability to recognize clues which may be very casual but which may lead to the discovery of important news.
3. The ability to recognize the relative importance of a number of facts concerning the same general subject.
4. The ability to recognize the possibility of other news related to the particular information at hand.

The following anecdote, possibly apocryphal, is told of Deems Taylor when he first became music critic for the New York *Times*. He is said to have arrived at the première of an opera only to learn that the prima donna had taken poison in her hotel room and the program had been cancelled. Taylor, it is hard to believe in view of the eminence he later attained, went home and to bed. He was awakened in the middle of the night by an outraged editor who told him every other paper in town had the suicide story on Page One. Taylor murmured, "Well, there was no opera performance to write about, so what else could I do but go home?"

Another, possibly fictitious, reporter was assigned to cover a speech which an important man was to deliver. He was instructed to follow the speech with the advanced copy in his hands to see if the speaker deviated at all from the manuscript. The speech, in the meantime, had been written up and its publication awaited only the actual delivery. The reporter strolled back to his editor's presence and reported that the speaker had cast aside his prepared manuscript and had talked extemporaneously. He said that it had been impossible to follow the speaker by means of the copy which he had. The reporter, however, had failed to take a single note on the speaker's impromptu remarks.

From these "classic" examples it is clear that common sense is indispensable for the reporter. Especially in these days of public relations counsel and press releases, making news sources often difficult to see, the reporter must ask question after question to draw out whomever he does get to interview to learn about less obvious but important phases of the subject at hand. He must, in other words, be inquisitive, perceptive and healthfully skeptical.

The reporter with a cultivated nose for news realizes that, although the same elements may be present in similar stories, they invariably are there in different proportions as to importance. For instance, in an automobile accident story the reporter always must find out the names of all persons concerned, the extent of the injuries, details of the collision, etc. In Story A, however, the name of a person injured may be most important. In Story B the most important element may be the name of a prominent person who escaped injury. No two accidents ever result from exactly the same cause. In one case it may be a defective brake; in another, a drunken driver; and in a third, a billboard obstructing the view. Often the cause of an accident is very unusual—as when a bee makes a driver lose control of his machine.

In the same accident story there may be other important features which the reporter could not know without considerable questioning of the persons concerned. Perhaps the same two persons had been in accidents together before. Perhaps one of them recently left a hospital where he was recuperating from a previous accident. Perhaps one of them was on his way to an important engagement, a sick bed or the scene of another accident.

The possibilities of a feature in a simple accident story have by no means been exhausted. Enough has been said, however, to indicate that to report a story "in depth" a reporter must be constantly "on his toes," as the expression goes. He has to think and think and think, and he has to ask and ask and ask. Good reporting consists in getting all the pertinent facts and then some more. Otherwise the story will not be complete and may be misleading because some of the important elements are left out. The reporter who learns to do a thorough job of delving into all of the potential angles of a simple "straight" news story is obtaining valuable training for interpretative reporting.

"Smelling a rat" is also an attribute of the straight news reporter and, especially, the interpretative reporter. For example, a reporter learned that a certain congressman was going to deliver a public address. He was sharp enough to inquire whether this meant that an important hearing over which the representative was to preside had been called off or postponed. Another reporter, unable to buy a certain game at several stores, investigated and learned that there was a new recreational fad in existence. Still another, noting that average school attendance in the elementary grades had gone up, investigated and came up with an article on the successful use of cold shots and other sickness preventatives.

This "smelling a rat" attitude should be the most valuable attribute of any kind of researcher, journalistic or academic. The truth-seeking reporter explores every possible avenue for information. If he is operating correctly he has no predetermined ends to seek, no hypothesis to prove—just the truth to be determined. The manner in which his information is transmitted is an important subject for scholarly research, and it is to gasp to conjecture what changes the development of electronics may bring. Nevertheless, the first essential step always will be the same: to seek and to obtain the facts.

WHAT IS NEWS?

Scholarly attempts to define news, for which the reporter is supposed to have a nose, correctly emphasize the fact that it is the account of an event, not the event itself. At any given moment billions of simultaneous events occur throughout the world. Someone dies, is born, gives a speech, attends a meeting, takes a trip, commits a crime and so on ad infinitum. All of these occurrences are potentially news. They do not become so until some purveyor of news gives an account of them. The news, in other words, is the account of the event, not something intrinsic in the event itself.

Professional newsgatherers judge the potential interest and/or importance of an event before deciding whether to render an account of it, thus making it news. These newsgatherers are men, not deities. They possess no absolutistic yardstick by which to judge what to report and what to ignore. There is nothing that cannot be made interesting in the skillful telling; and only God Almighty is qualified to say what is important.

Understanding of the nature of news is not improved by adding such words as "timely," "concise," "accurate" or the like to definitions, as all such adjectives require explanations which differ with the editors or the circumstances. Nothing is news until it is reported, no matter when it occurred. Nor is its nature changed by analysis of its effect on those who learn of it, regardless of whether the response is immediate or delayed. Valuable as the study of such factors as audience reaction may be for total understanding of social behavior, the first-rate newsgatherer acting as such persists in his search for truth. He does not ask himself what the potential use or effect of his information will be or how many "gatekeepers" will handle it; rather, his sole duty is to concentrate on discovering the truth.

THE NEED FOR INTERPRETATION

The successful journalist of the future is going to have to be more than a thoroughly trained journeyman if he is to climb the ladder of success. He must be capable of more than routine coverage and to interpret as well as report what is going on.

To interpret the news it is necessary to understand it, and understanding means more than just the ability to define the jargon used by persons in different walks of life. It involves recognizing the particular event as one of a series with both a cause and an effect. With their perspective the historians of the future may be better able to depict the trends and currents of the present, but if the gatherer of information is well informed, through his reading of history, his study of economics, sociology, political science and other academic subjects, and has acquaintance with the attempts of other observers to interpret the modern scene in books and magazine articles, he will at least be aware of the fact that an item of news is not an isolated incident but one inevitably linked to a chain of important events.

The interpretative reporter of the future should be as shock-proof as a psychoanalyst and a practical philosopher in his general outlook on life. He cannot succeed if he is hampered by prejudices and stereotyped attitudes which would bias his perception of human affairs. Modern psychiatry has proved that the first step in ridding a person of complexes is to make him aware of their bases. Hence, the newsgatherer should have a firm understanding of how men think and why, both to avoid pitfalls in his own search for so-called truth and to understand the behavior of those whose actions it is his responsibility to report.

What is this thing called public opinion which the newspaperman may think he is influencing? How explain a new political movement in terms of economic tendencies which give rise to such symptoms? What about the power which the demagogue of the moment seems to be able to exert? The interpreter of the news must see reasons where ordinary individuals observe only overt happenings. And he must study them as the scientist scrutinizes the specimen in his microscope, scientifically. He cannot be a participant in the events of which he writes or his viewpoint will be decidedly warped. Doing his best, he will err constantly; scientific method is nothing but being as approximately correct as possible. His mistakes, however, will be honest ones of an expert and not the blunders of an ignoramus. As Nathe P. Bagby, Texas newspaperman and journalism teacher, has said:

> Cultivation of the thinking habit will enable the reporter not only to handle his regular assignments in a manner more satisfactory and gratifying to his boss, but also make two stories grow where only one grew before he took to thinking. The best stories are not generally found near the surface. Only the reporter who cultivates the habit of constant, thorough thoughtfulness finds them.

A veteran newspaperman, William Little, associate editor of the Peoria (Ill.) *Journal Star*, wrote the author:

> My suggestion to young, old, middled-aged writers is: Think. I am convinced that most poor writing is committed by people who never think through what they want to say—and WHY they want to say it. You see it all the time. This guy doesn't know what he wants to say.
>
> Non-thinking is true in all phases of news writing. Ninety-eight per cent of all editorials would be better if the editorialist wrote out in so many words, "This is what I want to say. This is the reason I want to say it." This would necessitate crystallizing it in the writer's mind first of all— in short, thinking it through.
>
> This all seems elementary, but as I read papers day in and day out this is the biggest evil I see: does this guy know what he's trying to say? Frequently he doesn't because he never thought: What am I trying to say and why am I saying it?

THE GROWTH OF INTERPRETATION

The first important impetus to interpretative handling of the news was provided by World War I. When it broke out most Americans were surprised—dumfounded in fact—and utterly unable to explain its causes. In his doctoral dissertation at the University of Wisconsin in the mid-'30s, the late Maynard Brown suggested the extent to which the newsgathering agencies were responsible for this phenomenon. Brown wrote in part:

> Where the Associated Press failed most was in preventing its reporters from sending background and informative articles based on politics and trends. It smugly adopted the attitude of permitting correspondents to report only what had definitely transpired. It wanted no interpretation of events but the mere factual reporting of the obvious. Some of its correspondents were trained in foreign affairs, but too few were able to interpret or discern significant events and tendencies.

Not only the Associated Press but other press associations and newspapers as well learned a great lesson from the experience of being totally unprepared either to understand the final steps which plunged the world into war or adequately to report the war once it started. During the '20s and '30s they peopled the capitals and other important news centers of the world with trained experts qualified not only to report but also to explain and interpret factual occurrences. Among the best of these journalistic scholars were Walter Duranty, John Gunther, Vincent Sheean, Edgar Ansel Mowrer, Quentin Reynolds, William Shirer and M. W. Fodor. In newspaper stories, magazine articles, authoritative books and radio commentaries, they and others did such a thoroughly competent job that, by contrast with 1914, for years before World War II began in 1939, an overwhelming majority of Americans expected it or at least knew it was possible if not probable.

Reader demand for more than mere drab objective reporting of domestic news grew tremendously after the stock-market crash of 1929 and during the depression years of the '30s and the period of New Deal experimentation which brought with it nationwide awareness of the increased importance in the life of every citizen of the federal government. Readership of the recently created weekly news magazines, *Time*, *Newsweek* and others, skyrocketed; so did the circulation of *Reader's Digest* and a multitude of other monthly digest magazines. So did the number and readership of how-to-do-it and other easily read books, allegedly compendious accounts of how to understand what was happening in a variety of fields of human interest and activity. So also did newsletters for general and specialized audiences.

Slow to modify their basic news formula, newspapers nevertheless expanded their contents to include signed columns by political analysts, most of which were syndicated at reasonable cost so as to be available for moderate and small-sized newspapers. In the mid-'30s newspapers also experimented with weekly news reviews, many of which (notably that of the New York *Times*) have survived. They also tried out various forms of daily reviews, expanded Sunday magazine or feature sections and increased the number of supplemental articles to provide historical, geographical, biographical and other background information to help make current news more understandable and meaningful. A whole new vocabulary developed to categorize these writings. Instead of lumping them all under the general heading of "think pieces" as in the past, newsmen now talk of sidebars, explainers, situationers, wrap-ups, button-ups, blockbusters and other types of explanatory, enterprise, offbeat, background, subsurface, creative, speculative or interpretative reporting and writing.

Since shortly after the end of World War II, no subject has received greater attention at the meetings of the American Society of Newspaper Editors and similar organizations than has that of interpretation, no matter what it is called. Since 1947, when they were formed, a number of the Continuing Study committees of the Associated Press Managing Editors have stimulated heated discussions of the problem annually.

Especially at first, a considerable amount of attention was devoted to definitions to determine what difference, if any, there is between interpretation and explanatory material, background facts, editorializing and opinion. Fundamental, however, was the question of policy: whether to permit AP writers leeway to go beyond the mere objective reporting of the news. Typical of many strong committee statements was that of the Business and Financial Report committee as follows:

> There is a tidal wave of demands for more interpretative writing. The average American is worried. He is worried as a producer and he is worried as a consumer. He doesn't know or understand what is happening to him, or to the world he lives in. But he is aware that tremendous events are occurring. He wonders how the United States is going to make its postwar comeback. He wants to read about new products, new methods and new leaders.

Today, the debate is virtually over with only a few still arguing against the necessity for interpretative reporting. This means that to become more than a humdrum journeyman the future reporter must prepare himself to help meet the increasing need and demand for "subsurface" or "depth" reporting, to "take the reader behind the scenes of the day's action," "relate the news to the reader's own framework and experience," "make sense out of the facts," "put factual news in perspective," "put meaning into the news," "point up the significance of current events," and so on, to use the expressions of various authorities. As Marquis W. Childs has written:

> The interpretive reporter expands the horizon of the news. He explains, he amplifies, he clarifies....
>
> As contrasted with the sensationalist, the interpretive reporter must have a mature understanding of the importance and the responsibility of his function....
>
> One of the most important tasks of the interpretive reporter is to expand the peripheries of the news ... it is the special duty of the interpretive reporter to go behind the handout and the press conference....
>
> You will ask where these interpretive reporters are going to be found. They come out of growth and experience. They come out of the city hall and the state capital. They grow in knowledge and experience and in confidence.

Foremost defender of interpretative reporting against its critics has been Lester Markel, associate editor of the New York *Times*, who has written:

> Those who object to interpretation say that a story should be confined to the "facts." I ask, "What facts?" And I discover that there is in reality no such thing as an "objective" article in the sense these objectors use it—or in any sense, for that matter.
>
> Take the most "objective" of reporters. He collects fifty facts; out of these fifty he selects twelve which he considers important enough to include in his piece, leaving out thirty-eight. This is the first exercise of judgment.
>
> Then the reporter decides which of these twelve facts shall constitute the lead of the story. The particular fact he chooses gets the emphasis—which is important because often the reader does not go beyond the first paragraph. This is the second exercise of judgment.
>
> Then the editor reads the so-called objective story and makes a decision as to whether it is to be played on page 1 or on page 29. If it is played on page 1 it may have considerable impact on opinion. If it is put on page 29 it has no such emphasis. The most important editorial decision on any paper, I believe, is what goes on page 1. This is the third exercise of judgment.
>
> In brief, this "objective" news is, in its exponents' own terms, very unobjective, and the kind of judgment required for interpretation is no

different from the kind of judgment involved in the selection of the facts for a so-called factual story and in the display of that story.

In other words, just as the Constitution is said to mean what the Supreme Court says it means, so is news what newspapers and other media of communication decide it is to be.

How to Prepare

INFORMATIONAL BACKGROUND

The rule to follow in preparing for a career in journalism is: learn as much about as many things as possible and stay intellectually alert. The ignorant reporter is at a tremendous disadvantage. He annoys news sources, doesn't obtain all of the essential facts, and may make gross errors of fact as well as emphasis when he writes his story.

To cover intelligently a police station, criminal court, city hall, county, state or federal office, or political headquarters, one must understand the setups of government, the nature and functions of various offices. The reporter must be able to read and quickly digest the contents of legal documents. He must know the meanings of such terms as "corpus delicti," "habeas corpus," "injunction" and "certiorari." He cannot say "divorce" when he means "separate maintenance," or "parole" when he means "probation." He must be able to read a bank-balance sheet, know when a financial market is bullish and when bearish and what it means to sell short, hedge and stockpile. He must understand what it means to refinance a bond issue or liquidate the assets of a corporation. He doesn't confuse craft unions with industrial unions.

It is impossible for an interpretative reporter to write that the last obstacle to beginning a slum-clearance program has been removed unless he knows the procedure by which such projects are developed. He can't explain the status of a pending city ordinance unless he understands what the rules provide for future consideration of it. It is impossible for him to interview a prosecuting attorney regarding the course of action he may take in a particular case unless he knows what the alternatives are.

Although most editorial offices today are equipped with good libraries, or morgues as they often still are called, the reporter has to know which reference books and clipping files to consult to obtain historical and other explanatory information to "round out" a story. As he gathers experience he becomes a veritable storehouse of knowledge himself.

Aware of the nature of different organizations, public and private, he knows which ones to consult on which occasion and what each group's slant or interest is likely to be.

Without background knowledge in a field a reporter cannot fill out an account by declaring that the home run was the longest ever hit in the park; that this was the first time a certain ward gave a voting majority to the candidates of a particular party; that a fatal accident occurred at an intersection where the city council once refused to permit the erection of stop signs; that what seems to be a new proposal for civic reform really was resurrected from a decade-old report by an elder statesmen.

At a recent Associated Press Managing Editors meeting, Robert Paine of the Memphis *Commercial Appeal* cited the following story:

> Grand Junction, Tenn., Feb. 19.—(AP)—A smooth-working hound flushed seven bevies of quail in a three-hour trial yesterday for the top performance of the national championship.

Commented Paine:

> I imagine that every bird-dog owner in the country shuddered in horror at the word HOUND. That would be about the same as saying a cow won the Kentucky derby. They are strictly different kinds of dogs and bird-dog fanciers have a habit of shooting from the hip when one of their dogs is called a hound.
>
> Secondly, the word FLUSH is the exact opposite of the word that should have been used. That would be about like saying Babe Ruth won the game by striking out. Flush means to frighten the birds into flying away. The correct word is point.

It was not too many years ago that a journalistic ignoramus asked the Nobel prize-winning physicist, Dr. Robert Millikan, what cosmic rays were "good for." Those were the days when science was treated more or less as a joke in editorial offices and reporters assigned to science news stories were capable of little more than asking when the scholars expected to fly to Mars, find the missing link or take the smell out of the onion. No wonder that many scientists still are reluctant to talk to reporters.

The interpretative reporter "reads the fine print" of a news story in order to answer the reader's query, "What does it mean?" To keep a particular news event "in focus," the interpretative reporter shows its comparative importance. Darrell Huff began his *How to Lie with Statistics*, a book every journalist of whatever kind would find valuable reading, with a warning that widespread reporting of a particular type of news, such as crime, easily can create a distorted impression as regards a social situation.

"Statistical methods and statistical terms," Huff wrote in his introduction, "are necessary in reporting the mass data of social and economic trends, business conditions, 'opinion' polls, the census. But without writers who use the words with honesty and understanding and readers who know what they mean, the result can only be semantic nonsense."

Mere figures showing total numbers of different types of crime committed in two or more areas only suggest the real story. Explanations of why styles in lawbreaking differ in different places at the same time and at the same place at different times, are to be found in such variable factors as size and complexion of population, police policies and activities and many others.

To present anywhere near a true picture of the housing situation in any community, a reporter must consider the age of the community and of the dwelling units; the adequacy of zoning and building codes and their enforcement; the influx of newcomers and the effect, including that caused by prejudice against certain types of persons because of race, national origin, religion or other reasons; the extent of overpopulation; transportation and parking facilities; educational, cultural and recreational advantages; the income and cost of living indices; nearby urban and suburban growth and similar factors. With such data he can provide readers with an understanding of the situation and enable them properly to evaluate proposals for change.

Mere announcement that consumer credit outstanding at any given time is such-and-such means little or nothing unless the reader knows how the figures given compare with similar ones for comparable periods in other months or years. Tables, graphs and charts help show trends; the news magazine, *U.S. News & World Report*, makes very effective use of them. For a broader picture of the state of the economy as a whole, more than comparative figures in any one economic category is necessary. In addition to installment buying, price indices, extent and kind (savings or checking) of bank deposits and withdrawals, a breakdown of the types of depositors (by size of deposits), purchase and cancellation of government securities (with comparable breakdown) bank loans, mortgages, new businesses, business failures, growth of chains and monopolies and other similar factors must be considered.

Often the motives of persons in the news must be known to make their actions understandable. The more a spectator knows about the strategy involved in an athletic contest, for instance, the more enjoyment he derives from it and the better able he is to second guess the manager or be a Monday morning quarterback. If, on the other hand, he knows little or nothing about such strategy, he won't understand why a weak hitter was given an intentional base on balls in order to pitch to a weaker one, possibly one batting from the same side as that from which the pitcher throws and supposedly more likely to hit into a double play. Or he will not understand why a quarterback called for a play which could not help but lose ground on the third down in order to put the ball in better position to try for a field goal on fourth down.

Just as sports writers explain the strategy of coaches, managers and contestants, so could reporters dealing with political affairs explain that precinct captains who rival the positions of ward committeemen often are made candidates for judgeships in order to remove them from active politics. Often the interpretative reporter seeks and easily obtains attribution in such situations but, after he has "been around" long enough, he knows the "tricks of the trade" and can at least suggest probable causes for the behavior of many newsworthy persons. If he fails to do so readers are in the position of just not knowing "what's going on."

To write with the perspective of the cultural anthropologist or historian of a century means to be aware of "schools of thought," "climates of opinion" and social, economic and political trends. A journalistic scholar should know when the views of an educator are consistent with those of an outstanding scholar or organization or with what has been attempted elsewhere. He should know what "progressive versus traditional" in pedagogical methods means. If he covers social welfare he should know the difference between the missionary (settlement house or boys club) and the self-help (area or community project) approaches.

There is a correlation between the extent of a feeling of insecurity and attacks upon civil liberties. Quite naturally the "curves" fluctuate with periods of war and depression, although it always is dangerous to draw historical parallels without thorough consideration of all possible factors.

Of this the studious interpretative reporter is certain: nothing just happens. A wave of intolerance has a cause. So has a revival movement, excessive hero worship, a bullish stock market, an increase in superstition, or any fad, fashion, craze or mass movement. Sometimes what seem to be isolated phenomena in several different fields really stem from the same causal roots. At any rate, there always is an explanation for how we "got that way." At an Associated Press Managing Editors meeting, John L. Morrison of the Greenville (Pa.) *Record Argus* adversely criticized the press association's handling of the trial of Hungarian Cardinal Mindszenty. He said:

> There was likely a great deal of background involving two or three centuries of religious struggle and complications, and even without Soviet interference, there could have been a high tension requiring only a small thing to ignite it. There was a wide field for speculation and an exceedingly small supply of factual information.

ACADEMIC PREPARATION

Although there probably always will be exceptions, present trends indicate that future journalists will be college trained. Such, in fact, is already the case on most metropolitan newspapers and, except for old timers, most of the degree holders went to schools of journalism. The proportion of those with master's and other higher degrees also is increasing.

Modern journalism schools are not trade schools. From two-thirds to four-fifths of a student's class work is taken in the liberal arts or other divisions. Anything and everything that a future journalist studies has potential future value for him and it is frustrating not to be able to take the entire curriculum in the humanities, natural and physical sciences. Those who are ambitious to specialize ultimately in particular fields should do so, but the majority should strive for a thorough and well-rounded background in the social sciences: political science, sociology and economics in particular. The student should try to get in courses in public finance, criminology and labor problems among others. History courses give him perspective and psychology enables him to come closer to understanding both individual and crowd behavior.

In his advanced journalism courses the student should expect to be taught how to utilize the background and theoretical knowledge acquired all over the rest of the campus in reporting and interpreting the contemporary scene. On assignments, he observes "theory becoming action," and if he takes some philosophy he will be better able to comprehend and evaluate the immediate incident in terms of the general and eternal.

A strict journalism instructor, simulating the exactness of a hard-boiled city editor, can teach sound methods of research. The journalistic fact finder does not begin with a hypothesis for which he seeks factual proof. Rather, he is an open-minded seeker after truth who explores every possible avenue of investigation; and only after he has exhausted every chance to obtain additional information does he attempt to draw conclusions regarding the accumulated data. This objective approach to knowledge is much sounder than that practiced by many researchers in other academic fields. In the process, the student-reporter becomes familiar with the nature of reference or source material; he may learn how to read and understand a county board's budget or the complicated declaration filed to begin a civil law action.

Since World War II, a number of social scientists have become interested in quantitative analysis of various aspects of social behavior and in communication theory. They use the tools of the statistician and the language of the sociologist to examine the effects of various ways to influence human thought and behavior. Many of their findings are of value to the propagandist, advertiser, public relations counsel and others who have ideas or products to sell. Knowledge of what they are up to is important for the true journalist who is a protector of their potential victims.

CUB REPORTING

Fortunate is the school or journalism graduate whose first job enables him to write as well as report. He should avoid being "buried" in a press room on a beat where he merely phones in the news, or on a copy desk or in a radio or television newsroom where press association and newspaper leads are rewritten so as to be suitable for broadcast.

There is no better vantage point from which to observe a cross section of life "in the raw" than police headquarters or courts. There the reporter will meet novelists, playwrights and magazine-article writers as well as sociology, law, and other scholars and students observing and gathering authentic information for their own understanding and usage. It is the place to "get your nose rubbed in it," meaning to come face to face with the squalid side of life, social problems, human frailties and personality types. Few would care to remain on the police beat indefinitely but anyone who skips the experience is shortchanged.

Thorough preliminary journalistic training also should include some contact with politics and government as well as the mine run of general assignments: meetings, speeches, obituaries, accidents, interviews, routine business, society and similar news. After a few years of such varied experience the beginner is able to start thinking about settling down to specialize. Thereafter, however, he will be wise to arrange for "change-of-pace" interludes such as those which discerning publishers and editors provide editoral writers, columnists, foreign news editors and others when they send them on trips of observation and fact-finding and encourage them to stay out of the rut or ivory tower.

OCCUPATIONAL AIDS

Ability to use a typewriter is essential. Usually a short evening or summer course provides adequate training, provided one has not already taught himself too many bad habits to be corrected. Until recently, few reporters felt the need of shorthand since the task of translating notes, of which there was temptation to take too many, slowed rather than hastened the process of reporting and writing. Today, however, when it often is necessary to interview news sources in the company of other reporters or to attend news conferences at which only a few get to ask questions, a verbatim record of what transpired often is valuable. Testimony in court or at committee hearings also can best be taken down in shorthand; thus more and more newsgatherers who specialize in such kind of work are learning it.

Those who have not done so usually develop their own system of short longhand, and may know some of the commercialized systems which are based primarily upon abbreviations for common syllables and combinations of letters. The reporter who develops his own system uses abbreviations for frequently used words and phrases. For instance, "2" is used for "to," "too," and "two," and "c" for "see," "u" for "you," "r" for "are," etc. The reporter can use simplified spelling in note taking if not in actual copy and can make use of such common abbreviations as "rr" for "railroad," "inc" for "incomplete," etc. He may even use foreign words which are shorter than English, as the French "selon" instead of "according to." Instead of "capital punishment" he may jot down "cp" and instead of "labor union" he may write "lu."

Wire or tape recorders are coming into greater use at news conferences and public functions and even during some interviews as a means of protecting both interviewer and interviewee as to the accuracy of subsequent quotation. There is the danger, however, that such interviews can become too formal and stilted and that the presence of the electronic device causes the interviewee to become overly cautious in his remarks. The same is true if motion pictures or television recordings are made.

In such cases, of course, the reporter does not have to know how to operate the gadgets. On some small and medium-sized papers, however, he may be expected, on occasion at least, to be able to use a camera when a staff photographer is unable to accompany him on assignment. Labor union contracts may forbid his doing so in other places. In any case, it is unlikely that he will have to know more than how to take the pictures; the development and printing will be the task of others.

Fantastic predictions are made of changes to occur within the not-too-distant future in communications—facsimile, ultrafax, computers, communication satellites, computers that can translate languages, read handwriting or typewriting and change spoken words into written words on perforated tape. Future reporters of the news may dictate their stories into microphone-like gadgets for transmission to "voice setting" machines, which in turn will correct the words into "type" ready for the page form. Other machines may "think" their words and transfer them to their assigned space in newspaper pages, together with pictures and headlines, electronically and photographically. The words may go into international newspapers, facsimiles produced in the homes of readers, automatically translated into languages indigenous to the various countries in which they are circulated.

Before this or any other Jules Verne or Buck Rogers type of inventions occur or go into use, however, the news still will have to be gathered by human beings. And the most important "machine" will continue to be the human reporter whose training cannot be neglected while he becomes enamoured with the mechanical possibilities of tomorrow.

The Ethics of Journalism

In considering a possible life work, any young person with an adequate social conscience asks himself, "How much of my soul would I have to sell?" As regards journalism, he wants clarification of the accusations he has heard that the media are owned and run by conservative or reactionary businessmen whose interest is profit making rather than public service; that news and editorial policy is influenced too much by advertisers and powerful pressure groups, and that the individual reporter, to survive, must suppress, exaggerate, sensationalize and distort the news which he often gathers by means of dishonest practices, unjustly invading the privacy and betraying the confidences of those with whom he deals.

THE REPORTER'S PREROGATIVES

Flat denial of these and similar charges is impossible. Bad journalistic practices *do* exist in some places and it may not be much solace to know that a review of history reveals that the worst offenders ultimately succumb. There is a decided limit, however, to which the rank-and-file journalist deserves sympathy when he rationalizes his own sins and shortcomings by blaming his superiors. No editor worth working for requires any member of his staff to violate his moral standards or conscience. Any "dirty" assignments go to those who give evidence early in their careers that they are easy or perhaps eager to be pushed around. In few other occupations is it possible for hirelings to "talk up" to their bosses as much as in journalism. A careful fact-gatherer has a better-than-even chance on most publications if he undertakes to persuade his superiors to publish what he has found to be true. No matter how money-minded his publisher may be, the reporter on assignment is not so motivated. By contrast, a clerk or salesman is constantly aware of his responsibility to make a sale and even the smiles and courtesies with which he greets customers may be feigned. Lawyers cynically "cut corners" in the interest of clients. It is difficult to find the person who is qualified to "cast the first stone" at the working journalist.

NEWSPAPER POLICY

It is true that newspapers and other journalistic media are big business enterprises which means they are owned and operated by wealthy persons whose natural and sincere outlook is generally what is called conservative. Many of these publishers deserve more credit than they receive for their efforts to prevent their personal biases from distorting the fairness of basic news coverage. It is not true that on larger publications the advertisers dictate news and editorial policies. Especially as regards larger publications, the advertisers need the good will of the publication more than the publication needs them. Granting favors in the form of publicity stories for "sacred cows" or soft-pedaling unfavorable news is a decidedly shortsighted policy. The press' conservatism, which reflects itself mostly in endorsement of presidential candidates and attitudes toward national political issues, is derived honestly, no matter how unwisely, from the sincere beliefs of owners and publishers. They also are sensitive to reader and other criticisms as, witness the fact, that investigations of the handling of the 1960 and 1964 campaigns indicate extraordinary fairness following some bitter charges of bias in 1952 and 1956.

The American press is a patriotic one which means that often it is duped itself and misleads readers by rushing into print with statements by prominent public officials which later have to be modified or counteracted. Since the end of World War II, the overwhelming majority of American newspapers, magazines, radio and television networks and stations, and other journalistic media have been almost completely uncritical supporters of United States foreign policy. Any reader who peruses more than the streamer-headlined news, however, knows that American journalism has not succumbed to suggestions that it censor "the other side" of the news. Usually, when misinformation is disseminated, the original and most important offender is the news source, not the medium.

Certainly, at the beginners' level, newsgatherers are not instructed to fake or commit hoaxes. One beneficial by-product of the decline of competition, perhaps, has been the reduction of temptation to use unethical practices to obtain scoops. Few reporters any longer engage in picture stealing or misrepresent themselves as policemen or coroners' deputies. If they fail to give their readers more "inside dope" it usually is because they don't possess it themselves. A reporter is the last person to whom someone wishing to conceal facts unburdens himself. On the other hand, newspapers have expended huge sums of money, involving great expenditures of time and energy, to expose corruption or to verify or discover facts in the public interest.

INVASION OF PRIVACY

No legal or judicial clarification ever has been made of the extent to which any person possesses a right to privacy. Generally accepted is the fact that anyone who courts public attention, as the politician or entertainer, sacrifices much or most of his privacy. Others, such as witnesses to accidents, crimes and the like, lose it temporarily through no fault of their own. Few persons like gossip about themselves but fewer still fail to enjoy it when it involves someone else. Many newspapers suppress the names of juvenile first offenders, relatives of persons unfavorably in the news, innocent victims of rape and other offenses and the like. Such policies are determined at the journalistic summit and should be made clear to all newsgatherers who then know they will be supported by their superiors in their grass-roots decision-making.

REPORTORIAL DECISION-MAKING

The same is true as regards many other ethical or policy matters, as whether to play up or down an outbreak of interracial violence, sensationalism in the handling of news of sex or crime, the details or even the facts of suicide, identification as to race, nationality or religion and the like. The reporter can "pass the buck" to his superior when he knows he has operated in accordance with publication policy.

A troublesome decision which the reporter sometimes has to make for himself is whether to listen to "off-the-record" statements; that is, whether to receive information in confidence. Sometimes, by promising not to quote a news source, he can obtain facts which the public has a right to know, or he may get tips which he can follow up without implicating the tipster. At other times, however, he may find that he has allowed himself to be "conned" into suppressing something. It is difficult to set a rule which applies to all situations. One thing is certain, however: once given, a promise must be kept. Many journalists have gone to jail for refusal to betray a confidential news source.

FREEDOM OF THE PRESS

Properly to evaluate any journalistic performance, the original purpose of the freedom of the press clause in the first amendment to the Constitution must be borne in mind. On one hand, the founding fathers wanted to prevent any governmental interference with or censorship prior to publication of news in the public interest, as they recalled the centuries of struggle which it took in England to obtain such rights. On the other hand, freedom of the press also was intended as a positive instrument to bolster the chances of success for an experimental government of, by and for the people. It really was the "right to be informed" that was being protected. If the founding fathers had thought some form of governmental regulation would best serve that purpose, undoubtedly they would have prescribed it. However, they felt the opposite: that wide-open freedom for any and all to publish or speak as they chose, even untruthfully and unfairly, would, in the long run, serve the public interest best. Thus, freedom of the press is a means to an end, not primarily an end in itself.

In the light of this purpose, it is discouraging to read the results of Gallup and other public-opinion polls which show gross and widespread ignorance regarding names and events in the news. The blame, however, is hardly primarily that of the journalistic media which are there for the public to use. Rather, superficiality of interest in public affairs must be traced to failures in the homes, schools, churches and other places. Perhaps it is caused by the complexities and insecurities of our contemporary society. If the increasingly monopolisitic press furthermore gives only one point of view on major issues, there nevertheless exists a quantity of liberal and iconoclastic magazines, newsletters and other periodicals to which it is possible to subscribe. It is not necessary to be uninformed or befuddled in the United States, the most literate nation in the world; and it is unfair to scapegoat the press, despite its shortcomings, for any public apathy. Possibly, a more enlightened and vigorous defense of civil liberties and civil rights by journalistic media would help, but it would only go so far in combating undemocratic forces. Anything that the idealistic newcomer to the ranks of journalism can contribute to the improvement of the role of the news media in this respect is in the public interest. The opportunities for such service are greater than the young person would find most other places. He could, in fact, do no better than to attempt to live up to the code of the American Society of Newspaper Editors adopted in April 1923 as follows:

> The primary function of newspapers is to communicate to the human race what its members do, feel and think. Journalism, therefore, demands of its practitioners the widest range of intelligence, of knowledge, and of experience, as well as natural and trained powers of observation and reasoning. To its opportunities as a chronicle are indissolubly linked its obligations as teacher and interpreter.
>
> To the end of finding some means of codifying sound practice and just aspirations of American journalism, these canons are set forth:

I

> *Responsibility.* The right of a newspaper to attract and hold readers is restricted by nothing but consideration of public welfare. The use a newspaper makes of the share of public attention it gains serves to determine its sense of responsibility, which it shares with every member of its staff. A journalist who uses his power for any selfish or otherwise unworthy purpose is faithless to a high trust.

II

> *Freedom of the Press.* Freedom of the press is to be guarded as a vital right of mankind. It is the unquestionable right to discuss whatever is not explicitly forbidden by law, including the wisdom of any restrictive statute.

III

Independence. Freedom from all obligations except that of fidelity to the public interest is vital.

1. Promotion of any private interest contrary to the general welfare, for whatever reason, is not compatible with honest journalism. So-called news communications from private sources should not be published without public notice of their source or else substantiation of their claims to value as news, both in form and substance.
2. Partisanship in editorial comment which knowingly departs from the truth does violence to the best spirit of American journalism; in the news columns it is subversive of a fundamental principle of the profession.

IV

Sincerity, Truthfulness, Accuracy. Good faith with the reader is the foundation of all journalism worthy of the name.

1. By every consideration of good faith a newspaper is constrained to be truthful. It is not to be excused for lack of thoroughness or accuracy within its control or failure to obtain command of these essential qualities.
2. Headlines should be fully warranted by the contents of the articles which they surmount.

V

Impartiality. Sound practice makes clear distinction between news reports and expressions of opinion. News reports should be free from opinion or bias of any kind.

1. This rule does not apply to so-called special articles unmistakably devoted to advocacy or characterized by a signature authorizing the writer's own conclusions and interpretations.

VI

Fair Play. A newspaper should not publish unofficial charges affecting reputation or moral character without opportunity given to the accused to be heard; right practice demands the giving of such opportunity in all cases of serious accusation outside judicial proceedings.

1. A newspaper should not invade private rights or feelings without sure warrant of public right as distinguished from public curiosity.
2. It is the privilege, as it is the duty, of a newspaper to make prompt and complete correction of its own serious mistakes of fact or opinion, whatever their origin.

VII

Decency. A newspaper cannot escape conviction of insincerity if while professing high moral purposes it supplies incentives to base conduct, such as are to be found in details of crime and vice, publication of which is not demonstrably for the general good. Lacking authority to enforce its canons, the journalism here represented can but express the hope that deliberate pandering to vicious instincts will encounter effective public disapproval or yield to the influence of a preponderant professional condemnation.

2

Problems of Newsgathering

I INTERVIEWING
  1. Resourcefulness
  2. Perseverance
  3. Friendships on Beats
  4. Publicity Seekers
  5. Formal Interviews
  6. Denials

II THE INTERVIEWER

III PUBLIC RELATIONS
  1. Adverse Criticism
  2. In Defense
  3. Dangers

IV GOVERNMENT SECRECY

V THE INTERPRETATIVE VIEWPOINT

SOMETIMES A REPORTER IS PRESENT AT A NEWS EVENT OF WHICH HE writes, as a meeting, speech, court trial or athletic contest. More often he obtains his information second-hand, through interviewing eyewitnesses, authorities, and others, or from press releases, reports and documents. Even when the newsgatherer is at the scene he has to check facts and details with firemen, policemen, convention chairmen and the like.

Interviewing

RESOURCEFULNESS

Newspaper reporters not only have risked and lost their lives in the front lines during warfare, but they have braved danger in peacetime to cover floods, hurricanes, fires, strikes, crimes and many other kinds of stories. No editor expects a reporter to place himself in unreasonable jeopardy, but he does drill into every cub the fact that there always is more than one way to get any story. Resourcefulness by the reporter is imperative; the editor miles away cannot do his most important thinking for him.

Consider an experience with which the beginning reporter is likely to meet: arrival at the scene of an automobile accident after the crowd has disappeared, the injured persons have been removed and the wreckage has been cleared away. The unresourceful reporter probably would phone his office that he is unable to get the story. The resourceful reporter, however, makes inquiries at the stores and residences nearby. He tries to find the policeman on the beat who probably has the names of the persons who were involved. Unsuccessful in these attempts he hastens to the nearest garages to find the damaged automobiles. Succeeding in that, he makes a notation of the license numbers in case the garage proprietor is unable to give him names. He phones police headquarters to discover the owners' names and addresses. He also phones the nearest hospitals. From one of these sources surely he learns the identity and whereabouts of the individuals whom he wishes to see. If he knows that someone was killed, he investigates at the morgue or calls the coroner.

The experienced reporter possesses the knowledge of all the possible channels through which he can obtain the information that he desires. Unidentified persons can be traced by means of laundry and other marks on their clothing, by dental work, even by bodily scars and deformities. A suicide may be explained by friends of the dead person who recall conversations which at the time seemed unimportant to them but which later cast light on the deceased's motive in taking his own life. Often the reporter may recall some news story printed in his paper weeks or months previously which suggests a solution to the mystery at hand. The wise reporter makes a practice of reading his own and rival newspapers daily, and he preserves news items which may be of value to him later. When in doubt whether to clip a certain article, he follows the safer policy and clips.

PERSEVERANCE

When he has established contact with someone able to give him information, the reporter may be chagrined to discover that the news source is reluctant to cooperate to the desired extent. Maybe he just doesn't want to become involved in some matter, for fear of being summoned as a witness in court or of arousing the displeasure of public officials, gangsters and others whom he fears. Possibly he does not want to reveal his ignorance or to tip his hand regarding business or personal plans. The reasons why a news source slams the telephone or door or "clams up" may be many and diverse, but the obligation of the reporter is the same. It is his duty to discover any facts that it is in the public interest be made known.

In many situations perseverance usually is rewarded. If a person deliberately evades the press by refusing to answer the telephone or by locking himself in his office or home, he plays a losing game. If he is a person whose information or opinion the newspaper has a right to request, his refusal to grant an interview does not make him appear in a very favorable light to readers. The reporter must be careful in stating that a man has disappeared to avoid being interviewed or facing charges, but he can say that a person could not be reached. In fact, he should include such a statement in his story to let his readers know that he has made the effort. If a person grants an interview but still refuses to talk, his silence may be even more important news than any statement would have been. Once the reporter has questioned a person and has received a noncommittal answer or no answer at all, he can say that Mr. So-and-So refused to make any comment. Then readers can draw their own conclusions as to why Mr. So-and-So would not talk.

> Mayor Alvin R. Potter had nothing to say today regarding the accusation that city employees, including himself, obtain free gasoline from the city yards.
> The charge was made yesterday by Ald. Leonard Ball, chairman of the streets committee. The chief executive's only reply to inquiring reporters was: "I have no statement to make at this time."

Sometimes the reporter may be able to convince his subject that it is to his advantage to make some statement. If a person knows that the paper will run a story of his refusal to comment, he may be frightened into speaking against his previous resolution not to do so.

A person who becomes involved in the news in a way distasteful to him may hesitate to speak for publication for fear of being misquoted or misrepresented. The personality and sincerity of a reporter may suffice to cause such a person to talk. Everything depends upon the approach which the reporter makes and upon his own attitude during the interview. His purpose should be to convince his subject that he bears no malice, and that he is seeking an accurate and fair quotation. If the reporter can convince his subject of this fact, he may find the person grateful for the opportunity of at last being able to talk to someone who is sympathetic and who affords him the chance of making his version of a story understood.

Fortunate is the reporter who possesses some bit of information which his subject does not expect him to know. Skillful interjection into the interview of this information may bring to an end any attempt at bluffing or fabrication. If he does not possess knowledge with which to intimidate his subject, the reporter may himself start bluffing. It often is necessary to put on a bold front and to challenge statement with statement.

The reporter should realize at all times that he has a powerful organization, his newspaper, in back of him. If he "curls up" and permits himself to be browbeaten, he fails in his duty to his editor. If he is treading on ground where he has a perfect right to tread, he never should be humble. Men who have been in public life for any length of time realize the power of the press and respect it. This does not mean that the reporter should be overbearing or that he should resort to threats, except in extreme cases where such measures are justified. The reporter must be guided by his common sense and his understanding of what constitutes public interest in determining when to threaten and when to cajole.

The best kind of interview is that which proceeds in a natural, friendly, informal way. The reporter may inspire confidence and make himself attractive by not coming to the point of his visit at once, but by beginning the conversation with some general comment. If he can get his subject chatting about another matter, he may be able to lead the interview easily into the channel that he wishes it to take.

It is wise to take as few notes as possible during an interview of this kind. Often it is disastrous to take a single note. If the reporter can get his subject to forget that he is speaking for publication, he will obtain much more than if the person is constantly reminded that the interviewer is taking down verbatim what he is saying.

Sometimes the interviewee requests the reporter to take verbatim notes. Or the reporter at the end of an interview may remark, "By the way, would you mind spelling that name for me?" Or he may ask for exact figures, addresses, etc., which the interviewee will be glad to have him get correctly. The reporter must be careful in asking for such information, however, that he does not suggest to the interviewee that he had better start designating which of his remarks were for publication and which not.

The reporter must train his memory to recall, an hour or so afterward, all the important remarks of the interviewee. He should make immediate mental note of any startling statement which he will want to use verbatim, and should keep turning it over in his mind during the rest of the interview. He should seize the first opportunity after leaving the scene of the interview to write down such statements and to make any other necessary notes. If he has an hour or so before he must write his story, he will be surprised to find that, bit by bit, virtually the entire interview will come back to him.

Few editors today encourage deception on the part of reporters in obtaining interviews. Frankness and fairness are recognized as the best standards of conduct. The reporter should let the person know who he is and the nature of his visit, and then should attempt by any legitimate means within his power, or by more drastic means if forced to them, to obtain the information that he desires.

In writing an opinion interview, it often is wise, for the sake of authority, to mention that the statements were made during an interview. If so, "Mr. White stated in an interview today," is better than, "Mr. White told a News reporter today." The newspaper should not boast of an exclusive interview unless it has shown ingenuity in outwitting opponents.

FRIENDSHIPS ON BEATS

Because nobody is as grammatically correct while speaking as while writing, it is common practice to "fix up" unprepared oral statements of persons in the news so as not to embarrass them or create a wrong impression. The sense of any quotation must, of course, be retained. On occasion, it may not be in the public interest to protect a source. If, for instance, despite overwhelming evidence to the contrary, a public official declares that he "knows nothing" of a scandalous situation with which he should be familiar, it is not unfair to quote him verbatim. When such necessity arises, the beat reporter who has daily contact with the news source would be pleased to have a "special" or general assignment reporter sent over to handle that particular story. Often the beat man finds it wise to warn someone with whom he has made friendly contact that an unfavorable story is going to appear. In other words, a reporter cannot be effective if he makes enemies of those on whom he must depend for information. How to maintain personal relationships of friendship and at the same time fulfill his newsgathering obligations is one of the most vexatious problems with which the beat reporter has to contend. As one of them put it:

> A newspaper reporter, especially if he is assigned to a particular beat, enters into a very personal relationship with his news sources after a while. It can't be avoided, for these are the people you are talking with every

day. In contrast, the public for which a reporter is writing, and to which he is responsible, is always a very impersonal and nebulous thing. There is a constant danger of giving the human being the benefit of the doubt at the expense of some quite abstract body of readers. For example, the superintendent of schools gets himself into a bad situation. Knowing him, you understand that he had the best motives in the world, but simply made a mistake of judgment. You know he recognizes it is your duty to advise the public of his action. Or, a situation I actually ran into: a cop had been suspended for striking a prisoner. I found out about it. The cop was a guy I had talked with every day for nearly a year. He'd told me all about himself, his family, and his ambitions. The suspension had been ordered promptly and there was no doubt that he was being properly punished for his action. I wondered at the time what possible good it would do the public to know of the suspension. Who was the public, anyway? Of course, I wrote the story and spent much time trying to explain to the cop and to his superior why it was necessary that the public be advised. But the point is that the reporter is called upon often to make that kind of decision, and unless he is very careful, he will unconsciously find himself giving in to the very human appeal of his news sources. I think I've found this the toughest temptation to guard against in the business.

One of the greatest pitfalls the cub reporter must avoid is naïvete. No matter how pleasing the personality of the interviewee, nor how logical whatever he has to say, the reporter must realize that it is necessary to check, corroborate, diligently seek the other side and in general not be gullible. With complete sincerity a news source usually presents a one-sided version of whatever is at issue. A callow reporter may be tremendously impressed with the account given him of how a business, governmental unit or social agency operates if he relies entirely on what an interested party tells him. Omissions, misplaced emphases and distortions may become apparent only by interviewing other persons known to be critical. Otherwise the reporter may become only a messenger boy for press releases or one-sided "good" news. Probing, both by intensive interviewing of original news sources and of others, will not always end in complete reversal of original impressions, but it is a necessary precaution against error through excessive exuberance.

PUBLICITY SEEKERS

By no means are all persons reticent in granting interviews. The person who attempts to bulldoze reporters or to "hand out" statements to further his own interests, is ubiquitous. The reporter constantly must be on his guard against him. He must sift every statement and try to determine its truth. Entertainers or lecturers filling engagements in the community value any publicity they can obtain. They may, however, be reluctant to grant interviews. They take secretaries with them to receive reporters and to inquire the subject on which an interview is sought. Then stock answers to stock questions are produced, often in typewritten or mimeographed form. The reporter who asks a question to which the interviewee has a standard, prepared answer ought to and does feel foolish.

It may not be so easy to get to see other types of celebrities who are attending conventions or engaged in business. Often the reporter can obtain an interview with a person difficult to approach, by means of a letter of introduction from some other prominent person. Or he may wait out his party, accosting him in the lobby of the hotel or behind the scenes during a dramatic performance, concert or lecture.

In the majority of cases the interview can be obtained by the reporter's simply sending up his name or by phoning the person's room from the hotel office. If he has called at an inconvenient hour, he can request an appointment later. Usually he will get it, for the person will recognize the value of the publicity he may receive if he sees the reporter. Anyway, he will not want to offend an important newspaper.

A musician, scientist, writer, politician or any person who has become prominent, despises the reporter who betrays ignorance of his activities and reputation. Anyone with a specialty, furthermore, is bored to have to talk to another who is utterly uninformed concerning that field of interest. There are numerous biographical reference books which the reporter may consult to learn the outstanding facts about a person's life and achievements. The newspaper's reference department usually can supply clippings telling of what the person has done recently.

Without some knowledge of his subject, the reporter may fail in his interview. A famous person accustomed to being interviewed may become sympathetic toward the cub and may give him a few stock statements. But familiar, often-used material is not what the editor wants the reporter to get.

High school reporters may be excused for referring to notes while asking questions. The professional, however, memorizes his questions. These should be related to the interviewee's field of interest and yet should not be too elementary or questions which it is reasonable to suppose the person has been asked time and time again. The reporter should try to find some new angle of approach, some fresh subject upon which the person interviewed will be able to speak. He should not try to cover his subject's entire field of interest. To do so would mean failure to cover any aspect with any degree of thoroughness. The best stories following interviews with celebrities are on specific points about which the interviewer has questioned his subject thoroughly.

FORMAL INTERVIEWS

Persons who know that they are to be interviewed by the press often arrange for formal interviews at which representatives of all the newspapers and perhaps electronic and other media in the community are present. From the standpoint of the reporter, such an interview is undesirable because none of the information he obtains is exclusive.

An advantage of the formal interview, however, lies in the fact that there are several minds thinking up questions to ask. Frequently the person to be interviewed announces in advance that these questions must be prepared in writing and submitted some time before the hour of the interview. This procedure permits the reporter to know exactly what the subject matter of the interview is to be, but it also allows the interviewee to prepare guarded answers to questions which, if presented spontaneously, might bring forth answers more to the reporter's liking.

Even when interviewing a person in the company of other reporters, it is possible to obtain material on which to write a different story from those which the others will write. The keenest listener and the sharpest wit present writes the best story. Comparison of several write-ups based on a joint interview often discloses several different methods of handling the subject. One reporter plays up one statement and another reporter picks an entirely different one for his feature. Still a third writer concentrates on the personality of the interviewee rather than upon his remarks.

Sometimes it is possible to loiter for a minute or two at the end of a group interview to get a quick answer to an exclusive question.

DENIALS

Sometimes a person quoted in an interview as having made a certain statement, issues a denial. He may even aver that he never saw the reporter who wrote the story. This happens when a reporter plays up some extemporaneous remark of an interviewee's which the person would not have made in a formal interview.

A denial of the facts of an interview, of course, can be avoided by presenting the copy of the write-up to the subject, but few newspapers favor such a practice. To do so means that the interviewee will delete everything the least bit unfavorable to himself. It also means delay which a newspaper may not be able to afford, and a surrender of the newspaper's privilege to gather its information and write up its stories as it sees fit.

If the reporter is not guilty of misquotation he may "stick to his guns" and, if his newspaper stands back of him, defy the interviewee who has denied making a statement. In another story he reaffirms that his original story was correct. Then the public can believe whomever it pleases. Too often it chooses to believe the person interviewed when the reporter really was right.

Reporters frequently do not use remarks which they suspect the interviewee would deny. If he wishes to make sure that the interview will not be denied, the reporter can phone or call upon the interviewee again to obtain verification of whatever he wishes to write. When he does so, or even when he obtains his original interview, he may take a third person with him as a witness to the interview. This, however, seldom is feasible as the presence of a third person may prevent informality.

The Interviewer

The scientist in his laboratory and the author in his den can be as shy as a mouse in the presence of a cat, uncommunicative, embarrassed by the company of others, incapable of either social conversation or formal speech making—can be, in fact, an anthrophobe (one who fears people) and still be considered a personal success and a benefactor of mankind; the newspaper reporter must be an entirely different kind of person.

It is conceivable that the newsgatherer secretly may dislike most of those with whom his work brings him into contact, but he is forced to learn how to conceal any such feeling and to be able to meet people, all sorts of people, and to get them to feel so easy in his presence that he can obtain what he wants from them.

Because they are unaccustomed to dealing with them, many persons are suspicious of newspapermen, regarding them almost as some strange species of animal life not to be trusted or treated with the courtesy customarily shown those with other ways of earning a livelihood. Says Henry F. Pringle, veteran reporter: "The novice about to be interviewed for the first time assumes that all reporters are ghouls waiting for the emergence of the family skeleton." Such people think nothing of using methods of evasion and prevarication to hinder a reporter in his legitimate quest for information which they condemn in obstreperous terms if he himself tries.

What this amounts to is that the newspaperman must be an expert salesman. Good salesmanship is the basis of all good reporting, and fundamental to successful salesmanship are personality and tact. Although the timid, awkward cub may get what he wants by creating pity, it is the person who gives the impression of self-confidence, self-assurance, and self-respect whose success is enduring. It is in the presence of such persons that others feel most at ease.

It is impossible to lay down general rules on how to develop personality and tact. There are many types of newspapermen, all equally successful. On the whole, however, newspapermen are extroverts or compensated introverts with poise, self-assurance, and self-respect. Caspar Milquetoasts don't succeed in newspaper or any other kind of work calling for daily contact with the public.

A few specific suggestions to beginners are the following:

1. Don't conceal your identity. Begin an interview with a frank acknowledgment of who you are and of the purpose of your visit. Give the impression that you have an absolute right to obtain the information wanted and have no doubt of your ability to get it. Thus, it is wise to avoid negative questions, as "You wouldn't care to say anything on this matter, would you?"

2. Inspire confidence and even awe by directness in speech. Don't "beat around the bush" by informing a person, "We'd like to know if you will give us a statement—" Rather, ask, "What do you think about it?"

3. Be particularly careful in telephone conversations when the other party has the power to end the interview simply by hanging up the receiver. Don't say, "I wonder if—" "I'd like to ask you—" A good beginning is, "This is — of the *Daily News*. I'm calling to ask your opinion about—" and don't end a telephone conversation with "All righty" or "Oky doke" or some similar moronic expression.

4. Always give the impression of knowing more about a story than you really do or that you have other ways of obtaining information if the immediate source fails to cooperate. At the same time, don't make threats except as a last resort in special cases. Often a person can be induced to give facts by questions which make him believe the reporter has wrong information which he'll use if not corrected. From fear of having a wrong impression broadcast, he may open up and tell the truth.

5. Often, if a person is reluctant to talk, it is advisable to engage him in conversation about some unrelated subject, as an object in the room, his wife's picture, or an extraneous bit of gossip. After the "ice has been broken" and an attitude of friendship has been created, it is possible cautiously to bring up the real subject occasioning the visit.
6. Don't stop questioning until you have all the facts you want or flat refusals on the part of the news source to give them. Often a person's refusal to make a statement is better news than if he were to become voluble.

Public Relations

Most persons who quit newspapers or other journalistic media go into public relations work. Often this is because of the lure of a fatter paycheck, in which case the more basic reportorial experience the better. Others have been cynical failures in their attempt to find adequate means of self-expression where they were. Still others seek opportunities to promote causes in which they believe.

ADVERSE CRITICISM

Until recently, practicing journalists were almost unanimous in condemning public relations men as brazen if not unscrupulous space-grabbers and fakers. Today, this harsh judgment has been considerably modified, partly because of the impossibility of covering the wide range of potential news without assistance, and partly because of the considerable elevation of standards within the public relations field. Once they were mostly press agents, whose forte was the manufacturing of stunts and, more recently, they were mere publicity men whose success was determined largely by the amount of space their clients got in the legitimate news columns of the media. Now the best of them are skillful participants in top-level policy making who have the total "image" of their clients in mind. Instead of courting publicity they may, in fact, advise against seeking any journalistic mention. They concern themselves with internal problems of personnel and morale, advertising, product, salesmanship and total behavior. In their exalted positions they may be considered by some to be even more "dangerous" as hidden persuaders, pressure boys, masters of the invisible sell, space-grabbers, ballyhoo boys, hucksters or malicious engineers of public consent, to use some of the titles by which they are known to their detractors.

IN DEFENSE

In their own defense, the hundreds of thousands, if not millions, of persons who perform public relations functions contend that their activities are of great social benefit. To quote from an article, "A Working Concept of Public Relations," which the author wrote for the October 1958 *Library Trends*:

> They take credit for having converted business and industry completely away from the "public-be-damned" attitude and say that they have humanized business, helped give it good manners and, most important, a conscience; and that they have taught it that he profits most who serves best. They define public relations as simply doing the right thing and letting people know about it, applying the Golden Rule in everyday activities while not letting one's light shine unnoticed under a basket. To them, sound public relations means the daily application of common sense, common courtesy, and common decency in accordance with a continuous program of enlightened self-interest through good works which not only earn one a good reputation but cause him to deserve it as a good neighbor.

In further defense of public relations as it relates to news media, it is indisputable that almost every legitimate news item which appears in public print has publicity value for someone. Even unfavorable mention or scandal doesn't seem to be fatal to national heroes, especially in the entertainment world. Readers' memories are short and inaccurate and when they go to the polls the familiar name has advantage, no matter how unsavory the situation in connection with which it was publicized. Organized baseball and other professional sports are commercial enterprises which have thrived on free publicity, through good-sized sports sections, for generations. The same is true of the theater, book publishing, concert stage and other artistic enterprises which are not entirely philanthropies.

Since John D. Rockefeller I hired Ivy Lee early in the century, the policy of the public relations profession has been increasingly toward more cooperation with the newsgathering media rather than agencies to suppress unfavorable news or retard newsgatherers in their efforts to obtain it. Public relations departments of railroads, airlines and industries today are a great asset to reporters at times of fires, accidents and other disasters, whereas a generation ago exactly the opposite was the case.

The news or publicity division of a public relations department provides a quantity of legitimate news handouts, full texts of speeches by important people, notices of meetings and conventions, plans for changes in policies and operations of both private and public institutions, and other services which no newspaper or magazine could afford to obtain by means of its own paid employees. To some extent, the media are today at the mercy of the public relations people to keep them informed of what is going on in large segments of society.

DANGERS

The great danger is the extent to which public relations men erect a barrier between the reporter and original news sources. If all news is obtained through carefully prepared news releases, the reporter becomes little more than a glorified messenger boy. Good newspapers and magazines consist of more than such handouts with proper headlines and picture captions added by the editors. No matter how cooperative and sensible, the public relations man never can lose sight of the fact that his primary obligation is to his employer. The reporter, on the other hand, is a public servant in a democracy. There are bound to be at least occasional clashes of interest. News releases today are usually well written and reliable but often there are omissions and obscurities which can be corrected only by personal contact between newsgatherer and news source.

Large news conferences, especially with the President and other prominent public figures, can be extremely frustrating as no reporter present has the opportunity to probe deeply into any matter. Too often a reporter is limited to a single question so that as many as possible can have a turn. It's impossible under such circumstances to be thorough in one's fact-finding. Even if better conditions prevail, a public relations man may hover over the shoulder of the interviewee to advise, augment and correct his statements. Reporters often are infuriated and feel that their dignity has been insulted. Serving one's editor and the public is extremely difficult under such circumstances.

From their standpoint, public relations men recognize the value of good will on the part of reporters. Hence, they not only try to create the impression at least of the best cooperation possible, but they also make life easier in other ways. At meetings and conventions there are usually press tables and press rooms with ample refreshments, desks, telephones and other equipment. Media differ in the extent to which they allow staff members to accept favors from public relations men, public officials and others. Some even forbid the acceptance of free books to review, of passes to athletic, dramatic, and other performances, or of gifts on Christmas or other holidays. Others, however, allow and even welcome large favors such as trips and tours, even to foreign lands. The beginning reporter does well to learn what his superiors' attitude regarding all forms of what is opprobriously called "payola" happens to be.

A more subtle way of influencing news judgment is the awards which are given in recognition of stellar performance in a particular field. The decision in such a case as to what constitutes good journalism is that of the donor of the prize. Some newspapers are eager to wallpaper their offices with plaques and certificates, and some keep a careful tab on announcements of such honors-in-the-offing. Too much ambition, however, may develop into exaggerated emphasis on news of a certain character rather than unprejudiced evaluation of the happenings of the day. In other words, conscious efforts to please donors of prizes can badly warp good editorial performance.

Governmental Secrecy

From the standpoint of the public's right to know, even more serious than the censorship exerted by private public relations men, is that which exists at all levels of government. Beginning with the Truman administration, federal administrators were instructed to classify potential information as to its secrecy. The uproar this system caused among members of the American Newspaper Publishers Association, American Society of Newspaper Editors, Sigma Delta Chi and other journalistic groups, encouraged a House committee chaired by Representative John Moss of California to hold extensive hearings and to propose legislation intended to prevent unreasonable withholding of information. In June 1966 Congress passed and on July 4, 1966, President Johnson signed Senate Bill 1160, which established the right of the public, including the press, to inspect the Federal Register descriptions of the operations of federal agencies, their rules and records. Several kinds of information, mostly allegedly related to national security or privacy, are excepted, however, so the effects of the legislation may depend on its interpretation by those whom it was intended to force to be more cooperative with newsgatherers.

Under the impetus created by the Washington furor, inquiries revealed that various elements in state and local governmental units also practice censorship. Under goading from the journalistic organizations mentioned and state press associations, some states have passed new laws requiring city councils, boards of education, and similar bodies to hold only open meetings. Legislation also has been drafted to broaden the rights of reporters to inspect and use public records of all sorts. Since conditions vary so greatly from place to place, the beginning reporter must be certain to learn what his rights and privileges are as regards such matters and to get his information from official sources rather than taking the word of some bureaucrat. As he ferrets out the news and the news behind the news, he is truly an agent of democracy, a crusader for the right without which a free society cannot long exist—the right of the people to know.

The Interpretative Viewpoint

In gathering information about a news event, the reporter seeks answers to the *who, what, where, when, why,* and *how* of whatever happened. Of these, the first four are basic to virtually any account. The emphasis that they should receive under different circumstances will be discussed in Chapter 3. Offhand, it might be held that not all stories have a *why* or *how* element important enough to engage much of the newsgatherer's attention. Actually, exactly the contrary is the case. In delving into the *what* of most stories, the reporter really is asking "why?" even though the answers he receives may become part of the *what*.

The beginning journalist who aspires to the heights mentioned in the preceding chapter should be aware of this fact. Whenever he does a thorough job of interviewing for what may seem to be a minor or simple story, he is training himself for more penetrating assignments in the future. He is developing an attitude or frame of mind toward newsgathering. To illustrate:

Police arrested Carter Davis, 14, son of Mr. and Mrs. George Davis, 4513 W. Coral street.

Why?

Because he used a knife to stab his eighth-grade teacher at Tyler Junior high school, 1216 N. Marshall street. She is Mrs. Vivian Heller, 48, 5141 W. Falconer avenue.

Why did he do it?

The assault occurred just after she had told the boy that he would fail his course in English.

But other teenagers fail in their school work without committing violence against their teachers. *Why is this boy different?* The Behavior Clinic psychiatrist is examining him now in an attempt to find out. While waiting for the report, further facts can be obtained: the circumstances and sequences of the events, the victim's condition, police activities and so forth. Questioning of school authorities reveals Carter's academic and deportment records. Classmates tell of his behavior toward and reputation with his peers, expressing either surprise or the opposite as regards the immediate situation.

Further clues as to the answer to the *why* are obtained by a visit to Carter's home and neighborhood, by talks with parents and other relatives, neighbors and friends, and recreational and other workers with whom the boy has had contact.

The reporter is able to ask penetrating questions to a considerable extent because of his knowledge of modern thinking in the fields of psychology, social psychology, psychiatry and sociology. Not too many decades ago he would presume, with most everyone else, that there is a dichotomy of good boys and bad boys, determined largely by the individual's exercise of free will. A more lenient attitude would be to consider the social misfit a victim of some sort of demoniacal possession. In any case, harshness of punishment was the only known corrective. Police operated on the "catch 'em and kill 'em" philosophy and were goaded on by journalists who reflected the indignation of most of their readers whenever a particularly heinous example of misbehavior occurred.

Within a generation, the attitude of a majority of enforcement officers, judges, educators, journalists and others has changed. Today it is recognized that there is "something wrong" with a boy who commits an act like Carter's. Psychiatrists still are reluctant to discuss cases with newsgatherers until they have made their formal reports to whatever public authorities are involved. In the meantime, reporters must refrain from making medical diagnoses on the basis of their own investigations. They can, however, publicize such pertinent facts as that a misbehaving child comes from an underprivileged, broken slum home, or from a wealthy family where everything was lavished upon him except the most important ingredient of all—parental attention.

Why do some youngsters reared in the same neighborhood "go bad" whereas others do not? The answer concerns the behavior clinician who may conclude that the boy who does not act in accordance with group standards is the problem child rather than others who "go along" with the gang in committing antisocial acts. Human motivation is an extremely complex subject for scientific research, with multitudinous influences in and out of the home and other primary institutions affecting different children differently. The journalist should be warned against acceptance of "panacea" explanations such as broken homes, poverty, slum environments, and especially television, comic books, the movies and so forth, as providing easy answers to explain intricate situations.

Even if a reasonably clear picture emerges as regards an individual case, the probing reporter can continue to ask "why?" at several different levels of inquiry. If social statistics indicate that there are correlations between various factors, as slum conditions, racial, religious or nationality backgrounds, economic status, and so forth, for understanding it is necessary to ask "why?" as regards each item. What are the cause-and-effect relationships? And how explain the type of behavior which results? Why violence instead of suicide or something else? Because of the extreme frustration or sense of insecurity in the individual from whatever cause—an organic or biological reflex? Or because violence is an accepted or admired form of behavior in a group whose respect is desired? Or because there is violence in other aspects of the environment, including the international scene? These are matters which concern many different specialists in the social sciences whose erudition and research the newsgatherer cannot hope to duplicate. He can, however, solicit their information, assistance and advice. Most important, he can "get more" out of his assignments, both for immediate journalistic usage and for promotion of his general understanding, if he recognizes that the isolated news event is not really isolated.

It would be impossible and superfluous to attempt extensive probing into the broader aspects of every incident such as the hypothetical one of Carter Davis. Space will not permit usage of exhaustive analyses of every vagrant, jack roller, tough juvenile, prostitute or others of society's "problem children." There is no beat to compare with police, however, to provide an opportunity to begin cultivation of a querying attitude toward life. When he later attempts to fathom the causes of a depression, war or major issue of any kind, the experienced newsgatherer utilizes the habits of mind that he cultivated back in his cubhood. If he doesn't take advantage of the opportunities provided to him at the beginning of his journalistic career, his grandchildren will still be visiting him in the same press room where he got his start.

A quarter-century ago, Sidney Kobre wrote:

> What are the next steps in American journalism, if the newspapers are to be made an effective up-to-date social institution? Certain lines of development can be pursued.
>
> The materials with which the newspaper deals are fundamentally of a psychological, economic and sociological character. It is an oversimplification to handle this material as if it were ordinary routine stuff. All aspects of human life are being methodically investigated, instead of being viewed in the usual "common-sense" traditional manner. The human body is a complicated and intricate nervous and physical system. When it breaks down, only trained men can rehabilitate it. The stuff of which news is made is just as highly complicated because it relates to human behavior. Only specialized reporters with eyes sharpened in the social sciences can handle and interpret the facts intelligibly.
>
> The expert has been quietly emerging up to now from university halls and entering every field affecting industry and politics. Why not journalism?

3

Organizing the Facts

I Contemporary Trends

II The Inverted Pyramid Form

III The Lead

IV The Body
1. Spiraling
2. Unity
3. Block Paragraphing
4. Themes
5. Chronological

V The Reporter's Notes

Even before he has completed the task of gathering the facts concerning a particular news event, the reporter starts thinking of how he will organize them into a news story. The more experienced he is, the more automatic or unconscious this habit becomes. As new information is obtained he may modify earlier ideas regarding the theme or central idea coming out of the assignment.

Contemporary Trends

Since World War II, there have been numerous studies of the traditional methods of organizing a news story. At several annual conventions the Associated Press Managing Editors devoted considerable attention to ways of making news writing more readable. In part, they were motivated by the success of news magazines in presenting the news in brighter and livelier ways. Also, and perhaps more important, radio and television newscasters demonstrated how the gist of a story often could be presented in fewer words than were contained in the usual traditional newspaper story lead.

The press associations and some large newspapers employed experts in readability to analyze their practices. A few journalistic higher-ups became so enthusiastic over some readability formulas that they blamed widespread reader ignorance and indifference upon traditional styles of journalistic composition. Some others thought the answer was to be found in greater understanding by journalists of the philosophical and statistical aspects of the communication process.

Because they have been taught to journalistic novitiates for several generations, the five *w*'s often seem to be trite and academic. Nevertheless, no matter what writing or speaking style is used, the reader or listener's curiosity has to be satisfied as regards the *who*, *what*, *when*, *where* and *why*, as well as the *how* of a newsworthy occurrence. What has happened, largely as a result of the blandishments of the readability conscious and statistically conscious communication researchers, is a considerable loosening of the rigid rules regarding the structure of a news story. Whereas a generation ago it was virtually mandatory that as many as possible of the five *w*'s and *h* be mentioned in the first paragraph of a news story, today considerably greater freedom is permitted in presenting them.

The Inverted Pyramid Form

Despite the extensive experimentation that has taken place, the great majority of news stories still are written in accordance with the traditional rule that the first part—whether it be a conventionally written single paragraph or a half-dozen or more one-sentence paragraphs—contain a succinct résumé of the story as a whole.

The striking difference between news writing in the United States and other forms of written composition, such as the essay, poetry, drama, novel and short story, continues to be this: whereas the authors of these other forms of composition usually begin with minor or incidental details and work to a climax near or at the end of their compositions, the news writer reverses this plan of organization. That is, he begins with the climax or end of the story. Given a schedule of facts to arrange in the form of a newspaper article, he selects the most important fact or climax of the story he has to tell and puts it at the beginning. The second most important fact comes second, the third most important fact third and so on.

The traditional form of news writing is called the *inverted pyramid form*. It is said to have originated in Civil War days when correspondents used the telegraph for the first time. From fear that their accounts would not be transmitted all at one time, the war correspondents crowded as much information as possible into their first paragraphs.

Throughout the decades since that time, press associations, which transmit stories by telegraph, have perfected the system. Before the teletypesetter was introduced about mid-century, few leading stories ever were transmitted in one piece. Instead, a few paragraphs of several important stories were sent first and then the later paragraphs. Throughout a day's sending, there were numerous new or substitute first paragraphs (leads), inserts and additions.

Locally written news followed the press association pattern. The inverted pyramid form of organization was defended in several different ways, namely:

1. To facilitate reading. The reading matter of the average newspaper, if printed in book form, would fill a large volume. The American newspaper reader hasn't time to read that much daily. Neither is he interested in all the articles appearing in any newspaper. If the climax of each story is at the beginning, the reader can learn the gist of the news shortly, and if interested, can continue to the details of stories which attract him. He should not have to read any article to its conclusion to learn what it is about.

2. To satisfy curiosity. This is the natural way of telling an important item of news. If someone drowns while swimming, the average person would not begin telling of the incident by narrating the dead person's preparations for a visit to the beach with a group of friends. Rather he would tell the important news first—John was drowned while swimming. Then he would relate the supplementary details of how, when, and where it happened.

3. To facilitate makeup. In rectifying a page, the makeup editor often finds it necessary to cut the length of some articles. If the least important details are at the end of a story, he can do this without harming the story. The makeup editor should feel free to cut ordinary articles without consulting other editors.

4. To facilitate headline writing. The headline consists of the key words or their synonyms necessary to give an idea of what a story contains. If the story is well written, the headline writer should not have to look beyond the first paragraph or two to find these words.

A few years ago the Writing committee of the Associated Press Managing Editors cited the story in the right-hand column below as one of the best examples of news writing of the year. It was written in the traditional inverted pyramid style. In the left-hand column below the same facts, using the identical phraseology as much as possible, are rearranged in chronological order.

Chronological Style

About 1 A.M. today, Mrs. Harry Rosenberg was awakened by the sound of a car roaring out of the driveway of her home. She rushed to the living room where she discovered that her granddaughter, Judith Ann Roberts, 7, no longer was sleeping on the studio couch and that the front door was standing open.

Mrs. Rosenberg called her daughter, Mrs. Shirley Roberts, wife of a Baltimore attorney and labor leader, who was visiting her parents. Mrs. Roberts, the missing child's mother, notified police of her daughter's kidnaping at 1:10 A.M.

Police said the kidnaper sneaked into the home of the grandparents, stole the keys to the Rosenberg's car from the grandfather's trousers pocket and took the child away.

Four hours and ten minutes after they were called, police found the Rosenberg car abandoned in the strip of sandy land between Bayshore drive and the shore of Biscayne Bay. Its wheels were mired in the sand and the tire marks showed the driver tried frantically to get it out.

Judith Ann's nude and brutally battered body was found a block from the car in a clump of bushes off fashionable Bayshore drive. It was caked with blood and dirt, indicating she put up a brave fight for her life. The blue-eyed child had been raped and beaten on the head with a heavy instrument and a piece of gauze was knotted about her throat. Her flimsy seersucker nightgown, white with red polka dots, lay eight feet from her body.

Newspaper Style

Judith Ann Roberts, blue-eyed, 7-year-old daughter of a Baltimore attorney and labor leader, was kidnaped from the home of her grandparents here today, raped and beaten to death.

Police found the child's nude and brutally battered body in a clump of bushes off fashionable Bayshore drive five hours after her mother, Mrs. Shirley Roberts, reported her missing.

She had been beaten on the head with a heavy instrument and a piece of gauze was knotted about her throat. Her flimsy seersucker nightgown, white with red polka dots, lay eight feet from the body.

Judith Ann's little body was caked with blood and dirt, indicating she put up a brave fight for her life.

Police said the killer sneaked into the home of the grandparents, Mr. and Mrs. Harry Rosenberg, about 1 A.M., stole the keys to Rosenberg's car from his trousers pocket and took the child from the studio couch in the living room where she was sleeping.

Mrs. Rosenberg was awakened by the sound of the car roaring out of the driveway. She found the child missing and the front door standing open.

Police were called at 1:10 A.M. Four hours and ten minutes later, they found the Rosenberg car abandoned in the strip of sandy land between Bayshore drive and the shore of Biscayne Bay. Its wheels were mired in the sand and the tire marks showed the driver tried frantically to get it out.

Judith's body was found a block from the car.

"Note, please," the A.P.M.E. Writing committee asked, "the many fine points . . . 'the seersucker nightgown, white and red polka dots, lay eight feet from the body.'

"How many little nightgowns like that are all over this land? And *eight feet* . . . no guess-work there; the reporter was *seeing* it for you. Too, the killer sneaked in about 1 A.M. and 'police were called at 1:10 A.M.' The car was found *four hours and ten minutes later* . . . not simply later in the day."

Although few would argue with an unnamed telegraph editor with more than forty years' experience, whom the committee quoted as saying, "That Miami story is one of the finest writing jobs I've ever seen," the points cited by the committee indicate that the story's strength derived primarily from the fact that an extraordinary job of reporting, involving keen observation, had preceded its composition. In other words, *the most important step in communication is obtaining something worthwhile to communicate.* Stated still another way, the basis of all good journalism is thorough reporting. Shorter words, sentences, and paragraphs, desirable as they may be for clarity, cannot add important details to a journalistic account. *There is no substitute for good reporting no matter what writing style is used.*

The Lead

The Miami story was written in traditional inverted pyramid style. That is, the first paragraph contained the gist or skeleton outline of the entire story in a minimum of words. Subsequent paragraphs elaborated upon various aspects of the lead, making them more definite; or they supplied additional details in the order of their importance as the reporter judged them.

Since, for more than a half-century, this has been the orthodox form of news writing, the *lead* of a straight news story came to be defined as the first paragraph which contained all of the elements (five *w*'s and *h*) necessary for the complete telling of the essential facts.

This practice often led to long and crowded first paragraphs. The lead of the Miami story, for instance, might have read something like this:

> The nude and brutally beaten body of Judith Ann Roberts, blue-eyed, 7-year-old daughter of a Baltimore attorney and labor leader, was found by police in a clump of bushes off fashionable Bayshore drive here at 1 A.M. today after she had been kidnaped from the home of her grandparents, Mr. and Mrs. Harry Rosenberg, and raped.

In the effort to avoid such cumbersome lead paragraphs, and to increase readability, some newspapers have gone to the opposite extreme of invoking the "one-fact sentence" rule which would lead to something like the following:

> A 7-year-old girl has been kidnaped, raped and beaten to death.
> She was blue-eyed Judith Ann Roberts of Baltimore. Her father is a lawyer and labor leader.
> Police found the child's body in a clump of bushes off fashionable Bayshore drive.
> The body was nude and brutally battered.
> The child's mother, Mrs. Shirley Roberts, reported her daughter missing at 1:10 A.M.
> That was four hours and ten minutes before the body was found by police.

It is difficult to determine just exactly how many of the one- or two-sentence paragraphs of a story written in this manner constitute the lead, or first unit of the story. Each sentence relates to some word or fact in a preceding sentence, and it takes a half-dozen or more of them to present all of the information which once would have been crowded into half the space or less. This form of writing says less in more words but is scored as more readable. The original version of the Miami story was a compromise between the new and old extremes.

Since the inverted pyramid form still is adhered to, even in the staccato type of paragraphing illustrated above, in that facts are arranged in the order of their supposed importance, the traditional definition of a news story lead holds: the first unit of the story which performs the function of telling the entire story in epitomized form.

A good lead, no matter how much it is strung out, has the following qualities:

1. Answers all of the questions that a reader wants to have answered when hearing of a particular incident. These include: the cause and result (the *how* or *why* and the *what*), the *who* and often the *where* and the *when*. These elements are called the five *w*'s and the *h*. Not all of these must be present in every lead, but no important one should be omitted. (See Chapter 4.)
2. Plays up the feature of the story if there is one. (See Chapter 5.)
3. Is attractive and induces the reader to continue with the rest of the story. (See Chapter 6.)
4. Observes the canons of good news writing. (See Chapter 7.)

5. Suggests or gives the authority on which the news is printed. (See Chapter 8.)
6. Identifies the individuals mentioned in the story (or the story itself) by relating them (or it) to previous or contemporaneous news. (See Chapter 9.)

The Miami story fulfilled these requirements in this way:

Who—Judith Ann Roberts.
What—Killed.
When—July 7; time of day (1 A.M.) given later.
Where—Miami, Fla.
How—Kidnaped, raped and beaten to death.
Authority—Police and relatives obvious sources of information.
Identification—Seven-year-old daughter of a Baltimore lawyer and labor leader.
Feature—Kidnaped from home of grandparents.

The Body

In view of the tendency to reduce the first sentence of a news story to the fewest possible words, the function of the sentences and paragraphs which immediately follow is clearly to restate the facts of the first sentence so as to make them more definite. Loosening of the rule that the lead contain all of the five *w*'s and the *h* means that succeeding paragraphs often must supply some additional pertinent facts crowded out of the lead in the interest of brevity.

It doesn't make any difference what academic labels are placed on units of a news story, and it is difficult or impossible to chart news stories so that units do not overlap. If you wish, you can consider the extreme attempt at epitomized writing ("A 7-year-old girl has been kidnaped, raped and beaten to death") as the lead and call all the rest of the story by its traditional name, *body*. Or you can insist that the lead proper include as many sentences as are necessary to make the basic elements (five *w*'s and *h*) definite.

In either case, there often remain a number of additional paragraphs which can be labeled either "body" or "second part of body." If new details are added in the same sentences or paragraphs in which there is further amplification of the lead, telling exactly where the last unit of the story begins isn't easy.

SPIRALING

Perhaps a spiral with the broad part at the top would be a better simile than inverted pyramid to describe how a well-constructed news story today may unfold. Either by definite grammatical reference or linkage of thought, each well-written succeeding paragraph flows from the preceding one.

In the following example observe how each succeeding paragraph makes more definite an element of the preceding paragraph (words in italics) and in addition contains some new information.

> Aaron L. Engstrand, who recently completed a study of previously made civil service surveys for the city administration, will get a full-time city *job* July 1.
>
> He will become consultant to the city Civil Service commission, empowered to put into effect *recommendations* he submitted.
>
> They include "more realistic examinations" in the *selection of city employees*, and improvements in personnel relations.
>
> John S. Christopher, commission president, announced the appointment Friday. He said that one of Engstrand's first jobs will be to hire a *director of personnel* for the city.
>
> Engstrand, a veteran in public administration and social-service work, refused the personnel director job when it was offered him recently.

UNITY

A method of obtaining rhetorical unity as one short paragraph follows another is by use of *linkage* words. Note in the following example how their skillful use creates a flow and, at the same time, enables the writer to introduce new facts. This story could be cut at the end of almost any paragraph and there still would be a rhetorically complete account.

> BY *Associated Press*
>
> Mighty rivers on a late winter rampage surged through south central sections of Alabama, Georgia and Mississippi Wednesday, leaving wide trails of muddy ruin amounting to millions.
>
> *Except* around Jackson, Miss., the highest levels of the flooding rivers were spread largely across rural areas as they continued toward their common draining point, the Gulf of Mexico.
>
> *However*, more flood menace lies ahead for downstate residents, and even in ravaged mid-state sections where the worst is over, it will be days before the rampant rivers fall within their banks.

Alabama at Crest

At Selma in central Alabama, *for example*, the Alabama River reached its crest of 58.3 feet Tuesday night, but the muddy waters are not expected to creep back to the 45-foot flood level until March 9.

In hard-hit Selma and Montgomery and Demopolis, Ala., *as well as* Jackson, Miss., and West Point and Columbus, Ga., thousands in evacuation centers looked to more days of waiting for water to seep out of their homes.

To relieve the tension of Montgomery refugees, many facing their fifth night in shelters, the Red Cross put on recreation programs.

Damage to Alabama's public facilities *has already topped* $10 million in preliminary estimates. That includes only roads and bridges and county and municipal places—not homes, businesses, farmland and livestock.

Cattle Drowned

In central Alabama's Montgomery and Elmore Counties alone, a livestock broker estimates that about 2,500 head of cattle worth $500,000 have drowned *during the current flood.*

As the swollen Pearl River swirled around the Jackson, Miss., area Tuesday night and Wednesday, cutting a three-mile swath in some places, about 850 residents left their low-lying homes and most flocked to refuge centers.

[Tampa *Tribune*]

BLOCK PARAGRAPHING

In longer stories, regardless of whether the lead was one or several paragraphs long, or "straight" or spiraling, paragraphs are so written as to include a single subtopic each.

This type of paragraphing differs from the type which English composition students are taught is best. Because newspaper paragraphs of necessity (appearance) must be short, they do not follow the orthodox rule of rhetoric that each paragraph should include a complete thought or topic. Rather, in newspaper paragraphing the idea-unit is broken up into subtopics. In other words, news writers paragraph their paragraphs.

This type of paragraphing, called *block paragraphing*, is distinctly advantageous for news writing. It permits the insertion or deletion of paragraphs without disarranging a story. Frequently it is necessary, in the light of new information, to recast certain paragraphs, to add additional paragraphs, and to remove others. For example, note in the following story how additional information might be added without serious trouble. The paragraphs in italics quite conceivably could have been added after the story was written. Furthermore, several of them could have been inserted at other places in the story. Quite a few of the paragraphs, italicized or not, could be shifted around without destroying the effectiveness of the story. Often, different inserts are written by different reporters.

A five-alarm fire last night wrecked a big grain elevator in the 700 block West Jerome avenue, just west of Fort Alston.
Thirty-five pieces of fire equipment fought the blaze for three hours at the Northern Manufacturing company.
Damage was estimated at $225,000.
Flames and thick billows of smoke leaped high above the burning building as the blaze lighted the western sky. Periodically, a galaxy of sparks would burst from the roof, illuminating the entire area.
The wood-and-sheet metal building was still standing shortly before 1 A.M. but Patrick L. O'Hara, chief engineer of the Fire department, said the structure was a total loss.
One fireman was slightly injured when he ran a nail through his boot, but he was treated at the scene and returned to duty. No one else was reported hurt.
The blaze was discovered at 9:50 P.M. by Waldo Wozniak of the 2700 block Hazel avenue who was driving his children along Jerome avenue after showing them where he worked—the Key highway yards of the Keystone Steel company.
Mr. Wozniak said he saw flames through one of the elevator's windows.
He hurried west on Jerome avenue to Hurlburd street, the location of the No. 16 Engine company and the No. 18 Truck company. Mr. Wozniak told Firefighter Emerson Hudnutt what he had seen and led the first pieces of equipment to the scene.
The Police department sent sixteen motorcycle men and two radio cars to handle the traffic.
The fireboats *Mayo* and *Stirrup* quickly pulled into one of the Marble Point piers on the opposite side of Jerome avenue to supply additional water pressure for the land equipment's hoses.
Chief Mott and his men surrounded the burning elevator, which is about five stories high, and ordered them to direct their high pressure hoses against the building to keep the flames confined to as small an area as possible.
Three nearby tanks were scorched by the flames but received no further damage. Fire fighters watered down adjacent buildings to prevent them catching fire.

Themes

Some stories can be written around a central theme which is perceivable although not bluntly stated or restated throughout. The following story was written to explain the importance to the community of the news it concerns. This purpose is achieved in successive paragraphs which introduce and elaborate upon various aspects of the story as a whole.

J. R. MacDonald, president and chairman of the board of General Cable Corp., announced yesterday that the Tampa plant will manufacture a $4.8 million order of telephone cable to be shipped to Israel.

The order was believed by MacDonald to be the largest manufacturing order destined for export trade ever to be handled in Florida.

He saw it as a "harbinger" of Florida becoming a state doing an extensive manufacturing business in export trade.

To Add to Pay Roll

Fulfilling the order will mean the hiring of about 120 additional persons who will be kept busy for a year at the plant on E. Hanna St. Additional equipment is being installed in the Tampa plant and the hiring and training of the added personnel is underway.

All material going into the order will come to Tampa through its port and the finished product will be shipped from the port.

MacDonald said the quality of workmanship available at the Tampa plant and lower manufacturing costs here were reasons for Tampa facility making up the order.

Enough wire will be produced for the order that, if wrapped around the world, would circle the globe 10 times.

The order was negotiated jointly by General Cable and Automatic Electric International Inc., a wholly owned subsidiary of the General Telephone and Electronics Corp. [Tampa *Tribune*]

CHRONOLOGICAL

Still another widely used method of organizing the material after the lead is chronological, at least for a number of paragraphs, after which new facts can be added in block paragraph style. This type of organization is effective in stories in which action is described, as in the following example:

A gunman yesterday robbed the Eastwood Federal Savings and Loan association of about $7,000 while scores of noonday shoppers walked past the building at 118 S. Jeffrey street.

The bandit walked in at 12:45 P.M., normally the busiest time of day, and found the office empty of customers. A teller, Miss Virginia Kole, one of four employees present, asked the man if she could help him.

"Yeah. There's a lot you can do to help me," the man answered as he leaped up on the 4-foot high counter and pulled out an old rusty revolver.

"Get back, get back," he ordered from his perch. "I'm not fooling. I'll shoot the lady first. Don't step on the alarm."

Joseph L. Dierks, vice-president, said he was sitting in the back of the office and did not move, waiting to see what the man would do next.

The bandit jumped down on the floor behind the counter and ordered the four to a rest room in the rear. The other two workers were Howard K. Jacobs, secretary-treasurer of the association, and Robertson Evans, a teller.

As the holdup man was directing the group to the rear room, a customer came in. He was Walter Mather, 2130 W. Otis avenue, who also was ordered to the back room.

The robber closed the door on the five and went back to the front of the office where he rifled three cash drawers and the open safe.

When Mr. Evans heard the front door close, he hurried from the back room and ran to the front door hoping to see which way the bandit fled. The man apparently became quickly lost in the crowd and Mr. Evans could not see him.

Mr. Dierks said an early count indicated the stolen money totaled $6,829.15, but he thought the final tally would be higher, perhaps as much as $8,500.

The vice-president considered the holdup man an extremely lucky amateur. He pointed out that an experienced robber probably would have looked over the office several days in advance and would have realized that the association usually was busiest between 12:15 and 1:15 P.M. when many customers come in on their lunch hours.

Mr. Dierks said the gunman was probably a very athletic person, judging from the way he hopped about the office. He appeared to be in his early twenties, about 5 feet 6 inches tall, and weighed about 140 pounds. He wore a blue cap, green shirt, and khaki trousers.

What must be avoided is making the lead sentence merely a "peg line." For example, "Alderman John F. Gates today called Mayor Henry R. Penrose a liar" is superior to "An alderman today called the mayor a liar." It is inferior to "Alderman John R. Gates today charged that Mayor Henry R. Penrose lied when he said he never owned any west-side real estate." If by some grotesque error the former lead sentence were to appear alone, there would be considerable embarrassment if not worse. There is, in other words, a limit beyond which it is wise to be brief. Too often brevity necessitates being vague or indefinite, which requires more rather than less effort on the part of the reader who seeks the facts of a news story.

The Reporter's Notes

Prerequisite to a well-organized news story is a careful rearrangement of the reporter's notes. For the experienced reporter, the task of dictating a story over the telephone to a rewrite man from a handful of notes scribbled on copy paper while standing in a stuffy booth is an everyday matter. While he's learning, however, the cub reporter profits by an outline of the facts he has gathered. He has, first of all, to pick the feature to go into his lead; next, to be certain he has answered all of the essential questions which need to be answered and has sufficient identification and authority; then, to decide which phases of the lead need amplification in the first part of the body of the story and how it is to be provided and, finally, to arrange the other facts which he wishes to include.

Seldom, if ever, does the reporter jot down facts in the order in which he will use them in his story. As he learns more and more about the incident he is reporting, one or more lead possibilities strike his attention. There are few if any reporters, regardless of experience, who fail to profit by a study of all notes taken and an outlining of them, if only in the head, before beginning to write or dictate. The young reporter frequently finds it profitable to number the facts included in his notes in the order of importance.

The necessity for rearranging and discarding notes can be seen by imagining how the reporter who covered the Judith Ann Roberts case gathered his facts. If he were stationed at police headquarters, the first information he obtained was: Mrs. Shirley Roberts called to report that her child had been kidnaped from the home of her parents whose address was given. Either then or when policemen, accompanied by reporters, arrived at the residence, the mother gave a complete description of the child's appearance and habits. She and her parents told how the child's disappearance was discovered and the condition of the room, including the empty couch and open door. Mr. or Mrs. Rosenberg provided a description of their automobile: its make, model, color, license number, mileage and distinguishing features.

In the search for clues, police and reporters asked the three adults and other residents about the visit of the mother and child to Miami. They wanted to know how the family and child spent the preceding day, especially what they did during the evening. They asked about Mr. Roberts and whether either he or any of the others had any enemies who might wish them ill. They wanted to know whom Judith had met, talked with, played with, where she had gone, and so on.

Before the body was found, reporters made notes on the activities of the police: how many and who were assigned to the search, where they went and whom they questioned, what alarms were sent out, what clues, if any, they considered important, and the like. They inquired carefully into how discovery of the body was made—whether as part of a careful plan of investigation or by accident.

Bear in mind that the example given was written for a press association which means it was intended for publication in cities other than

Miami. In that city the story received much longer treatment with many additional details of interest to local readers.

To summarize: The first step in good news writing is good reporting. No story writes itself. The factual material must be gathered first. The person who doesn't know how to observe and gather facts never will be able to write a good news account.

4

Playing Up the Feature

I NEWS VALUES
1. Timeliness
2. Proximity
3. Prominence
4. Consequence
5. Human Interest

II THE 5 *W*'S AND THE *H*
1. The *Who*
2. The *What*
3. The *Why*
4. The *Where*
5. The *When*
6. The *How*

III RHETORICAL DEVICES
1. The Summary Statement
2. Conditional Clauses
3. The Substantive Clause
4. Phrases
5. The Cartridge Lead
6. The Punch Lead
7. The Astonisher Lead

IV MORE THAN ONE FEATURE
1. Separate Stories
2. The Crowded Lead
3. The "Shirttail" Method
4. Boxes
5. The 1-2-3-4-Lead

THERE IS NO EXACT "ONE WAY" TO WRITE ANY NEWS STORY. GIVEN THE same schedule of facts, equally competent writers will compose accounts which read differently, and an impartial judge might find it impossible to choose the best.

The first and most important step in news writing is selection of the lead. That requires the exercise of editorial judgment to determine what angle or phase of the total information available is to receive emphasis. It is not enough that the first part of a story answer as many of the questions, Who? What? When? Where? Why? and How? as the story demands be answered. These elements must be so arranged as to give proper emphasis to those which are most important.

The entire tone of a news story is determined by the feature which is emphasized in the lead, often in the first sentence or even the first clause or phrase of the first sentence. Giving proper emphasis to the different ingredients of a news story is a simple, standard *method of interpretation* which was practiced long before words were used to describe it. The reporter who develops facility in this regard is training himself well for the future.

News Values

Disregarding considerations of policy as a determinant of news judgment, newspapers and other media of communication, despite their differences, have similar criteria by which to determine the potential newsworthiness of the thousands or millions of occurrences from which they make their selection each day. Psychologically these criteria may be superficial or erroneous, but they have been tested by years of experience and, rightly or wrongly, are in vogue in all but a negligible number of news rooms.

Differing in arrangement, nomenclature and emphasis, the main determinants of news values, textbook writers and editors in the main agree, are these:

1. Timeliness.
2. Proximity.
3. Prominence.
4. Consequence.
5. Human interest.

TIMELINESS

Familiar to every newsman of the past half-century is the axiom that "nothing is so dead as yesterday's newspaper." Today, possibly, should be added, "or the radio or television newscast of an hour ago." Certainly the increased speed by which news is transmitted has increased the zeal of all who are engaged in the communication business to obtain and stress "latest developments first." The rule is always to bring a story up-to-date as much as possible before going to press or on the air and, if at all possible, to avoid using "yesterday" except in early morning reports.

This "last minute" effect often can be obtained by omitting the "when" from the lead, as in the following:

> A Circuit court judge has given the owners of a slum tenement 60 days to repair their building or face losing the property to the city.
> The action was taken Thursday by Judge Ernest L. Eberholtz in a case involving the five-story brick building at 2122 W. Ashberry street.

In reporting speeches, announcements and the like, this form can be used:

> Elimination of all overnight street parking is necessary to reduce Milltown's traffic accident rate in the opinion of Traffic Engineer L. Scott Updike.
> "Many pedestrians are being injured at night because parked cars obstruct the vision of drivers," Updike told the Milltown Executive club last night.

PROXIMITY

An event occurring within the territory of a newspaper's circulation is of greater interest than a similar event outside that area. It takes a very important foreign story to crowd out a fairly important local story. Readers have a primary interest in names of persons and places with which they are familiar and in situations and trends which may affect them. They want, first of all, to know what is going on in their own community. Examination of the front pages of newspapers published the same day in different cities shows that editors believe that the local story should be given first place. Metropolitan newspapers, however, feel the necessity of printing more national and international news than formerly. One result has been a rapid increase in the size and number of community and suburban papers devoted primarily to local news coverage.

Not only do people like to read of happenings in their vicinity of which they have no previous knowledge, but also, perhaps especially, do they look for accounts of events with which they are familiar. They like to see their own names in print and to read what the paper has to say concerning situations about which they already know something. When a person expects that his name, or the name of someone whom he knows well, is to appear in the newspaper, he looks first of all for the item containing it. He is eager to read the newspaper's account of a meeting that he has attended, an accident that he has seen, or an athletic contest at which he has been present. Logically, the contrary should be true: he should read first that which he already does not know. But he doesn't, and editors know that he doesn't. This being so, newspapers try to please as many readers as possible. If they feel that there is any chance of an appreciable number of readers being interested in an item, no matter how trivial it may be, they print the item.

This statement contradicts the supercilious attitude that it is only rural folk who delight in gossip. Just the opposite is true. We do not read in a New York paper that Mary Taylor is spending the weekend with relatives in New Haven merely because not enough people are acquainted with Miss Taylor. Those who do know her are interested in the item of her visit; if the name happens to be Elizabeth Taylor there is a strong possibility that the item will be published. There is no gossip about celebrities too trivial for publication in a metropolitan newspaper. No city reader has any right to laugh at readers of country weeklies who are interested to learn that Henry Jones has painted his barn red.

Writers are enjoined to play up the local as well as the latest angles of stories. For instance:

> Robert A. Brown Post No. 89 of the American Legion will be represented at the tenth annual convention of the state American Legion Monday, Tuesday and Wednesday at Neillsville, by a delegation of approximately 50 members, including 35 members of the fife and drum corps.

This is better than:

> The tenth annual convention of American Legion posts of the state will be held Monday, Tuesday and Wednesday at Neillsville. The local post, etc.

Newspapers rewrite or supplement the stories of press associations, correspondents and press releases, which carry general leads, such as the second, in order to meet the interests of local readers. They localize national stories, as illustrated by the following:

> The nationwide airline strike is having little or no effect on air mail service in Lincoln, Postmaster Kenneth Lewis said.
> He said that sufficient flights are available on nonstruck lines to ship air mail cargo from Lincoln.
> Problems, however, are occurring at the national transportation centers such as Denver, Kansas City and Omaha. National air mail deliveries are being delayed as much as 24 hours.
> Mail has been moving on airlines not affected by the strike and most of them have put on extra flights. But, William J. Hartigan, assistant U.S. postmaster general, reported that the emergency scheduling cannot be maintained and some of the extra flights will be canceled.
> Military mail for servicemen in Southeast Asia and in Europe has been proceeding on an almost normal basis because all airlines have maintained their military contracts. [Lincoln (Neb.) *Journal*]

PROMINENCE

All men may be created equal, but some are more newsworthy than others. This may be because of the positions they hold, their entertainment value, or because they have behaved so unusually in the past that they have created interest in whatever else they may do.

What is true of persons also is true of places and organizations. All other elements being equal, a newsworthy event, such as a fire or crime, is more important if it occurs in one's home town. The reader, however, does not have the same interest in all other places. Such large population centers as New York, Chicago and Los Angeles rate ahead of most small cities and towns. Among the latter, however, there are some considered more newsworthy than others, often because they have become associated with a particular kind of news. Among such places are Reno, Las Vegas, Hollywood, Tia Juana and Monte Carlo.

To the home-town editor, news of all potential subscribers is important, and he tries to use the names of as many of them as space permits. Newspapers often print long lists of delegates to conventions, guests at weddings and social events, committee memberships and so forth. Reporters are instructed to obtain as many names as possible and are cautioned to get complete names and their correct spellings. Last names seldom are enough. News media should use a person's name as he himself uses it in business and society generally. Sometimes a telephone book or city directory may give a full name whereas the person uses one or more initials or even a nickname. The only safe way is to ask the person.

If a widely known person figures in a news event, that fact may become the feature of a story, as in the following:

> State Sen. Lyle G. Fitzhugh and six other persons were injured last night when a row of temporary bleacher seats collapsed during the Milltown-Rushville basketball game.

CONSEQUENCE

Not only the prominence of persons, places, and things mentioned in news stories originating outside the community which a newspaper serves causes them to be published in place of local news; an equal or perhaps more important factor is the importance of the item.

To illustrate: News from Washington, D.C., is front-page copy in Chicago and San Francisco not primarily because it contains the widely known names of a senator or cabinet member, but because the problem with which those figures are connected vitally concerns the best interests of readers all over the country. Every American citizen is directly affected by an important piece of legislation before Congress. National or state political news often is more important than local political news. In a nuclear age one-world-mindedness is a necessity.

Stories concerning changes in the weather or fashions, and stories of epidemics and pestilences, are important because the immediate community may be affected indirectly if not directly. A coal strike in a distant state may lead to a local shortage of fuel; a new model of automobile will be on sale locally within a short space of time; an important scientific discovery may change a reader's way of thinking on a metal physical problem. The interest in such stories is very personal and very real.

In addition to localizing nationally important stories, newspapers emphasize the consequence of news by seeking the *tomorrow* angle on strictly local stories. This device serves to make the item seem timely and to point up significance. Emphasis is on results rather than causes, on explaining what the present continuing or probable future effect will be.

> Policemen, firemen and other city service employees would be allowed to live in the suburbs under an ordinance introduced Wednesday in the City Council.
>
> The cost of riding city buses in Lincoln is about to increase.
> The Nebraska State Railway Commission reported Thursday it has approved the application of Lincoln City Lines for a 5 cent-per-fare rate hike, effective Aug. 1.
> The change will boost the adult fare from 15 to 20 cents, and the fare for children under 12 from 10 to 15 cents.   [Lincoln (Neb.) *Journal*]

HUMAN INTEREST

Interest in human beings as such, and in events because they concern men and women in situations which might confront anyone else, is called human interest.

It is human interest, interest in the lives and welfare of others and in the well-being and progress of mankind as a whole, that causes us to read, with interest and sympathy, of loss of life and property in communities far removed from our own. When an earthquake destroys homes and takes lives in southern Italy or in Japan, there is little likelihood of our being affected directly, except perhaps as we are asked to contribute to the Red Cross relief fund; but we are interested in learning of such "acts of God" because other human beings like ourselves are involved.

It is this personal appeal which editors mean when they say that an item of news has reader interest even though it may not possess any of the other elements of news value: timeliness, proximity, prominence and consequence.

Strictly speaking, all reader interest is human interest. Because readers differ in their occupational, recreational, and other interests, some news which has a *personal appeal* to one reader fails to interest another. Any reader, however, no matter how cynical or self-centered has some *sympathetic interest* in the lives and well-being of other humans. This interest includes both extremes of the pathetic and humorous in everyday life, whatever causes a reader to feel sorry for or to laugh with or at some other fellow being.

Interest in accounts of disasters involving loss of life and property is sympathetic. There may be other elements of interest in stories of fires, wrecks, accidents and other catastrophes; but when individuals are mentioned in unfortunate situations, there also is sympathetic interest. Sickness, near death, suffering of any kind, loss of wealth, and the like create attitudes of sympathy in readers.

At the other extreme, ludicrous accounts of typical men and women touch a sympathetic vein also. Americans like to laugh and are amused at almost anything in any way incongruous. In most humorous stories there is someone who suffers some inconvenience, but this does not detract from the humor of the situation any more than does knowledge of injury to a person who has slipped on a banana peel and fallen suffice to suppress the smile which comes to one's lips.

Such incidents also involve *unusualness*. People everywhere, and perhaps Americans in particular, love thrills and anything with an "-est" to it. Unusual people, quaint and picturesque places, exciting adventures, all appeal to us. And when we cannot meet these individuals, see those places, experience romance ourselves, we like to read of them all the more. We take vicarious pleasure from stories of adventure and romance.

Once news of new theories and discoveries in the field of science was considered unusual. In the present nuclear age the element of surprise has disappeared, but the interest in *progress* continues. Likewise, unfortunately, the element of reader interest which probably outweighs all others—that in *combat*—also continues. Critical examination of the lists of "biggest" news stories of any year indicates that there is no other single element of reader interest which is present more frequently. Americans, it must be, like a good fight and consider life as a whole to be a struggle. The element of combat is found most prominently in stories of athletic contests, crime, politics, adventure, disaster and heroism. Man against man or man against nature always draws a big crowd, which usually roots for the underdog.

If there is *suspense* in the story of combat, or in any other story for that matter, the interest is heightened. Frequently, the attention of an entire nation is centered upon a single news event, as in the case of a mine disaster when rescuers work frantically to save human lives. Illness, especially of a prominent person or from an unusual cause, may be reported so as to emphasize the element of suspense. There is suspense in political campaigns, in law cases and in athletic contests.

The so-called human interest in any kind of story is enhanced if the principals include a *child*, an *animal* or a *woman*, preferably a good-looking young woman. Hieroglyphic warnings against the increasing immorality of youth have been discovered by excavators, proving that adolescence always has been a problem. Furthermore, since before the days of chivalry, the female sex has caused more worry than the male.

Times haven't changed much and "flaming youth" still is having its inning, with debutantes, co-eds, waitresses, and heiresses flaming perhaps a bit more brightly than ever before. The growth of newspapers and of newspaper photography has helped satisfy the desire for accurate information of just what our allegedly wayward sons and daughters are doing and how they look.

So-called middle age is, from the news standpoint, the drabbest of man's several stages. Precocious infancy and childhood and virile old age vie with hilarious adolescence in front-page importance: the little girl who calls on the mayor to let her doggie out of the pound, and the grandma who takes her first ride in an airplane. The thirties, forties, and fifties are the trying years if one is a publicity seeker. At those ages he really has to do something to get by the copy desk; or else he must employ an adroit public relations counsel.

Interest in animals is similar to interest in children and old age. Sometimes the reader is sympathetic, as in the case of a dog who refuses to leave his master's grave; sometimes he is resentful, as when a tame animal turns on someone and hurts him.

Stories of unusual intelligence in animals always are good copy, especially if the well-being of humans thereby is fostered. Also, anecdotes of admirable qualities, as faithfulness, have an appeal. Any freak from the animal kingdom attracts attention, as Barnum knew, and there is plentiful interest remaining in the disappearing sport of hunting, especially of big game.

The beginning reporter must learn to recognize the human interest possibilities of stories and to brighten up what he writes by giving it the twist which turns a drab yarn into a bright one without, of course, exaggeration or distortion.

The following are sprightly leads to factual news stories made so by adroitness on the part of their authors in picking and playing up phases lending themselves to human interest treatment or emphasis:

> Toronto—(UP)—John Brock, 32, began serving a two-year penitentiary term Tuesday because he hates women.
> He was convicted of assault for breaking into the ladies room of a downtown tavern and mussing up a young housewife who was fixing her makeup. The housewife told police that Brock crashed in and shouted, "I hate women and you're one." [Duluth *News-Tribune*]

> Roars and snarls of protest raged around the Denver zoo Friday, but the noise was emanating from the city and county building, not City park.
> The hubbub concerns the plans of Mayor Nicholson's administration to sign over management of the zoo to the Denver Zoological Foundation, a group of citizens long interested in the zoo's problems who believe they can operate it better than the city. [Denver *Post*]

These examples illustrate that it is possible to adhere to the rules regarding the news story form and at the same time avoid "wooden" leads.

The Five *W*'s and the *H*

The *who* or the *what* usually is the feature of a short one-incident (simple) news story. It often is difficult to determine which is more important, as most news concerns people and what they do. For instance, in the following short item many readers will be interested primarily in the young man mentioned as a friend or acquaintance. Others, however, will be interested chiefly because of the extent to which the local schools will be affected by the news. When the news is about a definite person the name usually comes first, as:

> Peter L. Clay has resigned his position as instructor in history in the local high school to accept a teaching fellowship in history at Booster college.

THE *WHO*

The *who* is unmistakably the feature in the following story:

> George L. Rose has been elected ninth vice-president of the American Council of Civil Service Employees.

Often the interest in the *who* comes from the kind of person involved (judged by his occupation, religion, sex, age, and so on, or by the circumstances in which he figures in the particular story), or from the number of persons involved, as:

> A private watchman shot a safecracker Tuesday when he and his accomplice resisted arrest.

The indefinite *who* is used increasingly as cities become larger and persons in the news are known to fewer other persons in proportion to the population as a whole.

THE *WHAT*

The *what* is more important than the *who* when the circumstance would be significant no matter who the persons involved, as:

> One man was shot and another was beaten today in an outbreak of violence as strikers tried to prevent operation of the Johnson-Smith corporation.

> A youth who went berserk with a butcher knife was captured and held by police tonight as a suspect in two recent murders in Milltown.

Press associations usually write their stories in this way, as names may not mean anything outside the immediate vicinity in which the event occurred. The writer of a news story always must decide which is more important, the name or the event.

Often a *what* lead begins with the *who* as an easier rhetorical method or to emphasize authority. Note in the following example that, although the *who* comes first, the *what* is more important.

> President Joseph E. Jennings today announced that the county board is able to pay off current expenditures as they arise, despite the fact that it has retired $568,910 in outstanding debts since he assumed office three years ago.

In the following example the *what* is unmistakably predominant:

> Vandalism against cars was reported in Southside Milltown Friday.
> Vice squad detectives began an investigation after auto windshields and windows were reported smashed on Haberkorn road, Lakeside drive, Alcott drive and Norton road, SW.

In action stories readers usually are interested in results rather than causes, as:

> A street-car bandit was killed and two others and a boy were injured in a robbery and raid early today. The boy was wounded when he got in line of fire.

THE *WHY*

Sometimes, however, it is the cause rather than the result that is the feature of the story, as:

> Trying to pass another car while traveling at high speed brought serious injury to two men last night when their automobile overturned twice on Washington boulevard at Potter avenue.

THE *WHERE*

In advance stories of meetings, speeches, athletic events, accidents, etc., the *where* must be very definite. Room numbers, street addresses, etc., should be given. In local stories, it is not always necessary to mention the name of the city or a street address. The immediate community is understood, as:

> Eight testing lanes on which motorists must submit their automobiles and trucks to examination for safe driving qualifications will be opened tomorrow.

The *where* may be the featurized element, as:

> In her 400-year-old ancestral home, the only daughter of an English general recently became the wife of a gypsy, who worked as a handyman on the estate.

In each of the following examples, the *where* definitely was the feature although, in the second example, the *when* rhetorically came first.

> A tract of approximately 30 acres at Forest boulevard and Kerwood avenue, assessed at $90,000, has been sold by Herschel Steel, represented by the Wray-Graw Co., to John L. Finch.

> Beginning today, parking will be permitted in the Underground Lakeside Exhibition hall of Citizen's hall by patrons of events at the hall and the Civic auditorium, at a rate of 40 cents per car.

When a place is more familiar than the names of those associated with it, the following style may be used:

> The operator of a candy store at 717 S. Ninth street pleaded guilty Monday in U.S. District court of the purchase, possession, and sale of 5 ounces of heroin.
> He is Andrew Solberg, 41, of 141 Oak street, who was arrested by narcotics agents last month.

THE *WHEN*

About the same may be said of the *when* as of the *where*. It ordinarily is included inconspicuously in the lead, as:

> Fur thieves hit two Milltown stores early Wednesday and got away with a total loot estimated at $230,000.

Frequently the *when* may be left until the second paragraph, as:

> Commissioner William Wheat has appointed a seven-man hospital committee to look into the situation surrounding construction of a countywide hospital for pay patients.
> The members were appointed at a Monday afternoon session with the commissioner.

Such omission of the *when* from the first paragraph is common practice with press associations, especially when preparing news of one day for use in the morning newspapers the following day.

The *when* may be a matter of "continuous action," as:

> A couple of perky oldsters who defied the wilderness for ten days on a can of beans, a bit of jelly and a small packet of powdered milk are recovering from exhaustion and hunger in Milltown hospital.

The *when* may be the featured element, as:

> Midnight tonight is the deadline for 1968 automobile license plates and vehicles in use after 12:01 A.M. tomorrow must carry 1969 plates, the Bureau of Motor Vehicles reminded automobile owners yesterday.

A type of *when* lead is the "duration of time" lead, as:

> After deliberating five hours last night, a Superior court jury returned a verdict of guilty in the steel purchase fraud trial of four Gruner county highway employees.

A similar type of *when* lead is the "since when" lead, as:

> After being gone for two weeks, "Duke," a wistful looking Collie-Spitz hybrid, decided he liked his old home better and trudged 40 miles to return to the residence of his former owner, Humane Officer Thompson Meredith.

THE *HOW*

By definition the *how* means details to explain how something occurred. Consequently, when the feature unmistakably consists in such details, care must be exercised to avoid wordiness.

Madison, Wis., July 25.—(AP)—An Air Force jet plane returned to its home base today—the hard way.

The fighter crash-landed in a corn field, mowed a path and popped out of the field, skittered across a busy highway beside Truax Air Force Base and slid home on a familiar runway.

The pilot, Lieut. John P. Curchill, 25, of Madison, N.J., was unhurt. His plane developed engine trouble and he was returning to base when the engine quit.

Sports stories frequently are given *how* leads, as:

St. Paul (AP)—Bobby Nichols, using his new "branding iron" putter and a different driver, shot a five-under-par Saturday to barge into the 54-hole lead in the Minnesota Golf Classic.

Rhetorical Devices

Skillful use of the ordinary rhetorical devices enables the news writer to play up a feature.

THE SUMMARY STATEMENT

Most news leads are mere summary statements consisting of simple sentences or of compound or complex sentences with the principal clauses first. Many examples given so far in this chapter illustrate how the feature of a story can be emphasized by means of such simple straightforward writing. Observe, in addition, the following example:

A 55-year-old River Forest contractor known by police to have built homes for several crime syndicate hoodlums, was found shot to death Wednesday.

CONDITIONAL CLAUSES

Often, however, it is difficult to get the feature into a main clause. This is so when the feature is present in addition to the main news idea which the writer must include in his lead. Features to be found in accompanying circumstances, conditions, coincidences in the *when*, *where*, and so on, often can best be played up by beginning the lead with a complex or complex-compound sentence with the conditional clause first.

In the following examples note how the conditional clause contains the feature, whereas the main idea which is the excuse for the story still is in the main clause.

Because Paul Gregg, 17-year-old high school boy, was caught as a stowaway and locked in the infirmary of the liner *Justice*, he started to burn the ship to seek his freedom, he admitted to steamship authorities here today.

This emphasizes the feature much more than would inversion of the clause order, as:

Paul Gregg, 17-year-old high school boy, today admitted to steamship authorities here that he set fire to the liner *Justice* to obtain his freedom after being caught as a stowaway and locked in the infirmary.

THE SUBSTANTIVE CLAUSE

The substantive clause usually takes the form of a "that" clause which has been much overworked by news writers because it is easy to write and is consequently taboo in many offices. Occasionally the substantive is forceful, as:

That the present legislative appropriation must be doubled if minimum essentials are to be provided relief clients, is the warning contained in the monthly report made today by Harold G. Todd, local relief administrator, to the State Department of Public Welfare.

Return to the pioneer days, when youths in their early teens could assemble a muzzle-loader and pick off game 50 yards away, was sought in a bill before the state legislature today.

PHRASES

Infinitive, participial, prepositional and gerund phrases and absolute constructions also may be used to emphasize a feature when it happens to be one of the minor *w*'s or *h*. In such constructions, the main clause contains the *who* and *what*, one of which is modified by the phrase.

Inverted sentence structure may be used to identify (tie-back) the news with previous news (see Chapter 9) and to identify persons, places and events. Use of phrases and of the absolute construction for different purposes is illustrated in the following examples:

WHEN

After a three-hour search by police and relatives, James Fillmore, 30, his wife and four children who had been missing since Saturday, were found early yesterday in a friend's home.

WHERE

Beside the Ring river, which he made famous in song and verse, the body of Feodor Vladik today was buried with only a handful of close relatives present.

WHY
Delayed somewhat by recent hurricane alerts, work to complete Harris Civil Defense Headquarters in the basement of the Carnegie Free Library was pressed anew last week.

HOW
Citing a permissive 1867 ordinance which never has been repealed, Henry Bucher today won the right to raise geese in his backyard at 10 Cheery Lane.

TIE-BACK
Disregarding three previous failures, Grace Slawson, 21-year-old grocery clerk, tomorrow will attempt to set a new record for swimming across Lake Malthusia.

THE CARTRIDGE LEAD

When war is declared or ends, a president or some other widely known figure dies, and on similarly important occasions, it is customary to tell the gist of the news in the fewest possible words, as:

Galvania has declared war on Powry.

Mayor Charles A. Brinshaw is dead.

The Maroons are conference champions.

Stories written entirely in such staccato fashion have a breath-taking quality. Consequently, the style should not be used too extensively but reserved for occasions of particular importance.

THE PUNCH LEAD

What has traditionally been called a punch lead performs a function similar to that of the cartridge lead, but it is not so short, abrupt or definite. Since World War II, it has grown in popularity and on some newspapers is used for almost any kind of story, not just stories of presumed extra newsworthiness. It has been called the "blind" lead because of its emphasis on situations rather than specific persons and details. It is a form of writing easily open to misuse: (1) in stories whose importance is thereby exaggerated, and (2) by being excessively indefinite or "empty." An example of the latter is: "Politics had a different look in Congress today," a sentence which tells exactly nothing. Paragraphs two and three of a well-written story with a punch lead should supply definite details.

A policeman has been suspended on charges that he deserted his school-crossing post.

78   PRINCIPLES OF NEWS WRITING

> Placed on indefinite suspension by Police Chief Patrick C. O'Brien Tuesday was Albert Murchison, 27, of 885 W. Strong avenue, attached to the Vickers station, 1412 E. Vickers avenue.
> Lieut. Ira Walters of the Vickers district said a routine check at noon Monday disclosed that Murchison was absent from his post at Bristol and Sacramento roads.

THE ASTONISHER LEAD

Beginning writers are discouraged in their use of superlatives and expressions of opinion. When deserved, however, superlatives should be used, as:

> The winningest rider of all times, Johnny Longden, makes his local debut as trainer Saturday in the $40,000 Beverly Handicap at Arlington Park.

More Than One Feature

So far, only stories containing simple features relatively easy to pick even though related to important events have been considered. Not infrequently, an item of news presents so many angles that the rhetorical devices described in this chapter are inadequate. There are several ways out of this difficulty.

SEPARATE STORIES

The easiest way is to write more than one story. When there are sidelights or interviews of opinion or features connected with a news event, the assignment usually is divided between two or more reporters. Some repetition usually occurs but is not discouraged; in fact, in some cases it is encouraged, and a paper may run several stories of the same event written by different reporters.

THE CROWDED LEAD

When the various elements of interest are of nearly equal value, a number of facts may be crowded into a single lead, as:

> Standing committees were appointed, the street-lighting contract was continued for one year and a proposed new ordinance regulating business licenses was referred to the Finance committee last night at the weekly meeting of the Board of Aldermen.

Succeeding paragraphs naturally would take up each item mentioned in the lead, providing full details.

THE "SHIRTTAIL" METHOD

To avoid crowded and vague leads, one item deemed the most important can be played up. Paragraphs containing mention of other items then can be introduced by such expressions as, "In other actions the City Council . . ." or "In a similar accident . . ." and so forth.

>Ald. Val G. Grauer (17th ward) has been elected chairman of the powerful Finance committee of the Board of Aldermen.
>Other standing committee chairmen, named at last night's board meeting, follow . . .
>The board also voted to continue for one year its contract with the Republic Light company for street lighting . . .
>In other actions, the board referred a proposed new ordinance regulating business licences to the Finance committee and rejected a request by Front street property owners that all-night parking be permitted in the 400 block.

BOXES

Often, statements, tabulations, data, side features, and the like can best be presented by means of a box set either ahead of the lead, within the main article or in an adjoining column. There are many other uses for the box, most of them connected with makeup. Material most frequently boxed includes:

1. Lists of dead and injured in accidents.
2. Telling statements from speeches, reports, testimony, and so on.
3. Statistics.
4. Summaries of facts included in the story itself or in two or more related stories.
5. Brief histories of events connected with the story.
6. Local angles on press association stories.

>After requiring 12 employees and six customers to lie face downward on the floor, three armed and masked bandits shortly after 8 A.M. today removed approximately $75,000 in currency from the cashiers' cages of the First National bank, 109 N. Main street, and escaped in a waiting automobile driven by a fourth man.

80   PRINCIPLES OF NEWS WRITING

> **FOURTH IN TWO YEARS**
>
> Today's burglary of the First National bank was the fourth in two years in Milltown. Others, together with losses and outcomes, were:
>
> March 3, 1966—First National bank, $17,451 cash, recovered upon arrest of Abe Mason, now serving a ten-year term in the state penitentiary.
>
> Sept. 21, 1966—Milltown State bank, $41,150 cash and bonds, recovered when sheriff's posse killed John "Gunman" Hays three miles south of town the same day.
>
> July 15, 1967—Citizen's National bank, $50,000 removed by blowing open safe at night. Still unsolved.

The men were described by Wilmer Asher, head cashier, as all apparently under 25 years of age. They wore blue overalls and caps which were drawn down just above the eyes.

THE 1-2-3-4-LEAD

After a short summary statement of the situation constituting the news, the different features can be emphasized by tabulation and numbering, as:

> The wishes of Mayor Louis T. Tupper were ignored by the new Board of Aldermen in several votes at its organizing meeting last night. Most importantly the board did the following:
> 1. Elected Ald. Val G. Grauer (17th ward), political rival of the mayor's, chairman of the powerful Finance committee.
> 2. Referred a proposed new ordinance regulating business licenses to Ald. Grauer's committee. The mayor has called the new ordinance unnecessary.
> 3. Continued for one year the contract with the Republic Light Company for street lighting. The mayor opposed the renewal in campaign speeches last month.
> 4. Rejected a property owners' petition for all-night parking in the 400 block on Front street which the mayor had approved.

The preceding lead, of course, is interpretative. It plays up the significance of the board's actions rather than merely reporting them deadpan. It does not editorialize for or against the board's insurgency, and the treatment probably could be adversely criticized only if it could be shown that each board action was taken despite rather than because of any attitude toward Mayor Tupper.

The article as written does not say the four actions indicated hostility by the board toward the mayor. Nevertheless, there is no mistaking the fact that such an impression is given. If, at a subsequent meeting, the board were to vote in favor of a number of measures sponsored by the mayor, the facts as they existed after the earlier meeting would have to be re-examined. If, however, the facts as stated in the first story are accurate, the reporter could not be accused of coloring his account. Certainly he provided his readers with background information whereby it would be possible for them to draw conclusions, whereas a strictly factual account of the actions of the Board of Aldermen, without attempt at any perspective, might have created a wrong impression.

It cannot be pointed out too often that essential for this kind of interpretative reporting is knowledge. Without it, the newsgatherer will consider as new something that is very old and will have news sources "revealing" and "disclosing" information that is common knowledge among a wide circle of readers.

In other words, you can't play up a feature unless you have brains enough to pick it.

5

Making It Attractive

I	The News Peg	IX	The Parody Lead
II	The Contrast Lead	X	The Quotation Lead
III	The Question Lead	XI	The Dialogue Lead
IV	The Descriptive Lead	XII	Cumulative Interest
V	The Staccato Lead	XIII	Suspended Interest
VI	The Figurative Lead	XIV	Sequence
VII	The Epigram Lead	XV	Direct Address
VIII	The Literary Allusion Lead	XVI	Freaks

If the first part of a news story answers as many of the five *w*'s and *h* as necessary (see Chapter 3) and gives the proper emphasis to the one which constitutes the feature (see Chapter 4), it is a good lead. If, in addition, the beginning of the news story is so interestingly written that the reader continues for that reason alone, it is a superior lead. No one reader is interested in a majority of the news items concontained in any single newspaper edition; it is the purpose of headlines to direct him to those stories in which he does have an interest. The lead of a story authenticates and supplements its headline and is sufficient for a large proportion of readers who get that far.

Each news story, however, is composed for the minority of readers who peruse it to its very end. Both its content and the way it is written determine its interest value. In Part II, the emphasis is on how to obtain completeness of detail in gathering information regarding a number of different kinds of events. The purpose of this chapter is to offer assistance to the beginning writer in how to attain rhetorical excellence without sacrificing news interest. The examples also illustrate how to give emphasis or perspective—elementary forms of interpretation—to otherwise routine stories.

The News Peg

When a lead is written in feature or semifeature style, either to play up a feature angle or for rhetorical attractiveness, the part which contains the kernel or more of news regarding the event which is the story's excuse for being, is called the *news peg*. The extent to which it can be made secondary to featured fact or language depends upon its importance. If it is of vital public interest, it must be given emphasis. If, on the other hand, the feature interest of the story outweighs its importance as public information, the news peg can be played down. In the following examples, however, despite the feature treatment, the news pegs are present in the leads:

> After dressing her three small daughters in their Easter finery and taking them to church where they were baptized, Mrs. Nora MacMahon returned yesterday to her Pineville home and strangled them.

> Milltown area police are in a race against death—and may already be too late—in their feverish search for Harold A. Dunraven, 58.
> They know what he has in mind—suicide.
> They hope to find him in time to prevent it.
> Dunraven is the Crestwood Community Chest director who disappeared a week ago.

The Contrast Lead

Sometimes the feature of a news story consists in the contrast between the immediate and a former situation or between the event at hand and another of which, for any of a number of reasons, it is a reminder. Note that the news peg is retained in the following lead though not so definitely, the emphasis being upon the unusual situation:

> Behind the same walnut desk which he used to dust 25 years ago as an office boy, Virgil F. Stimson yesterday received congratulations upon becoming president of Andalia Trucking company.

The Question Lead

Ordinarily the reporter should answer, not ask, questions in his news stories. To do otherwise merely delays telling the news, as in the case of a lead beginning "What causes delinquency?" followed by a summary of a new idea advanced by some authority. It would be much better to start: "Failure of teenagers to obtain jobs causes them to become delinquent in the opinion of . . ."

When the story concerns a problem of public interest or a matter likely to provoke debate among readers, however, it may be possible to obtain interest by means of a question lead, as:

> How does it feel to be buried alive?
> Edward Turner, 27-year-old laborer of 541 Green street can tell you. He learned first-hand when a bank of earth caved in on him at a construction project on W. Harmon avenue yesterday.

> Cheddar, England (UPI)—What does a man say when he learns he's broken the world underground endurance record?
> "Wow! Bless my little cotton socks. I've done it!" shouted 28-year-old David Lafferty in a cavern 400 feet below the surface.

The Descriptive Lead

The feature or key to the spirit of a story may be in its setting, the physical appearance of some person or object involved, or in an unusual phase of the action with which it deals. In such cases, a graphic or descriptive lead may be the most effective to give the tone or feeling necessary to proper understanding and appreciation. Before he can describe, the reporter must know how to observe; the best descriptive leads are written by eyewitnesses. To be avoided are superfluous and inapplicable adjectives, extraneous matter serving no purpose except, perhaps, to prove the writer's possession of an extensive vocabulary of trite and hackneyed expressions—clichés. The following leads to important stories avoid these hazards:

> A fusillade of gunfire shattered the quiet of a Milltown street shortly before midnight, and when it was over a young man lay dead.

> For more than a minute today the sun hung over central Minnesota like a twinkling, slate-blue Christmas ornament as the moon moved between it and the earth.
> In the awesome half-light that covered the area, hundreds of scientists and thousands of other persons had a perfect view of the total solar eclipse.
> [The New York *Times*]

The Staccato Lead

When the time element—either fast action or the intervals separating a series of related events—is to be emphasized, the staccato lead occasionally suffices. It consists in a series of phrases, punctuated either by periods or dashes and usually is a form of descriptive lead. The style suggests the tone of the story, its feeling.

> Hanover, June 23.—An ear-wracking roar followed by a series of cloud-burst demonstrations. A serpent's tongue of flame. Dense billows of black smoke thinning gradually into white. Movement made almost invisible by velocity.
> Thus the observer's brain recorded the spectacle of Fritz von Opel's rocket car blazing along the railroad tracks in the environs of this city today at a speed of 254 kilometers an hour—39 faster than has ever been achieved before by a vehicle running on rails.

> Thirty years ago—back in 1938—in a different era, in a different life, after 40 years of happiness in her simple home, the light went out for Mrs. Hattie Downs, of Gregoryville and she became blind—stone blind.
> Years passed—thirty of them—long and tortuous—and suddenly her prayers were answered, and Mrs. Hattie Downs could see.

The Figurative Lead

Triteness must be avoided in the use of metaphors, similes and other figures of speech, either in the lead or any other part of a news story. Many expressions have become so common through usage that they are hardly noticed by casual readers as figurative. Among them are "ax to grind," "shoe on the wrong foot," "attach his wagon to a star," "put all its eggs in one basket" and many more. If the writer uses such expressions naturally, without strain, possibly even without awareness that they are figurative, the result is more likely to be good than if he deliberately tries for effect:

> Knocked on the ropes by a wet and windy one-two punch, Milltown's July heat wave refused to call it quits Friday.

> Washington, June 27.—(AP)—The army is putting teeth into the new defense department directive which authorized a secrecy cloak for information when it bears the stamp "for official use only."

The Epigram Lead

The tone or moral of a story also may be emphasized by means of an epigram lead, in the writing of which bromides and platitudes must be avoided. The epigram is a concise and pointed expression, usually witty. The epigram lead may be either a familiar saying or a moral applicable to the story at hand, as:

Silence can be golden in more ways than one, Shortstop Tommy Jacobs of the Maroons has discovered.

After striking out three times against Bristol Aug. 12, Jacobs complained to his manager, Bucky Johnson, that he had been the victim of several debatable strike decisions.

"The trouble with you," said Johnson, "is that you spend so much time turning around to squawk that you're not ready to hit the ball. Just for the fun of it, forget to turn around and look at the umpire for any reason and concentrate on hitting the ball."

Tommy followed the advice and compiled the following record . . .

The Literary Allusion Lead

The writer with a normal background of knowledge in literature or history will have frequent chances to use it to advantage. Care must be taken to limit references to fictional or historical characters and to literary passages familiar to the average reader. The following examples illustrate how it is possible effectively to make use of one's general knowledge to improve his writing:

A motorist who thought he was performing a Good Samaritan act today almost went to jail for aiding a criminal to escape.

The mountain wouldn't come to Mahomet, so a chewing-gum maker is going to the false teeth manufacturers.

Philip K. Wrigley, president of the William Wrigley, Jr., Co., announced this milestone in scientific research Tuesday at its annual stockholders' meeting.

Ever since the advent of plastic dentures 12 years ago, he said, the company's laboratories have sought to develop gum that won't stick to them. . . .   [Chicago *Sun-Times*]

The Parody Lead

Popular song hits, bon mots by famous persons, titles of best-selling books or of motion pictures or new-coined phrases or expressions of any sort may be used while still fresh, usually in parodied form, to brighten an occasional news story lead. Well-established expressions may be used similarly. The following leads avoid the ever-lurking danger of triteness in such writing:

Sheridan, Wyo., Jan. 29.—Maybe it's a case of absence of water makes the heart grow fonder, but citizens of this northern Wyoming city have risen nobly to the call to help the flood-stricken dwellers along the Ohio River Valley.

Actor Charles Keller says you can't take it with you because the government takes it first.

The 77-year-old stage-and-screen star Tuesday urged outright repeal of the federal income tax, which he called an "economic cancer."

The Quotation Lead

In reporting speeches, public statements, and the like, it almost always is better to epitomize the feature in the reporter's own words rather than by means of a direct quotation.

Weak

"A sharp decrease in maternal mortality, medical progress, and greater economic prosperity have enabled welfare agencies to solve most of their problems except that of the emotionally disturbed child," Horace V. Updike, Council of Social Welfare director, said yesterday.

Strong

The emotionally disturbed child is the "No. 1 problem" facing welfare agencies today, Horace V. Updike, Council of Social Welfare director, said yesterday.

In news stories which are not accounts of speeches or documents, however, it sometimes is effective to begin with a direct quotation, as in the following examples:

"I just wanted to do something bad."
That, police said, was the only explanation 17-year-old Walter O'Malley could give for shooting and wounding two girls in a woodland ambush.

"Don't be an old grouch on the road!"
This advice for those who wish to stay alive although they drive in Labor Day weekend traffic comes from Francis Carroway, 18, judged Milltown's best teenage driver.

The following was the lead to a story judged best by 37 journalism professors and 32 city editors to whom nine writeups of an interview with an Ohio State university campus editor were submitted.

"To get ahead in journalism, you have to do a little more than people expect of you."
This is the advice Lantern Spring Quarter editor-in-chief Ron Shafer gave freshmen journalism students today.
"You may not think that anybody notices that extra work, but they do," Shafer continued.

The partial or broken quote often can be used to add authenticity without making the lead unwieldly, as:

> The city manager of Cresswood refused today to "commit myself" on revoking the liquor license of a saloon raided five times by sheriff's police in a year.

The Dialogue Lead

It is difficult, if not impossible, to begin a serious news story of an important event with dialogue. Minor court stories, with strong human interest, and occasionally stories of a more significant nature, however, can be handled effectively by means of a dialogue lead, as:

> "Wouldn't it be terrible," asked Hazel Muller, 22, of 1864 E. Payne avenue, "if I got locked in that record vault and couldn't get out?"
>
> "Ho, ho," replied Thomas Keyes, production manager of the Majestic Foundry company at 146 E. Belmont avenue, where Miss Muller is a secretary, "It couldn't happen."
>
> But it DID happen Tuesday and it WAS terrible.
>
> Here's a play-by-play account . . .

Cumulative Interest

Most of the examples given so far have been leads to news stories which otherwise conform to the standard rule that they be written to make possible the cutting of at least a few paragraphs from the bottom up, without sacrificing completeness.

There are three principal types, rhetorically speaking, of news feature stories which must be printed in their entirety to preserve the news interest. One is the cumulative interest story, the lead of which differs from those of the other two types because it contains some sort of news peg. In addition to emphasizing the tone or situation of the story as it progresses, this kind of story incites reader interest which cumulates as each succeeding sentence and paragraph makes for greater definiteness:

> Salt Lake City—(UP)—A 19-year-old salesgirl wants to wish a Merry Christmas to a Chicago soldier who provided an early holiday present when it was most needed.
>
> The girl, Barbara Swindle, Farmington, Utah, had left a department store where she worked when she found her purse had been robbed of $50, almost all her week's earnings.
>
> Next she found a tire on her car was flat. She couldn't find anyone to fix it.

She walked into a nearby bus station and was trying vainly to keep back tears when a soldier from Chicago persuaded her to tell him her troubles.

He handed her a $10 bill and told her to get some change so she could telephone home for help.

When she returned the soldier had boarded a bus for Chicago.

She does not know the soldier's name, but Barbara said, "I certainly wish that soldier, whoever he is, a Merry Christmas."

[Chicago *Daily News*]

Suspended Interest

This name is given to the news feature in which the writer "strings along" the reader to the very end before giving him the news peg on which the item is based. Such stories resemble magazine short stories in that they must be read in their entirety. Frequently, the climax may be a surprise; in any case, it satisfies the reader's interest which has been suspended because of the indefiniteness of early details. The lead of a suspended interest story is not so definite as that of a cumulative interest story:

> An ice-cream cone failed to have a cooling effect Saturday night on Patrolman Harry O'Brien.
>
> O'Brien, assigned to the burglary detail, was parking his car on Auburn street near Wilson avenue, when a man approached the car, mumbling incoherently.
>
> "What did you say?" O'Brien asked.
>
> Without another word, the man suddenly jammed an ice-cream cone into the policeman's face.
>
> O'Brien alighted, drew his gun, seized the man and was told, "You'll have to fight to take me in."
>
> With that, the prisoner slugged O'Brien in the mouth with his fist. O'Brien countered with an uppercut which knocked the man flat.
>
> At the Kenton Avenue Station the arrested man identified himself as Willis C. Solano of 1768 W. Tree street and said he thought policemen were "too hot" and he wanted to "cool one off."

Sequence

The sequence story differs from both the cumulative and suspended interest stories only in arrangement of material, the object in all three cases being to postpone the climax or satisfaction of the reader's curiosity until near the end. The distinguishing feature of a story written in sequence style is that the facts are arranged in strictly chronological order, as:

Three-year-old Byron Halpert, being an inquisitive little fellow, opened a second-story window Tuesday a few minutes after his mother had left to take her daughter to school.

Byron leaned out to see what he could see. But he leaned so far that he lost his balance, fell through the opening and wound up hanging from the window sill by his finger tips, 20 feet above a concrete walk.

Just then a police car came by. Officer William Watson, sizing up the situation, ran to the spot below the window just as little Byron let go. The boy landed squarely in the policeman's arms, unhurt but tearfully scared.

Direct Address

Beginning reporters are admonished to keep out of their own stories, only an occasional reference to the fact that a reporter asked a certain question or made an unsuccessful effort to obtain an important fact being permitted. Use of either the first or second person is discouraged. Columnists, special writers who sign their articles and writers of feature stories are exempt from this rule when effectiveness cannot be obtained otherwise. The following are examples to show how the first or second person occasionally may be used in an ordinary news or news feature story such as a beginning reporter might write:

Kids, when Ma and Pa take a look at your report card then start the sermon about how smart they were in high school, do you see red? Do you want to chew nails?

Relax, kids, you've got a friend.

He is Dr. F. H. Finch of the University of Illinois, and he takes your side today in a monograph of the American Psychological Association.

[Chicago *Daily News*]

If you haven't heard of it, and wouldn't believe it if you had, it probably will be on display today at the National Inventors' Congress in the Hotel LaSalle.

Window glass that can't be seen through, lamps that give invisible light and solid water pipes that have no hollow space for the water—those are some of the things you may expect to find.

Freaks

There isn't a rhetorical device which can't be used on occasion in writing for newspapers. The following are examples of unconventional leads which proved effective:

For sale: One college.

The board of directors of Pleasant View college at Fairview announced today that the school, consisting of four buildings and several acres of land, is looking for a purchaser.

Financial difficulties forced its closing at the end of the 1962 school year.

>   The turtle is a strange old bird,
>   He's often seen and never heard,
>   He's best in soup, the taste is swell,
>   But when he bites, he raises hell.
>   —Apologies to Otto Werkmeister

The sentiment in the jingle expresses the firm belief of Gustave Riebow, 3225 S. Illinois ave.

The other day, according to a traffic accident report by the police department to the safety commission, Riebow was driving on S. Illinois ave. near his home.

His only passenger was a snapping turtle which Riebow believed to be safely stowed away in a box on the front seat. Riebow whistled gaily at the thought of fresh turtle soup. It was not recorded what the turtle thought.

Anyhow, the turtle climbed out of the box, and, with mayhem in his heart, went after the first object in his path. That object was Riebow's leg and the snapper snapped his jaws down hard.

The pain threw Riebow into confusion. He yelled, swung the wheel and rammed into a tree.

"That," mused Dr. B. L. Corbett, executive secretary of the commission, "is the first time a turtle got 'in the soup' with the law in a traffic accident in Milwaukee." [Milwaukee *Journal*]

6

Making It Readable

I READABILITY FORMULAS
II OBJECTIONS TO FORMULAS
III NEWSPAPER STYLE
IV CONCISENESS
   1. Superfluous Details
   2. Superfluous Words
   3. Superfluous Phrases
   4. Superfluous Clauses
   5. Simplicity
   6. Passive and Active Voice
   7. Proper Emphasis

V AVOIDING BANALITY
   1. Figures of Speech
   2. Bromides
   3. Shopworn Personifications
   4. Journalese

VI CORRECT USAGE
   1. Grammatical Faults
   2. Parts of Speech
   3. Troublesome Words

MOST OF THE CHANGES IN NEWSPAPER STORY FORM AND STRUCTURE since World War II have been made on the advice of experts in readability employed to make surveys by some newspapers and press associations.

The changes all have been made to achieve brevity—shorter words, shorter sentences and shorter paragraphs—in the belief that thereby the average American, who has only a ninth grade education, will find the result easier to read and comprehend.

Readability Formulas

To test the ease with which a given piece of writing can be read and understood there exist numerous formulas. Among the best known are those of Rudolf Flesch of New York University and Robert Gunning, director of Readable News Reports of Columbus, Ohio. Following the recommendations of the former, the Associated Press reduced its average lead sentence length from 27 to 23 words and its average lead word sentence length from 1.74 to 1.55 syllables. Upon the advice of the latter, the United Press simplified its writing style so as to be suitable for readers with 11.7 years of education, whereas formerly it presumably was writing for those who had gone to school 16.7 years.

For the Associated Press Managing Editors, Flesch explained as follows:

> The formula is a statistical tool to estimate roughly the ease and interest with which a typical American newspaper reader will read the tested piece of writing. It was developed on the basis of reading comprehension tests and has been checked against numerous readership studies of newspaper and magazine material, as well as audience studies of news broadcasts.
>
> The formula estimates "reading ease" and "human interest." "Reading ease" is measured by the average length of words and sentences—the shorter, the easier to read. My studies have shown that an average word length of 1.5 syllables and an average sentence length of 19 words is a good standard for newspaper material.
>
> "Human interest" is measured by the percentage of "personal words" and "personal sentences." These include names, pronouns, and certain other words referring to people, and direct quotes, questions, "you" sentences, and other sentences indirectly addressed to another person. The more of these "personal" elements, the more interesting for the average reader. My studies have shown that 6 per cent "personal words" and 12 per cent "personal sentences" make a good standard for news writing.

On another occasion, Flesch told the same group how to use the formula:

> *1. The length of the average word.* This is measured by figuring the number of syllables per hundred words. You can do these easily for yourself: just read aloud and count. (What makes words hard to read are prefixes and suffixes like –ation and –osity; counting syllables is just an easy shortcut for counting prefixes and suffixes.) Naturally, the higher this count, the poorer the readability.
>
> *2. The length of the average sentence.* This is measured by counting the number of words and dividing by the number of sentences. Again, long sentences make for hard reading. So the higher the count, the lower the readability score.
>
> *3. The percentage of words that have human interest.* What counts here is names, personal pronouns that refer to people, the word people itself, and all words that have masculine or feminine gender. (Words that may be masculine or feminine, like teacher, do not count here.) The more of these "personal words" per 100 words, the better the readability.

4. The percentage of sentences that have human interest. Here I count all sentences that are addressed to the reader (questions, commands, requests) and all sentences that are addressed to one or more listeners and quoted in the text. If a quoted sentence is part of a large one, I count that one. To figure the percentage, I divide the number of these "personal sentences" by the total number of sentences. Quotations from written or printed stuff don't count, of course.

Gunning considers three factors:

1. Sentence pattern. It was found that difficulty begins when the average number of words per sentence exceeds twenty. *Time*, the news magazine, averages 16 to 18 words per sentence and *Reader's Digest* sentences average 18, suggesting that their popularity may depend more on the way they are written than upon what they contain. *Atlantic Monthly* averages 24 words per sentence and appeals to so-called "high brows."

2. Fog Index. This is a measure of complex or abstract words, as "prodigious expenditure" for "big expense," "undoubtedly" for "no doubt," "rendezvous" for "meeting" and so forth.

3. Human interest factor. This means that frequent use of names of people, referents to those names and other human interest words increases readability.

In *The Technique of Clear Writing*, Gunning enumerated the steps to find the Fog Index as follows:

1. Jot down the number of words in successive sentences. If the piece is long, you may wish to take several samples of 100 words, spaced evenly through it. If you do, stop the sentence count with the sentence which ends nearest the 100-word mark. Divide the total number of words in the passage by the number of sentences. This gives the average sentence length of the passage.

2. Count the number of words of three syllables or more per 100 words. Don't count the words (1) that are capitalized, (2) that are combinations of short easy words (like "bookkeeper" and "butterfly"), (3) that are verb forms made into three syllables by adding –ed or –es (like "created" or "trespasses"). This gives you the per cent of hard words.

3. To get the Fog Index, total the two factors just counted and multiply by .4.

Gunning presented the following key for practical judgment of Fog Index results:

READING LEVEL

Fog Index	By Grade	By Magazine
17	College graduate	(No popular magazine
16	College senior	this difficult)
15	College junior	
14	College sophomore	
13	College freshman	
DANGER LINE		
12	High school senior	*Atlantic Monthly*
11	High school junior	*Harper's*
10	High school sophomore	*Time*
9	High school freshman	*Reader's Digest*
8	Eighth grade	*Ladies' Home Journal*
7	Seventh grade	*True Confessions*
6	Sixth grade	*Comics*

Objections to Formulas

As an A.P.M.E. Readability committee once reported: "The virtue of the Flesch experiment is that it *has* made writers think more of their writing."

The same, of course, could be said of the Gunning and several other formulas. The principal effect of them has been a loosening of the rule that all five *w*'s and *h* should be included in the first paragraph or lead of a news story. Most newspapers now achieve brevity by playing up only the most important of these elements (usually the *who* and *what*), leaving the others for succeeding paragraphs or even omitting them. Furthermore, the *who* or *what* may be indefinite in the lead, being made more specific later in the story.

That these and other techniques to obtain brevity can be overdone is obvious. After what they considered fair trial, some newspapermen concluded that a new rigid formula merely was being substituted for another. One of the most outspoken of rewrite men who considered the new "strait jacket" worse than the old was Robert Faherty of the Chicago *Daily News* who wrote:

> The formula wastes writer-time, which costs money. It wastes writer-skill. It wastes writer-strength, cutting efficiency. It kills writer-creativeness, which some editors regard as desirable.
>
> It is often difficult to achieve a 14-word lead that expresses the news element and properly identifies a principal. It is often necessary to discard two or three attempts. A Formula 14W story about anything more complex

than a warehouse fire requires double or triple the time of a story written in normal-sentence flow.

The formula wastes space. A 14-word sentence very often becomes a 14-word paragraph. . . . Meager paragraphs waste space.

There is waste in the unavoidable use of surplus words. Subordinate clauses must be turned into full sentences by the use of introductory words such as "But Mr. Jones also was . . ." rather than the use of comma or conjunction.

The structural faults of sentences that have been cut abruptly to the formula give structural faults to the stories. Abnormality and artificiality are instantly evident.

Stephen E. Fitzgerald pointed out that many of the classics had a high Fog Index but managed to communicate. Of the "readability boys," this author wrote, "They threaten to put our words in a literary strait jacket, leaving us only the solace of an illusion . . . that by shortening our sentences, we have somehow clarified our thought."

Brevity, this and other critics contend, does not necessarily equate with clarity. A short word can be as vague as a long one, and a short sentence can be as misleading as a book. To strip writing down to the "lowest levels of understanding." Fitzgerald wrote, "is as though we were to insist on reducing all music to the primitive rhythm of a jungle beat, thus hoping to widen the audience."

Using the syllable-length criterion advanced by Flesch, such words as *beautiful, patriotism, vacation, prearrange, improbable, candlestick, bracelet, watermelon,* and other familiar ones would be considered difficult whereas use of *ohm, joule, watt, erg, baize, arn, tweak, volt* and *tort* would contribute to a high readability score.

Different from either the Flesch or Gunning system, in that it takes account of the reader's probable familiarity with words, is the system devised by Prof. Edgar Dale and Mrs. Jeanne S. Chall of the Bureau of Educational Research of Ohio State University. The Dale-Chall system takes into account average sentence length but also uses a list of 3,000 words familiar to fourth graders.

Dr. Dale discounts the value of counting affixes, suffixes and prefixes, as advocated by Flesch, by declaring that no two skilled judges ever get the same count. He also rejects Flesch's personal referent principle and is fond of citing a quotation from Koffka's *Principles of Gestalt Psychology* which contains personal pronouns equal to 5.8 per cent as follows:

> In the first case, real moving objects present in the field, the shift of the retinal pattern leads to behavioral motion of objects, whether I fixate a non-moving object or follow a moving one with my regard; in the second case, when my eyes roam stationary objects, such a shift will not have this result. . . .

That would be considered very readable by both the Flesch and Gunning systems.

Proper names, other critics of these formulas have pointed out, do not necessarily lead to greater understanding unless the reader knows the persons mentioned and understands the references to them. "He was as mad as Hamlet," for instance, is about as readable as you can get; but if the reader never has heard of Hamlet, its meaning is lost on him.

In reviewing Flesch's book, *The Art of Readable Writing*, Lester Markel, then New York *Times* Sunday editor, wrote, "The basic problem is not to humanize or to technicolor the news; it is to make the news understandable." According to Markel and his ilk, good writing is not mathematical or mechanical. Ease of reading depends, not on sentence length but on thought. It is his paucity of ideas and factual background information that gives a reader difficulty, not polysyllabic words. Popular magazines are read, not because the words and sentences are shorter but rather because the thought is simple. Even when news stories were written in allegedly ponderous style, readers devoured the sensational accounts and ignored the serious, each written in the same style. The problem, therefore, becomes one of supplying the reader with the necessary information to comprehend the immediate news account. Today, even the most erudite specialist, such as a scientist, needs to have the vocabulary of a fellow specialist in another field translated for him. In writing for the masses, newsmen long have adhered to the rule that they should not over estimate a reader's informmation nor underestimate his intelligence. It still is a good rule, and writing "A rose is a rose is a rose" merely because it scores high on a readability scale is futile if readers don't know what in thunder you're driving at.

The rise and fall of the readability fad should be recalled when evaluating the enthusiasm with which some more recent attempts to theorize regarding the communication process have been directed. This is particularly true of the esoteric declamations of Prof. Marshall McLuhan for whom "the medium is the message." Granted, as McLuhan elaborates in his *Understanding Media* and other books, television and other electronic devices have had a profound social effect. It does not necessarily follow, however, that the contents of a piece of writing are now unimportant. The essence of good journalism remains good reporting which means having something to say—the contents rather than the medium of the message.

The Reporter's Guide

In the opinion of many a newspaper editor, the typical reporter is a near illiterate who is dedicated to the proposition that the preposition is to end sentences with. To help the reporter overcome his ignorance, most newspapers provide him with a style book—and in their very diversity, newspaper style books make some of the most entertaining reading to be found anywhere.

The style books do not always agree on usage. The Indianapolis *Star* spells it "clew," the Indianapolis *News* "clue." Most papers capitalize Pope, but the Miami *Herald* does not. In most papers, rape is rape, but in the Memphis *Commercial Appeal* it is usually criminal attack. The Minneapolis *Star* and *Tribune* permit partial decommissioning of generals ("If it's Lt. Gen. John A. Jones in the first reference, plain Jones will suffice in later references"), but in the New York *Times*, once a general always a general. And no paper cares to folo the trail blazed by the Chicago *Tribune* into a virgin land of simplified spelling: altho, thru, sirup, burocracy.

All Women Aren't Ladies. Disagreements multiply in the areas of race and religion. The Miami *Herald* draws a careful distinction between white cops, who are always "policemen," and Negro cops, who are always "patrolmen." In the Memphis *Commercial Appeal* if a minister is white, he is "the Rev.," if Negro he is simply "Rev." The Denver *Post* is explicit on Roman Catholic ritual: "Mass is celebrated, said or read. High Mass is sung, never held. The Rosary is recited or said, never read." But the Miami *News* takes the easy way out: "Write it 'the mass (or rosary) will be at 7 P.M.' rather than having it sung, read, held, recited, given or said."

Matters of taste and the social amenities come under close style-book scrutiny. The Buffalo *Evening News* avoids "mention of hideous creatures or gruesome circumstances" and substitutes "glamorous" for "sexy"; the *Commercial Appeal* warns its reporters to "write nothing that will spoil the appetite." The Chicago *Tribune* permits "s.o.b.," but defines it as a "Trumanism." The Los Angeles *Times*, concluding that all women aren't ladies, ungallantly applies its conclusion: "A salesgirl or a saleswoman is not a saleslady, and a washerwoman is not a washlady, so a scrubwoman cannot be a scrublady." In Detroit, the *News* withholds the title of "Mr." from all males who are not Protestant clergy, dead, or the President of the United States. "However," cautions the *News*, "other cases may arise in which a tone of respect is desirable; in such cases Mr. may be used."

No One Loses Legs. Some style books draw exquisitely fine beads on proper form. The Salt Lake City *Tribune* explains the distinction between three cupfuls of sugar and three cups full of sugar, and softly suggests the typographical peril in such words as "shot, suit, short, shift, skit, etc." The Detroit *News* confidently calls a girl a girl until she reaches 21, when she becomes a woman; at 17 a boy becomes a youth, at 21 a man. "Beware of such relative descriptions as elderly, aged or old," says the Washington *Post and Times Herald*. "Few men under 70 would appreciate those adjectives, and few women this side of the morgue." On Denver's *Rocky Mountain News*, "animals may speak only with the special permission of the city editor." "Look out for people who lose legs or arms," say the Minneapolis *Star* and *Tribune*. "They really don't."

Too often the style books merely belabor the obvious and the picayune. Rare is the reporter anywhere who is not advised that cars do not run into trees (they crash against them). The *Commercial Appeal* demands that kerosene be identified as coal oil the first time the term is used; the Washington *Post* style book devotes 450 words to discussing the difference between optometrists, ophthalmologists, oculists, and opticians.

The Jewel. Are newspaper style books necessary? Some newspapers—and possibly thousands of newspaper reporters—think not. The New York *Herald Tribune*, the Boston *Record* and *American*, the Manchester, N.H., *Union Leader* and many other dailies don't have a style book. But the majority of United States dailies apparently agree with the Washington *Post*, which holds that consistency of style in a newspaper "is more than a jewel; it is a necessity."

[*Time* Magazine]

Newspaper Style

Long before readability became a cult, newspapers strived for many of the objectives which the researchers since have advocated. Disregarding criticism from literary purists, they developed an economical style well suited to the purposes for which it was intended. Characteristics of effective newspaper English in virtually every newsroom in the United States include the following:

1. Compact, usually short, sentences, each word selected and placed for maximum effect.
2. Short, terse paragraphs, each complete in itself and generally capable of being removed without destroying the sense of a story.
3. Conciseness, directness and simplicity, through elimination of superfluous words, phrases and clauses and through proper emphasis.
4. Factualness, without editorial opinion, puffs and boosts, unwise superlatives, adjectives, nouns or other dogmatic words.
5. Avoidance of "fine" writing, strong verbs and nouns being preferred to trite, hackneyed and obsolete words and expressions.
6. Observance of the rules of good grammatical and word usage.

What the readability experts did was shock many newspapers into the realization that they were not living up to their own rules. That a few should go to extremes to find new ways of doing so probably was to be expected. The readability fans placed too much emphasis on brevity without considering adequately other aspects of good writing.

Conciseness

The objective of effective journalistic writing should be to avoid cumbersomeness without becoming choppy or repetitious through the excessive use of referents.

SUPERFLUOUS DETAILS

Relaxing of the rule that all of the five *w*'s and *h* must be included in the first paragraph of a news story generally achieves the objective of uncluttering the lead.

Cluttered

Clifford Britt, 38, 1459 Grove street, and another passenger on an eastbound Mitchell boulevard street car were injured about 8 A.M. today when the car jumped the track and collided with a westbound car at Mitchell boulevard and Perkins street.

Scores of other passengers en route to work who filled both cars were heavily jostled and shaken up as the two cars came together, according to Mitchell boulevard police who also said another man was injured but disappeared from the scene of the accident.

Britt was taken to Municipal hospital with cuts and bruises on the head and hands.

Uncluttered

Two men were injured and scores shaken when two street cars collided at Mitchell boulevard and Perkins street about 8 A.M. today.

One car was going west and the other east on Mitchell boulevard.

Hitting an open electric switch, the eastbound car jumped the tracks, struck the other, and derailed it.

One of the injured men was Clifford Britt, 38, 1459 Grove street. Police said another man was injured but disappeared from the scene of the accident.

Britt received cuts and bruises on the head and hands. He was taken to Municipal hospital.

Both cars were filled with passengers en route to work. They were heavily jostled as the two cars came together.

SUPERFLUOUS WORDS

The articles *the*, *a* and *an* often can be eliminated, as:

WEAK: The Booster students who heard the talk—
BETTER: Booster students who heard the—
WEAK: It is for the men who make good.
BETTER: It is for men who make good.

Erling H. Erlandson warns against excess in adherence to this rule. Otherwise the result might be "nonsensical writing," as: "Cause of the dispute was the overtime clause. Union had demanded time and a half for work after 5 P.M." Says Erlandson: "Two words saved at the expense of communication."

Sentences may be shortened and made more forceful by making verbs more direct, as:

WEAK: The committee arrived at a conclusion.
BETTER: The committee concluded.
WEAK: The society held a discussion on the matter.
BETTER: The society discussed the matter.
WEAK: He put in an appearance.
BETTER: He appeared.

WEAK: They did away with the old building.
BETTER: They razed the old building.

Some words are unnecessary and even incorrect, as:

WEAK: She fell off of the roof.
BETTER: She fell off the roof.
WEAK: The case is a difficult one.
BETTER: The case is difficult.
WEAK: The man fell a distance of 50 feet.
BETTER: The man fell 50 feet.
WRONG: The actual fact is—
RIGHT: The fact is—
WRONG: The building was completely destroyed.
RIGHT: The building was destroyed.
WEAK: It reverts back to the former subject.
BETTER: It reverts to the former subject.
WRONG: It was plainly obvious.
RIGHT: It was obvious.
WEAK: He didn't know whether or not to go.
BETTER: He didn't know whether to go.

It is not necessary to include the state with the names of large cities, or to mention the state with the name of a city in the same state as that in which the newspaper is published.

WEAK: He lives in Los Angeles, Calif.
BETTER: He lives in Los Angeles.

But:

VAGUE: He lives in Springfield.
CLEAR: He lives in Springfield, Mass.

Don't waste words in giving dates, as:

WEAK: The Chemical society will meet on Saturday.
BETTER: The Chemical society will meet Saturday.
WEAK: The meeting will be held this coming Friday.
BETTER: The meeting will be held Friday.
WEAK: The meeting was held at 12 o'clock noon.
BETTER: The meeting was held at noon.

Sometimes a series of related facts can be presented in *series* form, in chronological order, as a word saver. In an article, "Condensation: A Check List of Current Techniques," in the Summer 1951 *Journalism Quarterly*, Robert G. Martin gave the following example:

He was born in Russia, reared in Austria, graduated in 1914 from the University of Vienna, and then served throughout World War I as an Austrian artillery officer on the Italian and Russian fronts.

Erlandson, on the other hand, correctly warns against misuse of this style, as "Born in Tennessee, he served on the Los Angeles Board of Education from 1935 to 1941." Wrote Erlandson: "When two unrelated facts are jammed together, it may be bright writing but it's also faulty subordination."

SUPERFLUOUS PHRASES

WEAK: The meeting was held for the purpose of discussing the matter.
BETTER: The meeting was held to discuss the matter.
WEAK: We met at the corner of Spring and High streets.
BETTER: We met at Spring and High streets.
WEAK: We reached him by the use of telephone.
BETTER: We reached him by telephone.
WEAK: The color of the cart was red.
BETTER: The cart was red.
WEAK: He will be here for a period of three weeks.
BETTER: He will be here for three weeks.

Often a strong verb, adjective, adverb or possessive form can be substituted for a phrase.

WEAK: A baby with brown eyes.
BETTER: A brown-eyed baby.
WEAK: The arguments of Brown.
BETTER: Brown's arguments.
WEAK: They assembled with little commotion.
BETTER: They assembled quietly.
WEAK: The howitzer went off with a boom.
BETTER: The howitzer boomed.

Before emulating the last preceding example, which was given by Martin, the writer must be certain that he has not distorted meaning. There is great temptation to use shorter action verbs which create a feeling of excitement not justified by the facts of the story. Some newspapers have been accused of offending considerably in this respect through frequent use of such words as *hits, slaps, traps, raps, rips, flays, slays, breaks, looms, dooms, lashes, kills, fires, cracks, nabs, grabs, quizzes, grills, curbs, blocks* and *foils*, to use a list compiled by Sydney J. Harris in the January 3, 1956, Chicago *Daily News*.

SUPERFLUOUS CLAUSES

WEAK: All citizens who are interested should come.
BETTER: All interested citizens should come.
WEAK: He will speak at the meeting which will be held Monday.
BETTER: He will speak at the meeting Monday.
WEAK: John Farrell, who is secretary of the Engineers' club, will be there.
BETTER: John Farrell, secretary of the Engineers' club, will be there.

On the other hand, clauses can be used effectively for word-preserving interpolations as in the following example given by Martin:

> Even though he lost them both, 8–6 and 9–7, he outscored Sedgman in earned points, 46–43, and his passing shots, often executed while he was running full tilt, were beautiful to watch.

SIMPLICITY

This quality is obtained in large part by avoiding "elegant" words when simple ones would do better.

about is better than *with reference to*
agreement is better than *concordance*
although is better than *despite the fact that*
before is better than *prior to*
body is better than *remains*
buried is better than *interred*
burned is better than *destroyed by fire*
city people is better than *urban people*
clear is better than *obvious*
coffin is better than *casket*
danger is better than *precariousness*
died is better than *passed away* or *succumbed*
dog is better than *canine*
farming is better than *agriculture*
fear is better than *apprehension*
fire is better than *conflagration*
forced is better than *compelled*
funeral is better than *obsequies*
horse is better than *domesticated quadruped*
if is better than *in the event of*
leg is better than *limb*
man is better than *gentleman*
marriage is better than *nuptials*
meeting is better than *rendezvous*
money is better than *lucre*
nearness is better than *contiguity*
normal is better than *traditional*
since is better than *inasmuch as*
theft is better than *larceny*
truth is better than *veracity*
understand is better than *comprehend*
well paying is better than *lucrative*
woman is better than *lady*

When two words are synonyms, brevity can be obtained by using the shorter, as

after for *following*   *expect* for *anticipate*
ask for *request*   *get* for *obtain*
buy for *purchase*   *try* for *attempt*
car for *automobile*   *use* for *utilize*

PASSIVE AND ACTIVE VOICE

The active voice usually is more emphatic than the passive. The passive should be used, however, when warranted by the importance of the grammatical object of a sentence. In the following sentences, for example, the passive voice is preferable to the active:

>Henry Binger has been appointed chairman of the County Republican campaign committee.

>Earl Kromer, prominent local merchant, was killed instantly early today when a bolt of lightning struck his home, 34 E. Wilson street.

>Increased rates for the Middletown municipal water works were ordered by the public service commission in an order issued Thursday.

In other cases the feature can better be played up by use of the active voice, as:

WEAK: The accident was witnessed by ten boys.
BETTER: Ten boys witnessed the accident.
WEAK: The report was received by the mayor.
BETTER: The mayor received the report.
WEAK: The keynote address was delivered by Governor Furman.
BETTER: Governor Furman delivered the keynote address.

PROPER EMPHASIS

Vagueness and indefiniteness are avoided, and clarity obtained, by placing important ideas at the beginnings of sentences. Also by playing up the action, significance, result or feature of the paragraph or story, by avoiding vague and indefinite words and eliminating superfluous details, words, phrases and clauses.

VAGUE: Some 50 persons were present.
BETTER: About 50 were present.
WORDY: People of Chester will be asked to contribute $4,000 to the National Red Cross campaign to relieve suffering in the drought area of the United

States, according to announcements made yesterday by John Doe, local chairman.

CONCISE: Chester's quota in the National Red Cross campaign for drought relief is $4,000, John Doe, local chairman, said yesterday.

WEAK: When asked what he thought of the compromise plan of unemployment relief, Senator Sapo today said that—

DEFINITE: Senator Sapo today condemned the compromise plan for unemployment relief as demagogic, unconstitutional and inadequate.

WEAK: The purpose of the Student Council meeting at 7 P.M. Monday in Swift hall is to discuss the proposal to limit student activities.

BETTER: The Student Council will discuss limitation of student activities at 7 P.M. Monday in Swift hall.

WEAK: It was decided by the Men's club at its meeting last evening to hold a smoker next Monday evening in the club room.

BETTER: The Men's club will hold a smoker Monday evening in the club room, it was decided at last evening's meeting.

Newspaper style books and journalism texts once admonished reporters never to begin a story with an article or indefinite pronoun. Like every other rule, this one could and should be broken on occasion. Such a lead as "There will be a meeting, etc." ordinarily should be avoided. Such effective writing as the following, however, should be encouraged.

> There was to have been a birthday party Saturday in the Ken Rose Rest Home, 6255 N. Kenmore. But instead there was quiet sadness.
> The party was to have celebrated the 102d birthday of Miss Frances Benson, a resident of the home.
> Miss Benson, a retired Chicago schoolteacher, died Friday after suffering a sudden stroke. [Chicago *Daily News*]

Avoiding Banality

The day of the grammatical purist is gone. Contemporary authorities recognize that language makes dictionaries and not vice versa. Many words in common use today were once frowned upon as slang or vulgarisms. Each year prominent writers coin new words or resurrect archaic ones which meet with popular acceptance. The fault of young writers as regards word choice is not so much selection of what might be called undignified words but tactless use of bromides, platitudes and clichés. What constitutes tactfulness in using slang, trite and hackneyed expressions is for the English department, not the school of journalism, to teach. Nevertheless, the journalism teacher and certainly the newspaper copyreader can spot a threadbare word or phrase used in a threadbare way.

There isn't a word listed below, as one to be used cautiously, which can't be used effectively on occasion. This is decidedly not a don't section, merely one of precaution.

FIGURES OF SPEECH

The following figures of speech generally should be avoided because they are likely to be misused. They are whiskered with age and mark their innocent user as callow.

a checkered career	old as Methusaleh
acid test	picture of health
alike as peas in a pod	pillar of the church
ax to grind	police combing the city
blessing in disguise	pretty as a picture
buffeted by defeat	rains cats and dogs
busy as a bee	round into shape
clutches of the law	sea of upturned faces
cool as a cucumber	silver lining
departed this Vale of tears	since Hector was a pup
devouring elements	slow as molasses
dull as dishwater	smell a rat
eyes bigger than his stomach	sober as a judge
flow like water	something the cat dragged in
hail of bullets	spread like a house afire
hangs in the balance	stormy session
heart of the business district	the crying need
Herculean strength	the great beyond
honest as the day is long	the wings of disaster
in the limelight	threw a monkey wrench into
innocent as a newborn babe	to swing the pendulum
long hours of the night	watery grave
loomed like sentinels	white as a sheet
met his Waterloo	won his spurs
never rains but it pours	worked like Trojans
nipped in the bud	

BROMIDES

Generally considered too trite or hackneyed for effective use are the following:

all-out effort
almost fatally injured
anyway, shape or form
as luck would have it
augurs well
bated breath
beaming smile
better half
bids fair
bigger and better
blushing bride
bright and fair
bright and smiling
broad daylight
burly Negro
crisp bill
dances divinely
departed this life
doing as well as can be expected
doomed to disappointment
dull thud
each and every
easy prey
fair maidens
favor with a selection
feature
few and far between
green-eyed monster
hale and hearty
head over heels
hectic
he-man
host of friends
in the offing
internal fury
laid at rest
last but not least
last sad rites
leering ghost
light fantastic toe
loomed on the horizon
many and various
method in his madness
music hath charms, etc.
no uncertain terms
order out of chaos
point with pride
powder keg
present day and generation
received an ovation
red-blooded
render a solo
resting comfortably
scintillating
sigh of relief
signs of the times
smashed to smithereens
sparkling eyes
thick and fast
trend of public sentiment
variety is the spice of life
view with alarm
vital stake
weather permitting
wild and woolly

SHOPWORN PERSONIFICATIONS

The following mythical characters have been introduced into all kinds of writing so often that they have lost their ability to impress or amuse:

Betty Coed
Dame Fashion
Dame Rumor
Dan Cupid
Father Neptune
Father Time
G.I. Joe
Grim Reaper
Jack Frost
Joe College
John Q. Public
Jupiter Pluvius
Lady Luck
Man in the Street
Mother Earth
Mother Nature
Mr. Average Citizen
Old Sol

JOURNALESE

Newspapers have not contributed so much as one might expect to the coinage of new words, but they have helped exhaust the

108   PRINCIPLES OF NEWS WRITING

effectiveness of a large number through indiscriminate repetition. Among these are the following:

blunt instrument	grilled by police	rush
bolt from a clear sky	gruesome find	sleuths
brutal crime	gumshoes	smoke-filled room
brutally murdered	hot seat	smoking revolver
cannon fodder	infuriated mob	solon
cheered to the echo	man hunt	speculation is rife
clubber	moron	swoop down
crime wave	mystery surrounds	thug
cynosure of all eyes	news leaked out	usual reliable sources
death car	police drag nets	war clouds
fatal noose	political pot boiling	while thousands cheer
feeling ran high	probe	whirlwind tour
focus attention	quiz	will be staged

Correct Usage

It is presumed that the student has completed a course in English grammar and composition and, therefore, that he knows the rudiments of good English. Although some reputable writers still split their infinitives without losing effect, few misuse "lay" and "lie," use "none" as a plural, get "don't" and "doesn't" twisted, misplace "only" or use "like" when they mean "as if." If the student of this book is deficient in his knowledge of grammar, he had better concentrate on it constantly. Cubs who cannot make their subjects and predicates agree and who can't spell ordinary words don't last long.

In every newspaper office some rules of grammar, word usage and punctuation are emphasized more than others. Most newspapers issue style sheets for the guidance of new staff members as to what kind of writing is preferred.

GRAMMATICAL FAULTS

Several years of correcting journalism students' papers have convinced the writer that the following are among the most common grammatical errors about which aspiring reporters need caution.

WRONG: Neither the mayor nor the city clerk are willing to talk.
RIGHT: Neither the mayor nor the city clerk is willing to talk.

WRONG: The Chamber of Commerce will begin their annual membership drive Monday.
RIGHT: The Chamber of Commerce will begin its annual membership drive Monday.
WRONG: Howard is not as tall as Harold.
RIGHT: Howard is not so tall as Harold.
WRONG: He gave it to John and I.
RIGHT: He gave it to John and me.

The next two examples do not illustrate infallible rules; in other cases these constructions may be better:

WEAK: He has always wanted to go.
BETTER: He always has wanted to go.
WEAK: He was ordered to immediately arrest Jones.
BETTER: He was ordered to arrest Jones immediately.
WRONG: Having arrived an hour late, the audience had begun to disperse before Smith began to speak.
RIGHT: Having arrived an hour late, Smith found his audience had begun to disperse.
WRONG: After Graham and Mitchell had shaken hands he turned to greet the senator.
RIGHT: After Graham and Mitchell had shaken hands the former turned to greet the senator.
STRONGER: After Graham shook hands with Mitchell he greeted the senator.

PARTS OF SPEECH

To obtain originality of expression, writers (not all of them journalists) sometimes change the part of speech of a word. In many cases the dictionaries have caught up with popular usage. For instance, it is proper to say "chair a meeting," "jail a prisoner," "hospitalize a sick person" or "table a resolution." Even such words as "alibi," "probe," "host" and "torpedo," to whose use as verbs objection often is heard, are listed as such. President Kennedy used "finalize" as a verb and the practice of inventing verb forms of nouns is widespread; thus we say "victimize," "contact," and the like indiscriminately.

In view of the dynamic character of the language, one hesitates to become crotchety when a newspaper columnist says someone "weekended" or "house-guested" another or that a dowager "lorgnetted" a stranger. In recent years such words as "babysit" and "moonlight" have come into common usage as verbs. Use of "wise" as a suffix (businesswise, timewise, bookwise, saleswise) still is regarded as somewhat flippant, however expressive.

Usually it is left to special writers who sign their stories, sports writers and feature writers to invent unusual word usages. Authors of formal stories are more conservative and wait until the dictionaries have sanctioned an innovation before using it casually. When Webster's *Third New International Dictionary* appeared, however, it created a storm for allegedly going too far in legitimatizing new usages. Among the leading liberal authorities in this field are Roy Copperud, who conducts a column for *Editor & Publisher*, and Prof. Bergen Evans of Northwestern University, who coauthored *A Dictionary of Contemporary American Usage* with Cornelia Evans. Defenders of the Webster dictionary pointed out that in 1800 such words as "banjo," "hominy" and "possum" were considered too slangy for its edition that year.

TROUBLESOME WORDS

No matter what the viewpoint regarding definitions, there can be no disagreement that words should be used to convey the meaning intended by their employers. Caution, therefore, is advisable in deviating from original usages.

The following are some words and expressions which often cause difficulty:

ABOVE Should not be used for *over* or *more than*.
ACCORD Do not use in the sense of *award*. *Give* is better.
ACT A single incident. An *action* consists of several acts.
ACTUAL FACTS All facts are actual.
ADMINISTER Used with reference to medicine, governments or oaths. Blows are not *administered*, but *dealt*.
ADOPT Not synonymous with *decide* or *assume*.
AFFECT; EFFECT *Affect* means to have an influence on; *effect* means to cause, to produce, to result in.
AGGRAVATE Means *to increase*; not synonymous with *irritate*.
AGGREGATE Not synonymous with *total*.
ALLEGE Not synonymous with *assert*. Say the *alleged* crime, but "He *said* he is innocent."
ALLOW; PERMIT The former means *not to forbid*; the latter means *to grant leave*.
ALLUDE Do not confuse with *refer*.
ALMOST; NEARLY *Almost* regards the ending of an act; *nearly* the beginning.

ALTERNATIVE Indicates a choice of two things. Incorrect to speak of *two alternatives* or *one alternative*.
AMONG Use when more than two is meant; for two only, use *between*.
ANTECEDENTS Do not use in the sense of *ancestors, forefathers, history* or *origin*.
A NUMBER OF Indefinite. Specify.
ANXIOUS Implies worry. Not synonymous with *eager* which implies anticipation or desire.
ANYONE OR NONE Use in speaking of more than two. *Either* and *neither* are used when speaking of only two. All take singular verbs.
APPEARS, LOOKS, SMELLS, SEEMS, ETC. Take an adjective complement.
AS THE RESULT OF AN OPERATION Avoid this expression. Usually incorrect and libelous.
AT Use *in* before the names of large cities: He is *in* New York, but the meeting was held *at* Greenville.
AUDIENCE An *audience* hears, *spectators* see.
AUTOPSY An *autopsy* is *performed*, not *held*.
AVOCATION A man's pleasure, while *vocation* is his business or profession.
AWFUL Means *to fill with awe*; not synonymous with *very* or *extremely*.
BALANCE Not synonymous with *rest* or *remainder*.
BANQUET Only a few dinners are worth the name. Use *dinner* or *supper*.
BECAUSE Better than *due to* in, "They fought because of a misunderstanding."
BESIDE; BESIDES The first means *by the side of*; the second, *in addition to*.
BY Use instead of *with* in such sentences as, "The effect was gained by colored lights."
CALL ATTENTION Do not use it for *direct attention*.
CANON; CANNON The former is a *law*; the latter is a large *gun*.
CANVAS; CANVASS The former is a *cloth*; the latter means *to solicit*.
CAPITOL The building is the *capitol*; the city is the *capital*.
CASUALTY Should not be confused with *disaster, accident, mishap*.
CHILDISH Not synonymous with *childlike*.
CHINESE Don't use *Chinaman*.

CLAIM A transitive verb. One may "claim a dog" but not that "Boston is larger than Portland."
COLD FACTS (or statistics). When is a fact hot?
COLLIDE To collide both objects must be in motion.
COMMENCE Usually *begin* or *start* is better.
COMPARED WITH Use *compared with* in speaking of two things coming under the same classification; use *compared to* if the classes are different.
COMPLETELY DESTROYED Redundant.
COMPRISE Do not use for *compose*.
CONFESS A man confesses a crime to the police, but he does not confess to a crime.
CONSCIOUS Not synonymous with *aware*.
CONSENSUS Don't say *consensus of opinion*; simply say *consensus*.
CONSEQUENCE Sometimes misused in the sense of "importance" and "of moment," as "They are all persons of consequence" (importance); "A matter of no consequence" (moment).
CONSISTS IN Distinguish between *consists in* and *consists of*.
CONSUMMATION Look up in the dictionary. Do not use in reference to marriage.
CONTINUAL; CONTINUOUS That is *–al* which either is always going on or recurs at short intervals and never comes (or is regarded as never coming) to an end. That is *–ous* in which no break occurs between the beginning and the end.
CONVENE Delegates, not a convention, convene.
CORRESPONDENT; CO-RESPONDENT The former *communicates in writing*; the latter *answers jointly* with another.
COUNCIL; COUNSEL The former is a meeting for deliberation. The latter is advice or one who gives advice.
COUPLE Used only when two things are joined, not of separate things.
CRIME Do not confuse with *sin* or *vice*. Crime is a violation of the law of the state; *vice* refers to a violation of moral law; *sin* is a violation of religious law.
CULTURED Don't use for *cultivated*.
CYCLONE Distinguish from *hurricane, typhoon, tornado, gale* and *storm*.
DANGEROUSLY Not *dangerously* but *critically* or *alarmingly ill*.
DATA Plural. *Datum* is singular.
DATE FROM Not *date back to*.

DEPOT   Don't use for *station*. A *depot* is a storehouse for freight or supplies; railway passengers arrive at a *station*.

DIE OF   Not *die from*.

DIFFERENT FROM   Not *different than*.

DIMENSIONS; PROPORTIONS   The former pertains to *magnitude*; the latter to *form*.

DIVIDE   Don't say, "The money was divided between Smith, Jones and Brown." Use *among* when more than two are concerned.

DOVE   Should not be used for *dived*.

DROPS DEAD   *Falls dead* is what is meant.

DURING   Do not confuse with *in*. *During* answers the question, "How long?" *in* the question, "When? At what time?" as, "We were in Princeton *during* the winter"; "We received the letter *in* the morning."

EACH OTHER; ONE ANOTHER   The former pertains to *two*; the latter to *three* or *more*.

EITHER; NEITHER   Use when speaking of two only.

ELICIT   Means to "draw out against the will."

EMIGRANT   Do not confuse with *immigrant*. An *emigrant* leaves, and an *immigrant* comes in.

ENVELOP; ENVELOPE   The former means to *surround*; the latter is a *covering* or *wrapper*.

EVENT   Do not confuse with *incident, affair, occurrence* or *happening*.

EXPERIMENT   Don't say *try* an experiment. Experiments are *made*.

FAIL   To *fail* one must try. Usually what is mean is *did not*.

FAKIR; FAKER   The former is an Oriental ascetic; the latter is a street peddler.

FARTHER   Denotes distance; *further* denotes time.

FINAL; FINALE   The former means *last*; the latter is a *concluding act* or *number*.

FRANKENSTEIN   In the story he was the monster's maker, not the monster itself.

FROM   A person dies *of*, not *from*, a disease.

GRADUATE, as a verb.   Colleges graduate; students *are graduated*.

GUN   Don't confuse with *revolver* and *pistol*.

HAD   Implies volition. Don't say, "Had his arm cut off."

HEALTHY   A person is *healthy*, but climate is *healthful* and food *wholesome*.

HEART FAILURE   Everyone dies of heart failure. There are several *heart diseases*.

HECTIC "Hectic flush" is the feverish blush of consumption. Not to be used in the sense of *excited, impassioned, intense, rapturous, uncontrolled,* or *wild,* except when a jocosity is intended.

HIGH Distinguish from *large.*

HOI POLLOI "The many." Do not use "the" before it.

HOLD Use advisedly. The Supreme Court *holds* a law constitutional, but one *asserts* that one man is a better boxer than another.

HUNG A criminal is *hanged.* Clothes are *hung* on a line.

INAUGURATE Does not mean *begin.*

INCUMBENT It is redundant to write *present incumbent.*

INDORSE Not synonymous with *approve.*

INFER; IMPLY The former means to *deduce;* the latter to *signify.*

INITIAL A man may sign his initial, but he does not make an *initial payment.* He makes the *first payment.*

INNUMERABLE Not synonymous with *endless.*

INVITED GUESTS Most guests are invited; omit the adjective.

LAST Not synonymous with *latest* or *past.*

LEAVE Don't confuse with *let.*

LEAVES A WIDOW Impossible. He leaves a *wife.*

LESS Use *less* money but *fewer* coins.

LIKE The slogan, "Winstons taste good like a cigaret should" has helped make the use of "like" legitimate as a substitute for "as."

LITERALLY Often the exact opposite, *figuratively,* is meant.

LOCATE A building is *located* when its site is picked; thereafter it is *situated.* A person is *found,* not located.

MAJORITY The lead over *all* others; a plurality is a lead over *one* other.

MATHEMATICS Singular.

MEMORANDUM Singular. *Memoranda,* plural.

MEND You *mend* a dress but *repair* a street.

MINISTER Distinguish between *minister,* a term used in Protestant churches, and *priest,* used in Catholic churches. Every *preacher* is not a *pastor;* a *pastor* has a church, a *minister* may not.

MUSICAL; MUSICALE The former means *rhythmic;* the latter is a *recital* or *concert.*

NAME AFTER The correct form is *name for.*

NEAR ACCIDENT There is no such thing.

NÉE Give only last name, "Mrs. Helen Kuenzel, née Bauman."

NICE Means *exact,* not *agreeable* or *pleasant.*

NOTORIOUS Different from *famous.*

Occur   Accidents *occur* rather than *happen*, but weddings *take place*.
Old adages   There are no *new adages*.
Over   Means *above*; *more than* means *in excess of*.
Partly completed   Has no meaning. The words are contradictory.
Past   Not synonymous with *last*.
People   Refers to population. Do not confuse with *persons*.
Per cent   Do not say "large per cent" when you mean "large proportion."
Politics   Singular.
Practically   Not synonymous with *virtually*. Different from *almost*.
Principle   Always a noun. *Principal* is generally an adjective.
Prone on the back.   Impossible. The word means "lying on the face." *Supine* is "lying on the back."
Provided   Not *providing* he will go.
Public   Singular.
Put in   You *occupy*, *devote* or *spend* time, never *put in* time.
Quite   Means *fully* or *wholly*. Do not, for example, write, "He is *quite* wealthy," but, "He is *rather* wealthy."
Raised   Animals are *raised*; children are *reared*.
Render   You *render* lard or a judgment, but you *sing* a song.
Rumor   It is redundant to write *unverified rumor*.
Secure   Means *to make fast*. Don't use it for *obtain, procure* or *acquire*.
Sensation; emotion   The former is *physical*; the latter is *mental*.
Ship   Cattle are *shipped* but corpses are *sent*.
So   Use in a negative comparison instead of *as*.
Someone, somebody, etc.   Take singular verbs.
Suicide   Do not use as a verb.
Sustain   Injuries are not *sustained* but *received*.
To the nth   An unspecified number, not necessarily infinite or large. Do not use for *to the utmost possible extent*.
Transpire   Means *to emerge from secrecy into knowledge, to become gradually known*. Not to be used in the senses of *happen, occur*, etc.; must not be followed by an infinitive.
Treble; triple   The former means *three times*; the latter means *three kinds*.
True facts   Facts never are false.
Try and   Use *try to*.

UNIQUE   Its adverbs are *absolutely*, *almost*, *in some respects*, *nearly*, *perhaps*, *quite*, *really* and *surely*. It does not admit of comparison. There are no degrees of uniqueness. It means *alone of its kind*. *Different* means *out of the ordinary*.

UNKNOWN, UNIDENTIFIED   The former means *not recognizable by* anyone; the latter means *not yet recognized*.

VARIOUS   Not synonymous with *different*.

VENDER; VENDOR   The former is a *seller*; the latter is a legal term.

WANT; WISH   The former means *need* and *desire*; the latter means only *desire*.

WE   Don't use the editorial *we*. Name the paper.

WELL-KNOWN   Usually *widely known* is meant.

WHETHER   Do not use for *if*. Don't add *or not*.

WIDOW   Never use *widow woman*.

YACHT   Do not say *private yacht*. There are no *public* ones.

7

Saying It Right

I DEFINITIONS

II UNFAMILIAR WORDS

III EDITORIALIZING
   1. Connotations
   2. Puffs and Boosts

IV EVALUATIVE WORDS
   1. Nouns
   2. Adjectives
   3. Verbs
   4. Adverbs
   5. Phrases

V IMPRESSIONISTIC REPORTING

DESPITE ITS LENGTH, THE FOLLOWING SENTENCE PROBABLY WOULD BE considered readable by the readability experts.

Many boys and girls are working at too young an age, for too long hours, too late at night, in dangerous and other undesirable conditions.

A general semanticist, however, would be quick to point out that no matter how clear the sentence may be, the information it conveys is vague and biased. How many is "many"? When you say "boys and girls" do you mean little children, such as used to work in sweatshops, or do you mean teenagers? What determines when one is too young to deliver newspapers, set pins in a bowling alley, run errands for a grocer, sew buttons or work on a lathe? How long is "too long" and how late is "too late"? What is a "dangerous" condition? Especially, what are "other undesirable" conditions?

Definitions

No experienced newsgatherer would fail to ask these questions if such a statement were made during the course of an interview. Often, however, such "glittering generalities," as the Institute for Propaganda Analysis (1937–1942) would have called them, appear in publicity releases and in public addresses, especially by politicians. They need amplification to convey important meaning to others, and it will be a happy day when editors toss them into the wastebasket unless it is possible to obtain such amplification.

On assignment, the interpretative reporter must be sharp enough to ask the proper questions to clarify vague statements and define "virtue" or "smear" words. Often, if not always, this requires more than the usual amount of knowledge on the reporter's part regarding the field of interest. In other words, the more one knows about a subject, the better able he is to interview someone regarding it. All the readability formulas and other aids to good writing cannot substitute for thorough fact-gathering.

"Pin the man down" should be the newsgatherer's first rule. If his subject talks about "progress," the reporter should ask him what he means by the term and for the facts and figures that justify its use. If the person being interviewed mentions "special circumstances," he should be asked what he means by "circumstances" and what makes them "special" and to give specific examples of what he's talking about.

Unfamiliar Words

If the words an interviewee uses are specific but nevertheless unfamiliar, the reporter had best overcome any sheepishness and ask for a little elementary shop talk from his subject. Otherwise, he might neglect to inquire deeply enough into the potential facts of the story at hand. Lacking such an opportunity for "depth" reporting, the reporter should consult dictionaries, encyclopedias and other reference works to fill the gaps in his own knowledge.

If a reporter has to ask or look up the meaning of an expression, he can be fairly certain that a goodly number of his readers will need explanation of it. Perhaps he can even avoid use of the unfamiliar word in his story. He can, for instance, say, "Union A is attempting to persuade members of Union B to change their membership from B to A." Then he can explain, "This is called 'raiding' in labor circles." Or, if he uses "raiding" in his principal statement, he can define it, perhaps in an italicized parenthetical insert.

"Jurisdictional strike," "mass picketing" and "secondary boycott" are among the other terms in a story of a labor dispute which may need explanation. In weather stories, it probably is wise to make clear the difference between hurricanes, tornadoes, cyclones and just plain gales or wind storms. Few readers probably remember what a nautical knot is or a French kilometer or an English mile. With the world becoming more complex daily and the areas of specialization growing, the need for such explanatory journalism is increasing.

Editorializing

Thorough reporting is the best safeguard against the misuse of words.

CONNOTATIONS

"The workers *won* a wage boost" has one connotation. "The workers *were given* a wage boost" has quite another. Only painstaking reporting can determine which is correct in any particular case. There can be no laziness or carelessness when the public interest is involved, as it usually is in stories pertaining to labor relations, governmental activities and the like.

Perhaps a news source condemns government "interference" when he really means he opposes government "regulation" in a particular area. Such words are loaded. Reportorial questioning should lead to specific details rather than vague charges or mere name calling. If loaded words are used from some necessity, they probably should be included in quotation marks or some explanatory matter should be added to indicate the alternative words for the same thought.

Newspapers propagandize if they use the labels of those with whom they agree editorially to describe pending legislation or situations. Examples of such editorializing would be "slave labor bill" for a measure regulating the mobility of the labor force in time of emergency; "dictator bill" for a proposal to increase the power of an executive; "goon" for labor union pickets; and the like. It makes a great deal of difference whether you write:

crop relief *or* farm dictatorship
foreign *or* alien
labor organizer *or* labor agitator
nonstriker *or* loyal worker
picketing *or* mass picketing
regulation *or* regimentation
U.A.W. chieftain *or* U.A.W. dictator
open shop *or* right to work

Sydney J. Harris, whose column originates with and is syndicated by the Chicago *Daily News*, is a fervid semanticist. The following, entitled "More Antics With Semantics," is typical of his writings:

Why is it that Our secret agents are "patriots," while Their secret agents are nothing but "spies"?

When I have one over the limit, I become "the life of the party"; when you have one over the limit, you become a "loudmouth."

I am "strongminded," but you are "opinionated."

My candidate's plan for the future shows he has "vision," but your candidate's plan for the future makes him a "wild-eyed dreamer."

I am about the only capable and careful driver on the road; all other motorists are either "stick-in-the-muds" or "reckless maniacs."

My failure to laugh at your dirty jokes shows my "good breeding," but your failure to laugh at my dirty jokes shows "stuffiness."

* * *

The British are too "reserved," and the French are too "effusive"; the Italians are too "impulsive," and the Scandinavians are too "cold"; the Germans are too "arrogant," and the Japanese are too "diffident"—surely God must be an American.

My new two-tone car is "gay," but your new two-tone car is just "loud."

I give an inexpensive present because "it's the spirit behind it that counts," but you give an inexpensive present because you're cheap.

My son hit yours over the head with a block because he is "playful," but yours hit mine over the head because he is "vicious."

A "sound" man is a man who sounds like me.

When I spread gossip, it is always a "harmless tidbit," but when you spread gossip, it is "malicious rumor-mongering."

A "realistic" novel is a novel that agrees with the idea of reality I held before I even opened the book.

* * *

My family, which is poor, lost its tremendous fortune during the Depression; but your family, which is rich, made all its money profiteering during the War.

Why is it that "modern" is an approving adjective for plumbing, but a disapproving adjective for art?

My wife's dress is "simple," but your wife's dress is "dowdy."

Likewise, my summer wardrobe is "casual," but yours is "sloppy."

Our relatives may "get into trouble," but your relatives have illegitimate babies, go to jail and take up dope. (Ours are, of course, "unfortunate," but yours are "bad.")

PUFFS AND BOOSTS

Against one type of editorializing most newspapers are sufficiently on the alert. That is the practice of making gratuitous complimentary remarks regarding a person or event rather than stating the facts and allowing them to speak for themselves. Some such expressions, obsolete in most newsrooms, are the following:

a big success	happy pair
a good time was had by all	in a very entertaining manner
a stellar performance	it beggars description
an enjoyable occasion	it bids fair
an impressive sight	likable personality
an interesting program was offered	prospects are bright
	proud possessor
attractive decorations	replete with interest
charming hostess	talented young man
everything went along nicely	the trip was the most popular ever taken
fills a long-felt need	

Such expressions are taboo if for no other reason than that they have been overworked.

Evaluative Words

In quite a different category are attempts to improve the reader's understanding by the use of qualifying adjectives, other parts of speech and expressions. Even some editors who have been outspoken in adverse criticism of interpretative reporting have for years allowed and encouraged their reporters to write, "One of America's *leading composers* will play his own compositions," "The two *top contenders* for the championship will meet in the first round," "An *unusual* workshop class in creative writing for talented children will be organized," "The court will hear arguments on the *complex, controversial and crucial questions*" and the like.

There is no denying that such expressions involve judgment and, to be socially responsible, the judgment must be based on adequate information. When a sports writer, for instance, writes that the outcome of a contest was "a stunning upset," he must know that leaders in the sports world and fans expected it to be different. No competent reporter uses superlatives without investigating to determine whether they are justified: "most devastating fire," "largest audience," "longest report," "rare appearance." Nor does he call every gruesome murder "the crime of the Century."

NOUNS

When, however, can you call a disturbance a "panic" or "riot"? When can you use such words as "catastrophe," "fiasco," "disaster," "climax," "zenith" or "debacle"? All you can say is that such terms should be used judiciously. To make common use of them would be to devitalize them. It would be like crying "wolf" when there was no wolf.

What, therefore, is judicious use? The experienced reporter who has covered many similar stories has a basis for comparison, and his own experience usually is better than that of most everyone else, especially ax-grinders with motives for hoping he uses this word instead of that. Competent reporting and integrity are more likely to give readers correct information than writing formulas and communication theories are.

ADJECTIVES

When is a girl pretty or beautiful? Not every time she gets into a newsworthy situation certainly. Since the development of photography, reporters have become more cautious over indiscriminate use of such descriptive adjectives. Since there is no similar restraining influence in other areas, the best that can be done is to advise caution in the use of such words as the following:

brave	ferocious	popular
brilliant	gigantic	remarkable
clever	happy-go-lucky	successful
cowardly	huge	tasteful
eloquent	illimitable	unpatriotic
enjoyable	impressive	valiant
exciting	nice	widely known

VERBS

Verbs must be exact. If a news source answers "yes" to a reporter's question, it is not always proper to say he "admitted" something. When he makes an announcement, he cannot be said to have "revealed" or "disclosed" something unless the matter previously had been kept secret intentionally. "Charge" is a strong word implying an accusation which the news source might have had no intention of making. "Claim" suggests that someone is trying to correct a wrong impression or obtain possession of something which he considers rightfully his. "Probe" implies detectives of some sort are afoot.

Since very few words are exact synonyms for each other, a good dictionary or thesaurus is a better companion for the writer seeking to impart correct information than Gunning's formula to determine the Fog Index. The practice of intentionally using a strong synonym for maximum visceral effect on readers instead of the word which comes closer to stating the situation correctly cannot be condoned.

Here is a list of verbs which the reporter should be hesitant about using:

allege	laugh	sneer
beg	object	squeak
confess	plead	threaten
flee	prowl	urge
grimace	roar	whine
implore	shout	whisper
insult	sneak	yell

ADVERBS

A properly placed adverb can change the entire meaning of a news story. Consider the potential power of the following:

accidentally	facetiously	jokingly
angrily	grimly	laughingly
boastfully	immodestly	mockingly
calmly	inadvertently	seriously
carelessly	intentionally	stupidly
casually	ironically	viciously

PHRASES

Evaluational phrases can "make or break" a news story and also, perhaps, some of the principals mentioned in it. Consider the potency of the following:

angry response
in an arrogant manner
in an unprecedented personal statement
in top oratorical form

pale with anger
shaking with grief
showing great dignity
under duress
with profound feeling

Impressionistic Reporting

In an address at the University of Missouri, Newbold Noyes Jr. of the Washington *Evening Star* advocated "impressionistic reporting." By it, he explained, he meant attempts by skilled and impartial reporters to create in the reader the same feeling about an important event as the reporter had as an eyewitness of it. In an article, "War, Peace and Journalism," in the April 16, 1949, *Nation*, Thomas Sancton pleaded for "gestalt journalism," which he defined as "journalism which seeks the whole truth in any given field of politics, deeming the whole truth, or even the more effort to discover it, greater and qualitatively different than piecemeal, selective reporting of its parts—gestalt journalism in this sense describes only what serious reporters have tried to do since writing began."

Sancton cited several news situations when "my on-the-scene notes contained, as a reporter's notes invariably do, more of the total mood and meaning . . . came closer to its 'gestalt' than their ultimate rewriting would ever have done."

To be impressionistic or to achieve a gestalt or to give correctly the atmosphere or essential reality concerning a news situation is primarily a task of fact-gathering. What the actual words shall be is dependent upon what needs to be written. After he cross-examined Senator Joseph R. McCarthy during the Army-McCarthy hearings, Chief Counsel Joseph N. Welch "went outside into the hallway where he broke down and wept," the Associated Press reported. Some managing editors objected to inclusion of this fact in the AP report. Others didn't like the statements, "Stevens bowed to the demands of McCarthy," and "Many spectators in the jam-packed steaming hearing room broke into loud unchecked applause after Welch denounced McCarthy." Still others thought it was bad to report during the subsequent Senate committee hearing that Senator Francis Case slammed down a report "with a force that scattered papers." A majority of those who expressed opinions, however, favored inclusion of such details in the interest of completeness and accuracy.

In the same edition of the A.P.M.E. *Red Book* in which appears the report of the discussion of the service's handling of the McCarthy hearings, there is also included a résumé of other parts of the Managing Editors' conference. The first few paragraphs of one section were as follows:

> Mary Margaret McBride, AP Newsfeature columnist, stole the show and the hearts of many of the editors when she matched them quip for quip in an hour of verbal sparring touched off by her contention that it is wrong to departmentalize all women's news under a "woman's page" label.
> This widely known writer, wearing a mink stole and a colorful orchid, beamed beneath an upswept hair-do as she prodded, argued, baited and cajoled while appearing at the two-part session on Newsfeatures, directed by Roderick J. Watts, of the Houston *Chronicle*, chairman of the Newsfeatures committee.
> On one occasion, Miss McBride even shouted. And the editors loved it. Some were seen to wipe tears of laughter from their eyes as their colleagues sought to match wits with Miss McBride in an unsuccessful attempt to beat her at her own game—the art of interviewing.

This obviously violated the Associated Press' own rules for proper sentence length, but everyone who read it probably caught the spirit of the occasion.

That the account includes "value" judgments there can be no doubt. The writer thought Miss McBride "prodded, argued, baited and cajoled," for instance. Quite possibly another observer might have thought she was becoming histrionic in the attempt to conceal inadequacy in the face of a barrage of questions.

The clever writer who attempts to convey his impressions of an occasion substantiates such statements as, "And the editors loved it," by reporting that "Some were seen to wipe tears of laughter from their eyes." Not always, of course, is there such tangible reportable evidence available. In such cases the reporter's experience, informational background, record of past achievement and, most of all, integrity are his weapons and his readers' protection.

Warren J. Brier gives scores of examples of good impressionistic journalism in an article, "The Lively Language of the Pros: A Glimpse at their Technique," in the 1963 *Montana Journalism Review*. Typical is the following from a UPI story about the Adolph Eichmann trial:

> Hausner, a small, hawk-faced, baldheaded man in a black legal gown, faced the defendant with both hands on his hips. An angry flush appeared on Eichmann's ashen-grey cheeks as the prosecutor pressed his attack.
> A nerve in Eichmann's jaw twitched and he licked his lips nervously between questions. His voice rose angrily as he answered some of the more pointed questions.

The future unquestionably will bring increased recognition of the necessity to develop newsgatherers of such high quality. The alternative is despairingly to retreat to so-called objective reporting which leaves the reader completely in the cold as to the meaning or significance of much of the news.

As the late Elmer Davis wrote in an article, "News and the Whole Truth," in the August 1952 *Atlantic*, later reprinted in his book, *But We Were Born Free*:

> But objectivity often leans over backward so far that it makes the news business merely a transmission belt for pretentious phonies. . . .
>
> There was not much objectivity in the American press through most of the nineteenth century; if a story touched on the political or economic interest of the editor or owner, it was usually written so as to make his side look good. Some papers still follow that practice, but most of them, for some decades past, have accepted the principle that they ought to try to be objective in the news columns, leaving arguments to the editorial page. Publish everything that is said on both sides of a controversial issue, and let the reader make up his mind. A noble theory; but suppose that men who talk on one side (or on both) are known to be lying to serve their own personal interest; or suppose they don't know what they are talking about. To call attention to these facts, except on the editorial page, would not, according to most newspaper practice, be objective. Yet in the complex news of today, how many readers have enough personal knowledge to distinguish fact from fiction, ignorance from knowledge, interest from partiality?
>
> This practice is perhaps not quite so prevalent now as it was twenty-five years or so ago—in the golden age of Calvin Coolidge, when it was the general opinion that things are what they seem. In those days, if the Honorable John P. Hoozis was an important person, you were likely to see him quoted at length in the newspapers, on almost any subject, with no indication that he had a strong personal interest in getting people to believe what he said—even if the editor who printed the story happened to know it. He was an important man; he had made a statement; and it would not have been objective not to print it. We have been getting away from that dead-pan objectivity of late years—or were, till the rise of Senator McCarthy.

In the address cited earlier in this chapter, Newbold Noyes Jr. emphasized the historical necessity for abandoning what he termed "journalism's adolescence":

> In 1900, when my grandfather, Frank Noyes, helped found the modern Associated Press and embarked on 38 years of service as first president of that news agency, he and his associates were pretty sure they knew the answer to our question, how to tell the truth. Their answer was a thing called "objectivity." It was a very good answer, too.
>
> Up to then, newspapers had been quite personal in their approach to the news. Most reporters fancied themselves as so many 19th century Westbrook Peglers. What they wrote was vastly entertaining, but they were not

nearly so concerned with telling people the truth as with telling people off. They faithfully promoted their own ends, and cudgelled their enemies with gusto, and a good time was had by all. But the truth, somehow, tended to get lost in the shuffle.

The Associated Press realized at the start that it couldn't possibly cater to the opinion whims of all the different publishers receiving its service. It set out to correct the situation by instituting the principle and practice of "objective" news coverage. Gradually, as time went by, this revolutionary principle became accepted as the Number 1 item in the creed of the responsible press all over the country. It wholly changed the face of the newspaper world, and it set the pattern for a full half-century of journalistic growth and progress.

The idea of objective reporting is second nature to all of us today—so much so that we have to stop and think when it comes to defining it. Fundamentally, however, to the men who first preached it, objectivity meant that the only safe thing in a newspaper—outside of the editorial page—was a fact. The reporter's duty was to supply his readers with the cold, hard barren details of what had happened—and with nothing more. If he *did* try to give them something more, he was moving into dangerous ground—for he was interfering with the reader's right to make up his mind on the basis of the facts alone.

In the early decades of this century, in short, our responsible press operated under the theory that it was better to take a chance on *not* informing its readers that it was going to take a chance on misinforming them. It tried, as we try today, to tell the public the truth. But it was afraid of trying to tell the *whole* truth. Its overriding concern was making sure that what it dispensed was *nothing* but the truth. It operated on the assumption that it simply was not feasible for a newspaper to attempt to tell the truth, the whole truth and nothing but the truth—all three at the same time.

The principle of strictly objective reporting was eminently sound. It provided an atmosphere in which the newspaper of this country could grow up out of its lusty and carefree youth into something like responsible maturity. The cult of objectivity, in other words, supplied the ground rules of a safe adolescence for American journalism.

But the day inevitably comes when an ex-adolescent must test for himself the forbidden fruits he has been taught are so dangerous. That time is hard upon us now.

8

Winning Reader Confidence

I How to Be Accurate
   1. Second-Hand Information
   2. Verification
   3. Qualification
   4. Systematic Checking
   5. Total Effect

II Authority in the News
   1. Direct Quotation
   2. Indirect Reference
   3. When Unnecessary

III Persistence

IV Obeying the Law

V Copyright

VI How to Avoid Libel?
   1. What is Libel?
   2. Dangerous Words
   3. Insinuations
   4. Damages
   5. Defenses
   6. Playing Safe

THE CHIEF COMPLAINT OF A NEWSPAPER'S CRITICS—THAT IS, EVERYBODY who reads it—is not bias through distortion and suppression. Nor is it sensationalism with its by-product, violation of the right to privacy. On the contrary, the American reader prefers the newspaper which gives him a point of view coinciding with his own and complains of prejudice only when he disagrees. His patronage of newspapers which specialize in lurid details, discounts any feigned distaste for them.

What the average American newspaper reader considers the cardinal journalistic sin is inaccuracy. Suppress news favorable to the other fellow and play up news favorable to your side but score the point through use of facts. It is a terrible letdown to be faced with irrefragable proof that something one wants to believe is false. Likewise, if the juicy sex story or other sensational yarn is shown to be untrue, it ceases to entertain.

Readers don't mean it when they say they don't believe anything they read in the newspapers; actually most of what they know is learned in that way. They apply the opprobrious term, "just newspaper talk," to a story unpleasant to believe, regardless of its truth.

Because editors are aware of these aspects of man's social behavior, and because there is no reason why a newspaper should be anything but one hundred per cent accurate in a vast majority of the stories it publishes, one of the first lessons the beginning reporter must learn is how to avoid making mistakes. There are some newsrooms even in large cities where a certain amount of carelessness is condoned, but not many. A standard of accuracy way beyond anything to which the recent college graduate has been accustomed in his English composition classes is maintained by a large majority of those newspapers worthy of being called first-rate. Lucky is the cub who starts his reporting career under an editor or desk man prone to "raising the roof" whenever he detects a misspelled word or incorrect middle initial in a piece of copy.

How to be Accurate

Although no news writer commits errors for personal enjoyment, a study of Professor Mitchell Charnley of the University of Minnesota revealed that altogether too many occur in at least three average American newspapers. Of 591 straight news stories which Charnley was able to verify through a questionnaire sent to persons either mentioned in them or in positions to know, only 319, or 54 per cent, contained no errors of any kind. Paper A was 52 per cent accurate, Paper B 53 per cent and Paper C 57 per cent. The inaccurate stories contained an average of 1.67 errors and, most revealing of all, only 34 per cent of the stories handled by reporters were correct whereas 62 per cent of the stories obtained from original sources, largely in the form of publicity releases, were without mistake.

Why this situation? Probably for several reasons which will be discussed in connection with suggestions of remedies.

SECOND-HAND INFORMATION

Most news is gathered by reporters second-hand. News sources unquestionably are responsible for as many if not more news story errors than reporters. Mistakes made by those giving out news may be intentional or unintentional. If intentional, the news source has reasons for wanting a half-truth or untruth to appear in print. If unintentional, the source was a faulty witness or has a poor memory. The errancy of testimony and the influences, including suggestion and what is popularly called wishful thinking, which make for errors in observation and recall, have been examined by psychologists and proved in the experimental laboratory so often as to leave no element of doubt regarding the really small chance the reporter has to get accurate answers during interviews for facts.

The reporter's weapons against inaccuracy, as a result of a news source's inability or unwillingness to give reliable information, are verification and honesty of purpose. If he does not rely on one person's say-so but interviews as many as possible, he invariably is able to correct many mistakes made in the first stages of gathering material about a news event. If he approaches the task of both reporting and writing his story without prejudice, whatever errors he does make will be at least unintentional. Fairness and caution both require that, when two persons interviewed differ greatly as to the truth, the statements of both be included in the news story. To achieve this objective, newspapers go to extremes of which the general public hardly dreams. The sentence saying that Mr. Smith could not be reached for a statement may have been added to a story after hours of futile effort to attain either accuracy or fairness or both.

Newsgatherers increasingly are up against what has been called "handoutitis," which means the refusal of many news sources to provide any more information than is contained in carefully prepared publicity releases. Between the reporter and a principal in the news is the public relations counsel, as publicity men and press agents like to call themselves today. On the whole, these intermediaries perform a useful function, as no newspaper could possibly employ staffs large enough to cover all a community's activities. They also can be helpful to the reporter who wants additional information not included in a press release or who is seeking an original story. It must not be lost sight of, however, that public relations men are employed to advance the best interests of their employers, which means that often ways to circumvent them must be sought. The reporter who is content with what is included in a mimeographed press release may become little more than a messenger boy.

VERIFICATION

Verifying a story means more than checking the statements of different news sources against each other. It also means making use of the standard books of reference to check spellings, addresses, middle initials and many similar details. In many newsrooms, reporters are required to write "All names verified" on their copy, and woe be it to them if such is not true. In many police and court stories more than the newspaper's reputation for accuracy may be at stake; innocence or carelessness is no defense against libel.

The newspaper takes a chance whenever it prints an unverified story. Mere rumor it generally can detect, but when a story contains something which seems improbable, it is safer to miss an edition than use the story before checking. Often men in public life say things to reporters which they later regret. It may seem to the layman that the newspaper should quote them regarding what they have let slip and then stand by its guns and insist upon its own accuracy. It is the same layman, however, who with few exceptions believes the important personage's denial even though it be a gross lie. For this reason many an editor has held up a story until he has had a chance to check on even a reliable reporter's work.

Telephone books, city directories, clippings in the newspaper's library and books of reference are available to the newspaper reporter for a purpose—so that they will be used. In interviews, it is possible to repeat information to be sure it has been heard correctly. Over the telephone, difficult words can be spelled in code: A as in Adam, B as in Boston, etc. If the reporter has profited by his high school and college education, he should avoid many errors which the uneducated might commit, such as giving a ship's speed as "knots per hour," the office as chief justice of the Supreme court instead of chief justice of the United States, the Court of St. James instead of the Court of St. Jameses, Noble instead of Nobel prizes, half-mast instead of half-staff, John Hopkins University instead of Johns Hopkins University, and many other "teasers," mastery of which is a journalistic prerequisite.

QUALIFICATION

When certain about the main facts of a story but doubtful about others, a way to make the earliest edition before complete verification is possible is to qualify what is written, as:

> A man believed to be Hillyer Swanson, 30, of Salt Lake City, was found by police today wandering in Forest Park, apparently an amnesia victim. Partial identification was made by means of a billfold and checkbook found in his possession.
>
> Fire thought to have resulted from faulty electric wiring in the coal cellar caused approximately $500 damage early today to the dwelling at 1514 Murphy place occupied by Mr. and Mrs. O. B. Ryan and their three small children.

Stories such as the following inspire the confidence in readers that newspapers attempt to give the truth as far as possible.

> Mayor Ezra Hawkins today intimated that he will not be a candidate for reelection, but Corporation Counsel Fred Bacon, who managed the mayor's last campaign, declared that "when the time comes the proper accouncement will be made" and that "friends of His Honor will be pleased by the announcement."

It is when the reporter guesses or takes a chance that he is most likely to err. Such careless habits not only are bad practice from the newspaper's selfish standpoint, but reprehensible ethically as well. The speed with which newspapers are produced and the other obstacles to accuracy in reporting make a minimum number of errors seem almost inevitable. If the newspaper is generous in publishing corrections of the most serious errors and if it gives evidence of striving to attain the ideal of absolute accuracy, the supercilious reader should not be "off" a newspaper for life because on one occasion it made a mistake in the middle initial of his great aunt's brother-in-law.

SYSTEMATIC CHECKING

Since the mid-1950s, the Minneapolis *Star* and *Tribune* have operated a Bureau of Accuracy and Fair Play "to deal courteously with any person who feels that he or she has not been justly treated in any news story or business dealing involving the newspapers." Every day stories are selected at random, clipped and mailed to persons mentioned in them with a request that the recipients answer the following questions: (1) Are names of persons and/or organizations spelled correctly? (2) Are addresses, ages, titles or other identifying information accurate? (3) Does the story present a factual and unbiased report of events? (4) Is all essential information included? (5) Is the headline accurate? Space is provided for both corrections and comments.

During one six-week period, 29 of 49 persons receiving the questionnaires responded. Most had no adverse criticism and complimented the paper involved. Those who did find something wrong fell into the following groups:

1. Those who found minor inaccuracies in names, addresses or job titles. These complaints are quite legitimate and are the part of the unending problem that everyone on a newspaper fights every day, never entirely successfully.

2. Those who found misinterpretation of the facts in headlines—also legitimate gripes, but probably inevitable considering the limitations with which copyreaders work.
3. The nitpickers. They were mad because the story didn't give just their side or didn't explain a detailed problem at great length or, as one respondent put it, the story must have been wrong because so many people got wrong ideas from it (a rather complicated story, apparently entirely accurate, dealing with an extremely complicated bankruptcy case). The Students for Democratic Society were angry about being identified as against the war in Vietnam because they do so many other things, too.
4. Those who fail to understand the newspaper process. Some people have no idea of how a news story gets written and the space and time limitations within which a reporter works. One reader complained because the story on his outfit didn't include information in a press release he had mailed to the editor—not to the city desk—some months earlier.

In no case did someone write, "You got everything all wrong in this story."

When received, the correction sheet goes to the managing editor and assistant managing editor of the paper involved, then down through the city desk to the reporter. Correction boxes on these errors are seldom printed, because there's a time lag of a week and more on most of them, and corrections listed are mostly minor. The sheets are used as a continuing check not only on accuracy, but on news processes and practices as well. When corrections are made, they are put in a box marked "Correction" and played at the top of an inside page. It is clearly stated that a mistake was made; there is no attempt to evade responsibility or cloud the issue.

TOTAL EFFECT

An account can be devoid of errors in facts, spellings and the like and still be inaccurate if the impression it gives as a whole is wrong. This, as has been pointed out several times already in earlier chapters, can happen when pertinent facts are omitted, when motivations are disregarded, when cause and effect relationships are not made clear, and in many other similar ways.

Thorough reporting is the best protection against unintentional distortion. For example, a story telling of an arrest for reckless driving could be error-free, but would it be accurate unless it were explained that the apparently careless motorist was trying to get to his injured child's side? Without the part after the "but" the following lead would have given an erroneous impression. The reporter obviously asked, "Why?"

> Chicago—The number of persons drawing unemployment compensation declined by 5,154 during the second week of this month, but indications are that more than 3,000 of them were off the rolls because their eligibility expired. [Peoria *Transcript*]

Prof. David Manning White of Boston University has warned the press against becoming "unwitting or unwilling accomplices in creating an atmosphere in which prejudice, half-truths and misinformation bloom with a noisome stench." He had in mind so-called "deadpan" reporting of unsupported charges by United States senators and others without attempt to allow simultaneous reply by persons affected by the charges.

The simple first step in avoidance of inaccuracy through total impression is to try to get the other side of every story that is in any way controversial. To print inaccurate statements merely because they were made by some newsworthy person is not accurate reporting. It can be irresponsible journalism.

The following example indicates a common method of presenting both sides, even when the original story comes from a press association:

> Cairo, Ill., July 14.—(AP)—William P. McCauley of Olney, American Legion rehabilitation commission chairman for Illinois, charged in a speech here today that the removal of cancer patients from the Veterans Administration Hospital at Hines, to the Chicago Loop Medical Clinic was "for no other reason than to make guinea pigs of war-veteran cancer victims."
>
> McCauley told the 5th Division American Legion convention that the clinic at Hines had resulted from many years of Legion effort, that the Legion had spent $7,000 for the first radium used there and that its work was responsible for recent addition of 500 beds there.
>
> (Informed of McCauley's charges, Charles G. Beck, Veterans Administration deputy director for the Midwest region, declared in Chicago:
>
> ("I think the statement that we're going to make guinea pigs of these cancer patients is, to say the least, ridiculous. The removal of which McCauley speaks has not yet taken place. It will not take place for at least a year.
>
> ("When we move our cancer center, the men will receive treatment at least as good as they have received at Hines. The entire clinic, its doctors, nurses, and equipment will be moved. How can that mean any change for the worse?

Idea Credited to Bradley

("It was the idea of Gen. Omar Bradley, head of the V.A., that these unfortunate veterans would be better served if they were located in the city, instead of 12 miles away from it.")

In another speech, Omar J. Mackin, Salem, State Legion commander, asked the state's 1,029 Legion posts to pass resolutions against the Ku Klux Klan, which he termed "un-American and contrary to the principles and the rights guaranteed under the Constitution." [Chicago *Sun*]

Authority in the News

Everything that has been said so far in this chapter goes to prove that the most convincing authority a newspaper can give to a particular story is its own general reputation for authenticity. If it has established itself as a publication ambitious to be accurate and fair, it doesn't have to resort to elaborate means to quote authority in every paragraph of every news story.

As a matter of fact, however, newspapers which are the most careful to relate every important fact in every story to someone enjoy reputations for coming closest to the truth. "Who said this?" bawls out the city editor of such a paper to the cub. "Why, Mr. Smith, whose name is in the lead as having given the speech," is no defense but merely provocation for a further remark such as, "You don't say he said this unquoted part down in the fifth paragraph. I know he made the statement in the lead, but the rest of your story reads like an editorial."

DIRECT QUOTATION

To avoid such reprimands, the smart reporter "documents" his stories. How to attain accuracy and authority in different types of news stories will be considered more fully in the chapters devoted to them in Part II. Including authority in the lead adds emphasis, satisfies the reader's curiosity, and partially protects the newspaper against criticism.

> Promotion of W. C. Fairchild, 2308 S. 10th street, lieutenant of the Superior Railroad police in the Milltown division, to captain of police of the Logan division, was announced today by Ronal Weber, superintendent of the Milltown division.

When the news consists in the fact that an announcement or statement has been made, especially if it is one which has been expected for some time, authority should be given the greatest emphasis possible by beginning the lead with it, as:

136   PRINCIPLES OF NEWS WRITING

> Mayor Herbert G. Van Duesen announced today charges of irregularities in the collection of business licenses made by the Chamber of Commerce will be referred to the Board of Aldermen Friday evening.

When someone in public life makes an attack on another, the lead should begin with that person's name, as:

> State Sen. Rollin A. Bishop today called Gov. Joseph B. Dilling a "crackpot" and described his plan to consolidate seven state departments as "the wild idea of a neophyte in public life."

This type of lead is much better than the following:

> Gov. Joseph B. Dilling is a "crackpot" and his plan to consolidate seven state departments is "the wild idea of a neophyte in public life," State Sen. Rollin A. Bishop said today.

It is the fact that Senator Bishop attacked the governor that is news; what he said is opinion unless he was much more definite than either lead would indicate. If he did make specific charges, then what has been said regarding efforts to obtain "the other side" applies.

In stories growing out of public reports, statements or announcements, mention of the authority may be delayed until the second paragraph but seldom should be any later than that:

> Milltown users of natural gas pay a higher rate than consumers in any other American city of comparable size, but local rates for electricity are among the lowest in the United States.
> These facts were revealed by a Federal Power commission report released today. . . .

Care, however, must be exercised to avoid a "tag line" type of lead which, standing alone, is misleading, as:

> Rep. Y. S. Owen could defeat Mayor L. L. Wood.
> That is the opinion of Judge K. K. Wendell who spoke at noon today.

Caution must be exercised so as not to declare as certain something which still is a matter of debate or further official action. For instance, a reporter erred when he wrote:

> Baxterville will have a new 20-story office building by next spring.
> Plans for it will be presented tonight to the City Planning commission.

In this instance the Planning commission disapproved the project which the reporter might have anticipated if he had interviewed more than its enthusiastic proponents. The hoary adage which applies is, "Never count your chickens before they hatch."

WINNING READER CONFIDENCE 137

The extent to which a careful newspaper goes to give adequate authority throughout a controversial story is indicated in the following example:

All ships of the North German Lloyd and Hamburg-American lines may be placed on the strike list of the International Longshoremen's association along with the Cunard White Star and Furness-Withy lines, *it was announced today* by Joseph P. Ryan, president of the longshoremen, when he learned a North German liner was scheduled to arrive at Montreal today.

If the ship is unloaded at Montreal by members of a union not affiliated with the I.L.A., *Mr. Ryan said*, his union will strike all German ships on the Atlantic coast from Portland to Newport News.

Although peace efforts continued in a three-way conference among I.L.A. officers, steamship officials, and representatives of the Montreal independent unions, plans were made for a protracted fight if necessary, *Mr. Ryan said.*

Threats of delay failed to halt the sailing of the Furness-Withy liner, Queen of Bermuda, which left her pier at 55th street and the North river promptly at 3 P.M. without tugs. The ship left behind more than a hundred tons of freight, but officers arranged to have crew members carry aboard the baggage of passengers.

The presence of 700 travelers in Bermuda awaiting return to New York caused the company officials to proceed without waiting for freight. Before the Queen of Bermuda sailed *Mr. Ryan declared* that if crew members carried aboard the baggage "they can continue doing it from now on." *He also said* that if tugs were used it would be "a long time" before the tugs would again take any ships out of New York. Two tugs were ready, but were not required because of the favorable tide.

A peace conference between Mr. Ryan and his associates and officers of the National Independent Longshoremen's Union apparently made some headway. *Mr. Ryan said* that he "told them what terms they (the Canadians) could have."

There are 700 passengers awaiting return from Bermuda, *it was said.*

The steamship officials regard the trouble as largely out of their jurisdiction because it revolves about an inter-union dispute. *They expressed* the hope that a quick adjustment could be made, and offered to sit in at the union meetings as "observers."

That efforts of the C.I.O. to organize waterfront workers is behind the I.L.A. move to assert its claims was indicated by *Mr. Ryan in a statement* protesting against C.I.O. inroads. [New York *World-Telegram*]

INDIRECT REFERENCE

Even the parts of the example just given which are not attached definitely to an authority imply that they were verified by a careful

138   PRINCIPLES OF NEWS WRITING

reporter. Note in paragraph 4, for instance, that the writer knew of "threats to delay" and that "officers arranged" to meet the situation. Possibly this paragraph and the first sentence of paragraph 5 were guesswork, but the careful inclusion of both cause and effect regarding each incident, plus the adequate authority given in other parts of the story, give the reader confidence in the correctness of the story as a whole.

No reporter should write a story supplied by an anonymous source, which means that practical jokers and persons with grievances who telephone and write to newspapers in the hope of giving news without disclosing their identity seldom are successful. When taking, over the telephone, information about which any question may arise, the reporter should obtain the informant's number, hang up and call him back. This practice often will expose impersonators, provided the reporter also checks the telephone numbers in the directory. Sometimes, at the request of high public officials, newspapers thinly veil sources of information by referring to "sources close to," "a source known to be reliable," "an official spokesman," "a high official," and the like.

> Washington—(AP)—Trevor Gardner was reported Tuesday to be ready to resign as chief of Air Force research in protest against the way the guided missile program is being handled.
>
> His detailed objections were not stated. But on the basis of reports from friends and his own past public statements, Gardner apparently wants more attention and money devoted to research and a more exact division of missile work among the three armed services.
>
> He was in Miami Tuesday to lay his case before Defense Sec. Charles E. Wilson, who is vacationing there. . . .   [Chicago *Sun-Times*]

It is irritating to any reputable reporter to have to write this way, and protests against the refusals of public officials to permit their names to be used as authorities are frequent. Such vagueness weakens the confidence of readers in any newspaper which practices it on its own volition.

Senator Joseph R. McCarthy once gave reporters a statement regarding monitored telephone calls, but insisted that it be used as emanating from "a person who declined to let his name be used publicly." Commented Russell Wiggins, Washington *Post* managing editor, "The press associations and the publishing newspapers allowed him to put out a transcript under conditions that it originated from an unprejudiced source." To this, Claude Ramsey of the Asheville *Citizen & Times* added: "Senatorial immunity is bad enough without being compounded with senatorial anonymity."

The President of the United States generally designates into which of four classes what he says at a press conference falls: (1) quotable directly as from the President, (2) quotable as from a reliable source in high governmental circles, (3) not quotable but valuable as background information for writers or (4) completely off the record. Reporters respect the President's wishes. In fact, newspapers guard jealously the identity of any news source who wishes his name concealed, provided they have agreed, before obtaining the information, that it is to be used anonymously. Editors and reporters have gone to jail for refusing to tell a judge where they obtained a particular item of news. Several states have passed laws protecting newspapers against being declared in contempt of court for so doing.

WHEN UNNECESSARY

In the average run of police, legislative and many other types of news it is possible to omit specific mention of the source of information. In such stories it is presumed that a reliable authority was interviewed, and the newspaper's general reputation for accuracy is the reader's safeguard, as in the following examples:

> The Keeler polygraph gave the lie today to Henry (Hank) Munson's denial that he shot and killed his nephew, Arnold Munson, Sunday in the rooming house at 717 Victoria place where they both live.

> The 95 boys and girls who came to Milltown to participate in the state spelling bee finals Friday will attend a banquet at 6:15 P.M. today at the Hotel Bedford.

One way excessive attribution can be avoided is by being careful not to cite authority for old, especially widely known facts. You wouldn't, for instance, write: "The capital of Wyoming is Cheyenne, according to Senator Blimp." Neither, unless there was uncertainty regarding it, would you give authority when mentioning the capital of Tibet, Afghanistan, or any other place. Such facts, though probably unfamiliar to most people, are easily obtained from standard reference books.

To cite authority for old facts can be misleading. It is likely to create the impression that the information is new. For example:

> To be eligible for low-cost public housing a person must not earn more than $3,600 annually, Theodore McCoughna, economist for the Public Housing administration, said today.

The statement would be bad if the $3,600 ceiling had been in effect for some time. It would be worse if "revealed," "announced," "admitted," or some similar verb had been used. When a statement of fact is inserted in a story as part of the background to enable readers properly to evaluate some item of news, it should not be attributed to any authority unless, in the newsman's judgment, it might not be accepted as true otherwise. Then dictionaries, encyclopedias, public laws and other authoritative reference works can be mentioned. Never use such vague expression as "statistics prove" or "authorities agree."

A lead which must be handled with caution is the "opinion here today" type. Seldom is such a lead based on an exhaustive survey of the "trend of public sentiment." The danger, from the standpoint of ethics, is the creation of what social psychologists call the "illusion of universality." It may be a gross exaggeration to write that "the entire city today mourned the death of Mayor Bull," or that "the world of music lovers was turned topsy-turvy," or that "business leaders today feared..."

In sports stories, which are written with a recognized good nature and prejudice for the home club, such leads may be condoned, but when used in political writing they generally are misleading. If it actually can be established that a majority of public officials or of any other group believe a certain way, there should be some indication not too long delayed that the news writer knows what he's talking about.

Persistence

A case study in the difficulties encountered by a medium-sized daily in its efforts to serve its readers is provided by Sherman Beinhorn of the Middletown (Conn.) *Press*.

The major portion of the story in the April 6, 1961, issue follows:

> The presidential stop order on development of a nuclear aircraft engine brought the first notice of job layoffs and transfers at the Connecticut Aircraft Nuclear Engine Laboratory, it was learned today.
> Mayor Clew said he had information that notices had gone out Wednesday and sources at Pratt and Whitney Aircraft in East Hartford later confirmed this fact.
> Pratt and Whitney would not say what the number of first layoffs would be.

In addition to sending out the pink slips, P&WA also sent out job relocation offers to employees faced with layoff at CANEL.

No information was available from P&WA as to the number of workers in this group. Neither would the company say what places in the United Aircraft Corp., of which P&WA is a division, are being held out to the CANEL people.

UAC had no comment to make today when asked what its president, William Gwinn, thought about a statement made earlier this week by Sen. Prescott Bush.

Little Unemployment

". . . I've also talked with the president of the United Aircraft about the decision," Bush stated. "From the assurance given me, I believe alternate job opportunities will be offered, so that little if any unemployment will result. I devoutly hope this will be the case."

Public relations people at UAC and at P&WA said the policy of the corporation has always been to transfer and relocate where possible.

President Kennedy asked Congress to knock out the nuclear-powered plane program March 28. Three days later came information from Air Force Maj. Gen. Thomas E. Musgrave that cancellation of the program meant elimination of 735 Air Force-financed jobs at CANEL. General Electric, Convair and Lockheed, all working under the nuclear plane contract, also were notified of the numbers of job elimination each faced.

While the fate of 735 CANEL jobs was sealed by the Air Force notice, no decision was made on the employment of 1,665 other CANEL employees, those under contract let by the Atomic Energy Commission.

The key to the future of these 1,665 was in the hands of a fact-finding committee that reached CANEL yesterday to hold discussions with UAC management.

Decision Shortly

Dr. A. J. Vander Weyden, deputy director of the AEC's division on reactor development and leader of the team, said today that a decision will be made shortly on the future of the local nuclear research facility.

He declared that a smaller operation, if one is approved, was in sight for the project under the new AEC program. . . .

Meanwhile, sources close to the plant indicated confusion among employees and continued rumors of mass layoffs.

Seeks Information

Mayor Clew said this morning that he is attempting to get information on the situation from Cong. Frank Kowalski. He was in touch this morning with public relations at UAC but learned nothing about the numbers given notice Wednesday.

The Unemployment Compensation Office in Middletown reported no applications for jobless pay from CANEL employees as yet. A staffer said the office understood that the CANEL employees were being given two-week notices. No applications could be made until the final two weeks of employment ended.

John Sullivan, business manager of the International Association of Machinists, said his office had no knowledge of notice of layoffs....

Regarding the difficulties of coverage, Beinhorn wrote:

This is an example of a story that will indicate a good deal made of nothing new. The story says several times that information to such and such question would not be given. In a sense, this is a story in frustration.
  I have been on this Connecticut Aircraft Nuclear Engine Laboratory since 1956. The lab is owned by the Atomic Energy commission and the Air department but is operated by Pratt and Whitney Aircraft. CANEL is a city unto itself. It is closed to the press. It has no public relations man of its own. Its manager says nothing. And there is no way to open the place up.
  Late in March, President Kennedy stopped work on the billion dollar nuclear aircraft engine program. This meant that the jobs of 8,400 people at CANEL were jeopardized. Naturally, the story was a big one for us.
  Luckily we got the first break. Kennedy's announcement broke on our time. But on almost all the other stories we have had to follow the bigger papers in Hartford, whose Washington bureaus can follow through at AEC or at the Pentagon. We have to rely on UPI which has other things to do, or go to our area congressmen and ask them to get news for us. It is all very second-hand.
  The very second-handedness of it made us blush badly when Kennedy made his announcement. Our Congressman Kowalski and Congressman Price of Illinois had assured us this program would go forward. They gave us a lead story one day only to have it come back in our faces. All this to tell you how difficult it is for the small city daily to handle stories that have an origin behind the federal curtain of secrecy.
  The instant story is also an example of giving substance to very little. We want to keep this news before the public and we also want to show the reader we are doing our level best. I think this shows through. This I think is important. "No comment" doesn't say very much. But it does indicate a try, which I feel the public appreciates.
  The difficulty in handling stories of this kind also has to do with standing fast against the rumor when there is nothing else. Everybody in town knows how many were laid off, from the barber on down to the street cleaner. On this story, I am convinced Pratt and Whitney public relations could have told us the number given notice on Wednesday, the number offered transfers, and where those transfers were to. This is all good information around here.
  It's tough. But if you can't get the core of the news today, at least shoot around it and get ready for tomorrow.

Obeying the Law

Unless he is forewarned, one of the first big surprises that the young reporter may have in his quest for authority is the discovery that he can invoke the freedom-of-the-press clause in the Constitution from morn to night and still be denied access to some documents which his naïveté might lead him to believe are public records open to all. Should he be able to break down certain barriers, he still might run the risk of being cited for contempt of court or sued for libel were he to use information thereby obtained.

It is regrettable that there is no place to which the reporter, or the editor either, can be directed for a clearcut statement of what his rights and privileges in particular instances are. Not only are the laws of different states different, but the same law is likely to have been interpreted differently by two or more courts of law in what would seem to be cases involving identical issues. As regards a number of important legal problems involving newspapers, there is little or no law, either statute or common. For this, newspapers themselves are partly if not largely to blame because they prefer to settle law suits out of court.

The principle generally observed, regardless of the clarity of state or municipal law, is that the public—which includes the press—has the right to inspect public documents except when the public interest thereby would be harmed. The frequent clashes between newspapers and public officials result from differences of opinion as to what constitutes a public record and what constitutes public interest. Some states have been careful to define public documents; others haven't. In either case, and regardless of the fact that there have been few tests in court, newspapers do not expect to be allowed to cover grand jury proceedings, executive sessions of law-making bodies, or to be shown records of unsolved cases in the police detective bureau, the report of an autopsy before it is presented to a coroner's jury, the report of an examiner to either a fire marshal or public banking official, or a number of other similar documents. In fact, public officials probably would be sustained by most courts were they to refuse the press access to many records now available to it. Pleading "public interest," the county clerk who refuses to disclose the names of applicants for marriage licenses, so as to protect them from commercial salesmen, probably is on sound legal ground.

The cub reporter should learn what both the law and general practice are in the community where he is to work, and the policy of his paper as to defiance or circumvention of public officials seeking to conceal news. Some editors encourage reporters to search for "leaks" whereby grand jury and executive session news may be obtained and they have defied judges' orders with resultant citations for contempt. Many years ago, the United Press forced the United States Senate to modify its rule regarding secret sessions after Paul Mallon obtained a secret roll call on the confirmation of a presidential nominee for a cabinet position. Over half of the states have passed "open record" and "open meeting" laws, many of them based on Sigma Delta Chi's "model" laws. Nevertheless, reporters continue to be frustrated by the evasive practices of some governmental bodies, such as city councils and school boards, which go into executive session and hold informal meetings in private places. Often important matters are decided at such clandestine rendezvous so that what transpires in public legally is merely a confirmation and leaves the newsgatherer ignorant of the factors which went into the decision-making.

It is the persistent clamor on the part of newspapers that has forced public officials to be as liberal as they are in what they make accessible to reporters. Since the fall of 1951, that clamor has increased in volume in opposition to presidential executive orders requiring federal agencies to classify news. Under President Truman's original order the classification were: top secret, secret, confidential, and restricted. Two years later President Eisenhower abolished the fourth class and greatly decreased the number of agencies permitted to withhold information. Neither order satisfied the American Society of Newspaper Editors, which established a vigorous Freedom of Information committee. Under its auspices, Harold L. Cross, prominent attorney, wrote *The People's Right to Know* which pointed out a considerable increase of information withheld at all levels of government. In late 1955, a subcommittee of the Committee on Government Operations of the House of Representatives, with Rep. John E. Moss of California as chairman, began hearings on federal government news secrecy policies. Its efforts led to the passage of the Freedom of Information bill in June 1966 (See page 44).

Copyright

Facts (news) cannot be copyrighted. The actual wording of an account of those facts, however, can be. A Conference of Press Experts called by the League of Nations in 1927 at Geneva stated the principle as follows:

> The Conference of Press Experts lays down a fundamental principle that the publication of a piece of news is legitimate, subject to the condition that the news in question has reached the person who publishes it by

regular and unobjectionable means, and not by an act of unfair competition. No one may acquire the right of suppressing news of public interest.

The Conference affirms the principle that newspapers, news agencies, and other news organizations are entitled after publication as well as before publication to the reward of their labor, enterprise and financial expenditure upon the production of news reports, but holds that this principle shall not be so interpreted as to result in the creation or the encouragement of any monopoly in news.

Although facts cannot be copyrighted, newspapers can seek redress for pirating of news as a violation of fair business practices. In the case of *Associated Press vs. International News Service*, the United States Supreme Court declared December 23, 1918:

> ... Except for matters improperly disclosed, or published in breach of trust or confidence, or in violation of law, none of which is involved in this branch of the case, the news of current events may be regarded as common property.... Regarding the news, therefore ... it must be regarded as quasi-property, irrespective of the rights of either as against the public.

A newspaper which wishes to rewrite or quote a copyrighted article appearing in another publication, either buys the copyright privilege or requests permission to quote. In either case, credit must be given to the publication which originally printed the material. If the copyright privilege is purchased, this credit line appears at the top of the article, as:

> COPYRIGHT, 1946, BY THE NEW YORK TIMES
> Honolulu, T. H., July 29.—Evidence of mounting animosity between the army air forces and the navy over the results of the atomic-bomb tests and their subsequent evaluation appeared here today as a high AAF officer attacked the "battleship mentality" of diehard naval officers and experts....

Otherwise, if permission to quote is given, the newspaper which copyrighted the article is given credit in the story itself. Unless permission is received, the paper using material in this manner is in danger of being sued for violation of copyright laws.

> Detroit, Aug. 3.—(AP)—The Detroit *Times*, in a copyrighted story, said today that a Wyandotte, Mich., grandmother has identified "Little Miss 1565," hitherto unidentified victim of a Hartford, Conn., circus fire, as her granddaughter....

Magazine articles and books usually are copyrighted, but a newspaper seldom cares to quote enough of such material to run the risk of violating copyright privileges. Often a magazine article or book contains an important fact which a newspaper wants to quote. Credit always is given to the original publication, as:

How lobbyists for the National Federation of Soothsayers defeated a bill which would have licensed their activities, is told in the May issue of Revelation, the organization's official publication.

A copyright runs for 28 years and can be renewed for a second 28 years. After that the previously copyrighted material passes into the public domain and can be quoted with impunity. In September 1966 a House Judiciary subcommittee approved a bill to revise the present law, which dates from 1909, to provide protection for "life plus 50 years" and to liberalize the "fair use" section to allow educators greater latitude in reproducing parts of copyrighted works. The bill had been in the making for 11 years.

How to Avoid Libel

As important as how to obtain access to public records is how to report the news they contain, or any other kind of news for that matter, so as not to involve one's newspaper in a libel suit. This problem is of personal importance to the reporter because any newspaper employee who had any hand in the preparation of a libelous news story is as subject to suit as the newspaper itself. Actually, it is seldom that action is brought against a reporter, but the chance that such might happen provides an added incentive to carefulness.

WHAT IS LIBEL?

The confusion already mentioned as regards the right of the press to obtain access to public records is even greater as regards libel. Succinctly, a libel is a written defamation as distinguished from a slander which is oral defamation. A more adequate definition which at the same time defines defamation is that given in the *American and English Encyclopedia of Law* as follows:

> A libel is a malicious defamation expressed either by writing or printing or by signs, pictures, effigies or the like; tending to blacken the memory of one who is dead, or to impeach the honesty, integrity, virtue or reputation, or to publish the natural or alleged defects of one who is alive and thereby expose him to public hatred, contempt, ridicule or obloquy; or to cause him to be shunned or avoided, or to injure him in his office, business or occupation.

It will be seen from this definition that cartoons, photographs and other illustrations are included.

Commission of a libel is a graver offense than slander because the written statement appearing in a publication with a wide circulation has greater possibilities of injury. In conversation, one may call another an opprobrious name and the effect be short-lived and restricted to a small circle of bystanders. Such statements made in print, however, have a far-reaching and more important effect.

In *The Rights and Privileges of the Press*, Fredrick S. Siebert deplores the distinction which formerly it was customary to make between words which are libelous *per se* (that is, libelous in themselves without the necessity of proving that their utterance or publication actually caused injury) and those libelous *per quod* (otherwise legitimate statements, libelous because of the circumstances under which made, so as to cause particular loss, as through declaring diphtheria to be prevalent at a summer resort). Instead of the old distinction, which he accredits to confusion resulting from the fact that only certain types of detraction once were regarded as actionable in slander, Siebert suggests a threefold classification of all questionable words as: (1) obviously innocent, (2) questionable, for the jury to decide; (3) obviously defamatory. It is the duty of the judge, he says, to indicate into which class the particular word, phrase or story falls.

That there is no reliable criterion by which to anticipate how either judge or jury will decide, Siebert indicates by many examples. So do others who have studied outcomes of libel actions. In their *Hold Your Tongue!* for instance, Morris L. Ernst and Alexander Lindey reveal the following absurd situation. It has been held libelous to call a man an "arch hypocrite," but not libelous to call him a "political hypocrite." In Tennessee one may, with impunity, call a woman a "hermaphrodite," but may not make the charge in Ohio. California holds "son of a bitch" not libelous and New York has legalized "God damn." On the other hand, however, while it is not libelous to say of a man that "he caught the pox," it is libelous to say that he "got the pox from a yellow-haired wench." In Minnesota, the statement, "You did rob the town of St. Cloud, you are a public robber," was held not libelous because the crime of robbery cannot be committed against a town; similarly, there was no redress for a church warden who was accused of stealing the bell ropes, because the warden is custodian of the ropes and cannot steal his own property. On the other hand, when it was said of a woman, "She did have pups," and when the accused sought to defend herself by alleging the inherent improbability of the accusation, an Indiana judge held that though the people are bound to know the law, they are not bound to know scientific facts and might therefore believe the charge a possible one. In New York, a similar statement, "She had a litter of pups," was held not libelous for exactly the reason that it could not be true.

These few examples should be sufficient to impress the young reporter as to the care he must exercise to avoid committing libel. While many of the cases to which reference has been made involved editorial comment rather than news stories, exactly the same inconsistencies are to be found in judicial decisions regarding other kinds of libel actions. It has been held both that the dead can and cannot be libeled, that a newspaper is and is not responsible for libelous statements in press association stories, and that a libelous headline alone is sufficient cause for action and that an article must be judged as a whole.

DANGEROUS WORDS

Despite this confusion, to be on the safe side, the reporter may expect that a court will consider defamatory statements that:

1. Charge that a person has committed or has attempted to commit a crime, or that he has been arrested for the commission of a crime, indicted for a crime, has confessed to committing a crime or has served a penitentiary sentence.
2. Impute that a person has committed an infamous offense, even though the words do not designate the particular offense.
3. Tend to diminish the respectability of a person and to expose him to disgrace and obloquy even though they do not impute commission of a crime.
4. Tend to disgrace, degrade or injure the character of a person, or to bring him into contempt, hatred or ridicule.
5. Tend to reduce the character or reputation of a person in the estimation of his friends or acquaintances or the public from a higher to a lower grade, or that tend to deprive him of the favor and esteem of his friends or acquaintances or the public.
6. Impute that one has a perverted sense of moral virtue, duty or obligation, or that he has been guilty of immoral conduct or has committed immoral acts.
7. Impute commission of fraud, breach of trust, want of chastity, drunkenness, gambling, cheating at play, violation of duties imposed by domestic relations, swindling, etc.
8. Impute weakness of understanding or insanity.

WINNING READER CONFIDENCE 149

9. Impute a loathsome pestilential disease, as leprosy, plague or venereal disorders.
10. Tend to expose a person in his office, trade, profession, business or means of getting a livelihood, to the hazards of losing his office or charge him with fraud, indirect dealings or incapacity, and thereby tend to injure him in his trade, business or profession.

Words and expressions the use of which has led to libel suits and which, therefore, must be used with great care by news writers, include:

abductor	extortionist	nigger
abortionist	false pretences	perjury
adulterer	false swearing	pettifogger
anarchist	forger	prostitute
arson	fornication	quack
bestiality	fraud	rape
bigamist	fugitive from justice	rascal
blackguard	gambler	robber
blackmailer	grafter	rogue
blasphemer	homicide	scandal monger
bribery	hoodlum	sedition
buggery	humbug	seducer
burglar	hypocrite	shyster
common drunk	imp of the devil	skunk
conspirator	incest	slacker
counterfeiter	indecent exposure	smuggler
criminal	informer	social leper
crook	insane	sodomist
dago	kidnaping	spy
dead beat	larceny	stock rustler
defaulter	leper	subornation
degenerate	liar	swindler
deserter	libelous journalist	thief
drunkard	libertine	traitor
embezzler	malicious mischief	villain
embracery	mistress	whore
eunuch	murderer	wop

It has been held actionable to publish of a butcher that he used false weights; of a jeweler that he was a "cozening knave" who sold a sapphire for a diamond; of a brewer that he makes and sells unwholesome beer or uses filthy water in the malting of grain for brewing; of a tradesman that he adulterates the article he sells; of a schoolmaster that he is an "ignoramous" on the subject he pretends to teach; of a clergyman that he is immoral or "preaches lies" or is a "drunkard" or "perjurer"; of an attorney that he offered himself as a witness in order to divulge the secrets of his clients or that he "betrayed his client" or "would take a fee from both sides" or that he "deserves to be struck off the roll"; of a physician that he is "empiric" or "mountebank" or "quack" or "vends quack medicines"; of a mechanic that he is ignorant of his trade; of a judge that he lacks capacity and has abandoned the common principles of truth; and of anyone in public office a charge of malfeasance or want of capacity to fulfill its duties.

H. W. Sackett in *The Law of Libel* cites the following published charges as having been held to be actionable: want of chastity (as applied to women, at all events) or adultery (charged upon either man or woman); the publication of the obituary of a person known to the writer to be living; a charge that a member of Congress was a "misrepresentative" and a groveling office seeker; that a juror agreed with another juror to rest the determination of the damages in a case upon a game of checkers; characterizing a verdict of a jury as "infamous" and charging the jurors with having violated their oaths; stating in the criticism of a book that the motives of the author are dishonorable or disreputable; calling a white man a Negro.

INSINUATIONS

It will be seen that a libel may be committed by mere insinuations. It is necessary only that the insinuation contain the elements of libel and that the readers of the paper understand it in its derogatory sense.

Likewise, allegory and irony may be libelous, as imputing to a person the qualities of a "frozen snake in the fable" or heading an article in regard to a lawyer's sharp practices, "An Honest Lawyer."

DAMAGES

Damages resulting from libel suits may be of three kinds: (1) general, (2) special and (3) punitive or exemplary.

General damages are awarded in cases of proof of libel when injury is recognized as the natural consequence of such publication. No proof of actual injury need be submitted.

A plaintiff may receive special damages when he can prove particular loss. When special damages are asked, proof of specific injury must be established by the plaintiff. Special damages may, however, be awarded in addition to general damages.

Punitive damages are inflicted as punishment for malice on the part of the offending publication. Proof of malice must be established by the plaintiff. Punitive damages may be awarded upon proof of gross negligence or if a newspaper reiterates its libelous statement after being warned that it is untrue.

DEFENSES

There are five possible defenses against libel:

1. Truth. In civil actions the truth of a publication is a complete defense, even though natural inferences of a defamatory character might be drawn which would be untrue. If malicious intent can be proved, however, truth may not be a defense. In criminal prosecutions, unless the publication was made for the public benefit or with good motives and for justifiable ends, truth is not a defense. The law in this respect differs in different states.

A publication must not only know the truth of what is has printed, but it must be able to submit legal proof. It is not a defense to claim that the libelous matter was printed upon the authority of another person. For example, publication of libelous statements made in a public address is not privileged, and the injured party can sue both the individual making the statement and all publications which reported it.

2. Privilege. Publication of the contents or of extracts of public records and documents for justifiable purposes and without malice, even though they contain libelous matter, is privileged by law. Publication of the contents of complaints or petitions before a public hearing has been held on them is not privileged; neither are publication of the proceedings of a private hearing, the contents of a warrant before it is served, confessions to police, news of arrests unless by warrant and many other exceptions.

The law on this subject reads as follows:

> An action, civil or criminal, cannot be maintained against a reporter, editor, publisher or proprietor of a newspaper, for the publication therein of a fair and true report of any judicial, legislative or other public official proceedings, without proving actual malice in making the report.

Another provision qualifies this as follows:

> The last section does not apply to a libel, contained in the heading of the report; or in any other matter, added by any person concerned in the publication; or in the report of anything said or done, at the time and place of the public and official proceedings, which was not a part thereof.

3. Fair comment. Authors, playwrights, actors, office holders and other public characters who invite the attention of the public to their work are liable to fair comment and criticism. This privilege, however, extends only to an individual's work and not to his private life, and there must be no malice.

In the case of office holders, comment or criticism must be confined to official acts or actual qualifications, and there must be an honest purpose to enlighten the community upon the matter under discussion.

The language of such criticism cannot be so severe as to imply malice, and the statement or comment must, in fact, be comment and not an allegation of fact. It, furthermore, must be on a matter of public interest, such as comment on public affairs, the church, the administration of justice, pictures, moving pictures, architecture, public institutions of all kinds, other publications and the like.

In 1964 the United States Supreme Court unanimously upset the conviction of the New York *Times* by an Alabama court based on an advertisement charging a "wave of terror" in the South. The court's decision prohibited "a public official from recovering damages for a defamatory falsehood relating to his official conduct unless he proves that the statement was made with actual malice," that is, with knowledge that it was false or "with reckless disregard of whether it was false or not."

4. Absence of malice. As indicated, malice is an important element of all libel suits. Its presence leads to larger damages than its absence. Malice is either *in fact*, which means that it springs from ill will, intent, hatred and so on, or *in law*, which is disregard for the rights of the person without legal justification.

Sylvan Meyer, editor of the Gainesville (Ga.) *Daily Times*, wrote in *Nieman Reports* for December, 1965:

> More than error is required to commit libel. Libel suits grow out of the atmosphere of a story or a campaign, out of the running relationship between the newspaper and the supposed victim of the libel. And, according to several astute editors, the gee whiz, slam bang stories usually aren't the ones that generate fear of libel, but the innocent-appearing, potentially treacherous minor yarns from police courts and traffic cases, from routine meetings and from business reports.

Absence of intent to libel is no defense, but proof of unintentional libel helps to mitigate damages. According to Sackett in proving absence of malice the defendant in a libel suit may show:

a. That the general conduct of the plaintiff gave the defendant "probable cause" for believing the charges to be true.
b. That rumors to the same effect as the libelous publication had long been prevalent and generally believed in the community and never contradicted by the accused or his friends.
c. That the libelous article was copied from another newspaper and believed to be true.
d. That the complainant's general character is bad.
e. That the publication was made in heat and passion, provoked by the acts of the plaintiff.
f. That the charge published had been made orally in the presence of the plaintiff before publication, and he had not denied it.
g. That the publication was made of a political antagonist in the heat of a political campaign.
h. That as soon as the defendant discovered that he was in error he published a retraction, correction or apology.
i. That the defamatory publication had reference not to the plaintiff, but to another person of a similar name, concerning whom the charges were true, and that readers understood this other person to be meant.

5. *Retraction.* Often a newspaper can avoid a suit by prompt publication of a retraction. If a suit does result, such retraction serves to mitigate damages, especially if it is given a position in the paper equally prominent to that given the previously published libelous statement. A few states have passed laws making complete retraction and apology a complete defense in libel cases.

PLAYING SAFE

Since truth is the best defense against a charge of libel, the primary responsibility of the reporter is clear; it is to be one hundred per cent accurate—which means carefulness and diligence of the type described earlier in this chapter. It is true that newspapers take many chances daily, especially in police news, but not in cases where the element of doubt is great. Among the precautions which the reporter should heed are the following:

1. Be sure that you have names and addresses correct.
2. Stop and think, "Will this defame anyone's character or hurt his business?"
3. Never call a man a crook, bootlegger, thief, forger or any other kind of criminal unless he is so proved in court. Don't anticipate what the court will do. Remember that an accused person is not a prisoner until after he is sentenced, and that he is innocent until proven guilty.
4. Only formal charges by proper authorities warrant their unqualified use by a newspaper.
5. The news of an arrest and the charge may be printed, but the reporter should obtain his information from the official police blotter and not from any other source. Testimony of witnesses also must be printed cautiously until made under oath.
6. "Police say," "it is alleged," "it is reported," and similar expressions are absolutely no protection, although insertion of such "softeners" may result in mitigation of damages.
7. Don't say someone is wanted "for the murder." Rather that he is wanted for questioning in connection with the murder or to answer a charge of murder.
8. Be careful to avoid imputing blame. It is better to say two automobiles collided than that one struck the other, unless, of course, one was stationary.
9. Verify all rumors, hearsay and comment.
10. Questionable statements always should be attached to an authority.
11. Remember that eyewitness testimony has been proven time and time again to err. Always interview as many eyewitnesses as you can.
12. If you doubt that a person has given his right name or address, write "—who gave his name as John Smith" or "John Smith who gave his address as—."
13. Be careful to say exactly what you mean. Avoid, for instance, saying that a man died "from" an operation when you mean "after" an operation.
14. Be careful of photographs gathered for the city desk. Many suits have resulted from improperly identified pictures.
15. Republication of a libelous statement from another medium is libelous. A newspaper is responsible for everything that it prints regardless of the source of its information or the authority upon which it prints it.

16. Never write anything when in a heat of passion or with the intention of injuring anyone, even though the statements that you make are true.
17. Forget your enthusiasm and personal opinions when writing a news story.
18. Avoid insinuations, innuendoes and irony.
19. Remember that a retraction is no defense in most states.
20. Copyread what you have written before turning it in.
21. When in doubt, leave it out.

9

Keeping Up-to-Date

I IDENTIFICATION
1. Persons
   a. *Making It Attractive*
   b. *Picking the Indentification*
   c. *Double Identification*
   d. *Synonyms*
   e. *Identification as the Feature*
   f. *Indefinite "Who"*
   g. *Delayed Identification*
   h. *Biographical Sidebars*
2. Organizations
   a. *By Type*
   b. *By Purpose*
   c. *By Achievement*
   d. *By Reputation*
3. Places
4. Events
   a. *Occasions*
   b. *Comprehensive Leads and Stories*
   c. *Predictions*
   d. *The Tie-back*
   e. *Coincidences*
5. Words

II THE FOLLOW-UP
1. The Second-day Story
   a. *New Information*
   b. *Cause—Motive*
   c. *New Development*
   d. *Opinion*
2. Featuring the Follow-up
3. Second-day Comment
4. Localization
5. Reminiscences
6. The Running Story
7. The Revived Story
8. Investigations
9. The Resurrected Story

III Rewrite
1. The Nature of Rewrite
2. Picking the Feature
   a. *Buried Feature*
   b. *Secondary Feature*
   c. *Follow-up Feature*
   d. *Comprehensive Lead*
   e. *Combined Stories*
   f. *Local Angle*

THERE IS NOTHING SO SHORT AS A NEWSPAPER READER'S MEMORY. No matter how carefully he reads a news story—and most newspaper purchasers read newspaper stories hurriedly if at all—when the next day's issue appears with news of later developments about any event, he finds that many if not most details of the first account have been forgotten.

As with events so also with persons in the news, no matter how prominent they may be. Results of current-events quizzes in which college students and other supposedly well-informed persons make bad "boners" are amusing, but instructions for such tests usually indicate that a very low score is "average." Names like faces may be familiar, but try to identify them! It is part of the interpretative reporter's responsibility to refresh readers' memories so that the immediate news account is more meaningful.

Identification

The obligation of the newspaper adequately to identify persons, groups, places and events in straight news stories is recognized in any efficient newsroom. The rule is never to presume that the reader has seen yesterday's story.

PERSONS

It is seldom that the name of a person is mentioned in a news story without some identification. Even the occupant of the White House is given his title, and other persons mentioned frequently in the news are identified by their news past or importance. Ordinary persons may be identified in several ways. The most common methods of identification include:

1. Address
2. Occupation
3. Age
4. Title
5. Nicknames
6. Race, nationality
7. War Record
8. News Past
9. Achievement
10. Life Span
11. Reputation
12. Relationship
13. Description
14. Occasion

Address. "Where do you live?" is one of the first questions asked anyone who is supplying information about himself. A man's address in a news story locates him, and the reader does not have to ask himself, "I wonder if that is the Newton Blue who lives in the next block?" Readers are interested in news pertaining to persons residing in their own or in a familiar neighborhood, even though not personally acquainted with them.

158   PRINCIPLES OF NEWS WRITING

Great care must be taken to get correct addresses. Libel suits have been started by persons with names similar to those of others mentioned in news stories. Rare cases have been reported of two persons by the same name living at the same address. It is important to ascertain whether it is "street," "avenue," "place," "boulevard," "terrace" and so on, as there may be both a Ridge avenue and a Ridge terrace. Whether it is East, North, West or South also must be mentioned.

> Peter R. Farrel, 159 E. Trembly place, was taken to Municipal hospital today after he had accidently cut his right foot while chopping wood.

Emmett Dedmon, executive editor of the Chicago *Sun-Times*, modified what he called "a journalistic shibboleth of long standing" with the following memorandum:

> The Sun-Times does not wish, as a matter of policy, to cause undue hardship or to invade the personal privacy of persons who are in the news through no fault of their own.
> While it is usually necessary to identify persons with their home address in a city as large as Chicago, The Sun-Times will refrain from doing so when good judgment would indicate such identification unnecessary or undesirable.
> In general the rule is: Don't use the address if it is secondary to the main point in the story, or if the address does not add to the identification of the individual.
> In all instances good judgment and clarity will be the criteria.
> Following are a few examples of situations where an address is not necessary:
> —John Smith is held up in his drug store. Use the address of the drug store but not his home address.
> —Mary Smith is posed in a weather picture.
> —Richard Rowe is a witness in a crime trial. His connection with the case is sufficient identification.
> —Five girls are arrested for prostitution at 1976 N. Dearborn. The Dearborn street address is sufficient.
> —John Doe, a printer, found the body, called police, gave the alarm, identified the suspect etc. As long as he is identified in some way the home address is not necessary.
> —A police officer captures a bandit. His station or section is sufficient identification.
> These examples are not meant to be a complete list but should give enough of an idea to explain the general rule. There are of course countless other situations which will have to be evaluated as they arise.

Occupation. "What do you do?" also is high up in the list of questions asked when data are being sought about a person. The reader wonders if Harry Snow, 1516 Chestnut street, is the carpenter by that name who worked on his new garage.

Donald C. Sorenson, 51, Edwardstown, district representative for the Common Laborers Union, Monday was sentenced to a two-year jail term and fined $1,500 for income tax evasion.

The occupation of a person mentioned in the news may be the feature, as:

A butcher today used his knowledge of animal anatomy to save the life of his hunting dog, Romeo, accidentally caught in a bear trap.

Sometimes the feature is in the fact that a person in a particular position has done a certain thing whereas the same thing done by another would not be so newsworthy.

An assistant postmaster general charged here today that Sen. Edwin F. Dietz has been talking out of both sides of his mouth in criticizing the Post Office department.

Age. It is customary to give the age of a person who is involved in a law suit or the victim of an accident. Otherwise, unless age has importance in the story, it may be omitted. Many persons do not like to have their ages known, but readers are eager to find out how old popular heroes and heroines are.

William Murphy, 16-year-old Greenwich high school junior, today identified John Pratt, 21-year-old bootblack, as the armed bandit who robbed him of his clothing and $15 in cash Sunday night on W. Totze avenue.

Age frequently is the feature, as:

An 18-year-old girl will marry a 73-year-old man on Saturday because "our common religious beliefs are of far more importance than the disparity in our ages."

Title. When a person has a title by which he is known, the news writer should use it. A short title is better placed before a name; a long title should be placed after a name, as:

City Clerk George Johannsen will deliver the commencement address at 10 A.M. tomorrow at Craven Junior High School.

James R. Wesley, commissioner of public works, will represent the city tonight at . . .

Nicknames. Nicknames seldom are used without first names; rather, they are inserted between the first name or initials and the surname. In sports stories and in feature articles, nicknames may be used alone. Often persons prominent in the news are better known by their nicknames than by their real names, as "Ike" Eisenhower, "Bing" Crosby, "Babe" Ruth, etc. When such nicknames become widely familiar, the quotation marks usually are omitted. It is a common practice with some newspapers to invent nicknames for persons mentioned in the news, frequently in crime stories. In doing so, care must be exercised so that the connotation given the nickname is not prejudicial to the proper administration of justice or otherwise socially harmful.

> William "Wee Willie" Doody, pint-sized killer-bandit of the 1920s, died Wednesday evening in the Stateville prison hospital. Death was attributed to a liver infection.
> The baby-faced killer, who got his nickname because he was only 5 feet 3 inches tall, was serving a life sentence for the slaying in 1929 of Berwyn's police chief. [Chicago *Daily News*]

Race, Nationality. Deciding when to pass copy containing "Negro," "Puerto Rican," "Polish-born," "of German descent," and similar identifications has caused many an editor many a headache. Members of racial and nationality minority groups understandably object to persistent use of such identifications in crime stories, especially in headlines: "Negro Rapist Sought," "Italian Gangster Shot." There is a slow but steady drift away from such practices, but the rule remains that race or nationality shall be used when pertinent. Determining just when that is often is not easy. When someone is in the limelight—as a politician, athlete or entertainer, for instance—his fans are eager to learn every picayunish fact regarding him, including his ancestry; certainly no injustice is intended when such details are given. For some people, as musicians and artists, a foreign background may be considered as an asset.

> Alfred M. Bowler yesterday became the first Negro to be elected to public office in Calhoun county since Reconstruction Days.

War Record. Under pressure from veterans' organizations, most newspapers have ceased identifying veterans as such in crime stories. Often, however, veteran status is a legitimate, even necessary, identification. It may, in fact, be the feature.

> Thomas Thomas, a former paratrooper, just couldn't get his training out of his head. He was sleeping in the apartment of a friend when he awoke and jumped out of a third floor window. He landed on a roof a few feet below the window sill. He was not hurt, and he explained that he had dreamed he was back in the army and had been given an order to jump.

News Past. After having once appeared in the news in connection with an important event, a person continues to be potentially more newsworthy than others. Should he become "copy" again, his former exploits are a means of identification.

> Miss Jane Boynton, 22, winner of a "most beautiful baby" contest 20 years ago, today filed suit against Dr. N. O. Holten, for $15,000, charging that his plastic surgery "disfigured her for life."

> Leon L. Desmond, star witness in the Fox-Delaney murder case four years ago, today was appointed chief deputy inspector of Raymond county by Sheriff L. L. Tyler.

Achievement. More than 40 years later, Charles A. Lindbergh still was being identified as "the first person to make a non-stop solo flight from New York to Paris." The achievement of one's early life may be his identification in later life or after death, as:

> Dr. Hal Foster, first Kansas City physician and surgeon to specialize in the treatment of eye, ear, nose and throat, died at 6 o'clock this morning at his home at the Brookside hotel, Fifty-fourth street and Brookside boulevard. He was 88 years old.

Life Span. Sometimes it is pertinent to identify a person in relation to the historical events or changes that have occurred during his lifetime especially as they relate to the news at hand.

> Julius C. Jacobsen, who joined the internal revenue staff 38 years ago, when relatively few persons paid income taxes, and stayed long enough to see virtually everyone pay, will retire Saturday. [Milwaukee *Journal*]

> Mrs. Eliza Addis, who was born in Philadelphia when City Council met in Independence Hall and City Hall was just a blueprint, is celebrating her 100th birthday today. [Philadelphia *Bulletin*]

Reputation. When identifying a person by means of his reputation, it is necessary to be careful that the reputation is deserved. It is possible for a newspaper to make or break a person by referring to him constantly as the foremost authority on a certain subject, or as a mere pretender or charlatan.

> James (Jimmy) Eder, reputedly the wealthiest and most successful jockey in the history of the Latin American turf, yesterday was named defendant in a suit for divorce or separate maintenance filed in Superior court by Mrs. Ruth Eder.

Relationship. A person's news importance may depend upon the prominence of a relative or friend. How much the families of persons important in public life or in the news of the day should be written up and photographed is another problem for debate by a class in newspaper ethics. Relationship may be used as identification even when the members of the family referred to are not of particular importance. Minors often are identified by parentage.

Legitimate use of relationship in identification is illustrated in the following examples.

> Maj. James R. Garfield, II, training officer of the 107th Armored Cavalry Regiment, Ohio National Guard, and great-grandson of James Abram Garfield, 20th President of the United States, is taking summer training at Fort Knox. [Louisville *Courier-Journal*]

> Robert Campbell MacCombie Auld, 80, a descendant of Robert Burns and an authority on the Scottish poet's life and Scottish history, died yesterday after a five weeks' illness.

A different kind of identification by relationship is illustrated by the following example.

> A 30-year-old father of five was stabbed to death Saturday night in a dispute on the street near his home in the Porterfield section of Avon. The victim was identified as . . .

Description. Sometimes the writer brightens up his identification by a bit of personal description, without which it often would be impossible to obtain a true impression of the story's importance. In the following example, note the use of descriptive identification throughout:

> Their shoes didn't squeak. They didn't talk out of the sides of their mouths. They showed no inclination to clip anyone on the jaw.
>
> Yet the dozen plain-looking fellows who gathered at the Hotel Sherman last night were honest-to-goodness private detectives. They were holding their first postwar meeting of International Investigators, Inc.
>
> Head man is Ray Schindler, world-famed New York detective. Other members include Leonarde Keeler, inventor of the lie detector; Dr. Le Moyne Snyder of Lansing, medical-legal director of the Michigan State Police, and Clark Sellers, Los Angeles handwriting expert and document ace who worked on the Lindbergh kidnaping case.
>
> Most of the men, unlike such movie detectives as Alan Ladd, Humphrey Bogart and Dick Powell, are in the 50s and 60s and are quite calm about their work.
>
> But one, at least, was not without a kind word for their movie counterparts. Said Harry Lewis of Sioux City, Iowa: "Those boys talk pretty tough and seem to run into an awful lot of trouble. But they get their job done and that's what counts." [Chicago *Sun*]

Occasion. A person's part in a news story must be explained no matter how else he is identified.

Prince Albert of Belgium, who is on a two-month study tour of the United States, will visit Chicago Oct. 12–13.

A mother, burned in a street car-gasoline trailer crash which killed 31 persons Aug. 14, 1967, won a $30,000 out-of-court settlement Monday.

Making It Attractive

It is not necessary that the identification always be formal and dull. In stories with considerable feature interest, all formal rules may be stretched or violated, as:

Vienna, April 22—(UP)—A beautiful 27-year-old widow named Aimona, of Mitrovitza, Yugoslavia, has lost all five of the suitors who made her the envy of the town's unmarried women, a dispatch to the newspaper Tagblatt said today.

In identifying persons prominent in the news, it is possible to brighten up the identification to avoid dullness, provided good taste does not forbid.

By George Lardner Jr.
Washington Post Staff Writer

Puffing on a Corona Corona and quoting Shakespeare as best he could, Julius Klein protested yesterday that he would never try to corrupt a United States Senator.

The portly, name-dropping publicist insisted to the Senate Ethics Committee that he had a "God-given right" to ask Sen. Thomas J. Dodd (D-Conn.) to help shore up his sagging image with his West German clients.

Dodd, he suggested, just needed more coaching than other Senators might.

"I don't call this pressure," he said.

He expressed much more satisfaction with the assistance he said he got from Sen. Jacob K. Javits (R-N.Y.).

"Senator Javits," Klein told the Committee, "is completely indoctrinated in this issue."

Flanked by two attorneys, Klein, a registered foreign agent, was the final witness in the first phase of the Committee's inquiry into misconduct charges against Dodd. . . .

Picking the Identification

The proper method by which to identify a person must be decided in each case. The appropriate identification should be sought in the case of a person with a number of achievements or a considerable news past, as:

Harold Bank, president of the senior class, today announced committees for class day.

Harold "Bud" Bank, football captain, will not be a candidate for the basketball team this winter.

The Associated Press Managing Editors once debated the propriety of identifying former New York Governor Thomas E. Dewey as "a two-time failure as a Republican presidential candidate" years after his candidacies and in stories which did not deal with national politics. The consensus was that in many instances recalling that part of Dewey's "news past" was poor journalism.

Often the occasion calls for special identifications for prominent persons, identifications which would be inappropriate at most other times.

Washington, Dec. 11—(UP)—President Eisenhower, who never voted before 1948, plans to transfer his voting residence from New York to Pennsylvania where he has a farm at historic Gettysburg.
[New York *Herald Tribune*]

Cleveland, July 25—(AP)—Federal Judge Paul Jones, once a football player himself, will hear injunction suits against Bobby Freeman and Jack Locklear, who jumped contracts with a Canadian pro team to join the Cleveland Browns. [Baltimore *Sun*]

DOUBLE IDENTIFICATION

Sometimes, especially in obituary stories, more than one identification may be crowded into the lead, as:

William Jay Schieffelin, retired chairman of the board of Schieffelin & Co., wholesale drug concern, and a crusader for government reform, education for Negroes and many other humanitarian causes, died Friday night at his home, 620 Park Avenue, after a long illness. He was 89 years old on April 14. [New York *Times*]

SYNONYMS

It is impossible, however, to use more than two or three identifications without making the lead awkward. One way out of this difficulty is to use the points of identification as synonyms for the person's name after the name itself has been used once. In this way, nicknames, reputation, news past, various titles and so on, can be brought in and repetition of the name or of personal pronouns avoided, as:

Former Alderman Guy L. Millard today charged that the local Fair Employment Practices commission is failing to perform its functions.

Chief backer of the commission when he was a member of the City Council, Millard now believes the agency's work is being sabotaged. The 78-year-old president of the Royal Dye Works said he has personally interviewed 20 local workers who had sought the commission's help in vain.

IDENTIFICATION AS THE FEATURE

When the achievement, reputation, occasion, or news past by which a person may be identified, seems more important or better known than the person's name, the identification should precede the name, as:

> Murray, Ky., July 28—(AP)—The man who wrote the official history of General Dwight Eisenhower's unified European command will deliver the commencement address at Murray State college's summer exercises next Friday.
> He is Dr. Forrest C. Pogue, commissioned by President Eisenhower to write a history of his World War II record, "Supreme Command."

INDEFINITE "WHO"

When the *what* of the story is more important than the *who*, the identification may be featured, names being delayed until the second paragraph, as:

> A 32-year-old Congregational minister has been named director of Youth Inc., a new nondenominational religious research agency.
> The Rev. Ernest S. Ernst, minister of the Westchester Community Church since 1963, will take over direction of the agency in January at Boone, Iowa.

DELAYED IDENTIFICATION

Similarly, overcrowding a lead already packed with important facts, can be avoided by postponing identification until the second paragraph, as:

> The eloquence of Reginald Burnett held a crowd of 1,200 farm delegates and their wives spellbound for an hour and 20 minutes here.
> The sandy-haired president of the United Plastic Workers amused and delighted his National Farmers Union audience Tuesday night with raps at big business, Wall Street and Secretary of Agriculture Freeman.

Biographical Sidebars

A quarter-century ago the J. David Stern papers developed a much-imitated practice of box inserts to provide additional information about persons, places, things and events mentioned in the news. Longer sidebars and feature articles also can be used to satisfy curiosity as to "Who is this fellow?" and make current news more understandable. Under the heading, "In College—and in Jail," the Chicago *Sun* used the following box insert at the time independent India was coming into existence:

> Pandit Jawaharlal Nehru, head of the newly formed Indian interim government, has had intimate contact with the British—first in college and then in jail.
>
> The 57-year-old leader of the All-India Congress Party received his education at Harrow and at Cambridge University in England where he became a barrister-at-law.
>
> Returning to India he joined the famous non-cooperation movement of Mohandas K. Gandhi in 1920 and became actively associated with native independence and peasant movements.
>
> He was president of the Indian National Congress in 1929 and 1936–37.
>
> He has been repeatedly imprisoned by the British for his political activities and his anti-war speeches.
>
> For many years, Nehru was sympathetic with the aims of the Soviet Union, although in political doctrine he was regarded as a Marxian Socialist rather than a Communist. In recent years, however, his leftism has become somewhat diluted.

ORGANIZATIONS

Organizations as well as persons must be identified adequately:

By Type

Directors of the Monument Builders of America, Inc., a national association of the retail monument dealers, today condemned as "a national disgrace" the unkempt condition of the Statue of Liberty.

By Purpose

Milltown's Transit Authority, set up to bring order out of the city's long existent transportation muddle, has ended a year of operation with a record of substantial accomplishments although difficulties still lie ahead.

The eight-man board held its first meeting July 29, 1967, in offices at

35 Elm street, beginning operations with the backing of a $200,000 fund made up of two equal contributions from the city and state, joint sponsors of the enterprise.

As a municipal authority, it has the power, fixed by state law, to acquire and operate transportation lines in and around Milltown.

BY ACHIEVEMENT

The Alameda County Fair, which has been America's "jockey incubator" since the close of World War II, has a record crop of apprentices on hand for its 12-day race meeting opening here Friday.

BY REPUTATION

The Milltown Associates, which for 23 years was the leader in promoting city beautification, will disband Jan. 1.

In stories related to important public issues—controversial matters—brief identification of an organization usually is not enough. The interpretative reporter may have to write a parenthetical paragraph, sidebar, or full-length feature to provide proper understanding of what is involved. Readers cannot judge the true nature of a group by a high-sounding title. Typical situations in which full-length identification of an organization may be necessary include the following:

1. When the name resembles closely that of another group whose outlook is different. Example: the National Council of the Churches of Christ in the United States of America and the American Council of Christian Churches.
2. When a powerful group takes a stand on a public issue, pending piece of legislation. In such cases it may be wise to point out whether the immediate action is consistent with previous activities by the same group. It may be possible to throw light on any selfish motives by revealing the business or other connections of the group's leadership or the general nature of its membership.
3. When a new group is organized, especially when its aims are expressed in semantically vague terms or it seems interested in only a single measure or matter of public interest. In such cases it may be a "front" organization for some other older interest group. Identification of the leadership may cast more light on the organization's real purposes than a quotation from its charter or constitution.
4. When an organization is involved in an act of force or violence. In such cases it may be necessary to seek reasons for the group's very

existence in the social, economic or political conditions that brought it into being. Such was done extensively as regards the Puerto Rican Nationalist party after some of its members attempted to assassinate President Truman in 1950 and shot several members of Congress in 1954. Otherwise the incidents would have seemed to be isolated ones by individual fanatics.

PLACES

Places must be identified when they are not widely known or when significant or the feature of the story, as:

> Purchase of the 1600 block on Palmer road for a new junior high school was announced today by the Board of Education. Twenty-three private dwellings, almost all of them condemned by the Department of Health, now occupy the site.

A place's news past or its proximity to another place previously in the news may be the best identification; often it is the feature:

> Within a few feet of the spot where once grew the elm under which George Washington accepted command of the Continental Army, 25 Boston University students yesterday organized the Army of American Liberation. Its purpose is to "wage incessant warfare against forces which are destroying American democracy."

Places, as individuals, have reputations which may be used to identify them, as:

> Sauk City, Minn., the "Gopher Prairie" of native son Sinclair Lewis' "Main Street" . . .

> Reno, Nev., divorce capital of the United States . . .

> Tarrytown, near which Rip Van Winkle allegedly took his long nap . . .

EVENTS

Events may be identified and explained:

1. By their significance (the occasion).
2. By their importance in relation to other events (comprehensive leads and stories).
3. By relating them to the "atmosphere" in the light, of which they must be understood (the situation).

4. By their probable consequence (prediction).
5. By definite reference to preceding events of which they are related (tie-backs).
6. By the coincidence between them and other events.

Occasions

Circumstances of a news event—purpose, importance, significance and so forth—must be made clear, as:

> The most crippling airline strike in the nation's history entered its 16th day Saturday and continued to strand travelers, disrupt tours and snag air freight service. [Lincoln (Neb.) *Journal*]

Often the feature of the story may be found in the purpose or importance of the occasion which is the subject of the story, as:

> Fort Washakie, Wyo.—(UP)—An age-old tradition was broken here when an Indian woman with white blood in her veins became a "chief" of the Arapahoe tribe.

The comparison between the immediate event and preceding similar events may be pointed out, either in the lead paragraph or shortly thereafter, as:

> For the first time in memory, neither political party has a contest for any office in Crow county in the April 8 election.

Comprehensive Leads and Stories

The comprehensive lead is correlative and explanatory. Used in straight news writing, it is not opinionated, however, because it deals with the incontrovertible.

One kind of comprehensive lead attempts to interpret the immediate news in the light of previous events, as:

> Six more witnesses Friday were called before the federal grand jury investigating the distribution of juke boxes in Farwell township.

> Further evidence that the voters of this city really elected a "reform" administration last month was provided by today's order by Mayor L. O. Oliver closing all amusement places in violation of municipal health ordinances.

A comprehensive lead emphasizes situations. When several stories related to the same general news event are received, they may be combined into one story and a general round-up or comprehensive lead be

170   PRINCIPLES OF NEWS WRITING

written. This type of lead is suitable particularly for election stories, stories of wrecks and other disasters, accidents, weather stories, etc. Facts on which a comprehensive lead and story of this sort are written usually are gathered by more than one reporter or correspondent.

PREDICTIONS

The significance of an event may be explained by pointing out the probable consequences or likely "next steps."

The City Council's Big 10 crime commission starts five days of public hearings Wednesday—probably the last hearings the committee will hold.

Drastic revision of the curriculum of Serena Junior High School will result if the Board of Education approves the unanimous recommendation of its Educational Policies committee.
Among the changes which Mrs. Rose Blakely's committee says should be made are the following . . .

THE TIE-BACK

The tie-back is the part of the lead of a story which shows the relation between the immediate news and some previous news event. In the following examples, the tie-backs are in italics:

Miss Colista Connor, 20, reputed heiress to a $500,000 fortune, *who disappeared mysteriously a week ago and returned Wednesday night to explain she was "on vacation,"* was gone again yesterday.

Five hundred and fifty-two *additional* influenza cases were quarantined in Will county today, *a slight increase over yesterday's figures,* while six deaths were recorded from flu and 14 *more* from pneumonia.

COINCIDENCES

The tie-back to a previous story may be made by emphasizing coincidence. In many cases, the immediate incident may be newsworthy primarily or solely because of the coincidence, and the prior event may have received no publicity.

A second tragedy within two months today deepened the sorrow of Mrs. Mary McKinley, 26.
On June 1, her husband, Thomas, 35, a tuckpointer, was killed in a 12-foot fall. Yesterday her son, Robert, 4, was crushed to death by a truck.

WORDS

Parenthetical sentences or paragraphs sometimes are necessary to define or explain the context in which unusual words or expressions appear. Rep. Clarence Brown of Ohio, for instance, sent reporters to the thesaurus when he accused the president of "ingannation." At that time, the Louisville *Courier-Journal* interjected the following in a United Press account:

> (The word is not in *Webster's New International Dictionary*. The United Press said it meant to confuse or bewilder, and the Associated Press reported solemnly, "On consulting a thesaurus, reporters found the word ingannation listed as a synonym for deception.")

When President Truman accused a senator of raising many "Macedonian cries or yells," the Chicago *Daily News* used the following italicized parenthetical paragraph:

> (A Macedonian cry is a cry for help, so called from Acts XVI, 9, "Come over into Macedonia and help us.")

When the president told the nation that it could achieve a production goal of $500 billion a year within ten years, the same newspaper explained as follows:

> (Five hundred billion dollars is half a trillion. A trillion is a 1 with 12 zeros behind it.)

Sometimes it is a legal term that needs explaining or a diplomatic proceeding, as the following which was once used when the United Nations received a plea for the application of sanctions:

> (Sanctions are positive measures that may be taken against aggressor governments under the U.N. charter, such as cutting off trade, communications, etc.)

The Follow-Up

Most of the news in any edition of a newspaper is related in some way to other news. It usually takes more than a single article to tell any story. After the first account has appeared, there usually are new developments.

Ability to sense phases of a news story which must be investigated further (followed up) is a valuable asset to a reporter or editor.

Newspapers are read carefully for stories which in their original form are incomplete or which should be watched for further developments.

THE SECOND-DAY STORY

The second-day story of any event may include: (1) new information not available when the first story was written, (2) causes and motives not included in the first story, (3) more recent developments, results and consequences since the first story, (4) opinions regarding the event.

Latest developments always are emphasized in follow-up stories, and the use of a tie-back is a rigid rule. Never should the writer of a news story presume that a reader has seen the previous story or stories. Just as each installment of a serial story is prefaced by a brief summary of what has gone before, so each news story related to a single event has a short reference to previous news stories.

The tie-back usually is inserted in the lead in the form of a phrase or dependent clause, but any grammatical device may be used; sometimes the tie-back is delayed until the second paragraph.

New Information

A 44-year-old Ardmore woman who was found unconscious on Coulter street near Sibley avenue, a block from her home, is in serious condition at Bryn Mawr hospital today while police searched for an unidentified man believed to have attacked her without motive.

[Philadelphia *Daily News*]

Cause—Motive

Four firemen who perished in a flaming back-draft that surged through the Backstage night club early Tuesday morning died while fighting a fire which was deliberately, criminally set.

That flat charge came yesterday from Fire Marshal Frank Kelly, chief of the San Francisco fire prevention and investigation bureau.

"The fire was not accidental," Chief Kelly declared following more than 24 hours of investigation.... [San Francisco *Chronicle*]

New Development

Hartford, Conn. (AP)—John T. Emmanuel, trapped six days in the wreckage of a small plane, died Wednesday in Hartford Hospital.

Emmanuel, who had been rescued Sunday from the slopes of Mt. Higby in nearby Middletown, was transferred Tuesday to Hartford Hospital from Meriden Hospital.

Opinion

Angry parents today charged the "L" system with neglect in the crossing death of an 8-year-old boy.

A system whereby one man controls two crossings at Flournoy and Lexington at Long endangers the lives of children in three schools, the parents declared.

Donald Kieft, 5227 Lexington, was crushed to death Monday when he attempted to cross the tracks at Flournoy on a bicycle.

The crossings are protected by gates. So many trains traveling at a high rate of speed pass the intersections in the residential district that the lone gateman keeps the gates lowered even when trains are not approaching. . . .

Metropolitan morning newspapers frequently use the follow-up technique on stories which broke for the afternoon papers the day before; afternoon papers do the same for stories the first news of which appeared in the morning papers.

FEATURIZING THE FOLLOW-UP

An important news story breaks too fast to permit investigation of its feature possibilities. By a later edition or the next day, however, the features are developed either in a rewritten story, or in supplementary stories (sidebars). If the reporter finds himself stuck with few new facts, he may simply retell the story in feature style:

Laramie *Boomerang*

A freak accident was investigated early this morning when an automobile belonging to Ralph Conwell, 803 Flint, crashed into a parked pickup belonging to C. H. Melvin, 657 North Eighth, and then crashed into the front of the Melvin home.

Police said apparently the Conwells were starting on a trip and after taking the car out of his garage, Mr. Conwell got out of the car to check if the garage was locked and the lights were out inside.

The car started creeping forward headed west on Flint. Mrs. Conwell, who was in the car and had on a safety belt, attempted to halt the car by applying the foot brake and

Laramie *Bulletin*

It was 4 A.M. Tuesday.

Mr. and Mrs. Ralph Conwell were parked in front of their home ready to leave for a vacation at their ranch near Daniel, Wyo.

Conwell started the car. Mrs. Conwell was secure in a new safety belt next to the driver's seat.

Conwell remembered he left the garage door open and left the car to close it.

The car began rolling.

Mrs. Conwell struggled to get out of her "secure" position, gave up the idea and reached for the steering wheel and the brake.

She got the wheel, but hit the accelerator with her foot.

inadvertently applied pressure to the accelerator.

The car surged forward hitting the curb and climbing it at the corner of Flint and Eighth and then headed north, striking glancingly on the outside of the Melvin pickup, also headed north, which was parked next to the curb, knocking the pickup upon the parking.

The Conwell car continued and jumped the curb to the right and came to a stop after uprooting a large lilac bush and smashing into the front of the Melvin home.

The impact of the car was just beneath the window of the bedroom where Mr. and Mrs. Melvin were sleeping. Although the wall was driven in about ten inches from the impact, the window pane remained intact.

Police said there were no injuries reported to them.

Around the corner she went, her husband running after her, the horn honking.

The car struck a parked ton truck, threw it 40 feet, jumped the curb, hit a 25-year-old lilac bush, threw it several feet, and smashed into the bedroom of Conwell's next door neighbor—Mr. and Mrs. C. H. Melvin.

Said Mrs. Conwell:

"It was the safety belt that saved me. You can never tell when an accident is going to happen."

Said Mrs. Melvin: "I thought it was a drunken driver."

Said Mr. Melvin: "My mother-in-law planted that bush here 25 years ago. I never thought it'd save our lives."

Mr. Conwell wasn't available for comment—he went back to the ranch, leaving his wife behind.

SECOND-DAY COMMENT

Whenever the President delivers an important message, the Supreme Court hands down a significant decision, a new scientific discovery is announced, or any one of a number of unusual events occurs, newspapers and press associations scour the country to obtain opinions from persons qualified to comment cogently. In such stories exaggeration must be avoided, as in the following piece in which generalizations were limited to the principals who are mentioned specifically.

By Robert E. Baskin
Washington Bureau of The News

Washington—Considerable controversy arose Thursday in legal and congressional circles over the propriety of Congressman Joe Pool's action in ejecting a New York attorney for the House Un-American Activities Committee's hearing.

Fellow attorneys of Arthur Kinoy charged that the House Committee was practicing brutality and intimidation of members of the bar representing "hostile" witnesses in the committee's inquiry into pro-Viet Cong activities in the United States.

Pool's colleagues on the committee, however, approved his action, although expressing regret that it became necessary to forcibly eject a lawyer from the proceedings, as was the case involving Kinoy.

An unofficial shorthand transcript of the incident gives some indication of what took place. [Dallas *Morning News*]

LOCALIZATION

A news item originating in a faraway place may have a local "angle," or it may cause readers to ask, "Could it happen here?"

Local parents need have no fear that babies in local hospitals will become confused and cause another Pittman-Garner baby mix-up a generation or so hence.

So thorough is the identification system employed in this community's three hospitals that their authorities consider mix-ups like Madeline Louise Garner-Pittman's in Georgia last month an impossibility.

Although many hospitals throughout the country supplement foot and palm printing as an added precaution, adequate supervision is the only real safeguard, in the opinion of H. James Baxter, superintendent of General Hospital since 1951....

REMINISCENCES

Similarly, readers may ask, "Has anything like that ever happened before?" Old timers draw parallels between the present and the past and relate anecdotes brought to mind by the immediate news item.

The slaying of eight South Chicago Community Hospital student nurses set a grisly all-time record.

It was the worst mass murder in modern Chicago history.

The previous record was set by the St. Valentine's Day massacre on Feb. 14, 1929, when seven men were gunned down by gangsters in a garage at 2122 N. Clark.

The seven men were either members of George (Bugs) Moran's beer gang or had the bad luck to be in the garage at the time.

They were lined up against a wall inside the garage by rival gangsters posing as policemen, and were gunned down with the help of Thompson submachine guns.

No one was ever tried in the St. Valentine's Day massacre, which nailed down Chicago's reputation as a gangster city.

The Fort Dearborn massacre, in August of 1812, occurred near 14th St. and Lake Shore Dr., and took the lives of possibly 52 settlers and soldiers, plus 25 Indians. But this was more than 20 years before Chicago was incorporated.

Mass murders—or a series of slayings by one person over several years —have plagued many parts of the nation.

In September, 1949, Howard B. Unruh, 28, a religious fanatic and ex-GI, walked down a street in Camden, N.J., and killed 13 persons with his German Luger pistol.

He was adjudged insane and committed to a mental hospital.

In 1958, Charles Starkweather, 19, went on a spree in which 11 persons were slain in Nebraska and Wyoming. At his trial he blamed girl friend Caril Fugate, 14, for one of the killings and called her the "most trigger-happy person" he ever met.

Starkweather was executed and Miss Fugate was sentenced to life in prison.

In 1955, John Gilbert Graham murdered his mother and 43 other persons by putting a time bomb in her luggage before she boarded an airliner at Denver. The bomb exploded aloft.

Graham was arrested by the FBI and later executed.

In 1960, 34 persons were killed when a bomb exploded aboard an airliner over Bolivia, N.C. One of the victims, Julian Frank, was accused of setting the bomb as part of a suicide-insurance plot.

The case of the Boston strangler was apparently closed in 1965 after 11 women had been strangled in the area since 1962. The prime suspect was "safely institutionalized." [Chicago *Daily News*]

THE RUNNING STORY

Newspapers continue to follow up stories as long as there are new angles or developments to investigate or until reader interest lags. Each succeeding story is written to bring the situation up to date.

In case of a flood, war, important court trial or political contest (to mention only a few of the possibilities), daily, almost hourly, stories are written to give the latest developments. A murder story frequently occupies the front page for weeks.

Note how the following story developed day by day, as shown by three successive leads from the Kansas City *Star*:

About 124,000 women here today are being given the opportunity to state whether they desire to serve as jurors. The ballots should be returned to the Jackson County courthouse by June 10.

Eighty-six ballots on jury service for women had been received this afternoon at the jury commission office in the Jackson County courthouse. Twenty-nine indicated a desire to serve on juries here. Fifty-seven declined to serve.

The number of women desiring jury service was increasing this afternoon when 314 of the 1,440 ballots received by the jury commission indicated that more than one in four women responding to the poll were willing to be jurors. The remaining 1,136 do not desire to serve on Jackson County juries other than federal.

THE REVIVED STORY

Days, weeks or months later a reporter may be assigned to find out "what ever happened to so-and-so" or regarding "such-and-such."

Five years ago Wednesday Dorothy Mae Stevens was brought to Michael Reese hospital, frozen stiff and brittle as an icicle.

Her body temperature was an unbelievable 64 degrees—so low, physicians had to use a chemical thermometer because regular clinical thermometers record only as low as 93. Normal body temperature is 98.4.

The 23-year-old woman had been found in an areaway at 3108 Vernon. She had been there about 11 hours.

When doctors examined Mrs. Stevens they found:

Her blood had congealed into a mud-like sludge.

Her breathing rate was three to five times a minute compared to a normal 18 to 22.

Pulse was 12 (normal is 70–80).

Blood pressure could not be recorded.

Her deep frozen condition attracted the attention of physicians everywhere. She was called the "human icicle," "deep-freeze girl," "frozen woman," and "human hibernater."

* * *

Mrs. Stevens was back in Michael Reese hospital Tuesday where she helped write medical history.

"She has been undergoing treatment in connection with her artificial limbs," a spokesman said. "She'll be here about two more weeks."

Physicians, about a month after she was brought to the hospital amputated both of her legs below the knee; all of the fingers on her right hand and all but one finger on the left.

* * *

Still in good spirits, Mrs. Stevens is keeping busy in the hospital reading and doing leathercraft. Now 28, she lives in a flat at 3800 Lake Park.

"I'm still a young woman and I have my whole life to live yet," she says. [Chicago *Daily News*]

INVESTIGATIONS

Often such assignments are for policy purposes, but the disclosures from the resultant investigations may be definitely in the public interest. Newspapers frequently keep after someone, particularly a public official, to correct an evil brought to light by some news event.

By Curtis Fuller

Doors still swing inward at Niles Center and Morton Grove taverns a year after seven persons, two of them Northwestern university students, burned to death in the Club Rendezvous. Doors still swing inward for bodies to pile up against, and do not even have exit signs to mark them.

Last year a week after the Rendezvous tragedy, two Daily News-Index reporters visited more than 15 taverns in the Howard street, Morton Grove, and Niles Center districts to discover if conditions existed which might cause other Rendezvous tragedies some day. They found fire hazards frequent. Sunday night the reporters visited the same taverns again, found the same conditions.

In three of a dozen Morton Grove and Niles Center taverns, doors comply with county fire regulations by opening out. In two of the three, exit signs direct customers to the doors.

The Cook county board April 4 passed a new fire ordinance to take effect April 30, ordering all taverns to have at least two exit doors that open outward, progress through which is unimpeded. Electrically operated catches for exit doors are prohibited by the ordinance. Other provisions included use of fireproof or slow-burning construction.

These regulations are not enforced. They are violated by more than half the taverns visited Sunday night.

Nowhere did we see fire extinguishers in plain sight. One of the ironies of the evening came as we sat in the Paris Gardens talking to the bartender. A man dashed in yelling that his car was on fire. There was no fire extinguisher handy, and the bartender handed him a seltzer bottle which the man took and dashed out. [Evanston (Ill.) *News-Index*]

THE RESURRECTED STORY

Sometimes a mystery is years in the solving, or a new fact is discovered which casts new light on some historical event or personage. In writing such a story the "tie-back" rule must be observed, although the lead seldom is adequate to supply all of the "resurrected" facts which must be told. For instance, if a criminal who has long evaded capture is arrested, the story may include a recapitulation of his crime and may even be accompanied by pictures and diagrams taken or made at the time of the crime. Later, when the person is brought to trial, the story may be repeated, and again if the criminal is put to death legally.

In every news office there are notations of stories which are said to be "hanging fire," and which may break at any time. Verdicts are withheld, a committee delays its report, there is a postponement in the filing of a suit, or an important person does not make an announcement of which he has hinted.

In the following examples, note the tie-backs to events of some time previous:

Ten cases of typhoid fever—one resulting in death—have been traced to a church wedding reception in suburban Rosehill last Nov. 1, Dr.

R. L. Edmonson, director of the Rosehill Health Department, disclosed today.

North Manchester, July 4.—Midnight lights burned by a Dr. Elies Ohmart prior to 1885 were explained here when Tom Richardson came across an ancient, handwritten record book in the attic of the John W. Ulrey home which he recently purchased.

The book contained notes of scientific inventions including a telephone patented by Bell in 1876, an electric arc lamp, the separation of aluminum from clay, a mechanical table of logarithms and an electric sign board.
[Fort Wayne (Ind.) *News-Sentinel*]

Rewrite

The day of the major newspaper scoop is gone. In the first place, except in a small and dwindling number of large cities, there is no competitor for the one surviving daily newspaper to scoop. Furthermore, the important day-by-day news of the world is gathered mostly by two press associations (Associated Press and United Press International) and transmitted simultaneously to all subscribers. Most important, radio and television have made it impossible for any periodical to be first with such news.

Newspapers and magazines amplify, explain and interpret the news, sometimes shortly after its occurrence; but, often, weeks, months or years later when new information becomes available or the passage of time gives new perspective. Newspapers today often are competitors of magazines in the attempt to obtain first rights to the memoirs of persons able to cast new light on old events.

THE NATURE OF REWRITE

Within newspaper offices the title rewrite man now is used to designate a person who spends his time in the office taking news over the telephone, mostly from the paper's own reporters. There persists, however, a considerable amount of rewriting in the old sense: "borrowed," with little or no attempt to obtain additional facts, from other printed sources.

Such sources include press releases, community newspapers, trade journals, house organs, public and private reports and announcements, newsletters intended for special interest groups and out-of-town newspapers (exchanges). Some papers run a column of news briefs or oddities from the exchanges or the day's wire report. Stories in the earlier editions of one's own newspaper may be rewritten for later editions, when new facts are obtained or for reasons of space, clarity, etc.

Usually, the rewrite man attempts to compose an item which will read as though it had been written up on original information. In his attempt to play up a new fresh angle he must avoid killing a good lead and burying an undoubted feature. Awareness of the extent to which radio and television have taken the edge off some of the news may lead to this error unless there is conscious effort to avoid it.

PICKING THE FEATURE

The rewrite man must obey the rules of good news writing which, among other things, means that the lead of his story must play up the feature of the item. The difficulty of the rewrite man is obvious when it is realized that this feature probably already was played up in the original story. The poorer the first story, the easier the task of the rewrite man who must do more than merely restate or reword the original lead.

The rewrite man, with no facts in addition to those of the original story, therefore, asks himself several questions, including:

1. Did the writer play up the real feature of the story or is it buried some place in the article?
2. Is there another feature of equal or almost equal importance as the one which the writer used, that might be played up?
3. Can I make my story read like a follow-up story by emphasizing the latest developments mentioned in the first story, or by suggesting the next probable consequence?
4. Can I write a comprehensive lead which will interpret this item of news in the light of other news?
5. Is there any other news today with which I can combine this story?
6. In the case of stories appearing in publications outside of the immediate community, is there a local angle that can be played up?

BURIED FEATURE

If the writer of the original story has missed the feature, the task of the rewrite man is simple, as:

KEEPING UP-TO-DATE 181

Original Story

The question of submitting to the voters of Milltown at a special election Mayor A. L. Hunter's proposal to issue $400,000 worth of street improvement bonds again was the major "bone of contention" at last night's City Council meeting.

Ald. Joel Oldberg, 15th ward, presented a list of streets which he said are badly in need of repair and urged the holding of the special election. Opposing him was Ald. Arthur West, 21st ward, who said the city already has too large a bonded indebtedness.

After three hours of debate the Council voted 21 to 17 in favor of Alderman Oldberg's motion to call a special election Sept. 14.

Rewritten Story

Milltown voters will decide Sept. 14 at a special election whether the city's bonded indebtedness shall be increased $400,000 to finance Mayor A. L. Hunter's street improvement program.

Decision to submit the matter to voters was made by the City Council last night after three hours' debate. The vote was 21 to 17.

The motion was passed over the opposition of Ald. Arthur West, 21st ward, who argued that the city already is heavily indebted. Maker and chief supporter of the motion was Ald. Joel Oldberg, 15th ward, who presented a list of streets which he says need repairs.

Secondary Feature

Note in the following example how the rewrite man found a second feature equally as important as the one played up in the original story:

Original Story

Loss of between $75,000 and $100,000 resulted from a fire which raged for three hours early today in the Central Chemical company plant at Calumet City. The plant, which manufactured nitric acid, was a subsidiary of Wilson & Co., packing firm.

Spontaneous combustion is believed to have been the cause of the fire which was noticed about 2:30 A.M. by two workmen, only occupants of the building at the time. In the attempt to save acid valued at about $50,000 in storage tanks, the two men, Abel Puffer and Jared Bean, shut off safety valves to the tanks.

Exact loss cannot be determined until the tanks are opened today and

Rewritten Story

Firemen of Hammond and Calumet City braved the dangers of huge stores of highly inflammable nitric acid yesterday to battle a fire which destroyed the Central Chemical company plant at Calumet City. The loss was estimated at $75,000 to $100,000.

The plant, a subsidiary of the packing firm of Wilson & Co., is devoted entirely to the manufacture of the acid. Quantities of acid valued at $50,000 were in storage tanks.

The blaze raged for three hours. The acid tanks will be opened today to determine whether water seeped into them and spoiled the stores.

Two workmen, the only persons

tests made as to whether water reached their contents. Because nitric acid is highly inflammable, Hammond and Calumet City firemen were in constant danger as they fought the fire.

in the plant, shut off safety valves to the tanks when the fire began, apparently from spontaneous combustion.

Follow-Up Feature

In rewriting the following story, the writer certainly was safe in assuming the next probable consequence. Note how this story contains a tie-back and reads as a follow-up story, although no new information is included:

Original Story

After strangling her three baby daughters with a clothesline, Mrs. Gilda Heyda last night hanged herself in her home at 423 S. Reba street.

The bodies of the three girls, Roberta, 4, Ruth, 2, and Hazel, four months, were discovered by Mrs. Sylvia Priem, mother of Mrs. Heyda, when she arrived about 8 P.M. for a visit. The children were lying on a bed with the body of their mother nearby.

The father and husband is Wilfred A. Heyda, unemployed carpenter, believed to be somewhere in the middle west on his way to Texas to seek employment.

Chief piece of evidence at the inquest which was to open this morning will be a note to her mother left by Mrs. Heyda, reading:

"It's pretty good! Wilfred has kids and can't even send them a card while on a trip."

Heyda left three weeks ago and was last heard from in Cincinnati from where he expected to go to Indianapolis, Chicago, Springfield, Ill., and St. Louis before heading for the southwest.

Rewritten Story

Somewhere in the middle west today tragic news followed a father who is in pursuit of employment to support his wife and three small daughters.

The young husband and father, Wilfred Heyda, unemployed carpenter, was sought by authorities who were to inform him his wife, Mrs. Gilda Heyda, strangled their three baby girls and then committed suicide last night in their home at 423 S. Reba street.

As an inquest opened into the deaths this morning, police expressed the belief that Mrs. Heyda had become despondent from loneliness. She left a note to her mother, Mrs. Sylvia Priem, saying:

"It's pretty good! Wilfred has kids and can't even send them a card while on a trip."

The last word from the father, who left home three weeks ago, was from Cincinnati. From there he wrote he was on his way to Texas by way of Indianapolis, Springfield, Ill., Chicago, and St. Louis.

The slain children were Roberta, 4, Ruth, 2, and Hazel, four months. Their bodies were discovered by

KEEPING UP-TO-DATE 183

Police believe Mrs. Hyda's act resulted from loneliness because of her husband's absence and failure to write more frequently.

Mrs. Priem lying on a bed when she came to visit. Nearby was the body of Mrs. Heyda who apparently had used a clothesline to strangle her daughters and then take her own life.

COMPREHENSIVE LEAD

The rewrite man's knowledge of recent news events is valuable. In the following example, the writer was able to supply additional information out of his memory. If time permits and the story merits the trouble, the rewrite man may consult the newspaper's library and reference department to obtain information of this kind.

Original Story

Virgil Miner, 17, son of Mr. and Mrs. Charlton Miner, 386 Coates street, last night won first place in the annual state high school extemporaneous speaking contest. Speakers from 11 other high schools competed at Beardstown Municipal auditorium.

Representing the local high school, Virgil drew "Neutrality" as his subject. All contestants were given 30 minutes in which to prepare and each spoke ten minutes. Judges were . . .

Rewritten Story

For the second time in five years, the Milltown high school entry won first honors in the annual state high school extemporaneous speaking contest when Virgil Miner last night was declared the winner at Beardstown Municipal auditorium.

Three years ago, Leland West, now a student at Booster college, won the contest which was held at Lincoln. By an odd coincidence, both boys drew the same topic, "Neutrality."

Virgil is the 17-year-old son of Mr. and Mrs. Charlton Miner, 386 Coates street, and a senior at the high school.

Rules of the contest give each entrant 30 minutes in which to prepare to give a ten minute speech. Twelve students competed last night. Judges were . . .

COMBINED STORIES

The following example shows how one rewrite man combined two items into a single story.

Original Stories

Losing control of his automobile when a butterfly flew against his face, Edgar Lewis, 33, 1301 Sherman

Combined Story

Insects were responsible for two odd automobile mishaps in Milltown early last evening.

street, crashed into a fire hydrant about 6:30 P.M. yesterday at the northwest corner of Simpson and Michigan streets. He was taken to Municipal hospital with only minor bruises.

Sylvester Finger, 28, 1428 Grove street, is in Municipal hospital today with two fractured ribs as the result of an automobile accident about 7 P.M. yesterday. Finger's car struck a telephone pole at the southeast corner of Michigan and Central streets after he took his hands off the steering wheel to drive away ants which were crawling on his ankles.

Ants crawling on the ankles of one driver led to a smashup which sent him to Municipal hospital with two fractured ribs. In the other accident, a butterfly flew against the driver's face and caused him to lose control of his machine.

The injured man is . . .

LOCAL ANGLE

The rewrite man who reads newspapers from other cities, official reports and documents, press agent material and the like, should look for a local angle to feature, as:

Original Story

PEORIA NEWSPAPER

A state-wide membership drive of the Fraternal Order of Leopards will be planned here next Thursday at a meeting of representatives of the eight original chapters in as many cities.

Goal of the campaign will be 25 chapters and 2,000 members before July 1, according to J. S. Kienlen, Peoria, state commander, who called the meeting.

Cities to be represented at Thursday's meeting and delegates are: Wayne Lueck, Danville; R. S. Kirschten, Cairo; Lowell Watson, Freeport; S. O. McNeil, Aurora; Silas Layman, Springfield; Richard Yates, Elgin; O. L. Moss, Bloomington; and Mr. Kienlen.

Rewritten Story

FREEPORT NEWSPAPER

Lowell Watson, 34 W. Bushnell place, commander of the local chapter of the Fraternal Order of Leopards, will attend an organization meeting next Thursday at Peoria to help plan a state-wide membership campaign for the order.

Representatives from all eight original Leopards chapters in the state will take part in the meeting called by J. S. Kienlen, Peoria, state commander.

Objectives of the proposed campaign are a membership of 2,000 and 25 Illinois chapters. To attend Thursday's meeting, in addition to Watson and Kienlen, are . . .

10

Giving It Substance

I Completing the Account
1. Factual Background
2. Eyewitness Accounts
3. Sidebars
4. Localization
5. "The Other Side"

II Interpretations
1. Causes and Motives
2. Significance
3. Analysis
4. Comparisons
5. Forecasts

III Providing Perspective
1. Résumés
2. Surveys
3. Investigations
4. Stunts
5. Situations and Trends

EXPERIENCED REPORTERS WHO DEVELOP SPECIALTIES OFTEN BECOME recognized experts. They write not only authoritative newspaper articles but magazine pieces and books as well. Their vast amount of background knowledge enables them to give meaning to current happenings. More than that, they become critics in their fields and can warn and forecast and even give advice to policy leaders, including heads of state. They may have a powerful effect upon public opinion.

Later journalistic success is determined by early experience. Nobody, that is, is catapulted into a top position of prestige and influence without having served a long apprenticeship during which he learned correct work habits and attitudes. Local reporting provides the first and best opportunity for the development of such essential traits as thoroughness, accuracy, resourcefulness and the like. The aspirant for future fame and fortune as an interpretative reporter and writer begins by becoming a superior gatherer of so-called "straight" news which he writes objectively. He "gets around" more than his competitors and digs deeper in his fact-finding. In other words, he does whatever is required and then a bit more, the key to success in most any area of endeavor.

The reporter who deals first-hand with the events which make news lays the foundation for a future as interpreter as well as chronicler of current affairs by conditioning himself to inquire regarding each assignment:

1. What happened? That is, what *really* happened—the complete story, not just the end results of a series of incidents.
2. Why (or how) did it happen? That is, what is the explanation?
3. What does it mean? That is, how interpret it?
4. What next? In the light of today's news, what may be expected to happen tomorrow?
5. What's beneath the surface? What are the trends, ideologies, situations and so on, of which one should be aware so that an overt news incident will make sense?

Completing the Account

FACTUAL BACKGROUND

When an event of major significance occurs, because of the mass of detailed information involved and from lack of time and space, first news stories may be in the straight news-writing tradition, leaving the interpretation for another edition or day. If, however, the reporter has an adequate knowledge and understanding of preceding events related to the one at hand, even his first story, prepared in haste, will have greater substance.

If there are both a morning and an afternoon newspaper, any news story inevitably breaks to the comparative advantage of one over the other. The publication with the earlier deadline will be able to print the story first, but the other paper should be able to prepare a more detailed account. For instance, the Peoria (Ill.) *Journal-Star*, a morning newspaper, once reported that an attempt by an alderman to have a painting contract awarded to the second lowest bidder was defeated when the mayor cast the deciding vote. The Peoria *Transcript*, that afternoon, with more time, cast new light on the incident by revealing that the alderman and contractor were brothers-in-law, that the alderman was attending his first meeting following election and that the mayor's vote brought about a tie, not a majority.

The knowledgeable reporter will recall the history of a bill or ordinance and of previous attempts to promote similar legislation. He knows whether lawmakers are behaving consistently, the identity of individuals and groups in support or opposition, and other facts of the same sort which enable readers to come to a better understanding of the immediate occurrence.

EYEWITNESS ACCOUNTS

To supplement the formal stories, it is common practice to ask victims of disasters (train wrecks, floods, fires) to relate their personal experiences. Often, such accounts are ghost written or are printed under the by-lines of the principals "as told to" some staff writer. Reporters themselves write eyewitness accounts of important scenes they have witnessed. Such stories are more informal than straight news accounts and usually provide graphic word pictures of what happened.

Photography, including motion pictures, has not yet made written description obsolete, nor is it likely to do so for some time, if for no other reason than that cameramen are not always present at news events about which it is necessary to answer, "What did it look like?" in order to present a complete account. Before he can describe well, a reporter must be able to observe. Careful observation means noting features which escape the untrained spectator. A bizarre vocabulary containing innumerable adjectives is not essential. The reader, in fact, will "see" best what the writer is describing if the words are familiar; ambiguous qualitative adjectives such as "handsome" or "delicate" are omitted and figures of speech, historical and literary allusions and other rhetorical devices used are easily understood.

In selecting anecdotes to relate and persons to describe, caution must be exercised so that they are either important in their own right or typical of a general situation. Otherwise a distorted impression can be created. A typical situation in which this might occur is a mine cave-in or flood or similar disaster. At the scene, probably accompanying rescue workers, the reporter is attempting to describe the reaction of victims and others so the reader can get the "feel" of the story. He must realize that one sobbing woman does not constitute an hysterical mob. The reader must be able to depend upon the integrity of the reporter.

That the best-intentioned newsgatherers will differ in their observations and impressions is inevitable. Carl Lindstrom, who quit the executive editorship of the Hartford (Conn.) *Times*, after a quarter-century, and wrote *The Fading American Newspaper*, and others point up the danger of permitting reporters to attempt to be interpretative. They cite the example of widespread differences in reports of a press conference with Dr. Otto John after he fled from West to East Germany in 1954. According to the Associated Press:

> He spoke nervously at first. Then he got over his first mild stage fright and was completely at ease. Pink-cheeked, he was the picture of German health. His low modulated voice was pleasing to hear, regardless of how one would react to the sentiments involved. He made many wisecracks that brought laughter, wisecracks appreciated only in his native German tongue which lost much of their salt in translation. Not all of the laughs came from the Communist press either.

What the United Press reporter saw was as follows:

> His press conference statement today was recited grimly and hurriedly, much in the manner of confessions made by the victims of numerous Red Purge trials.
>
> He gave the tell-tale evidence of Communist brainwashing tactics; He was wooden-faced and nervous at the conference. He never smiled, although some of his comments brought laughter from newsmen.

An International News Service writer in Washington, using material purported to be supplied by Allied counter-intelligence sources, wrote:

> These sources are convinced that, through use of a highly developed combination of hypnosis and hypodermic needles, Dr. John became a virtual "zombie" without a will of his own, capable of acting and speaking only at the dictates of his Communist masters.

Over the National Broadcasting company airways, Robert McCormick commented as follows:

> John handled himself with self-confidence and assurance. He definitely showed no signs of being drugged, beaten or tortured and, in fact, seemed quite happy. If anything, he looked more content than he looked in Bonn.

It is impossible to argue with the importance of attempting to describe Dr. John's attitude after his sensational act. No deadpan recording of whatever words he spoke would have sufficed to give readers a hint of the motives for his act. Equally obvious is the fact that at least one (which?) of those who attended the press conference was a thoroughly incompetent reporter. The example does not disprove the value or necessity of interpretative reporting. Rather, it provides argument for the fact that journalists, whether they report and write objectively or interpretatively, must be highly ethical.

SIDEBARS

Whenever an important story occurs, reporters often use sidebars to round out the complete account. A sidebar deals with phases of a story as a whole which conceivably could be included in the main account but not without either lengthening it too much or sacrificing some details. When an office building in Chicago's Loop exploded, among the anecdotal sidebars were the following: (1) 105,000 square feet of new glass being rushed to city to replace show-window glass broken, (2) analysis of city ordinances covering gas leakage which allegedly caused the blast, (3) description of army of glaziers at work in area, (4) police pass system to admit workers employed in area, (5) refusal of pass to a window washer, obviously because there were no windows left to wash, (6) symposium of eyewitness accounts, (7) narrow escape of nearby elevated tower operator, (8) instructions on how to enter area, (9) Red Cross activities, (10) list of buildings whose windows were blown out.

In such sidebars, the reader finds the answers to questions which naturally occur to him while reading the main story. A common rhetorical device is to pose the question presumably in the reader's mind and then supply the information necessary for formation of an answer.

When the news relates to a scheduled event, several reporters may be assigned to cover different angles. A woman reporter, for instance, may stay close to the wife of a visiting celebrity; at the same time, another reporter may concentrate his attention on the crowd, noting its size and nature, ever watchful for unusual personalities and incidents. Still another may observe the behavior of the police, marshals, secret-service men and the like, or he may interview members of the party of either the guest or the host or both. Someone else, who might not even need to be present, can compare the occasion with similar ones in the past, here and/or elsewhere. Some of the information obtained by members of a reportorial team may be used by whoever writes the main story of the event but each probably will have enough left for a separate piece.

LOCALIZATION

The effects of some news events are felt at considerable distances. Without mention of some of the repercussions, the original story is not complete. For instance, whenever the President of the United States or some other leader of government makes an important announcement, there are reverberations on Capitol Hill, where congressional leaders abandon or alter old tactics or institute new ones. The stock market may be influenced by mere rumor. A Supreme Court decision may affect governmental practices and legal procedures in the states and cities.

In all such and similar cases, the reader wants to know, "How will this affect me?" That is the perspective from which the interpretative reporter should approach his task. In that spirit, the Evanston (Ill.) *Review* figured out the average cost for every man, woman, and child in Illinois of a newly announced federal budget. Similarly, when the United States Supreme Court upheld the blue laws of some eastern states, the United Press International bureau in Topeka compiled a list of laws still on the books in Kansas regulating behavior on the Sabbath. The Baltimore *Sun* used a similar story to explain how a Supreme Court decision regarding motion-picture censorship would affect Baltimore and Maryland.

Many a newspaper has investigated to determine how long the local supply of coal or steel or some other commodity would last in the event a strike continued affecting the faraway source of supply. How a new federal or state law will affect the community specifically, probably always should be explained by the public-spirited local press.

> By Robert M. Lewin
> Daily News Labor Writer
>
> What will the new steel price increases do to the cost of things you buy?
>
> The price of steel used in a 30-gallon water heater will go up 21 cents, according to the arithmetic of Armco Steel Corp., the first to follow Inland Steel Co. in increasing steel prices.
>
> Armco's estimates also showed:
>
> The cost of steel in a home gas furnace will go up 32 cents; 23 cents in a washing machine; 16 cents in an automatic dishwasher; 28 cents in a refrigerator; 15 cents in an automatic clothes dryer, and $3 in an automobile.
>
> Armco contends that the increases of $2 and $3 a ton on the price of hot-rolled steel sheets and strip and cold-rolled sheets "are so modest they cannot be consequential."
>
> The auto and appliance industries are chief users of those products. The increases are scheduled to go into effect Wednesday. . . .
>
> [Chicago *Daily News*]

THE "OTHER SIDE"

Deadpan reporting of the contents of a report, speech or the like, even when the source is reputable, may be misleading in that it does not give readers the "whole" or "essential" truth. When the news source is irresponsible, grave disservice may be done the reading public. It certainly is newsworthy when someone important in public life attacks another person. Such news often cannot be ignored. It can, however, be put in better perspective if there is simultaneous opportunity for reply by the otherwise injured party. Readers want to know how those most affected by any news event react to it. Unless their curiosity is satisfied, the account is incomplete.

How "real objectivity" was attained by an interpretative reporter for the Memphis *Press-Scimitar* who merely filled in background and, without drawing conclusions, gave readers additional information by which to judge a current news story, was related by the editors of the April 1950 *Nieman Reports* special issue. The incident occurred during the campaign of B. Carroll Reece, Republican candidate for United States senator from Tennessee.

In a Memphis speech, Reece lambasted the "motley crowd" of Democrats in charge of the federal government for speaking "with such a variety of accents, all of them un-American, that they sound like the tongues of Babel." Continued Reece:

> These mixed tongues are chanting many themes that are utterly offensive to our American instincts. None is more offensive than their chant that "States' Rights might give way to human rights." Under this sweet-sounding slogan is a snake in the grass as vicious as any reptile we have ever encountered. Herein lies the efforts of men who are either recent immigrants to our shore or whose ideas of government are immigrant to our shore—to move in on our system of States' Rights for the kill. . . . We of the South shall throw the pretty phrases back in their teeth. We say to them that the South has always preserved human rights. . . .

Straight-laced reporting of this speech, the Nieman writers declared, would have appeared under some such headline as, "ALIENS CONTROL U.S. GOVERNMENT, WARNS REECE." However, the Memphis reporter included in his interpretative article the fact that in an earlier speech in Buffalo (N. Y.) Reece said:

> This element [the Southern Democrats] which of course stemmed from the slave-holding oligarchy which once plunged this nation into a bloody war to preserve the institution of slavery, is the group which still maintains itself in power in a large section of this country by the practice of outrageous racial discrimination, preventing millions of American citizens from exercising the right to vote. It is the element of the party which inaugurated Jim Crow laws; the element which had pushed discrimination into the North. . . .

The interpretative article was headed, "REECE VERSUS REECE."

Many American editors came to wish they had accorded the late Senator Joseph McCarthy of Wisconsin similar treatment.

There are, of course, a pro and a con regarding every public issue. The ethical newspaper considers itself a public forum for the airing of diverse opinions. The obligation, however, is not just to the person who wishes to express himself, but primarily to readers so that they can be fully informed. When a new curfew law for adolescents is under consideration, for instance, the paper should seek out persons who are in positions to have intelligent opinions on the subject. This is not the inquiring-reporter technique which often results in obtaining uninformed and unrepresentative viewpoints. Rather, it is a search for the best opinion available.

An example of how an experienced reporter can supply objective facts to make an important news story interpretative in spirit is provided by John W. Kole of the Milwaukee *Journal*. Its author does not consider it exceptional. "Instead," he writes, "it is what we strive for each day in the presentation of public affairs." Kole further explains: "We feel that the problems of local government, like those of our national government, become more complex each year. Interpretation is absolutely necessary to keep readers informed. In my mind, interpretative reporting of public affairs is simply the use of facts and the opinions of informed people to make a point."

The story, together with marginal notes by Kole, follows:

Switching more than three million dollars in street and sewer construction from cash to bond financing, the Milwaukee common council Thursday afternoon adopted a record city and school budget for 1960 of $142,554,153.

The budget, combined with the county budget, will require a tax of $58.20 per $1,000 of assessed valuation, which will mean a $35 higher tax bill for a typical Milwaukee home owner.

Obviously, huge financial figures mean little to a reader unless he knows what it will cost him. Thus, the $35 figure for the typical home owner.

The council reversed its finance committee by approving five controversial amendments. The actions so angered Ald. John H. Budzien, committee vice-chairman, that he resigned from the committee immediately after the wild three-hour meeting.

Mayor Zeidler said Friday he was "seriously considering" a veto of some of the council budget actions, especially the one switching the cash items to bonds.

"I am also disturbed by the impression left by the council that a group can get something out of line if it has a special pleader," Zeidler said.

He said he would confer with finance committee members and other city officials Friday afternoon before making his decision.

The $58.20 tax rate actually is lower than the $59.37 rate for 1959 purposes, but is based on 10% higher property assessments. Based on last year's assessments, the 1960 rate would be $64.02.

With an obvious eye toward next spring's election, aldermen cut the $50.08 combined rate proposed by the finance committee by $1.88, a move which will save a typical home owner $14.50 in 1960.

But because the cuts were made by slashing $3,250,000 from the cash program for streets and sewers and authorizing instead $4,250,000 for these items through bond financing, the typical home owner eventually will pay far more than the $14.50.

In contrast, county supervisors transferred more than three million dollars from the bond to the cash program during their budget hearings and recent budget adoption. This move will reduce their debt service costs in future years.

The city's budget examining committee had recommended the cash financing as a start in reversing a 10 year program of bond financing which has put the city more than

The aldermen were particularly careful to keep the tax rate down by cutting the cash program and increasing the bonds. We felt the reader should be told that this move would cost him more in the long run.

120 million dollars in debt. The committee was overruled by a 15 to 5 vote.

A disconcerting factor to some city officials was the lobbying success of two employee groups in getting special wage raises for city workers who the city personnel director said were no more deserving than others.

In four amendments, the council:

By a 17 to 3 vote, authorized a fourth week of vacation for 778 city workers with 25 years or more of service.

By a 19 to 1 vote, gave extra $25 a month pay increases to about 100 civil engineers who are college graduates and registered by special examinations.

By a 12 to 8 vote, gave extra $5 a month wage boosts to most of 1,084 workers in pay range 5, which includes ash collectors, forestry workers, janitors and others.

By an 11 to 9 vote, eliminated the position of the mayor's urban renewal coordinator, a job held recently by Sol Ackerman, now in private business.

The extra wage increases were on top of a 4% across the board boost given to all general city employees in the budget.

"The two extra wage increases amounted to succumbing to special pressure groups," Zeidler commented. "The actions create inequities which will create many problems in the near future."

[*Then followed 11 paragraphs mostly comparing the new with old budgets and with other details.*]

Only Budzien, Mortier and Richard B. Nowakowski voted against the fourth week of vacation after 25 years, an amendment proposed by Bernard B. Kroenke.

Extra wage increases were won by disturbing lobbying tactics. We used a statement by Mayor Zeidler (Milwaukee's mayor does not preside at council meetings; the executive branch is entirely separate) to bring this out.

But Meyers pointed out that the finance committee had granted a 4% instead of a 3½% increase while deciding to eliminate the fourth week proposal. Most of this new fringe benefit will be absorbed by various departments. The estimated additional cost for 1960 is $25,000.

Robert C. Garnier, city personnel director, said that although the county board granted a fourth week after 20 years of service, it was not general practice in either industry or government service.

General city employees next year will get 14½ paid holidays. Added to four weeks vacation, those with 25 years or more of service in effect will get one-half day short of seven weeks vacation, plus sick leave benefits. Firemen and policemen get less than half the holidays of general city employees.

The most curious action was the one granting most of the 1,084 workers in pay range 5 an extra $5 a month rise. This amendment also was sponsored by Kroenke.

Several hundred of the pay range 5 employees are represented by John C. Zinos, executive director of district council 48 of the American Federation of State, County and Municipal Employees.

Zinos and two of his staff members were busy buttonholding aldermen in the council chambers right up to the start of the meeting.

Typical of the argument in favor of the amendment was that of Ald. Clarence A. Heiden, who pleaded with his colleagues to "give the poor little scrubwoman a break."

(Actually, city scrubwomen will not benefit from the amendment because they are in a lower pay range.)

A fourth week of vacation was tossed in—contrary to the practice in most of private industry and despite the fact that city employees get twice as many holidays as most other workers.

Some more lobbying for pay raises. We point out that the lobbyists were at work right in the council chambers. And a parenthetical insert is used to show up an alderman who pleads, "Give the poor little scrubwoman a break."

[*Then followed 4 paragraphs of direct quotations on the amendment.*]

The $25 extra a month for graduate registered civil engineers was boomed by Atty. John J. Fleming, a former alderman and a leading city hall lobbyist. He represented the Association of Graduate and Registered Engineers.

The finance committee last June committed itself to special adjustments for engineers, but found as the wage hearings progressed that all of the higher income city ranges needed special attention.

But a motion to give extra raises in the higher brackets was defeated in committee, with only Mortier supporting it.

The result of Thursday's action, Garnier said, would be to give extra raises to 100 persons who deserved them no more than several hundred other persons in higher ranges.

"In fact, there are several other groups that need special attention far more than the civil engineers," Garnier said.

[*Then followed 5 paragraphs to explain what the amendment would cost and to give a few additional details.*]

The switch from cash to bonds was sponsored by Schmit, Heiden, Valentine V. Kujawa and Ralph F. Kelly, all of whom represent outlying wards where constituents pay comparatively high tax bills because they have newer houses.

Most of the improvements financed by the street and sewer bonds will be in those four wards.

All finance committee members except Mrs. Vel R. Phillips voted against the amendment. They were joined only by Hass.

An individual lobbying effort by an attorney who has powerful friends in the council, plus a comment by the city personnel director that the civil engineers were no more deserving of an extra pay increase than other groups.

A couple of paragraphs showing that the force behind switching cash improvements to bonds was especially concerned about property taxes, yet represented wards which get most of the improvements.

Interpretations

It decidedly is not true that "what you don't know won't hurt you." On the contrary, in a democracy it is essential that everyone have access to as many facts as possible so that he can form proper judgments and influence public affairs. Increasingly since the end of World War II, journalistic organizations have been alarmed at the extent to which secrecy *de facto* and *de jure* has led to distortions in the news. Sometimes it has taken days, weeks, months or longer to ascertain the truth regarding some major political decision or action. By then it may be too late to undo considerable harm.

At a recent meeting of the A.P.M.E., the veteran New York *Times* political writer, James B. Reston, declared:

> The whole future of reporting depends on telling intelligently what is going on in the world. The world is getting more complicated every year.
>
> Explanatory writing is the field in which we can excel. You cannot merely report the literal truth. You have to explain it.
>
> But you have to pay a price for explanatory writing. You pay first in the length of stories. You can't say stories should be brief and explanatory too.
>
> Explanatory writing is a matter of judgment. The judgment may be wrong from time to time. You have to give the interpretive writer leeway. You also have to pay in more time. If a man is tired by a day of work, he won't be in the mood to write an analytical piece late in the evening.
>
> The explanatory writer is the lens through which you see what is not obvious. He reads the "fine print" for you.

At the same session John Hightower, AP diplomatic writer, said:

> We have a terrific responsibility in writing the essential truth. I think that the AP must always stick to certain fundamentals. Our basic job is to tell people what happens. But there has been an increasing feeling that isn't all.

Foremost among those who advocated and campaigned for interpretation is Lester Markel, associate editor of the New York *Times*. The following extract from his article, "The Case for Interpretation," in the April 1, 1953, *Bulletin* of the A.S.N.E., is typical of his numerous comments on the subject:

> Interpretation, as I see it, is the deeper sense of the news. It places a particular event in the larger flow of events. It is the color, the atmosphere, the human element that give meaning to a fact. It is, in short, setting, sequence, and, above all, significance.

There is a vast difference between interpretation and opinion. And the distinction is of the utmost importance. Three elements, not two, are involved in this debate: first, news; second, interpretation; third, opinion. To take a primitive example:

To say that Senator McThing is investigating the teaching of Patagonian in the schools is news.

To explain why Senator McThing is carrying on this investigation is interpretation.

To remark that Senator McThing should be ashamed of himself is opinion.

Interpretation is an objective judgment based on background knowledge of a situation, appraisal of an event. Editorial judgment, on the other hand, is a subjective judgment; it may include an appraisal of the facts but there is an additional and distinctive element, namely, emotional impact.

Opinion should be confined, almost religiously, to the editorial page; interpretation is an essential part of the news. This is vital and it cannot have too much emphasis.

I see no difference between "interpretation" and "background." Of course, part of interpretation may be the setting out of some antecedent facts—and this many editors consider "background" as distinguished from "interpretation." But interpretation is much more than shirttail material; it is in addition to the presentation of the pertinent facts, present and past, an effort to assay the meaning of those facts.

CAUSES AND MOTIVES

The probing reporter keeps on asking "why?" as he seeks the news behind the news. He knows that official proclamations and carefully prepared press releases may conceal causes and motives which preceded the spot or "end result" news of the moment. So he digs beneath the surface.

Sometimes it is possible to conjecture. For instance, if a mayor and corporation counsel have disagreed frequently in public, the reasons for the latter's impending resignation would seem to be obvious. Too often, however, newspaper columnists and others, acting on rumors and tips from "persons close to" or "usually reliable sources," may be wrong. If, for instance, the mayor and corporation counsel announce after a conference that they have settled their differences and, in fact, now "see eye to eye," only a naïve journalist would accept the announcement on its face value. To obtain the "real lowdown," however, may be difficult or impossible. Perhaps the counsel threatened to make a public statement which would be embarrassing to the mayor. Perhaps he agreed to "go along" on some current matter in exchange for a promise of political support at some future date. Perhaps the mayor indicated he would withdraw some patronage from the counsel's followers. The possibilities are many and the responsible journalist must be careful not to give currency to gossip, rumor and surmise.

Once a large company with plants in several cities announced it intended to close its factory in City A and shift operations to City B. The announcement included a strong statement of regret by management, praise for City A and the like but explained that it had become necessary to retrench, operate closer to its supply of raw materials and avoid the necessity of investing in costly new machinery. This sounded reasonable but an experienced reporter "smelled a rat" and started snooping. Before long he learned that months earlier the company had negotiated a contract with a union local in City B at a wage rate much lower than that which prevailed in City A. The City B union accepted the deal as it would mean jobs for several thousand unemployed members. Further probing revealed that this act was considered by City A unionists to be a "sell-out" and was part of the campaign of a certain national labor leader to increase his strength. The City B union consisted mainly of his followers whereas those in City A belonged to a rival faction within the national organization. Facts such as these are necessary for a proper understanding of the news. The free press has been called a watchdog on government. It can perform no more worthwhile function than to scrutinize carefully everything which affects the public interest.

SIGNIFICANCE

Referring a proposal to a committee may mean either that its enactment into law is being accelerated or that it is being killed. The perspicacious newsgatherer should know which and should so inform his readers. The same for all other acts of all branches of government. Readers are able to understand the significance of parliamentary and diplomatic maneuvering, but it must be pointed out to them by someone who keeps close check.

When a convicted person is sentenced to a long term of imprisonment, it is customary to point out the minimum time that he would have to serve before being eligible for release on parole. When a deadline passes for filing or withdrawing a petition, it should be pointed out what thereby becomes possible or impossible. If a diplomat attends one function and boycotts another, there may or may not be significant repercussions. In some cases, in other words, it is not difficult to explain consequences objectively. In others, a certain amount of guesswork may be necessary, in which case the rule of caution must be invoked.

As Erwin D. Canham, editor of the *Christian Science Monitor*, has put it:

> Mere publication of spot news in newspapers is not enough, and most newspapers have acted on that assumption for some time. The news must be clarified, explained, interpreted and integrated with other news. The commentators do that on the radio too. But people still demand the printed word. They still can't quite depend on what they hear.
>
> Also, today's news is increasingly complicated. Therefore newspaper writers must be increasingly expert. They must be specialists in various subjects. Big news stories of the world can no longer be covered by a bright boy just off the police beat. Joseph Pulitzer recognized this fact half a century ago when he projected his post-graduate journalism school. This trend will greatly intensify. It takes a good man to explain to the lay reader the workings of the atomic bomb.

ANALYSIS

Long and/or complicated documents, including ordinances and statutes, must be analyzed so that they can be understood. This often is merely a job of tedious objective reporting to explain what now is forbidden, allowed or required and who will be affected in what way. Often the analyst will discover ramifications and repercussions which escaped even the lawmakers.

Speeches by important persons are analyzed almost immediately by journalists and later by scholars. What the speaker emphasizes, the number of times he mentions a particular matter, and what he omits are noted. Qualitative judgment enters into evaluating the importance of gestures, facial expressions, tone of voice, pauses in delivery and the like and also in estimating the reaction of a visible audience. It is not difficult to note the amount and duration of applause, of course, but the intangibles are so many that great restraint is needed by the reporter. The audience, for instance, may be easily identifiable as partisan to begin with. Nevertheless, how it reacts is part of the complete coverage.

Often explanation is needed for proper analysis. This is often true of crime records. Changes in the frequency of certain types of offenses may be seasonal. The population complexion of areas may change during a reporting period. Police departments have been known to alter their methods of reporting, even with the intention of making the results seem better than they should. An example would be to list automobiles as missing instead of stolen.

COMPARISONS

As with crime statistics, so with the budgets of public and private bodies, achievements of athletes, votes received by candidates and numerous other matters, the reader wants to know how the present compares with the past. Is something more or less, higher or lower, better or worse? Answers to such questions must be given with all possible influencing factors considered so as not to be deceptive. It would, for instance, be misleading to cite an expenditure as twice that for a comparable item some time in the past without taking into consideration changes in the value of the dollar, population increases, changing needs and demands and so forth.

Political party platforms can be compared with each other and with those of previous years. Faced with a vexatious local problem, public officials and newspapers may send representatives to other communities to study what steps were taken there by way of solution. Whenever a disaster of importance occurs, it is common journalistic practice to prepare sidebars, often in the form of charts or tabulations, to show how the immediate catastrophe compares in intensity with others of the past.

Old-timers are prone to draw historical parallels, to feel that some contemporary event is "just like" one they recall from years before; they feel they have "lived through this before," possibly when they observe a widespread practice which they consider undesirable, as excessive installment buying, stock market speculation, real estate booms and the like. There is no gainsaying the fact that history teaches many valuable lessons, but what may seem to be history repeating itself may not be that at all. Numerous cities previously tried and abandoned services which today are orthodox, as parking meters, traffic signals, one-way streets and off-street parking, to mention only examples in one area. Increasing populations and automobile ownership created new conditions for which new remedies no longer were premature.

Reform movements come and go in many communities. One reason for their failure to last often is the tendency of many supporters to become lackadaisical after the immediate first objective has been attained. History does prove that eternal vigilance is a prerequisite for a properly functioning democracy.

FORECASTS

Giving a news story a "tomorrow" angle often is a form of interpretation. Based on his analysis of an action by the city council, a reporter can predict new employment, building, police activities and the like. He can see "trouble ahead" for certain groups as the result of a sweeping court decision and business advantages to others. A drastic price cut by one retail establishment usually results in a price war among competitors. Tightening child labor laws may have the immediate effect of throwing a certain number of minors out of work.

When it comes to predicting beyond the immediate effect, as that the unemployed juveniles will become delinquent, the reporter may be merely speculating. He should draw on expert opinion and historical example and still be slow about making deductions. The death of a prominent figure may or may not clear the way toward a reconciliation between disputing factions, lead to a struggle for succession to a position of power or destroy the chances for achieving a certain goal. The expert can point out the possibilities but he should not forget that some pundits have lost the confidence of their audiences by excessive smugness which the future exposed as such.

Providing Perspective

News does not consist only in specific incidents which can be written up with clearcut inclusion of all of the five *w*'s. Ideas are news. So are ideologies, trends of thought, psychological situations and similar intangibles. It is not highbrow to believe that it would be a better world if more newspaper readers were aware of social, political, economic and other stresses and strains which often must be written about without definite news pegs. The "think piece" is a comparatively old journalistic device, but its use constantly is being broadened to include areas previously reserved for research scholars.

As Robert E. Garst, assistant managing editor of the New York *Times*, wrote in the *Nieman Reports*:

> Too much of past reporting has dealt only with the surface facts—the spot news—and too rarely has dug into reasons for them.
>
> A race riot, a prison outbreak, a bad slum condition—even a murder—has a social background, deeply rooted perhaps in the customs, traditions, and economic conditions of a region or community; but it is there and

discoverable. It's the newspaper's job, it seems to me, to discover it. Only with that knowledge can a remedy be found for many of the ills that affect us.

RÉSUMÉS

News weeklies, monthly digest magazines and weekly newspaper news reviews got their start during the depression years and appealed to persons in all walks of life who sought understanding in the midst of confusion. They have continued as an adjunct to quick spotnews reporting to provide recapitulations or résumés of series of fast-happening events. Few occurrences are treated as isolated happenings but as related to other events preceding and following them.

In addition to weekly news reviews, newspapers use "wrap-up" articles on running stories such as legislative assemblies, court trials, political campaigns and the like. In such stories, the expert reporter treats the events of a number of days, usually a week, as constituting material for a single story. Readers' memories are refreshed and relationships are pointed out. Often a condensed chronological recapitulation of the news is sufficient. In other cases, interpretation is added. This week, the observant reviewer may write, a certain objective came closer to realization because of this or that train of events. Defense strategy, another may explain, became clearer as cross-examination of prosecution witnesses continued in a court trial. A public official took two steps forward and one backward under observation by a knowledgeable journalist. And so on, all in the attempt to round up the events of a period into a comprehensive single story with proper perspective.

At the end of any session of the state legislature, a résumé of its activities is a journalistic must. Annual or semi-annual appraisals of the handling of his official acts by a public official are in the same category. The news reviewer often takes a second look at the cumulative record about each part of which he previously has composed separate accounts.

SURVEYS

When similar news occurs in a number of places, a journalistic medium may conduct a survey to find out what the over-all situation happens to be. Perhaps attempts to enact similar legislation were made in a number of states, in which case a compilation of the results is significant. Let disaster of any kind occur in one place and a follow-up survey reveals how widespread are conditions believed to have been its cause.

Newspapers have conducted surveys to determine the death rates on transcontinental highways, the outcomes of referenda on school bond issues, the use of prison labor on private projects, the attitude of condemned prisoners toward capital punishment, the extent of racial and religious discrimination in housing, schooling and job opportunities, the increase in the ownership of yachts, and on many and many other matters. Some of the material, though not quite so up-to-the-minute, might have been obtained from public and private research agencies.

In drawing conclusions from any kind of data, the press must avoid the error which professional researchers and pollsters also must avoid, that of inadequacy or lack of representativeness of the sample. It is incorrect to write, "Public opinion today here is that or that" unless one has exhaustively questioned persons in all walks of life, something it is rarely possible for a newspaperman to do. Even an impressive group of interviewees within a given area may not be typical. There is no field in which unanimity exists among experts. Quoting leaders is good journalism but minorities also should be contacted and exaggeration always avoided.

INVESTIGATIONS

Any newspaper with standing in its community is constantly being importuned to "look into" this or that, which usually means to uncover facts which it allegedly is in the public interest be known but which someone is attempting to conceal. The annals of American journalism are replete with examples of successful ventures of this sort. Many of them, in fact, have resulted in Pulitzer or other prizes for community service.

Annoying and time consuming as it may become to observe the rule, it is unsafe to ignore tipsters, no matter how unreliable or crackpot they may seem to be. Maybe the policeman whose neighbor cannot understand how he is able to afford an expensive car, *did* inherit a large sum of money. On the other hand, his affluence may be the clue to scandal involving others as well as himself.

No special attributes are required of the investigative reporter except a sharp inquisitive mind and familiarity with the area of his investigation. The investigative reporter seldom plays detective in the sense of shadowing persons. Rather, his quest more often takes him to public records where he uncovers information about which to query interviewees. In print, these facts usually speak for themselves. This was true as regards the assignment given Edward R. Cony, *Wall Street Journal* news editor, for which he was awarded the Pulitzer prize for reporting of national affairs. As the paper summarized it:

> In his prize-winning story, Mr. Cony disclosed that Carrol Shanks, then president of Prudential Insurance Co. of America, was in position to make a substantial saving in his income taxes as a result of a personal transaction with Georgia-Pacific. At the time, Mr. Shanks was a director of Georgia-Pacific, which had received over $50 million of loans from Prudential over a five-year period.
>
> The article told how Mr. Shanks had purchased 13,000 acres of Oregon timberland and then immediately sold it to Georgia-Pacific for the same price he paid for it, plus costs of financing the transaction. Mr. Shanks financed the purchase with a $3.9 million bank loan. Since interest on this loan would be tax deductible, it was estimated that Mr. Shanks might save as much as $400,000 on his tax bill over the five-year life of the loan.
>
> Mr. Shanks, while maintaining there was nothing unethical about the transaction, subsequently disposed of his interest in the financing and resigned from Prudential, citing as a reason "my highly publicized personal transaction" with Georgia-Pacific.
>
> The story also revealed the personal dealings which Owen Cheatham, chairman, and John Brandis, senior vice-president, of Georgia-Pacific, had had with the company.
>
> Shortly after the story appeared, Georgia-Pacific announced it had acquired Plywood Products Corp., a plywood concern which had been owned principally by Mr. Brandis, trusts settled by him, and members of his family. The Wall Street Journal story had detailed Plywood Products' extensive business dealings with Georgia-Pacific. Georgia-Pacific is currently facing a stockholder suit which charges, among other things, that when Georgia-Pacific acquired Plywood Products it paid Mr. Brandis and his associates a price excessive "by at least $2 million."
>
> Mr. Cony, in addition to interviewing Mr. Shanks in New Jersey and Georgia-Pacific officials in Oregon, spent many hours probing records in New York and numerous county seats in Oregon. Ray Schrick, manager of The Wall Street Journal's Portland bureau, aided Mr. Cony with research and reporting on the Oregon phase of the story.

Not all journalist investigations result in exposés or crusades. Sometimes exactly the opposite occurs and the public interest is served by revealing that rumors and charges are groundless. To avoid merely whitewashing, however, the reporter must not be so naïve as to accept uncritically whatever he may be told by interested parties. He must observe first-hand and check conflicting statements of fact and opinion against each other. At the same time, he must also avoid a chip-on-the-shoulder attitude so as not to give anyone the impression that he is out to "get" him regardless of the truth.

All of which just adds up to the advice: be thorough, be open-minded, be fair. There is no better advice which can be given to a newsgatherer whatever the assignment.

STUNTS

Often the best, perhaps the only way to investigate a situation is from the inside. Edgar May of the Buffalo *Evening News* won a Pulitzer prize for his series of articles after working for three months as a caseworker for the Erie County Department of Social Welfare. Ted Smart of the Chicago *Daily News* won several citations for his exposé of conditions in the Chicago Bridewell to which he got himself committed as a common drunk. Several official investigations resulted after Edward Williams, Milwaukee *Journal* reporter, spent ten days in the House of Correction posing as a vagrant.

Other reporters have obtained employment as guards or attendants in prisons, mental hospitals and other public institutions. The existence of illegal gambling has been exposed by investigative reporters who were supplied with money and told to find bookmakers with whom to place bets. Because of the growing complaint by teachers that students are unruly, reporters with the proper credentials have obtained teaching positions or have acted as substitutes in the classroom to observe first-hand.

The opportunities for such "undercover" journalism are boundless. Usually, some properly qualified official, as a judge or social worker, is "in" on the stunt, often to legalize it and, in any case, to soften adverse criticisms of entrapment or other unethical conduct. Certainly the responsibility is great not to yield to the temptation to merely "make a case" in the interest of a sensational story. It is easy to find that for which one earnestly is looking. The reporter and newspaper are vulnerable unless the highest principles of ethical journalism are observed.

SITUATIONS AND TRENDS

Getting his idea from an article on the subject in a national magazine, a city editor assigned a reporter to "find out how much moonlighting there is in this community." Other editors have sought the answers to such questions as, "What do we do for the mentally retarded in our town?" "What about juvenile delinquency among girls?" "Are there any independent grocers left?" "What's happening to our wild life?"

Often such assignments result in feature articles concerning little-known or off-the-beaten-path persons or groups. In other cases, there may be forthcoming broader expositions of current situations to which the journalistic limelight is applied. The net result is a better acquaintance with all aspects of the life of the community and possibly an arousal of civic interest in improvement where needed.

No reporter should start on an assignment of this sort without adequate preparation which should include, not merely examination of the publication's own clipping files but also the reading of books, magazine articles and other material to acquaint himself with the aspects of the situation which he should bear in mind during his fact-finding. When the reporter encounters someone with views contrary to those which he believes to be orthodox, he should avoid altercation. Instead, he should tactfully request his news source to comment on the viewpoint of "the other side" as he understands it.

Fortified with information from a number of other places, the perceptive reporter may conclude that what he is studying is not just a local phenomenon but part of a widespread trend. Farmers on the fringes of suburban areas, for instance, may be keeping land out of cultivation in expectation of selling their property to urban developers. "Blockbusting" to circumvent racial prejudice by real-estate interests, sit-in demonstrations, sympathetic picketing, panty raids by college boys, fads in games, dress, music, and the like may be national or international in extent. The locally written feature can stress home-town manifestations but would be inadequate if it did not mention the broader aspects.

Ora Spaid did a colossally successful job for the Louisville *Courier-Journal* when he investigated post-basketball game fights between rival gangs of high school boys. The following extracts, approximately the middle-third of the first of three articles, indicate how Spaid tackled the assignment, writing as the careful reporter and specialist-expert that he is, having been a social worker before he turned to journalism:

Athletics
One of those not-new conditions is overemphasis of athletics.

A high-school basketball game has become an orgy of emotionalism closely resembling a voodoo ritual. Big crowds pack into small gyms.

Drums pound a savage throb, and pretty little girls whip up frenzied partisan spirit that doesn't let up even when play begins.

Sportsmanship is usually evident—as in the exchange of "Hello" yells at the beginning. But it breaks down easily, as when a player from the other team steps to the line for a crucial free throw and the crowd jeers and shouts to distract him.

Coaches talk of the "home-court advantage"—the fact that the crowd is so partisan you can't expect a fair contest.

Emotions Stirred

Emotional pitch is built before the game in school-wide "pep assemblies," a practice that teachers consider "a necessary evil." A psychology teacher says pointedly that pep assemblies "are a real study in mass psychology sometimes."

The question is: Where does school spirit leave off and hysteria begin?

The concept of high-school sports for participation long ago lost out to the necessity of winning. Coaches build the equivalent of farm systems to produce material for winning teams. A coach becomes as much a victim of "ratings" as a television show; there's a tendency to enlarge the point spread over a defeated opponent to gain a higher rating.

Utterly lost is the grace of losing. High-school girls weep as if death had descended when their teams lose. Fathers grumble about ineffective coaches.

But gainsaying overemphasis of athletics is not enough. Why are athletics overemphasized?

It's a result, some say, of "urbanization." The exodus of people from the cities of recent decades and attendant flight to the suburbs produces a lonely-in-the-crowd society.

It also produces the big school, a factor that men like Richard Van Hoose, superintendent of Jefferson County schools, and Sam V. Noe, his counterpart in Louisville schools, hold as the root cause of many problems.

The Big School

Today's suburban high school of 2,500 or more students is almost what yesterday's college was.

Let Earl Duncan, principal of the 2,600-student Waggener High School, tell of some of the problems.

"In a school of 2,600, only 12 boys can play basketball, but certainly a lot more would like to," he said. "Only five youngsters can be elected to offices in a graduating class of 350. Think how many that leaves out."

It's a case of being lost in a big school.

A bright boy in a big suburban school came home last week with failing grades. He told his mother, "I'm not good at sports; I'm not in the band; I can't get on the school paper. I've just lost all interest in school."

Most young people don't lose interest—they plunge. If they can't find something they can participate in actively, they participate vicariously. The school is something they can belong to, something to "give them identity," as the psychologists say. So they become rabid fans, fanatic followers.

May Boil Over

But nonparticipation isn't too satisfying; there's not much opportunity to blow off steam, unless in violent rooting. And it's always possible that this pent-up steam may boil over into violence, particularly if there is some way to rationalize it, like defending the school's honor or avenging a lost game.

Big schools build up tension in ways other than pep assemblies—subtler ways, often overlooked.

Principal Duncan points out that when you have only one gymnasium and it is given over to varsity teams, there is no place for other youngsters to play. To "make the best use of facilities," in gym periods or after school, the play must be scheduled and organized. Regimentation is another word for it—constant supervision, no opportunity to just horse around.

Drop in at one of these big schools at noon hour and you will see long lines of students in the cafeteria. The sheer impossibility of feeding all students at once means they eat in shifts. And mark this: lunch hour usually lasts only 20 minutes. Not only that, but by the time a student gets his food, he may have only 10 minutes to eat it. Of necessity, he must "bolt his food" or miss his next class.

Difference Is Great

Compare this with the paper-sack days when pupils brought their lunches, ate leisurely and spent the rest of a long lunch hour dozing under a tree or breaking the tension of long hours at a desk in a make-up ball game.

This means that today's school children put in a 7-hour day with little let-up, seldom released from supervision. Even recess is now a matter of "supervised play," and in some schools, children are given a grade for lunchroom conduct.

Then there is homework. There always has been homework, but it seems to a lot of students that teachers are trying to close up the missile gap with Russia by the sheer bulk of homework they assign. The youngsters respond, not by learning from homework, but merely by "getting it done."

Getting it done means more hours under supervision, this time from a Mom or Dad anxious to see a good report card.

All this adds up to this: youngsters today are under greater tension than ever before but have less opportunity to dissipate it.

PART TWO

Handling Important Assignments

Hath Difficulties?
Behold the Editor

Consider the editor. He weareth purple and fine linen. His abode is amongst the mansions of the rich. His wife hath her limousine and his first born sporteth a racing car that can hit her up in forty flat.

Lo! All the people breaketh their necks to hand him money. A child is born unto the wife of a merchant in the bazaar. The physician getteth 10 gold plunks. The editor writeth a stick and a half and telleth the multitude that the child tippeth the beam at nine pounds. Yea, he lieth even as a centurion. And the proud father giveth him a Cremo.

Behold, the young one groweth up and graduateth. And the editor putteth into his paper a swell notice. Yea, a peach of a notice. He telleth of the wisdom of the young woman, and of her exceeding comeliness. Like the rose of Sharon is she and her gown is played up to beat the band. And the dressmaker getteth two score and four iron men. And the editor getteth a note of thanks from the SGG.

The daughter goeth on a journey. And the editor throweth himself on the story of the farewell party. It runneth a column, solid. And the fair one remembreth him from afar off with a picture postal card that costeth six for a jitney.

Behold, she returneth and the youth of the city fall down and worship. She picketh one and Lo, she picketh a lemon. But the editor calleth him one of our most promising young men and getteth away with it. And they send unto him a bid to the wedding feast and behold, the bids are fashioned by Muntgummery Hawbuck, in a far city.

Flowery and long is the wedding notice which the editor printeth. The minister getteth 10 bones. The groom standeth the editor off for a twelve-month subscription.

All flesh is grass and in time the wife is gathered into the silo. The minister getteth his bit. The editor printeth a death notice, two columns of obituary, three lodge notices, a cubit of poetry and a card of thanks. And he forgetteth to read proof on the head, and the darned thing cometh out "Gone to Her Last Roasting Place."

And all that are akin to the deceased jumpeth on the editor with exceeding great jumps. And they pulleth out their ads and cancelleth their subscriptions and they swing the hammer unto the third and fourth generations.

Canst thou beat it? [*Cowlitz County Advocate*]

11

Persons and Personalities

I GOSSIP IS NEWS
  1. The Personal Element
  2. Sources of Brevities
  3. Faults to Avoid

II TYPES OF PERSONAL NEWS
  1. Births
  2. Guests
  3. Newcomers
  4. Employment
  5. Trips
  6. Vacations
  7. College Students

III THE SOCIETY PAGE
  1. Types of Society News
  2. Elements in Society News

IV COVERING SOCIETY NEWS
  1. Style
  2. Receptions
  3. Coming-out Parties
  4. Engagements
  5. Showers
  6. Weddings
  7. Picking the Feature
  8. Style

V GOSSIP COLUMNS
  1. Anecdotes
  2. Night Life
  3. Entertainment Places
  4. Society

VI PERSONALITY INTERVIEWS

VII ETHICS

EVERYONE LIKES TO SEE HIS NAME OR THAT OF A FRIEND OR ACQUAINTANCE in print. This is as true of the city dweller as of anyone who resides in a small town or on a farm. Large newspapers do not refrain from publishing more items concerning births, newcomers to the community, trips, parties, engagements, weddings, illnesses and deaths, because they fail to recognize the reader interest in such events but merely because of lack of space. Gossip among urbanites still largely concerns such occurrences as they involve relatives, friends and acquaintances. Community newspapers within the large cities and suburban newspapers are capitalizing increasingly on the metropolitan press' inability any longer to devote much space to such news.

213

Gossip Is News

THE PERSONAL ELEMENT

In the country weekly, serving a community in which acquaintanceships are proportionately greater, the "personals" column never has ceased to be the chief reader attention-getter. Larger papers are using more and more news briefs after a short period during which there was a feeling that these were "hickish." Today, small and medium-sized newspapers are ceasing in the attempt to emulate their metropolitan betters and are concerned with how to serve better the needs of their own readers. Reader interest in gossip about "big shots" in the national field having been proved through the popular reception of syndicated columns from New York, Washington and Hollywood, local "It Happened in—," "Heard about—" and similar columns are growing in frequency.

SOURCES OF BREVITIES

Haunting the waiting rooms of railroad stations, hotel lobbies, clubrooms, floral shops and delicatessen stores and stopping to chat with friends on street corners or at their places of business still is excellent "breaking in" for the cub reporter. Not only does he receive items or tips for the "local happenings" or "news in brief" column but, while ostensibly in search for such comparatively trivial information, he comes across numerous first-rate stories.

Typical of the one-paragraph personals which the reporter may obtain just by "hanging around" or by telephone conversations with his friends, are the following:

> Mrs. Edwin P. Morrow of Washington, D.C., is visiting at the home of her son, Charles R. Morrow, 636 Sherman avenue. Mrs. Morrow is the widow of the late Edwin P. Morrow, former governor of Kentucky.

> Miss Eva Rathbone entertained her fellow members in the Puella Sunday school class of First Presbyterian church at dinner Friday night at her home, 133 N. Prairie avenue. During the evening, the girls worked on patch quilts to be distributed by the Women's Missionary society of the church.

> Five Milltown students at Augustana college will spend the Thanksgiving weekend with their parents here. They are . . .

Some papers which do not have a special column for short items of this sort use them as fillers; others restrict their use to the society page. In the country and rural town weeklies such items concern purchases of new farm equipment, planting and harvesting, unusual crops and the like. City dwellers may laugh at such news, but if they have moved to the city from the country or a small place, it is what they look for when the home-town paper arrives each week. And it's what they want to know about their friends in the big city.

FAULTS TO AVOID

The three most serious errors to avoid in writing short personals or brevities are: (1) underwriting, (2) overwriting, (3) stylistic banality.

Underwriting means writing as a brief what should have been a longer news or feature story, or not getting all the essentials into the brevity itself. The properly written personal really is a news lead. As such, it is good if it fulfills the requirements of a good lead and bad if it doesn't. Note how the following barren brevities might have been made more nearly complete and interesting while still remaining brevities:

Insufficient
A. L. Scobey, 1434 Ellis street, has returned from a two-week trip to San Francisco.

Insufficient
Mr. and Mrs. Edward L. Parkhouse, 683 Pulliam avenue, entertained 16 guests Monday night at a theater party.

Sufficient
A. L. Scobey, 1434 Ellis street, returned today from San Francisco with the prize given the delegate traveling the farthest distance to attend the annual convention of the Fraternal Order of Leopards there last week. Mr. Scobey represented the local Leopards lodge of which he is commander. The prize was a traveling bag.

Sufficient
To celebrate their 25th wedding anniversary, Mr. and Mrs. Edward L. Parkhouse, 683 Pulliam avenue, entertained 16 guests Monday night at a theater party. Formerly it was believed the Parkhouses had been married only 15 years, but they chose this belated occasion to reveal that they had been secretly wed for ten years before making an announcement.

It easily can be imagined how either of these, especially the second, could have been elaborated into a much longer story with considerable reader interest. Unfortunately, it is not presumptuous to imagine a beginning reporter's getting no more than the original items cited.

Articles have been written by despairing state or county editors on the inability of rural correspondents to sense news values. Reporters may be able to pick important names out of hotel registers, but they may miss the fact that the out-of-town visitor listed inconspicuously among those "in town for the day" is negotiating with the directors of a bank for its purchase, consulting with Chamber of Commerce officials about the establishment of a new industry, or applying for a position in the local schools or for the pastorate of a local church.

Overwriting, on the other hand, means going to the opposite extreme of including irrelevant and unimportant details of little or no interest even to residents or a small community. Such padding may be for the purpose of pleasing a friend or an advertiser, but too much of it alienates more general readers than it attracts. It should be paid for at regular advertising rates.

> Employment of an agronomist of high repute by the Ohio Sugar company is an innovation that will meet hearty appreciation by Henry county farmers.
> Mr. McLaughlin, an O.S.U. graduate, who has had supervision of the State Experiment station at Holgate for the past six years, and prior to that gained valuable experience at the Wooster experiment station, will have charge of this new department beginning Jan. 1.
> Mr. McLaughlin's advice to farmers and beet growers will be of incalculable benefit and every farmer is urged to avail himself of his wise counsel. There are so many perplexing problems that confront the farmer that no doubt this new department will be most heartily welcomed. Adaptability of the different Henry county soils to the various crops is one thing where Mr. McLaughlin's knowledge of agronomy will serve the farmer who seeks his advice most beneficially.
> While Mr. McLaughlin may, to a certain degree, specialize in beet culture, he is equally well informed on every phase of agriculture and his advice is free for the asking. The Ohio Sugar company is maintaining this almost solely for the benefit of growers and it hopes every farmer will avail himself of this service which is proffered free.

The most frequent criticism of personals, as used in country weeklies and small-town newspapers, is excessive informality and maudlin rhetoric. A chatty column is one thing; a banal one is another. Too much opinion, the extension of too many good wishes and insipid predictions are sickening to even the uneducated reader, although it is a remarkable fact that many persons who submit unsolicited personal items to large city papers often write them in such a manner. The following illustrative examples of misdirected energy were taken from small-town newspapers:

W. P. Nelson is again on the job at the bank following a siege with chicken pox. Walt had a real mixup with his "kid" disease and he says he was sure sick. Aside from being "well marked" he is okay.

The new band leader, Don Walters, put his Hubbard group through its paces last Saturday and again Tuesday and Wednesday of this week. The youngsters are all eager and ready to go to Iowa City this coming Saturday and do themselves and their community proud. Everything points to a good chance for them to come through with shining colors. The group expects to leave town about 7 o'clock in the morning so as to give the performers time to get some of the kinks from riding out of their system.

So let's cheer them on with three big rahs. All right, here we go—rah! Rah! RAH!

We extend congratulations to Mr. and Mrs. Dave Heden, who were recently united in marriage. We are not acquainted with the groom, but his bride, formerly Agnes Attleson, is well known here as this was her former home though she has been working in Chicago for several years. She has hosts of friends who wish her much joy, for she was a very nice young lady. They expect to make their home in Chicago, where the groom has employment.

Types of Personal News

BIRTHS

Characteristic of the growing frankness of newspapers in recent years is the prominence now given to announcements of impending parenthood on the part of prominent persons. The gossip columns, notably Walter Winchell's, were a large factor in breaking down the scrupulous rule against mentioning "blessed events" until they had occurred. Pregnancy, once a taboo topic, is even recognized today by motion pictures and television.

For the routine birth notice the reporter should obtain:

1. Names and address of parents.
2. Time and place of birth.
3. Weight of the baby.
4. Sex of the baby.
5. The name, if chosen.

The mother's maiden name may be included if she has not been married more than a few years, if the couple is living in another city and the girl's married name is unfamiliar locally, or if she uses her maiden name professionally. If the date of the marriage is mentioned, care must be taken to give it correctly. Libel suits have resulted from mistakes of this sort.

Since all parents are "proud," that fact is of no news value. And it never has been proved scientifically that newly born babies bounce. A baby's rosy cheeks, lusty lungs and dimpled chin may be taken for granted. "Daughter" or "son" is better than "baby girl" or "baby boy." Do not use "cherub" or "the new arrival to bless the home" and the like.

The name of the attending physician should not be included in a birth notice, or, in fact, in any story of illness or death. This rule is broken in the case of a person of great prominence and in stories in which the physician himself plays a part, as a participant in an accident, etc. Ordinarily, however, the name of the physician is left out, frequently at the request of the local medical society.

Whether the fact that "mother and baby are both doing nicely" is to be included probably is debatable. Ordinarily, however, it seems as though good health should be assumed; if either child or mother is in danger that fact may be included. Likewise, the number, names and ages of other children of the parents of a newly born baby may or may not be mentioned.

> Mr. and Mrs. Ralph Elsasser, 711 Renrose ave., became the parents of a daughter in Swedish-American hospital on Monday. Named Marie Lynette, the infant weighed 5 pounds, 5 ounces at birth. She joins a brother, Terry Lee, 12; and a sister, Vicki Lynn, 8. [Rockford *Star*]

> Mr. and Mrs. Jimmie Collins, Stonington, welcomed their first child, a son, at 4:56 (CST) o'clock Friday night in the St. Vincent Memorial Hospital. He weighed 6 pounds and 6 ounces. The mother is the former Anna Marie Jones. [Taylorville (Ill.) *Breeze-Courier*]

A frequent temptation to a beat reporter is to turn in a story telling of how some new father on his beat acted or announced the event to his co-workers. Such items must be adroitly handled to avoid the common fault of banality.

> It was cigars for everybody today in the office of Mitchell C. Robin, clerk of the Probate court. He explained that his wife, Mrs. Dorothy Robin, had given birth to their first child, a girl, at the Michael Reese hospital.

> Menlo Park, Calif.—(AP)—Sammy Yates showed up in the eighth grade at Central school with a cigar box.
> He opened it and passed out all-day suckers, explaining: "I'm a brother." [Chicago *Daily News*]

Siamese twins, triplets and quadruplets are unusual enough to rate considerably more than routine treatment. Quintuplets are the news story of the year! Unusual weight or size, physical deformity or the circumstances under which birth took place may elevate the event above the level of the routine birth notice, as was the case in each of the following stories:

Wenatchee, Wash.—(UP)—Mr. and Mrs. W. E. Robinson of Entiat Valley claim to be parents of the first baby born in an auto trailer in the Pacific northwest. A daughter, Kay, was born to them in March.

The fire department ambulance crew in charge of Lieut. Irvin Martin aided the stork early Wednesday and a baby was presented to Mrs. Callie Burns, 21, 1216 Freeman avenue. Mother and infant were then taken to the general hospital.

Some newspapers "play" births more prominently than others. One way is to obtain pictures of the newly born together with short feature stories in which source of the name, brothers and sisters, date of birth or some feature angle may be emphasized. The following is a typical entry from such a column:

Even if she is a girl, the first child of Mr. and Mrs. William Clifford Richards Jr., 1415 Ashland avenue, was named for her father and is called Billie Mae. Her second name is the first name of her maternal grandmother. Weighing 8 pounds 14 ounces the addition who has made the Richards family a threesome, was born Dec. 2 at Evanston hospital.

GUESTS

Whenever a visiting dignitary is entertained at the White House it is news from coast to coast. There is nationwide interest also in the travels of celebrities of all sorts. Just as important are the comings and goings of "ordinary" folk within the circle of one's acquaintance.

Mr. and Mrs. Ralph J. Peterson and daughter Linda are visiting here from North Hollywood, Calif. They are sharing their stay with Mr. Peterson's brother-in-law and sister in Salt Lake City, Mr. and Mrs. Cleon Anderson, 1851 Harrison Ave., and Mrs. Peterson's mother in Ogden, Mrs. Fred King. The coast matron is the former Phyllis King of Ogden.

Among those entertaining for them during their visit are Mr. and Mrs. Ferdinand Peterson, 1370 E. 9th South; Mr. and Mrs. Jess R. Jensen, 1621 Princeton Ave.; and Mrs. Ray Whitmeyer of Ogden.

The Californians will visit with their son Scott in Army training at Grand Junction, Colo., before returning to Hollywood.

[Salt Lake City *Tribune*]

NEWCOMERS

Even in crowded city apartments, a new family in the building or neighborhood is an event, especially if both households have children through which some of the adults are bound to become acquainted if only for the purpose of discussing discipline. The habit of calling on newcomers virtually has disappeared in the larger cities but is still proper etiquette in the small town. In places of all sizes, curiosity at least must be satisfied. The newspaper is in the best position to appease it.

A one-sentence brevity announcing the change of residence on the real estate page or telling of a newcomer to the community may be all a newspaper feels it can afford. On the other hand, some newspapers are subscribing to commercial services which collect data on new residents in the community and are using the information for editorial as well as business purposes.

A newcomer's column serves the purpose both of extending a welcome and of acquainting old-timers with the special interests of the arrivals. Organizations similar to those with which members of the new families were affiliated in their former cities of residence can follow such a column to learn of possible additions to their own rolls.

>   Newcomer to Phoenix is Ballerina Eileen Colgrove, native of London, England.
>
>   She and her husband, Michael Thoday, live at 35 W. Enconto Blvd.
>
>   Among Miss Colgrove's diplomas she holds a fellowship, or top degree, from the Imperial Society of Teachers of Dancing in London. This includes degrees in national, ballet, and stage branches. She is a graduate of teachers' course of Sadler's Wells ballet company, and also holds diplomas from the National Association and Midland Association.
>
>   Miss Colgrove has done radio and television work on ballet education programs in both England and Canada. She was recently a teacher at the National Ballet Co. summer school session in Toronto. At the summer session she taught children, professional ballerinas, and teachers of ballet.
>
>   During her career she has taught some children from the royal family, including the Earl of Uxbridge and Lady Henrietta Paget.
>
>   In Phoenix she will instruct at the Ruth Freethy School of Dancing, 16 W. Cypress, beginning Sept. 19.   [Phoenix *Arizona Republic*]

EMPLOYMENT

It is difficult to enforce any rule against "free publicity" connected with new jobs. It is news when a large corporation elects a new president

PERSONS AND PERSONALITIES 221

or chairman of its board of directors. Similarly it is news when a friend or acquaintance changes his employment.

Franklin R. Raynor today resigned his position as office manager of the Grayson Real Estate company to accept a similar position with the South Side Realtors. In his new position he succeeds Vincent L. Coke who died recently.

Miss Sylvia Waters, 574 W. Sequoia place, left today for Minocqua, Wis., where she will become director of a Girl Scouts summer camp.

TRIPS

Friends are interested when anyone takes a trip but may be bored when he returns and insists on relating the commonplace. Nevertheless, a skillful reporter should be able to keep a returned traveler off a textbookish account of the glories of Niagara, the Lincoln Memorial or Yellowstone and find something in the peregrinations of most everyone, regardless of how well traveled the road taken may have been.

When a person goes away, the purpose of his trip may be news, as he may be combining business with pleasure, attending a convention, or returning to the scene of an interesting former experience. If the journey is a short one, to be completed in a day, emphasis should not be on the fact that the traveler left but that he is in the other city.

WEAK: Carol Winters left Jefferson City today to visit relatives in Columbia.

BETTER: Carol Winters is spending the weekend with relatives in Columbia.

The shortest type of brevity regarding a trip resembles the following:

Mr. and Mrs. Fred N. Sigman, 1415 N. Cherry street, have returned from a two weeks' visit with their son, Fred, Jr., an intern in General hospital, Boston.

Often a returned traveler has experiences to relate or opinions to express which are newsworthy.

BY MARJORIE MACCABE

Instead of dining on such delicacies of the French provinces as matelot sparnassienne in Champagne or poularde truffe along the Rhone this spring, Mrs. Frank Timberlake was partaking of Madrid's unattractive oranges or indescribable squid in thick black sauce.

This is what came of the projected gourmet tour of France planned by Camille Timberlake and Mrs. Anne Cope Moulder.

But let there be no misimpression of the edibility of Spain's oranges and squid. Mrs. Timberlake, who is an epicure as well as a sterling cook, found the loss of the matelot sparnassienne and the poularde truffe more than compensated for by the oranges ("magnificent, despite their appearance") and the squid (called "calamares en su tinta, and very tasty").

The mis-meshing of schedules that were to have taken the two attractive matrons on their provincial motor tour served to send them off instead to the discovery of Spain holding hypothetical rain-checks for the gourmet tour. [San Francisco *Chronicle*]

VACATIONS

Resorts and other vacation places maintain publicity departments to keep faraway newspapers informed of the arrivals and departures of persons from their communities. They also provide articles and pictures of the social notables enjoying themselves (as swimming, tennis, skiing, and so on). Newspapers send their own society page columnists to report the activities of vacationing colonists. The following paragraphs from one such column are typical:

Making the most of their vacation days are Misses Virginia Barrett and Joan Chandler (Carl Walden photo), pictured here at Macfadden-Deauville Cabana club, where they take part in water sports.... Tennis also is included in their summer recreation program.... Joan, daughter of the Everett W. Chandlers, Miami Shores, is a student at Stephens college, and Virginia's parents are Mr. and Mrs. William Barrett, Miami Shores.

A trip through the Canadian Rockies then on to Alaska is included in the vacation itinerary of Mr. and Mrs. Frank E. Ellis, Miami Beach, who plan to leave next Monday.

They will sail from Vancouver, B.C., and after they return from Alaska they will go to New York. They also plan a sojourn at Hot Springs, Ark., before they return home.

Joining vacation travelers on Monday, Miss Phyllis Brettell left by plane for New York.... Phyllis, a daughter of Mr. and Mrs. Clinton Brettell, 1355 Biaritz dr., Normany Isles, will visit her aunt, Mrs. William Hafer, in New York and later will be the guest of Mrs. William N. Guthrie in Woodmont, Conn.... Also, she will visit Miss Maeve O'Toole, a Miami Beach winter resident, at her home in Forest Hills, L.I., and will go to Larchmont, N.Y., to visit other friends before she returns home in September. [Miami *Herald*]

Another typical handling of news of vacations follows:

By Marie McNair

Looking forward to an opportunity to "get away from it all," Mrs. Mitchell Palmer is leaving Sunday for Lake Racquet in the Adirondacks and Mrs. Francis P. Garvan's luxurious camp, open again for the first time since the war.

Train service being what it is to that rather remote section of northern New York, Mrs. Palmer will try a plane from New York to Utica this time and motor the 60 miles from there to camp. It's that or land there by train and arouse the family at 4 A.M.

For almost a score of years Peggy Palmer has been a summer visitor to the Garvan camp. She has known the three boys, Francis, jr., Peter and Anthony, and their sister, Marcia, as enchanting small fry; said goodby to the young Garvans as they went off to war and will be present at Marcia's marriage to Frank Coyle in September.

Wednesday, Francis, jr.—better known as Pat—will celebrate his birthday and a big party's planned. Francis, you may remember, married the lovely Hope Jackson, so well known in Washington. While her husband served in the Air Intelligence, U.S.N., Mrs. Garvan was studying voice, made her debut as an opera singer in the leading role in Tosca in Hartford, Conn., last spring, and according to critics, is definitely slated for greater heights. [Washington *Post*]

COLLEGE STUDENTS

Directors of publicity at the nation's colleges and universities won't believe it, but to the average newspaper of any size a news item telling of the selection for a homecoming committee of some student from the city has greater news value than the commencement speaker's name, an addition to the curriculum, a solemn pronouncement by the dean of women or even a routine football victory. When the boys and girls return for vacations, win scholastic honors, and approach graduation and on many other occasions, the news gets prominent play and pictures are used.

Jack Perry, son of Mr. and Mrs. S. L. Perry, is playing the co-lead part in the Cornell Summer theater's production of "Under Canvas," comedy-drama of tent-show days. The story concerns the hectic lives of a typical tent-show group. "Under Canvas" will be presented to the public on Friday and Saturday nights, July 5 and 6.

Mr. Perry, a freshman at Cornell, is studying journalism and dramatic art. [Clarion (Iowa) *Wright County Monitor*]

As much a puzzle to Booster college regulars as for four years it was to members of the Suburban Football league is the passing attack of Wayne "Bossy" Wilbur, half-back on the Booster freshman team.

Wilbur, the son of Nellie Wilbur, 148 W. Jackson street, was the mainstay of the Milltown high school football team for three years, two of which he served as captain. . . .

The Society Page

When New York newspapers near the end of the last century began printing the guest lists of parties attended by members of the so-called 400, they made journalistic history. At first this "invasion of privacy" was resented, but through "leaks" and gate-crashing, the news continued to be obtained. Today the problem of most society editors is not how to get news but how to satisfy everyone wanting "nice" notices on the page.

The original and enduring appeal of the society page has been twofold: (1) to the vanity of those considered important enough to receive mention, (2) to the curiosity of all others regarding the glamorous way of life of their social superiors. In recent years, an increasingly large number of newspapers have come to regard these values as fictitious and to criticize the undemocratic "snob appeal" of the society page. For this and other reasons—including the headaches entailed in arbitrarily deciding who is and who is not socially important—the society page is waning. Much of the space formerly devoted to it is being given to news of the activities of clubs and to news of interest to women at all economic levels. Whereas such news formerly was sandwiched in on the society page, the trend now is to squeeze society news in on the club page or women's page. The glamour appeal now is provided by movie stars and other entertainers who get full treatment on other pages. They are the modern public heroines or goddesses, not the society matron.

TYPES OF SOCIETY NEWS

The typical society page or section consists mainly of the following kinds of news:

Parties: birthday, reunions, anniversary, coming-out, announcement, showers, weekend, house, theater, card and miscellaneous.
Teas, luncheons, dinners, banquets, suppers, cocktail parties and picnics.
Meetings and announcements of meetings of women's organizations, if there is no club page.
Receptions.
Dances and balls.

Benefits, bazaars and the like.
Personal items, if not used in another part of the paper.
Engagements and weddings.

As this list suggests, the society page is written principally for women, although men are interested in many stories of engagements, weddings, parties and personal activities. A majority of society editors are women who have social rank themselves although many large papers have male society editors. Of whichever sex, the editor should be able to attend major social events on an equal footing with other guests, although only a few occasions require the presence of a reporter. A large majority of society page items are contributed by persons concerned or by social secretaries, either in writing or by telephone. The society editor must be ever on the alert for practical jokers sending or phoning in bogus announcements of engagements, weddings and other social events. Nothing should be used without verification. If the society editor needs pipelines, such people as chefs, florists, hairdressers and delicatessen store operators are among the best to utilize.

ELEMENTS IN SOCIETY NEWS

Most society events of any importance have elements in common which include:

Names. Host and hostess; guests of honor; members of the receiving line in order of importance; assistants to hostess in the parlor and dining room; members of committees; entertainers; musicians and their selections; prominent guests; relation of guest of honor to hostess or of assistants to either.

Decorations. Color scheme, its significance and how it was carried out; flowers, palms and ferns to make room resemble tropical garden, an outdoor scene and so on.

Refreshments. Distinguish between luncheon and tea and between supper, dinner and banquet. At receptions, always learn who poured and who served and ask if these assistants were selected for any particular reason (relatives, sorority sisters, officers of an organization).

Occasion. Is it an anniversary or an annual event? What will be done with any proceeds? Does the place have any significance?

It is difficult to achieve variety in writing similar accounts of social events. Consequently, the society editor welcomes any possible feature.

Covering Society News

STYLE

In writing routine society news, restraint should be exercised. Every hostess would like to see her party or luncheon mentioned as the "loveliest affair of the season." To avoid offending anyone, such superlatives must be subdued.

There is a tendency, however, toward more informality in longer feature stories concerning important social events. Much of the material on the society or club page is signed. Functions, the proceeds of which go to charity, frequently are given better writeups than private affairs.

The capable writer does not need to use hackneyed adjectives such as "gorgeous" and "exquisite." An accurate, impartial description of an object or an event conveys its beauty much better than does an article which makes indiscriminate use of adjectives. Only the writer who is not able to write better descriptions falls back on the old standbys.

A few additional words should be said about some of the more important kinds of stories classifiable as society news.

RECEPTIONS

The reception story should emphasize the name of the guest of honor, the occasion for the reception and the receiving line. Likewise, those who assist the hostess, entertainers, musicians and decorations.

COMING-OUT PARTIES

A debutante is presented to society by her parents, or, if they are dead, by a near relative. Some biographical data concerning the girl should be included, as well as a description of her dress. A possible feature may be found in the date or place or in the number or names of guests. In some coming-out party stories, the gowns of all the prominent women guests are described.

ENGAGEMENTS

Usually the parents of the bride-to-be announce their daughter's engagement. Sometimes the announcement merely takes the form of a newspaper notice. Often, however, an announcement is made at a social function. If such is the case, the manner of the announcement constitutes the feature. Especially if a girl chooses to announce her own engagement, the attempt is made to invent some novel method. For instance, the intended wife of a bank clerk uses as place cards or favors imitation bank books containing her fiancé's picture.

In the announcement story, the names of the bride- and bridegroom-to-be must be mentioned, and also their parents' names and addresses. Also the probable date of the wedding and the city in which the couple will live. The principals should be identified by their occupations and education. Sometimes the way in which the two met is interesting, as when a war veteran marries the nurse who cared for him in a hospital.

SHOWERS

Female relatives and friends of a bride-to-be are hostesses at showers. Guests are expected to bring gifts. Often the type of gift to be brought is designated. If it is, the shower should be referred to as a kitchen shower, linen shower and so on. Otherwise, it should be called miscellaneous.

WEDDINGS

The backbone of the society page is the wedding story. It is the longest and most difficult to write. Since most weddings are planned, it is possible for the society editor to obtain information about them and even to write them up in advance. In a majority of states a couple contemplating marriage must make application at least three days before the day set for the wedding. The city hall reporter gets the names of couples who apply for marriage licenses and, after including them in a short news item, gives them to the society editor.

The society editor writes an advanced story of the approaching wedding of a young woman who is prominent socially, often using a picture with the story. Many papers do not run such stories or pictures without charge. Ordinarily, the advanced story of a wedding is brief unless the principals are prominent.

After receiving the names of intended brides, the society editor of an average-sized newspaper sends a wedding blank to each bride about whose marriage she will want a story. This blank contains spaces for the girl to insert answers to the questions suggested. Use of the wedding

228   HANDLING IMPORTANT ASSIGNMENTS

blank eliminates the necessity of personal reporting and insures accuracy. Seldom does the society editor attend a wedding. Most wedding stories are written from the facts provided by the bride. A sample wedding blank follows:

WEDDING REPORT

Full name of bride..
Address of bride..
Full names of bride's parents or guardians...........................
Address of bride's parents......................................
Full name of bridegroom..
Address of bridegroom...
Full names of bridegroom's parents...............................
Address of bridegroom's parents.................................
Date of wedding........................ Time................
Place of ceremony...
Who will perform ceremony?....................................
Will bride wear a gown or suit?............ Describe...............
....
Will she wear a veil?.................. Is it an heirloom?..........
Describe the veil..
Will she carry a prayer book?....................................
Will she carry or wear flowers?........... Describe...............
....
Who will give the bride away? (name, address and relationship).........
....
Name of maid or matron of honor and relationship...................
Describe her gown and flowers...................................
Names and addresses of bridesmaids...............................
....
Describe their gowns and flowers.................................
Ribbon, ring or flower bearers....................................
Describe their gowns and flowers.................................
Name and address of best man...................................
Groomsmen..
Ushers..
Will ceremony be formal or informal?.............................
Musicians..
Musical selections:
  Before ceremony..
  As bridal party enters.....................................
  During ceremony...
  As bridal party leaves.....................................
Order in which bridal party will enter..............................
....
Decorations (color scheme and how carried out; significance)...........
....

Number of invitations sent out......... Probable attendance........
Will a reception follow?.............. Where?...................
How many will attend reception?................................
Decorations ....
Hostesses:
    In parlor...
    In dining room..
Will breakfast, luncheon, or dinner be served?........ Where?......
Will couple take a trip?....... Where?.......... When?........
When and where will couple be at home?..........................
Bridegroom's occupation and business address....................
Former occupation of the bride..................................
Bridegroom's education and degrees..............................
Bridegroom's fraternal connections..............................
Bride's education and degrees...................................
Bride's sorority connections....................................
Bridegroom's war record: service, rank, area in which served and duration,
    citations, unusual experiences, etc........................
    ....
Bride's war record..
Guests from away, names, initials and addresses.................
....
Other information...
....

PICKING THE FEATURE

The society editor welcomes any possible feature with which to lead off the wedding story. Possible features to give depth to the account include:

1. The romance. The manner of meeting or the length of the engagement if unusual. Sometimes childhood sweethearts are united after years of separation. Or there may be an Evangeline or Enoch Arden complication. Ordinarily, unless the bride is a widow, the fact of any previous marriage is omitted. Exceptions to this rule are persons prominent in the news, especially motion picture actors and actresses. In their cases it is common practice to write: "It is her third marriage and his fourth."

2. The place. Perhaps some relative of either party was married in the same church. Maybe an outdoor ceremony is performed on the spot where the betrothal took place. Sometimes a couple selects an unusual site for its nuptials, as an airplane or beneath the water in diving suits. Wedding ceremonies have been performed in hospitals, prisons and by long-distance telephone or radio.

3. *The date or hour.* It may be the anniversary of the engagement. Perhaps the bride's mother or some other relative was married on the same date. In an effort to make its wedding the first of the year or month, a couple may be married shortly after midnight.

4. *Bride's costume.* Often a bride wears her mother's dress or veil or some other family heirloom. There is an old superstition that a bride always should wear something old and something new, something borrowed and something blue; many modern brides adhere to this, and some article of a bride's costume may be unusual.

5. *Relationship.* If the scions of two old and prominent families are married, their family connections may constitute the feature. If either is descended from Revolutionary or Colonial ancestry that fact should be played up.

The feature, of course, may be found in any one of a number of other elements. Perhaps the bridegroom wears a military uniform or the bride cuts the wedding cake with her husband's sword. Maybe the minister is a relative. The attendants may be sorority sisters or representatives of some organization. Whatever it is, the society editor tries to find it and to feature it. Anything to drive off the monotony of the stereotyped wedding lead.

STYLE

The trite and hackneyed style of the "country" wedding story must be avoided. To this end, avoid use of such expressions as "blushing bride," "plighted their troth," "holy wedlock," "linked in matrimony." The word "nuptials" should not be overworked.

The easiest lead sentence is the straightforward: "A and B were married—." For variety, other possibilities include:

—exchanged (spoke) nuptial (marriage) vows.
Miss A became the bride of B—
Miss A was married to B—
First church was the scene of the marriage of—
A simple ceremony united in marriage Miss A and B—
The marriage of A and B took place—
—attended the nuptials of A and B.
Nuptial vows were spoken by A and B—
The marriage of A and B was solemnized—
Chaplain C read the service which joined A and B in marriage—
Chaplain C officiated at—

PERSONS AND PERSONALITIES 231

Some of these phrases may be appropriate in other parts of the story. When a page includes a half-dozen or more wedding stories, it is desirable to obtain variety. However worded, the lead of the wedding story should contain the feature, if there is one, the names of the principals with the bride's name ordinarily mentioned first and the time and place of the wedding. The principals usually are identified by addresses and parentage.

Writers vary the order of details in the body of the story. Most frequently, perhaps, the bride's costume is described right after the lead, and then the costumes of her attendants. The decorations or order of march, however, may come first. If there is a procession, the order in which it entered the church or home should be described.

The account of any wedding dinner or reception follows the account of the service proper. More nearly complete identification of the principals, the wedding trip and future residence and the list of guests come at the very end. Other elements which enter into the account are included in the sample wedding blank in this chapter.

Note in the following examples of well-written leads to wedding stories how the writers were able to find and play up unusual features. The leads are all from the Fort Wayne *News-Sentinel*:

> The Rev. Val Hennig, minister of St. John's Lutheran Church on the South Whitley Road, read the nuptial service, at which his youngest daughter, Katharine Alice, and Clarence Bade, son of Mrs. Chester Bade, 1721 South Hanna St., were united in marriage at 6 P.M. Saturday, June 29. Edwin Meitzler, organist, accompanied Howard Ropa, vocalist, who gave the musicale before the ceremony.

> Gold vases of white larkspur and Madonna lilies and palms decked the sanctuary of St. John the Baptist Catholic Church where Miss Eileen McGary and Robert John Wiltshire exchanged marriage vows this morning at 10 o'clock. The Rev. Leo Pursley officiated at the double ring ceremony and nuptial mass after a musicale of bridal airs given by Miss Frieda Winegart, organist, and Miss Mary Jo Kohl, who sang "Panis Angelicus" and "On This Day O Beautiful Mother."
> The bride is the daughter of Mr. and Mrs. William James McGary, 117 McKinnie Ave., and her husband the son of Mr. and Mrs. L. Wallace Wiltshire, 4225 South Calhoun St.

> In a quiet ceremony read in the presence of a few intimate friends, Miss Betty Ruth Beard, 2214 Winter St., and Lester Green, of Edgerton, O., were married last Saturday in the rectory of St. Peter's Catholic Church.

Gossip Columns

The avidity of readers for "inside dope"—intimate though perhaps inconsequential humorous, pathetic, unusual or anecdotal items—about friends and acquaintances and popular heroes worshipped at a distance, has resulted, not only in Washington, New York and Hollywood personal columns but also in a recrudescence of local "Around the Town," "On the Square" and similar columns.

The unusual new neon sign in front of a restaurant, the abnormally tall sunflower, the skilfully sculptured snow man, the practical joke played upon a dignified prominent citizen—many of these and other items which give substance to the local gossip column might be developed into separate brevity features. Collected and presented in the individualized style of a particular writer, however, their attention-getting value may be enhanced. Permitted greater stylistic freedom and a bit of friendly editorializing, the gossip columnist also can use a quantity of material which it would be difficult to work up into even an informal news feature.

ANECDOTES

After the Chicago *Sun* included in its "Chicago Briefs" column an item telling of the long eyelashes of one of the city's children, mothers actually fought with each other in the newspaper office for the privilege of having their offsprings' lashes measured and photographed. One subsequent item in the series was as follows:

> Move over, Mickey Cribben, Maureen Fitzpatrick, Dolores Wenk, Patricia Capetta and all you other lucky people with those long eyelashes!
> Make room for a newcomer—Patsy Ann Doyle, 5, who lives at 5149 Emerald av. Her mother claims Patsy's blond lashes are a mite over $5/8$ inches long, which is longer than Mickey's, Maureen's, etc. etc.
> [Chicago *Sun*]

Columns of anecdotes may be called "Chatter," "It Happened In—," "Evening Chat," "Informing You," "It's News to Me," "Front Row," "Personally Speaking," or the like. The Wakefield (Mass.) *Daily Item* heads its column "The Item Hears" and begins each paragraph anecdote with "That." Typical items follow:

That visitors to Wakefield from the West ran into what they described as a "gold mine" this week when they were permitted to visit a huge field of corn and select their own, fresh-picked ears for the unusually low price of 50 cents a dozen.

That a youngster 9 years old and his younger sister of Yale avenue, appeared at the police station Tuesday with a wallet they had found which contained $8. It was discovered at the station that the wallet belonged to a Melrose man.

NIGHT LIFE

In metropolitan centers the frequenter of night clubs has superseded the Social Registerite as copy for columnists who make the rounds after dark.

The following are extracts for a typical "It Happened Last Night" column by Earl Wilson in the New York *Post*:*

> When Jackie Gleason played Santa at the Lighthouse, he cracked, "I'm the only Santa Claus that didn't have to use a pillow" ... Comedienne Patsy Shaw reports this New England dialogue: "I hear you had an operation on your nose" ... "Yup, it was getting so I could hardly talk through it."

ENTERTAINMENT PLACES

Similarly, the night clubs themselves and other amusement places often are reviewed in the same manner as dramatic or musical events.

> By Elizabeth Rannells
>
> Soft lights, beautiful decor, hors d'oeuvres with the individual touch and solicitous service are the reasons the Town and Country room has become one of the town's quick-clicks. It is the spot for that pre-dinner, pre-show appointment, equally the place for the post-prandial, post-show meeting.
>
> Not for heavy appetites is this addition to the Palmer House. It is just for that lull in the late afternoon, or for that after-the-show session, where every table has its coterie of critics.
>
> And what is almost as important—the feminine guests feel like Powers' models, thanks to the bland and gentle illumination and the flattering colors of the room. They blend with all make-ups, thus putting the distaff customers in the cheerful mood. [Chicago *Sun*]

---

* Reprinted by permission from the New York *Post*. Copyright 1955, New York Post Corporation.

SOCIETY

To brighten the society page there is the society column, usually signed which, while newsy, is in keeping with the trend toward interpretative writing to give and explain the news behind the news.

> Effective formals seen recently include Nancy Wilmanns' (Mrs. Fred) strapless kelly green silk faille gown accented with a large pink rose at the waistline ... Carol Herzfeld in a gown of her own design with a high neckline black lace bodice atop a bouffant white organdy skirt with inserts of the black lace ... the strapless white dotted swiss dress of Carolyn Rowe (Mrs. Charles) ... Nancy Inbusch (Mrs. Ralph) in a black crepe creation featuring a peplum edged with white lace ... Betty Wright (Mrs. David) in a floral printed crepe gown in a patriotic motif—red, white and blue.
>
> Was Helen Fry's face red when she "gracefully" tripped over the full skirt of her formal at a recent affair and landed in a horizontal position!
> [Milwaukee *Journal*]

Personality Interviews

The growth of magazines, radio and television has made it more difficult for newspapers to obtain this type of interview. Celebrities and persons prominent in the news for the moment are offered such attractive prices for their life stories or opinions, by syndicates, that they hesitate to grant gratis interviews with newspaper reporters.

When a prominent person returns from abroad or is a visitor in the community, however, he hardly can avoid granting some kind of interview with the press. Such interviews often resemble interviews for opinion, although the subject matter may not be of immediate importance. When a member of Congress returns from foreign shores, of course, the statement which he gives out may be important. When an actress, athlete or public lecturer passes through the city, however, the reporter may be "hard put to it" to find questions to ask for a "between-trains" interview. The importance of knowing something about one's subject was impressed upon the Atlanta reporter who asked Vivien Leigh what part she had played in the motion picture version of *Gone with the Wind* when the actress showed up for the première of the re-issue of the 1939 Academy Award winner. Miss Leigh simply informed the reporter that she did not care to be interviewed by such an ignorant person.

Not only national celebrities but local persons who have won honors, taken new positions of importance, or been in the news prominently are the frequent subjects of reportorial inquiry. Reporters follow candidates for public office around during a day of campaigning to make a full report on their activities. Articles written after interviews with newly appointed school superintendents, bank presidents, chairmen of civic organizations, and the like may resemble the profiles (combined biography, character sketch and description) originally made popular by *The New Yorker*. The object is to give readers the "feel" of the person, not just statistical facts regarding him and his activities.

When a person is being written up primarily because of his information or opinions regarding a matter, personality traits and description should be kept to a minimum or ignored. If a man shouts, bangs on the table, hesitates before giving an answer or in some other way behaves so that proper understanding of his comments requires mention of such circumstances, they may be included. Unless such is the case, references to "the balding professor" or "the slight soft-spoken man" may be inconsistent and out of place.

Entirely the opposite is true when the object is to make readers thoroughly acquainted with the subject of the interview as a person. In such cases, the subject's opinions are secondary and are used to help build a total word picture. How a person appears, talks and behaves during the interview may be pertinent, especially if the reporter elects to write in the first person.

These rules are applicable to all kinds of subjects including the off-the-beaten-path "characters" who may be the subjects of feature articles: retiring lifeguards, octogenarians, persons with unusual hobbies or reminiscences, and the like. Pictures supplement and confirm written accounts in such cases, not the contrary.

Ethics

One of the most frequently heard criticisms of newspapers is that they unnecessarily invade the privacy of persons in the news. Sometimes, of course, the charge has validity. Increasingly, in a public relations-conscious society, however, the apparent victim of the invasion is getting exactly what he asked—or at least hoped—for. Acting in the belief that any publicity is valuable, persons in the public eye, especially entertainers, have been known to promote disturbances or engage in other kinds of behavior which the press could not ignore.

Reputable newspapermen gag at having to report the antics of publicity seekers who operate on the principle, "I don't care what they say as long as they say something," and whose only concern is that their names be spelled correctly. Readers get a distorted impression when there is deadpan reporting of something which should properly be exposed as manufactured news.

During the '50s a rash of magazines appeared to traffic in "inside dope" about public celebrities, mostly motion picture stars. Much of it verged on the scandalous and scurrilous and numerous libel suits resulted. This revival of "town topics" journalism became the object of widespread debate regarding the extent to which persons in public life are entitled to privacy. Admittedly, facts related to the character and capacities of public officials and other civic leaders are important for voters and patrons to know. No law ever has been written or probably could be written to draw a fine line between what is and is not permissible. The interpretative reporter knows that a person's actions frequently are understandable only when much is known regarding his background. On the other hand, a person's achievements, especially in the arts, often can be judged on their own merits. Pending the miracle of a legal definition in this matter, the ethical journalist must maintain a high consciousness of social responsibility and realize that a gossip-ridden society in which personal freedoms are minimized is not a good society.

1 2

Meetings, Conventions, Speeches

I MEETINGS
1. The Preliminary Story
2. The Follow-up
3. Style

II CONVENTIONS
1. The Preliminary Notice
2. The First-day Story
3. The Follow-up
4. Estimating Crowds

III SPEECHES
1. The Preliminary Story
2. The Follow-up
   a. *The Lead*
   b. *The Body*

MEETINGS, CONVENTIONS AND SPEECHES OCCUPY THE ATTENTION OF THE women's organizations mentioned on the society and club pages and of other organizations whose news is printed in other parts of the newspaper. It is impossible for any newspaper to give adequate coverage to any sizable proportion of the total number of groups seeking publicity. Those considered the most newsworthy are of the following types:

1. Those which take an active part in local, state or national political and governmental affairs, as the League of Women Voters, Chamber of Commerce, Daughters of the American Revolution, American Legion.
2. Those which have programs including widely known speakers, musicans, artists and so forth.
3. Those with large, nationwide memberships which hold elaborate conventions annually. Of this type are most fraternal lodges, routine news of which may be ignored but whose yearly meetings are first-rate shows.

In small city dailies, community and suburban newspapers, almost any organization is newsworthy. The initiative may be left to the group to send in its notices voluntarily, or the publication may follow a sounder policy of attempting to have complete coverage, especially of such organizations as the P.T.A., church groups, Boy Scouts, Girl Scouts, Y.M.C.A., Y.W.C.A. and so forth.

Meetings

THE PRELIMINARY STORY

Every meeting is held for a purpose and this purpose should be the feature of the preliminary or advanced notice. From the secretary or some other officer of the group which is to meet, the reporter should learn the nature of important business to be discussed, of committees which will report, speakers, entertainment and so on.

Note how the second of the following leads emphasizes purpose:

WEAK: The Cosmos club will hold a meeting at 7:30 o'clock Thursday evening in Swift hall for the purpose of discussing the question of whether or not undergraduate students should own automobiles.

BETTER: Undergraduate ownership of automobiles will be discussed by the Cosmos club at its meeting at 7:30 Thursday evening in Swift hall.

Other vague beginnings to avoid include:

There will be a meeting—
The purpose of the meeting—
At 7:30 o'clock—
The first meeting of the year—

The reporter should ask if the meeting is regular or special, business or social. He should inquire if a dinner or refreshments will precede or follow, whether any entertainment—dramatic, musical or otherwise—is planned. The main attraction of the meeting may be some special program. A meeting to elect or install officers, initiate candidates, hear a particular committee report or a speaker, or to celebrate an anniversary has an obvious feature from the news standpoint.

The reporter must be sure to obtain the following data:

1. The organization. Its exact name, and the name and number of the post or chapter. "Local Odd Fellows" is not enough; instead, write, "Keystone Lodge No. 14, I. O. O. F." That is the usual form: name of the local chapter first, then the number and finally the name or usual abbreviation of the national organization.

2. Time and place. In the preliminary story this information must be definite and accurate. A meeting scheduled for 8 o'clock should not be mentioned in the news story as to begin at 8:15. "Friday evening" is not enough; the exact hour should be given. Both the building and room should be given in stating the place.

3. *The program.* If there is a program of entertainment, the reporter should obtain it in detail. He must get names of musicians and their selections, names of casts and dramatic coaches, decorations, orchestras, committees in charge. Only the highlights of a program need be mentioned, and in order of importance, rather than in the order included in the program.

Note how purpose is emphasized in the following examples:

The American Legion Auxiliary's 5th District will meet at 8 P.M. Saturday in the Community club rooms, 1600 South Grand avenue, to hear annual reports by district chairmen and to elect delegates to the state and national conventions. Mrs. Martha Watkins, district director, will preside.

A score of California law-enforcement officials gathered here yesterday to discuss ways of living up to the new rule excluding illegally obtained evidence from criminal trials.

It was the first meeting of Attorney General Gerald L. Polk's committee on arrests, searches and seizures.

Polk announced that he will seek an immediate hearing before the State Supreme Court on five Valdavia narcotics cases that were dismissed as a result of the new rule, announced by the high court on April 27.

Sometimes the preliminary note may be the excuse for a historical sketch of the organization, as:

Having enjoyed a vigorous life for 80 years, the United Charities is pausing next week to give itself a birthday party. With a program as impressive as the occasion demands, the celebration will take place at the Palmer House the afternoon of the 16th.

Dr. Vance L. Howland is coming out from Escot to make the principal address of the party, and a pageant and tea will supplement the speeches.

As president of the group, Allan Fort will be chief host. Mrs. Stephen Lorch heads the committee in charge of the event, and is drafting a corps of her young friends who will act as ushers and hostesses in costumes their mothers used to wear as members of the organization.

Since 1888 when 23 Milltown business men founded the organization, it has been run largely by the same families. Victor G. Stoneking, Ernest I. Silsbee, James R. Leary, Austin H. DeZutter and Milo Morgan were some of the founders who named themselves the Milltown Relief and Aid society and obtained a state charter still in use.

They confronted the first big test of their efficiency in 1892 when Mayor William R. Trumbull turned over to them the job of looking after the thousands of Milltownians whose homes were destroyed in the April floods. Until then their chief means of relief had been money, but that spring, with O. A. Thayer as chairman of their shelter committee, they bought timber to build 9,000 homes, one of which still stands on the near southeast side.

Charles W. Riegel, the father of Mrs. Lee Diamond, was president of the society that year and wrote letters of thanks to people in the Hebrides, in Japan and Ecuador, and in more familiar places, for their contributions to Milltown's rebuilding fund.

It was Mr. Thayer's task to distribute building materials, food and clothes that came in from all parts of the country, and files in the present S. Savoy avenue headquarters still contain requests made to the shelter committee.

THE FOLLOW-UP

In the follow-up or story after the meeting has been held, the outcome or result should be featured, and the writer should look to the future. For instance, avoid:

Keystone Lodge No. 14, I.O.O.F. last evening voted to build a new million dollar lodge hall.

Rather, emphasize the future, as:

Keystone Lodge No. 14, I.O.O.F. will build a million dollar lodge hall, it was decided at last evening's meeting.

Or, better still:

A new lodge hall to cost one million dollars will be erected by Keystone Lodge No. 14, I.O.O.F., as the result of last evening's meeting.

Other beginnings to avoid include:

The Cosmos club met last evening—
At a meeting of—
There was a meeting—
The purpose of the meeting was—
One of the most interesting—
The outcome of the meeting—

The reporter should learn the disposition of each item of business. Some matters will be laid on the table or referred to committees. Others will be defeated outright. Some business, of course, will be concluded. If the meeting or business is important, the writer should include in his story, not only the result of balloting, but also the arguments presented by both supporters and opponents of each measure, both those that passed and those that were defeated.

The account of a meeting which has been held never should read as the secretary's minutes. The items of business are mentioned in the order of their importance, rather than chronologically as considered at the meeting.

It is important to obtain the exact wording of resolutions and the memberships of committees. It is not necessary to mention the presiding officer unless someone other than the president or usual chairman was in charge.

In the follow-up story, the time and place need not be stated so definitely. "Last evening" is sufficient as the exact moment at which the chairman sounded his gavel is immaterial. The name of the building in which the meeting was held is enough, especially if the organization has a regular meeting place. If the time of the next meeting is not fixed by custom it should be mentioned.

Names of everyone who took part in the program should be obtained if a complete account is desired. If a ladies' auxiliary serves a meal or refreshments, the names of the women who helped should be mentioned.

Note in the following example how the writer caught the spirit or importance of the occasion which he interpreted interestingly:

> The so-called conservative element in the labor union movement was successful in the annual election held Wednesday night by the Milwaukee Federated Trades' council.
>
> Herman Seide was reelected secretary by a vote of 458 to 169 over Al Benson, former sheriff and now organizer for the United Textile Workers of America, a C.I.O. affiliate.
>
> Anton Sterner, nominated to oppose J. F. Friedrick for the post of general organizer, withdrew. Friedrick was reelected by 624 votes.
>
> For secretary-treasurer, Emil Brodde was reelected with 458 to 164 for Severino Pollo. Frank Wietzke, sergeant-at-arms for more than 40 years, was reelected without opposition.
>
> In the contest between conservative and liberal slates for the nine places on the executive board, the same division was apparent. Those elected and their votes are . . . [Milwaukee *Journal*]

STYLE

Expressions such as, "Members are urged to attend," and "The public is cordially invited," should be avoided. If the purpose of the meeting is stated correctly, the former expression is superfluous. The latter expression is poor because of the "cordially." If an invitation is not cordial, it should not be extended.

Other expressions to avoid include:

—was the most important happening.
—was the main business transacted.
—was the topic of discussion.
—featured the meeting.
—was the principal transaction.

Conventions

Some organizations, such as the American Legion, W.C.T.U. and the D.A.R., are influential in state and national affairs. Consequently, when one of these organizations meets, what it does is of general interest. Such conventions frequently pass resolutions concerning vital political and business situations and recommend passage of certain laws by state legislatures and Congress. They even send lobbyists to state capitals and to Washington.

Conventions of other organizations which ordinarily are nonpolitical may be of widespread interest because of their large membership. Fraternal orders such as the Masons, Elks and Moose have chapters in all parts of the country, and their conventions attract thousands of delegates from all states. Church groups, businessmen's organizations, scientific and educational bodies consider matters of general interest. Frequently the first announcement of a new scientific discovery or theory is made in a paper presented at a convention of some scientific group.

Aside from the general interest which an important convention creates, there also is local interest, provided the locality is to be represented by delegates. If any local person is an officer or has a part in the program, the local interest is heightened. Many fraternal organizations hold drill team, band, fife and drum corps and other contests at conventions, and the local chapter may compete.

THE PRELIMINARY NOTICE

The first story of a convention usually appears a week or two before the opening session. Almost every important organization has a secretary or official who prepares notices for the press. The advanced notice emphasizes the business of the convention and the important speeches or papers to be given or read. Sometimes the nature of a report which a special committee will make is disclosed in advance.

Note in the following examples of leads of preliminary notices of conventions that the writer in each case emphasizes the most important plans from the standpoint of general interest:

> College training for women interested in the field of commerce and business administration will be studied and discussed at the 10th annual convention of Gamma Theta Phi, national professional sorority of commerce and business administration, tomorrow through Sunday in the Windmere hotel.

> The National Federation of Women's Republican Clubs will make congressional campaign issues the principal theme of the organization's third biennial convention in Philadelphia Sept. 26 and 27. Mrs. W. Glen Davis of Akron, president, will direct the sessions at the Bellevue-Stratford hotel. Several hundred delegates from 42 states and the District of Columbia are expected.

In addition to the general story of a convention, or even instead of it, a local newspaper may print a story playing up the "local" angle—the part that local delegates will play, as:

> With the hope and expectation of bringing next year's state convention to Milltown, 58 members of Keystone Lodge No. 14, I.O.O.F., accompanied by wives and families, are in Petersburgh today.
> Occasion is the 27th annual convention of the state I.O.O.F. in which several members of the local lodge will play prominent parts.

The First-Day Story

The story which appears just before the convention begins may emphasize the purpose and main business of the meeting, or it may play up the arrival of delegates, the probable attendance and the first day's program. Often a meeting of the officers or executive committee precedes the convention proper.

Some matter related exclusively to the internal organization of the group may be of sufficient general interest to be the feature, as when a rule changing the requirements for membership, or union with another organization is to be debated. Frequently an internal political fight is anticipated in the election of officers or selection of the next convention city.

> The leaders of the nation's banking fraternity, 8,500 strong, are arriving for the four-day annual American Bankers Association convention.
> The meeting, largest since the 1920s, will focus on the perplexing problem of the banker's role in curbing, while not blighting, the boom.

The program at the Conrad Hilton hotel will also include speeches on the farm price problem and the task of building the free world's strength through NATO and the nation's strength through a strong free enterprise economy.

In addition, a wide range of subjects, some of interest chiefly to bankers, others with a general scope, will be discussed.

While thousands of bankers and their wives flock to a private showing of the General Motors Corp. Powerama Sunday, other bankers on 22 special committees—such as those on credit policy and federal legislation—will buckle down to work.

But the committee which may prove to be the most controversial does not meet until Monday. That is the 50-member nominating committee, representing each state.

There's no doubt, short of catastrophe, who the next president will be. He's the vice-president, Fred F. Florence, president, Republic National Bank of Dallas. He'll take over automatically from Homer J. Livingston, president, the First National Bank of Chicago.

The rub will come when a successor vice-president to Florence is named. Observers think that for the first time in a generation there may be an open fight for control of the ABA, with the issue being state versus national banks.

The "state's righters" argue that they haven't had a president for the last seven years. Because they can't name one directly this year, their strategy is to name the vice-president who will move up to the presidency.

[Chicago *Sun-Times*]

A newspaper printed in the city entertaining a convention joins with the rest of the community in welcoming delegates. Reporters are assigned to gather side features and anecdotes unrelated to the serious business of the convention. Statistics may be included of the oldest delegate, the delegate who has come the longest distance, the delegate who has attended the most conventions, the delegate who flew to the convention by private airplane or arrived in some other unusual manner, the tallest delegate, the shortest and so forth.

The newspaper may take advantage of the opportunity to obtain feature interviews with important or picturesque delegates and speakers. At a gathering of editors of college newspapers, a reporter obtained numerous interviews regarding drinking in colleges, a subject entirely different from the business of the convention.

The following is a well written first-day convention story which "catches" the spirit of the occasion:

Cleveland, July 13—(AP)—The Shrine brought its big show to town today and made Cleveland an oriental oasis of parades, concerts, ceremonies and funmaking.

MEETINGS, CONVENTIONS, SPEECHES 245

Delegates were arriving by the thousands, by special trains, by automobile, by plane and by boat, and tomorrow between 60,000 and 100,000 nobles are expected here for the 57th annual convention of the Ancient and Arabic Order of the Nobles of the Mystic Shrine of North America.

Today was listed on the program as all-Ohio day, with 750 members of the six Ohio temples initiated into the order, but the arrival of delegations from all parts of the country came in for equal attention.

One thousand members of Medinah temple of Chicago, the largest in the order, arrived in spectacular fashion, on the Lake Steamer Seeandbee. The Chicagoans, bedecked in red, green and yellow uniforms and bright red fezzes, paraded from the dock behind Al Koran patrol of Cleveland, and tied up downtown traffic for a half hour.

Medinah sent a brass band, an oriental band, 500 uniformed men, and a headquarters company from its 23,000 members. This year a Chicago man, Thomas J. Houston, is to be elected imperial potentate and the windy city is a contender for next year's convention.

Lulu temple of Philadelphia sent the next largest delegation—900—and presented a quarter-mile long march of sound and color. Moolah temple, St. Louis, with 500 nobles, arrived on the Steamer Eastern States, while Iram temple of Wilkes-Barre, Pa., also came by boat, via Buffalo.

Abu Bekr, Sioux City, attracted attention with its white Arabian mounted patrol of 30 pure white horses. Syria temple, Pittsburgh, was represented by 700 nobles campaigning for the election of J. Milton Ryall for outer guard.

Band concerts, a lake cruise to Put-in Bay, patrol drills and the annual meetings of the recorders and the royal order of jesters, composed of men high in shrinedom, completed the day's program. Tonight was given over to a Mardi Gras and carnival, with Lakeside avenue roped off for the merrymakers.

San Francisco was unexpectedly put forward as a candidate for the next convention of the Shrine of North America. Pacific coast delegates got behind the move at a breakfast given by Leo Youngsworth, Los Angeles, past potentate of Islam temple. Previously Chicago had been the only city mentioned for next year's gathering.

Fourteen nobles of Hella temple, Dallas, came by airplane. Another long distance air delegate was Gerald Biles, postmaster of the Canal Zone, who flew from Panama to Cleveland.

Lou B. Windsor of Grand Rapids, Mich. is the oldest member of the imperial council present and is attending his 44th annual convention. He was imperial potentate in 1900. Another veteran in attendance is John A. Morrison of Kismet temple, Brooklyn, N.Y., known as the "grand old man of New York Masonry," who says he has attended every convention since "way back when."

Robert B. Kennan of Carnegie, Pa., the tallest delegate attending the Shrine convention, was listed by police today as the first "convention casualty."

Kennan, seven feet tall, was cut on the neck when a bottle of stench fluid was tossed in the lobby of the Hotel Winton. More than 100 persons were routed by the incident, which police blamed on hotel labor troubles.

THE FOLLOW-UP

After a convention begins, newspapers report its progress. Important speeches and debates are reported, and the outcomes of votes watched. Minor speeches, such as the address of welcome and the response and the humorous after-dinner talks at the banquet, may be ignored by press associations and correspondents, unless someone disregards custom and selects such an occasion for an important statement. Scientific papers and speeches must be written up so as to be understandable to the average reader.

Entertainment provided for delegates and their wives, the convention parade and minor business matters pertaining to the organization only, are not given much space. If the organization awards prizes of any sort, the names of the winners are desired by various outside papers whose readers are likely to be interested. Such prizes may be for the best showing in the parade, for the largest delegation, for the delegation coming the longest distance, for drill team, band, or fife and drum corps competition, for the chapter which has increased its membership the most during the year, for the chapter which has contributed most to a certain fund, and so on.

The results of the election of officers and selection of the next convention city usually are of general news interest. Papers in cities which bid for the convention or whose chapters have candidates for offices, frequently arrange for prompt coverage of elections, depending upon the importance of the convention.

ESTIMATING CROWDS

At athletic contests and other events to which admission is charged, there is no difficulty in obtaining accurate figures on total attendance. When the opposite is the case, especially when the audience or crowd is outdoors, the reporter often must make his own estimate of its size. Police usually estimate the numbers who watch a parade, take part in a demonstration or riot or similar event; but police are no more competent to do so than a trained newsgatherer.

The simple process for audience or crowd estimation is to separate it into sections. That is, count the number of persons occupying a particular area. This is easy when the spectators are seated in a grandstand or auditorium, as all that is needed is to multiply the number of seats in a row by the number of rows, then subtracting the apparent number of empty seats. Then cast the eye over the entire assemblage and see how many blocs of similar size there are.

The crowd-counting reporter has it easiest when he has an elevated position as a press box or platform. If he is on the ground he will do well to reach an elevated spot if possible. Otherwise, he will have to move about. He still uses the multiplied bloc system. The beginner can practice by estimating the attendance at athletic contests or the like so as to check his ability when the official attendance announcements are made. A skilled journalist comes very close to the mark.

Speeches

THE PRELIMINARY STORY

In obtaining information for a story about a speech to be given, the reporter must pay special attention to the following:

1. Adequate identification of the speaker.
2. The occasion for the speech.
3. The exact time and place.
4. The exact title of the speech.

Identification of the speaker in the lead may not be lengthy, but the body of the story should contain those facts about the man which indicate that he is qualified to discuss his subject. The opinions of other persons may be obtained and quoted to emphasize the speaker's ability, but the reporter himself should not say that "he is well qualified" or "is an authority on his subject." It is better to give an adequate account of the speaker's experience and let it speak for itself.

The speaker's name usually is more important than his subject and, therefore, should come first in the lead. Sometimes, however, the subject may be more important, but it rarely is advisable to begin with the exact title in quotation marks. Note in the second example below how the writer emphasizes the subject and at the same time the importance of the speaker:

WEAK: "Commercial Aviation" will be the subject of a speech to be given . . .
BETTER: The causes of several recent commercial airline accidents will be analyzed by . . .

Sometimes the occasion is more important than either the speaker or his topic, as:

> The 55th anniversary of the Milltown Salvation Army will be celebrated at 3 P.M. Sunday at the Municipal Opera house with Commander A. K. Asp delivering the principal address, a résumé of the Army's rise to second position among local charities.

In addition to a further identification of the speaker, the body of a preliminary speech story should contain the program of the meeting at which the speech will be given and additional details about the occasion.

In the following example of a well-written preliminary speech story, the lead emphasizes the speaker's name, and the body explains his importance and also the occasion on which he is to speak.

> State Sen. Charles H. Bradfield, Rushville, will speak on the state parole system at the monthly meeting of the Council of Social Agencies at 12:15 P.M. Thursday at Hotel Wolseley.
>
> A member of the joint legislative committee which recently recommended a complete overhauling of the existent parole system, Senator Bradfield has been a severe critic of Gov. Herbert Crowe for his failure to make a public statement on the committee's report.
>
> "It was Senator Bradfield, more than any other member, who was responsible for the recommendation that a board of alienists be substituted for the present board," declared Maurice S. Honig, president of the council, in announcing Thursday's meeting.
>
> The council's committee on legislation, of which Mrs. Arne Oswald is chairman, will report on the results of its study of the legislative committee's recommendations.

THE FOLLOW-UP

After the speech has been given, the emphasis should be upon what the speaker said, rather than upon the fact that he spoke. Never write:

> Bruce Paddock, Prescott city manager, gave a lecture Thursday on "Municipal Government" to the Kiwanis club of Greensboro.

Such a lead is vague and indefinite. It is only a preliminary story lead put into the past tense. It misses the feature entirely.

The feature should be found in something that the speaker said. The reporter must follow the orthodox rule of important details first and must disregard the chronological order of a person's remarks. No good speaker ever makes his most important point in his introduction. The reporter should play up the speaker's most startling or important remark, which may come at the very end of his speech. Such expressions as "The speaker continued" or "In conclusion the speaker said" do not appear in a well-written story.

Every speaker tries to make a point, and the news writer should play up the speaker's attitude toward his subject as a whole. This is not a hard and fast rule, however, as frequently it is better to pick for the lead some casual statement or remark that has strong local interest. In playing up an aside or incidental remark, however, care must be taken not to give a wrong impression. It is easy to misrepresent a speaker's attitude by picking a single sentence which, when printed alone, has a very different meaning than when considered as a part of the complete text.

The timeliness of a speaker's remarks may determine selection of the feature. If he refers to some vital public problem of the moment, his opinion regarding it may be more important than anything else he says. This, of course, is contingent upon his importance as an authority on whatever he may be discussing.

During political campaigns, it is difficult for a reporter who travels with a candidate to write a different story daily, because the aspirant for office gives nearly the same speech day after day. The same difficulty is met with in reporting public lectures by persons who speak frequently on the same subject. If the write-up of the speech is for local consumption only, the feature may be selected on its face value, provided an account of a similar speech by the same person has not been printed recently. The reporter, however, should not play up as something new and startling, a remark which actually is "old stuff" to both speaker and auditors.

As preparation for speech reporting, there is no substitute for adequate knowledge of both the speaker and his field of interest. A reporter with little or no background in science, for instance, would be completely unable to evaluate the relative importance of points made by a nuclear physicist, some of which might be of great potential general interest. An uninformed reporter in any field might write that a speaker "revealed" or "made known" something that could be found in elementary textbooks on the subject.

To localize the appeal of a speech means to play up any reference which the speaker makes to the immediate locality. Thus, if in the course of a lecture on geology, the speaker declares that the vicinity in which he is visiting is a very fertile field for research, that remark may be the most interesting, from the standpoint of his audience, of any he makes. The same speech, written up for a press association, might have an entirely different lead.

The time and place need not be stated so definitely in the follow-up as in the preliminary story, and the identification of the speaker should be brief.

THE LEAD

Possible rhetorical leads for a follow-up speech story include:

1. The speaker's name.
2. The title.
3. A direct quotation.
4. A summary statement of the main point or keynote.
5. The occasion or circumstances.

If there is reason for emphasizing the authority of the speaker, the story may begin with the name, as:

> Chief of Police Arthur O. Shanesy last night told members of the Chamber of Commerce at their monthly meeting that traffic accidents in the downtown business district are largely the fault of merchants.
>
> A prosecuting attorney today advocated the abolition of capital punishment.
>
> Instead of the death penalty, District Attorney Howard Crossman of Bristol county told a luncheon meeting of the Rotary club, the law should provide mandatory life imprisonment for convicted murderers.

Ordinarily, it is weak to begin with the speaker's name, because by so doing the importance of his remarks is minimized. For the same reason, the lead seldom should begin with the exact title unless it is stated in an unusual way or in a way which makes a title lead effective, as:

> "America's Weakness" is her failure to realize that the frontier has disappeared, according to Prof. Arnold L. Magnus of Booster college's political science department, who spoke on the subject last evening to the Milltown Lions club.

Opinion differs regarding the direct quotation lead. Jackson S. Elliott, of the Associated Press, once said, "Show me a news story that begins with a direct quotation, no matter how striking it is, and I will show you how it could be improved by taking the quoted statement out of the lead and placing it in the body of the story."

Other editors condone the direct quotation lead when the intention of the writer is to play up some startling statement rather than to epitomize the speaker's general attitude. Obviously, it is seldom that a speaker himself summarizes his entire speech in any one sentence contained in the speech itself.

The following is a fairly good use of the direct quotation lead:

> "World War III is inevitable within five years," Harold E. Paulson, professor of political science at Booster college, told the World Affairs club last night in Memorial hall.

The partial-quotation lead is a way to avoid lengthy direct quotations which would lack definiteness, as:

> Schools, by failing to develop to the full the "creativeness" of all their students, are responsible in large measure for "countless not fully developed humans," Dr. John L. Tildsley, retiring assistant superintendent of schools, told 1,800 art teachers and students yesterday. He spoke at the opening session at the Hotel Pennsylvania of the 28th annual convention of the Eastern Arts association.

The best lead for a speech story is one which summarizes the speaker's general attitude toward his subject or which gives the keynote of the speech.

> Kindergarten reading is out of place in high school and college, even if the students are coping with a foreign language.
> So a University of Illinois professor told his fellow teachers of French, Friday, in a national meeting in the Palmer House.
> "The books we're reading with our students in the first few years of French are far below their intellectual level, and below the seriousness of things they are reading in other classrooms," declared Prof. Charles A. Knudson, head of romance language at Urbana.
> "In short, in French classes we are reading tripe."
>
> [Chicago *Daily News*]

The lead may emphasize the occasion or the ovation given the speaker, the crowd or some unexpected circumstance which occurs during delivery of a speech, as in the following examples:

> Just six weeks after he was arrested for having in his possession a pamphlet of the American Workers' party, A. J. Muste, executive chairman of the party, last night explained its tenets to an audience of about 100 in the auditorium of Belleville city hall.

> A well-organized group of about 50 hecklers last night failed to persuade State Sen. Roger Parnell to discuss loyalty oaths for public employees.
> Instead, the Republican candidate for reelection stuck to his announced topic, "The State's Proposed Highway Program," and police evicted the troublemakers from an audience of about 500 in Masonic hall.
> The Vernon County Republican club sponsored the meeting.

If several speech stories are to appear on the same page, as a page in a Monday edition including stories of Sunday's sermons, there should be variety in the use of leads. The average sermon is difficult to report because there seldom is a well-defined feature or keynote. A "title" or "speaker's name" lead may be used for a sermon story.

Beginnings to avoid in writing a speech story include:

> The feature of the Chemical society meeting last evening in Swift hall was a speech by . . .

> Lieut. Amos Andrews spoke to members of the Chemical Society in Swift hall on the subject . . .

> "Shakespeare" was the topic of an address given last evening in Swift hall by . . .

> Speaking at a meeting of the Chemical society last evening in Swift hall, Lieut. Amos Andrews declared that . . .

> Pennsylvania limestone was discussed last evening at a Geology society meeting in Swift hall by . . .

All of these leads are vague and indefinite. They do not satisfy the reader's curiosity as to what the speaker thinks about his subject.

THE BODY

Prominent persons, as public officials, usually speak from prepared manuscripts, copies of which often are distributed to newspapermen before actual delivery. This enables a reporter to write part or all of his account in advance. The danger of going to press prematurely is obvious, as the speaker may make last-minute changes or digress from his text.

The safe way is never to publish a speech account until word has been received that delivery actually has begun. Even in such cases, and especially if it is impossible to obey the rule of delay, it is wise to use the identification, "in a speech prepared for delivery" on such and such an occasion in the first or second paragraph. This offers protection in case there are unexpected developments. If there are none, the reporter, manuscript in hand, can follow the speaker and make note of any modifications necessary in the story he already has written.

The second paragraph of a speech story ordinarily should explain the occasion on which the speech was given, if the lead does not do so. The rest of the body should consist of paragraphs of alternating direct and indirect quotation. The first paragraph of direct quotation well may be an elaboration of the indirect quotation lead.

If, as often happens, the reporter has an advanced copy of the speech, he has no difficulty in obtaining direct quotations. Otherwise, he must develop facility in taking notes.

The reporter needs to exercise his best judgment in selecting the parts of a speech to quote directly. Ordinarily he should quote directly:

1. Statements representing a strong point of view, especially if related to a newsworthy controversial matter. Often it is more forceful to use the material in indirect quotation first, possibly in the lead, as "Mayor Brinton will not be a candidate for reelection." Readers, however, like to know the exact words which a speaker used and they should be given in the body of the story even though a verbatim account appears elsewhere in the paper.
2. Uniquely worded statements, including ones which might become aphorisms or slogans, as "Lafayette, we are here," "I do not choose to run" and the like.
3. Statements of facts not generally known, perhaps in statistical terms.

Ordinarily, statements which are merely ones of evaluative opinion or which contain old or easily ascertained information can be summarized in a reporter's own words if they are newsworthy at all. It would be foolish, for instance, to quote a labor leader as saying, "Unions are the hope of America." If, however, the president of the National Association of Manufacturers were to say so, it would be a sensational news story lead.

Instead of quoting directly a statement containing an old fact, the reporter can say, "The speaker reminded the audience that white-collar workers are the most difficult to organize," or, "He recalled that the governor vetoed the measure two years ago."

How often a "he said" or synonym should be inserted in the body of a speech story depends on the length of the article. In paragraphs of indirect quotation a "he said" should be used as often as needed to make it clear that the ideas expressed are those of the speaker rather than of the writer. Direct quotations should be preceded, broken or followed by a "he said" or its equivalent.

The writer should try to use the most forceful synonym for the verb "to say." Any good dictionary of synonyms or a thesaurus includes many score. Since no two verbs have exactly the same meaning, great care must be exercised in their selection. If a speaker "roared," the interpretative reporter owes it to his readers to say so. If, however, the speaker merely raised his voice normally, grave injustice can be done by a reportorial magnavox.

Substance can be given to the speech story only by the reporter who knows something about the speaker and his subject. Otherwise it is impossible to comprehend the speech as a whole, to digest it with proper emphasis, or to convey the proper impression of the occasion on which it was delivered. A speech is an event and the superior reporter comprehends its significance. The factual material of a series of phrases in a sentence or paragraph may come from a half-dozen widely separated portions of the speech as a whole, yet be properly grouped so as to give a complete and accurate summary of the speaker's point of view. Note the understanding displayed by the writer of the following story:

> A brave new world is dawning in the United States today, "a world in which people will believe all other people are people."
>
> But this new desegregated world poses a tremendous problem for the teachers of America:
>
> How do you educate children to live in a world that no American has ever known?
>
> That problem and some suggested approaches to it formed the essence of a talk given here yesterday by Dr. Margaret Mead, New York anthropologist. Dr. Mead addressed the final general session of the Kentucky Teachers Association at Central High School.
>
> "A lot of the children you are teaching now," she said, "aren't living —in their minds—in the present world. They're off living in a 'galactic civilization'—which no girl and few boys over 16 can understand. (A galactic civilization in modern science fiction is one existing among all planets in a galaxy.)
>
> "They have already gone into outer space in their minds.
>
> "We must develop in ourselves a state of mind that realizes they are going into a new world right here. And we must convince our students that they can live in this new world that has never existed before."
>
> The first handicap teachers must shake off, she said, is the traditional American pattern of bringing up children to be "just like me" in preparation for "living in my world." That pattern of training, she said, will not prepare them for the new world.
>
> All through American history, she went on, the two major groups in the U.S. population (Negroes and white) have thought of each other as "something different."
>
> "How then," she asked, "are we to prepare them to think people they didn't think were people are really people?"

She suggested three lines of approach for teachers:

1. Think enough in terms of this new world so that "we don't pin our children down to our own world."

2. Seek out actively and find those children who believe they can do things that have never been done before. "Find one child who can do something no one in his grade has done before, and you can insult them all into doing it too."

3. Hunt for those individuals "who luckily already live in the world we're moving into, and let them lead the way."

"One of the tasks of teachers and superintendents is to identify individual children and parents who will have the trust to move into the new world. Trust is as contagious as fear. They will spread the trust to their groups and lead others."

People frequently ask her, Dr. Mead said, what it is that makes Dr. Ralph Bunche, famous Negro diplomat and scholar, so outstanding.

The main thing, she said, besides "his great brain and great character, is that he thinks white people are people. When I sit across a table from him at a committee meeting, I forget I'm white. With him, one feels like a human being."

She Takes Swipe at 'Mixed Snobbery'

During a question period after her address, Dr. Mead took a healthy swipe at the "mixed snobbery" of many teachers who snap, "Junior, put that comic book away!" and then the teachers "read all the comic books they confiscate."

"We must realize this is the way the ideas of the present are reaching our children. Teachers ought to know what is in comic books, they ought to watch the TV programs their pupils watch and listen to the radio programs, and maybe most of all read the backs of cereal boxes.

"We're teaching them about calories, the metric system, and letting them paper rooms (with pictures), and the new ideas are reaching them through all these other things.

"Sometimes I think teachers should spend much more time remembering their own childhood and comparing it with the childhood of today's children. That will keep them shaken up. And we need to be kept shaken up." [Louisville *Courier-Journal*]

13

Illness and Death

I ILLNESS

II MENTAL HEALTH

III OBITUARIES
1. Basic Elements
2. Circumstances of Death
3. Reviewing a Life
4. Evaluating a Career
5. Morgue Stories
6. Localization
7. Side Features
8. The Second-day Story
9. The Funeral Story
10. Follow-ups
11. The Obituary Blank
12. Language and Style

IV SUICIDES
1. The Motive
2. The Method
3. Inquests

V ACCIDENTS, DISASTERS
1. Elements of Interest
2. Picking the Feature
3. Precautions
4. Side Features
5. Perspective

IF HIS FRIEND, OR SOMEONE WITH WHOSE NAME HE IS FAMILIAR BECAUSE of its prominence in local or world affairs, is ill or dies, the newspaper reader is interested because of the personality involved. If an obscure person of whom he never before has heard has an unusual disease or makes a heroic struggle against affliction, millions of Americans "plug" for him mentally from edition to edition. If a new medical discovery is announced, everyone who may be affected beneficially as a result is pleased to learn of it. If a contagious disease threatens to become an epidemic, readers appreciate being warned of the danger.

Illness

Although the illness story may seem to be routine, it frequently is one of the most difficult to report and write. This is because the medical profession is reluctant to give out information about the condition of patients or about its own discoveries, unusual surgical performances and the like. Physicians hold that they are duty bound to protect the privacy of those under their care, and the ethics of the profession forbids anything suggesting personal publicity. They may feel that knowledge of his condition, gained through a newspaper account, will be detrimental to a patient's recovery, and they do not trust the average reporter to report medical news accurately.

Relatives of a prominent person who is ill usually can be persuaded to authorize the physician in charge to release periodic bulletins regarding the patient's condition, but these may be in scientific language which must be translated. Until newspapers can employ reporters capable of handling medical news with the same understanding that baseball writers handle their specialty, the only safe way is to ask the doctors themselves for popular "translations," or to consult a medical dictionary. Because in many cases they have gone to extremes in refusing cooperation with the press, physicians and surgeons must share part of the blame for any inaccuracies which occur in news concerning them. The press also has learned that attending physicians may not be entirely truthful in their discussion of the nature of an ailment when a prominent person, say a president of the United States, is involved. If the doctor has written a book, it can be consulted to detect differences between what the man writes and what he says.

Chambers of commerce also are a handicap to adequate coverage of medical news because of the influence they often have on editors to play down news of epidemics. Fortunately, few newspapers listen to such requests, holding their social responsibility to be too great and the loss of prestige they would suffer if the contagion reached sizable proportions to be an offsetting consideration. The paper with a sense of responsibility, of course, must take care not to frighten readers unnecessarily.

Most newspapers run a syndicated health column written by an outstanding medical expert who is cautious about diagnosing ailments on the basis of symptoms submitted by readers. Just as they discourage self-medication by patients, so do reputable doctors deplore sensationalism by the press in handling stories of unusual illnesses or treatments, as artificial hearts, organ transplants and the like. Newspapers provide the medium whereby public health officials advise the public on such matters as threats to the purity of the water supply, possible heat prostration and the presence of epidemic diseases.

HANDLING IMPORTANT ASSIGNMENTS

By Robert S. Kleckner

The misnamed hay fever season with its sneezes and tears—but no fever—is drawing near.

Some hypersensitive individuals already have manifested mild symptoms, although the culprit pollens have not yet appeared here in the atmosphere in measurable numbers.

Melvin Karau, director of allergenic products at Abbott Laboratories, said that, while normally the season begins in the area in the last week of July, a late spring and lack of rainfall early in the year delayed growth of ragweed and a few other plants whose pollens cause the suffering.

A Doleful Prediction

However, he offered the doleful prediction that, come Monday, the pollens might be showing up in amounts to be counted.

The delay, he added, will have nothing to do with possible intensity. The season usually lasts through the second week in September.

Hay fever sufferers, if they cannot get away to pollen-free areas, may get relief by staying in air-conditioned and air-filtered rooms. Certain drugs, doctors say, also are beneficial.

Roughly—and it is rough—some 7,500,000 persons over the nation are victims of the malady.

It also brings symptoms like runny and red eyes, itching, a stuffed nose and a tingle from the palate that climbs right up into the quivering nostrils.

See A Doctor

The allergy is nothing to be sneezed at. If you have it, you'd better see a doctor to prevent complications like asthma and respiratory ailments that can be serious.

Hay fever got its name in 1819 when Dr. John Bostock, a London physician and a victim of the disease, noted that the time of weeping and sneezing began at the start of the haying season.

It was not until 1831 that pollens were suspected. Twenty years later, Dr. Morrill Wyman of Harvard Medical School came up with proof that dust, train smoke and pollens were involved.

In centuries past, there were some pretty weird treatments. Dr. John Elliotson of Britain in 1831 advocated hypnotism. Also, before the 1800s, leeches were used to bleed patients. Some became so weak they could hardly breathe.

Some Drastic Cures

The archives of Charles Pfizer & Co., a pharmaceutical firm, show that the 1618 edition of the London Pharmacopoeia recommended a diet of fox lungs.

Thomas Sydenham, dubbed the English Hippocrates, recommended "purging of the brain" for strained breathing, although how this was done is still a mystery.

During the 19th Century, nasal surgery also was used. And some doctors suggested strong tobacco smoke and others cold baths.

Once asked by a patient if there was any cure for hay fever, Dr. Oliver Wendell Holmes of Harvard, answered: "Yes. Gravel . . . taken 8 feet deep."

Common Sense Rules

But with modern therapy available, such drastic treatment is not advocated.

There are some common sense rules, medical men say, that help avoid attacks. These include:

No smoking; no swimming in chlorinated pools; no spiced foods; don't garden, cut flowers or use powdered soaps or insecticides; don't drink alcohol—it tends to dilate blood vessels as pollens do; don't get in squabbles with the wife, children or others—emotional upsets can trigger attacks, and don't go for rides in the country.   [Chicago *Sun-Times*]

The following are a few precautions to observe in avoiding some of the grossest mistakes which otherwise might occur in medical news:

1. Be cautious about announcing cures for important diseases. The hopes of millions of cancer victims have been raised cruelly through newspaper publicity for discoveries which turned out to be false alarms.
2. Be certain that a newly announced discovery actually is recent. Cases have been reported of some cure or method's being ballyhooed as a startling find when it has been familiar to medical men for years.
3. Go easy on accrediting dogmatic statements to any medical researcher. Few of them ever speak in positive terms. Their efforts may be directed toward a certain goal, but they are extremely cautious about claiming credit for having reached it. Often they report to their scientific brethren on the progress of work they are doing; the newspaper should not credit them with having completed something which they have only begun.
4. Do not use without verification stories of miraculous cures.
5. Do not ascribe a pestilential disease to a person without absolute authority, as such a story, if untrue, is libelous.
6. Do not say a person died "from" instead of "after" an operation, as such a statement may be libelous.
7. Everyone dies of "heart failure." There are diseases of the heart and such a thing as a heart attack.
8. A person does not "entertain" a sickness; and not everyone "suffers" while under a physician's care.
9. Very seldom does a person "have his arm cut off." Rather it is cut off contrary to his plans and wishes.

10. Injuries are not "sustained" but are "received."
11. The nature of a diagnosis ordinarily should be stated unless there is weighty reason for omitting it.
12. Scientific names of diseases may be used provided the popular names also are given.
13. Attach statements of diagnoses and of the seriousness of an epidemic to an authority.
14. Do not mention the name of a physician except in stories of the illness of a prominent individual.
15. Avoid stories of medical freaks unless authorized by a medical association. Expectant mothers can be frightened dangerously by accounts which advance public understanding little or not at all.

Mental Health

The fastest growing field of medical knowledge probably is that of mental health. Although the supply of competent psychiatrists still is woefully inadequate, during the past few decades the thinking of many, within and without the medical profession, has been profoundly affected by discoveries and theories regarding the motivations of human behavior.

Among those most influenced by developments in the mental health field have been journalists. They have helped expose bad conditions in many hospitals for the mentally ill and have assisted psychiatrists, social workers, probation and parole officers, educators, judges and others in enlightening the public regarding the many ramifications of the newer knowledge. In its reporting of crime, juvenile delinquency, school problems and similar matters, the press has become much more understanding and consequently more intelligent in its exercise of news judgment.

For "depth" reporting in this field, considerable specialized knowledge is necessary. For a quarter-century, Dr. Sidney Kobre of Baltimore Junior College has advocated this form of journalistic specialization and greater knowledge by all newspapermen and newspaper readers. He did so in his first book, *Backgrounding the News*, in 1937 and in *Psychology and the News* and *News Behind the News* in 1955.

A typical error of the uninformed is to confuse feeblemindedness with mental illness. The former is lack of intellect, either from birth (amentia) or as a result of brain injury in later life (dementia). The feebleminded today are called "retarded" or "exceptional" and special schools exist for those who are educable—that is, the high-grade morons, not to be confused with lower-grade imbeciles and idiots for whom only custodial care is feasible. Under pressure from mental health authorities, newspapers generally have ceased using "moron" as a synonym for "sex pervert," which he is not.

The trend in mental health work is away from categorizing specific diseases—such as dementia praecox, schizophrenia, manic depression, catatonia, paranoia and the like—as long study reveals the existence of few pure types. Rather, the psychiatrist recognizes and speaks of symptoms of abnormal behavior. Long gone, of course, is belief in possession by evil spirits to be exorcised, malicious lunar influence, emotional suffering as a punishment for sin and similar unscientific and superstitious notions.

Although the teachings of Sigmund Freud, stressing the strictly behavioral aspects of mental disease, still influence modern psychiatric thinking more than those of any other scientist in the field, experiments continue in the search for ways to cure, or at least alleviate, symptoms through insulin, electric and other types of shock treatments, glandular extracts, tranquilizers and so forth. Newspapermen can do a great disservice by sensationalizing any results of isolated experiments. They also must be careful to distinguish between psychoses (major mental disorders whose victims lose touch with reality) and neuroses, of which most of us may be victims at times. Psychosomatic illnesses are physical disorders which have an emotional base; their understanding and cure progresses but has a long way to go.

Obituaries

BASIC ELEMENTS

The size obituary a person gets depends upon his importance as news. Even the shortest, however, must include these basic facts:

1. Name of deceased.
2. Identification.
3. Time of death.
4. Place of death.

Two other facts really are essential for even a one- or two-sentence notice:

5. Cause of death.
6. Age of deceased.

Unless death occurs in some unusual way the name (*who*) always is the feature of an obituary. Identification in the brief notice may be by address or occupation only. No authority need be stated unless the dispatch comes from an obscure place or is third- or fourth-hand. Then "it was learned here today" or some similar statement should be used. The paper must be on guard against false rumors of a man's death started by enemies.

In giving the age of a dead person some papers permit the form "Henry Baxter, 61, died today," whereas others object to this form on the ground that placing the age after the name indicates the present tense. Papers with this attitude prefer a phrase "at the age of 61 years" or a second sentence, "He was 61 years old."

> Rutherford Regal, 414 Oates street, a City Yards employee, died at 3 A.M. today at his home following a week's illness from pneumonia. He was 43 years old.

A man's importance or the achievement by which he will longest be remembered ordinarily should be used in identifying him, as:

> Atlanta—Collett Everman Woolman, who started the world's first crop dusting service and built it into Delta Air Lines, the nation's fifth largest, died yesterday. He was 76 years old.   [*Wall Street Journal*]

Sometimes a reporter discovers an interesting circumstance in the life of a relatively unimportant person who has died. Perhaps, for instance, he was present at the assassination of a president, was a pioneer of the locality, a former millionaire or in some other way a romantic figure, as:

> William Dickinson, 81, lifelong Milan resident whose grandfather laid out the village and founded and built the Presbyterian church here, died at 6 P.M. yesterday in his home on Dickson street.

> James Mauris, whose restaurant at 1464 E. 57th street has for many years been a rendezvous for faculty members and students of the University of Chicago, died suddenly of a heart attack last night. He was 70 years old.

See Warren J. Brier's "Delicate Art of Writing Obits," in the 1964 *Montana Journalism Review*, for advice on how to write colorful obituaries with dignity.

CIRCUMSTANCES OF DEATH

When a person is known to a large number of readers, the circumstance of his death should be related as that is one of the first things about which a friend inquires when he hears of another's demise. Circumstances of death include:

7. Bedside scene.
8. Last words, messages and so forth.
9. Account of last illness.

In a full-length obituary, according to the formula being developed, these facts usually follow the lead.

> Allen E. Schoenlaub, 57, cashier of the First National bank, died suddenly about 8 P.M. yesterday at his home, 1146 Elm street, from a heart attack.
>
> He was found in the kitchen by his wife after she heard him fall while in quest of a drink of water. About a half hour before the attack, Mr. Schoenlaub complained of feeling queer. He had spent a normal day at the bank and ate dinner with his wife, son, Robert, 22, and daughter, Flora, 18, apparently in excellent health. He had had no previous heart attacks nor any other recent illness.
>
> A physician whom Mrs. Schoenlaub summoned declared death was due to coronary thrombosis and that Mr. Schoenlaub probably died instantly.
>
> In addition to his wife and two children, he is survived by a brother, Herbert, Kansas City, Mo., and a sister, Mrs. R. S. Bostrum, Chicago.
>
> Mr. Schoenlaub was connected with the First National bank for 26 years, the last 18 of which he was cashier. He was born Jan. 30, 1901 at Ann Arbor, Mich., and was graduated from the University of Michigan in 1923. He moved here in 1932 after nine years as teller and cashier of the State Bank & Trust Co., of Dowagiac, Mich.
>
> Mr. Schoenlaub was an active member of the First Baptist church, having been president of the Men's club from 1946–53. He also was a member of Keystone Lodge No. 14, B.P.O.E., and of Milltown Lodge No. 150 F. & A.M.
>
> Funeral arrangements have not yet been made.

Note in the above the presence of three other important elements:

10. Surviving relatives.
11. Funeral plans.
12. Biographical highlights.

Sometimes the circumstances of death constitute the feature, especially in the case of an obscure person:

> Cleveland, April 22—(UP)—In a dingy one-room attic they shared, three men were found dead today amid evidence of a last struggle against either poisoning or coal gas fumes.
>
> The room was the same in which two of the victims were overcome by natural gas fumes and a third man was killed a year ago.
>
> The victims . . .

REVIEWING A LIFE

Often the news interest in a death is in the events in the life just ended which the occasion recalls. This is as true of a comparatively obscure person as of a prominent person. Note the emphasis upon the biographical in the following example:

Dr. Moses Hadas, world-famous classical scholar and Jay Professor of Greek at Columbia University, died early yesterday after a heart attack in Apsen, Colo. He was 66.

Renowned as an author and translator as well as a teacher, he was in Colorado to participate in a program of the Aspen Institute for Humanistic Studies when he was stricken Monday. With him was his second wife the former Elizabeth M. Chamberlayne.

Dr. Hadas looked every inch the sedate scholar with his pointed white beard. But his blue eyes twinkled as he startled his students with his modern and unorthodox approach to the classics.

He believed there should be continued revisions and fresh translations of classical works.

Space Age Teacher

"It's a little too much to expect a student to pick up a Victorian translation of the Iliad. He's got two strikes against him if he does. Let each age put down the classics in its own language, just so long as they keep the spirit of the original," he once said.

And he was not averse to making use of space age marvels in his teaching. In 1963, for example, he lectured on the origin of the Greek drama to 500 students in four colleges simultaneously by means of the telephone and Telstar, the communications satellite.

Dr. Hadas was a native of Atlanta and received his bachelor of arts degree from Emory University there in 1922. He joined the faculty of Columbia University as an instructor in 1926 and went on to earn his master's and doctor's degrees there.

Headed Department

By 1953, he had become a full professor of Latin and Greek. Three years later he was named Jay Professor of Greek, the University's oldest chair established in 1830 to honor John Jay, the Nation's first Chief Justice and a graduate of Columbia College. Dr. Hadas headed the Greek and Latin Department for two periods, the last as chairman from 1961 to 1964. He held a number of honorary degrees.

Dr. Hadas interrupted his teaching career during World War II when he served for four years with the Office of Strategic Services in North Africa and Greece. It was then he grew his beard.

It created much speculation among students when he returned to the Columbia campus. The most popular theory was that he grew it as part of a disguise. But Dr. Hadas soon straightened out its origin.

"Shave or Tea"

"It was a choice between a cup of tea and a shave. When the water supply got tight, there really wasn't much doubt about what went first," he explained.

Dr. Hadas was the author of more than 30 texts on classical subjects and he translated or edited many other works. He also translated about 20 books from German on classical literature and civilization. His books included "A History of Latin Literature," "Ancilla to Classical Reading" and "Old Wine in New Bottles," among many others.

He was the recipient of many awards. They included what he considered "one of the greatest honors," an invitation by the Parnassus Club, leading intellectual society of Greece, to deliver an address on Plutarch. He gave it in Greek.

Honored by Graduates

He also was twice honored by those he taught. In 1955, Columbia's Society of Older Graduates presented him with a "Greek Teacher Award" as "a skilled teacher who has the rare and happy gift of making his students enjoy the hard work of thinking."

In 1964, Columbia undergraduates honored him with the "Mark Van Doren Award" named for the Pulitzer Prize winning poet who had taught at Columbia for 39 years. It is given each year to a member of the faculty who shows "zealous scholastic leadership, devotion to intellectual development and humility."

Funeral services will be private. Columbia University will arrange for a memorial service after classes resume in September. [Washington *Post*]

EVALUATING A CAREER

The death of a nationally or world-famous person, one whom history will remember, is the occasion for an interpretative piece of writing which blends the details of death with attempts to evaluate the person's importance. Its purpose is to "place" the dead person in history with emphasis upon his importance and contributions. The interpretative obituary is not an editorial although it is impossible for a writer, qualified to pass judgment upon his subject, to avoid evaluation.

By Leonard Sloane

Bernard F. Gimbel was in the forefront of scores of new merchandising concepts during his 59-year career in retailing. Between 1907, when he joined the company founded by his grandfather Adam, and this year when Gimbel Brothers, Inc., reported record sales of $572-million, Mr. Gimbel played the major role in its growth. Under his leadership, Gimbels basement was established in New York as one of the pioneer low-price merchandising operations by a department store.

Long before discount houses reached their current stage of development, the basement at Gimbels, like that of Filene's in Boston and a few other stores throughout the country, established a reputation for selling inexpensive goods to people who had not previously been department store customers.

The stores in the Gimbel chain, moreover, were early proponents of such retailing techniques as the merchandising of private brands to complement national brands, the classification of merchandise into small categories for better profit control and the establishment of boutiques, or special shops, within a store.

In all of these developments, Mr. Gimbel, as president from 1927 until 1953 and as chairman of the board since then, was largely responsible for their implementation.

Two Major Decisions

Bernard Gimbel belonged to that generation of merchants who built great department store and specially store empires in the early decades of the 20th century. Among his contemporaries were such well-known retailing figures as Fred Lazarus Jr., chairman of Federated Department Stores, Inc.; Morton J. May, chairman of the May Department Stores Company; and Nathan M. Ohrbach, former chairman of Ohrbach's, Inc.

Mr. Gimbel engineered two major coups that were probably most responsible for making his chain a great one. The first was the decision to buy the land on which his New York store was located—thus affirming the company's desire to become a permanent fixture in New York, following earlier successes in Milwaukee and Philadelphia.

Overriding the determined opposition of his father, Isaac, and his uncle, Louis, two of the seven sons of Adam Gimbel, he persuaded them to purchase the property on which the Manhattan Gimbels store, built in 1910 now stands. The Herald Square site was purchased for $9-million and Gimbels soon became with its competitor, Macy's, the major retailing attractions of the area.

The second important feat accomplished by Mr. Gimbel was the purchase of the Saks stores in 1923. The following year, Saks Fifth Avenue opened between 49th and 50th Streets and a chain-within-a-chain was in the making.

During the depression, the Saks stores were the only ones in the company to make a profit, quickly proving the wisdom of the acquisition. Even now Saks Fifth Avenue is generally believed to contribute more than half of the earnings of Gimbel Brothers, while representing substantially less than half of its sales.

Not all of Mr. Gimbel's moves met with success. A $10-million, 15-story extension to the Philadelphia store was opened in 1925, but proved to be a white elephant and was sold in 1940 for $5-million.

The original Saks-34th Street store too proved to be a problem for the company, sandwiched as it was between the Gimbels flagship store and Macy's. It was closed in July, 1965 (E. J. Korvette plans to open there next year) and its three branches were converted into Gimbels stores.

Mr. Gimbel was long an admirer of Sears, Roebuck & Co. and Julius Rosenwald and Gen. Robert E. Wood, the two executives who led the giant retailing-mail order chain during its biggest period of growth. He named them as among the people who had the greatest influence on him and he adopted such Sears' policies as suburban-store building and decentralization of control for his own chain.

Going With the Times

In the last two decades of his life, Mr. Gimbel was a participant in the radical changes taking place in the department store industry he loved. The construction of branch units as the population moved to the suburbs, the increasing affluence of the average consumer and the development of new merchandise—both domestic and imported—all played a role in furthering the growth of his stores and those of his competitors.

A strong-willed person despite his affable exterior, he was constantly seeking out more information and learning whatever he could.

"You have to go along with the times," he said once in an interview. "If we're on the job, the business will continue to grow."

Bernard Gimbel continued to go along with the times and his business grew. His stores are a monument to a retailing giant whose name has become a household word not only in New York, but also throughout the United States. [New York *Times*]

MORGUE STORIES

The entire obituary of a famous person may be written after he has died. Newspapers have on file, however, biographical sketches of most prominent persons; it was because they once contained little else except such sketches that newspaper libraries came to be called morgues.

If it seems advisable, and if time permits, the morgue story is revised or edited to be a part of the obituary proper. More ordinary practice, however, is to add it at the end of the story of death with slight, if any, alterations. Events occurring in the man's life after the sketch was written are worked into the newly written first part.

The morgue story actually is an interpretative biographical sketch in which the writer attempts to evaluate the person and assign him his proper historical importance. In composing it, the reporter has an opportunity to do some of his best writing. The best source of material about the basic facts of a man's life is, of course, the man himself. Since the morgue sketch is prepared during its subject's lifetime, it usually is written following an interview. Also, the writer consults previously written material about the person and makes his own impartial estimate of the highlights of the career he is reviewing.

Emphasis in writing should be upon the outstanding characteristics, achievements and activities of the person. The temptation of the young writer is to begin with the fact of a person's birth and to continue with a chronological narrative of his life. In interviewing a person for material about himself it may be convenient to have him tell about himself in such a way but, in writing, the principle to be followed is the same as in all other news writing: most important facts first. The fact of birth seldom is the most important.

When only a short bulletin of an important person's death is received in time for an edition, the morgue part of the printed story may constitute almost the entire printed story, as in the case of the Moses Hadas obituary.

LOCALIZATION

When a famous person dies there is a chance for a localized feature based on the material in the morgue and interviews with local citizens. The following is the lead of a story telling of King Albert's visits to St. Louis. If this sort of story is not possible, an interview with someone in the community who had some contact with the dead celebrity could be written in almost any city, no matter how small.

> Albert I, beloved wartime king of the Belgians, visited St. Louis twice during his lifetime. The first time, in May 1898, he attracted little attention as he was traveling incognito under the name of "John Banks." On his second visit, of five hours' duration Oct. 21, 1919, he was acclaimed by a crowd said at the time to exceed that which greeted President Woodrow Wilson the same year.
>
> Many legends have arisen as the result of Albert's sojourn in America when he was crown prince. He is known to have denied a tale that he served as a newspaper reporter in New York, Minneapolis and other cities. In St. Louis he is said to have been entertained by the Belgian consul and other natives of his country.
>
> In interviews with reporters here in 1919 the triumphant monarch asserted that the reception accorded him by St. Louisans exceeded in cordiality and enthusiasm any other in scores of cities on his itinerary in the United States.
>
> Speaking of St. Louis, Albert I said, "One of the things I admire most is your wonderful activity, and the spirit of enterprise and the large scale of your industrial plants. This allows me to look for greater production. Without increased production, the world, I fear, will have a very difficult year."
>
> The king was accompanied upon his American postwar trip by Queen Elizabeth and Crown Prince Leopold, soon to become his successor to the throne. Heading the St. Louis reception committee were the late Governor Gardner and Mayor Kiel. Ambassador David Francis also rode in the automobile parade to the principal parts of the city and attended a 1:30 P.M. luncheon by the Chamber of Commerce at Hotel Statler. . . .
>
> [St. Louis *Star-Times*]

SIDE FEATURES

In addition to the obituary proper, a newspaper may print several other related items.

1. It is the habit of newspapers, for instance, to print encomiums of prominent individuals who die. Persons acquainted with the career and reputation of the dead man are solicited for statements which usually are included in a single story with a comprehensive lead. Many of these statements are prepared in writing by the persons quoted; others are written following interviews by reporters who express the interviewee's attitude if not his exact words. Expressions of appreciation of certain persons may be published as separate items. If the President of the United States makes a statement, it usually constitutes a separate item. Dispatches from foreign countries carry separate datelines.
2. Sometimes the death of a prominent person leads to an official proclamation by a public official, ordering flags to be flown at half staff or suggesting the cessation of business on the day or during the hours of the funeral.
3. When messages of condolence are received by members of the dead person's family, a newspaper obtains them for publication, either in place of or in addition to the statements that it gathers itself.
4. Resolutions of sympathy passed by organizations with which the deceased was affiliated usually are given to the press for immediate publication.
5. When a businessman dies, especially in a small community, those who had any dealings with him are interested to know whether the establishment will remain open. Newspapers print notices of how long, if at all, the business will be suspended, and whether other business places will close for any length of time as a gesture of respect.
6. The death of a prominent person is the excuse for a recitation of anecdotes of his life. Persons who were close to the deceased frequently write first-person reminiscences. In smaller communities, newspapers try to find citizens who were acquainted in some way with a prominent person who dies. In after years, on the anniversary of the famous person's death or birth or of some outstanding event in his career, more anecdotes are sought.

THE SECOND-DAY STORY

The second-day story is primarily the preliminary story of the funeral. When more than a day intervenes between death and the funeral, there may be two follow-up stories.

Details to look for in the funeral arrangements include:

Time and place.
Who will officiate?
Will services be public or private?
How many will attend?
Arrangements for handling a crowd.
Names of relatives.
Names of notables who will attend.
Will any club, lodge, etc. have a part?
Organizations to attend in a body or to be represented.
Names of musicians and selections.
Who will preach a sermon or deliver a eulogy?
Pallbearers, active and honorary.
Where will burial take place?
What will be the program of the services?

The second-day story also may include additional details of the last illness and death, additional panegyrics, letters of sympathy received by the family, resolutions, memorial services, and the floral offerings. If the family requests that friends omit flowers, the newspaper should include the request. If floral offerings are sent, the newspaper should obtain a list and description of the important pieces and the names of the individuals or organizations sending them. Sometimes potential senders of flowers are asked instead to contribute to some worthy cause.

In virtually every case of death, friends of the dead person are given an opportunity to view the body before the time of the funeral, or if the body is not placed on view, to visit with members of the family in a funeral establishment. Newspapers should find out when such visitations can be made. Organizations which will not be formally represented at the funeral may pay their respects in a group at any earlier hour.

When a member of Congress dies while in Washington, both houses pass resolutions and appoint committees to accompany the body home. Sometimes they adjourn out of respect. The practice of holding a separate memorial service for each deceased congressman has been dispensed with, and only one memorial service now is held each year at which all members of Congress who have died during the year are eulogized. Many clubs and lodges have a similar custom.

A few long-time friends of H. L. Mencken will join members of his family today at a funeral establishment to "speed him on his way."

Mr. Mencken, who died early Sunday, wanted no religious service.

His brother, August Mencken, said the gathering would be at 1 P.M. at an "unnamed mortician's place."

"One of the crying needs of the time in this incomparable republic is for a suitable burial service for the admittedly damned," H. L. Mencken wrote nearly 30 years ago.

Suggestion to Poets

He called on poets to concoct a service for the "doubting dead," saying: "What is needed, and what I bawl for politely, is a service that is free from the pious but unsupported asseverations that revolt so many of our best minds, and yet remains happily graceful and consoling . . . a suitable funeral for doubters, full of lovely poetry, but devoid of any specific pronouncement on the subject of a future life . . .

"Such a libretto for the inescapable last act would be humane and valuable. I renew my suggestion that the poets spit upon their hands and confect it at once."

Mr. Mencken's bawling apparently produced nothing to his taste.

Either August Mencken or Hamilton Owens, editor-in-chief of the Sunpapers, will address today's assembly briefly.

"Harry Left Instructions"

"We'll simply tell them Harry left instructions there was to be no religious service but he did want a few old friends around to speed him on his way," Mr. Mencken said.

Friends of the world-famous newspaperman and critic who are expected to be there include W. Edwin Moffett, who was a member of the old Saturday Night Club; Siegfried Weisberger, who ran the Peabody Bookshop; James M. Cain, novelist, of Hyattsville; Frank R. Kent, political columnist for The Sun and Mr. and Mrs. Louis Cheslock.

Mr. Cheslock, of the Peabody Institute, was another member of the Saturday Night Club and spent Saturday evening at the Mencken house at 1524 Hollins street.

Mr. Mencken died at home in his sleep.

His body will be cremated, and the ashes will be buried in the family plot at Loudon Park Cemetery next to those of his wife, who was Sara Powell Haardt. Mrs. Mencken died in 1933.

Mr. Mencken's survivors include August Mencken, the brother with whom he lived; Charles E. Mencken, another brother of Pittsburgh; and Anna Gertrude Mencken, a sister, of 5110 Gwynn Oak avenue.

Mr. Mencken, closely associated with the Sunpapers during his long career, left a box in the newspaper office with orders that it remain locked until he died. Managing editors of The Sun and the Evening Sun had keys to it.

When it was opened Sunday morning, it yielded a brief note requesting that news of his death receive as scanty coverage as possible.

[Baltimore *Sun*]

THE FUNERAL STORY

When a collection is made of the outstanding newspaper stories of history, it will include more than one account of a funeral. The story of the burial of the unknown soldier by Kirke L. Simpson of the Associated Press has become a classic, as have stories of the funerals of most of the Presidents of the United States. The following is a straightforward and dignified account of an important funeral:

By JAMES LATIMER
Times-Dispatch Staff Writer

Winchester—Quietly and simply, without pomp or eulogy, the last rites for Harry Flood Byrd were conducted here Sunday afternoon.

The former United States senator and governor, who dominated Virginia political life for 40 years, was laid to rest beneath a maple tree bright with the gold of autumn at Mt. Hebron Cemetery.

Vice-President Hubert H. Humphrey, Secretary of the Treasury Henry H. Fowler, Governor Godwin and five former Virginia governors, along with uncounted senators and congressmen stood silently and bareheaded with members of the Byrd family beside the grave.

500 In Cemetery

A crowd of perhaps 500 persons clustered into the cemetery for the 10-minute burial rite.

Earlier, more than 500 people had crowded into Christ Episcopal Church in downtown Winchester for the funeral service. Approximately 400 others stood on the sidewalks outside.

The Rev. John A. Baden, rector of Christ Church, and the Rev. David W. Cammack, rector of Grace Church at Berryville, officiated in following the Episcopal Order for the Burial for the Dead.

Vice-President and Mrs. Humphrey had flown by helicopter into the Winchester airport a few minutes before the service. They were met and escorted to the church by Governor and Mrs. Godwin.

The Humphreys had to hurry off from the cemetery to board their helicopter and transfer at Dulles airport to a plane that was to take them to Milwaukee, Wis., where the vice-president had a long-standing engagement.

They had not arrived in time to join other dignitaries in paying their respects to the family at Rosemont, the senator's home on the outskirts of Berryville.

Mr. Byrd's body had rested in a flag-draped mahogany coffin for nearly three days since his death Thursday at age 79 of a malignant brain tumor.

Inside the white-columned mansion, a profusion of flowers banked the walls.

Wreath From Rangers

One floral tribute stood out: a large wreath of many-colored leaves and berries against a background of rich green pine and spruce.

It had been fashioned by National Park Service rangers from the autumn foliage of Old Rag, the Blue Ridge Mountain that had been Mr. Byrd's favorite hiking ground since he was a boy of 15.

Mr. Byrd enjoyed the distinction of being the only honorary park service ranger, an honor bestowed on him a few years ago in recognition of his abiding interest in the national parks.

Another large wreath stood outside at the west entrance of Rosemont. It bore the figure "30" emblazoned in white against a background of red carnations.

This tribute had come from the Virginia Press Association and it symbolized an old newspaper way of saying farewell to a journalistic colleague.

It was a balmy October afternoon, and the trees around Rosemont glowed with the russet and gold colors of autumn as the funeral procession began shortly after 2 p.m.

Slowly, carefully, the pall-bearers carried the coffin down the steps of the west entrance.

At its front were two old friends and hiking companions, Speaker E. Blackburn Moore of the Virginia House of Delegates and Conrad L. Wirth, former director of the National Park Service.

Next were two United States senators, Mike Mansfield (D-Mont.) and John J. Williams (R-Del.); three grandsons, Harry F. Byrd III, Thomas T. Byrd and Richard E. Byrd Jr., and a nephew, J. Gray Beverley Jr.

The funeral cortege moved slowly over the eight-mile stretch of State Rt. 7 from Berryville to Winchester.

Inside the church, there were no flowers except for two vases of all-white blossoms—gladioli, snapdragons and carnations—at each end of the white and gold altar. The rites followed the classic Episcopal order.

There was a prayer, the responsive readings of Psalms 46 and 121, the brief lesson from Romans 8:14, and St. John 14:1 and the Lord's Prayer. There were no hymns.

Members of the family, the distinguished guests, and close friends along with employees of the Byrd apple and newspaper enterprises, filled the main floor of the church.

Former Govs. Colgate W. Darden, William M. Tuck, John S. Battle, Thomas B. Stanley and Albertis S. Harrison Jr. were among the many old friends and political associates who attended.

At the cemetery, Mr. Baden said the familiar prayers. A corner of the flag was turned back and the symbolic handful of earth was cast on the coffin. Two uniformed officers of the Virginia National Guard folded the flag and handed it to U.S. Sen. Harry F. Byrd Jr.

Out at Rosemont, looking east toward the Blue Ridge from the broad veranda where Sen. Byrd had welcomed President John F. Kennedy on a lovely Sunday in May five years ago, the skies were slightly overcast by light gray clouds.

A yellow leaf floated down beside the old sundial that for many years had stood by the white-columned mansion—a sundial that says in cast iron letters on its face "Time Takes All But Memories."

[Richmond *Times-Dispatch*]

FOLLOW-UPS

A number of other stories may grow out of that of a death. Virtually everyone who is worthy of an obituary has held some position which will have to be filled. Before a speaker of the house is buried, newspapers print stories speculating as to who will be his successor. Frequently there are changes in business organizations after the death of an executive. A smart editor reads the account of a man's death and notes the organizations, business, fraternal, and otherwise, in which he held an office, and assigns reporters to learn how the man's place will be filled in each case.

The courthouse reporter watches for the filing of wills and follows carefully each legal step up to and including the final settlement and discharge.

Memorial services may be held weeks or months after a person's death, schools and clubs may be named for him, monuments and tablets erected to his memory.

THE OBITUARY BLANK

The obituary may seem an important assignment, yet it is one of the first that a cub reporter receives. He is as likely to be sent out to gather facts about a death as to frequent a railroad station or hotel in quest of brevities. This is because few obituaries approach in importance those given as examples in this chapter, and because the elements of all stories of death are similar.

Most newspapers have an obituary blank for reporters who gather facts about deaths. These printed forms also are given to undertakers who cooperate in obtaining information for newspapers. A sample blank follows:

OBITUARY REPORT

Full name..
Residence...
Place of death.......................... Time...............
Cause of death..
Duration of illness..
Present at deathbed ....
Circumstances of death...................................
....
Date of birth.......................... Place...............
Surviving relatives: Wife or husband....................
Parents .... Address............
Brothers .... Address............
.... Address............
and
Sisters................................ Address............
.... Address............
Children.............................. Address............
.... Address............
.... Address............

Date of marriage..................... Place...............
Came to this country .... Naturalized..........
Residence here since.....................................
Previous residence and duration.........................
Last occupation...
Previous occupations ....
Education, with degrees and dates......................
Fraternal orders, clubs, etc..............................
Distinguished service, fraternal, educational, industrial, political, etc.....
....
....
....
Church affiliations..
War record: Division, war................................
When discharged..................... Rank ....
Honors ....
Time of funeral...................... Place ....
Who will officiate...
Organizations to attend in a body.......................
Body will lie in state: When .... Where..............
Active pallbearers ....
....
Honorary pallbearers ....
....
Music ....
....

Burial place ....
....
Prominent floral pieces ....
....
Attending from away ....
....
Additional information ....
....
....

No blank can include every question which a reporter may want answered, and so it is better not to rely entirely upon an undertaker but to interview the nearest living relative.

If he relies upon another to obtain his facts for him, the reporter may miss the feature of his story, especially if death resulted from violence or an accident. Possible features not suggested by the questions on the blank include: failure of a close relative to reach the bedside in time; a letter written by the dead person containing instructions for his own funeral; the last words of the deceased; some request made shortly before death; any coincidence in the date; place, or manner of death; and some other event in the history of the individual or his family.

LANGUAGE AND STYLE

The language of the obituary should be simple and dignified. The verb "to die" is the safest to use. No religious group can take offense at it but can interpret it to suit its own tenets. "Passed away," "passed on," "called home," "the great beyond," "gone to his reward," "the angel of death," "the grim reaper," "departed this life," and similar expressions should be avoided. Also, let it be repeated, attempts at "fine" writing may be only maudlin.

Suicides

In covering a suicide, the reporter seeks the same information about a man's career, funeral arrangements, when the body will lie in state, etc., as in the case of an ordinary obituary. Elements peculiar to the suicide story, however, include:

1. The motive.
2. The method.
3. The probable circumstances leading up to the act.
4. The coroner's inquest or medical examiner's report.

THE MOTIVE

A person who commits suicide usually is despondent because of financial difficulties, ill health, marital unhappiness, a mental disorder or a philosophic attitude of discouragement toward life in general.

If the person does not leave a letter explaining his motive, the reporter must investigate whichever motives seem most probable. A man's banker or doctor, his business associates, and his friends and relatives should be interviewed. The reporter should ask if the person made any previous attempts at suicide, if he ever mentioned suicide, if he appeared to be in good health recently, especially the day before he took his life. How did he take leave of his family and friends? Was there anything at all suspicious about his actions or remarks recently? If he had not consulted a physician recently, others who knew him can pass judgment upon his state of health. His appetite, sleep, recreation or hours of work may have been affected noticeably.

When there is no apparent motive, the news writer should say so and should quote those whom he has interviewed to that effect. He should not attempt to concoct a motive and must be particularly careful not to ascribe a suicidal motive when none was present. Legally, no suicide is a suicide until so called by a coroner's jury or a medical examiner's report, depending on the system in vogue. If there is a doubt, the account of death should be qualified by a statement as "thought to be suicide."

Even when the suicidal motive is present beyond a doubt, some newspapers hesitate to use the word. The editor of a paper in a small community may attempt to protect the feelings of surviving relatives by covering up the suicidal intent. Seldom is such an attempt successful, as an unprejudiced statement of the facts surrounding death indicates either suicide or murder. Only by deliberate fabrication is it possible really to "protect" the widow and other survivors.

It is doubtful, furthermore, whether the paper does as much good as harm in "hushing up" a suicide story. Anyone who knew the dead person will become acquainted with the facts anyway, and if he encounters an effort to deceive him as to what actually happened, he conjectures. The rumors which circulate as to the motive of a suicide usually are much more damaging to a person's reputation than the simple truth would have been. A frank newspaper account puts an end to rumors.

THE METHOD

The method by which suicide was accomplished usually is obvious. A newspaper should not dramatize the means of a suicide or print a story that might encourage another to take his life. A poison used for suicidal purpose should not be mentioned by name, and if suicide by any other method is prevalent, newspapers should cooperate with authorities by omitting the method.

The coroner or physician summoned to examine the body can estimate the length of time the person has been dead. Members of the family and friends can provide clues as to what actions preceded the accomplishment of the act. The reporter should try to find the person who last saw the deceased alive.

> Detroit (UPI)—The death of Mrs. Ethel Warren, an heiress to the Du Pont fortune and former wife of Franklin D. Roosevelt Jr., was ruled a suicide Wednesday.
> Dr. Edward S. Zawadzki, the Wayne County Medical examiner, ruled that Mrs. Warren, 49, committed suicide by hanging herself in the bathroom of her suburban Grosse Pointe Farms mansion Tuesday.
> "It was obviously a suicide," he said, "and no other element would enter into this."
> Zawadzki said Mrs. Warren had a "history of depression and so forth."
> Friends said twice-wed Mrs. Warren, mother of two sons by Roosevelt and a third in her second marriage, had been ill.
> Her body was found hanging by a braided belt of her dressing gown from a shower rod in the locked bathroom after a maid had become alarmed over her whereabouts.
> Police broke through the bathroom door. The maid, Martha Weber, said Mrs. Warren had appeared disconsolate when she was served breakfast in bed about 9 A.M.
> Miss Weber said when she returned for her tray about 40 minutes later, Mrs. Warren was gone. She said she then found the bathroom door locked and when Mrs. Warren failed to answer her calls, she notified authorities.
> Mrs. Warren was the daughter of the late Mr. and Mrs. Eugene I. du Pont.
> A brother, Eugene, is a board member of the family-founded E. I. du Pont de Nemours & Co. of Wilmington, Del.
> Funeral services will be held at 11 A.M. Thursday from Christ Episcopal Church in neighboring Grosse Pointe. Burial is to be at Wilmington, the Du Pont family home.
> Mrs. Warren's second husband, lawyer Benjamin S. Warren Jr., was called to her home at her death. The two had been separated.

Friends said Mrs. Warren had been looking forward to the marriage June 12 of Christopher du Pont Roosevelt, 24, one of her sons by her first marriage.

Christopher is to be wed to Rosamund Havemeyer of Huntington, Long Island, N.Y.

The other son from the first marriage is Franklin D. Roosevelt III, 27.

The son by the second marriage, Benjamin S. Warren III, 11, goes to private school in Eagle Brook, N.H.

INQUESTS

The coroner, a county official whose duty it is to investigate cases of unusual death, usually orders an inquest into a case believed to be suicide. Sometimes this is delayed until an autopsy is performed on the body and until circumstances of the death are fully determined. The coroner's jury may determine the motive as well as the manner of death. If in doubt, it returns an open verdict.

According to the National Municipal League elective coroner systems now exist statewide in only 13 states. Where it has been abolished, the office of coroner has been replaced by a medical examiner attached to the police department or some other law enforcement agency. It is his obligation to determine the cause of death in cases in which an attending physician cannot sign a death certificate. Neither a coroner's jury verdict nor a medical examiner's report has any more weight in a criminal case than a grand jury chooses to give it.

ACCIDENTS, DISASTERS

Part of the price which modern man pays for the benefits of a highly industrialized society is the danger he runs of sudden, violent injury or death. Automobile accidents result annually in about 50,000 deaths and many times that number of injuries. Wrecks of common carriers—railroads, street cars, buses, trucks, airplanes, boats—are fewer but are more destructive than in the days of slower speed and less delicate mechanics. Homes, public buildings, industrial plants and mines, are better protected against fire and explosions, but an undetected minor flaw may result in a catastrophe without warning. Because of lack of foresight on the part of our grandfathers, we who live in the United States today are facing a national crisis as to how to control floods, dust storms and soil erosion which cause tremendous losses of life and property and, some say, are turning our country into a desert. Other "acts of God," such as hurricanes, tornadoes, earthquakes and cyclones, continue to occur with their same frequency, and man has not yet learned how to protect himself adequately against them.

ELEMENTS OF INTEREST

Although they differ from each other by types, and although no two disasters of any kind are alike from the standpoint of news interest, news events pertaining to loss of life and property have in common numerous aspects which a reporter must bear in mind. Among the possible angles which no reporter can overlook are the following:

1. Casualties (dead and injured).
    a. Number killed and injured.
    b. Number who escaped.
    c. Nature of injuries and how received.
    d. Care given injured.
    e. Disposition made of the dead.
    f. Prominence of anyone who was killed, injured or who escaped.
    g. How escape was handicapped or cut off.
2. Property damage.
    a. Estimated loss in value.
    b. Description (kind of building, etc.).
    c. Importance of property (historical significance, etc.).
    d. Other property threatened.
    e. Insurance protection.
    f. Previous disasters in vicinity.
3. Cause of disaster.
    a. Testimony of participants.
    b. Testimony of witnesses.
    c. Testimony of others: fire chief, property owner, relief workers, etc.
    d. How was accident discovered?
    e. Who sounded alarm or summoned aid?
    f. Previous intimation of danger: ship or building condemned, etc.
4. Rescue and relief work.
    a. Number engaged in rescue work, fire fighting, etc.
    b. Are any prominent persons among the relief workers?
    c. Equipment used: number of water lines, chemicals, etc.
    d. Handicaps: wind, inadequate water supply or pressure, etc.
    e. Care of destitute and homeless.

ILLNESS AND DEATH 281

    f. How disaster was prevented from spreading: adjacent buildings soaked, counter forest fire, etc.
    g. How much property was saved? How?
    h. Heroism in rescue work.
5. Description.
    a. Spread of fire, flood, hurricane, etc.
    b. Blasts and explosions.
    c. Attempts at escape and rescue.
    d. Duration.
    e. Collapsing walls, etc.
    f. Extent and color of flames.
6. Accompanying incidents.
    a. Spectators: number and attitude, how controlled, etc.
    b. Unusual happenings: room or article untouched, etc.
    c. Anxiety of relatives.
7. Legal action as result.
    a. Inquests, post mortems, autopsies.
    b. Search for arsonist, hit-and-run driver, etc.
    c. Protest of insurance company.
    d. Negligence of fire fighters, police, etc.
    e. Investigation of cause.

In all stories of disaster there is human interest. In most of them, there also are suspense and a recognition of combat between man and the elements. Disaster stories, furthermore, are action stories and contain considerable details as to exactly what happened. If these details are not presented in chronological order, they at least are so arranged as to leave no doubt in the reader's mind regarding the sequence of the most important of them.

Few other types of stories offer the writer greater opportunity for descriptive writing. Although major disaster stories are illustrated, the writer does not rely upon a photograph to do the work of 1,000 or even 100 or ten words.

PICKING THE FEATURE

No formula for writing a disaster story—or any other type of story for that matter—should be accepted as absolute. In general, however, the lead of the disaster story should follow the orthodox rule of playing up the five *w*'s, giving identification and authority and playing up the feature. Any one of the elements listed may be the feature of the story at hand. Regardless of what is played up, the occasion must be identified in the lead by the amount of loss, either in lives or property. The reader judges the importance of the disaster by the size of the casualty list or the number of digits after the dollar sign. When the casualty list or inventory of property is long, it is impossible to be specific in the lead. Names, however, must be high in the story. If their number is not prohibitive, they should come immediately after the lead; otherwise, they should be included in a box either within or next to the story proper. If included in the story itself, they should be followed by explanations as to how each casualty or item of damage occurred.

PRECAUTIONS

The reporter must be careful not to assign blame in an automobile accident, the type of disaster story which he has most frequent occasion to write. Police reports are not adequate protection against libel in such a story as the following:

> Disregarding a traffic signal and a policeman's whistle, Alex Winser, 1421 Talcott street, crashed into an automobile driven by Miss Ruth Hazelhurst, 1191 W. Vilas court, at 11 o'clock this morning at Third and Hamilton streets.

The following is a much safer way:

> Two automobiles, one driven by Miss Ruth Hazelhurst, 1191 W. Vilas court, and the other by Alex Winser, 1421 Talcott street, collided at 11 o'clock this morning at Third and Hamilton streets. Neither driver was injured.

Some editors insist on the form, "the automobile driven by" or "the automobile in which the couple was riding," instead of "his automobile" or "the couple's machine." This is a precaution against possible libel action when the driver or occupant of a car is not the owner. Other editors consider the precaution unnecessary.

Care must be exercised in using "crashed," "demolished," "destroyed," and other descriptive verbs. The reporter should study the definitions of such words to avoid misapplying them. The makes of automobiles usually should not be mentioned.

It must be remembered that to collide two bodies must be in motion. Thus, if a moving automobile hits one which is parked at the curbing, there is no collision; rather, the car in motion strikes the other.

In the attempt to make drivers more careful and thus reduce

accidents, some newspapers print daily tables or charts to show the total number of accidents and casualties by comparison with the preceding year. Likewise, since a magazine campaign against automobile accidents a few years ago, newspapers have been more inclined to include frank details of such mishaps to emphasize their horror. Much more gruesome pictures also are being used than formerly.

In the belief that they are performing a public service as well as fostering both reader interest and friendship, some newspapers undisguisedly editorialize in accident stories, as:

> The danger of bicycle riding on public streets again was illustrated about 7 P.M. yesterday when Harold, 13-year-old son of Mr. and Mrs. Emil J. Bornstein, 636 Cabany street, was seriously injured in the 1200 block of Chicksaw avenue. He was struck by an automobile driven by O. S. Patrick, 802 Lunt avenue.

SIDE FEATURES

Any one of the elements which go to make up a complete disaster story conceivably could be played up in a sidebar: acts of heroism, miraculous escapes, rescue and relief work, coincidences, etc. It is customary to use boxes or separate stories for long tabulations of casualties or damages and for lists of previous catastrophes of a similar nature. Eye-witness accounts are provided by victims who had narrow escapes and by bystanders, rescue workers, reporters and others. When the disaster occurs outside the circulation area of the publication, it is customary to use a sidebar or in some other way play up the names of any local persons who were involved.

PERSPECTIVE

Many disasters can be prevented by such obvious precautions as straightening highways, repairing defective electrical wiring and posting warning signals. Others cannot be controlled without scientific study and analysis and action on a much broader scale. The media of communication can help the public understand why a certain type of disaster is prevalent in a community, area, state, or nation by "digging deeper" than the facts related to a specific news event.

Rufus Terral, St. Louis *Post-Dispatch* editorial writer, for instance, began an article, "In the Wake of the Floods," in the October 1951 *Survey* as follows:

Behind last summer's great natural catastrophe, the devastating floods in Kansas and Missouri, is a simple story. The sweeping tragedy of 44 persons killed, 500,000 persons displaced, 2,000,000 acres flooded, 45,000 houses damaged or destroyed, the teeming Kansas Citys gutted by water and flame, and a $2.5 billion loss is only an effect. Underlying it all is the tale of three dams that became lost in politics in Kansas and the District of Columbia, and never got built.

Sociological phenomena are interrelated. Why flood control projects are not constructed involves consideration of more than selfish political interests. The stories of the depletion of natural resources, chiefly forests and grazing lands, and of soil erosion and other bad consequences of unscientific methods of farming are intricate ones.

Slum area fires usually can be blamed on faulty building codes and/or their improper enforcement. Probing deeper, to obtain perspective, however, the interpretative reporter may discover the origin of overcrowded housing in the heavy migration of Negroes, Puerto Ricans or others into areas where segregation is enforced and programs for integrating newcomers into the economic and social life of the community are inadequate. The machinations of some real estate operators to reap personal profit by playing race against race or nationality group against nationality group may be revealed. Tracing the ownership of tenement property, often concealed by "dummy" title holders, may be enlightening and a first step toward removal of fire hazards.

At a different level, newspapers can lead the way in educating home owners and tenants in how to preserve and renovate property so as to remove hazards. The famous Baltimore Plan of urban renewal could not have succeeded without the vigorous support of the *Sunpapers*.

Those concerned with safety on the streets and highways still stress the *three E*'s: engineering, education and enforcement. Increasingly, however, researchers are paying more attention to so-called human factors. The psychology of the automobile driver is being studied with remarkable results. The causes of "accident proneness" often are deep-seated within the individual and, for proper understanding, may require study of social factors external to the individual. Only a start has been made toward understanding the interrelationships in this field.

The same is true of most other aspects of the problem as a whole. Too many explanations of why teenagers are more reckless drivers than adults are superficial and contradictory. Simple explanations and answers should be avoided until much more study has been completed.

In the meantime, the interpretative journalist can help keep the public informed as to the status of that research.

In 1966 the book, *Unsafe at Any Speed*, became a best seller and its author, Ralph Nader, was a key witness at Congressional hearings which resulted in legislation to compel the automobile industry to pay more attention to the safety of its products.

14

Police, Crime, Criminal Law

I LEARNING THE ROPES
  1. The Police System
  2. What Constitutes Crime

II ELEMENTS OF CRIME NEWS
  1. The Police Blotter
  2. Picking the Feature
  3. Juveniles
  4. Human Interest
  5. Other Police News
  6. Crime Statistics
  7. Situation Stories

III CRIMINAL PROCEDURE
  1. Arraignment
  2. Preliminary Hearing
  3. The Grand Jury
  4. Pleas and Motions
  5. Other Preliminaries

IV CRIMINAL TRIALS
  1. First Stories
  2. Picking the Jury
  3. Opening Statements
  4. Evidence
  5. Closing Statements
  6. Reporting Trials
  7. Verdicts
  8. Sentences
  9. Punishments

V THE ETHICS OF CRIME NEWS
  1. A Fair Trial vs a Free Press
  2. Understanding the Criminal

IF FOR SOME UNIMAGINABLE REASON A NEWSPAPER WERE COMPELLED TO remove all of its beat reporters but one, it would be the man at police headquarters who would remain at his post. This is so, not because crime news is considered so overpoweringly important, but because in addition to learning of homes that have been broken into, checks that have been forged and murders that have been committed, the police reporter usually is the first to turn in tips of accidents, attempted suicides, missing persons, rabid dogs, strikes and many other events about which newspapers carry stories.

Because the police are in close touch with more phases of everyday life than any other news source, the police beat affords excellent training for the beginning reporter and, fortunately, is one which he is likely to get. In the small community, covering police means visiting the police station two or three or more times a day, visiting the scenes of the infrequent important crimes which occur, verifying and amplifying the comparatively meager reports contained on the official police blotter or bulletin and writing all police news worth mention. In a large city, covering police means to remain all day at headquarters or at a district station, watching the steadily growing day's report and phoning tips of the most important items (perhaps 25 per cent of the total) to the city desk. When anything happens about which the paper wants more than the beat man can obtain from the police bulletin or by interviewing members of the force or witnesses brought to the station, an assignment man is sent out; the writing is done by rewrite men.

Neither the life of the police reporter nor of the average police detective resembles very closely that which the continuity strips and magazine short stories depict. After he has seen one sobbing mother, one hardboiled harlot, one repentant gunman, and one of each of the other types which frequent police headquarters, the reporter has seen them all. When this fact dawns upon him, and as he becomes accustomed to the intransigence of all parties concerned in the diurnal police drama, he may have to struggle against both cynicism and discouragement. A good turn at police reporting is the best hazing possible for the callow graduate and aspiring author of the world's greatest novel. There are few newspapermen of importance who did not take the test and pass. An attitude of detached studiousness will enable the beginning reporter to make his police reporting experience what it should be: the most valuable of his entire journalistic career.

Learning the Ropes

THE POLICE SYSTEM

The police reporter has got to know who's who and why at headquarters or at the district station which is his to cover. On the next page is shown the setup of the police department in an average-sized American city. In other cities, the organization may differ in details but not fundamentally. At the top is always a chief of police, superintendent of police, police commissioner or some other individual appointed either by the mayor with the approval of the lawmaking body or by a police commission so appointed. Whatever its title, this office is a

```
                        CHIEF
                          OF          ──── SECRETARY
                        POLICE
                          │
                     STAFF (TWO)
                          │
                       CAPTAIN
        ┌─────────────────┼─────────────────┐
   DETECTIVE            PATROL            TRAFFIC
    BUREAU             DIVISION           DIVISION
   LIEUTENANT   ┌────────┼────────┐      LIEUTENANT ──── Secretary
       │        │        │        │           │
   ┌───┼───┐   8 A.M.  4 P.M.  Midnight    Sergeant
Sergeant Sergeant Sergeant  —      —        —              │
   │    │    │   4 P.M.  Midnight  8 A.M.    ├── Accident Prevention Bureau
Police Auto Record      LIEUTENANT           ├── Educational Director
Women  Detail Bureau        │                ├── Inspectors
        │                Desk Sergeant       ├── Traffic Engineer
   Identification                            ├── Inspection Station
      Bureau           Telephone Operator    ├── Four Inspectors
                             │               └── One Patrolmen
   Detectives         ┌──────┼──────┐
                  Patrol    Foot    Motorized
                  Wagons  Patrolmen Patrolmen

                    Juvenile Officer
```

political one, and its holder may have little or nothing to say about the formation of general policies. If the higher-ups decide that certain "places" are to be allowed to remain open, they remain open until the word comes from above, either as a result of public pressure or for other reasons. Whenever any change in policy is made it is, of course, the chief who "fronts," making the announcements and receiving the credit; likewise, when something goes wrong, he is the scapegoat unless it is possible to "pass the buck" down the line to some underling.

This realistic picture of how the law enforcement system operates may be disturbing to young reporters with an idealistic or reformist nature, but until the public insists on an extension of the civil service system to include heads of police departments and upon strict observance of discipline and honesty throughout the entire system, the situation will not change. The trouble is that the element in the population which might favor an improvement either is unaware of the true state of affairs or is too indolent to do anything about it. The irate citizen who fulminates against the patrolman who looks the other way for a slight consideration or because of orders from above, is the same who, when he receives a ticket for parking his automobile overtime, starts on a hunt for someone who knows someone who knows someone. The practice of frightening children into proper behavior by threatening to call a policeman also is not conducive to a helpful attitude on the part of the same children when they become adults.

Despite modern training methods, many if not most policemen adhere to the "catch 'em and lock 'em up" school of criminology. Understandably, they want every arrest they make to lead to a conviction in court. They find it difficult to accept the principle of everyone's being considered innocent until proved guilty. They chafe under court restrictions regarding the gathering of evidence which forbid entering a place or searching a suspect without a proper warrant. They believe some eavesdropping, wire tapping and even entrapment to be necessary. They also want more time than the United States Supreme Court says they should have to question or "work over" a suspect before filing charges against him. The police reporter cannot allow himself, while making friendships, to adopt the policeman's psychology.

Paid more poorly than would be necessary to attract a higher type of public servant, "coppers" off their assumed dignity are pretty good fellows. Fraternizing with them, the reporter learns to like them. A policeman friend is a real asset and usually can be obtained through mention of his name creditably in connection with some story. Without friends in the department, the reporter is worthless as the formal reports and notations on the police blotter are grossly inadequate in case of an important story. In such instances it is necessary to talk to the policemen assigned to the case or to the principals; to see anyone in custody of the police, of course, requires permission.

A police captain is in executive control of a station which is organized in semimilitary fashion. In small communities, the chief may assume this responsibility or, as in the case of the city for which the outline is given, there may be a captain performing the function of chief at night. In large cities, each precinct station is directed by a captain. The lieutenants usually head up the different operating divisions, such as traffic, detective and patrol. The sergeant is a "straw boss" who may have charge of a switchboard over which he directs the activities of patrolmen on beats or may take charge of a small squad of patrolmen on some errand or duty. Inspectors may have roving assignments to check up on the operations of district stations or may perform the functions described as usually assigned to lieutenants; it is largely a matter of terminology. In the outline given, inspectors in the traffic division are an entirely different type, being responsible for investigating the circumstances of traffic accidents.

If there is more than one station in a community, all keep in touch with headquarters by means of a ticker or printer telegraph system, and a central record is kept of all important cases. Police departments even in small cities rapidly are installing two-way radio systems to enable headquarters to talk with cruising patrolmen in police automobiles. Bureaus of identification in which photographs, fingerprints and possibly bertillion records are taken and kept and ballistic and chemical studies made of clues also are increasing.

To check up on minor occurrences, the police reporter telephones the district stations at intervals throughout the day. For the most part, however, he watches the blotter or bulletin on which appears promptly everything of prime importance; assignment men are sent to district stations when necessary.

Entirely separate from the city police is the sheriff who is the law enforcement officer for unincorporated areas within a county. Theoretically, the sheriff can intervene in municipal criminal affairs, but actually he seldom does so except when invited or when local law enforcement breaks down. When such happens, it is extremely newsworthy and someone inevitably charges "politics."

Sheriff's raids are made mostly to break up illegal gambling establishments outside city limits. Sheriff traffic police also patrol the highways along with a limited number of state police. In states where the township unit of government persists, the law enforcement officer is the constable and the local judicial officer is the justice of the peace.

County prosecuting attorneys are called circuit or district attorneys or state's attorneys. They are elected locally but are responsible to the state attorney general in the enforcement of state law. Federal prosecutors are district attorneys; federal law enforcement officers are marshals; and preliminary hearings are conducted by commissioners.

WHAT CONSTITUTES CRIME

As important to the reporter as knowing police procedure is a knowledge of what constitutes crime. A breach of the law may be either a felony or misdemeanor. Since the law differs in different states the same offense may be a felony in one state and a misdemeanor in another; and a felony or misdemeanor in one state may not be considered a crime at all in another. A felony always is a serious offense, such as murder, whereas a misdemeanor is a minor offense such as breaking the speed law. Felonies are punishable by death or imprisonment, whereas a misdemeanor usually results in a fine or confinement in a local jail. A *capital* crime is one punishable by death; an *infamous* crime is one punishable by a prison sentence.

Crimes may be classified as follows:

1. Against the person.
    a. Simple assault: threatening, doubling the fist, etc.
    b. Aggravated assault: threat violent enough to cause flight.
    c. Battery: actually striking a person, a rider's horse, spitting on another, etc.
    d. False imprisonment: liberty unlawfully restrained by anyone.
    e. Kidnaping: stealing away a person; may use abduction for women or children.
    f. Rape: unlawful carnal knowledge of a woman forcibly detained; statutory rape occurs when girl is minor even though she consents.
    g. Maim (mayhem): the attacker disables or dismembers his victim.
    h. Homicide: killing when the victim dies within a year and a day.
        (1) Matricide: killing one's mother.
        (2) Patricide: killing one's father.
        (3) Fratricide: killing one's brother or sister.
        (4) Uxorcide: killing one's wife or husband.

        (5) Justified: in self-defense or in line of duty.
        (6) Felonious: either murder or manslaughter.
    i. Manslaughter.
        (1) Voluntary: intentionally in the heat of passion or as the result of extreme provocation.
        (2) Involuntary: unintentional but with criminal negligence.
    j. Murder.
        (1) First degree: with expressed malice and premeditation.
        (2) Second degree: no premeditation but intent to kill or inflict injury regardless of outcome.
    k. Abortion: interfering with pregnancy.
2. Against habitation.
    a. Burglary: entering another's dwelling with intent to commit a felony therein; often extended to include any building.
    b. Arson: malicious burning of another's real estate.
3. Against property.
    a. Larceny: taking and converting to use with felonious intent the property of another.
    b. Robbery: larceny with intimidation or violence against the person.
    c. Embezzlement: larceny by means of a breach of confidence.
    d. False pretenses: confidence games, impostures, swindles.
    e. Receiving stolen goods: for sale or concealment; recipient called "fence."
    f. Forgery: altering or falsely marking a piece of writing for private profit or deception of another.
    g. Malicious mischief: killing animals, mutilating or defacing property.
    h. Extortion: blackmail; obtaining illegal compensation to do or not to do any act.
4. Against morality and decency.
    a. Adultery: sexual relations between a married and unmarried person.
    b. Fornication: sexual relations between unmarried persons.
    c. Bigamy: second marriage without dissolving the first.
    d. Incest: sexual relations between persons so closely related that they are forbidden to marry.
    e. Miscegenation: marriage between races forbidden to intermarry.
    f. Seduction: inducing an unmarried girl to engage in sexual relations by false promises or deception.

g. Prostitution: promiscuous indulgence in sexual relations by women for profit.
h. Sodomy: homosexual relations between men.
i. Obscenity: anything offensive to one's sense of chastity.
j. Indecency: anything outrageously disgusting.
k. Contributing to delinquency of a minor: encouraging or permitting any waywardness in youths.
l. Sabbath laws: restrict commercial and other activities on Sundays.

5. Against the public peace.
    a. Breach of the peace: may cover disorderly conduct and a variety of nuisances.
    b. Affray: fighting in a public place to the terror of the public.
    c. Unlawful assembly: for purpose of planning or committing illegal act.
    d. Rout: occurs when unlawful assembly begins to move.
    e. Riot: occurs when assembly or rout becomes tumultuous or violent.
    f. Disturbance of public assembly: interference with legal meeting.
    g. Disorderly conduct: statutes stipulate acts forbidden.
    h. Forcible entry and detainer: illegal seizure or holding of property.
    i. Defamation: written is libel, spoken is slander.
    j. Concealed weapons: may be listed as disorderly conduct.
    k. Gaming: playing games for money or games of chance.
    l. Gambling: betting on outcomes of events over which bettors have no control.

6. Against justice and authority.
    a. Treason: breach of allegiance to country; giving enemy aid.
    b. Perjury: false testimony under oath in judicial proceedings.
    c. Bribery: attempt to influence public official in his duties.
    d. Embracery: attempt to influence a juror.
    e. Counterfeiting: making false money which is passed as genuine.
    f. Misconduct in office: extortion, breach of trust, neglect, etc.
    g. Obstructing justice: resisting arrest; refusing to aid arresting officer.
    h. Obstructing punishment: escape; prison breach.
    i. Compounding a felony: agreeing not to prosecute felon or assisting him in evading justice.
    j. Exciting litigation: stirring up lawsuits for profit; barratry; maintenance; champerty.

k. Election laws: fraud or illegal interference with voting.
l. Conspiracy: planning or plotting to commit crime.
m. Contempt: improper respect for court.
7. Against public safety, health and comfort.
　a. Nuisances: annoyances.
　b. Traffic regulations.
　c. Food and drug acts.
　d. Health regulations.
　e. Safety laws for common carriers, use of explosives, etc.

The police reporter must understand these popular definitions of criminal offenses, the names of which may or may not correspond to the statutory titles which differ somewhat by states.

Elements of Crime News

THE POLICE BLOTTER

Despite the quantity of news emanating from police headquarters which gets into print, much more that appears on the blotter or bulletin is disregarded by the police reporter. Whereas it is possible to give feature treatment to almost everything that is reported to police, there is so much sameness in most of the routine of law enforcement that such entries on the bulletin as complaints against peddlers, small boys or dogs, notices from the police of other cities to be on the outlook for a certain person or automobile, reports of suspicious characters and lost and found articles go unheeded. What follows is an almost verbatim copy of the entries covering several hours on the police bulletin in an average-sized city, together with the use made of the material by the police reporter:

Bulletin	*Newspaper Treatment*
The following were injured in auto accident at McCabe and Dunmore and taken to Municipal hospital: Joseph Muenter, 623 Center street, Massillion, Ohio, laceration to hand; Mrs. Ollie Richter, Peru, Ill., age 51, laceration to scalp.	Not used because minor and occurred outside city limits; no local citizens in any way involved. Reporter talked to traffic inspectors who investigated.
L. D. Donaldson, 117 Forest avenue, reports the loss of a male bull dog.	Ignored as trivial.

Bulletin

Grover Mack (c), 1835 Grey avenue, arrested for passing a red light on complaint of Robert A. Kirkhope, 118 N. Park avenue, Waukegan, in connection with accident. Case set for 9/23 and defendant locked up awaiting bond.

Attempts made to burglarize Royal Cafe, 1248 Chicago avenue, between 2 A.M. and 6:45 A.M. Used a one-inch drill on rear door. Entrance not gained.

Attempt made to burglarize Helen's Cafe, 523 Dempster street, between 2 A.M. and 6 A.M. Used a one-inch drill on rear door. Entrance not gained.

John C. Scale, 826 Sherman avenue, driving a Chevrolet coupe eastbound on Dempster street, at McCormick boulevard, backed into a Studebaker sedan driven by Lawrence G. Briggs, 1238 Oak avenue, and then continued east on Dempster street into city.

John C. Scale, 826 Sherman avenue, was arrested for driving while intoxicated on Dempster street. Locked up and case set for 9/23.

Hugh C. Collins, 809 Washington street, driving a Chevrolet coupe east-bound on Washington street, west of Elmwood avenue,

Newspaper Treatment

Combined with another report, below.

Two-paragraph story, as follows:

Burglars early today failed in their attempt to enter and burglarize two Evanston restaurants.

A screen over the rear window at the Royal Cafe, 1248 Chicago avenue, was torn but no entrance gained. The burglars also failed to gain entrance at Helen's Cafe, 523 Dempster street, after using a drill on the rear door, police say.

The following are paragraphs near the end of a general accident story, the lead for which was a serious accident, occurring after the reporter left police headquarters:

Two men were arrested on charges of driving under the influence of liquor yesterday after the car in which both of them drove was in two collisions. The men are: Hugh C. Collins, 809 Washington Street, and John C. Scale, 826 Sherman avenue.

Scale was driving the car when it was involved in an accident with one driven by Lawrence G. Briggs, 1238 Oak avenue, at Dempster street and McCormick boulevard, police say. He left the scene of the accident, police report, but was arrested a few blocks away.

His companion, Collins, drove the car toward his home, but it hit one owned by Richard Steele,

Bulletin

collided with a Ford coupe parked in front of 910 Washington street, owned by Richard Steele, 4730¼ Woodlawn avenue, Chicago.

Grover Mark (c), 1835 Grey avenue, driving a Pontiac sedan eastbound on Emerson street, at McCormick boulevard, collided with a Dodge sedan driven north by Robert Kirkhope, 118 S. Park avenue, Waukegan. Dorothy Brush, 1926 Noyes street, received a broken collar bone and was attended at St. Francis hospital.

Stephen Blake, 330 N. Kerr street, picked up around garage at 837 Dale avenue. Held for investigation.

Citizen reported someone in the St. Cloud Hat Shop, 106 Sherwin street. No one found. Store locked up.

Newspaper Treatment

4730½ Woodlawn avenue, Chicago, parked at the curb in front of 910 Washington street, police say. He continued to his home and was arrested by police on charges of driving while intoxicated and leaving the scene of an accident.

Both drivers in a two-car collision yesterday were arrested by police on charges of passing a red light when police were unable to ascertain which of the drivers passed the light. Grover Mack, 1835 Grey avenue, asserted he had the green light at the intersection at Emerson Street and McCormick road. Robert Kirkhope, 118 N. Park avenue, Waukegan, driving at right angles to Mack, said he had the green light. The cars collided causing approximately $300 damages.

Dorothy Brush, 1926 Noyes street, was attended at St. Francis hospital for a fractured collar bone.

Ignored as trivial.

Ignored as trivial.

More nearly complete records are turned in on regulation forms in all such cases, and these blanks may be consulted by the police reporter. Usually, however, he prefers to talk to the policemen involved if he can find them, or with the principals. It is not safe practice to rely upon the police bulletin as authentic because policemen are notoriously bad spellers and make numerous mistakes in names and addresses, some of which may be noted in the examples given. If attempts at verification fail, the reporter should accredit his story to the police bulletin. It is presumed, of course, that he knows the law of libel which offers him no protection if he uses the expression, "police say." It is not safe to print news of an arrest until a person has been taken into custody and booked on a certain charge; then the newspaper can relate only what has happened. It is impossible to say without risk that a person is "wanted for having fled the scene of an accident." Rather, the reporter should write the person is wanted "in connection with the accident..." Every item of police news should be verified before being used. As is seen from the examples given, for an adequate account of any item appearing on the police bulletin, more details than given there are needed.

PICKING THE FEATURE

All crime stories involve action. They relate to incidents which are potentially exciting when read about, provided the reporter has been resourceful and thorough in his newsgathering. Until a case reaches court, knowledge of law is secondary to ability to observe, describe and imagine all of the angles needing investigation and the sources from which information may be obtainable. The crime reporter, in other words, must possess some of the qualities of a good detective although his purpose is entirely different. He is not out to solve the crime but to learn all that it is possible to find out about it.

Because anything can and constantly does happen, the following list of potential elements of interest in news of crime cannot possibly be complete. It is only suggestive.

1. Casualties.
    a. Lives lost or threatened.
    b. Injuries and how received.
    c. Description of any gun play or fighting.
    d. Disposition of dead and injured.
    e. Prominent names among dead and injured.
2. Property loss.
    a. Value of loss.
    b. Nature of property stolen or destroyed.
    c. Other property threatened.
3. Method of crime.
    a. How entrance was effected.
    b. Weapons or instruments used.
    c. Treatment of victims.
    d. Description of unusual circumstances.
    e. Similarity to previous crimes.

4. Cause or motive.
    a. Confessions.
    b. Statements of victims.
    c. Statements of police, witnesses and others.
    d. Threats.
5. Arrests.
    a. Names of persons arrested.
    b. Complaint or policeman making arrest.
    c. Charges entered on police blotter.
    d. Police ingenuity.
    e. Danger incurred by police.
    f. Arraignment.
6. Clues as to identity of criminals.
    a. Evidence at scene of crime.
    b. Testimony of witnesses.
    c. Statement of police.
    d. Statements of victim and others.
    e. Connection with other crimes.
7. Search for offender.
    a. Probability of arrest.
    b. Description of missing persons.
    c. Value of clues.
    d. Contact with criminal through ransom notes, etc.

JUVENILES

Until fairly recently, most newspapers followed a policy of not using the names of juvenile offenders except in cases of major crimes, such as homicide. Since juvenile delinquency began to increase markedly in the post-World War II years, some modifications in this rule have been made in numerous newsrooms. The Peru (Ind.) *Tribune*, for instance, adopted a new policy after extensive consultations with the chief of police, state police, city police juvenile officers, the county welfare director and Circuit Court judges. The pertinent part of the statement of policy follows:

The *Tribune* will publish the names, ages, and addresses of all youthful offenders thirteen years of age or older provided:
1. in the opinion of the court there is no valid reason for such information to be withheld from publication
2. the offenses are not of an extremely minor nature
3. the offenders are actually charged with a specific offense

These facts will appear, along with all other pertinent facts of the case released by the proper authority.

The *Tribune* will follow up with stories which tell whether or not the youth charged has been found guilty or not guilty.

No names will be published unless and until charges are actually filed in juvenile court.

The *Tribune* will work closely with all law enforcing officials to make sure a consistent application of policy is adhered to at all times.

HUMAN INTEREST

In every community, no matter how small, there occur minor brushes with the law or situations reported to police which, in the hands of a skilled writer, can be made into extremely bright copy. In writing brevities originating on the police beat, the rewrite man is permitted considerable stylistic leeway as the emotional appeal outweighs the news interest.

The dire possibilities of equipping residential structures with an inadequate number of baths was demonstrated here today when two indoor bathers were arrested for causing a riot through the too-prolonged use of the only bathtub in the rooming establishment of which they were tenants.

Unfortunately, the two offenders chose Saturday night for a general overhauling. The operation consumed so much time that the regular weekly indulgence of the other ten guests, awaiting their turn outside the bathroom door, seemed in jeopardy. After a long wait, during which epithets of an uncomplimentary nature were hissed through the keyhole, disorder broke out among the would-be bathers, and soon took on such proportions that a riot call was sent into police headquarters.

When a sufficient number of patrolmen who were not at the moment taking their Saturday night baths could be corralled and sent to the scene, the two bath monopolists were taken into custody, charged with inciting riot and fined the goodly sum of $3, plus costs.

Leonard Rawlings, 45, of 1968 Winthrop avenue, stepped into a saloon Friday and, between beers, told a fellow he'd sure like to have a new car. And as a result, Leonard's $1,070 poorer.

The fellow, a character in a snappy sports jacket, said that it so happened he had a car to sell. If Leonard would meet him the next day at Division street and Wilmette avenue, he'd accommodate him.

Yesterday, Leonard showed up with his $1,070. The other showed up too, saying, "Let me have the money and I'll be back in a jiffy with the car."

That was at 6 P.M. By 10 P.M. Leonard got tired of waiting and trudged to the Central police station. He reported his loss to Sgt. Michael Thomason, who promptly informed Leonard that he undoubtedly had been swindled by a confidence man.

OTHER POLICE NEWS

Not all news originating in police headquarters has to do with lawbreaking. Police engage in a variety of noncriminal activities, many of which may be newsworthy. For instance, the missing persons bureau of any large department receives hundreds of calls weekly. Children who leave home in search of adventure, old people who wander off, and spouses and parents who desert their families often are news. The first intimation that a crime has been committed also may come from a report that a certain person is missing.

New traffic rules, warnings concerning dangerous intersections, demands that householders make better disposal of their garbage, and innumerable similar announcements come from police headquarters. Then there are additions to the staff, retirements, promotions, demotions, citations and social activities within the department itself. Monthly, annual and other reports contain statistics and other information of public interest.

CRIME STATISTICS

Since 1930, the Federal Bureau of Investigation, in cooperation with the International Association of Chiefs of Police, has published *Uniform Crime Reports*. Great caution, however, must be exercised in using the statistics therein contained because they are submitted voluntarily by local police departments. As the F.B.I. itself warns, "In publishing the facts sent in by chiefs of police in different cities, the F.B.I. does not vouch for their accuracy. They are given out as current information which may throw some light on problems of crime and criminal-law enforcement."

For several years, the crime figures for New York City were so patently inaccurate that the F.B.I. refused to include them in its reports. After the Chicago police department was reorganized under a new commissioner, its improved reporting system indicated crime had increased 85 per cent in a year. Newspaper investigation, however, previously had supported the Chicago Crime commission's contention that the old department had been officially reporting only about one-third of the crimes it actually handled. Among the devices used to minimize the situation were listing automobiles and other objects as lost instead of stolen, making burglaries seem to be larcenies, making grand larcenies seem to be petty larcenies by "writing down" the amount of loss and so forth.

"With reference to the volume of crime—number of offenses—pressures are always present to keep the figures low," the Chicago Crime commission warns. In addition, the same source declares, numerous known crimes never are reported, including: (1) various types of sex offenses because the victims wish to avoid the embarrassment of publicity, (2) those which private citizens fail to report because of lack of confidence in the police, (3) those unreported by citizens who do not wish to become involved in extended court actions, and (4) matters which are handled largely by private police or protective agencies.

Negroes and members of other minority groups are especially reluctant to summon policemen to their neighborhoods. This fact counterbalances, in part at least, the greater avidity with which police often arrest members of minority groups.

All these and numerous other factors contribute to making the best crime statistics of questionable validity. They suggest the caution with which newspapers should handle such news and the opportunity that exists for investigative reporting to uncover the truth.

SITUATION STORIES

One type of interpretative writing open to the police reporter is that in which he describes, not one or a number of specific crimes, but a situation related to anti-social conductor law enforcement of continuous public interest.

By Marjean Phillips

A woman's handbag is the sleek complement to a costume, a necessary sack to carry half the paperwork of a household, and an object of convenience, responsible for money, keys, identification and quick aids to beauty. True, it's useful, but this cache is a threat to woman's peace of mind. Why? The thing is always disappearing! Half the trouble, women agree, is due to their own forgetfulness. Also, there is the real danger of a purse thief, particularly now when stores and buses are more crowded with holiday shoppers.

What often happens, according to Miss Betty Lou Martin, retail store buyer, is that women put their purses and coats on a counter and turn away to a mirror to try on a blouse.

"They might not even leave the floor," she said, "but someone sees the temptation, picks up the purse, and is away before anyone notices."

An Easy Mistake

Occasionally, a shopper thinks her purse is lost when it's really on her arm, Miss Martin pointed out.

"With a lot of packages you can't get the feeling of where each item is located," she said. "It's natural to think the purse was left behind. Just like looking for glasses on the forehead!"

Lieut. Ora Gregg of the police department cautions that shoulder-type bags are easy prey for the pickpocket.

"If a woman has that style she should be sure to keep her hand on top," he said. "A pickpocket could bump her and easily flip the purse flag and get the billfold. Bumping is to distract the person. If a thief sees he is failing in an attempt, he is likely to go on and say, 'excuse me.'"

Sometimes a woman takes out her money purse, lays it on the counter, and thinks about something else. Then, it is hard to tell whether this is a lost article or a real purse theft, he pointed out.

"The best thing is to always hold on to the purse, as well as packages," he urged.

Lock Packages in Car

Lieutenant Gregg, who commands the general assignment unit of the detective bureau, also advises women to lock their purchases in the trunk of a car, instead of leaving them out in the back seat or floor. That merely tempts a thief to take out a screw driver and go to work.

The street is the scene of other trouble. A purse thief may approach women walking home alone late at night. Miss Margaret F. Richardson, 3304 Wabash avenue, former policewoman, has this advice: "Scream or throw a fit if someone bothers you."

Miss Richardson recalled an incident when she was surprised by a teenage boy, who worked as a team with another youth. He pulled on her purse (a box type hanging over her arm), and failed to take it because she kept jerking and yelling at him. Then the partner came up and asked to help her pick up a package she dropped in the struggle. Suspicious, she warned, "You get away or I'll scream again!" The two-man system is a common tactic, she explained.

Troubles in Offices

Office workers, Miss Richardson says, invite disappointment by leaving pocketbooks out on desks. The purses are safer in a locked drawer. If there is no lock, a secretary can place the handbag in a large manila envelope in the desk farthest from the office entrance. The noise of the drawer opening might alert others.

Women have worked out their own safety rules for homes, such as pulling down window shades before counting money. Also garage doors are closed when the homemaker drives out to go downtown.

It's an achievement for young mothers to get out of a grocery store with a child in one arm, parcels in another and the purse, hopefully, someplace in between.

Mrs. J. M. Bills, 7902 Fairway drive, manages by using a shoulder bag; the safest way is to place its closing side against her body. At home, she doesn't leave her purse in the kitchen where it could be spotted by an intruder.

Mrs. Bills recalled that a friend who frequently lost her purse had the unusual habit of going to the movie and placing her purse on the seat next to her.

Another example of carelessness was cited by Mrs. Ed G. Freed, 5820 the Paseo, who observed that women hang large handbags on the backs of their chairs in restaurants. Mrs. Freed keeps her purse on her lap.

Left on Busses

Handbags are numerous in the thousands of articles left on busses and streetcars. Of course, some never reach their owners again. Proof of honesty, however, are the 10,000 to 12,000 items returned by the lost articles department of the Public Service company each year. The clerks at the main office are Mrs. Mary Knight and Mrs. Georgia Ashenfelter.

"Operators turn in lost articles at the car barns each day," Mrs. Knight explained. "A quadruple record is made there and the objects are brought to the general office at Eighth and Delaware for thirty days.

"If there is identification, letters are written asking persons to come in. If unclaimed, after thirty days, the articles are sent back to the finder or the operator," she said.

Even Mrs. Knight has lost her purse . . . on a streetcar.

"Yes, I lost my purse and it beat me home. The person who found it on the street car took it to my home. I had gone back to look for it," she recalled. [Kansas City *Star*]

Criminal Procedure

When a person is arrested and charged with a crime, he is taken immediately to a jail or police station where he is held pending arraignment. If the arrest is made upon the complaint of another person, the magistrate or judge already has provided the arresting officer with a *warrant* which commands him to bring the defendant to court. Anyone seeking the arrest of another must affirm under oath that he has reasonable grounds for belief in the guilt of the accused. A *search warrant* permits search of a premise where there is reason to believe evidence of a crime may be found. Unless police on raids have search warrants, their testimony is worthless in court. By a *motion to suppress* the evidence the defense obtains the right to question the arresting officer as to the means by which he gained admittance to the place where the arrest was made. Even though the entrance was legitimate, the case still may be dismissed if *entrapment* (inducing someone to commit a crime) is proved.

ARRAIGNMENT

A person has a constitutional right to be brought into court promptly to be confronted with the charge against him. When that is done, he gives his legal answer to the charge. If he remains mute, a not guilty plea is entered. Then the court proceeds according to its authority.

> Andrew Konstans, 19, of 5700 Michigan avenue, stood mute on arraignment on a murder charge before Recorder's Judge W. L. Swanson. A plea of not guilty was entered for him and he was remanded without bond for examination Dec. 1.
>
> The murder charge resulted from the death of Policeman Arthur Kendricks, 44, of 156 South Wells street. Kendricks died of three gunshot wounds suffered when he interrupted the holdup of a grocery store Nov. 15.

PRELIMINARY HEARING

If the offense is one over which the inferior court does not have jurisdiction, it holds a hearing to determine whether there is enough presumption of guilt to *bind over* the case for grand jury action in the higher court. If it decides differently, it dismisses the case and frees the suspect. In such a case, either on a coroner's jury verdict or on the initiative of the prosecuting attorney, the case still can be presented to the grand jury. Persons charged with indictable offenses frequently waive preliminary hearing.

> Judge John A. Williams, sitting in Felony court, today ordered three women held to the grand jury under bonds of $15,000 each in the theft of checks from hallway mailboxes.

If the court in which the prisoner is arraigned has jurisdiction, it holds, not a preliminary hearing but a trial. Inferior court trials provide abundant human interest material, more than a paper can use.

> Frank Peterson, 30, of 2231 Wells street, was called "the lowest of criminals" today by City Judge Raymond C. Owens who sentenced him to a year in Bridewell for obtaining money under false pretenses.
>
> Peterson was found guilty of taking $10 from Mrs. Sarah Thornton, 619 Clybourn avenue, on the promise that he would go to St. Louis to seek her missing husband.

Pending hearing, the prisoner may be released on *bail*, usually requiring a bond of cash or security. Sometimes a person is released on a *recognizance*, which is merely his written promise to appear when wanted or forfeit a stipulated sum.

THE GRAND JURY

The grand jury must be distinguished from the petit jury. It does not try a case but merely investigates crimes which have been committed and decides where there is enough evidence to warrant the expense of bringing the accused persons to trial in the circuit or district court. The grand jury hears the evidence of the prosecution only, and, on the basis of that *ex parte* (one-sided) evidence, it may indict the accused.

An *indictment* may take the form of a *true bill* in case the evidence has been submitted by the prosecuting attorney. If the jury itself gathers evidence of a crime, the indictment is called a *presentment*. A grand jury is supposed to investigate the conduct of government in the territory served by the court and to consider conditions which it thinks should be remedied by law.

In some states, accused persons may be brought to trial upon *informations* submitted by the prosecuting attorney under oath and without a grand jury investigation.

Whenever a crime has been committed and the guilty person has not been ascertained, a *John Doe hearing* is held by the grand jury in the attempt to discover the identity of the person wanted. The prosecuting attorney has the power to summon witnesses to any grand jury hearing.

Grand jury proceedings are secret, but there frequently are leaks from which the reporter benefits. It is contempt of court, however, to publish the results of a grand jury action before it is reported in court. Often, newspapers withhold information even longer so that indicted persons not in custody of police can be arrested on a *bench warrant* (or *capias*) without tipoff.

The reporter should watch: (1) the number of indictments naming the same person, (2) the number of counts or charges in the same indictment, (3) the number of persons included in the same indictment. By standing outside the jury room, he can determine who the witnesses were and, on his past knowledge of the case, can speculate as to what their testimony must have been. The law under which indictments are returned and the punishment, in case of ultimate conviction, frequently should be obtained. Some states have immunity laws to permit a witness to testify without incriminating himself. The power of the prosecutor in determining what evidence shall be presented to a grand jury makes him a powerful political figure, and a trained reporter keeps an eye on his office as a public watchdog. In writing his story, the reporter must use great care to accredit every statement to the true bill.

Five police officers and six private citizens appeared before the special grand jury investigating police department activities in the jury's second consecutive meeting of the week, Tuesday night at East side court.

One of the first police officers to be called was Detective Sgt. Thomas Buzalka who remained closeted with the jury for more than an hour. While awaiting call, Buzalka chatted with Robert Hull, head of the police garage, and Patrolman R. L. Lincoln, who also appeared before the jury.

Emerging from the jury room, Buzalka left the building hurriedly with a brief "good night" thrown over his shoulder to those awaiting their turns.

Six indictments charging five companies and 14 individuals with illegally obtaining 800,000 gallons of cane syrup were returned by the federal grand jury yesterday before Judge Peter Ennis.

The indictments followed an investigation by the Agriculture and Justice departments to determine how the companies were complying with a supplement to the federal sugar rationing order.

PLEAS AND MOTIONS

When arraigned on an indictment, or at any time thereafter up to trial, there are numerous pleas and motions that may be made, chiefly by the defense. Those which merely seek delays are called *pleas in abatement*. One such is a *challenge of the panel* (or *to the array*) which contends that the grand jurors were selected or acted improperly. A motion for a *bill of particulars* asks that the charges be made more specific. A motion for a *continuance* is merely a request for a *postponement*. A *severance* may be asked so that a defendant will not have to stand trial with others named in the same indictment.

A *plea to the jurisdiction* challenges the authority of the court. A motion for a *change of venue* asks that the case be transferred to another court or locale or that a new judge be assigned to it. Motions which would stop all action are *pleas in bar*. One is a *demurrer* which contends that even though true, the acts alleged in the indictment do not indicate crime. A *plea of former jeopardy* is an assertion that the accused previously has been tried on the same charge.

The two common pleas, of course, are *guilty* and *not guilty*. A modified form of the former is *nolo contendere* by which the accused says he will not contest the charges. It is frequent after a test case when others awaiting trial realize that they have no chance to "beat the rap." It keeps the defendant's record clear of an admission but otherwise is the equivalent of a guilty plea. If any civil action is brought against the defendant, this plea cannot be used against him.

There is no legal plea of "innocent," but some newspapers use the word instead of "not guilty" as a precautionary measure. They fear that the "not" might get lost in the composing room, thereby committing possible libel.

The one important plea that the prosecution can make is *nolle prosequi* (*nol pros*) which means "do not wish to prosecute." It is made when new evidence convinces the prosecutor of the accused's innocence or when there is insufficient evidence to convict. If it occurs under any other circumstances, an alert newspaper should expose the fact.

> Fifteen to 60 years' imprisonment was in prospect for Frankie Waters, 24-year-old fugitive from a Georgia chain gang, who pleaded guilty yesterday to a charge of robbery in the first degree to cover a 15-count indictment alleging robbery and assaults on women passengers in taxicabs he had stolen.
>
> Waters entered his plea before General Sessions Judge T. L. Bohn. After the plea had been made by Waters' court-assigned counsel, Charles Shueman, Judge Bohn asked:
>
> "Do you realize that if you plead guilty I can give you no less than 15 years and up to 60 years?" ...

> Circuit Attorney Franklin Moore today dismissed in Circuit Judge Harry Jamieson's court, indictments against six precinct officials in the Fifteenth precinct of the Fourth ward, charged with fraudulent removal and secretion of ballots in the primary election, Aug. 7.
>
> The indictments were returned Nov. 3, but the cases have been continued from time to time by the defendants who said they were not ready for trial. The cases were originally assigned to Judge Charles R. Watson, but transferred to Judge Jamieson on a change of venue.
>
> The last continuance was sought Monday by the state, which said it was not ready for trial, in view of the fact that the State Supreme court had not yet acted on applications for permanent writs of prohibition to prevent the Madison grand jury from examining ballot boxes and other election records of the Fourth ward. Moore told a Journal reporter that the records were needed to prosecute the cases.
>
> Those indicted were ...

OTHER PRELIMINARIES

When a fugitive from justice in one state is arrested in another, he may be returned to the jurisdiction where he must answer charges by *extradition*. The procedure is for the governor of the state seeking custody of the fugitive to request the governor of the state in which he is apprehended to return him. It is newsworthy when such a request is denied, as it sometimes is by a northern governor reluctant to send a prisoner back south; or in the case of an ex-convict who has lived an exemplary life for years since a prison break. In federal courts, the equivalent of extradition is *removal* from one jurisdiction to another following hearing before a commissioner.

> A description of torture allegedly inflicted upon him in the Georgia State penitentiary was given yesterday by an escaped prisoner as he opened a fight against extradition proceedings to return him to that prison.
> He is Leland Brothers, 35, who was released Tuesday from the Stateville penitentiary after serving a one-to-three-year sentence from Brown county for armed robbery.
> Yesterday he filed a petition for a writ of habeas corpus in the Wayne County Circuit court.

In both criminal and civil cases, *depositions* may be taken with court permission when there is a likelihood that a witness will be unavailable during trial. A deposition differs from an *affidavit* because it is conducted by a court appointee, both sides are notified, and the rules of evidence are followed. In other words, the witness testifies under the same conditions that he would in court; the transcript of his testimony may be introduced as evidence.

Witnesses who do appear in court usually are there as the result of *subpoenas* (court orders) which either side may obtain as a matter of right. A *subpoena duces tecum* orders a witness to produce certain real evidence, usually documents and records.

Criminal Trials

Most criminal trials (same is true of civil trials) last only a few hours or minutes. Some, however, take days, weeks or months. The story the day before or on the day of trial may forecast its probable length, based on statements by attorneys for both sides and what the reporter knows of the probable evidence.

FIRST STORIES

The reporter should include in his story: (1) careful tie-back to the crime itself—time, place, names, events; (2) the charges as stated in the indictment; (3) the possible outcome, meaning the minimum and maximum penalties fixed by law for all of the possible verdicts in the case; (4) the probable evidence with names of witnesses and attorneys' statements, if obtainable, as to what they will attempt to establish; (5) any unusual angles, as possible difficulty in obtaining a jury—for instance, one side may be expected to favor persons of ages, occupations, religion or politics different from those favored by the other side. Maybe this is the first trial of its kind, or the first in a long time, or a new law may be applied to some part of the proceedings. The possibilities are limitless.

PICKING THE JURY

After the indictment has been read and the plea entered, and after any last-minute motions have been disposed of, selection of the jury begins. The jury of twelve is picked from a panel of *veniremen* prepared by the jury commissioners or its equivalent. They are questioned by attorneys of both sides and, if found unsatisfactory for reasons which are obvious, may be *challenged for cause*. In addition, each side has a stated number of *peremptory challenges* for which no reasons need be given; usually the defense has twice as many as the prosecution. The questioning of prospective jurors is called the *voir dire* (to speak the truth). Clues to future tactics may be obtained from the types of questions asked veniremen. If, for instance, the prosecutor does not inquire whether they are prejudiced against the death penalty, it is apparent he does not intend to ask for that punishment. If the original panel of veniremen is exhausted without a jury's being completed, additional persons are summoned; they are known as *talesmen* and in inferior courts may be brought in off the street or selected from courtroom spectators.

OPENING STATEMENTS

The state leads off with a statement of what it intends to prove and the nature of the evidence to be introduced. The prosecutor presents no evidence. The defense may make its reply immediately or may wait until after the prosecution's evidence has been presented.

EVIDENCE

First witnesses for the state are called for the purpose of establishing the *corpus delicti*, or proof that a crime was committed. All testimony is given in answer to questions by attorneys. After *direct examination* by attorneys for the side calling him, a witness is subjected to *cross-examination* by attorneys for the other side. They must restrict their questions to matters about which he already has testified and they often attempt to *impeach a witness* by catching him in contradictory statements. Objections to questions frequently are made by counsel; the judge is the arbiter. Occasionally, the jury is taken from the room while argument on admissibility of evidence is debated. A *jury view* is the taking of a jury to the scene of a crime or any other place outside the courtroom for the purpose of seeing anything pertinent to the case.

After it has presented all of its evidence, both through the testimony of witnesses and by exhibits, the state *rests*. Then the defense usually automatically makes a motion for a *directed verdict of acquittal* on the ground that the state has failed to prove its case. Most such motions are denied as automatically as they are made; when they are not, there is a news story. A *mistrial* can result in case of gross irregularity as an attempt to bribe a juror.

> The overzealous interest of a juror in a robbery case before County Judge Nova in Brooklyn caused a mistrial yesterday, and brought a reprimand from the court. The juror was William E. Rejall, 54 Tompkins place, Brooklyn, who had sat for two days in the trial of Joseph Fernandez, charged with holding up Felix Orrusti, 173 Washington street, Brooklyn.
>
> When the trial opened yesterday, Rejall stood up and asked if he might question the complainant.
>
> "I took the trouble to visit the scene and I want to ask the complaining witness how he could identify anyone in the dark," the juror explained. Judge Nova appeared surprised.
>
> "You are entitled only to the evidence that is submitted in court in the presence of the defendant," the court said. "You should not have gone to the scene. I must declare a mistrial." [New York *Times*]

All motions having been denied, the defense presents its case, beginning with its opening statement if not already made. Direct and cross-examination proceed as before. There follow *rebuttal* witnesses by the state and frequently the recalling of witnesses by either side for further questioning.

CLOSING STATEMENTS

The prosecuting attorney usually has the right to go first and then to follow the attorney for the defense with a brief rebuttal; frequently he

POLICE, CRIME, CRIMINAL LAW   311

waives his right to speak twice and lets the defense go first. These final statements by attorneys are argumentative. Then the judge *charges* the jury, explaining the law in the case, the possible verdicts it can return, and the meaning of each. Often the law stipulates the exact wording a judge must use in at least part of his charge. Judges have little right to comment on the evidence itself but by facial expressions, gestures and verbal emphasis they often can prejudice a jury without the fact being evident in a written transcript.

REPORTING TRIALS

In reporting trials of long duration, the reporter bases each new lead on the most important new development since his last preceding story. Factors to consider are:

1. Does some new testimony or other evidence contradict or supplement some preceding evidence?
2. Do the questions asked by defense counsel on cross-examination portend what the constructive defense case will be?
3. Is any of the evidence surprising; that is, has it been unreported in connection with either the crime itself or the trial?
4. How do the versions of what happened as presented by both sides coincide or differ?
5. Is there consistency of purpose in the types of objections raised by counsel and in the judge's rulings on them? Is the defense laying the ground for possible future appeal?

Seeking answers to these and similar questions involves an interpretative approach to the assignment. Much of the reporting "on deadline," however, is likely to be strictly factual. Often testimony can be presented in Q and A (question and answer) form if there is space; otherwise, it can be summarized briefly or the important parts quoted. The courtroom scene, including the attitude of principals, witnesses, relatives, friends and spectators is newsworthy, especially if there are any disturbances. In capital cases, the way the defendant acts when the verdict is announced is of interest.

> While Vincent Cilenti, 32-year-old ex-convict was in County Jail awaiting trial on a first-degree murder charge, he allegedly attempted to "shakedown" Mrs. Mary Carmigiano a second time in connection with the bombing of Angelo Pappalardo's home.

This was the testimony today of Albert P. Lauerhaus, alleged confederate of Cilenti, who is on trial for blackmail and bombing of the Pappalardo home.

The trial was interrupted shortly before noon when John Draggo of 3861 Montevista Rd., Cleveland Heights, a state witness, repudiated a statement he made to police in 1942 accusing Cilenti of "shaking him down" for $100.

Common Pleas Judge Alva R. Corlett excused the jury, summoned attorneys into his chamber and warned them he would not permit perjury in the courtroom.

Tells of Bulldozing

After the noon recess, Draggo reluctantly told a story of being bulldozed by Cilenti into signing papers which Draggo thought made him cosigner for a loan for purchase of an auto. Later, he said, he learned that he had actually been the one to sign the papers and that Cilenti had placed both car and license in Draggo's name, forcing Draggo to make the payments.

Lauerhaus, 32, said it was in November, 1942, while Cilenti was waiting trial in the murder of Peter Laduca (of which he was acquitted) that he sent for Lauerhaus to visit him at County Jail.

"I want you to see Mrs. Carmigiano," Lauerhaus said Cilenti told him. "She owes me some money. Go out and get it for me."

Q. What did you do then?

A. I went out and she said she didn't owe Cilenti any money. I didn't get any money from her.

Lauerhaus said he couldn't remember the exact amount of money Cilenti said she owed. Mrs. Carmigiano said in testimony yesterday that after paying Cilenti $300 she was approached for $600 more.

Lauerhaus confirmed Mrs. Carmigiano's testimony about how he drove her to see Cilenti in September after the Pappalardo home had been bombed.

Then James P. Hart, assistant county prosecutor, asked him: "Did you ever have any conversation with Cilenti about the bombing?" Lauerhaus said he did, talking to him about how Mrs. Carmigiano had complained that Cilenti had bombed the home without telling her about it or getting her approval.

"What does she think I am, a damn fool?" Lauerhaus said Cilenti told him. "Does she think I'd tell her when I'd be there so she could be in the window waiting for the explosion?"

Mrs. Carmigiano, 1392 SOM Center Rd., Mayfield Heights, yesterday told how Cilenti extorted $300 from her for bombing a neighbor's home without her knowledge or approval.

Mrs. Carmigiano, a real estate agent, said Cilenti first came to see her early in 1942, when she lived on Arrowhead Ave., about renting a house. Later, she related, he returned saying he understood she was having trouble with a neighbor.

Mrs. Carmigiano said she told him of arguments she had with the family of Angelo Pappalardo, 19408 Arrowhead Ave.

A. He said I should punish the people next door.

Q. What did you say?

A. Well, I don't know how to punish them. I'm only a widow. There's nothing I can do about it.

Q. What did Cilenti say to this?

A. He said: "I can take care of it for you." I asked him in what way. He replied: "Just leave it to me. We know how to take care of it for you." I told him I didn't want anybody hurt.

Mrs. Carmigiano moved from Arrowhead Ave. in May, 1942. The Pappalardo home was bombed July 8. She told De Marco she read of the bombing in the newspapers. Then Lauerhaus came to see her several times, she said, telling her: "Cilenti wants to see you."

On the second or third visit he came at night and pushed his way into her house, Mrs. Carmigiano said.

Q. What happened, then?

A. He took me in his car to 82d St. and Quincy Ave. He left me in the car awhile. I waited about an hour, so I went into a cafe and asked for Cilenti. They said they didn't know where he was. I went back to the car and someone came out and took me to Cilenti. Cilenti said to me, "The job is done. The boys want their money."

Mrs. Carmigiano said she asked: "What money?"

"They want $300."

"For what?"

"For the Pappalardo job," she said Cilenti replied.

Asked for Receipt

The interview, she testified, closed with Cilenti driving her home and telling her to get him the money by 2 P.M. that day. She said she borrowed the money from a friend, took it to Cilenti's home, accompanied by one of her sons. She said she gave the money to Cilenti and when she asked for a receipt she testified he told her:

"Oh, no. We don't do business that way."

Mrs. Carmigiano denied she was operating a still in 1941, but added that Cilenti's purpose in wanting to rent a house from her was to establish a hideout for operation of a still. S. M. Lo Presti, defense attorney, sought to show that the money transaction between Mrs. Carmigiano and Cilenti involved a bootlegging deal rather than a bombing.   [Cleveland *Press*]

VERDICTS

The jury leaves the courtroom and deliberates, with the foreman presiding. After the case is over, the reporter may find out, by questioning jurors, how many ballots were taken and how the vote stood each time. The length of time it takes a jury to reach unanimity is newsworthy. If no decision ever is reached, the jury is said to be *hung*, and there is a *mistrial*. Some indication of how a jury is thinking may be obtained if it returns to the jury room to ask further instructions or to have part of the evidence read to it again. The reporter's best tipster as to what goes on in a jury room is the bailiff standing guard at the door.

The defendant must be in court when the verdict is read. If a verdict is reached late at night, it may be written and *sealed* and left with a court official, so that the jurors may leave. All, however, must be present when the verdict is opened. The losing side may demand a *poll* of the jury, which requires each juror to declare that he concurs. If any juror changes his mind during such a poll it is "hot" copy.

> A Criminal Court jury Wednesday night convicted James Kyler, 22, of the murder of a milkman and set his penalty at 14 years in prison.
>
> The jury of nine men and three women deliberated 8 hours 55 minutes in reaching its verdict. The penalty it recommended is the minimum for murder under state law.
>
> Three boys, 8, 10 and 11 years old, were the chief state witnesses who connected Kyler with the slaying of the milkman, Jerome Giza, 30, of 1740 N. Mason, last Oct. 15. Giza was shot to death during a holdup attempt at 117 S. Rockwell.
>
> Kyler, of 2546 W. Monroe, testified at the trial presided over by Judge Joseph J. Drucker that he was in a friend's home at the time of the slaying. His attorney said he would appeal the verdict.
>
> Lennette Earl Brown, 35, of 2500 W. Warren, accused of participating with Kyler in the hold-up slaying of Giza, will go on trial for murder April 3. [Chicago *Sun-Times*]

SENTENCES

A jury's verdict is advisory only; the judge accepts or rejects it. He may grant a defense motion to *set aside* the verdict and grant a *new trial* if there have been errors which he knows would cause an appellate court to reverse the verdict and *remand* the case. A motion for *arrest of judgment* accompanies such motions to postpone sentencing.

The leeway permitted a judge in pronouncing sentence is established by statute for each crime. In some cases, he may have no choice at all; convictions on a certain charge may mean an automatic sentence of a certain kind. A *suspended sentence* is one which the convicted person does not have to serve pending good behavior. It is rapidly being replaced by *probation* which gives the convicted person limited freedom of action under the supervision of probation officials; if anyone violates the conditions of his probation, he serves not only the original sentence but an additional one also because of the violation. Probation is most common for minors and first offenders. It should not be confused with *parole* which is the supervised conditional release of prisoners who already have served part of their prison terms.

If someone is convicted on more than one count, he may serve his several sentences *concurrently* or *consecutively*. If the former, he serves only the longest of the several sentences; if the latter, he serves the accumulated total of them all. An *indeterminate* sentence sends a convicted person to the penitentiary for "not less than" a designated number of years, and "not more than" another number of years. The exact time of his release is determined by the state board of paroles. Usually he is not eligible to apply for parole until after at least one-third of his time has been served, so judges often give maximum penalties to run consecutively to make release on parole unlikely.

Clarence Whittle, 20, of 187 South Water street, was sentenced by Judge John S. Anthony in Criminal court yesterday to serve a term of not less than 10 years to life in the penitentiary for armed robbery.

Judge Anthony overruled a motion for a new trial before pronouncing the sentence. Whittle was convicted by a jury Jan. 10 of holding up a tavern at 1700 Ashland avenue, on Sept 1 and taking $190.

Whittle faces charges of murdering Michael Storms, 50, a tavern owner of 5800 Market street, on July 15. Four others have pleaded guilty to participating in the shooting of Storms and a fifth is under sentence of 20 years in prison.

Federal Judge John P. Altman today deferred a prison sentence for one of two men convicted of black market meat deals and reduced a fine against their company from $50,000 to $25,000.

He approved a stay of execution until March 15 for Martin Orton, president of the Orton Meat Packing company, on his penitentiary sentence of a year and a day.

Orton, who lives at 151 West Monroe street, and Walter Sherwood, of 989 Wells street, secretary-treasurer of the company, were given identical sentences by Judge Altman Sept 1.

The government charged them and the company with filing false subsidy claims with the government to obtain $155,000 and having sold meat at overceiling prices and failure to set aside 1,300,000 pounds for the armed forces.

On motions of Oscar Nethercott, attorney for the defense, Judge Altman granted the stay to Orton today so another man can be found to head the company, and reduced the $50,000 fine against the company to $25,000. Sherwood will surrender Monday to the U.S. marshal.

Assistant U.S. Attorney Bernard Whiteman opposed the motions, asserting the two had "at least $150,000 in black market money," and had refused to cooperate with the government in a costly investigation of their activities.

At the time I assessed the fine I wondered if it were not too drastic," Judge Altman said. "Now I think it was."

PUNISHMENTS

Despite the trend toward individualized treatment of law-breakers and the substitution of theories of reformation and protection of society for theories of retaliation and expiation, the criminal law still requires that a convicted person "pay his debt to society." To carry out any sentence is to *execute* it, although the popular connotation of the word limits it to cases in which capital punishment is inflicted. The death penalty rapidly is passing out because judges and juries are reluctant to impose it. It is within the power of a governor to *commute* any sentence: that is, to reduce it, as from death to life imprisonment. A governor also can issue a *reprieve* which, however, is merely a postponement of execution. A *pardon* is a granting of freedom. If absolute, it restores civil rights. If conditional, it prescribes limits to the ex-convict's behavior. Few states as yet have adequate systems for recompensing persons proved to have been imprisoned wrongly

The Ethics of Crime News

No ethical problem connected with newspaper publishing has been more thoroughly discussed by both newspapermen and laymen than the treatment of crime news. Upon his superiors' attitudes toward the problem depends largely the type of occurrences to which the police reporter pays particular attention and the manner in which he writes his articles. A few papers, notably the *Christian Science Monitor*, generally ignore antisocial behavior; others have experimented with leaving crime news off the front page or of playing it down in the writing. Familiar, on the other hand, is the type of newspaper which considers a sensational crime story as second to few other types in potential reader interest.

It is not so much a question of the amount of crime news but of how it is presented. Contrary to popular opinion, only a small proportion of the total offering of the average newspaper relates to lawlessness. Several years ago, for instance, Henry Fairfield Osborn revealed that whereas readers guessed from 25 to 50 per cent of the contents of their newspapers was crime news, scientific study showed the average space devoted to such news to be only 3.5 per cent.

A FAIR TRIAL vs A FREE PRESS

Some newspapers, magazines, and radio and television stations have been accused of inciting to crime by glorifying and making heroes of criminals; of assisting criminals to escape by relating detailed accounts of the activities of police; of interfering with the administration of justice by emphasizing the horrible aspects of brutal crimes, by quoting the prosecuting attorney as to the severe punishment he is going to demand and by editorial comment; of causing unfair suffering on the part of the relatives and friends of principals in a criminal case; and of offending public taste by relating lurid details of crimes and scandals.

By far the most important issue today is how much pretrial publicity there should be so as not to interfere with a defendant's right to a fair trial before an impartial jury in an unprejudicial atmosphere. Several United States Supreme Court decisions and adverse criticism of the press contained in the Warren Commission report on the assassination of President John F. Kennedy have intensified the debate. Although not liking the restrictions placed on them by the court, law enforcement officers have nevertheless become cautious about discussing cases with reporters and scrupulous in obeying the rules imposed upon them as regards questioning of suspects, especially that a suspect must be warned immediately of his right to remain silent and have a lawyer. On the other hand some newspapers toned down quite a bit after the United States Supreme Court ordered a new trial for Dr. Sam Sheppard of Cleveland on the ground that the Cleveland newspapers had made a fair trial for him impossible. Said the court in this case: "The press does not simply publish information about trials, but guards against the miscarriage of justice by subjecting the police, prosecutors and judicial processes to extensive public scrutiny and criticism." At issue, however, is how far the press should go in exercising this function without jeopardizing the rights of the defendant. Neither legal nor journalistic leaders are unanimous in their opinions on the matter or regarding the Warren Commission's statement that "the news media, as well as the police authorities . . . share responsibility for failure of law enforcement in Dallas."

In October 1966 the Advisory Committee on Fair Trial and Free Press of the American Bar Association issued a preliminary report which most newspapers felt recommended too-narrow restrictions on the press. Shortly before the report appeared the Toledo *Blade* and *Times* imposed upon themselves a code which included the following:

> Before a trial begins, the Toledo papers pledge to publish only the following data:
> ¶The name, age and address of the accused.
> ¶How, when and where the arrest was made.
> ¶The charge and the identity of the complainant.
> ¶The fact that a grand jury has returned an indictment and that a trial date has been set.
> The policy will be to provide detailed coverage so that information perhaps held back at the time of the arrest may be published later in the proceeding if and when it will not interfere with the judicial process.
> During the progress of the case, unless very special circumstances dictate otherwise, the following types of information will not be published:
> ¶Any prior criminal record of the accused.
> ¶Any so-called confession the accused may have made other than the fact—if it is one—that he has made a statement to the authorities, but with no indication of the nature of the statement.
> ¶Any statements by officials construed as detrimental to the accused.
> ¶Any statements by lawyers either detrimental to the accused or concerning any defense that is to be made during trial.
> ¶Any names of jurors selected for a particular trial.
> ¶Any arguments made in court in the absence of the jury, or evidence excluded from the jury.

UNDERSTANDING THE CRIMINAL

Perhaps the most important adverse criticism of the press in the past has been that it has not taken sufficient cognizance of modern criminological and penological thought. By advocating harshness of treatment as the only corrective, by labeling every sex offender (even before apprehended) as a moron (a scientific term meaning high-grade feebleminded), by pointing to every paroled prisoner violating his parole as proof of the unsoundness of the parole principle, by ridiculing leading thinkers as maudlin sentimentalists, and in other ways, the media, it is charged, are a sizable obstacle in the movement to replace a barbaric philosophy and methods of curbing antisociability with a scientific approach.

Following a scientific study of the life history of Giuseppe Zangara, the psychopathic immigrant who attempted to assassinate President-elect Franklin D. Roosevelt in 1933, Sidney Kobre said in part regarding the manner in which the American press handled the story:

Newspapers, in theory, print the news as it occurs, head it according to its significance, and comment on its important aspects. Here, certainly, was an opportunity for them to get at the root of a social evil—to insist, rather than on laws to prevent purchase of guns or enforce deportation of aliens, on the essential nature of the problem. Zangara, had the influences under which he labored been understood (and they might have been discovered when he entered the Italian army, when he passed through the immigration bureau, when he was admitted to citizenship, when he was a patient in a hospital), might have been headed off, his physical and psychological ailments corrected. Suggestions for the isolation and treatment of the class from whom are "recruited the criminal types and cranks" might have been made, along with emphasis on the fact that the class is not composed exclusively of aliens. . . .

The newspapers had opportunity to examine the impulse behind the shooting at its root. . . . For the most part they did not do so. Instead they seized upon the "red" stereotype, or proposed police or legislative methods of dealing with the evil once it had arisen, rather than psychiatric or medical methods of preventing it from arising. . . . Most American editors handling this story chose stereotypes and superficialities rather then the more subtle but certainly more fundamental implications. . . .

The American newspaper is the only agency which adequately reports such a case to the public. Because the attempted shooting of Roosevelt was dramatic news, attention was centered on a vital social problem. The newspapers had, therefore, an extraordinary opportunity to present the important news behind the surface facts—to mold public thought and action in a social, constructive pattern, if you will. The facts recited above show that they failed. And it should be noted that the Zangara case is but a single instance of a blundering habit—a habit that will repeat itself time and again unless newspapers can learn from it where their machinery is defective.

Since Kobre wrote this article, later expanded for inclusion in his *Backgrounding the News*, there has been considerable improvement on many newspapers. World War II awakened interest in psychiatry and acquainted millions with the fact that abnormal behavior does not necessarily result from malicious willful choice. Sociological research, furthermore, has proved that what is considered criminal in one environment may be perfectly normal in another, and that, particularly in large cities, there are communities in which the incidence of crime remains virtually constant although the racial or nationality complexion of the population changes many times. Gone is belief in "born" criminals, feeblemindedness as a major cause of criminal behavior, and many other unscientific explanations. Today, psychiatry is throwing light on the peculiarities of the individual offender and sociologists are examining slums, economic status, marital relations and other social factors which breed misbehavior.

In tune with the times, few newspapers any longer consult phrenologists, handwriting experts, fortunetellers, and other quacks whenever a major crime occurs. Instead, they interview scientists and they steadily are adding to their own staffs specialists able to do more than invent "cute" headline-fitting nicknames for murderers and their victims.

Indicative of the greater journalistic enlightenment are the first few paragraphs of a full-page article which appeared in the *National Observer* for August 8, 1966.

AUSTIN, TEXAS.
  The record will show that Charles Joseph Whitman was not a simple man.
  But who is?
  Whitman was, as the world knows by now, a good student, a conscientious husband, an Eagle Scout, a Marine Corps sharpshooter, a hard worker, handsome, strong, fun to be with, popular.
  Then last Monday, in the scorch of a 100-degree Austin day, from near the peak of a 341-foot building, he took a deer rifle and killed 13 people and wounded 31. This was a few hours after he had stabbed to death his pretty wife and shot to death his mother. Then police shot him to death.
  Gov. John Connally of Texas has announced that the state will convene in a few weeks a conference of psychiatrists and psychologists who will attempt to piece together the reason for such an action. They may never be able to explain Whitman fully, but perhaps their research will tell something more about the murderous mind.
  For never in the annals of mass murder has there been such a clean-cut example of a man run amok. If anything, the lesson of Charley Whitman is to remind us how delicate is the human mind, and how little we know of it.
  Reflecting last week on the rampage, a medical authority on mental health said he was not surprised that everyone who knew Whitman described him as such a pleasant person.
  "It is a sign of how superficial people are about other people," said the doctor. "We assume we know someone from the way he acts outwardly, but how many people get to know anyone well enough to judge his real being?
  "Perhaps a perceptive teacher or minister or friend might have seen the stress he was under. But casual friends did not. More people than we would care to admit have this hostility in them. Fortunately most can control it.
  "The common way of destroying someone [with this hostility] is over a period of 25 or 30 years. This boy just did it suddenly."

A Fierce Will Power
  It is only now apparent that Whitman's strains and vices were present all the time—suppressed, no doubt, by a fierce will power finally incapable of holding them in check, creating a pressure-pot that erupted beyond civilized understanding.

POLICE, CRIME, CRIMINAL LAW 321

Unfortunately, says one doctor, the whole story will never be known. The data are forever incomplete. There will be theories, but no one will be certain how valid any of them are.

Before the experts have a crack at it, here are a few of the pieces to the puzzle, some not widely known, which contributed to this deadly state of mind.

15

Courts, Civil Law, Appeals

I KINDS OF LAW

II THE COURT SYSTEM
1. Inferior Courts
2. County and Probate Courts
3. Courts of First Instance
4. Appellate Courts
5. Federal Courts
6. Officers of the Court

III CIVIL LAW
1. Starting an Action
2. Defending an Action
3. Civil Trials
4. Enforcing Civil Law

IV CIVIL ACTIONS
1. Damage Suits
2. Divorce
3. Foreclosures
4. Evictions
5. Condemnation Suits
6. Receiverships
7. Bankruptcy
8. Injunctions

V EXTRAORDINARY REMEDIES
1. Prohibition
2. Certiorari
3. Mandamus
4. Quo Warranto

VI PROBATE PROCEEDINGS
1. Filing a Will
2. Admitting to Probate
3. Contesting a Will

VII RULES OF EVIDENCE
1. Nature of Evidence
2. Burden of Proof
3. Presumptions
4. Judicial Notice
5. Qualifications of Witnesses
6. Privilege
7. Leading Questions
8. Hearsay Evidence
9. Opinion Evidence
10. Real Evidence
11. Circumstantial Evidence
12. Best Evidence

VIII APPEALS

JUST AS IT IS ESSENTIAL FOR A SPORTS REPORTER WHO COVERS BASEBALL to understand the rules of the game, so is it necessary for the reporter assigned to the courts to know the basic structure of American law.

Kinds of Law

Roughly, all laws can be divided into *public* and *private* (usually called *civil*), the distinction being whether the state (organized society) is a party to the litigation. The dichotomy is not exact because government can be a party to certain types of civil actions. In general, however, the distinction holds. Branches of public law include: constitutional, administrative, international and criminal, with the ordinary reporter, of course, being most interested in the last.

The two major divisions of private, or civil law, are *common law* and *equity*. The former is that law which was developed through the centuries in judicial decisions in English courts, and—roughly again—it can be divided into *real* and *personal* law. Real law relates to the possession of and title to property whereas personal law relates to attempts to recover damages for injuries received, to enforce a contract, to bring about the return of property and to similar matters. The two major divisions of personal law relate to *contracts* and *torts* (all injuries received other than by violation of contract). Equity law, as developed in the equity (or *chancery*) courts of England, begins where law leaves off. One does not go to equity to recover damages for injuries to himself or his property, but to compel someone to do or to refrain from doing something. Modern equity courts handle such matters as injunctions, foreclosures, receiverships, partitions, etc.

The law administered in the courts originates either (1) in the acts of Congress, of a state legislature, or of some other lawmaking body, such law being known as *statutory*, or (2) in the accumulated decisions of courts both here and in England, such law being known as *common law*. Courts adhere to the principle of *stare decisis* (let the decision stand), which means that lawyers quote at length from decisions in earlier cases in the attempt to show that the case in hand should be decided similarly. When there has been a pertinent decision by the Supreme Court of the United States or some state appellate court, the issue may seem clearcut. Usually, however, such is not the case. Either the matter at hand differs in some essential from the previously decided case, or the appellate court decision is limited in scope. Also, there may be conflicting decisions in apparently identical cases.

Young reporters should know that, despite the apparent inconsistencies in both the written (*basic*) law itself and common law decisions, and despite their ability to find citations to substantiate both or all sides of almost any argument, lawyers as a whole profess belief in the existence of absolute justice, and hold that the purpose of any court case is to find the abstract principle which applies. Such lawyers are not conscious rogues, whose main interest is to "play a game" and win a judgment for their clients at all costs. They have been trained to think in a precise specialized manner which makes it easy for them to rationalize their actions, even though to the layman the results may not seem tantamount to anything resembling common sense or justice.

The Court System

A knowledge of the court system of the state in which he works is essential to the reporter assigned to cover the courts. If he moves from one state to another he will discover that even the names of generally similar courts may differ. For instance, what is known as a circuit court in Indiana is called a district court in Nebraska, a superior court in Massachusetts and a supreme court in New York.

The jurisdictions of courts also differ, even between counties of different sizes within the same state. For instance, there may be a separate probate court in one county or state whereas probate matters may be handled by the circuit court or its equivalent in another place. One court may handle both civil and criminal matters or there may be different courts (*common pleas* courts are civil courts; courts of *oyer and terminer* are criminal courts). Similarly, law and equity courts may be separate or combined. The practice is growing of establishing special branches of courts to handle particular kinds of cases, and these branches may be referred to in news stories by their specialized names, such as Renters' Court, Juvenile Court, Traffic Court, Divorce Court. To the reader, it makes little or no difference that such courts really are only branches of a circuit, municipal or county court, but the reporter should know their nature.

It is particularly important that the reporter know which are *courts of record*; that is, ones which keep a permanent record of their proceedings. What happens in *courts not of record* is not privileged and the newspaper which covers them must be careful to avoid committing libel.

Differences in both the *substantive law* (defines what is and is not proper behavior) and *adjective law* (defines legal rules and procedures) also provide potential snares for unwary newsmen. For instance, in one state grand larceny may be defined as stealing anything worth more than $15 whereas in another state stealing anything worth less than $100 or $1,000 may be petty larceny. Since inferior courts generally can handle petty larceny cases but not grand larceny cases, the same offense committed in one jurisdiction will be tried in one type of court whereas if it happens in another jurisdiction, it will be tried in a different type court. In one jurisdiction, a civil action may be considered to have begun with the filing of a complaint, whereupon the reporter is safe in reporting it; in another, however, the action is not considered to exist until the other party has been notified. Similar rules may affect all motions by attorneys and court rulings.

Fortunately, the similarities between the 50 court systems are greater than their differences. Roughly, the typical system is as follows:

INFERIOR COURTS

These are the courts with the least amount of jurisdiction. Generally they can handle criminal cases involving misdemeanors for which the punishment is a fine only. Their jurisdiction in civil matters generally is limited to cases in which the amount of money does not exceed a few hundred dollars. Among the most common of such courts are the following: *justice of the peace* (townships); *police magistrates* (limited to a city or a section of a city); and *city* and *municipal* courts, which, however, in some larger places may have much greater jurisdiction.

COUNTY AND PROBATE COURTS

The jurisdiction of a county court depends upon what other state courts exist. Thus, it may be an inferior court or a court of first instance, with unlimited jurisdiction in civil and criminal matters. In other cases, it may operate mostly as a probate or juvenile court or as overseer of the election machinery and county institutions and agencies concerned with poor relief, adoptions and similar matters. Probate courts supervise the disposition of the estates of deceased persons and may also handle adoptions, lunacy hearings, commitments of feeble-minded and insane persons, and guardianships for minors and incompetents.

COURTS OF FIRST INSTANCE

The "backbone" courts are the circuit, superior, district, supreme, or whatever they are called. In them, all kinds of civil actions may be brought and, unless there are separate criminal courts, criminal matters as well. In some states, there are separate equity, divorce and other courts, but in a large majority of states the court of original jurisdiction either has separate calendars or branches for different kinds of civil actions. The criminal court may be set up separately or may be a branch of the circuit court. It may handle all kinds of criminal matters, or there may be separate courts for felonies (as the Court of General Sessions in New York). The number of circuit or district courts in a state is dependent upon the state's size and population. A large city or county may be a circuit in itself and may be permitted a large number of judges, the exact number being established by constitution or statute. Outside of thickly populated areas, a circuit may include two, three, ten or more counties and the judges may hold court at different times in different county seats. The number of terms annually and often their length is established by constitution or statute.

APPELLATE COURTS

These courts do not try cases originally, but only review decisions reached by courts of jurisdiction in the first instance when defeated parties, dissatisfied with lower court decisions, appeal to the higher courts. In smaller states, there is likely to be only one appellate court, usually called supreme, ranging in size from three to twenty-three judges, either appointed by the governor with the consent of the state legislature or elected (at large or by divisions). In larger states, there are intermediate courts of review, often called circuit courts of appeal, which, however, seldom if ever receive appeals involving constitutional or other important matters. Some of the decisions of the intermediate court may be appealed a second time to the highest appellate court, either as a matter of right or with that court's permission. The three, five, seven or more members of an intermediate appellate court may be appointed or elected, or they may be regularly elected circuit or district court judges assigned to appellate court duty by the supreme court. Appellate courts do not try cases as lower courts do; they merely pass on the arguments of attorneys in the case as presented to them in written form (*briefs*) and orally (at *hearings*). The practice is growing to permit new evidence not introduced in an original trial of a case to be presented to an appellate court, but this is not yet common practice. All appellate court decisions are by majority vote of the judges; there never is anything resembling a jury trial in an appellate court.

FEDERAL COURTS

Although it is growing in importance with the passage by Congress of an increasing number of laws defining as federal crimes certain offenses of which formerly only the states took cognizance, and with the establishment of additional federal court districts, the federal judicial system is outside the worries of the average small-city reporter. Anyone arrested in his territory for a federal offense is taken for arraignment to the nearest city in which a federal court is situated.

Despite the activities of the Federal Bureau of Investigation and its G-men in recent years, kidnaping is not a federal offense because Congress does not believe the Supreme Court would hold constitutional a law declaring it such. The so-called Lindbergh law makes the transportation of a kidnaped person across state lines a federal offense which, together with the federal law against sending ransom notes through the mails, allows the G-men to enter kidnaping cases.

Similar technicalities permit federal agents to participate in other criminal cases. For instance, automobile theft is not a federal crime but transporting stolen automobiles across state lines is prohibited by the Dyer act; seduction is not a federal offense but transporting a female across state lines for immoral purposes is prohibited by the Mann act. The notorious Al Capone was not convicted in a federal court for gangsterism but for failure to make a faithful federal income tax return.

In addition to those suggested, cases commonly handled by the federal courts include: (1) frauds against the federal government, including embezzlements from national banks; (2) citizenship and denaturalization cases; (3) violations of federal income tax and other revenue laws; (4) violations of post office regulations, including sending threats and other improper material through the mail, rifling mailboxes and other interferences with the mails; (5) violations of federal statues such as the food and drug acts, antitrust act, Securities and Exchange act, Interstate Commerce acts, narcotics act and Railway Labor act; and (6) bankruptcy proceedings.

OFFICERS OF THE COURT

Officers of a circuit court or a court with similar jurisdiction are as follows: (1) The *judge* presides during trials, decides points of law, rules on the admissibility of evidence, instructs juries as to the law, pronounces final judgments and sentences, and admits criminal defendants to probation. In fact, the judge *is* the court and even his oral orders are authoritative and violations of them constitute contempt of court. (2) The *clerk of court* receives applications and motions made formally to him for the record, preserves pleadings until used in a formal trial, prepares a court docket and trial calendar with the cooperation of the judge, during a trial records all motions and prepares records and orders of the judge, receives moneys paid to the court as fines, damages and judgments. (3) The *prosecuting attorney* prosecutes all civil and criminal actions in which the state is a party, defends actions brought against the county, examines all persons brought before any judge on habeas corpus, gives legal opinions to any county officer or justice of the peace and, in general, represents the constituency electing him in all legal matters. The prosecuting attorney usually is called *district attorney* or *state's attorney*. (4) The *public defender* is paid by the state to defend persons unable to afford private counsel; where no such officer exists the court often appoints a member of the local bar to serve in that capacity. (5) The *bailiff* acts as sergeant-at-arms, announces the opening of court ("Hear ye, hear ye," and so forth), keeps order in the courtroom, calls witnesses, ushers jurors from the jury room and acts as messenger. Many bailiffs really are *sheriff's deputies*, assigned to the courts. In justice of the peace courts the comparable officer is the *constable*; in federal courts it is the *marshal*. (6) The *masters, referees* and *commissioners* act as "assistant judges" in civil matters. They hear protracted testimony and make recommendations to the judge who has final authority. Masters act in *chancery* (equity) matters and referees in *common law* matters. Commissioners in state courts are appointed for particular tasks, mostly investigative; federal commissioners are examining magistrates in criminal matters. (7) The *court reporter* is not an elected official but a licensed stenographer authorized to take verbatim testimony and prepare notes in a transcript of evidence called a record. The court reporter may sell copies of his transcript to parties engaged in a trial; in cases of appeal, several copies of a transcript are necessary. (8) *A friend of the court* is a temporarily appointed adviser to the judge who serves during the particular case for which he is selected. (9) The *jury commissioners* make up a jury list or panel consisting of the names of a certain number of voters in the territory served by the court for each term of court. In smaller counties, the board of supervisors appoints the commissioners; in larger counties, the county judge does so.

Civil Law

Through codification and/or passage of civil practices acts, many states have simplified both the substantive and adjective law. Whereas formerly it was necessary to bring parts of the same action in different courts, in the federal courts and many state courts it now is possible to ask for both legal and equitable relief in the same action. For instance, you can ask for *damages* (legal relief) and for an *injunction* (equitable relief) to prevent continuation of the cause of injury in the same complaint.

The reporter must be warned, however, that such is not universally true. Several Atlantic seaboard states in particular still adhere to old common law and equity definitions and procedures. In those states one would not bring a simple action to set aside a contract or to force compliance with it or to recover damages because of its breach. Rather, one would bring an action in *covenant* (to recover money damages), or *debt* (to recover specific sums), or *assumpsit* (for damages if the contract was not under seal), or *detinue* (to recover specific chattels). Similarly, a damage suit (tort action) would be one in *trespass* (for money damages), or *trespass on the case* (if injuries were not the direct result of the action complained of), or *detinue* (to recover specific chattels) or *replevin* (a statutory right to recover both property and damages) or *trover* (damages in case the property is lost, destroyed or otherwise incapable of return) or *deceit* (damages for a wrong committed deceitfully).

STARTING AN ACTION

In noncode states a common law action is an *action at law* whereas a case in equity is a *suit in equity*. In federal courts and states with civil practices acts, there is just one *civil action*. To start it the *plaintiff* (he who brings the action) files a *petition* (also called *declaration* or *complaint* or *statement of claim*) stating clearly the alleged cause for action and the relief which he wishes the court to grant. Each paragraph of the complaint is numbered and is called a *count*. When he files an *answer*, as he must do within a specified period to avoid the plaintiff's winning a *judgment by default*, the *defendant* (often called *respondent*, with any third parties mentioned as equally guilty, being *co-respondents*) must admit or deny each count. In the old days, litigants could continue arguing a case on paper almost indefinitely. Under simplified procedures, the *pleadings*—as all such written arguments are called—are limited to two or three by each party.

There follows a typical complaint:

STATE OF ILLINOIS } ss
COUNTY OF COOK

IN THE SUPERIOR COURT OF COOK COUNTY

IRIS GARDNER,
    Plaintiff
    —vs—   NO. 42 S 10542
CHARLES W. WRIGLEY,
    Defendant

COMPLAINT AT LAW FOR
BREACH OF CONTRACT
JURY DEMANDED

Now comes IRIS GARDNER, plaintiff in the above entitled cause, and complains of the defendant, CHARLES W. WRIGLEY, as follows:

1. That the plaintiff was, on the 15th day of October A.D. 1937 temporarily sojourning in the City of Chicago, County of Cook and State of Illinois; and, on the date aforesaid, she was about to depart from said city, county and state, and return to her domiciliary city and state, to-wit: St. Louis, Missouri.

2. That plaintiff had a long social acquaintance and friendship with the defendant, CHARLES W. WRIGLEY, prior to October 15, A.D., 1937, when, on the date, aforesaid, she, the plaintiff, at the special instance and request of the defendant, CHARLES W. WRIGLEY, met the defendant, CHARLES W. WRIGLEY, in his offices, located at 400 North Michigan Avenue, in the City of Chicago, County of Cook and State of Illinois, and that at the place and on the date aforesaid, plaintiff entered into a verbal agreement with the defendant, CHARLES W. WRIGLEY, the substance of which agreement is hereinafter verbatim alleged.

3. That the defendant, CHARLES W. WRIGLEY, was then, and is now, engaged in the advertising business, and was then, and is now, reputed to have considerable material wealth.

4. That the plaintiff was then, and is now, a woman possessed of pulchritude, charm, and numerous other attributes and qualities to enchant, charm, and grace any person; or, in fact, any social circle.

5. That the defendant, CHARLES W. WRIGLEY, met the plaintiff, at the place and on the date aforesaid, at his special instance and request; and then and there the defendant, CHARLES W. WRIGLEY, was expressly charmed and enchanted by the plaintiff, because of plaintiff's charm, graciousness, and other womanly qualities and attributes and thereupon the defendant, CHARLES W. WRIGLEY, informed plaintiff that she was the person for whom he had been searching to assist him, socially and in his business. Whereupon,

the parties entered into a verbal agreement, which, in words, figures and substance, is as follows:

a. The defendant, CHARLES W. WRIGLEY, verbally agreed with the plaintiff to pay plaintiff the sum of One Thousand Dollars ($1,000) per month, either in cash, or by letters of credit, or in any other mode or manner the plaintiff might see fit, provided the said sum was paid in full to the plaintiff, before the expiration of each and every month, commencing on the 1st day of November, A.D. 1937, during the rest of her natural life; and the defendant, CHARLES W. WRIGLEY, further agreed, in order to protect plaintiff, in the event he predeceased plaintiff, to create a trust in the sum of Two Hundred and Fifty Thousand Dollars ($250,000.00), said trust to be evidenced by a trust agreement, the provisions of which trust agreement were to provide that the plaintiff would be entitled to receive the proceeds, rents, profits, and emoluments accruing therefrom, during the plaintiff's natural life.

b. That in consideration of the said verbal agreement, the plaintiff was to cancel her then imminent departure, as aforesaid from the City of Chicago, County of Cook and State of Illinois; and it was further agreed that the plaintiff should reside and domicile continuously in the City of Chicago, County of Cook and State of Illinois, during the natural life of the defendant, CHARLES W. WRIGLEY, in order to assist the defendant, CHARLES W. WRIGLEY, in his social activities, as the defendant might, from time to time, direct, which social activities, according to the defendant, CHARLES W. WRIGLEY, could be efficaciously performed only by the plaintiff, or by some other member of the fair sex with abilities co-equal to those possessed by the plaintiff.

c. That in pursuance of said verbal agreement, the plaintiff remained, resided and domiciled, and continues to remain, reside, and domicile, in the City of Chicago, County of Cook and State of Illinois; that the defendant, CHARLES W. WRIGLEY, in pursuance of the terms of said verbal agreement, obtained or rented an apartment on behalf of the plaintiff, at the St. Clair Hotel, and paid plaintiff (in cash or by check, or paid the expenditures of the plaintiff directly to plaintiff's creditors) the stipulated consideration thereof to-wit: One Thousand Dollars ($1,000.00) per month, including the rental for said apartment; and that the defendant, CHARLES W. WRIGLEY, continued to comply with the terms of said agreement until on or about the 30th day of May, A.D. 1943, on which date the defendant, CHARLES W. WRIGLEY, expressly repudiated the same, verbally informing and advising plaintiff that he would no longer continue payment, thereof, in view of his reduced financial status.

6. That in pursuance of the terms of said verbal agreement, the plaintiff heretofore has exerted much effort, and expended her youth, grace and charm, to the end of ameliorating defendant's social as well as esthetic, well-being.

7. That at the time the aforesaid agreement was entered into defendant was approximately twenty (20) years plaintiff's senior.

8. That the plaintiff has performed each and every condition of her contract with the defendant, CHARLES W. WRIGLEY, whether precedent or subsequent, and she is not in default thereof.

9. That the defendant, CHARLES W. WRIGLEY, has wilfully and maliciously, and without any just cause, but merely whimsically, breached the provisions of said verbal agreement.

10. That the plaintiff has sustained damages, by reason of the breach of said agreement by the defendant, CHARLES W. WRIGLEY, in the sum of Five Hundred Thousand Dollars ($500,000.00).

WHEREFORE, plaintiff brings her suit, and asks that a judgment be entered in her behalf and against the defendant, CHARLES W. WRIGLEY, in the sum of Five Hundred Thousand Dollars ($500,000.00) and costs.

This is how the Chicago *Sun* handled this news:

Suit for $500,000 charging breach of contract, was filed in Superior Court yesterday against Charles W. Wrigley, 71, brother of the late William Wrigley Jr., chewing-gum magnate, by a woman who described herself as possessing "pulchritude, charm, and manner."

She is identified in the bill as Mrs. Iris Gardner, 41, of the St. Clair Hotel.

Her complaint, according to the bill, alleges that Wrigley is not paying her $1,000 a month. He agreed to do this back in 1937, she said, and kept up the payments for six years before quitting.

Wrigley Indignant

Wrigley, head of an outdoor advertising firm, with offices at 400 N. Michigan av., indignantly denied the entire alleged transaction. Reached at his home, 10 Canterbury ct., Wilmette, he said:

"It's an outrage to file a suit like that. The lady's husband worked for me 15 years ago.

"She never worked for me. As to the payments of $1,000 a month, why, that's crazy! Where would I get the money? She started after me just after Charlie Chaplin's trouble."

Asserts Trust Fund Pledged

According to the bill, Wrigley, uncle of Philip K. Wrigley, owner of the Chicago Cubs, agreed to pay Mrs. Gardner $1,000 a month for life and, if he died first, leave a $250,000 trust fund to provide the income.

In return, the bill continued, Mrs. Gardner was to "assist him socially and in his business." The agreement, Mrs. Gardner said, was verbal.

Note: (1) the reporter obtained information other than that contained in the complaint, (2) he exercised great care in ascribing every fact based on the complaint to the complaint itself, by means of such phrases as "according to the bill," and "the bill continued." It is absolutely necessary never to allow any statement in a story based on a legal document to stand by itself, even at the risk of boring repetition of references.

During the course of his day the reporter watches for the filing of actions which are newsworthy either because of the persons or the amount of money involved or because of the unusualness of the charges. He should not be deceived, however, by exorbitant demands, especially in damage suits. Otherwise, he will be chagrined to learn that a $10,000 action was settled out of court for $250, as often happens.

A $18,000 damage suit was filed in Superior court yesterday by Mrs. Alice Allison, 50, of 179 North Shore drive, for injuries which she said she suffered when a truck collided with a car in which she was riding at McCormick boulevard and North Shore drive last May 1.

Eric Swanson, 55, of 2900 Milwaukee avenue, Mrs. Allison's nephew, was at the wheel of the car, the petition alleges, when a Petroleum Motor company truck violated traffic signals and smashed into it at high speed. The company and Ralph T. and Ernest J. Walton, its owners, are the defendants.

DEFENDING AN ACTION

A defendant who has been properly served by *summons* (law) or *subpoena* (equity) must answer within a prescribed time or at least file an *appearance*, which is an acknowledgment and indication that he will answer later. When the answer is filed the reporter scans it for its contents.

To avoid answering, the defendant may enter a *motion to dismiss* the action, contending that the plaintiff has no legal right to bring it. In such a motion, he may challenge the jurisdiction of the court or the sufficiency of the process by which he was notified of the beginning of the suit; or, most importantly, he may contend that the plaintiff has failed to state a ground for action. Under old procedures, he may enter a *demurrer*, which is a plea that, even if true, the facts alleged do not constitute a cause for action. He also may plead that the *statute of limitations*, which sets the time limit within which such action can be brought, has been violated.

To delay or postpone the case, the defendant may resort to dilatory tactics by a *plea in abatement* which may: (1) *challenge the array*—that is, question the procedure by which the panel of veniremen (potential jurors) was selected as the case nears trial; (2) ask a *change of venue*, which is a transfer to another court or branch of the same court on the grounds that judge or jurors are prejudiced; (3) ask a *continuance*, or postponement, for any of a variety of reasons, the merits of which the judge must decide; (4) be a *motion to quash* because the summons was defective.

A special kind of answer is one in *confession and avoidance* wherein the defendant admits the facts but declares he acted within his legal rights. A *counterclaim* is an answer in which the defendant not only denies liability but contends that the plaintiff is obligated to him. Counterclaims are frequent in damage cases involving automobile accidents; each driver blames the other.

When several actions related to the same incident are begun, the court may order that there be a *joinder of parties* or *joinder of causes*. On the other hand, on its own motion or that of one of the parties, the court may grant a *severance* when co-defendants make separate answers. A third party who believes his interests are affected by the action may petition the court for permission to file an *intervening* petition to become either a plaintiff or defendant.

> Complications in the divorce suit of Constantin Dantes against Mrs. Marie Busch Jones Dantes arose today with announcement by Carl Enger, attorney for Mrs. Gertrude Stuprich, Dantes' former wife, that he would file an intervening petition in the suit against Mrs. Marie Dantes.
>
> Basis for the intervening petition, Enger said, would be Dantes' failure to pay $7.50 a week for the support of his 17-year-old daughter, Bertha, as provided in the divorce obtained by Mrs. Stuprich in Circuit Judge James E. McLaughlin's court last Nov. 15. . . . [St. Louis *Post-Dispatch*]

So that he will understand what is going on, the reporter should be familiar with a few other types of motions: (1) a *bill of particulars* may be demanded by the defendant if the complaint is unclear or not sufficiently specific; (2) a *bill of discovery* may be asked if the defendant wishes to examine documents or other material in the plaintiff's possession; (3) either party may ask permission to submit an *interrogatory*, or set of questions, to the other to obtain necessary information; (4) scandalous, redundant, irrelevant or otherwise objectionable portions of any pleading may be eliminated if the court grants a *motion to strike*.

CIVIL TRIALS

Unless there is a *default judgment* (or *decree*) because of failure of the defendant to answer, or a *summary judgment* because the answer is inadequate, or a *judgment by confession* because the defendant admits the plaintiff's charges, the issue becomes joined and, upon motion of either party or the court itself, the case is placed on the trial calendar.

Most civil trials today are heard by a judge alone. In fact, it generally is necessary to make a formal request and pay a court fee at the time of filing a complaint or answer to obtain a civil trial by jury. Except for the preliminary step of selecting the jurors, theoretically the procedure is the same. The steps are as follows:

1. Opening statement by plaintiff, through his attorney, of what he expects to prove.
2. Opening statement by defendant.
3. Direct examination of plaintiff's witnesses.
4. Cross-examination by defendant of plaintiff's witnesses.
5. Direct and cross-examination of defendant's witnesses.
6. Redirect or rebuttal witnesses for plaintiff.
7. Closing statements by both sides, plaintiff speaking first, then the defendant, and, finally, rebuttal by plaintiff.

In actual practice, a hearing before a judge usually is informal. With all of the principals and their attorneys and witnesses clustered about the bench, the judge may interrupt, change the usual order of procedure and take a hand at questioning. Then he either takes the case under *advisement* (meaning he wants to think it over before deciding) or he enters a *judgment* for either plaintiff or defendant, in a law action, or a *decree* if the case is one at equity. Even if there is a jury, it can only recommend what *damages* are to be assessed against the loser in a law action; the final decision is up to the judge and, upon motion of the losing party or on his own initiative, he can disregard the jury's findings and enter a *judgment notwithstanding the verdict*.

Damages may be: (1) *general*, meaning they are the same as might be expected to compensate anyone for the type of loss proved to have been incurred; (2) *special*, those peculiar to the particular case; (3) *nominal*, which are trifling and for the purpose of moral vindication only; or (4) *exemplary*, assessed in addition to the general or *compensatory* damages, to punish the other party.

> A judgment for $119,358 against the Global Securities & Holding company as stockholders in the Acorn National bank, was ordered by Federal Judge Frick today in favor of Gerald Swayne, receiver of the bank. The amount of the judgment represented a double assessment against the company as holders of 1001 shares of the bank's stock and $9,358 accrued interest.

A civil action may end in a *nonsuit* if at any time the plaintiff fails to continue; such a judgment naturally is for the defendant. So is a *dismissal*, the difference being, however, that in case of a nonsuit the plaintiff may begin another action whereas a dismissal is a final disposition of a case, unless it is a *dismissal without prejudice* which usually comes upon request of the plaintiff himself. A *consent* judgment is entered when the court approves an out-of-court agreement between the parties. A *declaratory* judgment, obtainable in federal courts and some state courts, is an informatory opinion in advance of any legal action; by means of it the court declares what its decision would be in the event action were brought. Its use prevents much expensive and useless litigation.

An ordinary judgment or decree is either (1) *final*; or (2) *conditional*, which means certain acts (as exchange of property) must be performed before it becomes final; or (3) *nisi* (unless), which means it becomes final after a certain lapse of time if certain forbidden acts do not occur; or (4) *interlocutory*, in which case restrictions on behavior—as against remarriage—are designated.

ENFORCING CIVIL LAW

There is no imprisonment for debt in the United States, so a plaintiff may not be much better off after he receives a judgment against the defendant than before. By applying for a *writ of execution*, the judgment creditor can force sale of the judgment debtor's property to satisfy his claim, but if the debtor does not possess enough assets to meet the obligation, it is often better to allow the judgment to stand as a lien against what he does have until the day when it is wise to enforce it. To discover a debtor's assets, a creditor may obtain a court *citation* ordering the debtor to appear in court for questioning by a referee. Failure to comply means that one may be cited for *contempt of court* which, in some cases, may be punished by imprisonment. In such cases, however, the judgment creditor usually has to pay for the debtor's keep. The inmates of "alimony row" in the county jail are contemptuous divorcees.

Either at the beginning of a suit or after a judgment has been obtained, the plaintiff may obtain a *property attachment*, placing the defendant's assets under control of the court to prevent their conversion. A *body attachment* or *execution* is a court order to arrest a principal to prevent his untimely departure from its jurisdiction. A *ne exeat* decree is an order forbidding such departure. *Garnishment* proceedings are for the purpose of attaching a debtor's income, usually his salary, for the benefit of the creditor.

If a court becomes convinced that a supposedly closed case should be reopened, it can entertain a motion to *reinstate* a case which has been dismissed, to *set aside* a verdict, to *vacate* a judgment or to *review* a decree. A *writ of audita querela* stops execution of a judgment when new evidence is presented. A *writ of supersedeas* orders a court officer to stop execution which has not gone too far.

Many damage suits contain a *malice* count which means that the alleged injury was committed intentionally or because of gross negligence. If the court upholds the contention, the guilty defendant may be jailed if he fails to satisfy the judgment.

Civil Actions

There is a seemingly interminable number of kinds of actions. Judges and lawyers with years of experience pore over ponderous legal tomes for hours to refresh their memories regarding many of them. The lay reporter cannot be expected to master the intricacies of even an appreciable number of them. If he understands the basic differences between the major types of actions and can translate the most frequently used legal language, he can get along. There are several good law dictionaries which he can consult when he "encounters a new one." What follows are a few suggestions concerning some of the kinds of actions which are most newsworthy.

DAMAGE SUITS

The news interest usually is in the incident giving rise to the action: an automobile accident, a surgeon's error and so forth. If so, perhaps the paper carried a story at the time, which means the account of the filing of the complaint should contain a careful tie-back. The reporter should get: names and addresses of principals; the plaintiff's version of exactly what happened, all charges being carefully accredited to the complaint; the comments of the defendant on the charges; the amount of money demanded; is there a malice count?

> Harold Howard filed a $30,000 damage suit in Lancaster District Court Wednesday in connection with a fall he incurred while loading furniture belonging to the defendant, Harold McBride.
>
> Howard, who operates a long-distance moving firm, alleges that on Nov. 24, 1963, while in the process of loading the van to move McBride from Littleton, Colo., to Lincoln, he requested McBride to get him a ladder so he could inspect the load on top of the van.
>
> He contends that the defendant was negligent in setting up the ladder and, as a result, it collapsed and he suffered a fractured wrist.
>
> He alleges 20% permanent partial disability.   [Lincoln (Neb.) *Journal*]

DIVORCE

Distinguish between *divorce* and *annulment*, and between *separate maintenance* and *alimony*. What are the grounds (desertion, cruelty, and so forth)? Watch out for libel when reporting specific incidents cited as grievances (beatings, criminal behavior). The reporter should obtain: names and addresses of both principals; date of marriage and of separation; names and ages of children and what bill requests regarding them; suggested disposition of property; whether alimony is requested; whether wife asks court to authorize use of her maiden name. When a case comes to hearing, testimony, of course, can be reported; state whether defendant contests case or allows decree to be obtained by default.

> Two suits for divorce were filed in circuit court Thursday, Cruelty is charged in both cases.
> Sandra Neisen alleged James Neisen struck her several times. They were married Sept. 30, 1961, and separated Tuesday. She asked the court to order a division of the property in the residence at 26 South Granview, farm machinery and a checking account. She asked for the custody of three children and that a car be given to her.
> Rochelle Williams alleged James N. Williams struck her and ordered her to leave the house and not return. They were married Sept. 13, 1958, and separated in March, 1965. She asked that she be given her equity in real estate in New Jersey. [Quincy (Ill.) *Herald-Whig*]

FORECLOSURES

A person who defaults in payments on a mortgage stands to lose the property through foreclosure proceedings. In most states, however, he has an *equity of redemption*—a period of time in which to pay up, even though a court has awarded the property to the mortgage holder.

EVICTIONS

The Renters' Court always is a fertile source for human interest stories. The legal name for actions to evict is *forcible entry and detainer*. During housing shortages, renters' courts are crowded. The reporter does well to examine the statutes of the state for sections pertaining to the rights of landlords to evict or refuse to rent to families with children or pets. He also should read up on statutes and court decisions related to *restrictive covenants* whereby property owners are forbidden to sell or lease to Negroes, Jews or members of other minority groups, or are otherwise restricted in the use of property.

CONDEMNATION SUITS

When a new street or highway or public building is planned, the proper government agency uses its right of *eminent domain* to purchase —at a fair price—any privately owned land needed for the improvement. Property owners often resist such taking of their property or hold out for higher compensation. Public clamor may cause a change in official plans, as happened when property owners in Connecticut objected to the headquarters of the United Nations being established there.

RECEIVERSHIPS

Creditors or stockholders of a corporation or individuals in financial difficulties may apply to an equity court for appointment of a receiver to conserve assets and rescue the business. A chancery receivership, intended to put a going concern back on its feet, must be distinguished from a receiver in bankruptcy, who is in charge of liquidating a defunct institution. Many banks, hotels, transportation and other companies continue operating under receiverships for years. Often newspapers uncover scandals regarding political favoritism in appointment of receivers or companies with which they do business. Reporters should watch the periodic reports which receivers must make to the courts appointing them.

BANKRUPTCY

A financial failure may file a *voluntary petition* in bankruptcy, or his creditors may file an *involuntary petition* in his case. The reporter should examine the inventory filed with the petition, to obtain: total assets; total liabilities; nature of the assets (stocks, real estate, controlling interest in other companies, etc.); nature of liabilities, clues as to reasons for failure. Bankruptcy matters are handled by the federal courts. Each petition is referred to a *referee in bankruptcy*, a permanent court officer; the *trustee* is elected by the creditors and, if approved by the court, takes over the task of liquidating the assets and distributing them on a pro rata basis. Instead of dissolving a business, a company may undergo *reorganization* under a court-approved plan. Usually, some creditors are "frozen out" when such happens, and the legal jockeying between them to avoid that happening is newsworthy when the company is important. Since every action of a trustee must be approved by the court, the reporter can keep close to the situation.

INJUNCTIONS

Distinguish between a *preliminary restraining order*, which is issued by a judge on ex parte evidence only and without notice, and between *temporary* and *permanent* injunctions. The orthodox procedure is for the court to issue a temporary order to the defendant to appear in court and "show cause" why it should not become permanent. In the meantime, the alleged offensive conduct must cease. Injunctions are used to prohibit government agencies and officials from exceeding their authority; to test the constitutionality of a law; to restrain picketing and other activities by labor unions; to restrain corporations from acts injurious to stock- or bond-holders; to compel persons to keep the peace and not interfere with the civil liberties and other rights of others; to stop and prevent nuisances; and for other purposes.

BY EDWARD HUDSON

The Port of New York Authority brought suit against American Airlines yesterday to enjoin the airline from taking off or landing with its jets over Jackson Heights, Queens.

The action was taken in State Supreme Court in Queens, where Justice Nicholas M. Pette signed a temporary order restraining American from conducting such operations pending a hearing.

The hearing was set for 9:30 A.M. Wednesday. [New York *Times*]

Extraordinary Remedies

The equitable relief provided by an injunction originated as an extraordinary remedy, but has become so common it no longer is extraordinary. Almost the same is true of *habeas corpus*, whereby a jailer is required to produce a prisoner in court to answer charges against him. Dating from Magna Charta, it is one of the great Anglo-Saxon democratic protections.

Other so-called extraordinary remedies follow.

PROHIBITION

This is a writ issued by a superior court to one of inferior jurisdiction commanding it to desist in handling any matter beyond its authority to consider.

CERTIORARI

This also is an inquiry into the behavior of a lower court after it has taken some action. Thus, it usually operates as an appeal, to bring about a review of the lower court's action in the higher court. In granting a writ of certiorari or *writ of review*, as it is called, however, the higher court merely agrees to look into the matter. It may return the case later.

MANDAMUS

This writ is directed by a higher court to administrative officers, corporations or an inferior court ordering some action required by law. It does not specify what the action must be—as in a case where a required appointment is overdue—but it does demand that some action be taken.

QUO WARRANTO

By this writ, a higher court inquires into the right of a public official to hold office or of a corporation to exercise a franchise.

Probate Proceedings

When a person dies, the state supervises payment of his debts and distribution of his property. If he dies *testate* (that is, if he leaves a will), unless someone can prove that the contrary should be done, the court sees that its provisions are carried out. It usually appoints the *executor* named in the will to supervise settling the estate; that official, often a relative of the deceased, posts bond for about one-and-a-half times the estimated value of the estate and receives a commission when his work is done. If there is no will (deceased died *intestate*) the court appoints an *administrator*. In many states there now are public administrators. Either executor or administrator receives *letters testamentary* to authorize his work, which includes notification of beneficiaries named in a will or legal heirs if there is no will; advertising for bills against the estate; collecting money due the estate; preparing an inventory of the estate; and so forth.

FILING A WILL

The first step in probate proceedings is the filing of the will by whoever has it in custody or finds it. Reporters watch for such filings of wills of prominent persons recently deceased. In their case, it is news whether the estate is large or small. As a matter of fact, it usually is difficult or impossible to determine an estate's size from the will itself; it is not known with certainty until an appraisal is made months later. The first public information may come with the filing of an inheritance tax return.

> The estate of Henry B. Ritter, Milltown contruction contractor, totaled $3,062,182, according to an inheritance tax return filed Thursday with the Vernon County clerk.
> Ritter, uncle of former county treasurer Herbert C. Ritter, died Dec. 19, 1959, at the age of 77. He lived at 345 W. Fullerton.
> The estate was left in trust to the widow, Lillian, with a provision that upon her death one-half of it go to their children, Mrs. Marjorie O'Neil of 706 S. Sheridan, Barton, and Henry Jr., of 12 E. Scott.
> The federal tax on the estate was $358,659 and the state levy, $117,328.

An ingenious reporter in some cases can estimate value by determining the market value of securities, the assessor's valuations of real estate and by similar investigation. Frequently, the nature of an estate is newsworthy as a person may be revealed to be the owner of property which he was not known to possess. From the will, the beneficiaries can be determined and often they contain surprises. The first news story should mention when and where the will was drawn and possibly the witnesses. In small places, virtually every will is newsworthy; in larger places, only those of important persons or involving large estates receive mention.

ADMITTING TO PROBATE

The reporter must not confuse filing a will and admitting a will to probate which is done by court order upon petition of the executor or someone else. Before such a petition is granted it must be "proved" to be genuine and there also must be proof of heirship; usually referees supervise such routine matters. If anything happens to disturb the routine, it probably is newsworthy.

> The will of Richard W. Young, founder and chairman of the board of the Young corporation, who died March 1, at the age of 70, was admitted to probate today by County Judge Thomas Sullivan.

The executors are Thomas B. Young and R. L. Waters. Waters declined to place an estimate on the size of the estate, but it is generally understood to be in the millions.

Sets Up Trust Fund

The will sets up a trust fund on behalf of 11 relatives of the industrialist. The division is as follows:

On-sixth of the estate to Thomas B. Young, now president of the Young corporation, a nephew. One-eighth to Frank Young, a nephew. One-eighth to Ruth Young Stoddard, a niece.

One-twelfth to Louise R. White, a niece. One-twelfth to Margaret Rolnick, a niece. One-twelfth to Nancy Young, a niece. One-twelfth to Mary Sheridan, a niece. One-twelfth to Robert Carpenter, a nephew. One-twelfth to Richard Sheridan, a nephew.

One-twenty-fourth to Patricia Young, a grand-niece and one-twenty-fourth to Kent Young, a grand-nephew.

May Be Liquidated

The will provides that the Young Investment company, established by Young, may be liquidated within 12 months of his death and the assets distributed to the stockholders, this with the approval of the executors. It also provides that the entire estate shall be liquidated within 20 years and may be liquidated, if the executors approve, in ten years.

CONTESTING A WILL

By law an interval, which varies from three months to two years, must elapse between the time a will is admitted to probate and a *final accounting*. During that period, suit may be brought to break the will, perhaps by a disgruntled relative who was disinherited. Common charges are that the deceased was unduly influenced when he made the will, or was not in full possession of his mental faculties. Sometimes it is charged that the will filed was not the most recent. Such suits usually are filed in courts other than that handling routine probate matters.

Suit to contest the will of Mrs. Margaret W. Winchester, widow of Charles B. Winchester, an official of Scott & Co., whereby she left most of $100,000 to friends, was filed in Circuit Court yesterday by six relatives, including three sisters and a brother. Mrs. Winchester plunged to her death from a room in the Bacon House last July 27 at the age of 68.

The suit charges she was "eccentric and peculiar" and "susceptible to influence and blandishments," and that undue influence was put upon her in making the will. Attorney G. A. Yates, co-executor under the will, who was left a $20,000 bequest, was her close financial adviser, and Attorney Allan E. Mack, also left $20,000, was his associate, the bill points out.

Rules of Evidence

To "feel at home" as he should whenever he steps into any courtroom, a reporter must understand the fundamental rules of evidence.

NATURE OF EVIDENCE

Most evidence is in the form of testimony by witnesses. Other forms of evidence include objects and written material introduced as exhibits. Together they constitute the *proof* whereby it is intended to influence the court's decision. All evidence must be: (1) *material*—have a direct relation to the case; (2) *relevant*—pertinent; and (3) *competent*—authoritative. Otherwise, the court will uphold an *objection* to its introduction.

BURDEN OF PROOF

In a civil action, it is *preponderance of evidence* that counts; in criminal cases, the state must prove guilt *beyond any reasonable doubt*. At all times, the burden of proof rests with the side which must refute evidence which, if allowed to stand, would be injurious to it.

PRESUMPTIONS

The law presumes that any situation known to exist at one time continues to exist unless proof to the contrary is provided. Thus good character and impeccable behavior on the part of all citizens is presumed until disproved.

JUDICIAL NOTICE

Common knowledge—such as the organization of government, size and location of cities and countries, business practices and the like—need not be proved in court. Instead, the court "takes notice" of them, unless challenged for doing so.

QUALIFICATIONS OF WITNESSES

Children, wives, husbands, insane persons, felons, dependents, interested lawyers and other parties once were barred from testifying.

Today, the restrictions are much lighter. Almost anyone competent at the time of trial or hearing can be a witness; the credibility to be attached to his testimony is a different matter.

PRIVILEGE

The Fifth Amendment to the Constitution of the United States protects anyone from being compelled to testify against himself. In actual practice, refusal to testify because to do so might incriminate oneself often is a "dodge." No lawyer can be compelled to reveal what a client has told him in confidence. Similar protection is afforded physicians and clergymen in many cases and, in a few states, newspapermen.

LEADING QUESTIONS

Witnesses tell their stories in response to questions by attorneys. Those questions cannot be so worded as to suggest the answers desired.

HEARSAY EVIDENCE

A witness can testify only to that of which he has first-hand knowledge. He cannot draw inferences from the facts. Exceptions to the rule include dying declarations, spontaneous declarations, confessions and admissions against one's interest.

OPINION EVIDENCE

Anyone is an authority on matters which he has witnessed or which are within the knowledge of an ordinary person. Experts must be qualified before their testimony is considered credible. An expert's opinion often is obtained by means of a *hypothetical question* in which a situation comparable to that at issue is described.

REAL EVIDENCE

Clothing, weapons and objects of all sorts are introduced as exhibits. So are models and photographs.

CIRCUMSTANTIAL EVIDENCE

Correct inferences often can be drawn from evidence pertaining to a person's behavior both before and after a crime is committed and from his known capacities and predilections. A great deal of the evidence in both civil and criminal cases is circumstantial rather than eyewitness accounts.

BEST EVIDENCE

Copies of documents are admissible only when there is proof that originals are unavailable. In every case, the court demands the best possible evidence regarding any point.

Appeals

Since the trial judge passes on motions for new trials, not many are granted. Only in rare cases, however, does a judge refuse to grant a dissatisfied party the right to take his case to the appellate court. In criminal matters, no appeal is possible by the state in the event of acquittal, but a convicted defendant can appeal; and in civil matters either side can do so.

The distinction between *appeal* (of civil law origin) and *writ of error* (of common law origin) is virtually nonexistent today. Where it exists, it means that in the former instance a case is removed entirely from the lower to the higher court which then can review both the law and the evidence; a writ of error, by contrast, is an original proceeding, not a continuation of that in the lower court.

Appeals are either *as of right* or *by permission* of the upper court as the statutes designate. Common grounds on which an appeal can be made are: (1) irregularity of the submission of evidence; (2) new evidence discovered since the trial ended; (3) misconduct of the jury; (4) lack of jurisdiction of the court; (5) an error by the judge in instructing the jury; (6) incompetent witnesses; (7) excessive damages allowed (in civil cases); and (8) influencing or packing of the jury by the adverse party.

A *bill of exceptions* (also called *statement of the case* or *certificate of reasonable doubt*) must set forth clearly and completely the grounds on which appeal is taken. It may be accompanied by a *brief* in which the details are made more elaborate and the case as a whole summarized, although the trend is toward simplification of procedure so that only one document is necessary. Certified copies of *transcripts* and *abstracts* of lower court records also are submitted.

The party taking the appeal is known as the *appellant* or *plaintiff in error* and the other party (usually the winner in the lower court) as the *appellee* or *defendant in error*. It is good practice for a reporter always to ask a defeated party in an important case whether he intends to appeal. Otherwise, he first learns of such action by a *notice of appeal* filed in the appellate court. Today, such notice acts as an automatic *stay of proceedings* or *supersedeas* to hold up execution of any lower court judgment or sentence. In some jurisdictions, however, it is necessary to petition for such writs.

If the higher court's permission is necessary, whatever the court decides regarding a petition is news. If it agrees to review a case, it sets a date for *oral arguments* by attorneys. Then it takes the case *under advisement*. Each justice studies the case independently before the court meets to discuss it. After a vote is taken, the chief justice assigns one justice to prepare the *majority opinion* supporting the court's *decision*. Other members may prepare *concurring opinions* or *dissenting opinions*. Any part of a decision which deals with background not directly pertinent to the case at hand is called *obiter dictum*; it explains the mental processes by which the justices formed their opinions.

By its decision, the appellate court *upholds* or *reverses* or *modifies* the lower court's decision. A *mandate* is an order to a lower court to take any kind of action, and the upper court *remands* the case to the lower so that it can act.

Only an experienced reporter is likely to be assigned to cover appellate court proceedings. By the time he has mastered the art of handling lower court news, he will be thoroughly qualified to do so.

> The United States Circuit Court of Appeals took under review yesterday the criminal conviction of Henry Lustig, millionaire restaurateur, and two others on charges of having defrauded the Federal Government of $2,872,766 in income taxes owed by the Longchamps Restaurant chain.
>
> Decision was reserved after arguments for three and a half hours by former Gov. Nathan L. Miller, attorney for the appellants, and Bruno Schachner, assistant United States Attorney.
>
> Convicted last June 20 on all 23 counts of an indictment were Lustig, who was sentenced to four years in jail, and fined $115,000; E. Allen Lustig, his nephew, secretary of the restaurants, who received a three-year sentence, and Joseph Sobol, an accountant, who was sentenced to two years.
>
> Mr. Miller pursued the argument presented at the trial that the defendants were entitled to immunity from criminal prosecution because of an alleged voluntary disclosure made to William J. Pedrick, collector of internal revenue for the Second District, by Allen Lustig on March 26, 1945.

He told the court that the question to be decided was whether such immunity existed when a disclosure of delinquency had been made prior to the start of a government investigation and if such a self-incriminating disclosure could be used as a basis for criminal conviction.

Mr. Miller said that at the trial the question of fraud was not contested and that the only question litigated was whether a voluntary disclosure had been made before a Treasury investigation started. He said that a ruling by the lower court judge, Harold Kennedy, that the Treasury Department was not morally bound to keep a promise of immunity from prosecution had the effect of virtally decimating the verdict....

[New York *Times*]

1 6

Politics, Elections

I POLITICAL PHILOSOPHY

II POLITICAL PUBLIC OPINION

III POLITICAL ORGANIZATION
1. Local
2. Precinct and Ward
3. County
4. State, National

IV PRECAMPAIGN ACTIVITIES
1. Petitions
2. Registration
3. Primaries
4. Conventions

V CAMPAIGNS
1. Speeches
2. Strategy
3. Roorbacks
4. Issues

VI ELECTIONS
1. Predictions
2. Election Day
3. Election Results

VII "POST-MORTEMS"

THE AMERICAN POLITICIAN IS A PRACTICAL BUSINESSMAN. WHAT HE sells is his public service which the public purchases with its ballots. His remuneration is employment by the electorate with all the emoluments that the position entails. As a merchant, the politician is responsive to consumer demand and, in turn, attempts to influence that demand. Although independents in other lines of business have been able to withstand the competition of Big Business with its holding companies, chain stores and so on, the lone wolf in politics is virtually hopeless. Any success he attains is temporary; to get far he must align himself with one of the two large rival organizations which, since the Civil War, have divided the nation's political profits with very little loss to third parties.

Since communism and fascism began to threaten democracy in Old World countries and since the American New Dealers introduced a new note in our political life, newspaper readers have become more conscious of the broader aspects or philosophic bases of world politics. This awareness, however, still is predominately academic; all that the defeat of candidates standing for principles which formerly were popular means to the practical politician-businessman is that consumer demand has changed. The professor or student of political theory may be aware of national and international social and economic trends which are reflected in overt political events, but neither candidate nor voter has such breadth of vision. Should an aspirant for office also be a scholar he nevertheless, to be successful (that is, get elected), has to play the game as it is played.

Despite the increase in serious articles, usually Sunday features or those on the editorial page, discussing politics philosophically, the American newspaper remains as practical in its attitude toward the business of getting and staying elected as the politician himself. Because of consolidations, which have left few cities with fewer than 100,000 inhabitants with more than one newspaper, most newspapers today term themselves "independent" whereas formerly they prided themselves on being either Republican or Democratic. This change obviously was made for good business reasons so as not to alienate about 50 per cent of the potential subscribers. Political independence, however, is not tantamount to political indifference as to which party wins a particular election; rather, it means merely that the newspaper reserves the right to decide on which side it will be in each campaign. Theoretically, it is free to be Democratic one year and Republican the next or to support candidates of both parties for different offices in the same election. Once it has made its decision as to whom it will support, the allegedly independent newspaper may be as unfair in his behalf as the frankly aligned paper.

Truly interpretative political writing consists in explaining the immediate phenomenon in terms of long-range trends, national or international. Accepting the fact that practical politicians still do not operate with any appreciable awareness of such trends, pragmatic interpretative political writing consists in identifying leaders with movements and "seeing through" motives and actions to discover their probable meaning and effect upon political fortunes.

From whichever angle he regards the political scene, the political reporter, to "keep his feet on the ground," must see beyond the externals which the politician hopes, usually successfully, will be all of which the average voter is aware. What benefits this overcoming of naïveté will be to the reporter, outside of the extent to which it furthers his education, is dependent upon the attitude of his superiors. No matter what they profess, newspapers *are* involved in politics and, all the statistical evidence to the contrary, both candidates and voters act as though the press is an important factor. Any aspirant for any office welcomes the support of any newspaper, and any newspaper is glad to have a political friend in public office. As long as a newspaper attacks a politician it advertises him; the most effective journalistic weapon is to ignore a person. Although there have been numerous instances in which exactly that was done, it is not common practice if for no other reason than to avoid "one party press" criticisms which result when a newspaper does not seem to be giving rival candidates for an office equal treatment.

In small cities, the primary interest is local politics inasmuch as the small newspaper has little to gain directly from state or national politics. Local political news is written by staff members whereas material regarding state or national politics is obtained from press associations, syndicates and political headquarters. That all of this news, regardless of how obtained, is presented impartially except in rare instances, is obviously absurd to believe. Hence, the reporter seeking to do a meaty objective job is handicapped. In no field of writing is the merely narrative more impotent in serving any public purpose nor absence of bias more difficult of attainment. Early in this book, the distinction was made between intentional color and honest interpretation. It should be the responsibility of readers to see that newspapers provide the latter.

In preparing himself to derive the most benefit from his experiences, the newspaper political reporter should: (1) know something about political philosophy; (2) be a student of public opinion, its nature and manipulation; (3) understand practical political organization and election machinery; and (4) be sufficiently on the "inside" to distinguish the bunkum from the realities of political phenomena.

Political Philosophy

Plato, in describing a highly disciplined perfect state in which philosophers would be kings, Aristotle, in advocating a balanced democratic government, and political theorists ever since, expressed points of view which the enlightened political reporter will detect in substance in the arguments of contemporary seekers for public office. Heaven forbid that the college-trained reporter should be a pedantic idealist passing judgment upon twentieth-century practical men of affairs in terms of his favorite thinker of the past. Nevertheless, historical perspective is indispensable in enabling one to "make sense" of modern affairs. Being conversant with the history of political thought, especially with how it has been affected by practical considerations, at least provides the political reporter with the tools for making his work personally instructive.

In the writings of many contemporaries, the aspiring political reporter will find plentiful interpretative analyses of the modern scene. A superabundant amount of material concerning democracy, communism and fascism, of course, exists. The average person may not be able to tell the difference between these and other political theories, but no political writer can be so ignorant. He should at least know when a demagogue is incorrect in branding an opponent as socialistic or fascistic or the like.

Political writers are a potent force in educating the public regarding the pros and cons of such matters as the two-party versus multiple-party systems, permanent registration, proportionate representation, the direct primary and the like. Nobody, however, can write on such subjects without deep understanding of them.

Political Public Opinion

Before formulating an opinion about the nature of public opinion, one must understand what is meant by each word. What is a public? And what is an opinion? Unless one knows the results of scholarly attempts to answer these questions, his own conclusions are invalid. Consequently, a minimum of training in sociology and psychology, or in the dual science, social psychology, is essential to the political writer. From a good course or textbook he will learn that few modern thinkers in the field share the faith formerly held in instincts or a group mind as the explanation of why men behave similarly. Instead, inspired by the revelations of the behaviorists, psychoanalysts, anthropologists and other specialists, they are tending toward placing the emphasis upon habits and attitudes as the answer.

The politician as a psychological phenomenon has been treated by Harold D. Lasswell in *Psychopathology and Politics*, by A. B. Wolfe in *Conservatism, Radicalism, and the Scientific Method* and by many other writers. Walter Lippmann's *Public Opinion* and *The Phantom Public* resulted from his observations as a newspaperman. Lincoln Steffens' momentous *Autobiography* was inspired similarly. There is a sizable library on modern propaganda, including political propaganda, and abundant reading material on all other phases of the subject.

Failure of the professional pollsters to predict correctly the outcome of the 1948 presidential election gave impetus to research into the motivations of voting behavior. Paul Lazarsfeld and associates at Columbia University stress the effects of group interrelationships (*The People's Choice, Voting*). Louis Bean emphasizes longtime economic trends (*How to Predict Elections*). Samuel Lubell thinks the effect of nationality and cultural background has been underestimated (*The Future of American Politics, The Revolt of the Moderates*). Angus Campbell and associates demonstrate in *The American Voter* that voting preferences are consistent with a person's total personal and cultural conditioning.

Political Organization

LOCAL

Municipal political affairs in recent years generally have become dissociated from major party organizations. Candidates for mayor and other city offices run as independents but may be identified in state and national politics as members of established parties which tacitly lend them support. In smaller communities, the rival groups in a municipal campaign are more likely to cross established party lines and to be dissociated from all but strictly local issues.

Because of the nonpartisan character of municipal elections, it should be the newspaper's function properly to identify candidates by the interests of the persons or groups backing them. Local political groups may take names as the People's Party, but these have little or no meaning until party members have held office and given indication of what they represent. A local candidate's backing may be racial, religious, economic, geographic or in some other way classifiable. In preparing slates of candidates, political parties try to have as many of the important elements as possible represented. Furthermore, it is customary to run a Catholic against a Catholic, a Jew against a Jew, someone of Swedish extraction against another with similar ancestry and so on. In this way, awareness of nationality, racial and other backgrounds is kept alive as well as taken advantage of politically.

The author of the following article attempted to interpret the candidates and issues in their geographical setting:

By Jacques Nevard

Contrasts abound on Manhattan's Upper West Side, where mink-clad matrons live next door to out-at-the-elbows clients of the Welfare Department and one of the nation's greatest universities casts its shadow on tenements that shelter illiterates.

Possibly because such contrasts are familiar, Upper West Siders appear to be paying little attention to the campaign in the 20th Congressional District—a race in which the candidates' views on major issues show more clear-cut differences than most in the metropolitan area.

According to William F. Ryan, who has represented the district since 1960, the election next Tuesday is nothing less than "a test of liberalism versus conservatism."

Mr. Ryan, a Reform Democrat who has Liberal party support as he seeks his fourth term, is an outspoken political liberal.

Both of his challengers hold strongly conservative views. They are Norman C. Harlowe, a one-time Democrat who is the Republican candidate, and Mrs. Caroline S. Weller—who says that in her heart she is a "Taft Republican"—the Conservative party candidate.

Ryan Favored to Win

Despite Mr. Ryan's view that the election will test political philosophies, most observers believe the results will hinge more on political practicalities, and by any rule-of-thumb of practical politics, Mr. Ryan is an odds-on favorite for re-election.

The Democratic incumbent is an experienced and well-known campaigner. Neither of his opponents has ever before run for office, and in addition to a tendency to pull support from each other, neither appears to be widely known in the district which runs from 86th Street north through Marble Hill to the Bronx County line, west of the low-lying north-south ridge that forms the geologic backbone of Manhattan.

Historically heavily Democratic, the district returned Mr. Ryan to Congress in 1964 with 124,128 votes, while a Republican got 23,409 votes and a Conservative 2,994.

Largely a residential area, the Upper West Side has an estimated population of 475,000 persons. Approximately 45 per cent are Jewish, 15 per cent are of Irish extraction, 15 per cent are Negro and another 15 per cent are Spanish-speaking, mainly Puerto Rican. Of the remaining 10 per cent, the largest single ethnic group is of Greek origin.

White Backlash Factor

While an upset is considered unlikely, few observers are predicting that Mr. Ryan will repeat his 5-to-1 victory. This year that margin will be subject not only to the usual reduction that befalls members of the President's party in non-Presidential election years, but also to the white backlash against both Negro civil rights gains and Negro demands for still more gains.

In New York City, according to Mr. Ryan, white backlash has gone on the ballot in the form of the referendum on the Police Department's Civilian Complaint Review Board.

Mr. Ryan has strongly advocated retention of the review board, which he calls vital for reducing tensions in minority ghetto areas. Both Mr. Harlowe and Mrs. Weller want the board abolished, on the ground that it reduces public safety by inhibiting police freedom of action.

There is similar division on the question of Vietnam. Mr. Ryan opposes escalation of the war there and has urged the United States to work toward a diplomatic and political settlement. His opponents favor vigorous prosecution of the war until Hanoi is willing to discuss peace at a conference table.

Divided on Inflation

Still another contrast appears on the question of inflation. Mr. Harlowe and Mrs. Weller advocate the reduction of Government spending to fight inflation. Mr. Ryan says that inflationary pressure is not the result of Federal spending but of the booming economy, in which the residents of slum areas are not sharing equally.

Mr. Ryan, 44 years old, a lawyer and former assistant district attorney, was the Reform Democratic candidate for Mayor last year. Born in Albion, N.Y., near Rochester, he was graduated from Princeton and Columbia Law School. He is married and has four children.

Mr. Harlowe, 49, also is a lawyer. Before entering private practice he was an enforcement attorney with the Office of Price Control and the City Rent Commission, and an administrative attorney with the Department of Labor. Born in the Bronx, he was graduated from New York University, where he also earned his law degree. He is married and has a son.

Mrs. Weller, 57, is a food importer and broker. Graduated from Barnard College, she attended the College of Physicians and Surgeons for several years. A widow, with a grown daughter, she was born in Warwick, in Orange County. [New York *Times*]

PRECINCT AND WARD

To assist the party to power in elections involving established political parties, cities are organized by wards and their subdivisions, precincts. The lowest rung on the political organization ladder is that of precinct worker who carries the responsibility of ringing doorbells, talking to voters, handing out campaign literature, watching at the polls and assisting voters to and from polling places. Ambitious workers are conscious of their positions between elections and "talk up" the party or some of its prominent members on all occasions; intensive work, however, is only during the few weeks or months before an election.

Procedure for selecting precinct and ward captains differs, but ordinarily both are elected by registered members of the party in the sections. It may be, however, that only the ward or township captain or chairman is elected and given the responsibility of appointing precinct captains. A precinct, created by the election board, usually contains from 500 to 2,000 voters, and it is the precinct captain's job to carry his precinct in both primary and general elections.

Precinct workers are paid for their work during campaigns by the precinct captain, who gets the money from the ward leader, who gets it from the city or county committee, which raises part of it and gets more from the state or national committee. Original sources of the millions spent annually to assist candidates to get elected are the candidates themselves, public office holders and others who have obtained employment with the assistance of the party and interested outsiders who believe they have more to gain by a certain candidate's being elected than if his opponent were to win. Some large donors, bidding for the friendship of whoever occupies an important political office, may contribute to the campaign funds of both major parties.

The precinct captain generally is credited with "controlling" at least fifty voters among his friends and relatives, the families of those whom he helps obtain positions on election day as judges and clerks at the polls and others for whom he has done political favors. Unlike the ordinary worker, the precinct captain is active between elections, obtaining minor favors for voters in his precinct, such as assistance when they run foul of the law, financial help in case of illness or death, advice on how to obtain employment, and any other services which the strength and wealth of the organization permit. John Salter tells it well in *Boss Rule*.

Although the nonpolitically minded person doesn't realize it, if the power of a political party machine is to be broken it must be done in the primary. In the general election, the voter merely has a choice between two or more machine-picked slates. Under any circumstances, bucking the efficiently organized party is virtually impossible; so-called reform slates result from fusions of political cliques or parties out of office at the time and with no hope of victory without each other's cooperation. The history of such fusion movements is one of temporary successes only. The primary laws in many states, furthermore, make starting a third party virtually impossible.

Most candidates for public office at the local level who receive regular party endorsement, earned the reward by hard work in the precincts. Not always, however, is this the case. Sometimes, a ward committeeman becomes jealous of the growing popularity of one of his subordinates and maneuvers to get him into a public office where he will be less of a personal power threat. Usually, this means a judgeship or some appointive job whose incumbent is required by the Hatch act or other laws, or by tradition, to minimize his politicking.

COUNTY

County chairmen usually are elected by ward and township leaders, some or all of whom constitute the county executive committee. No political leader whose concern is a unit smaller than the county merits the unofficial title of "boss." All bosses, furthermore, are not office holders or even party officials; they may be influential dictators who prefer to operate in the background. By whatever type of person occupied, the political boss' office is the clearing house for finances and information. Reporters may obtain tips from underlings but seldom get anything official except directly from headquarters.

"Getting next to" a political boss is not impossible, as Lincoln Steffens discovered. How to do it, however, is an individual matter dependent upon the reporter's particular personality. Just as the boss must be cautious about making promises but scrupulous about keeping them once made, so must the political reporter become resigned to learning more "off the record" than on and to not learning anything about a great deal of important party business. Frank Kent has aptly defended newspapers for not giving more "inside political dope" by explaining that newspapers are unable to obtain such information. Furthermore, to get what he does, the reporter cannot incur the displeasure of his source. Instead, he often must report seriously what he knows to be the insincere remarks of some demagogue, overlook his personal foibles, correct his bad grammar and in general "cover up" for him. The alternative is openly to defy and fight the party machine; a newspaper finds it difficult to take that attitude against all political groups without discrimination.

STATE, NATIONAL

State and national committees nominally exist continuously but are quiescent most of the time, arousing from their lethargy about a year before an election. Most active are potential candidates who are "pulling strings" to obtain machine backing when nominating time comes around. With feigned modesty, the aspirant gets some friend or group of backers to "front" for him so that the suggestion that he run for office may seem to emanate from someone other than himself. To reporters, he is evasive and unambitious and is so quoted by a press which, of course, knows better. Until an official announcement is made, however, it is dangerous to go too far in surmising anyone's intentions.

Pre-campaign Activities

PETITIONS

To have his name placed on the printed ballot as a candidate for office, a person must obtain the signatures of a certain proportion of the voters on nominating petitions which must be filed before a certain date with the proper public official—city clerk, county clerk, secretary of state and so on. Because top positions usually are given to candidates filing their papers first, candidates stand in line waiting for the hour at which it is legal to file them.

It is news both when petitions are taken out and when they are filed. The candidate's name, address, occupation, political experience and general background are included in the first story about his intentions. Sometimes he already has prepared a statement or platform regarding his candidacy although generally that comes later. In city elections, the first petition stories should contain information as to the deadlines for filing, the number of signatures needed and possibly something about the position at stake. The names of prominent signers of a petition are newsworthy.

> The next clerk of the Milltown Municipal court will be either the incumbent, Andrew L. Ziegler, or Constable Eustace L. Cohen for whom nominating petitions, containing the required number of signatures, were filed yesterday, the deadline, in the office of City Clerk Jerome Z. Day.
>
> Mr. Ziegler, who has been court clerk since establishment of the municipal court three years ago, filed petitions containing 1,416 names, 11 fewer than the maximum permitted. Cohen's petitions contained 1,043 names. Minimum number of names required was 892, or 5 per cent of the vote cast at the last general election.
>
> Graham R. Olson, 146 Arnold avenue, insurance man who took out petition forms last week, failed to file. His name appeared on one of Cohen's petitions. Feature of Ziegler's petitions was one sheet containing only the names of Milltown's 16 aldermen.
>
> Until late yesterday, it was believed petitions would be filed for a candidate backed by the Milltown Democratic organization which took out blanks several days ago.
>
> The election for Municipal court clerk will take place Nov. 3 at the same time as the state and national elections. There will be a separate ballot, however, for the office.

REGISTRATION

Eligibility to vote differs by states but some sort of registration usually is required. On certain specified days, all otherwise eligible voters (those who have resided in the state, county and precinct a sufficient length of time, have paid certain taxes, given evidence of literacy, and so forth, as the case may be) appear at their polling places to have their names recorded. Such registration may be quadrennial, annual or permanent; for municipal elections no registration at all may be necessary. Voting by affidavit also may be permitted in case a voter is unable to register on the designated days. If there is permanent registration, the voter merely notifies election officials of a change of address.

The total number of voters registering is news. Knowing that only about 60 per cent of the nation's eligible voters take the trouble to register, crusading editors often investigate abnormally large registrations. Pulitzer prizes have been won by newspapers which checked registration lists to discover "ghost" votes from empty lots abandoned buildings and transient hotels.

> Despite the all-day rain, Saturday's registration of voters for the Nov. 3 election was slightly higher than normal for a first registration day when 21,678 Milltown voters registered, according to City Clerk J. M. Blackburn.
>
> John A. Burgess, Republican township committeeman for Milltown, declared that this total should be 340 greater, to include additional registrants from the Seventh ward; the clerk's office, however, reports that its figure is accurate.
>
> The 21,678 total represents about 70 per cent of the total vote cast in Milltown in 1966. A registration of 65 per cent of voters normally is expected on the first registration day. Final registration day this year will be Tuesday, Oct. 6, when the polling places again will be open from 6 A.M. to 9 P.M. Registration is essential in order to be eligible to vote in November; no affidavits will be accepted.
>
> According to the city clerk's office, Milltown's registration by wards was as follows . . .

> Ghosts also walk in the Eighth ward, at least on municipal election day.
>
> To be specific, Tuesday, April 2, at least three nice spooks materialized in the southernmost ward of Milltown and helped the voters there select their aldermen and other city officials.
>
> One of them called himself Hugh Hillis and gave 130 Elmwood avenue as the apartment building he haunts.
>
> The second and third identified themselves as Thomas Long and Nicholas Reding and claimed to be neighbors in the closets of 333 Howard street, also an apartment building.

Thus it is seen that the ethereal denizens of the Eighth ward differ from those of the Fifth ward, where you will recall from my article of last Friday, the dusky unrealities preferred empty lots as their mundane habitats for the day.

This is not surprising, of course, when it is realized that the Eighth ward is predominately an apartment house section, whereas the Fifth ward is punctuated with wide open spaces.

Here is the dope on Spooks Hillis, Long, and Reding . . .

PRIMARIES

With the notable exception of the national tickets every four years, most candidates for important office are chosen by party primaries instead of by conventions as formerly. Any citizen may enter a primary election as a candidate for the nomination of any party. A voter, however, can participate in the primary of one party only. The names of only those candidates who have filed nominating petitions appear on the printed ballot, but the voter can add the name of anyone else. It is seldom, however, that a "write-in" candidate is elected.

In some states run-off primaries are held of the two or three candidates receiving the most votes. In a majority of states which have primary laws, a plurality at a single primary is sufficient to nominate.

If there is little contest in his own party, in most states a voter may vote in the primary for another although he intends to vote for his own party candidate in the general election. If too many voters desert it in a general election, however, the party may not receive a large enough proportion of the total vote to receive a place on the ballot at the next election.

CONVENTIONS

Adoption of a direct primary law does not mean the end of state party conventions, but such conventions (or conferences) are held outside the law and for the purpose only of recommending and endorsing candidates to receive the party's nomination at a primary election. Often rival factions within a party hold separate conventions and endorse different slates.

The news writer can estimate the strength of candidates at a state or national convention by comparing the instructions given to delegates. Delegations sometimes support "favorite sons" from their localities and may deadlock a convention by refusing, after the early ballots, to change their votes to one of the leading candidates. Some delegations from states with open primaries are uninstructed.

Knowledgeable political editors suspect deals whenever stubborn delegations suddenly change their positions. Possibly appointment to a cabinet position or judgeship or some other office has been promised someone; or support has been pledged in some future campaign. Maybe the compromise involves stands on issues to be involved in anticipated legislation.

A party convention is called to order by a temporary chairman who gives a prepared keynote speech. Then a permanent chairman is elected and he also gives a speech. Usually the committee's recommendation for permanent chairman is taken, but sometimes rival factions may nominate different candidates. The vote for permanent chairman then may be an indication of how delegates will vote later on other important matters.

The group in control of a state or national committee has the advantage of obtaining a personnel to its liking. Through its committee on credentials it determines which delegates are eligible for seats, if rival delegations from the same locality claim recognition.

Vote on the platform submitted by the committee on resolutions is conducted by a roll call of delegations. After the platform is adopted, with or without amendments, the next procedure is the election of candidates. Often, several ballots are necessary for a choice. When a deadlock continues after several ballots, a "dark horse," someone not among the leaders, may be elected as a compromise candidate.

A party convention frequently is interrupted by the demonstrations of different delegations. When the time to nominate candidates arrives, the roll call begins. Each delegation either nominates someone or passes its turn or permits some other delegation, whose turn normally would come later, to use its opportunity. In addition to the principal nominating speech there may be several other speeches to second a nomination. Each speech is the signal for an outburst of enthusiasm by supporters of the candidate.

A party *conference* is for the purpose of discussing an important matter. A party *caucus* differs from a conference because all who attend it, by their attendance, pledge themselves to support the opinion of the majority. Insurgent members may stay away from party caucuses, because they do not wish to commit themselves to the support of what the majority will favor.

Campaigns

SPEECHES

A campaign really gets underway with the first speech of the candidate. In the case of a presidential candidate this is the speech of acceptance of the nomination formerly made at a formal notification ceremony, but in recent years more often at the nominating convention. Although presidential candidates usually have fresh speeches for every important occasion thereafter, in the case of candidates for less important offices the opening or keynote speech may be the pattern for all others delivered during the campaign. The political reporter traveling with the candidate may be hard put to it to obtain a fresh angle in reporting the day's forensics, but the local news writers who hear the candidate only once are not so handicapped.

When candidates start calling each other names, hurling challenges, answering each other's arguments, and raising new issues, the political reporter's problem is easy. Otherwise, he may be forced to rely upon the press releases of political headquarters. If he travels with a candidate he tells of the crowds, the opinions of local leaders, the reception given the candidate and the like.

In reporting and writing up a political speech the reporter should observe the orthodox rules for such occasions as described in Chapter 12.

STRATEGY

Newspapermen have this in common with politicians: there are no two groups which come in for more indiscriminate damning than those to which they belong. Just as there are highly ethical editors and publishers, there also are politicians, in and out of office, who desire wholeheartedly to serve the public good. The "system," however, invariably demands that before he can be a statesman a man must be a politician and get himself elected to office. The process of becoming elected and of assuring oneself of re-election involves compromise, evasion, equivocation and other "expediencies" which are distasteful to the reputable public servant and shocking to the callow political reporter.

The plight of the high-minded man in politics, of the newspaperman and of the public may be inferred from the following summing up by Frank Kent in *The Great Game of Politics*:

No candidate and no campaign are exactly what they seem. The part that is open and above board is always less vital than the part that is secret. The voters see the performance but not the rehearsal. They completely lack information of the real movements by which the candidate becomes a candidate. They are in the dark as to how the issues are evolved and why, when and by whom. They see and know nothing until the curtain goes up and there before them is the smiling candidate, playing his part in complete makeup and wearing a full set of false whiskers. . . .

It is not a reflection upon many honest and sincere men who hold elective offices or who seek such offices. It is merely a statement of facts, and the point is that, under our system, complete frankness with the voters is not possible, because there is no way of obtaining complete frankness from both sides in a political fight. A downright, outspoken candidate, who honestly, openly and fearlessly expresses exactly what he believes to every group of voters on every issue, declining to dodge or evade, and refusing to appeal to prejudice or cater to class, would be overwhelmingly beaten by the candidate on the other side who would promptly take advantage of such honesty to gather for himself the large number of voters alienated by the other fellow.

To give voters the "feel" of a campaign a reporter interviews rival candidates and accompanies them as they "make the rounds."

By Dan Morgan
Washington Post Staff Writer

The foghorn voice of Robert Campbell, a mustached auctioneer and politician from Annapolis, blared over the din of dining Democrats:

"Issues? Why confuse the voters with a lot of election garbage? Why should George Mahoney argue when he's holding four aces?"

The speech-making had just ended. A few feet away George P. Mahoney, smiling and back-slapping, was edging his way through a crowd of admirers who had turned out for the rally Thursday night at Dairyland Restaurant near Ft. Meade.

His just completed, off-the-cuff speech had been a rousing success— a flamboyant, tumultuous, emotional speech in the favorite style of the Democratic candidate for the governor of Maryland.

He had told his listeners that their homes were their castles. He had promised to "protect" Anne Arundel County if elected. And he had jested over his argument with a newspaper reporter the night before:

"I told him, 'If you don't let me go I'll punch you in the nose.' Now what was wrong with that? Do I have to give up being red-blooded?"

His listeners raised the roof applauding from their places behind long rows of tables loaded with pitchers of beer.

Earlier in the day, Mahoney headquarters had run off hundreds of mimeographed copies of the candidate's stand on the "issue of the day" —the need for tax reform. But at the Dairyland rally, he never mentioned his tax program. And his audience of Anne Arundel Democrats heard nothing of his stand on his issue of the day before (education), nor of the day before that (crime).

Nobody among the Mahoney supporters seemed disappointed.

"I just don't think it was a program-type meeting," said one man dressed in plaid hunting shirt and dark suit.

It had been a day that put in sharp focus the differing campaign styles of the volatile Democratic candidate and his Republican opponent, Spiro T. Agnew, who has shunned emotional appeals and slogans.

In public appearances—large or small—Agnew consistently bids for votes in terms of detailed programs for State problems. Transportation, education, air pollution are topics that he raises before the voters.

Strictly Business

At coffee sessions and mass rallies alike, voters are asked by Agnew to support him for what he wants to do, not for a knack to excite the glands.

Agnew's approach is crisp and businesslike. It is one, however, that prompted one observer to say that Agnew resembles a teacher more than a politician at times.

It is not that Agnew lacks personal appeal or wit. But he insists—despite warnings from some staff members—on sticking like glue to discussion of issues, concrete proposals and specifics.

That style can have its drawbacks. Only 150 persons turned up at a well ballyhooed rally in Dundalk the other night. Even Agnew conceded it "was a floperoo."

But he has no plans to shift tactics. Right or wrong, he says, he will follow his conviction that voters "should be given the opportunity to decide on issues, not personalities or gimmicks."

His opponent, however, has been fighting a different war. All week he waged a personal campaign stressing people, people, people.

"I'm the most humble man in the world," he devoutly told a group of giggling girls who wished him well at Dairyland.

Other Side of Coin

In contrast to his personal triumph there, he had been stiff and ill at ease earlier in the evening as he read a position paper to the United Women's Club of Maryland.

Cocktails, not beer, were served. The women wore tailored suits and corsages, not department store dresses.

Mahoney stumbled over parts of the text, which contained his only reference all day to his tax stand.

At the end of it, he declared, "And Gov. (J. Millard) Tawes is going to help me with the speech—I mean what's in it."

The applause was polite, not tumultuous. But down at Dairyland half an hour later, he didn't use a prepared speech. And when he said, "All I want to do is be your public servant number one," they stood up and cheered.

Afterwards, as the shouts died down, Holly Stratton, a 50-year-old variety store owner from Glen Burnie shook hands with the candidate. He was wearing a "Mahoney for Governor" tie left over from Mahoney's unsuccessful bid for the job in 1950.

He was going to vote for George Mahoney in 1966, too, programs or no programs.

"There's no point talking about issues. I'm satisfied he will be out with his program in time," said Stratton, heading back to the buffet where cold macaroni salad and ham were being served. [Washington *Post*]

ROORBACKS

The word "roorback" entered the dictionary as a common noun following the presidential election of 1844 during which a last-minute attempt was made to defeat James K. Polk by newspaper publicity for a fictitious book by a nonexistent author named Roorback supposedly telling of Polk's having bought and branded a number of Negro slaves.

There is a difference between raising false issues and plain lying. The former is for the purpose of misdirecting attention from important to insignificant matters; the latter is sheer falsehood. Roorbacks generally appear as late as possible to be effective and yet permit the opposition insufficient time for an answer. The political reporter always should be wary of a new important issue raised late in a campaign unless it is one which couldn't have been brought up earlier.

May it be said to the credit of newspapermen that they generally have the intelligence to "see through" political humbug, but they are stymied as to what they say, for the reasons which have been enumerated in this chapter. The political reporter who is "taken in" by political bunk is inadequate for his job, which is one for seasoned and not callow men.

ISSUES

The interpretative reporter talks not only to candidates and political leaders, but also to representatives of civic, business, labor and other groups and with ordinary citizens in the attempt to determine the issues upon which the outcome of an election depends.

Nobody has developed this technique better than Samuel Lubell whose periodic series of articles on the political thinking of "the man in the street" are supplemented by his uncannily correct forecasts of election results. Lubell's methods confound the professional pollsters and academic political analysts who go to elaborate extremes to be certain those whom they interview represent a correct cross-sectional sample of the electorate as a whole.

Lubell studies election results. When he notes similar significant changes in voting behavior, even in precincts thousands of miles apart, he follows his nose for news to the areas to determine the cause. He has "pet" precincts and blocks and even residences in all parts of the country based on past experience of their value as political weathervanes, enabling him to make generalizations. Lubell's main interest is in discovering the reasons for voting behavior rather than merely straw voting. Too much political writing to explain the issues of a campaign derives from the writers' ideas or desires as to what they should be. Neither these pundits nor the politicians determine the issues. Rather, the voters do so, and they favor those candidates who they think hold views closest to their own.

Another and more conventional method of determining the issues of a campaign is by historical perspective. The following is typical of the way *The Christian Science Monitor* often handles such stories:

BY ROBERT BLANCHARD
Special to the Christian Science Monitor

Helena, Mont.—Montanans, having witnessed one of the most vigorous state primary elections in recent times, are beginning to sense an equally active general election campaign is under way.

It has been said often here that in Montana "men are men, Democrats are Democrats, and Republicans are Republicans"—after the primary elections. If this ever was true, it was this year.

While the primary election was a "battle of the giants," or individuals—with "conservatives" and "liberals" within each party splintering the loyalties—the campaign which ends Nov. 8 is almost strictly the battle of the issues.

The intraparty splints have been mended, for the time being, and the historical divergent poles in Montana politics are tugging as never before for those magic "independent" votes around the political equator.

Deep Roots

Montana's extreme political polarization came to light as early as 1878 when the Butte Miners Union was formed to fight a threatened wage reduction for copper miners. It spread to the rural areas when Montana was singed by the post-World War I political prairie fire of discontent—the ultraliberal Nonpartisan League.

A farmers' organization founded in North Dakota, the league sponsored state ownership and operation of grain elevators, flour mills, packing plants, and utilities. It appealed to many eastern Montana wheat growers, suffering from low prices. Former Senator Burton K. Wheeler, a candidate for Vice-President on the Progressive Party ticket in 1924, was an early league representative in Washington.

The wedge between the two dominant political groups deepens more each year as automation increases in mines and on farms; as domestic copper production decreases; as the eastern half of the state grumbles over market conditions and as "family farms" disappear; as neighboring states bypass Montana in highway construction; as property taxes continue to rise, even though vital school bond issues are defeated and as teachers leave the state because its salaries stand 30th in the nation and next to last in the region; as the state's unemployment fund reaches rock bottom and small businesses pay more and more to keep it alive; and as the state's general fund pays day-to-day bills with paltry sums borrowed from other state funds with no letup in sight.

The major issues in this campaign include each side's solutions and blame for the problems. . . .

There followed a series of paragraphs comparing the Democratic and Republican attitudes toward such issues as taxation, highway finance, right-to-work laws, education, finance, unemployment compensation funds and the like. The last section of the article compared the rival candidates.

Elections

PREDICTIONS

As election day approaches, reporters who have followed the campaign more objectively than candidates or party leaders, usually are better able to predict its outcome than they. It is customary for large newspapers which assign reporters to travel with candidates, to "switch assignments" at least once as the campaign progresses; that means, one writer will travel with Candidate A for a few weeks or months and then shift places with the reporter who has been covering Candidate B. Straw votes among political writers have shown them much better able to predict election outcomes than publishers, editors or editorial writers.

In 1956, the New York *Times* spent a huge sum of money to send more than thirty of its best reporters all over the country to see if they could correctly predict the outcome of the presidential election, state by state. The experiment was a success but some critics asked whether the main function of the press in such a campaign is prediction. Rather, some contended, it should be to clarify issues and put candidates "on the spot" regarding them. The *Times* never repeated the experiment and no other paper has emulated it.

A phenomenon of elections in the '60s has been the accuracy with which national television networks have been able to project early returns to predict probable winners, but such does not occur until after the polls have closed.

ELECTION DAY

The size of the vote, violence at polling places, amusing anecdotes, the circumstances under which the candidates cast their ballots, last-minute statements and predictions and methods used to get out the vote or persuade voters on their way to the polls, furnish news on election day before the ballots are counted.

Ordinary newsroom routine is upset on election day as there are extras to get out and extra help to obtain to assist in collecting returns. A newspaper may use its news carriers or other employees to wait at polling places until the votes are counted or may receive its returns through campaign headquarters. Often, the police gather returns and release them to reporters.

In national elections the three television networks and the two press associations pool their efforts to gather the returns rapidly. As the results come in by isolated districts they are tabulated, and the political writer prepares a trend story for the first edition. Some outcomes can be predicted comparatively early; often, in a close race, the result is in doubt until the last vote is counted. When the result is apparent, campaign committees and candidates issue statements claiming victory or conceding defeat. Losers send messages of congratulations to winners, and everybody poses for pictures.

If an outcome is close, a loser may demand a recount. Some elections are protested by defeated candidates who charge fraud, stuffing or tampering with ballot boxes and other irregularities. All candidates are required to file statements of campaign expenditures. Investigations of alleged violations of the corrupt practices act during an election are not infrequent.

The mid-election day story should include the number voting and a comparison with previous elections.

> Candidates were being nominated in today's statewide primary elections for United States Senator and Representatives in Congress, and for some state and local offices in St. Louis and St. Louis county. In the city and county, balloting was generally light, indicating one of the smallest off-year primary votes in years.
>
> By 4 P.M., it was estimated 61,889 ballots had been cast in the city, following 10 hours of balloting in the 784 precincts. This was 18 per cent of the total registration of 343,830.
>
> In the county, an estimated 9,936 ballots were cast by 4 P.M., nine hours after the 7 A.M. opening of the polls. The estimated vote was 7.9 per cent of the 125,782 registration.

St. Louis polling places will close at 7 p.m. Those in the county will close at 8:07 P.M. with the exception of those in University City, where the closing time is 8 P.M. The hours given are daylight saving time.

Special Watch on Two Wards

Special deputy election commissioners are on duty in all precincts of the Fifth and Sixth Wards, in which a recent recanvass of the registration indicated efforts to pad the lists. Chairman Frank L. Rammacciotti of the Election Board, said the deputies were stationed in the two downtown wards to guard against any election irregularities.

Ballots and registration lists for the two wards were not delivered to the polling places until early today. Rammacciotti said this was done because many of the election officials resided outside of the wards and they did not have adequate means to care for them. These were the only two wards where this was done, the ballots and voters' lists having been delivered to election officials in all other wards last night.

The special deputies in the Fifth and Sixth Wards were instructed specifically to guard against ballots being marked openly instead of in the regular voting booth, and to see that all ballots were counted by Republican and Democratic poll officials working together instead of dividing ballots for a separate tabulation by each party's officials.

Two Ballots in City

City voters received two ballots at the polls, a party primary ballot and one for the two amendments to the City Charter and the proposed $4,000,000 bond issue for rubbish collection facilities, each calling for a Yes or No vote.

Proposed amendment No. 1 would permit . . .

[St. Louis *Post-Dispatch*]

ELECTION RESULTS

When all or nearly all returns are in, so that the outcome is known, the news feature naturally is who won. The story also should emphasize: (1) by how much—in total votes and proportions; (2) areas in which different candidates were strongest and weakest; (3) upsets—incumbents with long services who were defeated, candidates on a party slate who lost whereas most of the others won; (4) whether results coincide with predictions; and (5) statements by winners, losers and party leaders, and similar matters.

"Post-Mortems"

A great deal of post-election interpretative writing is of the "I told you so" or "We should have known it" type. By analyzing the vote in different sections where the electorate is predominantly of one type—

workers, members of a particular racial, national or religious group—it is possible to imagine which campaign issues or attitudes antedating the campaign were most effective. The skilled political writer analyzes results in the search for trends. Often, he has to compare local with state and national results to interpret correctly.

When a new office holder or party takes over a city hall, county building, state or national capitol, the citizenry expects that "there will be some changes made." Party platforms and campaign speeches provide clues as to what they will be, but voters have become suspicious of politicians' promises. Personality sketches and reviews of the past records of successful candidates are valuable.

The author of the following piece made no attempt to disguise his biases. In fact he made quite clear the criteria by which he examined the political scene.

By Bob McCarthy

The whiskered Democratic Party machine in the State of Virginia was shaken all the way to the bottom of its ancient foundation last week with two election upsets and a near upset in the State primary.

This is the organization shaped and directed by Senator Harry Byrd. Conservative in philosophy and dedicated to resisting the new, the Byrd Democratic organization is and has been completely alien to the national image of the Democratic Party and its liberal leadership.

That was good enough to win any election in Virginia up until now, but the party ancients have been successfully challenged by two younger political leaders. They don't hold with the moss-covered views of their elders, and history will record that in 1966 they started the process that will at last dismember the Byrd organization.

This, of course, has implications far beyond the confines of the Virginia Democratic Party. This split in the Democratic ranks will strengthen the Virginia Republican organization, which up until recently was a light weight political outfit that only won elections when the State was voting for president.

This will no longer be true. The Republicans will be formidable foes for the Virginia Democrats beginning this Fall, for their conservative candidates will be a lot more welcome to old line Virginia Democrats than the young Democratic firebrands who so unceremoniously kicked two Virginia perennials in Congress right into political oblivion.

The newcomers are 45-year-old State Senator William B. Spong Jr., who edged incumbent U.S. Senator A. Willis Robertson, age 79, out of office, and State Representative George C. Rawlings, 44, who knocked over 83-year-old Congressman Howard W. Smith. Smith is chairman of the House Rules Committee and he has used his position whenever he could to circumvent every civil rights proposal, all social reform legislation and every Democratic president in the 36 years he has been in Congress.

In the long run, Virginia is going to miss these two political relics like it will miss the plague, and the Democratic Party leadership in Washington will miss them even less. Only Senator Byrd's son, who succeeded him when he stepped down a few months ago because of poor health, survived the youth movement in Virginia politics last week.

The fact that he was willing to admit that the Twentieth Century has arrived, something his father never seemed to acknowledge, may have saved young Byrd from the embarrassment suffered by Robertson and Smith.

It is significant that the "upstarts" who knocked over Robertson and Smith appealed openly for Negro and urban support and ran as political moderates. Spong ripped into Robertson during the campaign as a reactionary who fought progress in the name Southern tradition. Rawlings showed about the same respect for Smith's record in his campaign.

Nomination on the Virginia Democratic ticket, however, is no longer assurance of election. This division in the Democratic ranks will mean the Republicans can make a fight out of it in the Fall. In fact, don't be shocked if the Republicans win both seats.

What is happening in Virginia and the rest of the South is due for the most part to the new Negro registrations and the shift of the population from rural areas to the cities. The Negroes have been registering in the Democratic Party and the swelling of urban area populations has brought Virginia city dwellers face to face with the need for Federal funds and social legislation.

That is why the obstructionist tactics of Robertson and Smith no longer appealed to the majority of Virginia Democrats. To be sure, the majority edge of the winners is a slim one. Spong won by 764 votes and Rawlings by 364, but it's a majority nevertheless.

It is this very narrow lead that these newcomers won by, however, that creates so much doubt about the outcome of the Fall elections. The Republican candidates are sure to woo the disenchanted Democrats who voted for the old line traditionalists in a losing cause. You can just bet that they'll offer the Virginia voters that same kind of conservatism that Robertson and Smith gave them, and that sort of campaigning won't fall on deaf ears in Virginia.

In the years to come this will be repeated over and over again in Virginia and many other Southern states. The Southern Democrats are dividing into liberal and conservative camps and a two-party South is just around the corner. But instead of shedding tears over it, American should welcome it, for Dixie has needed a two party system for a long, long time.

[Penn Hills (Pa.) *Progress*]

17

Government

I City Government
1. Mayor
2. City Council
3. City Clerk
4. Corporation Counsel
5. Public Works
6. Finances
7. Other Offices and Boards
8. Urban Renewal

II Schools and Education
1. Integration
2. Religion
3. Delinquency
4. Exceptional Children
5. Automation
6. Academic Freedom

III County Government
1. County Board
2. County Clerk

IV State Government

V Federal Government

VI The Weather
1. Elements of Interest
2. Writing the Story
3. Interpretations
4. Definitions

As population increases and all phases of life become more complex, "closing the gap" between governed and governors becomes a major problem in a democracy. The media of communication have a great opportunity and responsibility to stimulate interest and participation on the part of the citizenry in governmental affairs.

Journalism's first obligation is to report fully the activities of public agencies and officials. Since all public issues ultimately are decided by public opinion, the duty includes presentation of the pros and cons of all important matters and expert analysis of them. In other words, interpretative reporting and writing are essential in the field of governmental affairs.

To prepare himself for the role of expert in this field, the aspiring interpretative reporter must be thoroughly grounded in political history

TYPICAL MAYOR-COUNCIL CITY GOVERNMENT

and theory. He must understand the nature and purpose of all governmental agencies and the political connections and motivations of public officials and their backers. No matter how public spirited or socially conscious they may be, office holders are candidates for re-election or reappointment; they do not cease to be politicians and become statesmen suddenly the day they take office.

The interpretative reporter who specializes in governmental news makes use of all of the devices of the interpretative reporter anywhere. To place an immediate occurrence in proper perspective, he may give its historical background. Even before legislators or administrators take action, he may describe the existence of a problem. When a proposal is pending, he explains its nature, the argument pro and con and the political alignment as regards it. He describes the functions of various offices and officers and reviews the records of the representatives of the people.

City Government

Closest to the average newspaper and its readers is city government. On the previous page is shown the outline of the government in a typical middle-sized American city having the mayor-council plan of government. If the city had the commission plan, instead of the aldermen there would be two, four or six commissioners, usually elected at large, and fewer appointive officers, the duties usually performed by them being assigned to the full-time commissioners. If the city had the city manager plan, the important officer would be not the mayor but the city manager who would perform the duties, in a small city, of many appointive officers under the mayor-council plan. Under the city manager plan, the office of the mayor, if it were retained at all, would be little more than that of presiding officer at council meetings. A city manager runs a city as a general superintendent operates a business or as a superintendent of schools directs a school system. He is chosen for his expert knowledge of municipal business affairs and is not necessarily a resident of the city at the time of his appointment.

MAYOR

Under the mayor-council plan, which still exists in a majority of American cities, the mayor is chosen as is a governor of a state or a president of the United States, by popular election every two or four years. A significant change has taken place in recent years, however, in that city politics has been divorced from state and national. Except in the larger cities, candidates for mayor generally do not run as Republicans, Democrats or Socialists but as independents, their backing crossing party lines.

As the executive head of the city, the mayor is the chief news source in the city hall. He should be aware of every important occurrence in all city departments, most of them headed by persons whom he has appointed with the approval of the city council. For details, the reporter should see the department heads themselves, or subordinates in closer touch with the news at hand.

Because the mayor is called upon to take part in most important nongovernmental activities in the city, he is a potent source of miscellaneous tips. He is visited by delegations of all sorts and receives letters of complaint and inquiry; he buys the first Red Cross button, proclaims special days and weeks, welcomes convention delegates, attends meetings and gives speeches.

If he is a strong mayor, he has a program for the city which he reveals in his reports, messages and remarks to the city council. Usually he is close to certain aldermen who introduce motions, resolutions and ordinances embodying his ideas. Unable to speak on legislative matters without leaving the presiding officer's chair, the mayor who is a leader has spokesmen in the council who present his point of view for him.

An alderman Wednesday proposed that Chicago, Evanston, Skokie and Lincolnwood join in development of a new recreation area.

The land involved is along both sides of the Sanitary District channel between Touhy and Howard.

* * *

Ald. Jack I. Sperling (50th) showed a tentative plan for building a fieldhouse, ball diamonds, playgrounds and tennis courts on the now vacant land.

In a resolution prepared for introduction to the council, Sperling asked Mayor Daley to call a meeting of officials involved.

These would include officials of the Sanitary District, present owner of the land, the city and the suburbs.

Sperling said his plan has the backing of Mayor Daley.

* * *

Recently the Sanitary District rejected a proposal that the land be leased at 7 cents a square foot for industrial purposes.

Sperling described the area as "ideally located" and "desperately needed" for recreational purposes.

The city boundary touches on the area. Details for acquisition of the land have not yet been explored fully, Sperling said.

[Chicago *Daily News*]

City Council

Councilmen or aldermen usually are elected by wards, geographical units into which the city is divided. They devote only part time to their official duties, possibly doing little more than attend weekly or semimonthly meetings. Committee meetings are held council night before the general session and may be closed to reporters. Chairmen of important committees, such as finance, streets and relief, are compelled to give some attention to their aldermanic duties throughout the week, at times at least, and may be interviewed in case of important news. A typical order of business for a city council meeting follows:

Roll call by the city clerk
Minutes of the last meeting
Communications read by the city clerk
Standing committees (reports called for in alphabetical order)
Special committee reports
Call of wards (each alderman brings up any matter pertaining to his ward which needs council or executive attention)
Miscellaneous business, including mayoral reports
Adjournment

The rules for covering a city council meeting do not differ from those which apply to any other type of meeting. Because of the importance of council meetings, however, it frequently is necessary to write two or more stories adequately to play up different matters affecting the public. It is seldom that a reporter can write his story entirely from the notes he is able to take as motions are made and argued and matters are referred to different committees. Usually he must verify names, the wording of motions and resolutions, the outcome of votes and other matters by consulting the city clerk or his stenographer at the end of a meeting.

In an advance story of a council meeting, the nature of business likely to come up should be emphasized. The experienced reporter usually can anticipate the nature of debate and the lineup of votes. He also should attempt to interpret the significance and possible aftermath of any controversial matter.

> The plan to build a $20,000,000 city airport at Pratt and Sumner will be disposed of by formal vote of the common council tonight.
> If the lineup of councilmen remains unchanged, the so-called southeast site will go down to defeat by a vote of 5 to 4.

Councilmen Howard, Lane, Otis and Cade favor the northwest airport. Councilmen Moore, Kole, Blede, Masse and Walz are opposed.

Mayor Wants Action

Mayor McCartney, who also favors the southeast site, has promised that he will try to get a final decision before Jan. 31—the date on which the offer of a gift of 650 acres at the site expires.

Regardless of the outcome, few observers had any hope that tonight's action would be final.

Arthur Schuman, secretary of the Metropolitan Civic Airport Trust, today was on the verge of conceding defeat. He said the would-be donors of the $750,000 for land at the southeast site would have their money returned to them at once.

"Nothing short of a miracle can save it now," Schuman declared.

"They have kicked this around for ten years and now the airlines have moved to St. Martin. I'm all through.

"If the city wants a modern airport now, let the city department heads get one. It's their job from here on. Apparently they don't want the aid of the industrial groups."

Will Seek Ballot

Councilman Otis will attempt to keep the southeast site alive even though voted down tonight. He said he would seek a ballot proposition on the question at the next election, probably in June.

If the northwest site is turned down tonight, St. Martin County Airport will remain as the city's "major interim airport," according to a council resolution already adopted.

Making reliable contacts and keeping friendships while reporting fearlessly is the main problem of the city hall reporter. Clerks and others like to give tips to favorite newsmen but often do so in confidence which must be respected. It frequently requires great reportorial ingenuity to wheedle information out of others while concealing the source of one's knowledge. Often it is best for the city editor to assign a special reporter to a particular story so that the regular man on the beat will not alienate his sources.

Strong papers and state and national press associations have waged vigorous fights in the post-World War II years to end or prevent secret meetings of city councils, village boards and similar groups from which reporters as well as the public are excluded. Some state legislatures have been persuaded to pass laws requiring open sessions. Then the problem becomes one of discovering and exposing the subterfuges which may be used, as informal and unofficial get-togethers, possibly at lunch or in a private home. The newspaper which fights secrecy is acting on the democratic principle that the public's business should not be transacted in private. If it persists it usually wins its campaign because of the public support it generates.

The writer of the following article concentrated on the highlights of the matter under consideration in order to simplify them for readers:

> Skokie's village fathers Monday night adopted the largest money bill in the village's 83 year history—a giant $9,959,101.
>
> That's the maximum the trustees can spend between now and next Apr. 30.
>
> It is almost $1.2 million more than was authorized a year ago, and includes these highlights:
>
> —Total salaries to more than 400 employees of $3,299,838, an increase of some $296,000 over 1965–66.
>
> The increases resulted from most employees earning their five per cent merit hikes this year, plus an almost three per cent cost of living increase across the board.
>
> —An overall increase in the corporate (housekeeping) fund of $800,000 (which includes the bulk of the pay hikes).
>
> —A $650,000 decrease in projected spending within the water department.
>
> —The appropriating of $885,800 to cover acquisitions of buses—and land for a terminal—for the projected Intra-Skokie Mass Transit Demonstration Project.
>
> About $550,000 will come in the form of a federal grant.
>
> —A reduction in the library's operating budget of some $250,000, resulting from the voters turndown of the library board's proposal to buy land adjacent to Old Orchard junior high.
>
> —An expected cost of $456,000 to replace or add to the auto-truck fleet.
>
> —An expected $400,000 surplus in the water revenue account which may be transferred to the corporate fund.
>
> —Some $1,226,000 made available to acquire land for bus terminals, fire stations, and water department use.
>
> The entire appropriation ordinance is printed elsewhere in The News today.
>
> However, appropriating money for a given project should not be construed as spending the money, Mayor Smith said.
>
> Mayor Smith said that the ordinance is the legal tool the board must approve before it can spend any money—and then it can spend for only those items included in the ordinance.
>
> "If our revenue projection is correct, this is our program for the use of those funds," he said. [Skokie (Ill.) *News*]

The same paper did a splendid job of presenting the "news behind the news" of an important local personnel change:

> Ben Marsh has accepted the city manager's post in Anchorage, Alaska, effective Sept. 15, and will step down as Skokie's manager Sept. 1.

Mayor Albert J. Smith made the announcement at Monday's meeting to a handful of spectators about two hours after more than 100 residents along and near Crawford ave. had left the council chambers.

Marsh said he was leaving because the Anchorage position:

—Will add to the variety of his professional experience.

—Offers a chance to improve the economic situation for his family, and

—Satisfies his desire for adventure.

He said that only "three or four managerships in the U.S. could meet those specifications and persuade me to leave the association I have found so enjoyable."

He told the board that the Alaskan city has a population of 50,000, the hub of a metropolitan area of nearly three times that size.

"It has 900 municipal employees (more than twice what Skokie employs), an annual budget of $18 million (about $2\frac{1}{2}$ times Skokie's), and operates the telephone, power and water utilities, the port authority, the airport, parks and recreation program and the library."

Marsh, for all practical purposes, has been Skokie's only village manager though historians count him the third.

Arthur Lowther of Denver was hired in early 1958, turned out to be a Milquetoast-type, terrified by the political machine then in power.

Lowther lasted about eight months then simply left the village hall one evening and returned to Denver as if he had been commuting regularly.

Supt. of Public Works Henry Weber, who retired only three weeks ago, was named acting manager and served until Ben Marsh was hired.

Marsh arrived in Skokie Apr. 1, 1959, exactly seven days before voters "threw the rascals out" and gave the Caucus Party its first opportunity to run the village.

That incoming administration—including trustees Albert J. Smith and William Siegel—were skeptical about Marsh who had been hired by "those guys."

A true pro, Marsh went to work and let the politicians worry about the politics.

In two years time, the voters felt the Caucus Party had lost its sheen, tapped Myron (Mike) Griesdorf to head the new administration, and gave it a four-year lease on the village hall.

One of the subrosa pledges Griesdorf and his supporters made to one another was to unload Marsh at the first opportunity.

That opportunity never came—though there were many times when it sounded like it was knocking on the door.

But Mike Griesdorf learned early in his term that Marsh was an excellent buffer between irate citizens and the administration, that he was more than competent at his job, and that he, like Griesdorf, really wanted "to make a record."

Rather than fire him, Griesdorf came to the realization that he and his chief administrative aide complemented one another.

So he stayed on. . . . [Skokie (Ill.) *News*]

CITY CLERK

This elective officer might be termed the city's secretary. He attends council meetings and takes minutes, receives communications addressed to the city, issues licenses (dog, beach and the like), receives nominating petitions, supervises elections and preserves all city records.

CORPORATION COUNSEL

A lawyer, he is legal adviser to the city and its representative in court in major matters. In smaller communities his duties are performed by the *city attorney*, who, in larger places, is the prosecuting attorney in criminal cases; much of his work relates to minor court cases. His title may be *city solicitor*.

PUBLIC WORKS

The tendency is toward consolidation, under a *commissioner of public works*, of the departments of streets, water, public buildings, local improvements and the like. If the offices are not consolidated, the commissioner of public works has charge of new construction of streets, sewers and so on, whereas the *street commissioner* has the responsibility of seeing that the streets are kept clean and in repair and usually has charge of garbage collection. The *city engineer* works under the commissioner of public works.

The newspaper has it within its power to interpret the activities of these departments for tax-paying readers. One way is by an eyewitness description of their functionings.

By Charles B. Cleveland

A uniformed policeman noted the pile of garbage strewn in the alley; walked around to the apartment with an arrest book in his hand.

This is a frequent scene in Chicago now as every ward has a policeman assigned to arrest garbage violators who litter alleys and who fail to employ refuse cans.

Let's walk along with Officer Peter Miller, a veteran of nine years at the Fillmore Station, as he enforces laws on refuse in the 29th Ward.

Here's an alley in back of 509 South Keller av., with rubbish and garbage piled alongside the building. There are no refuse cans.

"This alley was cleaned yesterday," Vito Marzullo, ward superintendent said, "now look at it—"

Miller knocked on the apartment door and Mrs. Yolanda Nania, a tenant, answered.

"I think it is a good thing you are doing, trying to keep the alleys clean," she said. "But we have no cans. We had some before but somebody took them."

"Did you dump your garbage in the alley?" she was asked.

She shrugged. "Yes. What else can we do?"

"Notify the owner to get some cans for this building," Officer Miller warned. "I'm going to check here on Saturday and if there are no cans, I'm going to issue a summons and he'll have to go to court."

In back of 4101–03 W. Van Buren st., a pile of rubbish lay alongside a half-filled can. The landlord, Daniel King, was brought down to look at the litter.

"I don't know about it," he said. "That didn't come from our place. Somebody must have come along and dumped it there."

A man came up to the reporter as he watched the scene. "You looking at the alleys?" he asked. The reporter nodded. "How about telling that landlord over there," he pointed across the street, "to get some cans. The people have to dump in the alleys."

A youngster, Barney McCarville, of 4157 W. Van Buren st., also watched the scene. "Our alley doesn't look like that," he said proudly. "We've got cans and we use them and we keep the alley clean."

"We've got seven-day service," Marzullo said, "but if the people won't help—" [Chicago *Daily News*]

The nature of issues that are being debated by public officials can be brought home to the ordinary citizen by emphasizing his stake in the outcome.

By Marion Porter

The man on the street doesn't know and doesn't care whether he is riding on "batch-mix" or "continuous-process" asphalt.

But right now exponents of the two different schools of mixing are having a dignified controversy on the subject.

Because J. W. "Bill" Goose of the Jefferson Construction Company is a continuous-process man, he has not yet been awarded contracts on street jobs on which he was low bidder. City specifications call for the batch-mix method. The contracts are held up pending the arrival of Law Director Gilbert Burnett, now on vacation, who will decide whether the city should, or should not, let contracts to "a nonconforming" bidder, even though he be low bidder.

May Get Court Decision

"I'm going to get a decision from the Court of Appeals, if necessary, before I do anything," Goose said yesterday. "I'm going to find out if one man can set up specifications as to method of mixing—if specifications of the ingredients are all right, of course."

Works Director James B. Wilson said that the Jefferson Construction Company probably won't get four of the street contracts it bid on, but none of the other recent bidders will get them either, because the City plans to do the work itself.

The company, however, may get two other street contracts on which it was low bidder because they involve street-construction work at property-owners' expense. Burnett will have to rule on this also.

Either method of making asphalt is acceptable to the State Highway Department, said Harry Eads, Anchorage, senior material laboratory aide for the Highway Department. The Jefferson Company now has a State contract for resurfacing sections of Broadway. The Highway Department inspects every carload of the material.

"It's just two different methods of reaching the same conclusion," said Eads. "We don't care how they make it as long as the results are right. If the sprockets and feed gates are set right the continuous-process is just as accurate as the batch-mix; and likewise, if the operators accurately weigh the ingredients in the batch-mix method, it is just as accurate as the continuous-process."

Weigh Ingredients First

To the layman, the chief difference in the two methods is in the preliminary steps. The batch-mix people weigh the ingredients first. Everything is done by machine in the continuous-process method. One side claims that the machine process is more accurate since it is not subject to the human element of skill, fatigue, and indifference. The batch-mix people lean toward placing trust in man rather than machine.

The Jefferson Construction Company's expensive, gigantic Barber-Green mixing plant on Crittenden Drive is flanked by piles of gravel, rocks and sand. The material is picked up in automatic containers with wickets on them, passed along through a series of conveyor belts; stewed, boiled, stirred, screened and sprayed and comes out as the finished product, untouched by human hands, at the rate of 6 tons in five minutes . . . [Louisville *Courier-Journal*]

FINANCES

The elected officials are usually the mayor, city clerk and city treasurer; other city officers also may be chosen by the voters but usually are appointed by the chief executive with the approval of the council. It is the duty of the *city treasurer*, of course, to collect taxes and other moneys due the city and to pay bills upon executive order. There also may be a *city auditor*, who keeps detailed records of the city's financial setup and acts as financial adviser. Also there may be a *city collector*, who is chiefly a desk clerk to take in money, and a *purchasing agent*, in charge of buying material authorized by the city council.

The financial setup of a city requires study to be understood. The reporter struggling to comprehend it has the consolation of knowing that many city officials don't know what it's all about. State law limits the taxing power of a municipality, usually by restricting the rate at which each $100 of assessed valuation of real and personal property can be taxed for each of several different purposes. The city's budget cannot call for expenditures beyond the total tax collection possible for a given purpose, such as streets, parks and libraries. The financial operations of a city furthermore are limited by state laws, restricting the city's bonding power. A city, for instance, may be allowed to issue tax anticipation warrants to only 50 or 75 per cent of the total amount which would be realized from the collection of taxes if all were paid. Financial houses which purchase these warrants, however, may not be willing to approve the issuance of as many as the law would permit. In Illinois, a city's bonding power is limited to $2\frac{1}{2}$ per cent of assessed valuation.

The reporter with a good grounding in economics and commerce courses has an advantage in comprehending municipal finance. Any reasonably intelligent reporter, however, can grasp it if it is explained clearly to him. He should not feel embarrassed to ask some city official qualified to do so—the city treasurer, auditor or chairman of the council finance committee perhaps—to give him an hour's time to outline the basic principles of the system. Once he has mastered the essentials himself he will be in a position to perform a valuable public service by making each story related to city finance a lesson in an important phase of government for tax-paying readers. With training, he may even be an authority on the finances of his own city at least.

At least three financial stories annually are of "sure fire" interest. They are: (1) announcement by the assessor of the assessed valuations of real property; (2) announcement of tax rates; and (3) passage of the city budget.

The assessment story may not be an annual one, as many places have new assessments biennially or quadrennially. There invariably follow interminable appeals to the board of tax appeals by property owners seeking reductions, and there always is at least one additional news story regarding the quantity of such suits. It is in the public interest that those who pay taxes understand the procedure by which they are levied.

The interpretative reporter's function is to translate proposals and actions into terms that the ordinary taxpayer can understand, usually to point out how the reader will be affected personally.

By Dick Herman

Operating on the wholly absurd theory the Lincoln school district and Lancaster County's government won't certify a need for any more property tax money to operate in the coming fiscal year than they did in 1965, State Tax Commissioner George Dworak's proposed 42% increase in Capital City real estate values should cost the average homeowner between $2.50 and $3 next year.

It wouldn't even be that much, had not the 1965 Legislature seen fit to continue a series of fixed special property-tax mill levies, rather than appropriate set dollar amounts to operations financed from those levies.

The Lincoln Journal asked real estate men to point out three typical Lincoln properties—two homes and a vacant lot—and supply their current market price.

With that as a start, The Journal researched these properties' county and city tax valuations and applied mill levies against the valuations for 1964 and 1965.

Inequities in Lincoln

A by-product of the brief study was documentation of real estate valuation inequities in Lincoln.

A house now on the market for $17,750 is valued by the county assessor's office at $9,985, while another house with a sale price of $13,950 is on the assessor's tax books for $10,756.

A vacant lot on the market now for $4,500 has an actual value on the county assessor's records of $1,345.

Assessed value—the value on which property tax mill levies are computed—is 25% of actual value.

The state tax commissioner's office says it is aware of many inequities within Lancaster County real estate valuations—one compared to another.

But the state's position is that it is the sole responsibility of county officials to guarantee intracounty equalization.

Theoretically, as valuations rise and governmental tax needs remain the same, mill levies go down proportionately.

This, of course, is theory.

It doesn't always work out that way.

For example, of the current 11.73 mills of the state property tax levy, 4.3 mills make up the total of special, fixed levies.

General Fund Changes

These 4.3 mills will remain the same whether the State Board of Equalization accepts the tax commissioner's recommendation, increases it, lowers it or rejects it completely.

Only the general fund portion of the state levy—7.43 mills last year—is subject to any rise and fall, based upon valuation adjustments.

[Lincoln (Neb.) *Journal*]

When he knows the valuation placed on his property and the legally adopted tax rate (the amount he will have to pay for each $100 worth

It's going to cost city taxpayers $2,328,672 in principal and interest payments for fiscal 1966–67. This is the figure proposed in the 1966–67 city budget and compares with $1,714,160 for last fiscal year.

However, the debt service payments on the city's general obligation debt in the tax supported portion of the city budget is $557,538 which is 5.823% of the total tax funds budget.

The $557,538 is needed, according to city officials, to pay the principal and interest on auditorium and storm sewer bonds and also the new city hall bond issue which is being collected for the first time.

Following is a breakdown of the proposed total city's principal and interest payments for the next six fiscal years:

Schedule of Principal Payments on Bonded Indebtedness for Fiscal Years Indicated Below

	1966–67	1967–68	1968–69	1969–70	1970–71	1971–72
General Obligation Bonds	$ 365,000	$ 375,000	$ 380,000	$ 385,000	$ 395,000	$ 410,000
Special Assessment Bonds	398,000	319,000	319,000	320,000	320,000	330,000
Revenue Bonds	387,000	479,000	512,000	534,000	712,000	736,000
Grand Total	$1,150,000	$1,173,000	$1,211,000	$1,239,000	$1,427,000	$1,476,000

Schedule of Interest Payments on Bonded Indebtedness for Fiscal Years Indicated Below

	1966–67	1967–68	1968–69	1969–70	1970–71	1971–72
General Obligation Bonds	$ 192,538	$ 136,170	$ 125,750	$ 114,995	$ 105,550	$ 96,318
Special Assessment Bonds	174,201	161,178	150,445	139,675	128,925	119,515
Revenue Bonds	811,933	799,293	782,688	764,688	750,823	714,584
Grand Total	$1,178,672	$1,096,641	$1,058,883	$1,019,358	$ 975,298	$ 930,417

[Lincoln (Neb. *Journal*]

of assessed valuation), the taxpayer can figure out his own tax bill. Taxpayers' suits to set aside a tax rate in whole or part on the basis that some item in the city budget is improper are frequent. Usual practice in such cases, and when appeals are pending from the assessor's valuations, is to pay the tax under protest. If the protest is allowed, often after an appellate court decision, refunds are made. To postpone tax collections until after all appeals are decided would be to deprive the city of revenue.

On page 385 is an example of how a trained reporter can make other aspects of municipal finance comprehensive to laymen.

OTHER OFFICES AND BOARDS

The police and fire departments and the courts already have been discussed and schools will be the subject of the next section. There remain the offices of the building commissioner, commissioner of health, superintendent of playgrounds and recreation, other minor officers (sealer, purchasing agent and so forth) and the numerous official and semi-official boards and commissions.

The first requisite of the city hall reporter is to be aware of the existence of these offices and boards and of their functions. In no two communities is the setup exactly alike, although generally to be found are the following: civil service commission, zoning board, park board, board of tax appeals, library board and planning commission. The number of land clearance commissions, urban renewal and housing authorities is increasing.

In some cities, these groups are active and newsworthy; in others they are dormant, their existence seeming to serve little purpose other than to provide the mayor with the opportunity to appoint minor political followers to prestige positions. A live chairman, however, can make any one of the groups a vital factor in municipal affairs. The civil service commission, for instance, can cease being the rubber stamp for political appointments that it is in many places and can become a real watchdog of the merit system by insisting that all jobs which should be filled by civil service examinations are so filled, that the spirit of civil service not be defeated through repeated temporary appointments in lieu of holding examinations to fill vacancies, that too much weight not be given in the final ratings of candidates to the "intangible" qualifications as contained in the recommendations of political friends, that dismissals from city employment be for valid reasons rather than as a result of trumped up charges and that the conduct of examinations be absolutely honest.

Civil Service examinations for seven city positions now filled by temporary employees will be held next month. They will be given in the Board of Health building, 19 W. Market street, Ralph Williamson, secretary of the Civil Service commission, announced yesterday.

The highest paying position is that of deputy city treasurer with an annual salary of $7,750. The examination will be given at 9 A.M. April 2. The present deputy is John Cooper.

Examinations for three jobs as assistant supervisor of operations at Municipal Airport will be held at 9 A.M. April 12. The incumbents are Roy Brody, Mitchell Arnold and Herbert Small.

Dr. Peter Orthcott, president of the board of health, telegraphed 30 more hotels and restaurants yesterday, warning that those with unsanitary conditions must correct them immediately or be closed.

Nine restaurant operators were summoned before the board yesterday for unsanitary food conditions. Five agreed to close until corrections were made. Three others said corrections were being made and inspectors were sent to check.

The ninth, Joe's Grill, 90 East Wabash street, had cleaned up since Wednesday's inspection. The restaurant was allowed to remain open with a warning not to repeat the violations.

The five restaurants which closed voluntarily, and the violations reported by inspectors were as follows . . .

URBAN RENEWAL

No aspect of local governmental operations in the large cities has grown more in importance in recent years than slum clearance and urban renewal. Federal, state and local funds are involved and many metropolitan centers are undergoing wholesale renovations costing into the millions or billions of dollars. Whereas a generation ago the strength of a political machine was its ability to act as a welfare and relief organization—the Tammany Hall method—today municipal political leaders feel that their strength comes mostly from their ability to remake the appearance of their bailiwicks by tearing down and rebuilding. Mayors and their planning, housing and land clearance boards trot to Washington to seek approval of "workable plans," the first step in obtaining federal funds for any program. There follows an interminable number of steps, including legislative and administrative action at three levels of government, condemnation proceedings, letting of contracts, demolition, housing of dispossessed tenants, haggling over plans for buildings, streets, the location of parks, schools and the like. Civil libertarians and human relations groups often are apprehensive over the futures of Negroes and members of other minority groups who are most frequently affected by slum clearance projects. The movement of whites to the suburbs means that the proportion of nonwhites within the big city limits is becoming greater. Political as well as social and economic upheavals often results.

So intricate and important has this field of activity become that large newspapers increasingly are hiring or training reportorial specialists to keep up with developments.

Some critics, notably Jane Jacobs in *The Death and Life of Great American Cities*, contend that federally supported urban renewal programs are destructive of small independent businesses and are a weapon used by large commercial interests in central business districts to combat the growth of suburbs and outlying shopping centers. If so, this explains why so many otherwise-Republican businessmen support big city Democratic mayors and their machines which are adept at obtaining federal subsidies.

In *The Federal Bulldozer*, Martin Anderson wrote that during the 1950–60 decade 126,000 dwelling units—25,000 of them in good condition—were destroyed to make way for urban renewal projects which resulted in public or private commercial construction. Only 28,000 new housing units were built in the same areas. Anderson predicted that by 1972 over four million persons will be displaced and that the overwhelming majority will have worse rather than better living accommodations as a result.

A balanced appraisal of the problem is to be found in *Urban Renewal and American Cities* by Scott Greer, Northwestern University sociologist.

Schools and Education

Routine coverage of school news is not too difficult. It consists of watching such items as enrollment figures, bond issues, faculty and curriculum changes, new buildings and equipment, commencement and other programs, student activities and the like. Such stories as the following are commonplace:

> The Baltimore County Board of Education yesterday announced that construction on a new elementary school building, needed to serve several

rapidly growing communities in the Lansdowne-Baltimore Highlands section, will begin this week.

To be known as the Riverview Elementary School, the structure will be erected on a site situated south of the proposed extension of Hollins Ferry road in the Landsdowne area. The low bid for the school was $744,900.

Pupil Overflow

Need for the new school is evidenced by the fact that a 230-pupil overload already exists at the two elementary schools at Lansdowne and Baltimore Highlands that now serve this section of the county.

A pupil overflow at Lansdowne is housed in the school library and in two rented churchrooms. The Baltimore Highlands school utilizes a basement room as a temporary classroom. Regular classrooms are generally overcrowded at both schools.

The new facility is situated within a 1,200-unit housing development only part of which is now completed.

The school will contain eighteen classrooms that will normally accommodate 630 pupils. It will also include a library, remedial instruction room, multipurpose room, cafeteria, health suite and administration office.

Grimm Comments

Preston L. Grimm, statistical and research expert for the county school system, explained that the new Riverview school is designed to offer only interim relief for enrollment gains in the Baltimore Highlands school district.

"Long range plans envision the construction, at some future date, of a new elementary school at Baltimore Highlands, for which a site has already been acquired," Mr. Grimm said.

"This is expected to occur when the area is sufficiently developed to justify its erection." [Baltimore *Sun*]

Helping citizens—over 50 per cent of whose local tax dollar goes to maintain the public schools—understand what's going on educationally is a different matter. Since the children of World War II veterans began reaching school age in the early fifties, there has been hardly a school district in the United States which has not found it necessary to expand its educational facilities. Nevertheless, in many places there persist grave shortages in buildings, classrooms, equipment and teachers. As the total tax burden—federal, state and local—has grown during the Cold War period, taxpayers have been increasingly reluctant to approve school bond issues and little progress has been made toward obtaining financial aid from the federal government. Whereas formerly school elections aroused only meager interest, by the mid-'60s exactly the opposite was coming to be the case in many places.

In addition to the basic problem of finances, other educational issues have become controversial and, consequently, newsworthy.

INTEGRATION

The court action and violence which followed the United States Supreme Court decision outlawing racial segregation have made headlines the world over. Since only token integration has taken place in most southern cities, this will continue to be so for some time to come. Outside the south, segregation exists *de facto* if not *de jure* in many places as a result of housing segregation. Some bond issues for the construction of new schools have been defeated in the suburbs in order to discourage migration of Negroes and other minority groups. On the other hand several northern cities are providing bus service, mostly for Negro children, to implement their no-segregation policies. The National Association for the Advancement of Colored People and other groups pressure school boards to redraw district lines so as to encourage integration. Other groups violently oppose such proposals.

RELIGION

Parochial schools, mostly Roman Catholic, have increased greatly in number and enrollment in the post-war years, disrupting public school attendance in some places and relieving congestion in others. Bitter local campaigns have resulted when Catholics have sought membership on public school boards. Defeat of bond issues for public schools sometimes has been blamed on Catholic voters. At the national level, the Catholic church has opposed federal aid to education unless its schools share in it. The parochial schools believe their children should benefit from free bus transportation and similar benefits. Released-time programs, whereby children are excused from school to take religious instruction elsewhere, may be highly debatable locally. Also very controversial is the more recent trend toward shared-time programs whereby parochial school students take some of their classwork in nearby public schools.

If there is one thing above others that the average newspaper wants to avoid it is stirring up religious controversy. Consequently, handling of such matters usually is gingerly and only when the circumstances compel any mention at all.

Newspapers comment editorially on United States Supreme Court decisions outlawing prayers and Bible readings in the public schools, but they have not been aggressive in consideration, one way or the other, of proposals to amend the United States Constitution to upset the Court's decisions.

DELINQUENCY

From one standpoint, the history of public school education in America could be written to show how, step by step, the schools have assumed responsibilities formerly considered the prerogative of the home, factory or other institutions. Most of broadening of the curriculum has resulted from outside pressure, including statutes requiring that this or that—American history, the dangers of dope addiction, automobile driving, and the like—be taught. As a consequence, the student's free choice is limited, especially if he is among the increasing number who seek to meet college entrance requirements. Were it not for compulsory attendance laws, the already serious "drop-out" problem would be greater. Problem children are mostly ones in revolt against regimentation, real or imagined. In the huge high schools of today, potentially disturbed adolescents develop intense feelings of revolt. Despite physical education and intramural athletic programs, participation in varsity sports is limited to an increasingly smaller proportion of the student body, with resulting frustrations. The same is true of other school activities, with opportunities to become officers or star performers restricted to the minority. In several large cities, post-athletic contest riots between fans representing rival schools have become serious. The emphasis which rooting alumni insist colleges and universities place on sports, especially football, sets a nationwide pattern. Exposures of widespread professional gambling activities, which include attempts, successful and otherwise, to bribe players, occur frequently. Even if the schools solved all the problems suggested in this paragraph, of course, the problem of juvenile delinquency would continue to exist because its social and economic causes are mostly outside, not inside, the school walls.

EXCEPTIONAL CHILDREN

Counselors, psychologists, psychiatrists and other advisers deal with individual problems of disturbed and other children. Special classes or instructions exist for physically handicapped children—the deaf, dumb, blind, crippled and mentally retarded—and the gifted child is attracting more and more attention. Opinions differ as to whether children should be grouped according to potential ability, usually determined by intelligence or other tests, or achievement. On the one hand, the consciousness of being labeled superior, medium or inferior is considered disturbing to some children who will have to compete in a world of unequals. On the other hand, it is contended that fast learners are held back if instruction has to be kept at the level of the slowest. The pros and cons of this matter have been debated by educators and parents for a number of years in many parts of the country.

AUTOMATION

Related to this issue is the controversy over the extent to which instruction should be standardized in the interest of reducing teaching burdens. Under the influence of teachers' colleges during the past generation, testing of many kinds—intelligence, aptitude, achievement and so forth—has developed considerably. The results are used for placement of students in classes in the grades and high schools and by colleges and universities to determine admissions. Criticism is growing that if improperly used these tests result in "giving a student a number" at an early age and prejudice teachers' attitudes toward actual classroom work. Also and more seriously, it is contended that the tests do not measure a student's ability to organize his thoughts, his total understanding of a topic, imagination, ingenuity or originality. Devised for fast grading by machines, the tests require the student merely to put an x after which of three or four answers to a question is correct. University professors, especially in the professional schools such as law and medicine, complain that students are coming to lack the ability to express themselves and that automatized teaching makes for conformist robots. Teaching machines, airborne television programs and the like ease the teacher problem, it is admitted, but stultify initiative and creativeness.

ACADEMIC FREEDOM

There is hardly an American community which has not had a "case" involving a teacher with allegedly heretical ideas, a reading list which someone does not like or a textbook or magazine under attack by a patriotic or other pressure group. This situation unquestionably has made teaching less attractive to many young men and women and has contributed to the development of the strong administrator type of school superintendent. As in all other aspects of contemporary complex society, rules and regulations and forms and reports have multiplied in the school system. Teachers often complain that they are left too little time to teach and that they have increasingly less to say about the determination of educational policy. In huge school systems, not only pupils but teachers as well run the risk of becoming merely numbers.

Lengthy as it may seem, the foregoing discussion has by no means exhausted the subject. Educational news by contrast with school news requires the attention of journalists with specialized knowledge and understanding. It is a great field for the interpretative reporter.

County Government

The county building is what ordinarily is known as the courthouse because the county court is the most important room in it. The same building probably also contains the circuit court and possibly the municipal court, if there is one, and the court of a police magistrate or justice of the peace. There also are other offices of county officials.

COUNTY BOARD

Corresponding to the city council (or *board of aldermen*) of a city, is the county board, also called *board of commissioners* or *board of supervisors*, which is the governing body of a county. Its president (or chairman) may either be elected by the voters or selected by the board members who are elected by townships or at large. In smaller places, the board may meet infrequently, as bimonthly or semiannually; in large places it meets almost as frequently as the city council. Its powers are limited because the county is primarily an agent of the state in collecting taxes, enforcing laws, recording documents, constructing and maintaining highways, providing poor relief, administering rural schools, supervising nominations and elections, guarding public health and performing other similar functions. These duties are the responsibility of the elective county officers.

COUNTY CLERK

Secretary of the county board, the county clerk also issues licenses (wedding, hunting and the like), accepts nominating papers, supervises the printing of ballots, receives election returns and keeps county records. If there is not a separate elective officer, *a register of deeds*, he also records articles of incorporation, receives applications for corporation charters, and keeps all other records and documents of private transactions. It is to him one writes for a copy of his birth certificate or to prove ownership of a piece of property.

Duties of the *sheriff*, *prosecuting attorney* and *coroner* and the operation of the county court already have been explained. The sheriff usually has his office in the county jail and the coroner may be a practicing physician or undertaker with a private office.

The *county treasurer* is an agent of the state, collecting taxes which he forwards to the state capital. He pays county employees out of funds reallocated to the county from the state and meets other obligations in similar fashion. The *county assessor* assesses the value of property in the county, prepares maps to show real estate ownership and reports his findings to the state.

The *county highway commissioner*, *county engineer*, *county surveyor*, *county superintendent of schools*, *county health officer*, *county agricultural agent* and other county officials perform duties suggested by their titles.

With the "population explosion" into the suburbs, county government has had to pay more attention to unincorporated areas because they inevitably are involved in problems related to water supply, transportation, recreation, policing and the like. Counties also operate poor farms, homes for the aged, jails, general hospitals, special hospitals for the tubercular, mentally ill and others, nursing homes and other institutions which cities and states also maintain. The awarding of contracts must be watched carefully as well as the quality of service performed. Illegal operations, as gambling, banned from the cities, may flourish in nearby areas.

An authoritative interpretative reporter may goad public officials to take action at the same time he enlightens readers regarding a governmental function.

BY LEN KHOLOS

Erie County commissioners' refusal to enter into regional planning with the city is not only hampering efforts to attract new industry, it is actually costing Erie taxpayers extra thousands of dollars.

In an interview with The Erie Dispatch last week, J. Cal Callahan, of Morris Knowles Inc., disclosed that the federal government is willing to pay half the cost of developing a workable program when more than one community is involved.

"The federal government feels that regional planning is the only sensible vehicle for progress, not only to promote orderly growth of an area but to prevent mistakes that will be costly in future years," Callahan said.

* * *

How is refusal of the county leaders to cooperate costing Erie taxpayers money?

Before the government will forward funds for redevelopment, whether it be for industrial or residential purposes, the communities involved must prepare a workable program.

Erie has already spent $5,000 and has contracted to spend $25,000 more to prepare this progam in order to become eligible for federal planning money.

Assuming that the cost of work within the city would cost the same amount in a regional planning setup, the federal government would then have paid $15,000 plus half the costs incurred outside the city limits.

* * *

Can the individual communities in the county do anything to protect their own futures?

County Solicitor Jacob Held has told county commissioners that they cannot spend any money for planning. This came as a surprise to local government observers.

Held may also claim that the boroughs and townships are not allowed to spend money to plan for themselves.

On the other hand, the government will pay half the costs of preparing a workable program for communities of less than 25,000 population or, if they join in the city's planning efforts, half of the cost of the joint project.

* * *

We have explained why the federal government wants communities to have a workable program before it will forward funds for redevelopment. Now, here is what a workable program includes:

1. Sound local housing and health codes, enforced; an end to tolerating illegal, degrading, unhealthy substandard structures and areas.

2. A general master plan for community development, an end to haphazard planning and growth, a road map for the future.

3. Basic analysis of neighborhoods and the kind of treatment needed, an inventory of blighted and threatened areas upon which a plan of treatment to stop blight in its tracks can be developed.

4. An effective administrative organization to run the program, coordinated activity toward a common purpose by all offices and arms of the local government.

5. Financial capacity to carry out the program, utilizing local revenues and resources to build a better community for the future instead of continuing to pay heavily for past mistakes.

6. Rehousing of displaced families; expanding the supply of good housing for all income groups, through new construction and rehabilitation, so that families paying premium prices for slums can be rehoused.

7. Full-fledged, community-wide citizen participation and support, public demand for a better community and public backing for the steps needed to get it. [Erie *Dispatch*]

State Government

Unless he works in one of the 50 state capitals, the beginning reporter has little contact with state governmental offices. If he is ambitious to become the state capital correspondent for a metropolitan newspaper as a possible step toward a similar position in Washington, D.C., covering the city hall and local politics furnishes excellent training.

Although he does not attend legislative sessions or visit the offices of state officers, some member of the editorial staff of the small city newspaper follows what is happening at the state capital as the local community is certain to be affected. City officials, civic organizations and other individuals and groups discuss state governmental matters and make known their opinions to their representatives in the legislature. Often it is necessary to obtain passage of a state law before it is possible for the city council to take some desired action; the corporation counsel may write such laws which members of the legislature from the district introduce and push to adoption.

The following are examples of how to localize what is happening at the state capital so as to emphasize its importance and the role played by local persons:

> Mayor Walter E. Lewis today urged State Rep. Oscar R. Fall and State Sen. James L. Born to support the bill pending in the state legislature which would permit Milltown and other cities in the state between 25,000 and 100,000 population to establish a municipal court.

> All doubt as to the legality of Milltown's compulsory automobile testing station was removed today when Gov. Dale O. Hart signed the enabling act prepared by Corporation Counsel V. K. Kenwood and passed unanimously last week by both houses of the legislature.

> Representatives of The Crib, Milltown's foundling home, will go to the state capital tomorrow to join the lobby fighting passage of a bill which would establish a state department of public welfare. The bill is considered a threat to the local institution because it is believed a state department with power to direct all such establishments would insist upon regulations which The Crib could not meet and continue to exist.

> Killing of the remaining state library appropriation in Springfield last night in the term-end jam by a legislature anxious to adjourn late tonight,

will deprive Milltown of the purchase of books and periodicals to the amount of $6,000 during the next two years, Miss Edith Delancey, city librarian, revealed today.

Local newspapers use, often by rewriting to play up the local angle, press releases from state offices. State representatives often write weekly newsletters to summarize legislative activities. Press associations in state capitals handle special queries from newspaper clients regarding matters of special interest. Only the largest papers, however, can afford to maintain bureaus in the capitals, either while the legislatures are in session or at any other time. Such assignments almost invariably go to reporters with experience covering local politics and government.

Federal Government

Of the major divisions of the executive department of the federal government—those represented in the president's cabinet—only one has a permanent peacetime representative in the city or small town. That is the post office department. In moderate-sized cities, at least for a few days before April 15 each year, representatives of the Internal Revenue division of the Treasury Department occupy space in the post office or federal building to assist local taxpayers in preparing their federal income tax returns and to collect taxes.

A record high in the number of federal income tax returns filed and payments received was reported yesterday at the office of the collector of internal revenue here.

The approach of the midnight deadline brought thousands of persons to the office and there was sufficient extra help to take care of taxpayers who needed assistance in filling out the forms. Extra cashiers were on hand to accept payments. Because taxpayers had familiarized themselves with their problems, comparatively few had to wait long in line.

The peak in the day's business came in the early afternoon, but there were long lines in the early evening. Early closing of offices and manufacturing establishments, as well as the complete shut-down for some for the entire day, also help make easier the trips of the last-minute visitors to the tax offices.

Payments in cash, money orders and checks totaling $150,000,000 were received yesterday. One check was for $1,000,000. In the two previous weeks $50,000,000 had been paid in person and through the mail.

In the internal revenue offices there were hundreds of bags of mail waiting to be opened. The opening of this mail, containing millions of dollars in checks and money orders, will begin tomorrow and will be finished by the end of the week.

With the exceptions noted, the federal government as a local news source in a small city hardly exists. As its power increases and that of the states declines, however, the lives of American citizens are more and more affected by it. Whereas the press associations and special column writers from Washington must be relied on for interpretations of major current events in the national capital, intelligent handling of much local news requires an understanding of national political issues and events.

Work for the unemployed, for instance, in depression years was provided through funds supplied by the federal government. In wartime there was the Office of Price Administration. Financial assistance also has been obtained through such federal agencies as the Home Owners Loan corporation and the Federal Housing administration, and the bank deposits of most everyone today are insured through the Federal Deposit Insurance corporation. Most far reaching, perhaps, is the federal Social Security act which provides for old age pensions, unemployment insurance, aid for dependent children, widows, the blind and other needy persons, and the Fair Labor Standards (wage and hour) act.

To write about how the local community is affected by these and other federal governmental activities without understanding them is not conducive to effectiveness.

> It was the suburbs' turn today to absorb some criticism from the United States Public Health Service.
>
> Milk sanitation conditions in several of them were found to be below a high standard set by Milltown, the federal agency said in a report released by the Advisory Committee of the Milltown-Wayne County Health survey.
>
> Richmond had a rating of only 75.01 per cent for raw milk from 40 dairy farms under control of its health department and 73.15 per cent for three pasteurization plants, the report showed.
>
> This compared with Milltown's rating of 91 per cent compliance with conditions set up in the recommended USPHS ordinance and code.
>
> "The weighted rating for all milk sold in Richmond was 86.74 per cent," the surveyors declared, "the increase being due to the fact that 80 per cent of the milk sold in the city was being produced under the control of other agencies maintaining a more efficient control.
>
> "It is advisable that Richmond adopt the standard ordinance and limit sale of milk to Grade A pasteurized in order to be in line with the state, Milltown, and other communities in the county."
>
> Sanitation control of milk also was found to be "less than satisfactory" in Bluffs, Blytheville and Lakeside.
>
> Milltown's milk control was praised by the surveyors, and the report commented, "there has been no communicable disease epidemic traced to the Milltown milk supply since 1936."

Nevertheless, the USPHS declared improvement in inspection services is needed immediately "if these high standards are to be protected."

The report also criticized an ordinance recently adopted by the county commissioners requiring all milk and milk products to be pasteurized, but not specifying grading.

The Weather

Another important federal governmental office, purposely omitted from the preceding section because the news emanating from it is not classifiable as governmental, is the Weather Bureau, a part of the Department of Commerce. If, as is often the case in small places, there is no local representative of the Bureau to provide official information, the newspaper obtains the most reliable data available from other sources. Possibly a college or high school can provide it; if compelled to rely upon it own resources, the newspaper at least can make certain that its thermometer is properly set up. As any conversationalist knows, the weather is interesting even when there are no hurricanes, floods or droughts. Since man lived in caves his everyday life has been dependent to a large extent upon the behavior of the elements; the machine or power age has not reduced man's dependency in this respect. In fact, in many aspects of life, it has increased the dependency, as delicate machines may require certain atmospheric conditions for proper operation.

ELEMENTS OF INTEREST

It is not necessary to read a newspaper to know that it is abnormally hot or cold or that there has been a thunderstorm, but the reader does expect his newspaper to supply authentic statistics about the weather, the widespread consequences of any unusual climatic condition and predictions as to a change in the situation.

To meet this reader demand, newspapers print weather reports and forecasts daily. The maximum and minimum temperatures for the preceding twenty-four hours and the next day's forecast frequently are printed on the first page with detailed hourly readings, reports from other cities, wind velocity, rainfall and other details on an inside page. If the weather becomes unusual in any way, a full-length news story is written.

When the weather becomes extreme, the reporter should seek information including the following:

1. Statistics and Explanation.
    a. Maximum and minimum for day.
    b. Hourly readings.
    c. Comparison with other days during the season.
    d. Comparison with all-time records for the same date, month and season.
    e. Comparison with situations in other localities.
    f. Humidity, wind velocity, etc.
    g. Predictions: when relief expected.
    h. Official description of nature of phenomenon.
2. Casualties.
    a. Illness and death directly caused by the weather.
        (1) Heat prostrations.
        (2) Freezing.
        (3) Lightning.
        (4) Tornadoes, cyclones and hurricanes.
        (5) Floods.
        (6) Sleet and hail.
    b. Injuries and deaths of which the weather was a contributing cause.
        (1) Drownings.
        (2) Spoiled food.
        (3) Accidents from slippery pavements, snow, wind, etc.
        (4) Fires.
        (5) Heart disease from heat exhaustion.
3. Property damage.
    a. Telephone and telegraph wires.
    b. Water craft sunk.
    c. Bridges and highways, pavements buckling.
    d. Farm buildings and animals.
    e. Automobiles, buses, and other public conveyances.
4. Interference with ordinary life.
    a. Transportation.
        (1) Railroads.
        (2) Buslines and streetcars.
        (3) Airlines.
        (4) Highways and bridges.
        (5) Private automobiles.
    b. Communication.
        (1) Mail service.

(2) Telephone.
(3) Telegraph.
(4) Cable.
(5) Radio.
(6) Stoppage of food and other supplies.
  c. Public utilities.
    (1) Electric lights.
    (2) Gas pressure.
    (3) Water supply.
    (4) Fuel shortage.
5. Methods of seeking relief.
  a. Increased demands on water supply.
  b. Bathing beaches and parks.
  c. Trips.
  d. Sale of fans.
  e. Children cooled by hydrants, hoses, etc.
6. Methods of handling situation.
  a. Police activity.
  b. Volunteer groups: Boy Scouts, Legionnaires, etc.
  c. Red Cross and other relief agencies.
  d. Use of ashes and other materials.
  e. Public warnings on driving, diet, etc.
7. Freaks.
  a. Narrow escapes.
  b. Undamaged property surrounded by desolation.
  c. Unusual accidents.

WRITING THE STORY

Because the weather affects every reader in his daily activities, no matter what unusual features are included or how the story is written, the reporter must include in his account as many of the preceding elements as are pertinent. Emphasis should be on the effects of an unusual weather condition—casualties, damage, disrupted service—and upon the basic statistics such as temperature, inches of rain or snowfall and wind velocity.

    New Yorkers who prayed for rain to relieve the heat and humidity of the week end received their fill in varying degrees yesterday when Sunday's freak thunder showers were followed by a steady downpour.

The chief sufferers were those in the suburbs, particularly in Westchester, where residents bailed out flooded cellars and were left for short periods without power in their homes. Motorists felt the weight of heavy rains in Westchester, where parts of the Bronx River, Hutchinson River, and Saw Mill River Parkways were washed out and detours outlined by state police.

Those in the city escaped with only a wet day that recorded 1.58 inches of rain at the United States Weather Bureau atop the Whitehall Building at 17 Battery Place. But in Dobbs Ferry, N.Y., 20 miles up the Hudson River, a precipitation of 6.6 inches resulted in the 24 hours ended at 7 P.M. The New York Board of Water Supply reported that the Kensico Reservoir at Valhalla went up 5.24 inches.

Flying conditions were also affected by the weather. Rain, fog, low ceilings and poor visibility forced 122 cancellations of flights at La Guardia Field during the day. They included fifty-nine in-bound and sixty-three out-bound flights.

When rain subsided at 6:40 last night, Benjamin Parry, chief meteorologist at the Weather Bureau here, predicted something better for today. He said it will be cloudy and cool, with intermittent rain until this afternoon, fresh northeasterly winds and a high temperature of 65 degrees. Yesterday's high was 68 at 3:15 A.M. with 66 prevailing between 10 A.M. and 3 P.M., a noteworthy drop from Sunday afternoon's 82.5.

The 1.58 precipitation here brought the month's total to 5.79 inches, which is 2.95 above normal, but still far below the May, 1908, record of 9.1. The year's total is 13.91, a deficiency of 3.28 below normal.

The storm, Mr. Parry reported, originated several days ago in the West, looped south to Oklahoma, then turned northeast. Thunderstorms within the parent storm, he pointed out, hit parts of New York and New Jersey between 4 P.M. and 7 P.M. on Sunday. He said it missed the weather station at the Battery completely, since his gauges there did not record any rainfall until 3 A.M. yesterday.

It hit Dobbs Ferry hard enough at 5:15 to record 2.78 inches in the first 30 minutes. Reports from Fairfield County in Connecticut also told of a heavy rainfall of four inches at 8 A.M.

The sections of highway washed out in Westchester were the Bronx River Parkway intersections at Palmer and DeWitt Avenues in White Plains, the Hutchinson River Parkway between Mamaroneck and Westchester Avenues in Mamaroneck, and the Saw Mill River Parkway north of the traffic circle at Hawthorne.   [New York *Herald Tribune*]

The effects of weather often best can be explained by eyewitness descriptive accounts.

Tragedy struck in the little railroad village of Butler Tuesday night. Lightning struck the village baseball diamond, killing the manager of the Butler American Legion baseball team and two members and injuring five other team members.

The bolt hit at 6:45 P.M., out of an overcast sky. The blow made the entire village tremble. Window panes rattled. Children ran screaming to their mothers. The bolt hit like a broadside from a battleship, and there was a blinding flash. Then the rain came down in solid sheets, bent back and forth by hammering winds.

Several seconds later another bolt struck a transformer in the North Western road yards, throwing part of the village in darkness.

On the baseball diamond the victims of the bolt lay scattered in the dirt.

The bolt that hit the diamond struck at the shortstop position, tearing open a trench four inches deep and three feet long. The bolt ripped the clothing and shoes off the three victims. Peter Hillstrom, 14, was standing only a few feet from where the bolt hit.

William Simerlein, 16, was in left field, about 40 feet away. Raymond Phillips, 40, was about 50 feet away. The players who escaped with injuries were standing farther away. The only player who was not knocked down was Marvin Huberty, 17, who was batting out flies.

Two other Butler boys, Emil Wruck, 19, and James Murray, 16, were sitting in an automobile alongside the diamond. They were shaken up by the crash.

Wruck jumped out of the car and ran into a nearby tavern, yelling, "Get the fire department! Call an ambulance! Some guys are hurt on the baseball field."

The siren of the Butler volunteer fire department began wailing. Firemen ran in the rain for the firehouse. At nearby Hampton Heights the volunteer fire department also responded to the alarm.

On the baseball diamond, just east of N. 124th st., and two blocks south of W. Hampton av., the players who could move began picking themselves up.

Dazed, James Gundrum was one of the first to get up. His first thought was to give artificial respiration to the victims. He trotted over to Hillstrom. Patches of Hillstrom's hair had been burned off his head.

The back of his head was crushed. Gundrum realized that Hillstrom was dead. Gundrum walked over to Phillips and Simerlein. They lay in nude heaps. Gundrum knew that they, too, were dead. . . .

[Milwaukee *Journal*]

INTERPRETATIONS

Public curiosity concerning unusual weather conditions is a form of scientific interest. To satisfy it, the media of communication cannot be expected to define each meteorological term as it appears in a news account, as many of the most common must be used almost daily. When occasion seems to demand, however, parenthetical inserts, sidebars and longer feature articles can be used, mostly for the benefit of middle-aged readers who went to junior high school before its curriculum was enriched by elementary instruction in this field.

After many decades of stubborn refusal to popularize its vocabulary, the United States Weather Bureau has relented in recent years. It takes cognizance of popular usage now by permitting such phrases as "unusually fine weather" and "clear and bright" in its forecasts, and it no longer uses "alert" in official storm notices unless danger immediately threatens.

Explanations of natural phenomena can be given in scientifically accurate but easily understood language.

> Washington—(UP)—A Weather Bureau spokesman said Wednesday that the mid-continent's scourge of tornadoes was "unusual" in scope but otherwise "typical."
>
> He said the conditions that produced the wind barrage were "a classical arrangement" of warm and cold air masses. This occurs frequently in April and May.
>
> Cold air masses from the Pacific and Canada tangled with masses of warm and moist air from the Gulf of Mexico. Tongues of cold air pushed out on top of lighter warm air.
>
> Result: tornado-breeding turbulence along a line or "front" where the conflicting air masses ran afoul of each other.
>
> * * *
>
> Except for the great extent of the tornado area, the weather conditions were "typical for April and May."
>
> When the turbulence is not too great, the result is thunderstorms. When it becomes "extraordinarily severe" tornadoes develop.
>
> Radar observation of some of Tuesday's storm areas showed violent updrafts surging as high as 40,000 to 50,000 feet. When only thunderstorms develop, the updrafts usually go no higher than 20,000 or 30,000 feet.
>
> * * *
>
> Reports received here, the Bureau spokesman said, indicate the tornado warning system worked well except for a few storms.
>
> The bureau's "severe local storm warning service" is headquartered at Kansas City.
>
> It gets storm reports from thousands of volunteer and professional observers. When tornado conditions appear, the service issues warnings that may cover as many as four or five states.
>
> It cannot pinpoint communities where tornadoes actually may appear. Tornado conditions may blanket an area of 10,000 square miles or larger.
>
> * * *
>
> The bureau pins its hope of perfecting tornado warning on radar. Radar can spot storm conditions for 150 miles in all directions.
>
> Radar warning systems are operating in several Texas communities and a few others elsewhere, including Kansas City, Oklahoma City and Wichita, Kan.

GOVERNMENT 405

There are none in Michigan, the worst-hit state in Tuesday's storms.

Eventually, the bureau hopes to have radar coverage from South Dakota to Mexico and east to the Allegheny Mountains.

[Chicago *Daily News*]

DEFINITIONS

To write understandable weather accounts, the reporter must know the meaning of the most important meteorological terms. The following list was prepared especially for this chapter by J. R. Fulks of the Chicago office of the United States Weather Bureau:

Barometer. An instrument for measuring atmospheric pressure. There are two types. In one, the mercury barometer, pressure is measured as the height (commonly expressed in the United States in inches) to which the atmosphere will lift mercury in a vacuum. An average height of the barometer at sea level is about 29.9 inches, and in the lowest several thousand feet one inch less for each thousand feet above sea level. The other type of barometer is the aneroid which measures air pressure by the expansion or contraction of one or more metal vacuum cells. Pressure is also measured in millimeters of mercury, but the international unit used by meteorological services is the millibar (1 millibar equals 1000 dynes; 30 inches of mercury equals 1015.92 millibars). An airplane altimeter is a high-precision aneroid barometer. Ordinarily, when the barometer is around 31 there will be good weather for 24 hours or more. When the barometer goes below 29, wind and rain are likely.

Ceiling. An aviation term used in the United States to designate the height above ground of the lowest opaque cloud layer which covers more than half the sky.

Cold wave. A sudden drop of temperature. Defined by the United States Weather Bureau for each region and season. A typical wintertime cold wave in the central United States is a drop of 20 degrees (from the temperature 24 hours earlier) to below 10°F.

Cyclone. Same as a *low*. The term cyclone refers to its system of rotating winds. It is a moving storm, usually accompanied by rain or snow.

Fog. A condition of lowered visibility caused by minute water droplets suspended in the air. It is a cloud resting on the ground.

Forecasts, weather. Statements of expected weather, prepared by specially trained professional meteorologists. They are based on weather data collected rapidly over a large portion of the world. To obtain the most probable expected weather, the forecaster makes physical computations, considers statistical factors, and applies judgment based on long experience. Specific forecasts are generally for periods of one to three days at the most, but the Weather Bureau issues both five-day and monthly forecasts of *average* conditions. Weather forecasts are of many types, such as public, aviation, marine, agricultural and forest-fire weather.

Front. A boundary between two different air masses, one colder than the other. A *cold front* moves toward the warmer air, a *warm front* toward the colder air. When a cold front overtakes a warm front, they form an *occluded* front.

Frost. A deposit of ice crystals on outside objects caused by condensation of moisture from the atmosphere on clear cold nights. Killing frost is defined as the first frost of autumn sufficient to kill essentially all vegetation in the area.

High. An area of high barometric pressure, usually several hundred to a thousand miles or more in diameter. In the Northern Hemisphere, winds blow clockwise about a high center. The approach of a high generally means improving weather—the ending of rain or snow, then clearing, colder and finally somewhat warmer as a result of sunshine. The weather in highs, like lows, varies from one high to another and will differ depending on where the center passes. A slow-moving high may cause fog, and often accumulation of air pollution, in and near its center.

Humidity. A general term applying to any of various measures of the amount of moisture in the atmosphere. See *Relative humidity*.

Hurricane. The name applied in the Caribbean Region, Gulf of Mexico, North Atlantic and eastern North Pacific (off Mexico) to a tropical cyclone in which the strongest winds are 75 miles per hour or greater. The same type of storm in the western Pacific is called a typhoon.

Lake breeze. A relatively cool breeze which frequently blows, on warm afternoons, from a cool lake onto adjacent warmer land. It may extend less than a mile or as much as several miles inland.

Lake effect. A general term which applies to any effect of a lake on weather. Near the shores of the Great Lakes a sometimes spectacular effect is that of heavy snowfall over a small area (perhaps a county). It is caused by moisture-laden air in winter moving from the lake onto the land, the air having been originally very cold, probably much below 0°F, before it moved onto the lake.

Local storm. Any storm of small scale, such as a thunderstorm. *Severe local storms* are those likely to cause damage, including severe thunderstorms, damaging hail, and tornadoes.

Low. An area of low barometric pressure usually a few hundred miles in diameter. In the Northern Hemisphere, winds blow counter-clockwise around a low center. Typically, the approach of a low means worsening weather—increasing cloudiness and finally rain or snow, but the pattern of weather varies for different lows and will be different depending on how far away the center actually passes. The low may affect weather up to several hundred miles from its center. Usually, as a low approaches, the weather becomes warmer, then colder as the low passes; this is typical of a low that passes to the north, but there may be little or no warmer weather if the low passes to the south.

Mean temperature. The average temperature over any specified period of time, such as a day, month or year. The Weather Bureau uses the average of the lowest and highest temperature of each day as the mean temperature—an approximation that is very close to the true mean.

Mist. A condition intermediate between fog and haze—a thin fog. Also, in the United States, often applied to drizzle (fine rain).

Precipitation. Water droplets or frozen water particles falling to the ground. It includes rain, drizzle, freezing rain, freezing drizzle, snow, snow pellets, snow grains, hail, ice pellets (in the United States, sleet) and ice needles. The term *precipitation* is applied also to total measured depth of precipitation for which purpose any frozen form is first melted.

Relative humidity. A commonly used measure of atmospheric humidity. It is the percentage of moisture actually in the air compared to the amount it would hold if completely saturated at the given temperature. High humidity contributes to human discomfort at high temperatures but only slightly so if at all at low temperatures.

Shower. A rain of short duration, such as with a thunderstorm. Typically, showers begin abruptly and the intensity of precipitation varies considerably. There may be many separate showers on a day of showery weather. The term is also used with other than rain, for example, *snow shower* or *sleet shower*.

Smog. A contraction of the words "smoke" and "fog." It is, however, applied commonly in large cities or industrial areas when the pollutants may include other types in addition to smoke and fog.

Squall. A strong wind which begins suddenly and lasts a matter of minutes—somewhat longer than a gust. Also, especially in nautical usage, a sudden strong wind and an accompanying cloud mass that may produce precipitation, thunder and lightning. A *squall line* is a line or band of active thunderstorms.

Storm. Is a general term that may mean a cyclone, thunderstorm, wind storm, dust storm, snow storm, hail storm, tornado, hurricane and the like.

Storm warning. Can be a warning of any type of storm, but is applied more specifically to warnings for mariners. Marine storm warnings are of four types: *Small Craft* (less than 39 mph), *Gale* (39–54 mph), *Whole Gale* (55–73 mph) and *Hurricane* (74 mph and greater). The figures refer to wind speeds.

Temperature-humidity index. A measure of human discomfort in warm weather. It takes into account the effect of both temperature and humidity. Exactly, THI equals 0.4 times air temperature plus wet bulb temperature, plus 15, all in degrees Fahrenheit. With a THI of 70, nearly everyone feels comfortable; at 75, at least half the people become uncomfortable and, at 79 or higher, nearly everyone is uncomfortable. Fewer people, however, are uncomfortable if there is a good breeze.

Thundershower. A thunderstorm accompanied by rain.

Tornado. A small, violently rotating storm, commonly a few hundred yards in diameter. It accompanies a thunderstorm, but only a very few thunderstorms have tornadoes. Direction of rotation is usually the same as a Low, and the strongest winds range generally 100 to 300 mph.

Water vapor. Water in gaseous form. The atmosphere always contains some water vapor, but the amount varies greatly. In hot humid conditions, it sometimes constitutes as much as 2 per cent (by weight) of the air. At low temperatures, the amount is much less. Water vapor is invisible, but when it condenses it forms water droplets that become visible as clouds or fog.

Wind direction. The direction *from* which wind blows.

18

Business, Finance, Labor, Agriculture

I THE BUSINESS BEAT
1. Routine News
2. Stressing the "Why"
3. Localization
4. Trends

II FINANCIAL NEWS
1. Stock Exchanges
2. Seeking Explanations
3. Definitions

III PROBLEMS AND POLICIES
1. Secrecy
2. "Puffery"
3. "Payola"
4. Codes

IV THE *Wall Street Journal*

V LABOR
1. Labor Laws
2. Covering Labor
3. Labor Problems
4. Stressing the Public Interest
    a. *Union Affairs*
    b. *Policy Statements*
    c. *Management Agreements*
    d. *Union Demands*
    e. *Strikes*

VI AGRICULTURE
1. A Neglected Field
2. Political Power
3. Federal Policy

SINCE THE END OF WORLD WAR II, THE NUMBER OF SHAREHOLDERS OF publicly owned corporations in the United States has more than tripled to a total of more than 25 million. This does not mean that control of the management policies of American businesses and industries has passed into the hands of housewives, widows, factory workers and middle-class shopkeepers. In fact, in monetary terms, the total ownership of stocks and bonds by small investors still is but a minute fraction of the invested wealth of the nation. It does mean, however, that millions of newspaper readers who formerly ignored the financial and business pages now have a vested interest in them. As a result, such pages are being expanded and their contents geared to appeal to the average reader and not just to the broker or banker. The phenomenal increase in general readership of the *Wall Street Journal* and the popularity of some syndicated columns in this field have helped inspire many newspapers to give greater attention to business and financial news, and specializing in this kind of journalism has become much more attractive to active newspapermen, especially beginners.

Whereas a generation ago ability to read a financial ticker tape, bank statement and annual report of a corporation was about all that was required of him, today's business or financial page reporter must be able to explain as well as report what goes on in his field of activity. Several developments have made almost nonexistent the strictly local business news story. Among these have been the growth of retail chain stores which are parts of nationwide operations, the mushrooming of shopping centers serving more than one community, the specialization of factory production so that few products any more are manufactured all in one plant, the growth of dependency of small industries upon large ones for subcontracts and of large industries upon the federal government for orders, the increase in foreign trade and investments, government aid to underdeveloped countries and other similar trends which add up to this: what happens almost anywhere else in the world today can affect the prosperity of the small town, which is no longer self-sufficient economically as it may have been in grandfather's day.

The Business Beat

Despite the trend toward localization of as much as possible of what appears on the business-financial pages, there is no business beat as such. That is, the reporter's day is not spent making regular "stops" comparable to those which other newsgatherers make at police headquarters, city hall and so on. Rather, covering a story for the business page, means mostly investigating a tip or following up an idea, and each assignment may require making contacts with an entirely different set of news sources. Thus, the business page reporter must be fully conversant with the public and private agencies from which information of all kinds can be obtained.

ROUTINE NEWS

Publicity departments of businesses, industries, trade organizations and governmental agencies voluntarily supply the bulk of the routine news in this field: new advertising campaigns; new products; stock sales; production figures; expansion programs; comments on pending legislation, court decisions, or other events affecting business; big orders received; reports on dollar sales; new models; personnel changes in partnerships, corporation officials, managerial appointments, promotions and the like; new building or other expansion plans; moves to new locations; public shows and exhibits.

Trade associations and institutes make reports covering entire industries monthly, quarterly, semiannually and annually. The weekly reports on department store sales issued by the twelve Federal Reserve banks are regarded as a "holy index" even though they do not include suburban stores or discount houses. Transfer of the service to the Department of Commerce has been announced and seems to be imminent. Federal Reserve bank monthly reports are an index to the state of the over-all economy and usually include profiles of particular industries. The monthly index of industrial production gives information regarding the outputs of mines, mills and so on. Even more up-to-date are the reports put out by some state agencies—for example, the *Illinois Business Review*, a monthly summary published by the Bureau of Economic and Business Research of the College of Commerce of the University of Illinois. Its summaries are made public from two to six weeks after the data are gathered whereas government figures may be two or three months old. Similar first-rate reports are put out in Indiana and Texas, among other states.

Other good over-all business and economic indicators are monthly and weekly reports on carloadings; reports of shipments of folding paper cartons; reports on shipments of collapsible metal tubes; weekly Edison Electric Institute reports on electrical production and percentage changes. Gross national product reports (dollar values of all goods and services produced) are widely used but price increases and inflation will affect this index and possibly give a false picture of the nation's real output.

Since so much of this news originates or at least is announced in New York or Washington, it first reaches local newspaper offices throughout the country via press association financial wires. The business page editor must be highly selective and naturally considers the particular interests of the readers in his circulation area. It is easy to clutter a page with indiscriminate use of commodity market reports—livestock market prices, dairy, poultry, produce, grains, prices of various futures, dividends and earning tables and the like.

Typical examples of how the business reporter obtains information would be the following: a railroad shipping clerk knew that a company which was close-mouthed was on the decline because its shippings had fallen off; a city assessor provided information on plans for a major shopping center with which the reporter confronted the developer who persuaded him to postpone publication in exchange for a promise of an exclusive story eventually; a department store official had an informed guess on the sales volume of a statewide chain which did not disclose sales or earnings; a paragraph in a routine quarterly report of a company indicated a major change in marketing plans; a union official confirmed rumors of a reduction in a plant's production as indicated by the laying off of a large number of employees. Frequently, a business reporter can persuade a company to talk even though it at first declares, "We don't want to say anything for competitive reasons," by pointing out that he can dig out the information he wants from Dun & Bradstreet reports or from other sources available to competitors as well as everyone else.

STRESSING THE "WHY"

Even in the case of a routine story, the explanation may be the feature. For example, businesses have been known to move to avoid the disturbance caused by jet airplanes. A concern once changed location because the vibrations from trucks on nearby highways interrupted the manufacture of delicate parts. More significantly, a major appliance store pulled out of a shopping center, saying that shopping habits had changed and customers did not care to hunt for major durable goods in the midst of other commodities.

A routine story could be written:

XYZ Cola reported lower earnings, etc.

More significant would be:

The coldest weather in 79 years cut XYZ Cola sales to the lowest in 20 years, etc.

If stories are written in this way, one leading business and financial editor commented, "Aunt Jane with her $1\frac{1}{2}$ shares of XYZ Cola stock won't be so prone to seek to oust the dumb bunny management."

The following is a typical *Wall Street Journal* lead which offers explanation as well as facts:

> Prices for most major commodity futures declined yesterday. July and October copper, "M" coffee, and all deliveries of corn, lard, and July oats at Chicago fell to new season lows.
>
> Continued selling of cash corn by the government was responsible for the decline in corn prices. It was the fifth session in the last six that prices dropped to new season lows. The government is selling corn to keep market prices low and penalize farmers who did not participate in the 1961 crop reduction program.
>
> The market price for corn declined despite news that a large export business is pending. Egypt yesterday was in the U.S. market for one million bushels of corn. From one million to two million bushels of corn are expected to be sold this week to European nations. The United Kingdom is also scheduled to buy U.S. corn.
>
> The price for scrap copper was reduced $\frac{1}{4}$ cent a pound yesterday. The London copper market also was down. Last week the smelters reduced their buying price for scrap copper $\frac{1}{2}$ cent a pound.
>
> A lack of export buying and slow domestic consumer demand for lard brought active selling into the futures market. Declines ranged to $\frac{1}{2}$ cent a pound.
>
> Livestock prices generally weakened because of a seasonal increase in marketings.

The reporter must not be so naïve as to accept uncritically whatever he is told. An electric plant once moved out of the state saying that the "labor climate" was unfavorable. Several months later it advertised its plant for sale, citing as an advantage, "skilled, stable labor." One Wisconsin business editor has this warning note:

> Business executives pressed for "why?" usually tell reporters that it's all due to high taxes, unreasonable wage demands by labor, too much government interference, not enough tariff protection and spiraling costs of goods and services. Never mentioned in public (it's been called the "conspiracy of silence") is the fact that other factors may have had a more important part in lower profits, salary cuts, layoffs, production cutbacks, plant moves and shutdowns, etc. The other factors include bad guesses by management on product acceptance, excessive production costs, poor scheduling, bad design, insufficient market research, lack of quality control and/or generally poor management.

LOCALIZATION

Famine in India, an earthquake in Japan, revolution in Venezuela or the peaceful overthrow of a government anywhere can affect local business conditions. This it may do directly if an industry sells or buys abroad, or indirectly if anyone with whom it does business is directly affected.

Local opinion should be sought whenever important new legislation is proposed, introduced, passed or tested in the courts. Always the desideratum should be, "How will this affect us locally?" The same is true of work stoppages from strikes or for other reasons. If the commodity is coal, oil, steel or some other basic which is used locally by manufacturers or the public, estimates of stockpiles should be obtained.

The direct relationship between the politics of a foreign nation and an American business was stressed by Donald K. White in the following column in the San Francisco *Chronicle*:

> Gillette Co. looks sharp, feels sharp and is sharp as a result of the Tory victory in the British elections last month.
>
> The company's stock was down to $66.37½ a share the day before the election and the prognosis was for a rough go if the voting went against the Tories.
>
> But it didn't and investors took heart and brought the stock back up to $72.50 a share last week.
>
> On the surface there doesn't seem to be much connection between elections in Britain and razor blades, the Friday night fights, VIV lipstick, Pamper shampoo and Toni home permanents. The last three items are also Gillette products.
>
> The connection becomes clear when you realize Gillette got 43 per cent of its net profit from overseas sources last year. And the bulk of that profit came from the clean-shaven British, who voted back into office the party Gillette investors felt was better for their interests.

Similarly, in the Milwaukee *Journal*, Harry S. Watson explained the ramifications of a new congressional action as follows:

> Business executives across the country Friday will start to wrestle with a new cost increase that for some will run into tens of thousands of dollars a year.
>
> The boost in costs will come in the form of increased postal rates, which go into effect at midnight Thursday. The increase will amount to an estimated 33% in over-all postage costs.
>
> For the individual person, the postage increase probably won't be too costly, but for companies that make extensive use of mail, the added expense will run up into sizable chunks of cash.
>
> Some firms, such as utilities, banks and insurance companies, say they will just have to "take it." They use first class mail for bills, statements, premium notices, and invoices and see no way—at the moment—to avoid the added 1¢ postage charge.
>
> **Scramble to Trim List**
>
> For other firms, which depend heavily on bulk mailings for promotion, advertising and selling efforts, it means a scramble to prune mailing lists, revise promotional literature and catalogs and investigate other advertising media.

One Milwaukee manufacturer, who has depended almost entirely on direct mail advertising for sales, is planning to change back to a salesman-distributor setup, gradually eliminating the direct mail effort.

"The postage increase comes at a bad time," a direct mail advertising specialist said. "Business isn't good and that's just the time when you step up promotional literature and advertising. But now we're going to get hit with an increase in a fixed, uncontrollable cost."

Effects of the rate increase will be felt heavily next month by such firms here as Northwestern Mutual Life Insurance Co., the First Wisconsin National bank, the Wisconsin Telephone Co. and the Electric Co.

$230,000 on First Class

Northwestern Mutual mails from seven to nine million first class letters annually through its central mailing office. Last year, it spent $230,000 for first class postage. The Aug. 1 rate increase will add about $24,000 to the bill for the remainder of this year, and about $69,000 each year thereafter. . . .

TRENDS

Any old-timer knows that methods of doing business have changed considerably during his lifetime. It requires journalistic perception, however, to become aware of a new development when it is still new. In the early sixties it was apparent that speedier transportation, including "piggy backing" by trucks and railroads, had made it expedient for local businessmen to maintain smaller inventories than formerly. Both the Chicago stockyards and railroad passenger service were in decline, much more foodstuffs of all kinds were being rushed in refrigerator cars from place of origin to place of consumption, one-industry towns were disappearing, chambers of commerce were more intent on attracting diversification and other changes were occurring which affected the entire social as well as the economic life of communities.

Two of the most significant new businesses were retail discount houses and leasing companies. The former originated shortly after the end of World War II in New England in abandoned factory towns, most of them depleted as industries moved south, often as a result of strong state governmental inducement, to obtain cheaper, usually nonunion labor. Some smart operators bought the distress merchandise of retailers who faced bankruptcy and made fortunes. Through their operations it was learned that customers take to self-service in department stores as well as in groceries and this type of merchandising spread, mostly in the suburbs where automobile parking was made available. Pegging his story to the remarks of an authority, the financial editor of the St. Louis *Globe-Democrat* told about discount selling as follows:

By James A. Cockrell
Globe-Democrat Financial Editor

—Discount house selling, the shrill and beshambled dimly lit merchandising experiment of a few years ago, is growing.

—But discount selling no longer will be a fight between the "new merchants" and established stores. These latter figures are joining the discount evolution in force and are armed with their own merchandising skills.

—Discount selling techniques will affect all department store, supermarkets and chain drugstore selling in the future.

These predictions come from an expert on discount selling, Richard G. Zimmerman, publisher of Super Mart Merchandising, and The Discount Merchandiser. This week-end, Mr. Zimmerman was in St. Louis to address the Sales and Marketing Executives of St. Louis.

Many diverse interests are entering the expanding discount field, he pointed out, including department stores, mail order firms, Wall Street financiers, real estate men, soft goods manufacturers and others.

Among these new entries, he said, are Spartan Industries, a manufacturer of soft goods with sales of $43,000,000; Mangel's Stores, a specialty apparel chain with sales of $65,000,000; Interstate Department Store (which recently joined forces with Montgomery Ward), and Katz Drugs.

Discounters today, he continued, are "gaining increased prestige among the Wall Street fraternity."

And well they might: Mr. Zimmerman reports that "a return of 30 per cent after taxes is not exceptional" for some discount operations!

This, he added, is about three times what traditional retailers are getting.

And what is a discount house?

It goes, he explained, by many names, such as bargain store, closed-door shopping center, factory outlet, mill store, promotional or self-service department store, soft-goods super market, and others.

Mr. Zimmerman offered the description suggested by the Council on Consumer Information: "A retail store whose policy is to sell nationally advertised, trademarked, and branded goods below the suggested list price or fair trade price to all consumers on a continuing basis."

The discount formula in the beginning, he declared, seemed "temporary." To the retailing profession, discount operations looked a "shambles, with dimly-lit interiors, roughly handled merchandise, no service of any kind, barkers shouting bargains over the public address system and similar 'primitive' features," he continued:

But how big are discount operations in the totaling retailing scene?

In one sense, they are still quite small.

Last year, the nation's some 1985 discount centers had sales of $2,900,000,000, compared with super markets' $35,000,000,000; department stores' $14,000,000,000; drug stores' $7,000,000,000, and variety stores' $4,000,000,000.

But this year, some 2400 discount centers, it is estimated, will have a volume of about $4,100,000,000—a sales increase in one year of 41 per cent.

Similarly, the Chicago *Daily News* ran a "round-up" piece to highlight the increasing importance of leasing:

By Dale Morrison

A growing Chicago firm counts among its assets a fleet of airplanes, ocean-going vessels, a pickle washer, a fortune cookie machine and a hog farrower.

It will soon add a strudel dough machine to its holdings.

What's more, as it name indicates, Nationwide Leasing Co. doesn't use any of the diverse items it carries on its books—it leases them to people who do.

"Long-term leasing isn't new in itself," said Robert Sheridan, Nationwide's youthful president. "What's new is leasing as a business in its own right."

Sheridan's 4-year-old company was the first general leasing firm headquartered in Chicago. The first in the nation—U.S. Leasing Co.—was founded in San Francisco only nine years ago.

Nationwide now has offices at 11 S. LaSalle and in New York, Boston, Houston, Wichita, Kan., St. Louis and Dallas.

In essence, what Nationwide and similar firms do is put up money for expanding enterprises.

Take the case of a cooky cutter manufacturer who wants to set up a new plant. The company has land and buildings, but lacks equipment and capital.

The company doesn't want to tie up its commercial bank credit with a long-term loan for fixed assets.

By turning to a leasing company, the firm can order cooky cutters of the type it wants from the manufacturer it chooses. The leasing company foots the bill, then collects rent from the cooky firm for use of the equipment.

A variation of the standard leasing arrangement is sometimes useful to companies that have all the equipment they need, but are hungry for working capital.

They can sell some of their equipment to the leasing company, pay rent on it and use the ready cash from the sale.

Nationwide currently leases about $25,000,000 in equipment to more than 2,000 firms.

"The big companies have seen the advantages in leasing," Sheridan said. "And the smaller companies sometimes haven't had anywhere else to turn.

"The middle-sized firms that we feel could really benefit from our service are just beginning to come around."

418   HANDLING IMPORTANT ASSIGNMENTS

Among Nationwide's biggest lessees is RCA, which rents about $3,000,000 in defense and other equipment.

Most of Nationwide's leases run from five to 10 years, during which the equipment is amortized and Nationwide collects its markup (about 6 per cent a year), Sheridan said.

When the original lease is up, it can be extended on a year to year basis at reduced rentals.

Besides being a financing tool, Sheridan said leasing has become a potent aid to selling. About half Nationwide's business comes to it through manufacturers' representatives who direct their sales prospects to the firm.

How big will leasing get?

"It's growing at 40 per cent a year now, and we're just getting started," Sheridan said.

Sheridan has been invited to speak Tuesday at a meeting of the American Gear Manufacturers Assn. in the Edgewater Beach to explain the merits of leasing as a way to beat equipment obsolescence.

Financial News

Until they broadened their scope to include business news, most newspaper financial pages contained little more than listings of transactions on the New York and/or other stock exchanges. Such charts still are used and every editor must exercise judgment as to what items to include in the limited amount of space at his disposal. He does so by editing the listings transmitted by the press associations or obtained from local brokerage houses to include those securities in which his readers have the greatest interest, because they are those of outstanding nationally known companies or of companies which have plants or do business in the community.

STOCK EXCHANGES

Elementary is ability to read stock quotations. A typical line as follows:

High	*Low*	*Stocks*	*Div.*	*Sales in 100's*	*High*	*Low*	*Close*	*Net Change*
$26^7/_8$	$18^5/_8$	Jeff.	1	278	$20^3/_4$	$19^1/_8$	20	$-1^1/_4$

This means that the highest price for which one share of Jefferson company stock sold during the current year was $26^7/_8$ and the lowest price was $18^5/_8$ per share. The "1" means that the stock paid $1 per share in dividends last year. This day, 27,800 shares were sold on the exchange, at prices which ranged from $20^3/_4$ to $19^1/_8$ per share. The day's last sale was for $20 which was $1^1/_4$ less than the closing sale the preceding day.

This is the raw material on the basis of which the financial reporter describes the "ups" and "downs" of the market. Since perhaps 90 per cent of all stock trading takes place in New York, what happens on the New York Stock Exchange is, of course, of primary importance. There are also, however, the American Stock Exchange, with about one-quarter the amount of trading as the New York Stock Exchange, the Midwest Stock Exchange in Chicago and numerous small exchanges in different cities throughout the country. Before its securities can be listed on an exchange, the corporation must register under the Securities and Exchange act of 1934 which means it must meet minimum standards of financial soundness. Then its application must be approved by the exchange's board of governors. This act does not guarantee the value of the stock but, because of the double scrutiny by federal government and exchange, listed stocks generally are considered more secure. Over-the-counter sales, however, more than double the accumulated total of sales on all the exchanges combined. They are sales made by their issuers either directly to the public or through some agents other than an exchange. The securities are mostly those of companies with less than $300,000 annual gross sales which means they are not registered with the S.E.C. The salesmen are supervised by their own self-regulatory agency, the National Association of Securities Dealers, which provides information to the press, as does the National Quotation bureau.

The advantages of a stock exchange are said to be: (1) to provide financial facilities for the convenient transaction of business, (2) to maintain high standards of commercial honor and integrity; and (3) to promote just and equitable principles of trade and business. This is decidedly not to say, however, that most other trading is unethical, dangerous or otherwise undesirable. As a matter of fact, the extent to which what happens on the large exchanges actually reflects the state of the nation's financial health is a matter of considerable dispute. Certain it is that the exchanges respond emotionally to political and other news and the prices of particular securities may fluctuate wildly within a matter of hours or minutes. Some skeptics say that a great deal of what goes on is just dignified or aristocratic gambling.

SEEKING EXPLANATIONS

Whatever the truth may be, the financial reporter has the responsibility to seek reasons for important fluctuations. He is aided in the first instance by the Dow Jones & Co. ticker-tape news service which continuously transmits selected stock quotations, late news on the grain, meat and foreign markets, sometimes baseball scores and top national and international news. Its most important function is reporting business news of all kinds and its averages of what stocks are doing in accumulated major categories—industrials, railroads, utilities—are widely accepted as indices of the financial market as a whole. How the averages operate was described for lay readers by the Chicago *Daily News* as follows:

By Joe Beckman

Ask a broker, "How's the market?" and you'll usually hear him say something like, "The Dow Jones industrial average was up about 3 points the last hour."

Everyone connected with the securities market discusses the Dow Jones average, but just what are they and how are they computed?

Dow Jones & Co., operator of the news service known to LaSalle Streeters as "the broad tape," compiles averages on several different types of investments.

Those watched by most market followers are the industrial, rail, utility and composite stock averages, reported each hour and at the close.

But while the averages have many followers, they also have many critics.

The critics charge that using an average of 30 or 65 stocks hardly can tell you what the more than 1,100 common stocks on the New York Exchange are doing.

Their criticism is well taken from one point of view, because occasionally the average will move in one direction while the bulk of stocks in the market will go the other way.

Even so, as Dow Jones itself says:

"The purpose of the averages is to give a general rather than precise idea of the fluctuations in the securities markets and to provide a basis of historical continuity of security price movements."

In a sense, the investor should use the averages as a doctor uses a thermometer. It is an important diagnostic tool, but certainly it is not the only one.

Of the stock averages compiled by Dow Jones, the industrial average is the one investors most carefully scrutinize.

The industrial average is made up of the stock prices of 30 industrial corporations, generally regarded as "blue chips."

These are: Allied Chemical, Aluminum Co., American Can, American Telephone, American Tobacco, Anaconda, Bethlehem Steel, Chrysler, Du Pont, Eastman Kodak, General Electric, General Foods, General Motors, Goodyear, International Harvester and International Nickel.

Also included are International Paper, Johns-Manville, Owens-Illinois Glass, Proctor & Gamble, Sears, Roebuck, Standard Oil of Calif., Standard Oil of N.J., Swift, Texaco, Union Carbide, United Aircraft, U.S. Steel, Westinghouse Electric and Woolworth.

The average goes back to Jan. 2, 1897, when Dow Jones began publication of the daily average closing prices of 12 active stocks. This continued until 1916 when the list was increased to 20. This list was increased to 30 on Oct. 1, 1928.

The stocks in the average now and then are changed to stay modern. Otherwise, the average today might have a buggy whip manufacturer among its components. Substitutions also are made when a stock becomes too inactive or its price is too low.

To compute the average, you would think that Dow Jones would simply take the 30 stocks' prices, add them up and divide by 30.

Not so, though this is the way it was done in the beginning. When stocks were split or a stock dividend was declared, the divisor had to be changed.

Dow Jones at first multiplied the price of each split share by the amount of the split to get away from the distortion that would otherwise have been caused.

In 1928, it adopted the method still used. The night before a split is to take effect, the average is worked out in the usual way.

Then the stocks' prices are added up again, but with the stock that is about to be split included as if the split were already a fact. This total is divided by the average already calculated.

The result is the new divisor, which today is 3.09 for the industrial average. It won't be changed again until a component is split or a stock dividend is declared.

The history of the railroad average also dates back to Jan. 2, 1897. Originally it was comprised of 12 railroads, but this was increased to 20 on March 7, 1928.

The roads in the list now are the Santa Fe, Atlantic Coast Line, Baltimore & Ohio, Canadian Pacific, Chesapeake & Ohio, Chicago & North Western, Rock Island, Delaware & Hudson, Erie-Lackawanna, Great Northern, Illinois Central, Kansas City Southern, Louisville & Nashville, New York Central, Nickel Plate, Norfolk & Western, Pennsylvania, Southern Ry. and Union Pacific.

The rail divisor now is 5.34 and it is not changed if the stock split, stock dividend, or substitution causes a distortion of less than 2 points in the railroad average.

The Dow Jones utility average was started in late 1929 and was made up of 20 stocks, but five stocks were dropped from the list June 2, 1938.

It is comprised of American Electric Power, Cleveland Electric Illuminating, Columbia Gas System, Commonwealth Edison, Consolidated Natural Gas, Detroit Edison, Houston Light & Power, Niagara Mohawk Power, Pacific Gas & Electric, Panhandle Eastern Pipe Line, Peoples Gas, Philadelphia Electric, Public Service Electric & Gas and Southern California Edison.

The utility average divisor currently is 7.91.

The composite average is an average of the 65 stocks making up the other three stock averages and its divisor is now 16.47. The average was begun Nov. 9, 1933.

Many people, both in and out of the market, err when they report an average "up $3." Correct terminology is in points, not dollars, since the changing divisors ruin direct dollar-point relations.

The following article by the same writer shows how this background information is utilized to make the day's news comprehensive:

By Joe Beckman

"This type of market is the kind that separates the men from the boys."

That's a customer's man in one of Chicago's major brokerage houses talking about the Friday market. His comment also was applicable to other sessions this week and the way they've been going the last several weeks—since Labor Day, in fact.

In some ways the market seemed like a boat that had lost its rudder. It took directions from the latest news reports.

Tax selling in many stocks took its toll.

One LaSalle Streeter complained, "Is the tax-selling over with now in (a particular stock) and the 'smart money men' moving in? Or is the tax-selling still to hit?"

These cross-currents hurt.

But there was more to consider than just tax-selling.

International tension mounted, the business recovery was running behind the expectations of many observers and some third quarter earnings reports were less than exhilarating.

Chicago's Inland Steel nearly tripled its earnings from the year-ago period, as did Bethlehem Steel. But Jersey Standard Oil, General Motors and Chrysler all reported lower earnings, the last named showing a $4,800,000 loss.

Technically, the Dow Jones industrial average stayed in its narrow 690–710 trading range.

Will it break below 690? One analyst said there was a 50–50 chance. If it does, he felt the DJI might fall another 20 points or so.

For the week, the DJI was off 0.62 at 129.52 and 65 stocks off 2.24 at 241.28.

The more comprehensive Standard & Poor's 500-stock index slipped only 0.14, indicating the market was really better off than you might guess, looking only at the Dow Jones averages.

Volume rose to 16,990,958 shares from 16,801,760 the week before.

Jersey Standard was the week's most active issue, gaining $1\frac{3}{8}$ to $46\frac{1}{8}$ on 265,400 shares.

Of the 1,463 issues traded on the New York Exchange this week, 744 declined while 563 advanced. A total of 103 stocks touched new 1961 highs while 95 touched new lows.

Among Chicago stocks, Commonwealth Edison was off $1\frac{1}{8}$, Fansteel, planning a stock split and dividend hike, off 1, Brunswick off $1\frac{3}{4}$, International Harvester off $1\frac{1}{4}$ and Admiral up $1\frac{1}{4}$. . . .

Tax selling occurs near the end of the year when investors get rid of securities to establish a loss for income tax purposes, which suggests the importance to the financial reporter of understanding the effect tax laws have on market operations. The layman often is mystified by sales of what from all indications are profitable businesses, for instance. Often they occur so that the seller can pay a capital gains tax of 25 per cent on the difference between the value of the property when he purchased it and its value at the time of his own sale. This, his financial advisers have figured out, means a greater long-run return on his investment than staying in business and paying the graduated corporation income tax. Put in laymen's language this means it sometimes is bad business to be too successful provided one wants to stay in the same line of work.

Many in the financial world consider the Standard & Poor ratings and analyses a better clue to the economy as a whole than the Dow Jones averages. The latter are based on a formula devised a long time ago and do not include electronics, airlines and some other more recently developed industries. Standard & Poor uses a list of five hundred stocks which is more modern.

In 1966 two significant new stock market indices were begun by the American Stock Exchange and the New York Stock Exchange. Both use rapid computers to include all stock transactions, not just those of selected stocks. The American Index reflects the average price changes of more than 950 common stocks, and the New York Exchange Index does the same for approximately 1,250 common stocks.

Another valuable source of business and financial news is Dun & Bradstreet which, among other things, issues a monthly report on business failures based on data from 25 large cities. The emphasis is on explanation as is also true of the Dun & Bradstreet annual and other reports.

The possible assignments for the business-financial page are interminable. The alert interpretative reporter constantly asks "why?" especially when any form of behavior seems to become widespread, as investing capital abroad, establishing branch banks, splitting stock, purchasing government bonds or shares of an investment club or mutual fund rather than investing directly in common stocks, and so forth. The following is a round-up article regarding a then-current trend:

By Gerd Wilcke

Does the recent wave of industry mergers in Europe and Japan foreshadow the return of powerful cartels of prewar fame?

Or will the mergers serve the avowed constructive goal of helping national industries stay competitive on a global scale?

A survey conducted by this newspaper in a number of industrial nations confirmed that new industry line-ups are indeed very much on the minds of business executives and government officials. There was less agreement on what the regrouped mammoth organizations should be called. A dispatch from Germany last week raised the question whether cartels were on the verge of a major comeback.

Webster's New Collegiate Dictionary describes a cartel as an "association of private business organizations bound by contract to cooperate in regulating production and marketing of products, thus tending to restrict world markets and fix prices."

Major Findings Cited

These were some of the major findings of the survey:

In Japan the influence of cartels has been strong in recent years and has been supported by the Government to promote the national industrial boom.

The French Government has conducted a drive toward concentration to meet competition within Europe and with the United States, although a junior economic official said jokingly he hadn't heard the word cartel in five years.

The Italian Government, through a liberal fiscal policy, has greatly facilitated the process of industrial mergers.

For the Common Market as a whole the trend is definitely toward bigger companies but, its officials insist, this does not mean that cartels are coming back.

Approved in Japan

In Japan, the Government has sanctioned the establishment of "anti-depression cartels" in 17 major fields last year to counter the effects of the economic recession that now seems to be drawing to a close.

A correspondent reports that now, with the Government under increasing pressure to liberalize the still severely restrictive entry of foreign capital, Japan's big business interests are said to be pushing hard for the formation of industry federations, pooling of resources by financial institutions and other large-scale cartelization steps. The influential Japanese Committee for Economic Development is backing the drive.

The Ministry for International Trade and Industry, the correspondent reports, has long been a proponent of strong industrial associations to limit excess production and maintain prices.

The chief argument heard is that Japan's industry must operate at maximum effectiveness to compete in important world markets with giant combines of other nations.

On the other hand, Finance Minister Takeo Fukuda has stressed that once the economic lag is overcome, more free competition must be promoted.

A report from Paris recalls that in 1961, the then Premier Michel Debré gave the six French shipbuilders two years to merge into two companies. It took a little longer than that, but there are two today.

This year, a wave of mergers or associations has taken place under Government pressure, involving such key industries as banking, chemicals, autos and electronics. The French news media is calling the results "de facto cartels." Newspapers cite the steel industry as a de facto cartel of another kind, since it has set up a joint corporation to distribute investment capital raised by the Government.

All this, the correspondent says, is much desired by the de Gaulle government to develop units big enough to support modern research, development and marketing.

A report from Rome stresses that the recent merger of Edison and Montecatini into a new chemical combine was expected to pave the way for other mergers. However, most of them are expected to be on a smaller scale.

Though the Edison-Montecatini merger was facilitated by a liberal fiscal policy, that policy contained safeguards against an abrogation of the freedom of competition. Currently a more extensive study is under way dealing with the question of competition.

Politically, mergers in Italy are approved by the left wing in the Government, provided that such mergers lead to lower production costs. However, the left wing has been the strongest force to push the bill to safeguard free competition.

Trend Toward Bigness

A report from Brussels, the "capital" of the Common Market, notes that the trend toward bigness was well-established, and that the European communities fostered it to promote technological advances and to make Europe competitive with the United States.

The market's Executive Commission is currently studying ways to make more feasible mergers of companies in different member nations. Companies in the coal and steel industry, whether in the same or different countries, must get prior approval to merge from the High Authority of the Coal and Steel Community.

The correspondent stressed, however, that the communities zealously watch out for cartel-type arrangements, notably market sharing and price fixing, whereby companies might diminish competition across member state boundaries.

In the last year, for example, investigations by the Common Market commission have led to the dissolution of market sharing agreements in soap, sand and chemical fields. [New York *Times*]

DEFINITIONS

Because of the injury that might otherwise result, the business-financial page reporter must be deadly accurate. Among other precautions he must observe is not to use business or financial terms unless he thoroughly understands their meaning. He should not hesitate to ask a news source to define and explain unfamiliar words and expressions. Among the fundamentals in his lexicon are the following:

Arbitration. Submitting a dispute to a third party to decide and agreeing to abide by his decision.

Articles of incorporation. The charter granted by the state permitting the organization of a corporation. It usually contains details relating to such matters as the purpose or purposes for which the corporation is formed, its principal place of business, the number of its directors and the amount of its capitalization.

Audit. Verification of records and accounts.

Balance sheet. The report of a company's assets and liabilities, profits and losses.

Bankruptcy. Abandonment of one's business and assignment of his assets to his creditors which discharges the debtor from future liability, enables the creditors to secure title to all the debtor's assets and provides a pro rata distribution of the assets among all creditors. A petition in bankruptcy may be voluntary if initiated by the debtor, or involuntary if initiated by the creditors.

Bear. (Stock or produce exchange.) One who believes the market will decline and contracts to sell securities or commodities at some future date at a certain price in the belief he will be able to buy them for resale at a lower one. In a bear market, the average price of all stocks drops because of widespread selling.

Bonds. A bond is a formal promise, always under seal, by the maker, usually a corporation, to pay a principal sum of money at a specified time and interest at a fixed rate at regular intervals. *Registered bonds* are paid only to the party named in the instrument and recorded on the corporation's books. A *coupon bond* is payable to bearer and may be transferred by mere delivery.

Broker. A financial agent who buys and sells securities for others, usually on a commission basis.

Bucket shop. A phony securities exchange which really engages in speculation or gambling on the ups and downs of the market.

Bull. (Stock or produce exchange.) One who expects, or tries to effect, a rise in prices. Sometimes a great number of people decide more or less at the same time to buy stocks. Such general buying action raises the average price of all stocks. If the price rise is big enough and lasts long enough, it is a bull market.

Call loans. Subject to payment upon demand.

Check off. Reduction from employee's pay checks of union dues which the employer then transmits to union officials.

Clearing house. A device to simplify and facilitate the daily exchange of checks and drafts and the settlement of balances among associated banks.

Collateral. Stocks, bonds and other evidences of property deposited by a borrower to secure a loan, as a pledge or guarantee that the loan will be repaid at maturity.

Collective bargaining. Bargaining between an organized group of workers and an employer instead of between each individual worker and an employer.

Conciliation. The attempt to settle a dispute by consultation with rival parties who do not pledge themselves to abide by any third person's decisions.

Controlling ownership. A controlling owner is one who owns sufficient shares to give him stockholder voting control which may sometimes be less than 50 per cent of the total stock.

Corporation. Any body consisting of one or more individuals treated by the law as a unit. The rights and liabilities of a business corporation are distinct from those of the individuals which comprise it.

Craft union. A labor organization of skilled workers doing similar work. Called a horizontal union because no one craft union would include all workers in any one large industry.

Credit. Postponed money payment; a promise to pay money or its equivalent at some future time.

Curb. A market for securities not listed on any regular exchange.

Debenture. Similar to a bond except that the security is the company's earnings only.

Deficit financing, debt management. Financial arrangements by United States treasury, companies operating at a loss to borrow new cash, consolidate debts, shift from short to long term loans, refinance and so forth. The objective generally is to reduce interest charges, put loan repayments on regular basis, assure enough funds to meet payroll costs and bills for raw materials.

Depletion. Exhaustion or using up of assets, such as raw materials used for production.

Depreciation. Loss of value through use or disuse.

Discount. Receiving payment on an acceptance or note from bank for a consideration. The indorser still is responsible in case the maker of the note or acceptance defaults.

Discount rate. The interest charged for discounting a note.

Dividend. The share of the surplus distributed to a stockholder.

Dumping. The sale of products abroad at prices lower than those charged at home.

Escalator clause. A provision in a union contract whereby wages fluctuate with the cost of living.

Feather bedding. Union rules to slow up or reduce work and to prevent speed up so as to protect jobs and avoid unemployment.

Federal Reserve banks. Banker's banks dealing only with member banks and the government, the purpose of which as set forth in the preamble of the act creating them is, "to furnish an elastic currency, to afford means of rediscounting commercial paper, to establish a more effective supervision of banking in the United States, and for other purposes."

Foreign exchange. A clearing house to adjust balances between countries.

Futures. A contract for future delivery.

Hedging. To sell or purchase a security or commodity to offset the purchase or sale of another security or commodity.

Holding company. A corporation which produces nothing for the market but merely invests in the securities of other corporations.

Income, earnings or profit. Must be used with modifiers: net, gross, operating, nonoperating, etc. Net profit is figure most people interested in. Gross profit is sales less cost of selling the goods. Operating profit is gross profit less operating expenses (overhead). Net profit is operating profit less income taxes, any other charges or extraordinary expenses.

Index numbers. An index number represents the price of a group of commodities, or the average price during a given period, which is used as a basis or standard with which to compare the prices of these commodities at other dates.

Industrial union. A labor organization in which membership is open to all workers, skilled or unskilled, within any industry. Called vertical instead of horizontal because of its inclusiveness.

Insolvent. Unable to pay one's debts.

Insurance. A contract whereby one party, for a consideration, promises to indemnify another party in the event a specified loss occurs.

Interest. The price paid for the use of capital.

Interlocking directors. Individuals who are on the boards of two or more corporations which do business with each other.

Investment club or house. Small investors pool their resources, usually by monthly payments, for the purpose of purchasing securities. They profit in proportion to their investment.

Jurisdictional strike. Members of one union refuse to work if those of another union are employed.

Liquidation. Conversion of available assets into cash.

Lockout. The wholesale exclusion of workers from a plant by an employer.

Maintenance of membership. Workers must remain union members during life of contract with employer.

Majority owner. One who owns 50.1 per cent or more of the stock of a company.

Margin. To buy securities on margin means to do so without putting up the full purchase price in cash, with a broker lending the rest.

Mediation. Third party attempts to end a dispute by persuasion.

Monopoly. That substantial unit of action on the part of one or more persons engaged in some kind of business which gives exclusive control, more particularly, though not solely, with respect to price.

Mutual fund. A corporation which invests members' capital in securities and pays dividends on the earnings.

Net income. See *Income.*

Nonprofit. No dividends or financial advantage to owners.

Odd-lot investor. A broker who combines small requests for sales or purchases by several customers to be able to make an adequately sized bid on the exchange.

Open and closed shop. An open shop is one in which both union and nonunion workers are employed. A closed shop is one in which either nonunion or union workers only are employed.

Option. The right to have first chance, as in the purchase of property, usually obtained by a money payment which is not returnable if the deal falls through.

Overhead. Expense of equipment, stock and maintenance which is relatively constant regardless of production.

Premium income. In insurance, the income of an insurance company from premiums paid by policy holders. Interest and dividends from investments are the other major source of revenue.

Prime rate. The interest rate charged by banks to customers—business firms and individuals—who have the best credit ratings and solid collateral. Prime rate generally is one percentage point higher than the discount rate—the interest rate which federal reserve banks charge on loans made by commercial banks from the reserve bank.

Profit and loss statement. It summarizes income and expenses of an organization or business, to show net profit or loss for the fiscal period covered.

Profit sharing. Sharing with workers the profits of good years; in effect, a bonus based on profits.

Proxy statement. A signed document to give another authority to act for the signer. Proxy fights develop at stockholders' meetings when rival groups solicit proxies from absent stockholders.

Receiver. A temporary court-appointed officer to conduct a bankrupt business in the interest of the creditors.

Receivership. Operation of a business by the creditors when the debtor otherwise would be bankrupt or in danger of bankruptcy.

Rediscounting. The purchasing by one bank of a note or bill of exchange held by another.

Rent. The price paid for the use of land or anything else.

Reserve. Lawful money or other liquid assets which a bank must keep on hand to insure prompt payment of its deposits and liabilities.

Revenue. Generally, the cash received in any fiscal period. It may include cash from sales of goods or services (operating revenue) and cash from investments, sale of property or from other sources such as patent rights, royalties and license agreements (nonoperating revenue).

Right-to-work laws. Open shop laws.

Sabotage. A conscious or willful act on the part of workers intended to reduce the output of production or to restrict trade and reduce profits by the withdrawal of efficiency from work and by putting machinery out of order and producing as little as possible without getting dismissed from the job.

Scab. A strikebreaker.

Sell short. To contract to sell securities one does not own in the expectation of being able to buy them later more cheaply.

Speculation. Taking a risk when making a purchase in the hope future developments will make the deal profitable.

Stock certificates. A stock certificate represents one or more shares of the corporation's capital. Its price is determined by the market, usually a stock exchange, where securities are bought and sold. *Preferred stock* holders have a prior claim on the company's assets before the *common stock* holders in the event of bankruptcy. *Cumulative stock* arrears are paid before the common stock receives a dividend in case dividends are omitted at certain periods. *Participating preferred stock* entitles the holder to a share in the profits, in addition to the stated dividend.

Stock split. To increase the total number of shares of stock, usually by doubling the number and dividing the par value of each share. This has the same effect as a stock dividend but is treated differently for taxation purposes. It enables small investors to buy more easily.

Surplus. The equity of stockholders in a corporation above the par value of the capital stock.

Sweetheart contract. One between management and a labor leader which benefits them at the expense of the rank and file.

Trust. A company which deals in capital and handles funds that are principally inactive, thus conserving existing wealth.

Trustee in bankruptcy. Court-appointed officer who converts a bankrupt's assets into cash and pays the creditors.

Underwriting. To insure against loss, to guarantee to meet an obligation if the original party fails to do so.

Wildcat strike. One not authorized by union officials.

Yellow dog contract. A contract for labor in which the worker is required to promise not to join any labor union during the term of his employment.

Problems and Policies

As the scope and consequently the readership of the business-financial page increases, so do the problems of the editor and the need for a strong sense of social responsibility. Tips are received from many sources—brokers, lawyers, union leaders, competitors, shipping agents, trade associations and the like—and some of the tipsters may be motivated by other than pure public-spiritedness. Misinformation or injudicious handling of news may be injurious to innocent persons. Premature disclosure regarding a pending real estate transaction, for example, may ruin a potential deal. And then there is the little old lady who reads a story about the profits being made by raisers of soybeans and wants to cash in her small savings to speculate on the grain market. She calls the editor for further information and advice.

SECRECY

Increasingly, the business reporter is likely to be stymied because of federal government security regulations which make it impossible for even the most cooperative official or public relations counsel to provide information. Often the editor suspects that there is too much "hush-hush" about what happens to be common knowledge in his community, so he may contact the Freedom of Information Committee of the American Society of Newspaper Editors or some such group to see what can be done about "knocking some sense" into the heads of some Washington bureaucrats. Seldom, however, does he dare defy requests from officials with proper credentials.

"PUFFERY"

Biggest perpetual problem is how to distinguish between legitimate news and free publicity. "Business Office Musts" from the advertising department are distasteful to any editor who wants to use only the yardstick of legitimate public interest. This means that he wishes to keep no blacklist of nonadvertisers whose news is to be ignored or played down and he resents any successful attempt to persuade him to use a spurious story whose only effect is to increase someone's sales.

Especially in the sections devoted to real estate and main business district news, the business-financial page may seem to be a booster page and its editor to be interested in promoting the best interests of the community—much as the sports editor usually promotes the success of the home-town team. Emphasis on innovation and progress, however, does not mean excessive "puffery" provided there is plenty of legitimate news available which almost always is the case. How to teach this lesson to business executives and their public relations representatives, however, is not often easy.

Special real estate and similar sections are a thing apart. The copy between the advertisements may be unashamedly free publicity. Most of it is handout material, although some papers strive valiantly to localize and legitimatize it. Advertisers generally believe that such "good will" material enhances the value of their advertisements. Many skeptical newspapermen believe that a good obituary or other legitimate story would serve their purposes better; but they are still to be convinced.

Businessmen who employ expensive public relations men want to be relieved of responsibility. They expect the highly paid help to maintain relations with the press and both boss and public relations men resent it when a journalist attempts to circumvent this line of authority. Often, however, it is imperative to do so. One of the best places is the cocktail party. This is a genteel type of "payola" to which many business enterprises are addicted. The business reporter may be as bored as the society reporter who attends a tea party a day, but he might otherwise not get the opportunity to rub elbows with top executives. More naïve than their public relations men, these officials often provide tips and information of importance, and possibly exclusive as far as the imbibing newsman is concerned. It is a constant source of amazement to newspapermen how ignorant those who make the news usually are as regards its reporting and editing. They do, however, understand that any business enterprise must operate in accordance with rules and, although not understanding, are often prone to accept the explanation, "That is not done," when a reporter diplomatically rejects a suggestion.

"PAYOLA"

How far the reporter should go in accepting favors from news sources is a stickler. Many of them can afford expensive gifts at Christmas or on other occasions and may be offended if a friendly newspaperman refuses to accept their largess. Most editors wish there were an easy rule applicable to all occasions. Some forbid their staff members to accept any presents, even passes to public entertainments and certainly not expensive junkets by airplane to be present at the dedication of a new plant or on some similar occasion. Others are willing to accept anything which does not cost more than a fifth of whisky. Still others will take whatever a news source is handing out to other friends. Whatever rule is adopted, difficulty arises in enforcing it without making exceptions.

CODES

What follows are extracts from a memorandum on "Business News Policy," issued to the staff by Creed C. Black, then executive editor of the Wilmington (Del.) *News-Journal*.

> One of the traditional and thorny problems of newspapers is distinguishing between legitimate news of the business world and free advertising. Wilmington has its share of both legitimate business news stories and space-grabbers. The aim of our newspapers is to get the legitimate news in and keep the puffs out.
> Our policy is based on the premise that the decision on whether an item will be published will rest with the news departments.

Advertising salesmen have been instructed to explain that they have no connection with the news departments, and advertisers are being requested to deal directly with our city desks when they have stories they consider newsworthy.

Our decisions will be based solely on news value. If it's news, no amount of advertising will keep it out of the paper; if it isn't news, no amount of advertising will get it in.

To follow such a policy successfully, consistency is absolutely essential. If we slip up in one instance, we're putting ourselves in a position that's hard to explain the next time somebody wants similar treatment and wants to know why we won't do thus-and-so for him when we did it for so-and-so . . .

There will be no attempt here to set down a comprehensive list of hard-and-fast rules, for that's obviously impractical. But here are some general guidelines on various types of items we encounter:

Personnel Changes. Appointments, promotions, resignations, etc., are news up—or down—to a point, depending on how important the job is. Obviously we can't cover all personnel changes in the business and industrial community, so we must be selective.

Probably the biggest problem here, just because of the sheer weight of numbers, is with the Du Pont Company. I am told that the public relations department there does a good bit of screening in its releases. But if you are in doubt about the importance of a Du Pont position, consult the PR people. Ditto for Hercules, Atlas, etc.

New Businesses. A new business or a change in ownership is news. So is a major expansion of an established firm, or a major remodeling project. Let's not get sucked in, however, by somebody who's just added another showcase or finally put a badly needed coat of paint on the walls.

And when pictures are justified, let's strive for something besides ground-breakings and ribbon-cuttings.

Giveaways. Everybody who's giving something away seems to think we should provide full coverage, including photos of the jubilant winners. We shouldn't and we won't.

Our first consideration here is the lottery laws. If anything must be bought to make one eligible for the prize, the drawing is legally a lottery and we can't touch the story.

Beyond that, our general policy is that we aren't interested in giveaways unless there's something unusual enough to give the story an angle that will enable it to stand on its own as a readable human interest feature. And even when a story is justified, the name of the firm giving away the prize should be only an incidental part of the story.

Business Anniversaries. The fact that a firm has been in business for x number of years hardly excites our readers, even though some businessmen have the idea this qualifies as big news every 12 months. We will not report such anniversaries except on special occasions—such as a 50th, 75th, or 100th anniversary.

Dealerships. It is not news when a men's clothing store adds a new line of shirts; it is news when an auto dealer takes on a new car. The distinction (and it can be applied generally) depends on both the nature of the product and the type of business. A clothing store, for example, handles scores of products; an auto dealer handles only one or two lines, and usually he is the exclusive dealer for these.

Company Awards. If a company could get newspaper coverage of awards it makes or prizes it gives its own employees, there would be no limit on the number of plaques, scrolls, certificates and gold keys gathering dust in Wilmington households. So let's help fight the dust menace by covering only very special awards within a company—a recognition of 50 years of service, for example—or genuine honors bestowed by professional organizations embracing more than a single company.

Special Sections. Special sections are somewhat of a case apart, since their aim is frankly promotional. Even so, no editorial content will be devoted to a special section event unless participation in it is broad enough to give it general interest. And in *all* special sections, remember, the editorial content is as good—or as bad—as *we* make it. If it sounds like advertising, that's our fault.

Trade News. Strictly apart from the question of what is and what is not a legitimate business news story, there's the problem of whether to use commercial names of businesses or products in other news stories.

No pat rule is possible here. A good general guide is to use commercial names only when the story would be incomplete without them. You don't have to say, for instance, that thieves looted a Buick parked in front of the Wilmington Dry Goods; a car parked on Market Street would do. But if an elevator falls in a store, name the store; if a man jumped out of a hotel window, name the hotel.

There has been a tendency in our papers to go out of the way not only to describe a car as a compact car but to name the make as well. Only if the size of the car is an important element of the story is it necessary to designate it as a compact, and the make is almost never relevant. . . .

We will not use stories on the sale of individual homes unless historic interest or something similar makes them especially newsworthy. The sale of such a home or of commercial property should be reported immediately and not saved for the real estate pages. Prices are permissible if known.

Stories and photos on the real estate pages should be confined to developments or general trends instead of to individual homes for sale. That is, a picture of one home in a new development would be permissible, but we would want to avoid using a single home that's come on the market in an established neighborhood. Price ranges of homes in a development are permissible.

Let's be sure we don't use repeated pictures or stories on the same development and let's also avoid follow-up stories on crowd turnouts at individual developments and stick to general roundups on the state of the real estate market.

Several years ago, the Atlanta newspapers got together to draw up a statement as to how to reduce the "puff" evil to a minimum. In part, the agreement read as follows:

The following items are specific types or publicity which we will NOT carry in the future:

a. Fashion shows, cooking schools, garden schools or any similar promotion of any kind originated by or which has any commercial connection with any business.
b. Beauty specialists.
c. Pictures of salesmen or managers who change jobs or pictures of new members of organizations.
d. Pictures of buyers.
e. Pictures of either the exterior or interior of stores except in those cases which might be considered in the light of real estate news.
f. Interiors of buildings.
g. Special promotions such as the "Bell Ringers," "Hour Glass" teasers, etc.
h. Luncheons or store promotions.
i. Entertainment of prominent people by stores.
j. Receptions for authors in book departments.
k. Pictures of merchandise. It is understood that this not only includes retail but distributors' publicity; as, for example, pictures of distributors holding a can of beer, etc.
l. Pictures of grocery chain new members.
m. Santa Claus promotions.
n. Robots and trick automobiles disguised as locomotives, etc.
o. All promotions on the part of stores which feature the Junior League, the debutantes or other social celebrities.
p. All commercial promotions such as state fairs, carnivals, auto races, flower shows, etc. This does not apply to civic enterprises or those enterprises which are operated strictly for charity, as for example, Scottish Rite hospital, but it is understood that where publicity is given these promotions the names of no retail or commercial organizations are to be used.
q. Photograph contests, dancing schools, insurance stories, stories and pictures of used car lots.
r. Elimination of travel, resort publicity.
s. Any paid local ads simulating news matter must take the word "Advertisement" spelled out in 8-point black.
t. No automobile publicity will be carried in daily paper. All must go Sundays.
u. All special sections for advertisers cannot carry over 30 per cent publicity.

Special: Photographs of meetings of business organizations, which hold conventions in Atlanta; pictures will be used of men of prominence who attend. These will be run in one column cuts only.

Publicity on wrestling matches will be limited to 3 inches on week days and 3 inches on Sunday before the match, but story after the match will be based on news value as determined by sports department.

Advertisers should not be given preference over any other teams in soft ball leagues. No requests will come from business office on soft ball stories.

In addition, according to *Editor & Publisher*, unwritten understandings between news executives on the papers included, in substance, the following:

Mention of meeting places (such as restaurants and department stores) is to be considered part of the story in advance material, but not to be used in stories appearing following the event.

Stories about airlines, railroads, bus lines and other transportation services are "out," except in cases of change of regular schedules, when brief stories are permitted, or of revolutionary changes in services offered the public. (Air-conditioning not included in the latter category.)

No definite rule promulaged on bowling. The commercial angle, however, should be subordinated as much as possible and individuals rather than commercial teams played up.

In stories of skeet shooting events, names of powder companies, cartridge and shot gun manufacturers and hardware stores eliminated.

Stories about lectures, concerts, recitals, football and baseball games and other musical, educational and sports events shall not contain location of the place where tickets may be purchased, nor the price of tickets.

No publicity shall be given music or dancing teachers, except, perhaps, in the case of annual concerts.

Stories having to do with the arrival of athletic teams or so-called notables shall not mention the hotel at which they are stopping.

In stories about benefit dances by organizations, the name of the orchestra shall not be used, except in the rare cases when nationally-known orchestras are brought to the city.

Identification of persons in stories of all types to be eliminated as far as possible where identification mentions name of some commercial organization.

Brief stories about merchants' associations and similar business-promoting organizations excepted, provided commercial affiliation of members is eliminated.

In stories about changes in price of gasoline, names of all companies must be eliminated.

Stories about changes in law firms and changes of location are "out." Changes which affect the titles of prominent firms are approved, however.

Names of undertakers shall not be used in connection with ambulance calls to accident or crime scenes. Use of undertakers' names in death stories left to the individual editors, but the consensus is that names of funeral directors should be used prior to the funeral and not after it has been held.

The Wall Street Journal

Few newspapers interpret news as consistently and successfully as the *Wall Street Journal*. The national business daily's in-depth, analytical coverage has played a major role in its circulation climb to more than a million from 500,000 in 1958 and less than 250,000 in 1953.

Wall Street Journal stories are generally well reported, tersely written and highly accurate. Inside pages are crammed with spot news stories of corporate profits, mergers, proxy fights, the stock, bond and commodity markets, government actions affecting business and the like. Most such stories have a limited readership. The showcase for articles of broader interest is page one, where each day the *Journal* runs three painstakingly researched pieces. One, named an A-head after its headline, runs in column four. Usually 700 to 1,000 words, it deals with such topics as a new clothing fad, a civil rights development, a Madison Avenue trend. A-heads are less significant than the two other in-depth stories. These appear in columns one and six and are called leaders. Most leaders are 1,200 to 1,500 words, although a few run to 3,000. Nearly any topic of broad interest with a clear-cut theme is leader material: automobile sales, medical advances, taxes, overseas developments, law, education, space, war, Washington and even religion. Some topics that seem unrelated to business may affect business and businessmen indirectly. Businessmen are also consumers, and the *Journal* feels they should be interested in consumer-oriented stories. Most leaders pinpoint trends not yet widely reported. A few are exposés; muckraking stories won Pulitzer Prizes for three enterprising leader writers in a recent five-year period.

One of every ten or twelve leaders is a national roundup. It is put together by a rewriteman in New York from reports filed by bureaus around the country. From 50 pages of copy, the rewriteman must draw intelligent conclusions as to the significance of the reporters' findings, add pertinent background data and come up with a comprehensive, comprehensible five-page story. Roundups are mostly concerned with heavy economic topics, such as home building, capital spending, inventories, credit and advertising outlays.

The vast majority of leaders are conceived, reported and written by a single reporter. The *Wall Street Journal* reporter typically devotes half his time to inside spot news coverage and half to page-one stories.

A typical leader will take four to six weeks of such half-time effort—the equivalent of two to three weeks of fulltime effort. The completed leader, unless pegged to a news development, is allowed to mellow in the page-one editor's drawer in New York for another four to six weeks. Then it passes to a rewriteman. If the story is in good shape, he may merely sharpen the lead, rearrange some paragraphs, make some cuts, and ask the reporter for clarification or elaboration on a point or two. However, if the story is below grade, it will be bucked to the inside of the paper, returned to the reporter for more reporting and re-angling or killed outright. Casualties often result because a staffer, discovering part way through his reporting that the theme that had seemed strong when he started is really too weak to support a leader, decides to take a chance and finish the story, rather than abandon it in midstream and chalk up the misspent time to experience.

An increasingly popular leader topic is the company profile. Usually the company selected is a major factor in its industry or a maverick. The profile gives the reporter a chance to dig deeply into a company's operations and to assess its place in its industry. While most company profiles are friendly—it is difficult to report one without the company's cooperation—they mustn't be puff pieces. The surest way to avoid that is for the reporter to talk to as many people outside the company— competitors, customers, suppliers, former employees—as in it.

In profiling the *Reader's Digest*, a veteran *Wall Street Journal* reporter went through an elaborate warm-up before interviewing anyone at the magazine itself. First, he read what he could find on the *Digest*, including a 20-year-old profile in the *New Yorker*, a 15-year-old cover story in *Time*, more recent but less comprehensive articles in other magazines and newspapers, sections of a book on the history of American magazines and back issues of two house organs for *Digest* employees.

He had telephone interviews of five to fifty minutes each with seven advertising agency executives (on the *Digest's* advertising policies and practices), twelve editors and circulation and production experts on other magazines, four free-lance contributors to the *Digest*, two book club officials (on the *Digest* Condensed Book Club), two union officials (for their reaction to *Digest* labor coverage), a doctor (for his reaction to *Digest* medical coverage), a psychologist (for his opinion on the *Digest's* phenomenal appeal) and twelve other assorted sources. An ex-*Digest* editor talked off-the-record for three hours about his unhappy stay at Pleasantville.

The main benefit of these interviews was to deepen the reporter's knowledge of the *Digest* and sharpen the questions he would put to *Digest* people. He interviewed 17 *Digest* staffers by phone and 15 in person. One four-hour session with the two top editors wasn't interrupted even when lunch of cream cheese and jelly sandwiches arrived. Back at the *Journal,* the reporter spent two days sorting his voluminous notes and making an outline before touching the typewriter.

Wall Street Journal editors encourage reporters to outline a leader before writing it. Cataloging all points to be made helps assure that the principal points will appear high in the story, before the reader's interest flags. The outline helps the reporter pick the best quote, statistic or anecdote to support each point. It helps him decide what is least important and can be left out. It helps him avoid spiraling—covering the same ground twice in slightly different language.

The *Reader's Digest* profile, two months of half-time effort in preparation, ran a month later after being cut from 4,000 words to 3,000 on rewrite. Reaction at the *Digest* was mixed. Advertising and circulation executives liked it because it showed the magazine to be big and successful and still growing. The editors, stung by criticism of their sweetness-and-light and ultra-conservative approaches to many stories, and displeased by details on how they "plant" pieces in other magazines before "reprinting" them, were put out. Pleasing everyone all the time, the reporter consoled himself, is often incompatible with doing the job right.

Labor

The history of the American labor movement is as much that of a struggle of different ideologies for supremacy within the ranks of labor itself as it is that of a fight between capital and labor for a share of the national wealth and income. In its early stages, organized labor was handicapped because of its control by leaders of foreign birth or influence and by native born intellectuals who lacked experience as workers and were discredited further because of their known unorthodoxy in other fields.

In the middle half of the nineteenth century, labor was too prone to espouse every new economic or political theory that offered a possible step upward on the economic scale. Agrarianism, idealistic cooperative plans, greenbackism, the single tax, free silver and syndicalism were among the ideologies with sizable followings within the ranks of labor.

Until the American Federation of Labor emerged as powerful under the leadership of Samuel Gompers late in the nineteenth century, organized labor hardly was an important permanent factor in American economic and political life.

The A.F.L.'s triumph over the Knights of Labor represented a victory for the craft union as opposed to industrial unionism. Gompers and his followers believed in working within the existent capitalistic system, seeking through unions of craftsmen organized horizontally throughout industry as a whole, to obtain the maximum benefits for the workers. The Knights of Labor had admitted unskilled as well as skilled workers.

Craft unionism remained dominant until 1936, when, under the leadership of John L. Lewis, the Committee (later called Congress) for Industrial Organization began to organize many large basic industries, such as the mining, motor and steel industries, in which large masses of unskilled workers were not eligible for membership in craft unions. C.I.O. unions were industrial or vertical unions because membership in them was all-inclusive within a given plant in which there might conceivably be numerous craft unions.

In December 1955, the two big organizations reunited as the A.F.L.-C.I.O. but a decade later many old units of each, at all levels from international to local, still operated with virtually unchanged autonomy. Also, still independent were the railway brotherhoods and a number of other large groups, as the miners and teamsters and several mavericks which were expelled as left-wing by the C.I.O. in 1949.

Despite the comparative contemporary strength of the labor movement as a whole, not more than one-fourth of the entire labor force belong to unions. Little progress ever has been made among white-collar (professional) workers whose proportion of the total labor force continues to grow with the expanding service industries and as mechanical automation reduces the ranks of the blue-collar workers.

In the United States, with its rugged individualistic frontier tradition and its democratic open class social system, there never has developed strong class consciousness at any social or economic level. Despite considerable demagoguery to the contrary, socialistic and communistic ideas never have attracted any appreciable number of rank-and-file working people. There is no political labor party as in many other parts of the world, and organized political activity by labor always has been condemned by the rest of the populace. Because of the absence of class consciousness as a welding force, there has developed a strong type of labor leader in the United States. Whoever happens to be the leading labor figure at any time is bound to be considered a "public enemy" by antilaborites. Regardless of the justice involved, this has been true of such widely different labor leaders as Samuel Gompers, Eugene V. Debs, John L. Lewis, Sidney Hillman, Walter Reuther, James Petrillo, Harry Bridges and James Hoffa.

Because it never has enjoyed the confidence of an appreciable proportion of the American people, organized labor has been faced with the problem of avoiding mistakes which are more costly to it than similar ones are to any other segment of the population.

LABOR LAWS

The National Labor Relations (Wagner) act of 1935 was called labor's *magna charta* because it gave federal protection to the right to organize and bargain collectively and to maintain closed shops. It was mostly under its protection that the C.I.O. became established in the mass production industries, using the Gandhi-inspired sit-down strikes strategy. The Taft-Hartley act of 1947 and the Landrum-Griffin act of 1959 considerably weakened the basic law from the standpoint of labor. Among other things the former outlawed jurisdictional strikes (one union against another), secondary boycotts, strikes for union recognition and the closed shop except by majority vote of eligible employees. It also stipulated penalties for breaches of contract and boycotts by unions, forbade union contributions and expenditures for political purposes, forbade the services of the National Labor Relations board to unions which had not registered financial information and filed anti-communist affidavits for all its officers, allowed employers greater freedom to campaign against unionization of workers, gave the federal government the power to use injunctions to compel an eighty-day "cooling-off" period before a strike could be called.

The Labor-Management Reporting and Disclosures act (Landrum-Griffin) of 1959 was aimed at racketeering labor officials. Among other things it required annual reports from all unions, gave the F.B.I. power to enter cases of suspected violations, forbade "hot cargo" pacts in which a trucker, for example, refused to handle cargo from another trucker if the union labeled it forbidden, outlawed extortion or blackmail publicity, outlawed "sweetheart" contracts between unscrupulous employers and labor leaders and provided for secret ballots in union elections, machinery for ousting crooked union officials and a ban against arbitrary raising of union dues or assessments without a secret ballot vote of the members.

In the 1950s, several states adopted "right-to-work" laws. These were a misnomer for open shop as they guaranteed nobody a job and were intended to forbid closed union shops under any circumstance. In its behalf, organized labor increased agitation for the guaranteed annual wage, shorter work week and strengthening or recovery of old protections as maintenance of membership clauses, seniority rights, check-off systems for the collection of dues, pensions, longer vacations, profit sharing plans and the like.

COVERING LABOR

Important as all these other factors indisputably are, the basic issue involved in most contract disputes is wages. As in the case of business, there is no regular labor beat. The smart labor reporter notes in his futures book the dates of expirations of contracts between important unions and industries and, weeks or months in advance, starts interviewing both management and labor officials to determine what exactly will be at stake when the new contracts are up for negotiation.

Newspaper headlines naturally emphasize conflict, especially when it leads to strikes and lockouts. It is easy to overlook the fact that the overwhelming majority of labor-management affairs are conducted harmoniously and that there are numerous companies and even entire industries in which there has been little or no trouble for decades or longer. Labor leaders have traditionally charged that when matters do come to a point of conflict, the press underplays its side of the story. During the day-by-day account of a strike, the issues causing it often become lost because of the emphasis given incidents of violence, hotheaded statements by leaders and human interest accounts.

LABOR PROBLEMS

Understandable today is the contention that any major or protracted shutdown in any part of the American economy would be catastrophic throughout the entire economy, so interrelated have all parts of it become. How to preserve the dignity and freedom to work or not to work guaranteed all Americans in the Thirteenth amendment to the Constitution and at the same time protect the innocent masses from the repercussions of a strike or lockout is a major social and political issue.

Through its Mediation and Conciliation service, the federal government investigates and provides leadership in bringing about peaceful settlements of most disputes. During periods of comparatively full production and high prosperity, as during a Cold War with huge government expenditures to keep industry going, its successes far outnumber its failures. Organized labor has been a strong supporter of American foreign policy and local unions prod employers to be diligent in seeking good government contracts to maintain full employment. If such a condition continues, organized labor may be expected to devote more of its energy to worker education programs and to plans to assist workers to participate in community affairs.

Greatest obstacle to such activities continues to be the matter of racial integration. A.F.L. unions were discriminatory against Negroes and the unskilled foreign born. The C.I.O. forbade such discrimination, but unions must share with management the blame for the slowness with which Negroes and members of other minority groups obtain equal job opportunities, are upgraded and are given seniority rights, not to mention managerial positions.

STRESSING THE PUBLIC'S INTEREST

In covering many aspects of labor news, the reporter should consider the public interest as paramount.

Union Affairs

Aside from the same reader interest that exists regarding the activities of any large organization, in the cases of unions there is the additional public interest as regards their control and policies.

Policy Statements

Organized labor is a political force. Consequently, it is significant news when a large union or prominent labor leaders comment upon some current matter of widespread interest.

Management Agreements

In the field of labor, as in all others, it is conflict that attracts attention although, as in other fields, such as marital relations and law observance, strife is the exception rather than the rule. Nevertheless, changes in wages and hours and working conditions of thousands of employees affect a whole community.

With increases of $15,000 in appropriations ($10,000 from the city and $5,000 from the county), the Chattanooga Public Library has prepared a schedule of salary increases for its overworked staff.

In an administrative committee report to the board of trustees yesterday, Mrs. Griffin Martin, chairman, said, "The completion of a salary scale and scheme of service by the staff association (members of the library staff) and the adoption of this by the board of trustees is an outstanding accomplishment of the year."

The increases will leave the public library here below other comparable libraries in salaries, but the new scale is expected to help the library fill several vacancies for which competent librarians could not be secured at the salaries previously within the scope of the library budget....

[Chattanooga *Times*]

Higher retail meat prices faced housewives today as butcher shops prepared to hike pay for their workmen $10 a week.

The agreement providing for the pay increase, which is retroactive to Oct. 1, was accepted last night at a meeting of 4,000 members of the A.F.L. Amalgamated Meat Cutters and Butcher Workmen in Carmen's Hall.

The session was called by Emmet Kelly, international vice-president of the union and secretary-treasurer of the Chicago local....

[Chicago *Daily News*]

UNION DEMANDS

When management balks at union demands, a strike is always a potential threat. State and federal conciliators may step in to attempt mediation; one side may offer to arbitrate. In all such cases, the reporter should seek the versions of both union and management as to the issues: what the union asks and what management offers. This involves comparing the new conditions sought with existing ones. A résumé of the past history of relations between the particular company and the union may suggest the possibility of peaceful settlement in the current situation.

STRIKES

Unless it is a "wildcat," a strike is preceded by a strike vote of the membership. Maybe this vote may be taken long in advance of the actual walkout and may consist in authorizing the officers to use their own discretion. In states with "cooling off" periods it may be necessary to file notices of intention to strike weeks or months in advance. One result of such laws may be that a union keeps an industry under almost perpetual notice, as was the case frequently under the wartime Smith-Connally act.

After a strike begins, the reporter describes factually what happens: (1) how many members of what unions walk out, when and where; (2) what is the status of picketing—number engaged, location and activities; (3) police handling of the situation and comment by both union and management of the handling; (4) violence or threats of violence; (5) the effect upon the public because of curtailed production or services; and (6) efforts to settle the strike. A fair treatment of labor disputes requires constant contact with both sides and equal space to comments. Also, good reporting consists in frequent reminders as to the issues involved; that is, the union's demands and the company's counter proposals. Too often tempers become so inflamed that by the time a strike ends, nobody remembers what it was all about in the first place. The newspaper which never forgets that nobody, including the participants, really wants a strike, contributes toward peaceful settlement by not contributing to the incipient ill will.

By Don Stillman
Staff Reporter of The Wall Street Journal

Florence Nightingale all of a sudden is sounding like Samuel Gompers.

As a result, there are real crises at hospitals across the nation—from New York to San Francisco, and including such scattered places as Oak Ridge, Tenn., and Youngstown, Ohio. Some registered nurses are on strike right now. Nurses at 30 or more West Coast hospitals are scheduled to hand in their resignations Friday and walk out later this month if their demands aren't met. And nurses at scores of hospitals in other areas are confronting administrators with their stiffest demands ever; if these demands aren't met, say some of these groups, they, too, will quit.

The registered nurses have long wanted more money and better working conditions. Only recently, however, have they become militant. Some have elected to affiliate with established labor unions while others have organized on their own. At the same time, the American Nurses Association, a professional organization, is arming its members with economic data and bargaining techniques so they can make a strong showing in negotiations.

"We're on the front page and we're going to stay there until the public realizes that dogcatchers make more money than nurses," declares a gray-haired registered nurse from Evanston, Ill. "It's a revolution," says Ralph Hartley, chief negotiator for the California Nurses Association. "Nurses have been kicked around so long in every way that nobody ever dreamed they would do this."

Hitting When Foe Is Down

The nurses are hitting hospitals when they're down. There already are severe nursing shortages across the country. An estimated 21% of the budgeted positions for fulltime nurses in Federal hospitals are vacant. The nationwide shortage is so bad, say nurses, that it may be contributing to the death of some patients. One possible example: A doctor administered medication to a heart attack victim in the crowded emergency ward of a New York hospital, then left the ward's one registered nurse in charge. "By the time I got a chance to look at the patient again, he was dead," she recounts bitterly.

One new hospital in New York has had to delay opening many of its facilities because of a shortage of nurses, and a unit of Frankford Hospital in Philadelphia has been closed temporarily because it can't find nurses during the summer vacation period.

What's more, the nursing militancy has arrived concurrent with the start of medicare, which will require a sharp increase in the number of registered nurses. One Government estimate says 850,000 registered nurses will be needed by 1970, up from the 621,000 now practicing. Among other things, the Government-sponsored medical care for the aged allows persons 65 and over a total of 100 free annual visits at home by a registered nurse.

"But a patient can't receive 100 visits by a nurse if there aren't any nurses available to visit him," notes one nurse caustically.

What Should Be Done?

Hospital administrators are split on what to do about the new militancy. The current problem is "as much the hospital administrators' fault as the nurses'," says Mark Berke, administrator at San Francisco's Mt. Zion Hospital and president of the California Hospital Association. "If we don't want to see the nursing profession really unionized, we're going to have to sit down and really listen to what they are saying—to treat them as if they already were unionized."

Nursing has finally found its voice, says the director of nursing for one big hospital, but "like a child learning to climb steps, we're trying to get to the top too fast." George Wood, executive vice-president of Oakland's Peralta Hospital, says bluntly: "I don't think 'informational picketing' is ethical. It's an unhealthy trend that will damage the profession." In "informational picketing," being conducted at several hospitals, nurses don't strike but do picket the hospital with signs telling of "intolerable" working conditions.

Most administrators, however, agree with Martha Johnson, director of nursing for the American Hospital Association, who says, "I don't know of a single hospital administrator who wouldn't pay his nurses more if he could." ... [*Wall Street Journal*]

Agriculture

An area of potential news which is generally neglected by city daily newspapers is the rural, farm or agricultural sector. Generally such papers rely on the press associations to cover Washington and state capitol developments regarding farm legislation. Some press releases from agricultural organizations are rewritten to stress local angles and, especially in smaller places, columns written by local county agents are sometimes run. By comparison with the treatment given business and/or labor, this coverage is meager.

A NEGLECTED FIELD

Secretary of Agriculture Orville Freeman has charged that the press is neglecting its responsibility by ignoring changes that have occurred in farming. "Too many of the daily papers," he told farm magazine writers, "run farm news as if it were a running battle between farmers and the secretary of agriculture or between farmers and town people—or between farmers themselves."

Most newspapers which formerly gave greater coverage to farm news have long since ceased the attempt to instruct farmers in how to farm, leaving that area to the farm magazines. Commenting on Freeman's criticism, B. B. Watson, farm editor of the Hannibal (Mo.) *Courier-Post*, emphasized a "conflict of objectives" as follows: "Farm news as such is primarily local or at least regional in character, is pedantic, repetitious, highly compartmentalized and is seldom productive of advertising revenues in proportion to other elements in the news."

Other editors explain that agricultural news is slanted to interest the public as a whole. As Stanley Lantz, farm editor of the Bloomington (Ill.) *Pantagraph*, puts it, it is "not written in 'farmer talk' to the mythical man in the overalls and straw hat."

That such a man is mythical is seen in the statistics regarding changes in rural America since the country's origin. Whereas in colonial days 90 per cent of the population was rural, today about 10 per cent is. American farm units reached their all-time peak of 6,800,000 in 1935. In the mid-'60s there were only about 3,500,000 units, and approximately half of them were marginal and not needed to supply the nation's food supply.

POLITICAL POWER

Several recent United States Supreme Court decisions cannot help but cause greater changes in the rural-urban balance of political power. States have had to reapportion congressional and legislative districts in accordance with the equal representation rule: one voter, one vote. Previously, through gerrymandering and refusal of the rural-dominated legislatures to reapportion, the farm areas were represented way out of proportion to their population strength. For instance, a Georgia farmer's vote was 62 times more effective than that of a Georgia city man. A typical situation existed in Michigan where an upper peninsula congressman represented 177,431 persons whereas a Detroit congressman spoke for 802,994.

Logrolling by members of the Farm Bloc, representative of noncompetitive agricultural interests as cotton and cattle, wheat and vegetables, no longer will be so effective with total rural representation reduced. Cities should find it easier to obtain needed laws from state legislatures and possibly be able to rely less heavily on Washington. The effort of the farm lobbies should diminish. The Big Three of such lobbies are: the American Farm Bureau of over one million members, generally sympathetic to the larger and wealthier farm owners; the National Farmers Union with about 100,000 members, a gadfly New Deal-born organization of small and independent farmers; and the National Grange, whose 700,000 members regard it mostly as a social group instead of as a militant political force as it was when it began shortly after the Civil War.

FEDERAL POLICY

Today's federal agricultural policy is still substantially the same as that established in early New Deal days by Henry A. Wallace and associates. The essential feature is to keep farm income high by payments to farmers for participation in the Soil Conservation program whereby part of their acreage is kept idle and by loans through the Commodity Credit Corporation secured by products which can be forfeited in case the market price stays low.

These and similar efforts are geared to what is called parity, the relationship between the well-being of the farmer and nonfarm population using the period 1910–1914 as the base. Devised years ago by the American Farm Bureau, it has been called a statistical monstrocity, and the Bureau in recent years has favored reduction or elimination of federal farm supports. The small independent farmers, however, insist that the present policy is necessary for their continued existence, even though the large corporate farms admittedly benefit more from it and do not need it to survive.

Critics of the present policy correctly point out that it is handicapped in achieving its aims because it still is based on acreage rather than productivity. Today an hour of farm labor produces five times as much as was true a generation ago and crop production by acres is up about 75 per cent. All of this has been accomplished by the technological revolution which began in the late nineteenth century with the threshing machine, reaper and similar machines and by the experimental work of the land grant agricultural colleges which have made higher education an essential for farming today. Contemporary farming is Big Business and expensive. The family farm is becoming obsolete.

Today more workers are engaged in transporting, processing and selling food than are engaged in producing it, and the farmer receives only about 35 cents of every dollar that the housewife spends in the grocery store.

A typical interpretative news summary for "city slickers" is the following:

By Tom Littlewood
Sun-Times Bureau

Washington—A recent government study has pointed up the "inordinately high" costs of distribution as the chief factor behind rising bread prices.

Bread prices went up two cents a loaf this week in Chicago.

The national commission on food marketing reported that the price of bread has about doubled since 1947. During that period, however, the price received by farmers for the wheat that went into the bread stayed about the same. The farm value of wheat in a loaf of bread is now about 12 per cent of the retail price.

Distribution Costly

Distribution of bread is inordinately costly, the commission report stated, because of small-lot deliveries and shelf-stocking by bakery driver-salesmen.

In the last decade, bakers' costs shifted significantly, it was emphasized.

Costs of selling and distribution went up by more than one-third—far more than other cost increases.

Ingredient costs remained about the same. Manufacturing costs rose 17 per cent. All but 15 per cent of a 40 per cent increase in hourly wage rates were offset by higher labor productivity.

"Moving the bread from the bakers' platform to the consumer in a retail store costs almost as much," the commission said, "as it does to grow the wheat, mill the flour, and bake the bread."

Almost Double

"A loaf of bread that costs 11 cents at the baker's dock sells for around 20 cents in the retail store.

"It is not unusual for five or six different wholesale bakeries to deliver to a supermarket each day and for the driver-salesmen to stock the shelves and remove the stale items. This duplication of service contributes to high delivery costs."

Wholesale bakers' profits as a percentage of sales have been cut almost in half since 1947, the commission reported.

The rate of increase in bread prices will be stemmed, said the report, only when efficient mass production and distribution techniques replace outmoded methods. The commission said driver-salesmen have tried to cling to the conventional selling commission of 7 per cent or more of the wholesale price.

A year ago, bakers and other wheat processors engaged in a massive lobbying campaign to defeat the administration's proposed "bread tax." That was an effort to shift part of the cost of subsidizing wheat prices for the farmer from the federal Treasury to the processors. The millers and bakers prevented the shift by warning that higher bread prices would result. [Chicago *Sun-Times*]

19

Religion, Science

I RELIGION
1. Promoting Understanding
2. Church and Politics
3. Religious Group Pressures
4. Religious Controversy
5. Correct Nomenclature

II SCIENCE
1. Changing Attitudes
2. Space Age Glossary
3. The Newspaper's Responsibility
   a. *Don'ts for Writers*
   b. *Hints for Editors*
   c. *Some Ethical Problems*
4. Reaching the Reader
   a. *Elements of Interest*
   b. *Humanizing the Copy*

A REGULAR FRIDAY OR SATURDAY FEATURE IN MOST NEWSPAPERS IS A column or page of church notices, listing the times of Sunday services and possibly sermon subjects and announcements of meetings of church organizations throughout the week. Special events, such as installation of a new pastor or dedication of a new building, are written up on either the church page or in the regular news sections, often with pictures. Meetings of missionary societies, weekday Bible classes and similar activities receive attention on club pages or in other parts of the paper.

Religion

Handling all of this routine church news is time-consuming and easy to the extent that church authorities cooperate in preparing material adequately and on time. Personal acquaintanceships between reporter and news sources are important so that ill will does not result from mistaken ideas regarding deadlines and space limitations.

Covering all of the sermons delivered any Sunday in any place of any size is impossible. Some papers ignore them all. Others "take turns," reporting a minimum but different sample each week. Still others run "A Reporter Goes to Church" piece written by a staff member who attends a different church each week. Sometimes these pieces are more than accounts of particular services and include historical background regarding the church and possibly an explanation of the major tenets of the denomination. Always, however, great care is taken not to offend, to explain dogma and ritual sympathetically from the standpoint of the believer.

PROMOTING UNDERSTANDING

This practice accentuates the fact that religious controversy is mostly a hush-hush matter, journalistically as well as among friends. As Gustavus A. Myers details in *A History of Bigotry*, religious intolerance has been severe throughout American history, with virtually every one of the 260-plus denominations which exist in this country having suffered from some sort of discrimination at one time or another. On the whole, however, freedom of religion and separation of church and state, as guaranteed by the Constitution, have worked well for almost two centuries and nobody, least of all the press, wants to stir up trouble.

Most people know little about religions other than their own. Helping them understand the faith of others, however, never has been considered to be a function of periodical journalism. About the only occasion on which this rule is broken is on a religious holiday.

By Edward H. Eulenberg

Symbolism at many levels attends the celebration of Passover, the Jewish holiday that will begin at sunset next Friday.

Some of the symbols are visible, touched, and tasted—the matzoth, bitter herbs, and red wine.

Others are in the spoken word in home and synagog services.

Some are expressed, others implied, denoting a tie with the past, reponsibility to the future, regeneration, hope.

Though the eight-day holiday is marked by synagog services on the first two and last two days, the central service is the seder (pronounced sayder) held in Jewish homes on the first two nights.

(Only seven days and a first-night seder are observed by Reform Judaism and by Jews in Israel.)

The holiday and its services are based on the Biblical story (in Exodus) of the Israelites' liberation from Egyptian slavery.

The seder, often with two or three generations of a family present, portrays much of the symbolism.

The service starts with blessing of the wine—traditionally red—the first of four cups served during the seder in commemoration of God's four promises of freedom to Israel.

A fifth cup of wine—to which no lips are touched—is set on the table. This is dedicated to Israel's most beloved prophet, Elijah, who according to legend will herald the Messiah—symbol of hope for a world of peace and righteousness.

Other visible symbols, displayed on an ornamented tray, are explained. Some are tasted.

These include the roasted lamb's shankbone (symbol of the paschal lamb); vegetable greens (symbols of the holiday's origin in an earlier spring festival); and bitter herbs (recalling the bitterness of slavery).

Best known is the matzoth, or unleavened bread (recalling the hastily baked bread prepared by the Israelites as they fled into the desert).

Matzoth are eaten during the entire Passover period, instead of bread.

The youngest member of the household prompts recital of the Passover story by asking the four questions—starting, "Why is this night different from all other nights?"

In response, the story is read from the Haggadah (the book of the seder service).

The narrative fulfills the commandment of Exodus that "in every generation it is man's duty to regard himself as if he had gone forth from Egypt," and for every man to "tell his son" the story.

Thus is symbolized the sweep of history that links every Jew to his past and obligates him to transmit his heritage to future generations.

At the final synagog service, renewal of life is represented in the reading of the Song of Songs with its hopeful note:

"For lo, the winter is past; the rain is over and gone; the flowers appear on the earth...."

This Biblical book is still as well-beloved as when the revered Rabbi Akiba, centuries ago, called it the "holy of holies" of the holy writings.

[Chicago *Daily News*]

The expertise needed by a religious journalist was stressed by Sanche de Gramont in an article, "Covering the Ecumenical Council," in the September 1965 *Nieman Reports*:

The reporter must penetrate the mechanism of the council, learn its vocabulary, be alive to the significance of an apparently trivial event such as a change in the order of seating (at first, the patriarchs were seated after the cardinals, then, across from the cardinals, to make it clear that in rank they were not less than the cardinals, a clarification of Vatican policy), and build up sources who can fill in the omissions in the daily communique. The historian must consider the day's story in terms of church evolution. A vote allowing married men to become deacons seems pointless unless one knows what the Catholic position on ecclesiastical celibacy has been over the centuries. The much abused term "collegiality" is meaningless outside the context of papal infallibility voted at the First Vatican Council in 1870. The theologian must consider collegiality in terms of the apostolic succession, that is Christ's passing on the succession of his church to Peter and the apostles. He must also reconcile the Pope's supreme and total authority with the powers handed down to the bishops. The prophet must evaluate the impact of collegiality on the church, and show how the existing institutions will be modified when the bishops' share in the government of the church is defined.

CHURCH AND POLITICS

As any political or journalistic insider knows, religious peace is more apparent—because of the hush-hush policy—than real. For more than a century, religious controversy was at a minimum because the United States was predominantly a Protestant nation. Split into 267 sects, Protestants could proselyte each other but, except for the Know Nothings just before the Civil War and the Ku Klux Klan immediately afterwards, few felt great alarm over Roman Catholicism. In the mid-twentieth century, however, there is visible evidence of the extent to which the two major divisions of Christianity are pulling even. Church statistics of all sorts are extremely unreliable, because of different methods of counting communicants. The best available indicates that between the two campaigns, 1928 and 1960, in which Catholics were nominees for the presidency, the American Roman Catholic population increased from 19,000,000 to 40,000,000. In most large cities today, Catholic parochial school attendance almost equals that in public schools and the religious affiliations of candidates for public office are considered important by political parties.

Because the Republicans were entrenched among the upper economic classes, during the second half of the nineteenth century, the Democrats made strong appeals to the immigrants who came in waves and settled in the large urban centers to do the most menial work. The social welfare services, developed by Tammany Hall in New York and by other urban Democratic organizations, resulted in the recruitment of most of these new citizens into the Democratic party. They were predominantly from southern Europe and were Roman Catholics. Today, their grandchildren run the city governments of virtually every large city in the United States, although the exodus of the older white elements to the suburbs is increasing the importance of the urban Negro voter. The relationship that exists between parishioners and their church is suggested by the appellation usually given the local

Catholic archdiocese office. It is Powerhouse, and its opposition to any important public issue jeopardizes its success. Public health commissioners do well to clear promotional matter related to venereal diseases, birth control and some other matters so as not to risk public chastisement. The hierarchy is concerned over assignment of judges to such courts as Juvenile, Divorce, Domestic Relations and Family, and with the attitudes of social welfare workers, hospital administrators and the like.

RELIGIOUS GROUP PRESSURES

At all levels of government, the activities of religious groups interested in censoring motion pictures, plays, magazines, books and the like are opposed by civil libertarians, most strongly represented by the American Civil Liberties Union. A generation ago it was Protestant groups which were most active, censoring books in Boston and fostering laws forbidding the teaching of Darwinism in the South. Today, Catholic groups, as the Legion of Decency and the National Organization for Decent Literature, bring pressure on motion picture theaters, libraries and bookstores and advocate the establishment of official censorship boards. The revival of Sunday blue laws, forbidding certain commercial operations, as the sale of used automobiles, is more economic than religious in origin. Such groups as the Jews and Seventh Day Adventists, however, are in opposition for religious reasons.

The schools probably are the battleground for more religious controversies than any other institution. In the late forties the United States Supreme Court ruled that school properties cannot be used for religious instruction but that so-called released-time programs, whereby children are excused from school to go elsewhere for religious instruction, are legal. Originally supported by Protestants who feared the effect of the decline in Sunday School attendance, released-time programs now are also approved by Catholics, especially in areas where there are no parochial schools. Jews are unalterably opposed. Still to be tested in the United States Supreme Court are shared-time programs whereby parochial school students take some of their work in public schools.

Although the state and federal governments already contribute considerable sums to local boards of education, through such programs as those which provide hot lunches and through the National Defense act and similar legislation, "federal aid to education" is a controversial phrase whenever a bill is before Congress to provide large-scale federal expenditures for school building construction, teachers' salaries or other services. Catholics oppose such federal aid unless it is provided parochial as well as public schools and have succeeded in blocking several proposals, even when they were endorsed by the nation's first Roman Catholic president. Catholics argue that free transportation for parochial school students and similar benefits are proper governmental expenditures as they are made to benefit children rather than churches. Under President Johnson's War on Poverty programs such grants have multiplied but not without protest from such organizations as Protestants and Other Americans United for Separation of Church and State. That group also is attacking sales or gifts of public property to religious institutions and much tax exemption of church-owned property, especially that not used for strictly religious purposes.

United States Supreme Court decisions outlawing a New York Regents Prayer and compulsory Bible reading in public schools have been followed by attempts, so far unsuccessful, to amend the United States Constitution to permit such practices.

Other controversial matters which may have local angles include compulsory flag salutes or other patriotic exercises to which Jehovah's Witnesses and others may object; vaccination and other health requirements repulsive to Christian Scientists; what religious emphasis should be given to Christmas programs, so as not to offend Jews; the propriety of Catholics' serving on public school boards; inspection of the quality of education in parochial schools; and the like. Most editors would prefer to ignore them, but such is difficult to do when large groups rally, parade, petition and go to court. In such cases, the only choice is to "bring it all into the open" where it is going to have to be decided ultimately.

RELIGIOUS CONTROVERSY

No matter how hard-boiled they may be otherwise, editors and reporters handle both church and religious news reverently. To do the opposite doubtless would be to commit commercial suicide. Nevertheless, many newspapers run daily horoscopes despite the protest of those who say astrology, in addition to being made obsolete by astronomy, involves fatalistic concepts inimical to religious ideas of free will and individual responsibility. Some papers also like to play up claims of visions, revelations and apparently miraculous escapes. Journalistic critics assert that when someone says that the "Man Upstairs" heard his prayers and was responsible for his escape from death, the implication is that others who prayed in vain deserved the fate that befell them and is a blasphemous assumption. Nevertheless, some newspapers feature such claims and may be prone to inquire of anyone who confronts disaster or experiences sorrow whether he or others involved had premonitions. Superstition may be perpetuated by the treatment given Friday the 13th, Ground Hog day and similar occasions. A frequent problem is how to handle the remarks of a public speaker who insists that God is on his side and condemns others as irreligious, sacrilegious or atheistic. So many prominent men of affairs take this line that it is difficult to edit their remarks to delete all such unfounded, unfair and unprovable expressions.

Since Paul Blanshard's *Catholic Power and American Freedom* appeared in 1949 and the Vatican became more vocal in international affairs, the convictions of many who are concerned over possible serious religious strife in America perhaps have deepened, even though the majority remain indifferent. In that year, the American Catholic Trade Union movement was mainly responsible for a purge of left-wing unions in the Congress of Industrial Organizations and President Truman had to accede to Protestant protest and abandon plans to name an ambassador to the Vatican. During the '50s, as usually happens during a period of insecurity following war or depression, there was a wave of revivalism, led by Billy Graham, and church attendance boomed. Protestants and Other Americans United for separation of Church and State also increased in membership and activity, and the National Conference of Christians and Jews did little more than persuade some white congregations to listen to Negro preachers during annual Brotherhood Week. Any lessening of anti-Catholicism in the United States probably resulted from the outspoken opposition of the Vatican to the spread of Communism, despite the fact that outside the Soviet Union—in such nations as Italy, Hungary and Poland—the majority of Communists were also Catholics. During this period the American Catholic Church became the principal financial support of worldwide Catholic missionary efforts and contributed heavily to other causes operated from headquarters in Rome. In all this, many fundamentalist Protestants and others saw cause for alarm. Newspapers in general leave it for magazine and book authors to discuss the ideological issues involved.

Then came John F. Kennedy, the first Catholic president, who contributed a great deal to the destruction of the fears of rabid anti-Catholics. More important, then also came Pope John XXIII, and the "breath of fresh air" which he frequently let into the church meant considerable liberalization of Roman Catholic practices. One visible effect was greater participation by priests and nuns in civic affairs, notably the civil rights and peace movements. Catholic leaders became much more outspoken on public affairs, often in defiance of their immediate superiors. Such behavior destroyed a great deal of the fears of those who thought that the Church of Rome is a monolithic and authoritarian institution. The Vatican Council II, the visits of Pope Paul VI to New York and of the Archbishop of Canterbury to Rome furthered the cause of ecumenism.

Holidays, such as Christmas, Easter and Thanksgiving, provide opportunity for writing which catches the religious atmosphere without revealing denominational basis. Such stories emphasize the attendance at commemorative ceremonies, the extent and nature of charitable activities, possibly extracts from sermons or statements by church leaders, anecdotes of moral or ethical behavior, specific incidents to promote peace and/or good will among men.

CORRECT NOMENCLATURE

When he was religious news editor of the Nashville *Tennessean*, the Rev. James W. Carty Jr., professor of journalism at Bethany (W. Va.) College, prepared the following warning:

> Incorrect use of titles in the reporting of church news discourages reader interest, but correct use helps build confidence in the reliability of the news, feature and interpretative articles.
>
> In fact, the wrong designations can draw some hot protests. The appropriate bring grateful letters or phone calls.
>
> A reporter has to be cautious lest he use the wrong synonym for the sake of variety.
>
> An example concerns the different designations for the spiritual heads of the church. Many terms are available. They include the Reverend, Rabbi, priest, minister, pastor, evangelist clergyman, father, brother. Actually, these concepts have different meanings. Some are interchangeable with different denominations; others are not.
>
> A Catholic priest would be called the Reverend or Father and lives in the rectory. A Monsignor is the Rt. Rev.; a bishop, the Most Reverend; a nun, Sister.
>
> Christian Science has practitioners, lecturers, readers. A title would be Reader John Jones.

The words reverend, pastor, doctor, or clergyman would not be used for the Church of Christ minister or evangelist. Two other correct terms for addressing them are preacher or brother.

An Episcopal clergyman, a deacon or priest, would be called the Reverend, and lives in the rectory. A dean is the Very Reverend. A bishop is the Right Reverend; an archbishop, of which there are none in the United States, would be called the Most Reverend.

A Jewish clergyman would be called Rabbi or Doctor if he holds that degree.

The Lutheran designation would be Pastor John Jones or the Reverend.

A Methodist pastor, minister or preacher also would be called the Reverend. The episcopal head is Bishop John Jones, never the Right or Most Reverend.

Seventh-day Adventist pastors are addressed as Elder.

Presbyterian ministers also are called the Reverend Mister. Their residence is the manse.

Groups also are concerned about their title. Most resent being called a sect.

America's two largest indigenous groups, the Christian Church (Disciples of Christ) and Church of Christ do not want to be called denominations. They prefer brotherhood or religious movement.

Other groups are careful about stating the power of conventions. For example, Southern Baptists and Christian churches (Disciples of Christ) are careful to point out that the convention resolutions are not binding on congregations, which are autonomous. Both groups use the title the Reverend for pastors, preachers, ministers.

And editors, remember also not to displease women. Don't call their presbyterial a presbytery.

Science

As the awful power of science to make the planet uninhabitable became apparent, the absolute necessity for everyone's understanding something of the implications of scientific progress (?) became recognized.

Even before the atom bomb and sputniks, newspapers had awakened to their social responsibility as regards science. The remarkable improvement, in completeness of coverage, in accuracy and clarity of writing and, in general, social purpose followed years of misunderstanding and consequent inadequate cooperation between scientific writers and scientists. Out of the name-calling came a mutual decision to "get together" in a common program to protect the public against false science and to assist it in obtaining the maximum benefit from what the experimental laboratories and the scholars' studies are revealing daily, almost hourly.

CHANGING ATTITUDES

The change in emphasis from the spectacular in science to the practical was inevitable in an age in which the average man tinkers with his radio, automobile and household electrical equipment, takes motion pictures, dreams of owning his own airplane and uses scientific language unknown to his grandfathers.

Professor Hillier Krieghbaum, of the Department of Journalism at New York University, has said:

> The public reads science news and wants more. A survey for the National Association of Science Writers and New York University, financed by the Rockefeller Foundation, dramatically demonstrated this recently. This survey of 1,919 American adults, conducted by the Survey Research Center at the University of Michigan in the spring of 1957, showed that 37 per cent of the respondents read *all* of the newspaper items dealing with medical news and 28 per cent read *all* of the nonmedical science news stories. This is an over-all average of one out of every three adults reading *all* the science news that gets into print.

On the other hand, Dr. Frank Fremont-Smith, of the Josiah Macy Jr. Foundation, expressed the views of a growing number of scientists as follows:

> It seems to me that the medical profession, the universities and hospitals have ignored too long the fact that they can be successful only with genuine public support and they are going to get genuine public support only if their story, their very dramatic and thrilling story, is appropriately told to the public. There is no better group to tell this to the public in terms that the public can understand—because, God knows, we cannot make ourselves understood to the public—than the intelligent, thoughtful science writers.

SPACE AGE GLOSSARY

One paper, the Atlanta *Journal* used this United Press International piece under the heading, "Fallout of Words Follows Orbiting":

> Washington, March 7 (UPI)—The bird, fueled by lox, roared off its pad at Mach 4. At T plus four, the astronaut began to fly by wire but by the time it reached the Van Allen radiation belt, the bird's sun-seeker took over and directed it toward the moon.
>
> A passage from some weird new "Alice in Wonderland"? Not at all. It's a sample of the massive fallout of strange words resulting from man's conquest of space and the rockets he uses to get him there.

Translated it means:

The rocket, fueled by liquid oxygen, took off from its launching site at four times the speed of sound. Four minutes later, the space pilot took manual control. By the time the vehicle reached a belt of high-energy particles trapped by earth's magnetic field, a navigation device keyed to the sun assumed control and steered the rocket toward the moon.

All of this has been a bonanza for the word experts. They have come up with a variety of glossaries. Most are being published by the government or scientific societies for the benefit of persons working in space or related fields.

Ablation—Melting of nose cone materials during reentry of a spacecraft into the earth's atmosphere.

Abort—Failure of a space vehicle to accomplish its purposes for any reason other than enemy action.

Aeropause—An upper region of the atmosphere in which the air ceases to function for manned or unmanned flight.

Agravic—Weightlessness.

Apogee—The point or position at which a satellite in its orbit is farthest from the earth.

Barber Chair—An adjustable seat that can quickly position the occupant to increase his tolerance to high acceleration.

Beta Rays—Electrons given off by radioactive atoms.

Ferret—A vehicle equipped for detection, location, recording and analyzing electromagnetic radiation.

Hot Configuration—A test missile equipped and ready for firing.

Moon—A man-made satellite.

Node—Either of two points at which an orbiting body intersects the orbit of the earth.

Pad Deluge—Water sprayed on launch pads during launch to reduce temperatures.

Perigee—The point at which a satellite in orbit is closest to earth.

Rad—A unit of an absorbed dose of radiation. It amounts to 100 ergs of energy per gram of the affected material.

Scrub—To cancel a scheduled test firing.

Silo—A missile shelter consisting of a hardened vertical hole in the ground with facilities for launching.

Spatiography—The geography of space.

Terrella—A self-contained, manned spaceship in which crew life is maintained during flight by a close-cycle breathing system.

X—Symbol for experimental.

Y—Symbol for prototype.

By assigning to scientific news, men with sufficient training to talk the language of those whom they must interview, newspapers have broken down much of the reluctance of inventors, medical men and theoretical scientists to give information to the press. Whatever hesitancy to cooperate remains results from several factors: fear of being considered a publicity seeker, fear of revealing the nature of an experiment before absolute proof has been obtained, a feeling that one's fellow scientists deserve to hear of a new scientific fact or theory for the first time at a learned gathering, fear of being misquoted, doubt of the reporter's ability to translate a technical matter into popular terms, fear that improper emphasis will be given to sensational, unimportant aspects of a news item.

On the other hand, partly through the pressure of well-intentioned journalists, many leading scientists have come to realize the value to them of sharing their findings with the public, of their social obligation to do so, and of the sincerity of a vast majority of present-day newspapermen in attempting to do a completely honest and creditable job. Scientists and writers cooperate to combat "quacks."

The two leading press associations and most large newspapers today have science editors. Several of them were among the few who knew the real nature of the "Manhattan Project" before the atom bomb tests in New Mexico. Not only did they keep the great confidence placed in them, but they also produced an amazing amount of brilliant writing which made it possible for the ordinary newspaper reader to understand fission, isotopes, electrons, plutonium and many other terms which he considered recondite or boresome when encountered in classes at school. The newspaper handling given atomic energy, radar, space exploration and other recent scientific topics makes it difficult to recall that newspapers of the past virtually ignored Robert Fulton, Samuel F. B. Morse, Charles Darwin and the Wright brothers.

Professor Krieghbaum reports:

> A poll of several hundred newspaper editors a year ago, on the first anniversary of Sputnik I, showed that three editors out of every four reported their dailies were giving at least half again as much space to science developments as before the Russians launched their first satellite. Almost half of this group indicated that their papers were using twice as much space. Not a single editor reported that his daily was using less space for science news during the first year of the Space Age.

THE NEWSPAPER'S RESPONSIBILITY

In the stories of sufferers from virulent diseases who have been given pathetic false hope because of premature announcements of new cures, of lives and fortunes which have been lost because of misplaced confidence in inventions, and of persecution and injustice resulting from unscientific superstition, are implied the social responsibility of the newspaper as regards scientific news. Likewise, for that matter, is implied the duty that the reputable scientist has not only to maintain proper caution himself but to discipline his fellows as well.

The rise of science, since primitive man thought the sun was alive, moving across the sky each day, and attempted to cajole the unseen forces to his own gain, has been one of overcoming the obstacles which ignorance and tradition have put in the way of knowledge. The present, however, truly is a scientific age and a major theory or discovery in any branch of science may have tremendous effect upon man's way of living and his manner of thinking.

Don'ts For Writers

To the late Dr. Edwin E. Slosson, first director of Science Service, a news agency dealing only in scientific news, goes much of the credit for having made American newspapers scientific-minded. The following are extracts from a list of "Donts for Would-Be Writers of Scientific Articles for the Public Press" compiled by Dr. Slosson. They emphasize the newspaper's responsibility:

> Don't overestimate the reader's knowledge and don't underestimate the reader's intelligence. He may not know as much as you about this particular thing—let's hope not anyway—but otherwise he may be as bright as you are—let's hope so anyway.
>
> Don't try to tell all you know in 500 words. Leave some over for another time. The clean plate rule does not apply here.
>
> Don't think that because a thing is old to you it is known to the public. Many of your readers are still living in the nineteenth century; some of them in the eighteenth. Anything new to your readers is "news" to them if hung on a timely peg.
>
> Don't leave out the human interest. Your reader is a human being even if you are only a scientist.
>
> Don't forget that your reader is interrupting you every ten lines to ask, "Why?" "What for?" or "Well, what of it?" and if you don't answer his tacit questions he will soon stop reading. . . .
>
> Don't say "this discovery is interesting" unless you can prove that it is, and if you can prove it, you don't have to say it. . . .
>
> Don't define a hard word by a harder word. Vladivostock is a hard word, but when a press correspondent arrives at Vladivostock he goes right on inland without stopping to explain that "this is a city south of Khabarovsk and east of Tsitsikhar." So, if you want to say "calorie," say it, but don't make it worse by "explaining" it as "the quantity of heat

necessary to effect a rise of temperature of one degree Centigrade of a cube of water each dimension of which is one tenth part of the length of a bar of platinum and iridium alloy lying in the observatory of St. Cloud." If you think you must define the calorie say casually something like this, that 100 calories of energy can be derived from three cubes of sugar or from a small pat of butter, or explain that a man needs to expend 100 calories an hour to keep his body running, and 160 calories if he is working hard.

Don't think you must leave out all the technical terms. Use them whenever necessary without apology, and if possible without formal definition. People are not so easily scared by strange words as you may think. They rather like 'em. . . .

When the Great War broke out everybody had to learn a new language for which there was no dictionary. But the war correspondent wrote without hesitation: "At zero hour, the barrage was raised and the poilu and the doughboy sprang over the top, sticking their bayonets into the boche." And the man in the street read it without batting an eye, although the sentence contained a half-dozen words not to be found in his vocabulary before. But if this sentence were being written by one of our conscientious scientists he would word it in this fashion:

"At zero hour—to use the military term for the time set for the beginning of an offensive—the barrage—that is to say the line on which the artillery fire is directed—was raised and the poilu—this is a French slang term for soldier, meaning 'hairy' and corresponding to our 'rough-neck'—and the doughboy, this is an American slang term for infantryman derived from the round buttons worn in the Civil War or the 'dobe' huts inhabited in the Mexican War or the pipe-clayed belts of the Revolutionary War or because the secretary of war was named Baker—sprang over the top—that is to say surmounted the parapet of the entrenchments—sticking their bayonets—a weapon invented at Bayonne, France, in 1650 —into the boche—a contemptuous term referring to the Germans, probably an abbreviation of *caboche* or *blockhead* originally applied to Alsatians."

HINTS FOR EDITORS

Watson Davis, successor to Dr. Slosson, has compiled a list of "Stories to Be Careful Of." It follows, together with Dr. Davis' introductory paragraph:

> Stories on this list should, in general, *not* be used, at least until they are thoroughly checked and investigated by several competent specialists in the subject. These are not forbidden stories for some of the impossible things of today may become possible tomorrow, but scientific discoveries rarely come nowadays from accident or inspiration. They are usually the result of systematic research of many investigators.

General

Any "secret" scientific or technical process.

Any process or preparation, where the essential element is not disclosed, bearing a coined name.

Announcement of the sudden achievement of "what scientists have long sought for in vain," and rediscoveries of "lost arts."

Complaints of "a conspiracy of silence" against the inventor or other evidence of a persecution complex.

Sweeping claims of any sort.

"Supernatural" Stuff

Telepathy and mind reading.

Spirit manifestations of any sort.

Long range weather forecasts in general.

Long range weather forecasts based on animal habits.

Astrologists and horoscopes.

End of the world predictions for the near future.

Evil or beneficial influence of the number 13.

Evil or beneficial influence of the number 7.

Evil or beneficial influence of any number.

Stars affecting human events or destinies.

Phrenology.

Numerology.

Predictions based on lines of hand, shape of nose or bumps on head.

Intelligence or character reading based on size and shape of features, handwriting or hands.

Charms, amulets, lucky coins and other such survivals of savagery.

Rediscoveries of lost prophetic books.

Animals that "think," "read minds," etc.

Medical

Universal germ killers.

Any absolute cure of any disease.

Unauthenticated treatments of cancer, tuberculosis, colds and such diseases.

Cancer "cures."

Cures of deafness, blindness or baldness.

Doctors who advertise.

Cures for "male and female weakness."

Drugs for curing obesity and underweight.

Rejuvenation.

Electrical treatments for serious disorders.

Electric belts.

Electronic treatments by the Abrams or other such methods.

Spinal adjustments.

Whiskey as an antidote for snake bite.

Mad stones for snake bite.

"Marking" of children by experiences of mother before birth.

Determining or controlling sex before birth.

Mineral waters as cures for disease.

Cure of rabies by a stone or by shooting the dog.

Physics and Mechanics

Perpetual motion.

Machines that produce more energy than they use.

Fuelless motors.

Chemicals that greatly increase gasoline mileage.

Fluids that recharge storage batteries.

Methods of burning water or ashes.

Chemicals that make coal burn hotter.

Rediscovery of supposed lost arts, such as hardening of copper.

Death rays.

RELIGION, SCIENCE

Physics and Mechanics (Contd.)
Engine stopping rays.
Divining rods.
Intuitive methods of discovering water, oil and minerals.
Transmutation of metals.

Animal and Plant World
Creation of life.
Spontaneous generation of life.
Sea serpents.
Seeds that grow after more than 300 years, especially that old chestnut about wheat in mummy cases.
Superhuman intelligence in animals.
Prehistoric and gigantic animals living today.
Gigantic snakes in temperate zones.
"Hearts," "nerves" or other animal-like organs in plants.
Record-breaking new species of rubber plants.
Inheritance of acquired characters.
Absolute proof or disproof of evolution.
Hybrids between unlike plants or animals: e.g., goat and pig, or carrot and beet.
Toads or frogs enclosed for many years in stones or rocks.
Living "Missing Links."
Man-eating trees.

Miscellaneous
Discovery of prehistoric men of gigantic or dwarfed size.
Ozone in seaside, mountain or prairie air; radium water.
Messages from or to Mars or other planets; inhabitants of other planets.
"Moron" as synonym for "sex offender."
People living to extreme ages, as 115 or 120 years.
Skeletons or mummies of "giants" (more than 7 feet tall).
"Squaring" the circle; trisecting the angle.
Moon's influence on weather, crops or people.
Influence of sunspots on animal propagation, death rate, etc.
Children "brighter than Einstein."
Discovery of the secret of the pyramids, sphinx or other ancient monuments.
Discovery and interpretation of ciphers in old books or manuscripts.
Lost continents, such as Atlantis and Mu.
Equinoctial storms.
Earthquakes are necessarily accompanied by volcanic eruptions.
Mound-builders as a "mysterious lost race" (they were just plain Indians).

Dr. Watson has also deplored the publication of horoscopes by newspapers. He believes that cigaret smoking and habitual use of alcohol should be discouraged; that medical nostrums, food fads and dangerous and useless cosmetics should be campaigned against; that the lack of public protection against diseases that can be prevented by immunizations should be protested and the situation brought to the attention of readers, public health officials and doctors; that antivivisection propaganda should be resisted as a barrier to essential medical research; that fluoridation of public water supplies should be supported; and that birth control should be upheld as personal privilege and a needed world population policy.

Others believe that the press performs a disservice when it takes seriously most flying saucer findings or when it plays up claims of extrasensory perception.

SOME ETHICAL PROBLEMS

What scientists deplore is reporting which they consider "shallow, inept and totally lacking in scope and understanding," to use the phraseology which Dr. Jonathan Karas of the Lowell Technological Institute applied to the radio and television handling of the first manned Soviet orbital space flight. Dr. Karas said:

> Apparently, most networks and local stations had done little background scientific research in preparing for an event that was inevitable and sent anyone available to interview local scientists. Consequently, the public, eager to learn the details of what had happened, was subjected to answers to shop-worn questions such as: "Is this significant?" "When will the Russians land on Mars?" "Does this mean that the United States is behind in space travel?" Such questions, to which obvious answers are apparent, left some of the scientists being interviewed staring in amazement.
>
> The reason was obvious. Newscasters well qualified to report on fires or conduct man-on-the-street interviews were suddenly asked by their stations to interview scientists about a scientific feat—they found themselves good reporters caught in the wrong league so they pulled out the standard questions—nondefinitive and lackluster....
>
> Since 1957, radio and television stations have been informing the public about lack of a definitive educational plan, lack of American understanding, and other changes which must be made. Yet these same stations have made no moves to obtain scientific counsel in preparing to report scientific news to the public. They should learn a lesson from the progressive newspapers and periodicals who recognize the value of science writers and editors to cover and report on scientific news.

Scientists are appalled when some journalist refers indiscriminately to a new scientific announcement as a "major breakthrough" or "major advance" or "a key to life." They deplore journalistic playing up and exaggerating the significance of a medical or scientific contribution.

The greatest post-war force in improving science reporting has been the National Association of Science Writers whose membership approximates 500 and whose annual conventions attract more than 1,000.

Its bimonthly *News Letter* is a forum for discussion of problems of scientific newsgathering.

In many fields today, the science writer is faced with the problem of government-imposed secrecy. Also, government publicity men can make the science writer's task difficult by extravagant announcements of innovations in the nation's missile and other programs. Many launchings at Cape Kennedy have been conducted in a carnival atmosphere. Hundreds of journalists, seated in bleachers, have had less opportunity to observe details than television watchers. The reporter must be on the alert to distinguish between a publicity or political propaganda stunt and a genuinely important event.

Noting a trend among magazine advertisers to hire newspapermen, including science writers, to compose endorsements or what amounts to endorsements of their products, the National Association of Science Writers passed a resolution that:

> 1. A science writer shall take all necessary measures to insure that the information he purveys to the public is accurate, truthful and impartial.
> 2. A science writer should not for any remuneration by a commercial organization permit his name to be used to promote a commercial service, a commercial product or a commercial organization. Such activity shall be considered prejudicial to the best interest of this association.

REACHING THE READER

With both scientist and reporter realizing the necessity of "writing down" so that scientific news will be effective, and realizing also that, although familiar to a scholar, some item of scientific interest may seem new and even startling to most average readers, the first problem of scientific news writing concerns the elements of reader interest involved.

Elements of Interest

An item of scientific news seldom appeals to the nonscientific reader because it happens to relate to geology, astronomy or psychiatry but because of its emotional value to him as an individual. This value may be: (1) purely personal, to the extent that the revelations of the laboratory are utilized to increase human comfort, improve health, extend the lifespan, increase productivity and affect ways of thinking; (2) the result of curiosity, either ordinary or scholarly, concerning the nature of the past, of the universe and of man himself; (3) because of an interest in progress and the future, regarding which scientists in all fields issue warnings and make predictions; or (4) romantic, interest in the doctor who risks his life in his experimentations, the explorer who braves danger to become a popular hero and the like.

To elaborate on each of these interests and to classify the news which satisfies each longing:

1. Personal interest.
    a. Comfort.
        (1) Communication: telephone, telegraph, radio, etc.
        (2) Transportation: automobile, airplane, etc.
        (3) Entertainment: motion pictures, mechanical toys, ferris wheel.
        (4) Machine-made products: furniture, homes, etc.
        (5) Power: electricity, water, etc.
    b. Health.
        (1) Infant and maternal mortality.
        (2) Preventive medicine.
        (3) Research into the cause of disease.
        (4) Sanitation, smoke control, etc.
        (5) Noise abatement.
        (6) Birth control.
        (7) Eugenics, sterilization, etc.
        (8) Mental hygiene.
        (9) Safety devices in industry.
        (10) X-ray, vitamins, violet rays, sun baths, etc.
        (11) Synthetic food and diets.
        (12) Difficult operations and cures.
    c. Productivity.
        (1) Machinery to increase production.
        (2) Robots and labor-saving devices.
        (3) Scientific agriculture.
        (4) Scientific business methods.
    d. Ways of thinking.
        (1) Darwinism and Mendelism, etc.
        (2) Relativity.
        (3) Reconciliation of science and religion.
        (4) New metaphysical and philosophical creeds and theories.
        (5) Psychoanalysis and psychiatry.
2. Curiosity.
    a. Nature of the past.
        (1) Excavations of evidence of former civilizations.

(2) Fossils and remains of prehistoric animals and men.
(3) Research among primitive tribes of today.
(4) Proof or disproof of biblical stories.
(5) Origin of the white race, American Indian, Negro, etc.
  b. Nature of the universe.
    (1) Eclipses, comets, meteors, etc.
    (2) Theories concerning life on Mars, the moon, etc.
    (3) Nature of the atom and electron.
    (4) Speed of light, curved space, quanta.
    (5) Discovery of new planets, stars, universes.
    (6) Discovery of new elements, mutation of elements.
  c. Nature of man.
    (1) Evidences of evolution.
    (2) Search for the "missing link."
    (3) Origin of life and the age of man.
    (4) Mental tests, inferiority complexes, etc.
    (5) Glands and personality.
3. Progress.
  a. Warnings of science.
    (1) Race suicide.
    (2) Overpopulation.
    (3) Necessity of birth control.
    (4) Susceptibility to disease.
    (5) Waste of natural resources.
    (6) Ascendancy of insects.
  b. Predictions and theories.
    (1) Elimination of manual labor.
    (2) Improved aviation, television, etc.
    (3) Exploration of other planets.
    (4) Skyscrapers and city planning.
    (5) Constructive use of nuclear energy.
    (6) Control of elements, weather, etc.
    (7) Scientific criminology and penology.
    (8) Selective breeding.
    (9) Electrogenesis.
    (10) Scientific government.
4. Romantic.
  a. Heroism.
    (1) Sacrifices to research.
    (2) Exploration.

(3) Bravery in adversity, bad health, etc.
(4) Struggle to save life.
c. Adventure.
(1) Hardship at the poles, in the jungle, etc.
(2) Stratosphere flights.
(3) Deep sea diving.
d. Unusual.
(1) Theories concerning other worlds.
(2) New inventions.
(3) Animal and plant freaks.

Humanizing the Copy

A point the scientists have conceded, in the face of evidence, is that dramatizing an item of scientific news does not destroy its educational value. Austin H. Clark, eminent biologist, for instance, once confessed that he would not object to a newspaper article beginning:

> Those unfeeling mothers who leave their babies on the doorsteps of prosperous people's houses have their counterparts among the birds, etc.

as a popular translation of a scientific paper in which he might declare:

> Most cuckoos, the honey-guides of Africa, the weaver finches, some hang-nests, our cow birds, the rice-grackle, a south American duck, and, according to recent information, one of the paradise birds, lay their eggs in nests of the other birds which hatch these eggs and raise the young.

Dr. Dael Wolfle, executive officer of the American Association for the Advancement of Science, has lamented: "The chief thing wrong with science news writing is the audience. The average reader does not know enough about science to let the reporter do his best job."

That is the challenge. That is the opportunity.

20

Sports; Reviewing and Criticism; Features

I SPORTS
1. The Sports Reporter
   a. *Remaining Cool*
   b. *Following Plays*
   c. *Knowing the Rules*
   d. *Knowing the Records*
   e. *Talking the Language*
2. Writing Sports News

II REVIEWING AND CRITICISM
1. The Reporter-Critic
   a. *Essayists*
   b. *Formulas*
   c. *Reviewing*
   d. *Criticism*
2. Handling the Assignment
   a. *Motion Pictures*
   b. *The Stage*
   c. *Books*
   d. *Music*
   e. *The Dance*
   f. *The Fine Arts*

III FEATURES
1. Featurized News
   a. *Oddities*
   b. *Converted Assignment*
   c. *Situations*
   d. *Events*
2. Straight Features
   a. *Familiar Places*
   b. *Obscure Places*
   c. *Familiar Persons*
   d. *Obscure Persons*
   e. *Occupational Types*
   f. *Historical*
   g. *Stunts*
   h. *Situations*

THE COUNTRY CLUBS WITH THEIR GOLF COURSES, TENNIS COURTS, swimming pools and other athletic facilities have proved to be fascinating places. Churches, boys' clubs and other organizations engaged in social service work have discovered the value of sports in character building. Schools have acquiesced to criticism and pressure and are developing intramural as well as interscholastic or intercollegiate sports programs. As a result of these and other influences, Americans—men, women and children—are playing games much more than they did a decade ago, and even metropolitan newspapers are devoting more space to amateur athletics than formerly. At the same time attendance records at professional contests of all sorts—baseball, football, basketball, hockey, golf, tennis and the like—keep being broken.

Sports

Knowledge of the fine points of a game which comes from having played it oneself increases a person's interest in the skill of experts at the sport. Baseball became established as the national sport at a time when it was the most common sandlot pastime; in later years, the boys who played it vicariously relived the thrills of their adolescence through the achievements of Christy Mathewson, Babe Ruth, Ted Williams and others. Today, with young and old enjoying golf, tennis, bowling, swimming and other sports, interest in professional experts in these fields is growing.

With all professional sports and many amateur sports, such as college football, conducted for profit, the miles and miles of space devoted annually to sports news in the nation's newspapers is actually unpaid for advertising. It is free publicity, however, which newspapers are not reluctant to give because, for a large number of readers, the sports page is the most interesting in the paper. A few editors have experimented in reducing the space devoted to sports news but have been forced, by reader pressure, to abandon the attempt to make those who profit from sports pay for their advertising.

THE SPORTS REPORTER

High value is put upon the experience gained in writing sports, generally for two reasons: (1) only the critics and reviewers have anywhere near comparable freedom as to both what they say and the manner of saying it, and (2) there is no audience more critical than that which consists of sports fans who demand of a writer absolute accuracy and soundness of critical judgment.

REMAINING COOL

Everyone who attends an athletic event does so in quest of pleasure—that is, everyone except the sports reporters. This does not mean that sports reporters do not enjoy their work; it does mean that they cannot permit their enthusiasm to approach that which the fan displays. The press box is not a cheering section because its inhabitants have all they can do to follow closely what is happening so as to explain the difficult plays and decisions for fans who were too busy spurring on alma mater to notice exactly what happened. It is pleasant for the reporter to view sports events from the best seats and without paying admission, but he never is able to assume the carefree attitude of the casual fan.

Following Plays

From his superior vantage point, the sports reporter should be expected to observe accurately. In many sports, the action is so fast that spectators cannot always follow it. The news story should let the bleacherite know what kind of pitch went for a home run or should tell the fans in the cheap seats how the knockout blow was struck. At major sports events, the work of newspapermen is facilitated by the assistance of an official scorer who decides whether a hit or error is to be scored. There also will be statisticians to prepare details in addition to those going into the official score book. At minor events, however, the reporter usually has to compile most of his own statistics. If, in addition to a general story of an event, a play-by-play account is desired, customary practice is to assign two reporters. An indispensable part of any featured sports story is a summary or box score, as the particular sport requires, which is run separately or at the end of the story proper. To the fan, the summary or box score is a complete account in itself.

Knowing the Rules

The sports fan not only attends contests but receives considerable pleasure from discussing the past performances and future chances of players and teams. A favorite pastime is to second-guess the coach or manager and to pass judgment upon the abilities of referees and umpires. Just as popular among fans is criticism of the writeups of sports reporters. In other words, the sports writer has to "know his stuff" just as much as do players and officials. It is inconceivable that a reporter not understand the rules of the game he is covering. Writers of business news can make mistakes which only economists recognize; sports writers produce copy for readers who think they know as much as they.

Knowing the Records

To keep up with what is expected of him, the sports reporter not only must understand the rule book but also must know the record book containing the statistics of what players and teams have done in the past. Otherwise, he will not know whether a particular achievement is unusual. The reporter whose mind is a storehouse of information regarding the history of sports is in a position to enrich his copy considerably. He can compare players of today with those of yesterday and frequently may remember "way back when" something, recalled by an immediate event, occurred. At his disposal, in case his memory is weak, are numerous sports record books in the newspaper's morgue.

Talking the Language

A New York sports writer of a generation ago, Charles Dryden, is given credit for having been first to introduce on the sports page an informality and originality of language which would scandalize readers if found in the regular news sections. The credit for genius due Dryden has been dimmed because of the banal depths to which thousands of imitators, consciously or unconsciously, have sunk since then. Stanley Walker has been quoted as saying: "If it is true, and it appears to be, that Dryden was the father of whimsical baseball reporting, then the man has a great deal to answer for. He may have freed some reporters and afforded them the chance to do their gorgeous word-painting with a bold and lavish hand, but for every one he liberated he set demons to work in the brains of a dozen others—demons which made American sports writing the most horrendous mess of gibberish ever set before the eyes of a reader."

Today the desideratum in effective sports writing is informality and originality without triteness. Expressions which fans use in discussing a game cannot be considered hackneyed, but overuse of any word weakens any news story, sports or otherwise. For every sport there is a vernacular used by players and fans, familiar examples being "love" in tennis and "fore" in golf, with which the sports writer must be thoroughly familiar. It is in his use of shopworn synonyms to describe typical plays that he must be cautious. The following is a list of expressions which must be used with considerable discrimination or not at all:

bingle	it augurs well	run roughshod
brand of ball	keen battle	rung up a victory
brilliant rally	keystone hassock	salary arm
cagers	looms	scintillating play
charges	lost its stride	seasoned team
concentrated practice	made his debut	sent to the showers
concerted effort	many surprises are in	show up well
crush	store for—	slam
department of play	mermen	sock
flash	moundsman	strong bidders
flipper	much heralded	superb guarding
fork hand	netted a gain	tap the apple
forms the nucleus	old platter	tidal wave of
fracas	pellet	enthusiasm
functioned smoothly	performed well	tough going
got off on wrong foot	pigskin	triple threat
	pile up a total	usual brilliant
gridders	pilfered sacks	playing
homer	pill	vanquished
horsehide	populated bases	warriors
hot corner	prospects are bright	wealth of material
in the thick of action	run riot	*win* as a noun

WRITING SPORTS NEWS

One advantage the sports writer has over the reporter who specializes in political, governmental, business, scientific or any other type of news: the rules are definite and, despite minor occasional changes, remain the same year after year in all parts of the country. This situation, which contributes to the ease of sports reporting, also may lead to monotony. It is the belief of many successful writers that the opportunity to develop an individual writing style which sports reporting affords more than any other kind of newspaper work, exists up to a certain point only, after which the sports reporter should do the more serious writing for which his work has trained him. On the other hand, however, there are scores of first-rate sports writers whose copy seems just as fresh as ever after years of writing. Outstanding is Walter (Red) Smith, whose syndicated column originated with the New York *Herald Tribune* and survived the paper.

In reporting amateur or local sports, the sports reporter almost invariably supports the home team. Any criticism of local heroes is constructive and usually is consistent with what a large number of fans believe. The tendency to "build up" local players may be overdone to the detriment of both the players and writer when performances do not square with predictions. The sports writer has a friendly attitude and makes it clear that he, as well as his readers, wants the home team to win. On the other hand, he must never forget that he is writing for readers and must not act as a virtual public relations man for a coach or manager who may wish to use him to send up deceptive trial balloons to confuse opponents, or to promote his own interests.

Although all contests of a particular sport are played according to the same rules, the major news interest of an individual game might be any one of a number of potential elements. In determining the feature of a game, the sports reporter considers the following:

1. Significance.
   a. Is a championship at stake?
   b. Effect of the result on the all-time records of the contestants.
   c. Effect of the result on the season's records of the contestants.
   d. Are the contestants old rivals?
   e. Are they resuming relations after a long period?
   f. Will the outcome suggest either contestant's probable strength against future opponents?
2. Probable outcome.
   a. Relative weight and experience of contestants.
   b. Ability as demonstrated against other opponents, especially common ones.
   c. Improvement during the season.
   d. New plays, tactics, etc.
   e. New players, return of injured players, strength of substitutes, etc.
   f. Former contests between the two contestants.
   g. Weather conditions favorable to either contestant.
   h. Lack of practice, injuries and other handicaps.
   i. Tradition of not being able to win away from home.
   j. Recent record, slumps, etc.
3. How victory was won.
   a. The winning play, if score was close.
   b. The style of play of both winner and loser.
   c. Costly errors and mistakes of judgment.
   d. Spurts which overcame opponent's lead.

4. Important plays.
    a. How each score was made.
    b. Spectacular catches, strokes, etc.
    c. The result of "hunches."
    d. Penalties, fouls, etc.
    e. Disputed decisions of umpire or referee.
5. Individual records, stars, etc.
    a. Records broken.
    b. High scores.
    c. Players who "delivered" in pinches.
    d. Teamwork.
    e. Players not up to usual form.
6. Injuries.
7. The occasion or crowd.
    a. Size of crowd; a record?
    b. An annual event?
    c. Enthusiasm, riots, demonstrations, etc.
8. The weather.
    a. Condition of track or playing field.
    b. Effect of heat or cold.
    c. Effect of sun on fielders, etc.
    d. Which side was more handicapped? Why?
    e. Delays because of rain, etc.
9. Box score, summary and statistics.

Reviewing and Criticism

If he is not ambitious to become a foreign correspondent or a sports columnist, the college-trained cub reporter is likely to want to be a critic—motion picture, dramatic, musical, literary or other forms of art. Unfortunately for the youngster with talent which might lead to success in such writing, the average small newspaper offers him inadequate opportunities either for experience or editorial guidance. As a result, many—including some of the best that the schools of journalism turn out—redirect their energies into other channels.

This section is intended both for the few who create opportunities for themselves, perhaps by developing a column of motion picture or book criticism in addition to their other work, and for the regular staff members who draw the assignments to cover the annual high school play, the local art club's exhibits, the occasional Broadway cast which makes a one-night stop, and the home talent Gilbert and Sullivan light opera.

THE REPORTER-CRITIC

Essayists

The lure of critical reviewing, in addition to free tickets, probably is the opportunity it seems to offer for self-expression. The great critics, including Matthew Arnold, Stuart Sherman and George Bernard Shaw, also have been creative artists and social philosophers. In addition to explaining to their readers how some muralist, playwright or composer regarded life, they have chronicled their own reactions.

To prevent his "spouting off" too much on the basis of only textbook knowledge and classroom discussions, it is perhaps fortunate that the beginning reporter is hampered in his critical writing. Before he can be a competent critic he must first serve an apprenticeship as a reviewer. When he covers a dramatic, musical or any other kind of aesthetic event, he does well to accept the assignment as one in straight news reporting. That is, while he is learning.

The purpose of the average member of a small town audience at a motion picture, play or concert is pleasure seeking. A safe guide for the tyro in criticism, therefore, is the reaction of audiences; no matter how high he rises in critical writing, it supplies an element of news interest of which he always must take cognizance. What got applause? What evoked laughs? Regardless of what the reporter thinks of the audience's taste, to make a fair report of the occasion, he must mention what indisputably were its high points from the standpoint of those for whom it was presented.

This advice is not tantamount to condoning the practice of building a review upon fatuous sentences or short paragraphs lauding each performer, but it is intended as a brake for those who might be tempted to use a night at the opera merely as an inspiration for an essay upon the fallacies of hedonism as demonstrated by "Faust" or a dissertation on the evidence regarding Hamlet's insanity.

The following is an example of a straightforward, objective report:

By Olin Downes

Lenox, Mass., Aug. 6—"Peter Grimes," the opera by the librettist, Montagu Slater, and the composer, Benjamin Britten, designated by Serge Koussevitzky before the curtain as the opera that came "first after Carmen," was given its American premiere by the students' orchestra, chorus and soloists of the Berkshire Music Center this evening in the Opera Concert Theatre at Tanglewood.

The performance was conducted by Leonard Bernstein, who had as collaborators Eric Crozier and Frederick Cohen, stage directors; Richard Rychtarik, stage designer; Hugh Ross, choral director, and Boris Goldowsky, director of the opera department. Mr. Britten had come from London to attend this production, supervised dramatically by Mr. Crozier, who had directed the world premiere of the work at Sadlers Wells on June 7.

It is known that this score had been commissioned of Mr. Britten by Dr. Koussevitzky, representing the Koussevitzky Musical Foundation which he established in memory of his late wife, Natalie Koussevitzky, to whom the opera is dedicated. Mr. Britten had said to Dr. Koussevitzky: "This opera is yours." Dr. Koussevitzky related his reply: "No, this opera belongs to the world." He said finally that he had been asked to remind the audience that the performers at this premiere were students. . . .

[New York *Times*]

FORMULAS

The critic with a bias is as dangerous as the political or labor reporter whose prejudices forbid his interpreting fairly the activities or viewpoints of more than one side in a controversy. In criticism, application of a formula as to what an artistic form should be often results in conclusions as grotesque as condemning a cow for not being a horse.

An example of a critic with a formula is one who believes art should exist for art's sake only and that no artistic form ever should be utilized for propagandic purposes. As a result, if the hero of a motion picture or play happens to be identified with a particular racial, nationality, economic or other type or group, the critic is likely stupidly to condemn the entire production as propaganda even though it be an honest and perhaps brilliant attempt to describe sympathetically a certain segment of life.

Even worse than the opponent of propaganda is the exponent of it who is sympathetic only when a certain theory is promulgated by the particular art form under review. Such critics dismiss books, plays or other artistic creations with (to them) derisive adjectives, as "romantic" or "too realistic," with a condescension which, in the small community at least, cannot but brand them as supercilious or, as the critics' critics may put it, "half-baked high brows."

The critic with a formula is bound to be mostly a negative, carping, constantly dissatisfied one. Because a Hollywood production does not square with his conception of what the old Globe players would have done, he sees no good in the result. Regretting that some artistic hero of his did not execute the idea, he is likely to make absurd comparisons between what is and what might have been.

The essence of competent reviewing of any kind is understanding an artist's purpose so as to interpret it to others. Any art form—painting, drama, the novel, music—is a medium of communication. No artistic creation should be condemned merely because of inability to understand its language although those who hold that the artist should use a vocabulary which it is possible for others to learn have a valid point.

The duty of the reviewer or critic, in addition to that of describing a piece of art or an artistic event, should be to assist his readers in an understanding of the artist's motives to enhance their enjoyment of it. This obligation is prerequisite to that of passing expert judgment upon the artist's success in his undertaking; the role of evaluator is one which the critic-reporter should postpone until he has reached maturity himself in objective understanding, and not even then if his public consists largely of laymen. The greatest service the newspaper which gives space to artistic news can perform for both artists and spectators or auditors is to interpret the former to the latter. The educational background that such service requires easily may be imagined.

The writer of the following example attempted to explain motives without passing judgment:

> Under the auspices of the Adult Education council and the cooperation of the Greek people and the Greek Orthodox churches of Chicago, Vassos and Tanagra Kanellos, directors of the Institute of Hellenic Chorodrama at Athens, presented in Orchestra hall last night a program of music, dance and drama drawn in great part from ancient Attic sources.
>
> The performance brought the Chicago observance of the Greek Orthodox Easter week to a climax and was intended also as a tribute to the University of Athens, which is now celebrating its centennial.
>
> From a purely cultural standpoint the prime purpose of the program was to reproduce, as accurately as possible, the blend of the arts which distinguished ancient Greek drama. To this end excerpts from Aeschylus' "Prometheus Bound" and Euripides' "The Trojan Women" were presented in what was announced as a close approximation of their original form. A vast amount of scholarship has gone into the process of determining just what that form was. [Chicago *Daily Tribune*]

Reviewing

The difference between reviewing and criticism has been implied in the discussions under both previous headings. No matter how critical he may become with experience and expert judgment, no writer of the arts can overlook his duty to supply the answer to the question, "What is it like?" to the reader who has not read the book, attended the play or viewed the exhibit in question.

Is it a book about Russia or about how to raise puppies? A farce or a tragedy? A painting in imitation of Cezanne or one suggestive of Paul Cadmus? The reader who must select the books he reads, the motion pictures, plays and musical events he attends, expects the newspaper to tell him the answers. He wants, furthermore, an honest, fair statement, not an advertiser's blurb; and he doesn't want his pleasure spoiled by being told too much. That is, if the success of the playwright or novelist depends upon an unusual plot incident, it is unfair to both the artist and his audience for the writer to reveal its nature. How to convey an adequate impression of the nature of an artistic creation without spoiling one's fun demands only that quality known as common sense.

WOMAN OF VIOLENCE. By Geula Cohen. Translated by Hillel Halkin. 275 pp. New York: Holt, Rinehart and Winston. $5.95.

REVIEWED BY
EMILY C. MCDONALD

"Woman of Violence" is the story of Geula Cohen and the life she led as a member of the notorious Stern Gang—which fought for the liberation of Palestine from the British. The gang—also known as the Lechi—was composed not only of terrorists, but also of idealists.

Geula Cohen was no exception.

She left her comfortable family life while still a student to join the freedom fight. First she tried the sanctioned organization—Betar. Then she turned to the more revolutionary Estel. Still not satisfied, she finally let herself be "recruited" into the Lechi.

From that day on her life changed completely. She went underground and rarely emerged from hiding except under cover of night. Geula learned to fight, to hide, to recruit, and—perhaps most important of all—to put dreams and ideals into action.

Finally, Geula became one of the "voices" on the Hebrew underground radio. Her voice brought news and inspiration to thousands of Jews eagerly awaiting news of the freedom fighters.

Although her work was dangerous, she never feared the danger. Her family was under surveillance, her friends were captured and put to death —still she went on with her broadcasts.

Then she too was captured. Through the Lechi underground, however, her escape was planned and finally brought about. She immediately returned to work.

Geula's memoirs end on the eve of Independence Day, 1948. Her active work in the Lechi ended then, too. She watched the celebrating but couldn't take part in it. The independence gained was not the Lechi ideal. As she put it:

"But I would remain outside. An ancient, heady melody that had started long ago would continue to resound far beyond these voices and frontiers." [Nashville *Banner*]

CRITICISM

To pass judgment on the merits of a book, play, painting, musical number, motion picture or any other attempt at art demands expert judgment. To be an expert, one must have a specialist's education and training. This does not mean necessarily that the newspaper critic must be able to produce masterpieces himself to be qualified to pass judgment on the efforts of another, but it does mean that he must have a thorough-going understanding of the field about which he writes.

It is not peculiar that supposedly expert critics often do not agree. Neither do political theorists, economists or scientists. A difference of opinion among specialists, however, is based upon sound principles whereas philistines have as their premises only stereotypes.

The critic who wins the respect of readers usually is one who has proved his ability to report correctly an artistic event and to review fairly the nature of a piece of art. If he can observe correctly and interpret with understanding, he also may be trusted as an artistic "tipster." If he lacks either of the other qualities, however, his starred selections will be ignored.

These, then, are the three responsibilities of the finished critic, which the ambitious beginner would do well to master one at a time in order: (1) to describe objectively an artistic object or event; (2) to explain what the artist intends it to convey; and (3) to pass expert judgment on the artist's success in achieving his purpose.

Note in the following example how the writer, although passing critical judgments, remained aware of his role as reporter:

By ALBERT GOLDBERG
Times Staff Writer

The difference in technique among dancers qualified to be principals in such an organization as the Bolshoi Ballet are generally so minute as to defy anything except pedantic expert analysis.

But the difference in personalities can be enormous and readily apparent, and it was this factor, with six changes of cast in the leading roles, that made the Bolshoi's second performance of "Don Quixote" in Shrine

Auditorium Thursday night a much livelier and more convincing affair than the one of the previous evening.

Type casting is not ordinarily one of the basic principles of ballet, but it was utilized to maximum advantage by placing Ekaterina Maximova and Vladimir Vasiliev in the roles of Kitri and Basil the Barber. Seldom has a couple—they are Mr. and Mrs. in private life—been better matched in every respect than this irresistible pair of handsome youngsters.

Their Youth

Naturally they capitalize on their youth and beauty, but their skills go far beyond the physical aspects. Though quite different in other respects, Miss Maximova has something of the radiance of Margot Fonteyn. She lights up the stage with her petite, mischievous sparkle, and she dances with a buoyancy that completely reflects her personality....

It is characteristic of the ensemble principle on which the Bolshoi operates that Natalia Bessmertnova, the troupe's third-ranking ballerina, should turn up unannounced in the comparatively minor part of the Queen of the Driads. Though brief, she made its opportunities count with a serene elegance of style and technique that aroused anticipation of more extended roles.

Alexander Lavreniuk took over the Toreador with a welcome addition of refinement and aloofness, and Rimma Kerelskaya, the Queen of the Driads on opening night, injected more variety and less routine into the street dancer. Maya Samokhalova, the previous street dancer, did the first variation in the last act, but we'll have to take that on faith.

[Los Angeles *Times*]

HANDLING THE ASSIGNMENT

Two factors which the reviewer-critic must bear in mind are the following: (1) Are those upon whose work he is to pass judgment professionals or amateurs? (2) Is the performance (dramatic or musical), production, presentation or object of art an original creation or a copy or imitation?

It is unfair to judge an amateur by professional standards. The home talent cast usually gets as much fun out of rehearsing and acting as do the relatives and friends who witness the result. Generally, amateur events should be reported objectively with the audience's reactions as the guide.

Whereas Broadway first-nighters are as interested in the work of a playwright as in the excellence of actors, when the local dramatic club puts on something by Oscar Wilde or Somerset Maugham, it is stupid to place the emphasis in the review upon the familiar plot or problem with which the dramatist was concerned. Rather, it is the acting and staging which should command attention.

The broader the critic's background, the better able he is to make comparisons between immediate and past events. If he has seen several actresses play the same part, he can explain the differences in interpretations. When a motion picture is adapted from a novel, short story, or stage play, he can point out the changes made in plot and artistic emphasis. The same orchestra under different conductors behaves differently in rendering the same musical masterpiece; two authors handling the same subject may have little in common as to either method or conclusions.

MOTION PICTURES

There are few places large enough to support a newspaper which do not also have a motion picture theater. For the assistance of small-town editors, motion picture producers issue publicity material descriptive of their films and performers. Obviously, however, much to be preferred is the locally written review or criticism composed from the standpoint of the audience rather than that of the advertiser; fearlessness is a quality without which motion picture reviewing is likely to be jejune.

THE STAGE

What has been said about the motion picture applies also to the legitimate stage. If the play is a much-acted one, the reviewer should not devote any appreciable amount of space to relating the story of the plot or to describing the general motive. Rather, he should perform the difficult task of distinguishing between the acting and the actor's role and should consider stage management and direction. Obviously, to criticize effectively he must have some acquaintance with the technique of play production.

If the play is a production, the critic rightfully evaluates the playwright's success in achieving his purpose. Is there proper congruity in settings, costumes, language and plot? Is the action logical or is the happy ending arrived at by a series of unnatural coincidences? Are exits and entrances merely artificial devices to get characters on and off the stage?

If the production deals with a problem, is it met squarely or is it falsely simplified? Are the characters truly representative of the types they portray or are they superficial or caricatures? Is the play propaganda? If it points a moral, is the playwright sincere or naïve or bigoted? Is anything risque just smut for smut's sake or is it essential for dramatic completeness?

These are just a few of the questions the critic must ask himself. For whatever conclusions he reaches he must give sound reasons.

Truly great dramatic critics have been students of life as well as of the drama. "Ideally," according to Norman Nadel, critic for the old New York *World-Telegram*, "the theater critic should be a Renaissance man." As explained in *Editor & Publisher* for April 23, 1966, his idea of such a man is one "with a knowledge of architecture, sculpture, painting, music, government, history, philosophy and other liberal arts subjects." Nadel suggests that college students finish their four-year course with a good classical and historical background so as "to have perspective and to understand the art form in relation to the world as it exists." He urges a knowledge of philosophy because "people turn to a play to express a philosophical question," and a knowledge of history of the theater and playwriting "to recognize a play's originality and importance and to acquire an intellectual appreciation of the play form."

Walter Kerr, long with the New York *Herald Tribune* and now drama critic for the New York *Times*, believes a drama critic must have an extensive background in dramatic literature on a broad humanistic base. John Mason Brown feels that critics should be able to "feel, touch and have sight of the world." He advises students aspiring to be drama critics to get a thorough knowledge of history. Richard Watts of the New York *Post* emphasizes the value of studying the English language as well.

BOOKS

The first task of the editor of a book review page is one of selection of those few of the 20,000 or more volumes published annually which are to receive mention. Harry Hanson, veteran newspaper and magazine book reviewer, told an *Editor & Publisher* interviewer:

> The daily book review lifts a book from an overtowering mass of printed material and makes it an integral part of life. It often becomes news of the first order. Between the covers of all these volumes there may be an authoritative voice touching on our vital problems, and if this is true, that voice certainly deserves a hearing. The book reviewer's job, it seems to me, is to sort this flood of titles, find the one that fits in the day's news, and then write about it as news.

That the first duty of the writer about books is to assist readers to select those they wish to read also is the viewpoint of another leading reviewer, Joseph Wood Krutch, who said:

The best review is not the one which is trying to be something else. It is not an independent essay on the subject of the book in hand and not an aesthetic discourse upon one of the literary genres. The best book review is the best review of the book in question, and the better it is the closer it sticks to its ostensible subject. . . . However penetrating a piece of writing may be, it is not a good review if it leaves the reader wondering what the book itself is like as a whole or it is concerned with only some aspects of the book's quality.

As to the style of book reviewing or criticizing there is no formula. The writer is free to use virtually any method he chooses, the only test being the effectiveness of the style used. Somewhere in the review or criticism the writer should be expected to classify the book as to type— fiction, philosophy, biography—to describe its contents, communicate something of its quality, and pass judgment upon it.

The writer should be warned against misuse of clichés and omnibus words, especially adjectives such as "vigorous," "amazing," "haunting," "powerful," "gripping," "thrilling" and the like.

Music

The reporter who is timid about covering a musical event because he lacks technical training in music, at least has the consolation that by far a majority of his readers, both those who attended the event under review and those who didn't, know no more than he. The superior musical review, of course, is written for both the professor of music and the music-lover. The qualities demanded of the musical critic were summarized as follows by the late Lawrence Gilman, long music critic for the New York *Herald Tribune*:

> The best music critic is a good newspaperman. Of course, he must know music, deeply and thoroughly and exactly; he must know what he is talking about. But the first and indispensable requirement of any article written for a newspaper, no matter on what subject, is that it must be readable—it must be interesting as well as clearly intelligible to the lay reader of average education. A professional musician might be able to write a competent, technical account of a composition or a musical performance. But his review would probably be interesting only to other musicians.
>
> The chief aim of a newspaper critic must be to interest the general reader. And if he can interest those readers who have not heard the performance, as well as those who have, he is entitled to call it a day. Quite apart from its value as a report and estimate of a musical performance, his criticism must be able to stand alone as an interesting, readable story.

It is the musician with whom the musical critic primarily is interested because only occasionally, even in the large cities, is he required to pass judgment upon a new symphony, opera or other musical creation. Thus, if the audience includes musically trained auditors, he may well take his cue from their reactions as to the merits of the performance. If he is woefully lacking in musical training, he can make his entire story descriptive of the audience or the personalities of the musicians.

The Dance

Whereas music is written with complete directions by the composer to guide the virtuoso, and whereas rules for the playwright, novelist, painter and sculptor may be found in textbooks, no way as yet has been devised to score the movements which characterize what, historical evidence proves, was one of the first if not the original form of art. Motion picture recording may prove the way out for future teachers of the dance who wish to convey the qualities of the work of a Harald Kreutzberg or a Martha Graham.

The medium of the dance is motion, but motion may be either abstract or pantomimic, rhythmic or natural. Folk dancing, being pantomimic, reflects the customs of the people participating in it. Natural dancing consists in such normal movements as running, walking, skipping and leaping without studied posing. What is called the German school of dancing emphasizes strength, endurance and precision of movement. The ballet is rhythmic and repetitious. Greek or classical dancing, revived after World War I by the late Isadora Duncan, is symbolic and involves the entire body, not just the head, arms and legs. Miss Duncan considered her art interpretative of poetry, music, the movements of nature and of moods and emotions; as such, it defied analysis.

To review a dancing entertainment with any intelligence, the reporter must understand the principles superficially sketched in the preceding two paragraphs. A sympathetic attitude perhaps is more essential than in reviewing any other form of art, if for no other reason than that it is the form with which the average person has the least everyday contact.

The Fine Arts

The camera was to a large extent the cause of the contemporary "war" in the field of painting which has repercussions among the sculptors and architects as well. Dadaism, futurism, surrealism and other recent "schools" of art are revolts against the formal, and a popular explanation given laymen is that the day of the portrait painter is gone and with it a theory as to the purpose of art. It is argued that the role of the twentieth-century artist is to communicate an idea or an emotion; the extremes to which some go in upsetting tradition is dumfounding to laymen. In the works of such painters as Grant Wood and Thomas Benton, so-called "regional" artists, is found an abandonment of the photographic purpose but the models still are recognizable. Some abstract art has as many interpretations as there are interpreters.

Current tendencies in painting, sculpture and architecture are not new. The history of art reveals that throughout the centuries every conceivable theory has been tried out. Likewise, the search for a definition of art is as old as artistic criticism; upon his answer to the question depends largely the nature of what an artist produces.

Through reading and fraternizing with artistic people the reporter can become educated in the meaning of art to the different "schools," the work of whose representatives he is called upon to review. In no other field is the responsibility for interpreting the artist to his public greater than in that of the manual arts. In fact, such interpretation is about all there is to this kind of criticism.

The opportunity and responsibility of the newspaper today were explained by Herbert Kupferberg, then editor for the arts of the late New York *Herald Tribune,* in an article, "The Art of Covering the Arts," in *Nieman Reports* for March, 1965. His final paragraph was as follows:

> For better or for worse, the world of the arts today is wider than it has ever been. It encompasses not only the patron of the art galleries on New York's Fifty-seventh Street, but the housewife who finds Van Gogh and Renoir reproductions amid the breakfast foods and beauty aids at her local supermarket. It includes the teen-ager buying his first Beethoven symphony at the discount record counter no less than the dowager with a subscription to the Metropolitan Opera. It even touches the millions of visitors who rode the moving platform past Michelangelo's Pieta at the New York World's Fair without being fully aware of whether they were undergoing an artistic or touristic or religious experience, but recognizing that for a brief moment they had entered a realm of beauty. Today a newspaper that makes any pretense at reflecting the life around it, or at appealing to the broad interests of an alert readership, no longer has any real option as to whether it will cover the arts. Its only choice is whether it will cover them badly or well.

Features

The difference between news and feature stories is largely one of intention. Numerous examples in preceding chapters have illustrated how unorthodox journalistic rhetorical methods, customarily associated with feature writing, may be used to improve ordinary news stories in which the writer's purpose is to be informative about overt happenings. On the other hand, a feature article emphasizing human interest may be composed according to the standard rules for formal news writing.

In addition to designating those stories of events which might have been written up in straight news style, the term "feature" also is used to include human interest stories related to or suggested by news events, a quantity of different types of articles only slightly or not at all connected with any news item, and a growing number of special informative articles and regular columns of advice and instructions.

FEATURIZED NEWS

"Make it into a feature," the reporter says to himself or is told by the city editor when he has a schedule of facts about something which actually has happened of little public importance but of considerable potential reader interest.

ODDITIES

One of the milestones in the evolution of the modern newspaper was when the James Gordon Bennetts began printing accounts of happenings which previously had been considered too trivial to merit attention. Today, without consciousness of the loss of any dignity, the average newspaper balances its offering of serious matter by a liberal sprinkling of "brighteners," usually brief, cleverly written feature items of relatively unimportant happenings. Some papers group a number of such shorts each day in a column headed, "Oddities in the News," "Strange as It May Seem" or some similar title.

> Columbus, Ohio—(UP)—Exasperated by the endless questions of 3-year-old Harold Thompson, a neighbor who was painting his house painted the child red "from head to foot" and sent him home.
>
> The child's mother, Mrs. Lester Thompson, scrubbed him clean—except for a few red splotches—and sent him out to play again.
>
> A few minutes later, she charged in a police complaint, the child returned. This time he was painted a battleship gray.

It was her last day in Williamsville, and Mrs. Mary McLain, who has lived 50 years there, was saddened at the thought.

But she was willing to leave. Her husband, James, 75-year-old city employee retired, wanted to go back to St. Louis, the home town he had left more than 50 years before.

He had retired a year ago, and his old home had been in his thoughts ever since.

And so they were leaving. The house at 678 Thorn ave., had been sold a week ago. The moving van, loaded with their furniture, was in front, ready to take their goods and their life to St. Louis.

Only one piece of furniture—Mrs. McLain's old worn rocking chair—had been left out.

It remained on the porch, where she had rocked contentedly in it ever since a stroke five years earlier had paralyzed her legs. There, on the porch, she would rock quietly, exchanging greetings with her neighbors. But now she was leaving.

"I'm going to sit down in my good old chair for the last time," Mrs. McLain told her husband, and her voice was sad.

"We've been very happy, haven't we, James?" she murmured as she closed her eyes to fix forever in her mind the sight of the street she was leaving.

After a few moments her husband shook her gently.

"It's time to be going, dear," he warned.

Mrs. McLain did not answer. She had gone on already.

The doctor who examined her said that Mrs. McLain had died of a heart attack.

Converted Assignment

Often a reporter goes out on what he believes to be a serious assignment and encounters a situation lending itself much more readily to feature than straight news treatment. Or he may be instructed, "If it isn't worth a news story, write a feature about it," such an order implying what every city editor believes—that a competent reporter should be able to write a feature story about anything. Decision to give feature treatment to what otherwise might be a regular news story may be influenced by another newspaper's having published an earlier account in orthodox style. This happens frequently when the article is of an evening event for an afternoon newspaper and a morning newspaper already has had a story about it.

This is the story of the conversion of a newspaper reporter.

Traditionally he's a hard nut to crack anyway, but when religion is concerned, he's doubly so. Last night he entered the Salvation Army building at Sherman avenue and Greenwood street with a cuss word in his eye and leering sarcasm on his face.

Inside was a big tent, staked out in the regular canvas oval camp-meeting style. The reporter could hear the evangelistic exordium coming from the female in the pulpit.

Pushing back the tent flap, he trod down the sawdust aisle. The female was leading a hymn. He snorted in contempt and looked disdainfully at the weaklings all around him who had religion. The girl in the pulpit attracted his eye—he wasn't an old reporter. She was dressed in the Army's trim uniform and wore the black-ribboned bonnet. There was an aura of something almost celestial around her. It quieted the reporter's disbelief.

Looks Around Him

He looked around him. A carnival procession of lights were stretched over a bar nailed across the tent pole in the rude semblance of a cross. Overhead the canvas top was billowing in a draft, almost as though a prairie wind had struck it. Late visitors came in, like shades of Gypsy Smith and Billy Sunday. They shuffled down the sawdust aisle, stirring up a smell of fresh pine shavings.

The varnished seats down in front that resembled the dismantled rows of some ancient nickelodeon were filling with other shades. There were Adam Goa and his congregation from the holy thinking plains of Kansas. From somewhere came the dulcimer tones of a piano and the muffled percussion of a drum. The reporter wanted to join in the inspired hymn. The tent was billowing above again, and down in front Adam Goa's shades had risen and were whooping up an old chantey....

The reporter, with a bursting chest, seized the hymn book. It was titled "Fralsnings—Armens Sangbok." It wasn't enough to erase the vision of Adam Goa down there in front. Then came the sounds of creaking wagon wheels and grandfather Jewel lived again. He was straight and stalwart and was handing down Miss Mary Ann, with an arm around her waist.

Other late-arriving rustics were gathering outside making noises, and the prairie wind was blowing over groves of trees wherein the young folk paid homage to Eros.

The reporter strove to shut out all this. It was religion, that of his old home state, and it wasn't becoming to his profession. Uncle Jimmy, another famed Kansas exhorter, was stumping up to the pulpit preparatory to the revival meetin' rogations. And there was the shade of Beulah Woolson, the soul who had been inside the gates of heaven. Oh Lord!

The reporter, half blinded, broke suddenly up the sawdust aisle. They were singing a hymn behind him.

> O neighbors have you seen old Rummy,
> With a scowl upon his face?
> I saw him on the street this morning,
> And he's going to leave the place!
> He's going to leave the place!
> Old Rummy's going to pack his baggage,
> For it's getting mighty warm!

494 HANDLING IMPORTANT ASSIGNMENTS

The reporter dashed past the poster advertising the Army's sunshine brigade. In the street again, he shook his head clear.

"Cripes," he muttered, "that old-time religion in Evanston, and it almost got me, too!" [Evanston (Ill.) *News-Index*]

SITUATIONS

Not a single event but a series of them may suggest a featurized situation story to a reporter or editor. Such articles have a strong element of news interest as they summarize and possibly explain what "everybody" is doing or talking about. They are not concocted features but are based upon recent events. In their *Pathways to Print* the late Harry F. Harrington and Lawrence Martin explained the difference between the situation feature and the interpretative article as follows:

> The situation feature differs from the strictly interpretative story mainly in that it is content to assemble the evidence pro and con—or at most to offer a symposium of opinion, leaving the interpretation largely to the individual reader. This type of feature article creates nothing essentially new; it simply analyzes and coordinates, smoothing out difficulties and hazy impressions which waylay a reader who is not in a position to understand all of the hidden implications of a series of events. In its fullest expression, the situation story is a fusion of the past, present and future.

A situation story explains the "atmosphere" in which an immediate incident or series of incidents must be understood. It may be known as a "round-up" story.

BY KATHY GOSNELL
Staff Writer

Motorcycles are here to stay.

They come in all shapes and sizes and so do the people who buy them.

Teenagers buy them because they are cheaper than cars. Business men buy them because they outmaneuver cars.

Some people buy them for the feeling of "the wind in your hair," says Jack Koske of Koske Import Motors in Palatine.

The growing popularity of cycles had brought growing concern about safety problems.

Sen. Vance Hartke (D-Ind.) two weeks ago told the United States Senate of an "epidemic of motorcycle accidents."

The National Safety Council figures show 1,580 cyclists killed in 1965, as compared to 1,118 in 1964 and 882 in 1963.

On both state and national levels there is talk of safety regulations ranging from mandatory wearing of crash helmets to special tests and licensing for cycle drivers.

But increased publicity noting climbing death tolls and the possibility of regulation are apparently not daunting the spirit of the cyclists.

Two million cycles and scooters are registered in the United States and some five million people are driving them, according to the Motorcycle, Scooter, and Allied Trades Association.

In Illinois 56,753 cycles were registered last year.

One possible form government action might take is the establishment of special tests and licensing for motorcycle drivers in addition to the present requirements for a driver's license.

Such action would probably make special instruction mandatory. Some dealers do instruct buyers now; others don't care.

Koske said he refuses to sell a cycle to anyone until he is sure of the buyer's ability to handle the machine.

This training has paid off. "As far as we know there has never been an accident involving a bike we've sold," he said.

Koske said he would be "100 per cent behind" regulation of licensing and testing for cyclists, saying dealers who are not concerned with safety are committing a "severe injustice." ...

John Lemme, 23, has been driving a cycle for nine years and racing for seven. He is in his fourth year of professional racing and will participate in the national short track championship race at Sante Fe track in Hinsdale this month.

Cyclists should wear heavy clothing, preferably leather, to prevent minor cuts and wounds in case of a fall, Lemme said.

Crash helmets and face masks should also be worn, he said.

When driving on the road, cyclists should keep their headlights on to help other drivers to notice them. Too often people driving in cars do not see cycles, Lemme said.

The most important thing to remember, he advised, is to stay alert at all times.

Lemme attributes the increase in accidents in part to the "different kind of people who are riding motorcycles." ...

[Arlington Heights (Ill.) *Herald*]

Events

"Go out and see what is going on at—" the city editor may say. His purpose is not investigation, certainly not exposé; rather, he wants a news feature on an organization or activity not lending itself to straight news treatment but of public interest or importance.

By Emery Hutchison

Forty children who know prejudice only as a big word were frolicking in the spray arching from a fire hose.

The sight, a typical one at Camp Reinberg, near Palatine, is a recommended antidote to anyone who has been reading the lynch news from Georgia.

The skins of half the children were dark.

The experiment in inter-racial summer camping is one of the first of its kind.

Ninety-six youngsters, 48 of them Negroes, are enjoying a 10-day outing at the camp under the auspices of two Chicago community houses.

They are the fifth of seven groups from low income families who are taking turns in sharing the fun of outdoor life at the camp.

Watching the bathing youngsters from the shade of a tree was William Brueckner, 47, the outing supervisor and head resident of Emerson House, 645 N. Wood st.

"The children mix well," he said with satisfaction. "Even the smallest, and we have them as young as 5, discuss their differences in color, but that's all it is to them.

"And we hope that's all it ever will be."

A barefoot Negro boy about 10, stepping as gingerly as a tight-rope walker on the rough grass, headed for his cottage, then stopped with a grimace.

"Mr. Brueckner!" he cried, "How'm I gonna walk in these old sickle-burrs?"

Brueckner lifted the boy to one shoulder and carried him on his way.

A 5-year-old Negro boy, slightly envious, decided he also wanted to play "horsie," and an 8-year-old white youngster obliged.

"I got lost today—twice," the "horsie" boasted to his rider.

Henry Cameron, 26, one of the counselors from Parkway Community House, 5120 South Park Way, looked on with a grin.

Cameron, a Negro, is a visiting student from Georgetown, British Guiana.

"They play like brothers," said the lanky youth. "Whatever we cultivate in them here," he added, his face becoming serious, "will be to their advantage later in life." [Chicago *Daily News*]

STRAIGHT FEATURES

Not related to any current news event, the straight newspaper feature article originates as an idea with a reporter or editor. In gathering material for it, the feature writer may stumble upon newsworthy information which lends weight to his story; the origin of his quest, however, was a desire to supplement rather than expand upon the day's regular news budget.

Familiar Places

To make the commonplace attractive is a popular feature assignment. Although the average citizen uses the public parks and beaches, knows the names of the city's leading industries and the locations of important buildings, monuments and other landmarks, he may not be acquainted with the "inside" regarding them—their origin, history, laborious upkeep. The skilled feature writer should be able to find a new interesting angle about the city's most widely known institutions.

By Herb Owens

Milo, Ia.—Seventy-five years ago, in the late years of Pope Pius IX, "some of the boys" in a German Catholic farm settlement about seven miles southeast of here were celebrating the Fourth of July—and they decided the community needed a church.

Enthusiasm sprouted up immediately. Anthony Keller hauled stone out of the hills for a foundation. Michael Ripperger had a tract of good timber. Someone else had a sawmill outfit. All got together and built a church on the brow of a hill, opposite the Rosemount postoffice.

That spirit of enthusiasm and co-operation, carried down through the years by families of the original builders, still thrives around the Church of St. Mary's of Perpetual Help, more widely known as "Rosemount church."

Anniversary

The diamond anniversary will be celebrated on the church grounds next Thursday starting with a mass and continuing through a schedule of games and entertainment. It will end with a dance at night. Last year, approximately 3,500 persons, many coming "home" from many miles away, were at the celebration.

The church now has only one member who was alive when the original Rosemount church was constructed. He is Hubert Keller, 84, son of the farmer who hauled stone for the foundation.... [Des Moines *Tribune*]

OBSCURE PLACES

Straying off the beaten path, the roving reporter finds sections of his own community which neither he nor the "other half" realized exist. Such a reporter is able to make the "ole home town" much more interesting than heretofore.

We visited two nudist camps in New Jersey recently to see just what happens there and what kind of people nudists are.

Both camps—Goodland, a mile and a half from Hackettstown, and Sunshine Park, three miles from Mays Landing on the main road from Philadelphia to Ocean City—are affiliated with the American Sunbathing Association, the leading nudist organization in the country with 35 clubs in 15 states. Two states, New York and Ohio, have anti-nudism laws, though there are some nudist camps in upstate New York.

Both camps are strict about admitting visitors. Starers are thrown out on their ears, and single men are allowed at Sunshine Park only if accompanied by a woman member of their families, or by their fiancees. No liquor or beer is permitted at either of the two camps.

Both Goodland and Sunshine Park are small resort communities where members may own or rent small cottages. Accommodations are also available for transients. As at ordinary resorts, the main activities at nudist camps are outdoor sports: swimming, volleyball, boating, sunbathing, etc.—and in the evening games like bridge or ping-pong. The only difference is that at nudist camps you do most or all these things naked.

Going without clothes is not required, but at Sunshine Park almost everyone wears nothing at all, or at most shoes and a sunhat, from getting up time in the morning until retiring at night. At Goodland, clothes are worn at meals.

Before visiting a nudist camp, we were worried about what our reactions might be. We needn't have been. After a few minutes, going without clothes seems the most natural thing in the world. Our experience, and one of the old hands said it had been his too, was that at first we were conscious only that everyone else was not wearing clothes. Later we remembered we didn't have any on either.... [PM]

Familiar Persons

When a person enters the public limelight for the first time he is worthy of a write-up to satisfy curiosity regarding him. Thereafter, as long as he continues successful or interesting, he is the potential subject of innumerable articles. What is he like? How did he do it? To what does he accredit his success? If he had it to do over again, how would he behave differently? These questions suggest only a few of the many angles from which a widely known citizen may be re-introduced to readers. Frequent practice is to run a series of "who's who" articles on the community's leading figures.

Brentwood, Calif.—At first glance, there's nothing shocking about the freckle-faced woman peering through her brown-rimmed glasses. There's something a bit odd, perhaps: Her walk suggests a skinny duck in its cups; her bony legs, hugged by canary-colored stretch pants, resemble yellow pipe cleaners; her white-straw-blond hair—she calls it "tweed"—shoots out in all directions like the hirsuite hide of an anemic porcupine. Even so, she might be something you'd run into at a suburban laundromat.

The shock doesn't come until Phyllis Diller sprawls onto a sofa and belabors your eardrums with that ... that.... SOUND. Surely there is nothing like it in the darkest reaches of the Brazilian jungle. After that first deafening note, the Sound slumps, catches a second wind, and bounces up and down a few times in what could be roughly described as a tired cackle. She is, you realize, only laughing.

The Sound, of course, is only half of the Diller shock effect that has been rocking audiences for 11 years. The Sight is the other half. When Miss Diller's improbable shape is swaddled in one of the most bizarre outfits ever conceived—a poniard-like, bejeweled cigaret holder clenched between pearly teeth, her hazel eyes disguised by lavender or blue or green contact lenses—she looks like something even Fearless Fosdick might put down. She has been variously described as "the Brigitte Bardot of the Geritol Set," "the Liz Taylor of the Twilight Zone," and "Batwoman." Her beauty secret: Saddle Soap.

"I started out to become Queen of the May, just like all the other broads," she admits to her guests. "But I never got past February. A-A-A-ha-ha!"

We're in the high-ceilinged Bob Hope Salon—"it would be just a living room if we had no class"—of Miss Diller's sprawling 50-year-old "rural French" home in this posh residential community on the way to the ocean from Hollywood. She's entertaining on what may be the last free afternoon she'll have before becoming totally immersed in the filming of her first TV series, *The Pruitts of Southampton*. In the situation comedy, premiering in September on ABC-TV, Miss Diller stars as the zany matriarch of a high-society family that somehow maintains its elegant facade even though it's dead broke and owes $10,000,000 in back taxes.

Today the famous Sound is there but not the Sight. Barefoot, without makeup, dressed in slacks and a blouse with the shirttail out, Miss Diller looks like any housewife who has been working all morning with interior decorators furnishing a 22-room house. But there's nothing out of character about the hair-do—or, if you prefer, the hair-don't. It looks just the way it does each time Miss Diller appears on the TV or movie screen, on the stage, or in a night club. Every strand is a stringy assertion of independence.

The coiffure is truly a dazzling sight that elicits looks of wonderment and frequent queries. And Miss Diller is always ready for them. "Anyone can achieve the same effect," she advises. "Just comb your hair with an electric toothbrush." She named her hair style "D-D." Why? "Are you ready for this: 'Half Diller, half Dirksen.' A-A-A-ha-ha!"

"It Happened Naturally"

A nosy guest, his ears still ringing, pursues the point, and Miss Diller waxes serious for a moment: "Actually, it happened naturally, like most things in my life. My hair was in such bad shape that I went to a scalp clinic and they gave me a curry brush, and told me to lean over and brush my hair to make it grow. I brushed it like that all the time, and just left it that way." Yet on rare occasions, when Miss Diller gets dolled up, she miraculously whips that mop into a coiffure that looks downright sexy. Anyway, that's what she says.

Bloody Marys finished, it's time for a whirlwind tour of the antique-filled house, which Miss Diller bought several months ago. Just off the roomy Bob Hope Salon is the cozy, bay-windowed Gothic Alcove, wherein squats the "Hope Chest" (Bob has long been her idol), a Seventeenth Century Italian traveling chest decorated with hand-carved pictures of people under a waterfall.... [Daniel Greene in *National Observer*]

Obscure Persons

Likewise in every community are scores or hundreds of persons, not so much in the limelight, who nevertheless have had picturesque lives or unique experiences. In fact, there probably is nobody about whom an interesting feature article could not be written by a skillful interviewer.

By Cal Turner
Evening News Staff Writer

Bessie and Carrie Bonawitz rolled up their sleeves this morning and, over a bowl of cereal, watched the new day break. The calendar on the wall still said some nice things about molasses and the clouds with big muscles whispered of rain.

With or without it, Bessie, 44, and Carrie, 42, would cut the day in half and tidy up the crumbs.

Operating a 115-acre farm off of Red Top Rd. in South Hanover Twp., by themselves, the sisters have known no other world than the farm.

"It's been in family for 85 years now," said Bessie, lean and tanned as Carrie, slightly taller, but with the same brown eyes and a smile that tries to back up. "We share the work and it's up every morning at 5 and in bed about 9:30."

Sitting at the small kitchen table while the spotless pale green linoleum on the floor caught a handful of daylight, Bessie admitted each day was "work" and when it came time to sit down "and turn on the teevee" there just wasn't "much to talk about."

The sisters began operating the farm by themselves when their father died in 1959 at the age of 79. There had been four boys and seven girls.

"But everybody moved away," said Bessie, smiling slightly. "Found better paying jobs."

Corn, wheat, barley and grass for hay are the principal crops on the farm, which tags the eye like a bright child's toy tucked in the green and brown dip of the hills.

The house, barn and milking room are white as a sheet, trimmed in green. In the shadows of the bean trees, two large, old dogs growl at a mad fly that springs from the heavy, pungent odor of the barn. Near a dilapidated corn crib, the blade of a plow is polished by the sunlight.

"I'm plowing now for barley," said Carrie, grinning . . .

[Harrisburg (Pa.) *Evening News*]

Occupational Types

In addition to whatever news interest he may have as an individual, everyone is the potential source of a feature article because of the way in which he earns a living. When hard put to it to find a personality easily worked up into a story, the reporter can seek out someone engaged in a job about which what he has to say can be used effectively.

So you think that certain streetcar conductor is a pretty nice looking girl, eh? So you wink slyly and snap your sleeve garters at her when you think nobody is looking, eh? Here, then, is some good advice:

Next time you feel in a flirtatious mood on that streetcar, it might be prudent to look to the front of the trolley, where the mirror reflects the motorman's face. If he has fastened a baleful eye on you, get off the streetcar and transfer to one going in the opposite direction.

Now hold your seat for just a moment and we'll explain this advice. During the war many motormen were in service and their wives, needing supplementary earnings, were given jobs by the Cleveland Transit System. And even when the landlords were not in service, help was sometimes so badly needed that wives were persuaded to go to work on the streetcars.

Many of these women have retired to domestic life, but others are still working—and doing a fine job, C.T.S. officials aver.

Six Man-and-Wife Teams

In some cases, the husbands and their mates preferred to work on different cars. But from the Denison Avenue-W. 73d station alone there are six couples who prefer to work on the same streetcar.

"I hardly ever saw my husband before I went to work as a conductorette," said one of the wives. "Now we can go to work together and I can talk intelligently about his work and sympathize with his problems. It's a dandy arrangement." . . . [Cleveland *Plain Dealer*]

HISTORICAL

The familiar or unusual place or person feature quite frequently is historical, as there is no community without a building or citizen associated with some important event of the past. Old-timers like to recall events of yesterday. If possible, the historical feature should be illustrated with pictures taken at the time of the event being recalled.

The mystery of an old sign painted on the upper portion of the west wall of a four-story building at 414–18 Market street, was partly solved today by two St. Louisans who are keenly interested in the history and architecture of the city's oldest buildings. They are John A. Bryan, research architect at the Jefferson National Expansion Memorial, and Dr. William G. Swekosky, a dentist whose hobby is the history of old buildings.

The sign which caused them to delve into old city directories advertises "Crow & Farrell, Dry Goods." Who Crow and Farrell were and the years when they did business have perplexed many persons. Recently, however, Bryan and Swekosky, working independently, decided to find out for themselves.

Bryan, using an old city directory, said he found that the dry goods establishment occupied the ground floor at 418 Market about 1864, but he was unable to identify either Mr. Farrell or Mr. Crow. The latter, he says, is not the Wayman Crow who was a former member of the legislature and a leader in the establishment of Elliott Seminary, now Washington University. Wayman Crow's dry goods firm was on Main (now First) street, Bryan said.

Dr. Swekosky said the firm of Crow and Farrell was in the wholesale and retail dry goods business and rented space at the Market street address from 1868 to 1876. The firm was headed by William F. Crow and John Farrell, he said, and later was at the northwest corner of Fourth street and Washington avenue, but he was unable to identify the two men any further.

The sign is in black letters on a white background painted on the rough brick wall. It was uncovered when the adjoining five-story commercial structure, on the southeast corner of Market street and Broadway, was torn down last year. The site today is a parking lot. . . .

[St. Louis *Post-Dispatch*]

STUNTS

The stunt reporter courts adventure and finds it in submarines, airplanes, ambulances, breadlines, slums, morgues, police patrols and all sorts of out-of-the-way places. Reporters impersonate beggars, unemployed persons, street-corner Santa Clauses and criminals to obtain feature stories about the reactions of others and an insight into how certain types of individuals exist.

Riding alongside a milkman on his early morning route. It sounds calm enough, yet if the precautions a dairy owner takes are any indication, it is more hazardous than sailing aloft thousands of feet in the air or clanging through the city to a fire on a hook and ladder.

After producing a signed statement to the effect that in case of some dire mishap the company would be absolved from all blame and responsibility, I was allowed to climb up on the high narrow seat next to Joseph Plenn.

"I've never had an accident," Mr. Plenn assured me, "in the 12 years I've been with the company."

Nevertheless, one wagon a week meets with some accident, sometimes while it is standing still. Motorists are notably reckless in the wee small hours.

"Besides, you might get pneumonia," I was warned, "with ice and water under your seat."

By three o'clock yesterday morning, Mr. Plenn had Fanny hitched and our wagon loaded with great piles of cases holding icy quarts and pints and half-pints.

In the eerie blackness that enveloped the city, there was something cheery about the bright little white wagon with its gleaming candle light, something comforting about the stinging swish of Fanny's tail over my foot. Even the rattling of hundreds of milk bottles as we jogged down deserted streets was pleasant in the deep and sinister silence.

Drowsy householders don't care so much about the clatter of milk bottles or the whistle of a milkman. And occasionally when he calls on his second trip of the day, which starts about eight o'clock, he is severely scolded for his noise.

Sometimes he is scolded for lack of noise. Many families use the milk-wagon in place of an alarm clock and if the wagon is too quiet or is late, their whole day's schedule is thrown out of whack....

[Philadelphia *Bulletin*]

SITUATIONS

Differing from the round-up story of a series of current news events, the straight situation feature article is "trumped up" by an investigating reporter. What happens to discarded automobiles? What name appears most frequently in the city directory? How do college students earn their tuitions? What pets are most popular in the community? Do men and women differ in what they look for in apartments? These questions suggest the types of assignment which originate as "hunches." Factual, even statistical in content, the written stories nevertheless, were "manufactured."

BY DALE MORRISON

As you mull over your income tax forms this weekend in a last minute rush to meet the April 17 deadline, you may wonder where it all goes.

Not the money, everybody knows where that goes.

But what about Form 1040 or 1040A or 1040W or Schedule G, or the other monuments to documented confusion that Americans use to keep their government in the green?

When John Q. Taxpayer drops his tax return in the corner mailbox he launches it on a seven-year trip to oblivion with a few interesting way points.

Before it's forgotten, it's processed, probed and purged by a small army of experts.

The government's first processing step, naturally enough, is to remove returns from their envelopes.

It may not sound like much but it's a big job.

This week the Chicago office of the Internal Revenue Service has 140 employees doing nothing but opening envelopes, taking out forms, and noting on the return the amount of money sent in.

Harold R. All, district director of the I.R.S. here, said his office is expected to receive about **600,000** pieces of mail a day early next week.

From Jan. 1 to the week of the tax deadline it receives an average of 80,000 returns a day.

Once the envelope is opened, returns and money—in the form of checks, currency or money order—part company.

At the end of each working day the receipts from the 26 northern Illinois counties served by the Chicago office are deposited in the I.R.S. account of the Federal Reserve Bank of Chicago.

Deposits from personal income tax payments average $11,000,000 a day during the height of the season and total about $2 billion a year.

Uncle Sam can tap the I.R.S. account to meet current expenses the minute the money is in the bank.

Meanwhile, the incoming returns are broken down into more than 20 categories.

Mailing lists are made up from each category—wage-earner, small businessman, farmer, etc.—so that next year each taxpayer receives the same series of forms he filed this year.

At this stage, raw material for statistical surveys is drawn from the forms.

In the next processing step, the arithmetic in each return is checked.

I.R.S. auditors say that of the 2,800,000 taxpayers who file in the Chicago area, many have divergent views on the sum of 2 and 2.

About two-thirds of the returns are checked by hand and eye.

A skilled Comptometer operator can work through 35 returns an hour.

The other third—returns filed on punched card (Form 1040A)—are shipped to the I.R.S.'s service center in Kansas City, Mo.

There, electronics data processing machines check addition hundreds of times faster than flesh and blood processors.

Next comes the check for what revenue men delicately call "irregularities."

Highly trained agents scan each return, looking for those little apparent inconsistencies that frequently send poor John Q. scurrying for his records and sometimes send tax cheats to jail.

More often an agent's curiosity is aroused by what appear to be exorbitant business or medical expenses. The taxpayer is then asked to come in and give documentary proof of his claims.

Occasionally agents pick a return at random and ask the taxpayer to justify it.

Once over the checking hurdles returns are divided into two classes: those that will cost the government money and those that need a bill for the taxpayer.

Of late, the I.R.S. has gone to some pains to get out refunds before it sends out bills.

If a refund is due, the government must pay before June 1 or face 6 per cent interest charges. Interest from taxpayers who owe money starts the day the return is due.

Once accounts are squared the returns are confined to filing cabinets covering some 25,000 square feet of the main Chicago I.R.S. office.

After three years of dust-gathering there, they are moved to the two-square block federal records building at 78th St. and Deamington, where they gather more dust for another four years.

With the expiration of the statute of limitations at the end of seven years, the returns are just so much scrap to the government, just as well forgotten.

The forms are bundled and either sold to scrap dealers or burned.

[Chicago *Daily News*]

Becoming proficient as a feature writer is excellent preparation for interpretative reporting and writing of more significant happenings in city, state, nation and the world.

Index

A

Academic freedom, 392–93
Academic preparation, 22–23
Accidents, 11–12, 32, 279–85, 290
Account, completing the, 186–96
Accuracy, 129–35
Achievement, 161
Address, 157–58
Adjectives, 122
Adverbs, 123
Age, 70, 159
Agriculture, 447–51
American Bar Association, 317–18
American Newspaper Publishers Association, 44
American Society of Newspaper Editors, 8, (code) 29–30, 44, 144, 197
Analysis, 200–201
Anderson, Martin, 388
Anecdotes, 232–33
Appeals, legal, 346–48
Appellate courts, 326
Arraignment, 304
Associated Press, 15, 92, 179, 188, 250, 272
Associated Press Managing Editors, 16, 19, 21–22, 49, 51, 53, 124–25, 164, 197
Associated Press vs. International News Service, 145
Astonisher lead, 78
Attractive, making it, 82–91; identification, 163
Authority in news, 135–40
Automation, 392
Avoiding banality, 105–108

B

Background, factual, 186–87
Bagby, Nathe P., 14
Baltimore *Sun*, 190, 284
Bankruptcy, 339–40
Beinhorn, Sherman, 140–42
Biographical sidebars, 166

Births, 217–19
Black, Creed C., 433
Blanshard, Paul, 458
Blank, obituary, 274–76
Block paragraphing, 57–58
Body of story, 55–60; speeches, 252–55
Books, 487–88
Boosts, 120–21
Boxes, 79–80
Brevities, sources, 214–15
Brier, Warren T., 125, 262
Bromides, 106–107
Brown, Rep. Clarence, 171
Brown, Maynard, 15
Buffalo *Evening News*, 206
Bureau of Accuracy and Fair Play, 132–33
Buried feature, 180–81
Business, 409–18
Byrd, Harry Flood, 272–74

C

Campaign, political, 362
Canham, Erwin D., 200
Capone, Al, 327
Career, evaluating, 265–67
Cartridge lead, 77
Carty, James W. Jr., 459
Case, Sen. Francis, 124
Causes and motives, 198–99
Certiorari, 341
City clerk, 380
City council, 376–79
City government, 372–73
Civil law, 329–40
Civil trials, 334–36
Chall, Dr. Jerome S., 96
Charnley, Mitchell, 129
Checking, systematic, 132–33
Chicago Crime commission, 301
Chicago *Daily News*, 171, 206
Chicago Loop, 189
Chicago *Sun-Times*, 158

510 INDEX

Children, exceptional, 391–92
Childs, Marquis W., 17
Christian Science Monitor, 316, 366–67
Chronological organization, 59–60
Church and politics, 455–56
Clark, Austin H., 472
Clauses, 75–76; superfluous, 103
Cleveland crime news, 317
Closing statements, legal, 310–11
Code, A. S. N. E., 29–30; business, 433–37
Coincidences, 170
College students, 223
Combat, 69–70
Combined stories, 183–84
Coming-out parties, 226
Comment, second day, 174–75
Comparisons, 201
Comprehensive leads, 169–70, 183
Completing the account, 186–96
Conciseness, 99–105
Condemnation suits, 339
Conditional clauses, 75–76
Confidence, reader, 128–55
Connotations, 119–20
Consequence, 67–68
Contemporary trends, 49–50
Contrast lead, 83
Conventions, 242–47; political, 360–61
Converted assignment, 492–94
Cony, Edward R., 205
Copyright, 144–46
Corporation counsel, 380
Correct usage, 108–16
County government, 393–99
County politics, 357
Courts, 324–28
Cowlitz County Advocate, 212
Credo, newspaperman's, 2
Crime, 291–321
Criminal, understanding the, 318–21
Criticism, 479–85
Cross, Harold L., 144
Crowded lead, 78–79
Crowds, 246–47
Cub reporting, 23–24
Cumulative interest, 88–89

D

Dale, Prof. Edgar, 96
Damage suits, 337
Damages, libel, 150–51
Dance, 489

Davis, Elmer, 126
Davis, Richard Harding, 6
Davis, Watson, 465–67
Deaths, 261–79
Decision making, reportorial, 28
Decorations, 225
Dedmon, Emmett, 158
Defenses in libel, 151–53
Definitions, 117–18; financial, 425–31; weather, 405–408
de Gramont, Sanche, 454–55
Delayed identification, 165
Delinquency, 391
Denial of interview, 38–39
Description, 162
Descriptive lead, 84
Dewey, Gov. Thomas E., 164
Dialogue lead, 88
Direct address, 90
Direct quotation, 135–37
Disasters, 189, 279–85
Divorce, 338
Don'ts for science writers, 464–65
Double identification, 164
Dryden, Charles, 476
Duranty, Walter, 15

E

Editor & Publisher, 2
Editorializing, 119–21
Education, 207–209; news of, 388–93
Effect, total, 133–35
Eichmann, Adolph, 125
Elections, 367–71
Elliott, Jackson, 250
Employment, 220–21
Engagements, 226–27
Entertainment places, 233
Epigram lead, 85–86
Essayists, 480
Estimating crowds, 246–47
Ethics, 25–30; crime news, 316–18; science, 468–69; society, 235–36
Evaluative words, 121–23
Events, feature, 495–96; identification, 168–69
Evaluating a career, 265–67
Evanston Review, 190
Evictions, 338–39
Evidence, rules of, 344–46; trial, 309–10
Exceptional children, 391–92
Explanations, financial, 419–25

INDEX 511

Extraordinary remedies, 340–41
Eyewitness accounts, 187–88

F

Facts, organizing the, 49–62
Factual background, 186–87
Faherty, Robert, 95
Fair comment, 152
Fair trial vs. free press, 317–18
Familiar persons, 498–99; places, 496–97
Faults to avoid, 215–17
Features, 491–505; identification the, 165; more than one, 78–81; picking for rewrite, 180–84; picking for society, 229–30; playing up, 63–81
Federal Bureau of Investigation, 300
Federal courts, 327
Federal government, 397–99
Federal policy, agriculture, 449–51
Federal Register law, 44
Figurative lead, 85
Figures of speech, 106
Finances, city, 382–86
Financial news, 418–31
Fine arts, 489–90
Finlay, Dr. John, 8
Fitzgerald, Stephen E., 96
Five W's and H, 71–75
Flesch, Rudolf, 92–94, 96–97
Floods, 284
Fodor, M. W., 15
Follow-up, 471–79; feature, 182–83
Forecasts, 302
Foreclosures, 338
Formal interviews, 38
Formulas, reviewing, 481–82
Freak leads, 90–91
Freedom of Information bill, 144
Freedom of the press, 28–30
Fremont-Smith, Dr. Frank, 461
Freud, Sigmund, 261
Friendship on beats, 35–36
Funerals, 270–74

G

Garst, Robert E., 202–203
Gilman, Lawrence, 488–89
Gimbel, Bernard, 265–67
Giving it substance, 185–209
Glossary, space age, 461–62
Gossip, as news, 214–17; columns, 232–34
Government, city, 192–96, 372–93; county, 393–96; federal, 397–99; state, 396–97; secrecy, 94–95
Grammatical faults, 108–109
Grand jury, 305–306
Greer, Scott, 388
Guests, 219
Gunning, Robert, 92, 94–95, 123
Gunther, John, 15

H

Hadas, Dr. Moses, 264–65
Hanson, Harry, 487
Harrington, Harry F., 494
Harris, Sydney J., 119–20
"Hath Difficulties?" 212
Hightower, John, 197
Historical features, 501–502
How, 74–75
How to Lie with Statistics, 19–20
Huff, Darrell, 19–20
Human interest, 68–71; crime, 299
Humorous, 69

I

Identifications, 157–71
Illness, 256–60
Impressionistic reporting, 124–27
Indefinite pronoun, 105
Indirect reference, 137–39
Information, second-hand, 129–30
Informational background, 18–22
Injunctions, 340
Inquests, 279
Insinuations, 150
Institute for Propaganda Analysis, 117
Integration, school, 390
International News Service, 145, 188
Interpretation, 197–202; need for, 13–14; growth of, 15–18; viewpoint, 45–48; weather, 403–405
Interviewer, 39–41
Interviewing, 31, 39–41; personality, 234–35
Invasion of privacy, 27
Inverted pyramid form, 50–53
Investigations, 177–78, 204–206
Issues, political, 365–67

J

Jacobs, Jane, 388
John, Dr. Otto, 188
John XXIII, 459

512 INDEX

Johnson, Lyndon B., 44
Journalese, 107-108
Journalism, today and tomorrow, 3-5
Jury, grand, 305-306
Jury, selection, 309
Juveniles, 298-99

K

Karas, Dr. Jonathan, 468
Keeping up to date, 156-84
Kennedy, John F., 317, 458-59
Kent, Frank, 357, 362-63
Kerr, Walter, 487
Krieghbaum, Hillier, 461, 463
Krutch, Joseph Wood, 487-88
Kupferberg, Herbert, 490
Kobre, Sidney, 48, 260, 318-19
Kole, John W., 192

L

Labor, 440-47
Language, obituaries, 276
Lantz, Stanley, 448
Law, 313-14; obeying the, 142-44; labor, 442-43
Lead, 53-55; speeches, 250-52
League of Nations Conference, 144-45
Lee, Irving, 42
Leigh, Vivien, 234
Lerner, Max, 2
Libel, 146-55
Life span, 161
Lindstrom, Carl, 187-88
Literary allusion lead, 86
Little, William, 14-15
Local angle, 184
Localization, 175; 189-90; business, 413-15; obituaries, 268
Louisville *Courier-Journal*, 171; 207-209
Lubell, Samuel, 353, 365-66

M

Making it attractive, 82-91; readable, 92-116
Malice in libel, 152-53
Mallon, Paul, 144
Mandamus, 341
Markel, Lester, 17, 97, 197-98
Martin, Lawrence, 494
May, Edgar, 206
Mayor, 374-75
McBride, Mary Margaret, 125

McCarthy, Sen. Joseph R., 124, 138
McCormick, Robert, 188
McLuhan, Marshall, 97
Mead, Margaret, 254-55
Meetings, 237-42
Memphis *Press-Scimitar*, 191-92
Mencken, H. L., 271-72
Mental health, 260-61
Method, suicide, 278-79
Meyer, Sylvan, 152-53
Millikan, Dr. Robert, 19
Milwaukee *Journal*, 192-96, 216
Mindszenty, Cardinal, 22
Minneapolis *Star* and *Tribune* Bureau of Accuracy and Fair Play, 132-33
Moorman, John L., 22
Morgue stories, 267-68
Moss, Rep. John, 44, 144
Motion pictures, 486
Motions, criminal, 306-307
Motives and causes, 198-99
Motives, suicide, 227
Mowrer, Edgar Ansel, 15
Music, 488-89
Myers, Gustavus, 453

N

Nadel, Norman, 487
Nader, Ralph, 285
Names, 225
National Association of Science Writers, 468-69
National Broadcasting Company, 188
National Observer, 320
Nationality, 160
New York *Post*, 233
New York *Times*, 16; libel case, 152; 367
New Yorker, 235
Newcomers, 220
News, nose for, 10-12; what is, 12-13
News magazines, 15-16
News past, 161
News peg, 83
News reviews, 16
News values, 64-71
Newsgathering problems, 31-45
Newspaper style, 99
Newspaper work, 5-7
Newsweek, 15
Nicknames, 159-60
Nieman Reports, 191, 202-203
Night life, 233

Nomenclature, religion, 459–60
Nose for news, 10–12
Notes, 60–62
Nouns, 122
Noyes, Newbold, Jr., 124, 126–27

O

Obeying the law, 142–44
Obituaries, 261–79
Obscure persons, 500; places, 497–98
Occasions, 162, 225; identification of, 169
Occupation, 158–59
Occupational aids, 24–25; types, 500–501
Oddities, 491–92
Officers of court, 327–28
One-two-three-four lead, 80–81
Organizations, identifications, 166–68; political, 353–58
Organizing the facts, 49–62
Osborn, Henry Fairfield, 316
"Other Side," 190–96

P

Paine, Robert, 19
Paragraphing, block, 57–58
Parody lead, 86–87
Parts of speech, 109–10
Passive and active voice, 104
Paul VI, 459
Payola, 433
Peoria (Ill.) *Journal-Star* and *Transcript*, 186
Perseverance, 32–35
Persistence, 140–42
Personalities, 213–36; interviews, 234–35
Persons, 213–36; identification, 157–66
Personal element, 214
Perspective, 202–209; disasters, 283–84
Peru (Ind.) *Tribune*, 298–99
Petitions, political, 358
Philosophy, political, 351–52
Phrases, 76–77, 123
Picking the identification, 163–64
Places, identification, 168
Playing up feature, 63–81
Pleas, criminal, 306–307
Police, 281–91
Policy, newspaper, 26–27
Political power, farm, 448–49
Politics, 349–67; and church, 455–56
Precautions, accidents, 282–83
Precincts and wards, 355–57

Predictions, 170; political, 367
Preliminary hearing, 304
Presidents, 139
Preparation for journalism, 18–25
Prerogatives, reporter's, 26
Press, freedom of, 28–30
Pressures, religious, 456–57
Primaries, 360
Pringle, Henry F., 39
Privacy, 235–36; invasion of, 27
Privilege, 151–52
Probate proceedings, 341–43
Problems, labor, 443–44; newsgathering, 31–48
Procedures, criminal, 303–11
Prohibition, 340
Prominence, 66–67
Propaganda Analysis, Institute of, 117
Proper emphasis, 104–105
Providing perspective, 202–209
Proximity, 65–66
Public opinion, political, 352–53
Public relations, 41–44
Public works, 380–82
Publicity seekers, 36–38
Puffery, 121–22, 432–33
Pulitzer, Joseph, 7
Punch lead, 77–78
Punishments, 316

Q

Qualifications, 131–32; reportorial, 7–18
Question lead, 83–84
Quotation, direct, 135–37; lead, 87–88, 250
Quo warranto, 341

R

Race, 160
Ramsey, Claude, 138
Readability formulas, 92–98
Readable, making it, 92–116
Reader's Digest, 15
Receivership, 339
Reception, 226
Recorders, tape and wire, 24
Reece, B. Carroll, 191–92
Reference, indirect, 137–39
Refreshments, 225
Registration, voters, 359–60
Relationship, 161–62
Religion, 452–60; and schools, 390–91
Remedies, extraordinary, 340–41

INDEX

Reminiscences, 175–76
Reporter's notes, 60–62
Reporting, impressionistic, 124–27
Reputation, 161
Resourcefulness, 31–32
Responsibility, newspaper, 463–64
Reviewing, 479–85
Reston, James B., 197
Résumés, 203
Resurrected story, 178–79
Retractions, 153
Reviewing a life, 264–65
Revived story, 177
Rewrite, 179–84
Reynolds, Quentin, 15
Rhetorical devices, 75–78
Right, saying it, 117–27
Roberts, Judith Ann story, 51–55, 61
Rockefeller, John D., 1, 42
Roorbacks, 365
Roosevelt, Franklin D., 318
Running story, 176

S

Sackett, H. W., 150
Sancton, Thomas, 124
Saying it right, 117–27
Schools, 207–209, 388–93
Science, 19, 460–72
Second-day story, 172–74
Second-hand information, 129–30
Secondary feature, 181–82
Secrecy, 431–32; government, 44–45, 144
Semantics, 120
Separate stories, 28
Sequence, 89–90
Sex, 70
Sheean, Vincent, 15
Sheppard, Dr. Sam, 317
Sheriff, 290–91
Shirer, William L., 15
Shirttail method, 79
Shopworn personification, 107
Shorthand, 24
Showers, 227
Sidebars, 189; biographical, 166
Side features, accidents, 283; obituaries, 269
Siebert, Frederick S., 147
Sigma Delta Chi, 44, 144
Significance, 199–200
Simplicity, 103–104

Simpson, Kirke L., 272
Situations, 206–209; features, 494–95, 503–505; crime, 301–303
Slosson, Dr. Edwin E., 464
Smart, Ted, 206
Smith, Walter "Red," 477
Society page and news, 224–34
Space age glossary, 461–62
Spaid, Ora, 207–209
Speeches, 247–55; political, 362
Spiraling, 56
Sports, 473–79
Staccato lead, 84–85
Stage, 486–87
State government, 396–97; politics, 357–58
Statistics, 20; crime, 300–301
Stock exchanges, 419
Students, college, 223
Stunts, 206, 502–503
Style books, 98
Style, meetings, 241–42; newspaper, 99; obituaries, 276; society, 226, 230–231
Substance, giving it, 185–209
Substantive clause, 76
Suicides, 32, 276–79
Summary statement, 75
Superfluous details, 97–100; words, 100–102
Suspended interest, 89
Surveys, 203–204
Suspense, 70
Systematic checking, 132–33

T

Taylor, Deems, 10–11
Terral, Rufus, 283–84
Themes, 58–59
Tie-back, 170
Time, 15, 98
Timeliness, 64–66
Title, 159
Toledo *Blade* and *Times*, 318
Total effect, 133–35
Traits, valuable, 9–10
Trends, 206–209; business, 415–18; contemporary, 49–50
Trial, fair, 317–18
Trials, civil, 334–336; Criminal, 308–13
Trips, 221–22
Troublesome words, 110–16
Truman, Harry S., 44, 171
Truth in libel, 151

U

Unfamiliar words, 118–19
Uniform crime reports, 300
Unions, 440 ff.
United Press International, 93, 125, 144, 171, 179, 188, 190, 461
U.S. News & World Report, 20
United States Supreme Court, 152
Unity, 56–57
Unnecessary attribution, 139–40
Unusualness, 69
Urban renewal, 387–88

V

Vacations, 222–23
Values, news, 64–71
Verbs, 122–23
Verdicts, 313–14
Verification, 130–31

W

Wall Street Journal, 205, 438–49
War records, 160
Warren Commission, 317
Watson, B. B., 448
Weather, 399–408
Weddings, 227–29
Welch, Joseph N., 124
What, 72
When, 74
Where, 73
White, David Manning, 134
Whitman, Charles Joseph, 720–21
Who, 71–72; indefinite, 165
Why, 73; business, 412–13
Wiggins, Russell, 138
Williams, Edward, 206
Wills, 342–43
Wilmington (Del.) *News-Journal,* 433
Wilson, Earl, 233
Winchell, Walter, 217
Winning reader confidence, 128–55
Wolfe, Dr. Dael, 472
Women's pages, 224–31
Words, 226; dangerous, 148–50; evaluative, 121–23; identification, 171; unfamiliar, 118–19
World War I reporting, 15
Wrigley, Charles W., 330–32

Z

Zangara, Giuseppe, 318–19